BETTER PRACTICES: EXPLORING THE TEACHING OF WRITING IN ONLINE AND HYBRID SPACES

PERSPECTIVES ON WRITING
Series Editors: Rich Rice and J. Michael Rifenburg
Consulting Editor: Susan H. McLeod
Associate Editors: Johanna Phelps, Jonathan M. Marine, and Qingyang Sun

The Perspectives on Writing series addresses writing studies in a broad sense. Consistent with the wide ranging approaches characteristic of teaching and scholarship in writing across the curriculum, the series presents works that take divergent perspectives on working as a writer, teaching writing, administering writing programs, and studying writing in its various forms.

The WAC Clearinghouse and University Press of Colorado are collaborating so that these books will be widely available through free digital distribution and low-cost print editions. The publishers and the series editors are committed to the principle that knowledge should freely circulate and have embraced the use of technology to support open access to scholarly work.

Recent Books in the Series

Genesea M. Carter and Aurora Matzkel (Eds.), *Systems Shift: Creating and Navigating Change in Rhetoric and Composition Administration* (2023)
Michael J. Michaud, *A Writer Reforms (the Teaching of) Writing: Donald Murray and the Writing Process Movement, 1963–1987* (2023)
Michelle LaFrance and Melissa Nicolas ((Eds.), *Institutional Ethnography as Writing Studies Practice* (2023)
Phoebe Jackson and Christopher Weaver (Eds.), *Rethinking Peer Review: Critical Reflections on a Pedagogical Practice* (2023)
Megan J. Kelly, Heather M. Falconer, Caleb L. González, and Jill Dahlman (Eds.), *Adapting the Past to Reimagine Possible Futures: Celebrating and Critiquing WAC at 50* (2023)
William J. Macauley, Jr. et al. (Eds.), *Threshold Conscripts: Rhetoric and Composition Teaching Assistantships* (2023)
Jennifer Grouling, *Adapting VALUEs: Tracing the Life of a Rubric through Institutional Ethnography* (2022)
Chris M. Anson and Pamela Flash (Eds.), *Writing-Enriched Curricula: Models of Faculty-Driven and Departmental Transformation* (2021)
Asao B. Inoue, *Above the Well: An Antiracist Argument From a Boy of Color* (2021)
Alexandria L. Lockett, Iris D. Ruiz, James Chase Sanchez, and Christopher Carter (Eds.), *Race, Rhetoric, and Research Methods* (2021)
Kristopher M. Lotier, *Postprocess Postmortem* (2021)

BETTER PRACTICES: EXPLORING THE TEACHING OF WRITING IN ONLINE AND HYBRID SPACES

Edited by Amy Cicchino and Troy Hicks

The WAC Clearinghouse
wac.colostate.edu
Fort Collins, Colorado

University Press of Colorado
upcolorado.com
Denver, Colorado

The WAC Clearinghouse, Fort Collins, Colorado 80523

University Press of Colorado, Denver, Colorado 80202

© 2024 by Amy Cicchino and Troy Hicks. This work is licensed under a Creative Commons Attribution-NonCommercial-NoDerivatives 4.0 International License.

ISBN 978-1-64215-224-1 (PDF) | 978-1-64215-225-8 (ePub) | 978-1-64642-622-5 (pbk.)

DOI 10.37514/PER-B.2024.2241.

Produced in the United States of America

Library of Congress Cataloging-in-Publication Data

Names: Cicchino, Amy, 1987– editor. | Hicks, Troy, editor.
Title: Better practices : exploring the teaching of writing in online and hybrid spaces / edited by Amy Cicchino and Troy Hicks.
Description: Fort Collins, Colorado : The WAC Clearinghouse ; Denver, Colorado : University Press of Colorado, 2024. | Series: Perspectives on writing | Includes bibliographical references.
Identifiers: LCCN 2024013158 (print) | LCCN 2024013159 (ebook) | ISBN 9781646426225 (paperback) | ISBN 9781642152241 (adobe pdf) | ISBN 9781642152258 (epub)
Subjects: LCSH: English language—Rhetoric—Web-based instruction. | English language—Composition and exercises—Web-based instruction. | Blended learning. | LCGFT: Essays.
Classification: LCC PE1404 .B478 2024 (print) | LCC PE1404 (ebook) | DDC 808/.0420711—dc23/eng/20240501
LC record available at https://lccn.loc.gov/2024013158
LC ebook record available at https://lccn.loc.gov/2024013159

Copyeditor: Don Donahue
Designer: Mike Palmquist
Cover Photo: RawPixel Image 2963427. Licensed.
Series Editors: Rich Rice and J. Michael Rifenburg
Consulting Editor: Susan H. McLeod
Associate Editors: Johanna Phelps, Jonathan M. Marine, and Qingyang Sun

The WAC Clearinghouse supports teachers of writing across the disciplines. Hosted by Colorado State University, it brings together scholarly journals and book series as well as resources for teachers who use writing in their courses. This book is available in digital formats for free download at wac.colostate.edu.

Founded in 1965, the University Press of Colorado is a nonprofit cooperative publishing enterprise supported, in part, by Adams State University, Colorado State University, Fort Lewis College, Metropolitan State University of Denver, University of Alaska Fairbanks, University of Colorado, University of Denver, University of Northern Colorado, University of Wyoming, Utah State University, and Western Colorado University. For more information, visit upcolorado.com.

Citation Information: Cicchino, Amy, and Troy Hicks. (2024). *Better Practices: Exploring the Teaching of Writing in Online and Hybrid Spaces*. The WAC Clearinghouse; University Press of Colorado. https://doi.org/10.37514/PER-B.2024.2241

Land Acknowledgment. The Colorado State University Land Acknowledgment can be found at landacknowledgment.colostate.edu.

CONTENTS

Foreword vii
    Miranda Egger and Scott Warnock

Introduction. 3
    Amy Cicchino and Troy Hicks

Chapter 1. Using Push Notifications to Establish Teacher Presence in Hybrid/Online Courses 27
    Theresa (Tess) Evans and A.J. Rivera

Chapter 2. Using Structural Examples to Promote Creativity and Engagement. 53
    Brielle Campos and Candie Moonshower

Chapter 3. Peer Review in Online, Real-Time Learning Environments 71
    Meghalee Das and Michael J. Faris

Chapter 4. Scaffolding for Collaboration and Multimodal Assignments. . . . 93
    Ashleah Wimberly, Amanda Ayers, Amory Orchard, and Michael Neal

Chapter 5. Annotation and Rhetorical Analysis with Discussions Hosted in Flip 119
    Ana Contreras and Troy Hicks

Chapter 6. Teaching Textual Analysis through Collaborative, Online Annotation. 139
    Valeria Tsygankova and Vanessa Guida Mesina

Chapter 7. #WriteTeachChat: Social Media for Writing to Learn and Learning to Write. 161
    Jessica Eagle, Michelle Falter, and Caitlin Donovan

Chapter 8. Fishing for Online Engagement 187
    Ingrid K. Bowman and Briana Westmacott

Chapter 9. Cripping Writing Processes: Composing (Neuro)Divergently . . 211
    Ada Hubrig and Anna Barritt

Contents

Chapter 10. Creating Cultural Awareness, Building Community: Encouraging Student Writer Identity Through Purposeful Assignment Design..235
    Jennifer Burke Reifman and Jessie Borgman

Chapter 11. Promoting Social Justice through Multimodal Composition in the Hybrid Writing Classroom...................259
    Syndee Wood and Mary K. Stewart

Chapter 12. Open-Media Assignment Design to Address Access and Accessibility in Online Multimodal Composition...............279
    Amory Orchard, Michael Neal, Ashleah Wimberly, and Amanda Ayers

Chapter 13. Accessible Multimodal Social Media Projects..............303
    Alex Wulff, Christina Branson, and Cecilia Ragland Perry

Chapter 14. Reflective Learning in Data Storytelling 325
    Christopher E. Etheridge and Heidi Skurat Harris

Chapter 15. Retooling Decision-Making in A/Synchronous Online Literacy Instruction 349
    A. Chase Mitchell and Rich Rice

Chapter 16. Iterative Processes for All: Rewards and Risks in Contract Grading..371
    Shawn Bowers and Jennifer Smith Daniel

Chapter 17. The Radical Equity of Grading Contracts in Online Writing Courses..393
    Kevin E. DePew and Kole Matheson

Chapter 18. Learning to Unlearn: Grading Contracts in the Online Classroom 419
    Michelle Stuckey and Gabriella Wilson

Chapter 19. Dialogic Assessment Agreements: A New Genre For Building Trust and Mitigating Risk in Online Writing Instruction.......447
    Kate Pantelides, Samira Grayson, and Erica Stone

Appendix. Alignment Between *Better Practice* Chapters and National Position Statements......................................475

Contributors 481

FOREWORD

Miranda Egger
University of Colorado Denver

Scott Warnock
Drexel University

Before you is a collection of chapters describing better online writing instruction (OWI) practices (also, often termed online literacy instruction, or OLI). Amy Cicchino and Troy Hicks use the term *better* in this collection deliberately. As they point out in their introduction to *Better Practices: Exploring the Teaching of Writing in Online and Hybrid Spaces*, educators have debated the usefulness and accuracy of adjectives to describe their practices: Are they "best"? "most effective"? Or, should teachers accept that we're on a developmental continuum, like an asymptote that moves toward a curve of idealized/best teaching but never quite gets there?

    In short, *better* is this book's target, and we think it is a useful and empowering aim. Teachers work constantly to improve, to provide something that helps students a little more than last class, last term, last year. There's always more to be done. As Ingrid Bowman and Briana Westmacott point out, "This is the beauty of being an educator—we are, in fact, innovators, continually working to solve problems" (Chapter 8, this collection). That is especially true with OWI/OLI, which doesn't hold a monopoly on innovation, but its foundation in digital teaching invites the use of technologies that are always changing and, thus, always opening new opportunities for educators and students.

    This perpetual change, while exciting, can be a source of stress for educators new to OWI/OLI. It is not unusual to hear teachers say they are confused by changing technologies or hesitant to learn new interfaces well enough to put them into practice, but that's part of the power of this book: Its 19 chapters and six themes show readers how innovative, better teaching and learning practices to achieve focused goals can often be accomplished with accessible technologies. And it is imperative that we describe and share these practices, as Cicchino and Hicks say: ". . . our current context demands closer attention to the kinds of pedagogies that can improve student writing, no matter the course modality" (Introduction, this collection).

    The many authors included in this volume are clearly skilled all around as teachers, yet we are struck that they do not lose sight of their role as online educators. If we intend to get better at OWI/OLI, we must continue to invest in the specific thread of scholarship that is demonstrated in this volume. We must acknowledge the legitimacy of OWI/OLI as its own learning space: The value this expanded approach to the delivery of education brings to students, the scholarship informing our practices, the rigor of inclusive and accessible course design in digital spaces, and the desire our students have to be challenged to meet the world's latest exigencies.

WE ARE ALL ONLINE TEACHERS

The pandemic heavily underscored the fact that, if we were not before, we are now all online teachers in some manner. Anyone who uses an LMS, has flipped their classroom, or relies on any technological tool to teach a lesson is an online teacher who could benefit from OWI/OLI-specific professional development. While the pandemic has been devastating to so many lives and livelihoods, it has also been maieutic in focusing our attention on what we wish we'd seen more clearly all along: OWI/OLI is a mainstay of education and teaching with some virtual component that fosters improved learning will continue to be the norm. To dismiss that reality limits ourselves and our students' options.

Cicchino and Hicks describe three goals for this book:

1. to bring together diverse online writing educators to make their teaching practices more explicit,
2. to feature a set of replicable *better* practices that show ideas articulated by professional organizations in national statements in-action, and
3. to validate online teacher-scholars and make their intellectual contributions to writing studies more visible.

This collection offers a jumpstart for teachers to engage in those goals and seek specific classroom practices that meet the field's highest standards as well as for administrators looking for professional development in their earnest (yet often nascent) effort to support their departments. We, Miranda and Scott, have done much of that sort of administrative support of new and new-to-online teachers and find that a community of well-intentioned educators with clear ideas to share is one key ingredient necessary to foster the confidence needed to step into that virtual classroom space. This volume evokes a form of grassroots professional development that features teachers teaching teachers (a long-standing National Writing Project principle[1]) by sharing detailed ideas throughout. Here is a menu of such ideas.

---

1   Please learn more about the National Writing Project at https://www.nwp.org.

Foreword

This book welcomes all writing teachers—and their students—into the world of OWI/OLI. Some chapters reify, clarify, and expand commonly accepted tenets of better practices (Brielle Campos and Candie Moonshower's use of templates, Chapter 2, this collection; or Shawn Bowers and Jennifer Smith Daniel's application of ungrading to OWI/OLI, Chapter 16, this collection; or Syndee Wood and Mary Stewart's application of multimodality as a means of promoting social justice, Chapter 11, this collection) while some challenge those tenets (Anna Barritt and Ada Hubrig's description of neurodivergent approaches to the writing process, Chapter 9, this collection; or Kevin DePew and Kole Matheson's use of grading contracts in online courses to promote radical equity, Chapter 17, this collection). Meanwhile, other better practices offer new ways to achieve accepted goals (Tess Evans and A. J. Rivera's use of push notifications to foster teacher presence, Chapter 1, this collection). Of note, while there are indeed big, provocative conversations in OWI/OLI's journals, conferences, and books among the teacher-scholars of the field related to antiracist languaging, accessibility, transfer, and the proper place for and subject of first-year writing, this book converts many of those conversations into actionable classroom practices.

FRESH APPROACHES TO BOTH CONTENT AND DELIVERY

Chapters are solidly grounded in key OWI/OLI principles and composition position statements, but the book also takes fresh, and in some cases unique, approaches to its construction and delivery. First, the editors invited an unusual type of collaboration among co-authors: They asked an OWI/OLI "expert" specializing in a theoretical approach to pair with a "colleague teaching the approach for the first time" to collaboratively write explorations of practices anchored in OWI/OLI research and expertise "delivered across multiple institutional contexts." These expert-novice labels were productively complicated throughout, and we found it interesting to consider what exactly constituted an expert and a novice—even in our own writing partnership. The editors initially asked Scott to write this foreword and provided suggestions for a collaborator who was newer to the field; however, when he asked Miranda, whom he knew from other OWI/OLI contexts (especially her heavy-lifting work when the Global Society of Online Literacy Educators offered resources to instructors during the pandemic's onset[2]), it was apparent immediately that while she may have just earned her doctorate, she was a long-experienced, talented educator, administrator, and

---

2   Learn more about GSOLE at https://gsole.org/

scholar. You will see similar complexities in the chapters that follow, as ostensible differences in experience produce interesting conclusions throughout.

Second, the editors not only invited co-author teams but also supported them through the composition process by providing structured times during an eight-week period to meet and collaborate with one another and with the editors. The editors nurtured the collaborative writing process, in an online setting, using tools similar to those the authors themselves use in their own teaching practices. Interestingly, although writing instruction is a pillar of our professional lives, we often create our own texts in opaque, enigmatic ways. Cicchino and Hicks, however, chose to exercise our field's *better* practices by supporting the authors through the complicated collaborative writing process, helping demystify the process of drafting scholarly texts.

Third, the chapters open with vignettes that help focus these better practices around student experiences. These vignettes, stories of people, remind us consistently of the importance of humanistic approaches to OWI/OLI. The practices are designed explicitly with individual students in local contexts in mind. In many chapters, student experiences are not just assumed to be present and valuable: Teachers seek student input, too. At the end of "Scaffolding for Collaboration and Multimodal Assignments," for example, Ashleah Wimberly, Amanda Ayers, Amory Orchard, and Michael Neal say,

> Taking the time to articulate what we wanted our students to learn and how we wanted to help our students to learn is what inspired our re-visioning of this course. The ongoing reflection and discussions we had amongst ourselves and with students helped us make decisions that centered student experiences, scaffolded their learning, and fostered collaboration . . . (Chapter 4, this collection)

There is a risky honesty at work here, as Wood and Stewart point out: They notice "most 'best practices' articles tell a positive story" in which "authors' pedagogical goals and intentions were met and the students experienced valuable learning," but their work "found a much more complicated reality." Many chapters comfortably linger in that "complicated reality," one that reifies the need to travel asymptotically toward idealized teaching rather than adhere to a simple linear model in which we learn a practice, succeed, and move on.

Finally, following the guiding lights of "better," "innovation," and "individuality," the book offers different paths—themes that structure the reading experience around specific OWI/OLI topics and goals. The editors codify and organize a variety of pedagogical experiences: Choose your adventure!

ELIMINATING DISCIPLINARY UNCERTAINTY

Cicchino and Hicks call for us to be aware of OWI/OLI's precariousness. We could all write books and articles and deliver presentations and lectures worrying about precarity, but they do something about this problem. This book grounds us in a more clearly articulated sense of better practices, rooted in OWI/OLI principles, as applied in humanistic fashion (teachers seeking student input throughout), and it is the kind of solid footing we think will help eliminate disciplinary uncertainty. This book gives us all a strong place from which to enter critical conversations in our scholarship, and we think the audience will be pleased to discover that the scholars sharing their work show new ways to enact *better* practices in their teaching—and overtly invite readers to do the same with their own.

REFERENCES

Conference on College Composition and Communication. (2023). *CCCC Position Statements*. https://cccc.ncte.org/cccc/resources/positions.

Global Society of Online Literacy Educators. (2023). *Welcome to GSOLE!* https://gsole.org.

National Writing Project. (2023). *Who we are*. https://www.nwp.org/who-we-are.

BETTER PRACTICES: EXPLORING THE TEACHING OF WRITING IN ONLINE AND HYBRID SPACES

INTRODUCTION

Amy Cicchino
Embry-Riddle Aeronautical University

Troy Hicks
Central Michigan University

Online writing instruction (OWI) is professionally and pedagogically precarious.

This precarity occurs on many planes, all at once. As online writing educators, we find ourselves working with colleagues who hold various ranks and thus are valued differently by their institutions: graduate teaching assistants, staff, contingent and term-limited faculty, those on full-time fixed terms, and those who are tenured or tenure-track. We find ourselves moving across teaching different modalities. We find ourselves still questioning both the "what" and the "why" of teaching online writing courses, from the traditional thesis-driven essay in a word-processed document to the possibilities of multimodal composing, with text, image, audio, and more being combined in new genres and forms.

Prior to the pandemic, the proliferation of online learning had already exacerbated challenges that have vexed writing instructors and writing program administrators for years, if not decades. These challenges include broad concerns about K–12 educational inequity manifesting in postsecondary writing courses, placement testing and tracking of students, student persistence in online learning, and the need for teacher professionalization for online learning. Also, there are the very specific needs of those teaching writing courses online that are above and beyond the normal challenges of composition courses, which will be explained more throughout the collection. It is with these concerns in mind that we issued a call to our colleagues to share their online writing practices; we did so in an effort to recenter conversations about what it means to teach writing online, in this moment and in the future.

New kinds of precarity continue to arise, such as the widespread use of generative artificial intelligence (AI) writing platforms and how they will impact what we teach in writing courses. While AI is not explicitly taken up in this collection, the responses that we see in this moment—panic towards edtech solutions such as AI-related plagiarism—is not new. Instead of edtech platforms policing students, we offer a stance that anchors this collection: intentionally designed assignments and activities that center student learning in context, reflection,

DOI: https://doi.org/10.37514/PER-B.2024.2241.1.3

and engagement. We hope we've provided a heuristic for scholars to continue exploring teaching/learning in more responsive, thoughtful, and critical ways.

DEFINING TERMS

Before exploring the intersections of professional and pedagogical precarity in OWI, we want to define anchor terms for this collection. A number of scholars—many of whom we call colleagues and some of whom are even featured in this collection—have offered definitions of OWI. Yet, in an effort to clarify and condense these many ideas, we define OWI as: **A specialized field within writing studies in which educators adapt principles of effective writing instruction—such as modeling the writing process, composing across modes and media, and providing timely feedback—to meet students' needs in networked learning environments, both in real-time, synchronous, or any time/asynchronous formats.**

We also identify instructional practices taken up in four modalities. For clarity, we have asked the authors in this collection to note their primary modality and adaptations for other modalities amongst the four listed below:

- **In-Person, Real-Time Learning:** traditional class sessions at scheduled times, where some students may join in real-time session via "hyflex" video call, but a majority of students attend in-person.
- **Online, Real-Time Learning:** where all students are expected to join scheduled video calls during regular class sessions.
- **Online, Any Time Learning:** online learning with minimal or no real-time attendance or interaction, and most work is self-paced with scheduled deadlines.
- **Hybrid Learning:** the whole class fluctuates between scheduled, in-person meetings and various forms of online learning.

Of note, the CCCC OWI Standing Group released a (2021) "State of the Art of OWI" report that further expanded on five different online and hybrid learning modalities that includes elements of location as well as time. As another example, a report from a provost's office (privately shared with us from another institution), featured seven different modalities. Some institutions are being more particular about listing modalities in course catalogs, and some are not. This is to say teaching and learning modalities are yet another inconsistent, precarious reality in OWI that will continue to change.

Finally, as we consider the terminology in which we discuss our work, we want to make a clear distinction: we opt for the term **better practices** instead of "best practices." We explore our rationale for this choice—striving always to be "better" in our teaching as compared to offering a single "best" practice—below.

BEST VS. BETTER PRACTICES

As we think about meaningful OWI practices—those that include consistent teacher presence, active communication, opportunities for exploring content in different ways, and authentic assessments—we know that there is no single set of "best practices." In fact, throughout educational scholarship, the very idea of "best practices" has been contested. Though captured in a blog entry and not a formal article, the highly regarded educational historian Larry Cuban describes concerns about the concept of "best practices" being transported from the medical field into education. He contends that policy makers are encouraged to adopt "best practices" for "classroom management, professional development, and school working conditions" that do not account for variations in students, schools, and communities, and that best practices "has become a buzzword across governmental, educational, and medical organizations" (2010, para. 2). We agree, noting that the rhetoric of naming something a "best" practice suppresses any need to question that practice or critically reflect upon it. Jory Brass (2014), speaking to the field of English Education—yet certainly in line with concerns about college writing instruction—argues that a series of neoliberal educational reforms that include phrases such as "best practices" and "evidence-based education" should be seen as threats to teachers' autonomy and professionalism; also it can signal a shift toward "networks of policy entrepreneurs, state governors, philanthropists, foundations, for-profit and non-profit vendors, and edu-businesses" (p. 126). In this sense, the phrase "best practices" can be a disguise for the reforms that will ultimately undermine practices that contribute to high-quality teaching and learning.

To further this point, in the introduction to a volume of articles from scholars working in international and comparative education entitled "Working with, against, and Despite Global 'Best Practices': Educational Conversations Around the Globe" (2015), Sarfaroz Niyozov and Paul Tarc critique the inherent generalizability of "best practices," stating that these practices may appear neutral, but do not properly consider diverse individuals and contexts nor teach educators how to adapt purportedly "best practices" to meet the unique needs of their students and courses. While Niyozov and Tarc are critiquing the concept of "best practices" in light of global education, their argument aligns with the fact that the many contextual factors in any given post-secondary composition classroom—whether in-person, real-time learning; hybrid; online, real-time learning; or online, any time learning—also matter a great deal. Julian Edge and Keith Richards (1998) similarly critique the "insidious" abstractness of the term "best practice" and highlight its potential to contribute to inequitable power dynamics instead of forwarding "emergent praxis," self-reflection, and iterative processes of teacher development (pp. 572–573). Though a deeper dive into critical theory and contesting the idea of "best practices" could be had here, we summarize by simply stating that these scholars remind us that there is no single, set version of a "best practice" that works in any writing classroom at any given moment.

Furthermore, the pedagogical precarity of online writing instruction, in general, and online writing educators, as individuals, further destabilize the idea of a one-size-fits-all best approach to online teaching and learning. Put another way, a pedagogy that has been studied in one institutional context with a particular student population may fail to be equally effective in a vastly different teaching and learning context. Thus, online writing educators must adapt "best" practices to their local contexts. Yet, due to the genre and space limitations, position statements by professional organizations often fail to make explicit the educators' labor that is required when adapting broad principles to the unique institutional contexts and student populations. As a result, new online writing educators might try and struggle when implementing supposed "best" practices without consideration for their local contexts.

Instead of promoting "best" practices, then, for all the reasons noted above, we propose an approach to teaching and learning that seeks to do "better" with the teaching and learning practices that we use across modalities. In our spring 2021 call for proposals, we noted that as teachers "continue to extend and adapt their teaching practices in a post-pandemic world, we know that there are still no 'best' practices, yet we continue to get better." We invited co-authors—"an expert in online writing instruction specializing in the particular theoretical approach alongside a colleague teaching the approach for the first time"—to work together to create chapters that explored authentic practices anchored in research and expertise in OWI, and that were delivered across multiple institutional contexts.

Our vision for "better practices," then, enacts theories and ideas captured in national statements by professional organizations in writing studies like the Conference on College Composition and Communication (CCCC), the Global Society of Online Literacy Educators (GSOLE), the Council of Writing Program Administrators (CWPA), and the National Council of Teachers of English (NCTE). In particular, we asked our co-authoring teams to draw from the following professional resources:

- *Framework for Success in Postsecondary Writing (2011)*[1]

---

1 Available at https://wpacouncil.org/aws/CWPA/pt/sd/news_article/242845/_PARENT/layout_details/false

- *A Position Statement of Principles and Example Effective Practices for Online Writing Instruction* (OWI) (2013)[2]
- *Principles for the Postsecondary Teaching of Writing* (2015)[3]
- *Online Literacy Instruction Principles and Tenets* (2019)[4]
- Also, many authors reference the Personal, Accessible, Responsive, Strategic framework, created by Jessie Borgman and Casey McArdle (2019).[5]

Thus, chapters in the collection explicitly link each OWI practice to specific statements and principles so that readers can see the connection between principle, theory, and practice demonstrated in-action in online and hybrid writing contexts. A matrix provided in the collection's appendix maps how each principle or framework is used in specific chapters.

THE PURPOSE OF THIS COLLECTION

We need to continue to develop representations of what online writing instruction looks like as it is enacted by OWI practitioners in their local contexts. The teaching strategies featured in this collection have been adapted from evidence-based "better practices" and delivered across learning modalities so that readers can understand how to adapt these strategies for their own instruction at the course level or their own OWI professional learning at the programmatic level.

REVIEWING THE LITERATURE

Through our review of the literature and in the process of collaborating with the co-authors of this collection—as described in the section "The Process for Building *Better Practices*" below—we identified five sections. By necessity, this literature review is merely a snapshot, not a comprehensive review. These sections highlight the dual foci of this book: to articulate the professional and pedagogically precarious contexts in which we find ourselves working and, more importantly, to imagine "better practices" that can be shared as a way to rethink the work that we do.

These sections are:

- The Role of Professional Organizations in Effective OWI
- The Need to Professionalize OWI Educators

---

2 Available at https://cdn.ncte.org/nctefiles/groups/cccc/owiprinciples.pdf
3 Available at https://cccc.ncte.org/cccc/resources/positions/postsecondarywriting/summary
4 Available at https://gsole.org/oliresources/oliprinciples
5 Available at https://wac.colostate.edu/books/practice/pars/

- Issues of Student Access and Equity in OWI
- The Precarity in Educator Labor and Status in OWI
- And, as in nearly any collection that is now examining the state of teaching and learning in an endemic world, The Effects of Emergency Remote Teaching during the COVID-19 Pandemic

Before tracing the history of OWI, we take a moment to introduce the guiding statements we draw from by professional organizations on effective writing and online writing instruction.

THE ROLE OF PROFESSIONAL ORGANIZATIONS IN EFFECTIVE OWI

As a distinct field of study, OWI has its own established theories and practices. Namely, scholars have explored the pedagogical practices, processes, and activities shown to be effective for online learners in the context of college-level composition courses. Moreover, they emphasize the importance of intentional online course design, expertise in online learning, and adequate institutional support. They discourage efforts to move in-person writing instruction to online spaces without significant consideration for the affordances and limitations of the online learning environment. Professional organizations like CCCC and GSOLE have similarly articulated "best practices" in online writing instruction, including recommendations for supporting OWI programmatically and institutionally. This section will briefly discuss some key aspects of effective OWI, as described by these scholars.

Numerous position statements have been created to guide OWI, most notably CCCC's *A Position Statement of Principles and Example Effective Practices for Online Writing Instruction (OWI)* (2013). When it was released a decade ago, such a statement was greatly needed as previous national statements in writing studies—which did describe the "habits of mind" a postsecondary writer would need—lacked attention or provided minimal guidance related to online learning (e.g., CCCC *Principles for the Postsecondary Teaching of Writing*, 2015; CWPA/NCTE/NWP *Framework for Success in Postsecondary Writing*, 2011). This 2013 CCCC's statement was based on a survey of those who self-identified as "online writing instructors"—in whatever capacity they defined that role—and then crafted by an expert panel to articulate 15 foundational principles and effective practices for OWI. Practices and principles range from instructional to administrative and institutional. Importantly, the CCCC statement situates the role of technologies as something that should enhance the learning in OWI courses, not serve as additional barriers. Principle 2, for instance, argues that the center of OWI is writing, not technology, and Principles 3 and 4 note the importance of designing instruction around the "unique features of the online instructional environment," importing "onsite composition theories, pedagogies, and strategies" only when they are appropriate to the context for the course.

With the founding of Global Society of Online Literacy Educators (GSOLE) in 2016, the work of OWI then broadened to include "literacy" and not just "writing." A few years later, GSOLE adapted and updated their founding principles in their *Online Literacy Instruction Principles and Tenets* (2019). The first principle identifies a commitment to accessibility and inclusion, which should be shared by administrators, educators, tutors, and students. The second principle extends arguments for instructors' professional learning to advocate for regular processes of professional development and course and program assessment. The third principle links recurring professional development to iterative processes of instructional design with opportunities to reflect on how instruction enacts "current effective practices." And the final principle promotes active conversations and research across the online literacy instruction community through webinars and an annual conference. Combined with opportunities found through CCCC and CWPA, GSOLE's regular professional development opportunities and research support grants offer online writing educators support from a professional organization devoted specifically to the field of OWI. To those ends, GSOLE has created a Basic OLI Certification, a series of OLI focused modules that provides participants with a foundation of theories, research, and practice in OWI (Cicchino et al., 2021). The certification modules are taught by OLI educators from across the globe, centering the idea that the most qualified people to train online literacy instructors are other practicing online literacy instructors from their discipline.

In 2020, 2021, and 2023 publications from Borgman and McArdle introduced their "Personal, Accessible, Responsive, Strategic," or PARS, approach to OWI. The first co-authored book (2020) outlines PARS as a practical framework for designing and evaluating online writing course design while the edited collection (2021) features online writing educators putting PARS into practice. The third book in the PARS series (2023) focuses on programmatic strategies for implementing online instruction.[6] Borgman and McArdle additionally created the Online Writing Instruction Community,[7] a website that shares OWI resources and hosts open access professional development through its OWI symposium. Of note, the PARS framework is grounded in the user's experience and

---

6   All three PARS books are available through the WAC Clearinghouse under the Practices and Possibilities series: https://wac.colostate.edu/books/practice/

7   Learn more about the Online Writing Instruction Community at https://www.owicommunity.org/

critically examines usability across three layers: design, instruction, and administration (Borgman & McArdle, 2020, 2021, and 2023). PARS is part of a larger OWI repository organized by Borgman and McArdle under the OWI Community banner.

Because professional statements and frameworks are meant to be a directional charge for writing programs and because they come from committees staffed by scholars who engage with and conduct research in effective writing instruction and use that research to inform their recommendations, we have asked authors in this collection to link their better practices to position statements and frameworks from writing studies created to guide writing instruction.

While position statements and professional organizations advising the delivery and administration of OWI exist, writing program administrators and individual educators have expressed difficulties in enacting such principles locally. Melvin Beavers (2021) noted that first-year composition programs have higher rates of contingent faculty, restricted budgets for faculty development, and increasing online offerings creating a scarcity in the resources and time needed to create and sustain meaningful OWI professional development. Writing from a technical and professional communication (TPC) perspective, Lisa Melançon's (2017) study of contingent, online TPC faculty found that these faculty often lack both access to adequate professional development and training as well as the autonomy to impact the instructional design and delivery of their online courses. Thus, we argue that our abilities to enact the practices recommended by the professional organizations above relies heavily on OWI educators' labor conditions and on institutional and programmatic attempts to offer sustained professional development specific to both online and writing contexts. To put a finer point on it, "best" practices require "best" resources and "best" working conditions, yet the multi-faceted precarity experienced by OWI educators and administrators is rarely acknowledged as a limitation to enacting such practices in real life.

THE NEED TO PROFESSIONALIZE OWI EDUCATORS

Online and networked elements are commonplace fixtures in higher education with the analog classroom as a largely anachronistic concept. Digitally enhanced education using, at the very least, learning management systems (LMSs), word processors, and discussion forum software allow every kind of course to have online spaces for file sharing, communication, and dialogue. A few data points are relevant here:

- A 2017 study conducted by Educause found that nearly every institution has an LMS in place (Pomerantz & Brooks, 2017).

- A 2019 report by the National Center for Education Statistics identified that over 7.3 million students were enrolled in online education before the pandemic.
- The Integrated Postsecondary Education Data System (IPEDS) reported that "Almost all public 4- and 2-year colleges (96 and 97 percent, respectively) offered" distance education courses and programs (Ruiz & Sun, 2021, para. 3).

Given this reality, Jason Snart explores the potential advantages of the online-enhanced classroom in *Hybrid Learning: The Perils and Promise of Blending Online and Face-to-Face Instruction in Higher Education* (2010), sharing practices for building virtual presence and bringing blogs, wikis, and social bookmarking into hybrid and on-campus courses. While these online and networked elements have become ubiquitous in higher education, educators have not always been prepared to use digital technologies to effectively achieve their learning goals.

The need to adequately support online writing educators has been a longstanding call to action in writing studies—a call that echoes the perpetually missing or underdeveloped support of education professionals that has led to the creation of professional organizations (like NCTE, CCCC, CWPA, and GSOLE, to name just a few). Two decades ago, Kristine L. Blair and Elizabeth A. Monske (2003) stated that institutions might be eager to create online courses but "often forget to create structures that help faculty in the process" of designing online courses and "fail to revise tenure, promotion, and merit documents . . . to account for increased instructor labor" (p. 447). Sadly, many of these challenges remain.

Still, we trace a formative moment in OWI educator preparation to Beth Hewett and Christa Ehmann's (2004) book, *Preparing Educators for Online Writing Instruction: Principles and Processes*. Hewett and Ehmann justify OWI as a theoretically distinct field within writing studies and argue that educators need to be properly trained to teach writing online, whether those are either "online, real-time" or "online, any time" learning environments. Since the publication of Hewett and Ehmann's book, experienced OWI scholars and educators have provided writing studies with theoretical and practical guidance related to teaching writing online. Scott Warnock's (2009) *Teaching Writing Online: How and Why* defines and describes online writing pedagogy for new-to-online writing educators. Warnock includes such on-the-ground practices as communicating with students, organizing online learning content and introducing students to this organizational structure, and fostering student-centered conversations around writing and learning. Warnock advises online writing educators against adopting too many technologies, reinforcing the importance of clarity, usability, and ease as students encounter the course and its assignments. Building on this emerging set of ideas, Hewett and DePew's (2015) edited collection *Foundational Practices of Online Writing Instruction* echoes many of these recommendations. Chapters are written by experts in the field, including many members of the CCCC Committee for Effective Practices in OWI. Hewett and DePew offer a primer in OWI and guidance for OWI pedagogy, administration, and practice.

The longstanding need to professionalize OWI educators is represented in both 2011 (Hewett et al.) and 2021 State of the Art of OWI reports (CCCC Online Writing Instruction Standing Group, 2021), completed by the CCCC Standing Group for Best Practice in OWI. Researchers note that professional development is a persistent problem with 29 percent of the 235 respondents in 2021 noting they were offered mandatory online faculty development, a decrease from the reported 48 percent in 2011. Surprisingly, this situation did not improve much as shocking details from the 2021 report include the following: 27 percent of respondents received no online-specific training and 59 percent of respondents who did receive online-specific training were not compensated (p. 9). Percentages across the 2021 and 2011 reports showed a decrease in the role subject area experts played in course development processes (decreasing from 81% in 2011 to 77% in 2021) (2021, p. 27). One possible reason researchers identify for this decrease in disciplinary experts is the outsourcing of course design to non-discipline-specific instructional designers (p. 10). While limited in the number of respondents, these data suggest OWI professionalization is not just a persistent need but a significant area where we are moving further away from meaningful, discipline-specific OWI professional development.

STUDENT ACCESS AND EQUITY IN OWI

While online learning once generated enthusiasm for its potential to increase access to education, it has also encountered criticism due to student attrition and issues of access. A large-scale (2007) study by Lin Y. Muilenburg and Zane L. Berge identified eight barriers to online learning and retention, with some barriers addressing cost and access to the hardware necessary to engage with online learning and others complicating notions of "access" (which had previously been limited to the hardware, software, and internet connectivity) to include a broader definition of access that includes the academic and technical skills needed for students to be able to self-monitor their learning in online courses. June Griffin and Deborah Minter (2013) note that, because online writing courses lack the shared in-person classroom discussion that frequently reviews and reinforces important course criteria in in-person learning, OWI courses equate to higher "literacy loads" for students. Put another way, because so much of the interpersonal communication that happens in in-person, real-time learning occurs online through course announcements, emails, discussion boards, and other written formats, students need to spend much more time reading. As the section below will go on to explain, OWI scholars have theorized pedagogical approaches that attend to student engagement, support, and retention, arguing that online learning can be just as effective as in-person learning when properly designed and supported. Others have considered how equity-driven pedagogies developed for in-person writing instruction can be critically adapted for the online learning environment, such as Angela Laflen and Mikenna Sims' (2021) chapter on ungrading in OWI. Further, critiques of access and equity are not limited to online learning modalities and often reflect larger systemic inequities impacting higher education more broadly.

An important step for inclusion in online learning is accessible course design. We are continuing to learn about universal design for learning and other teaching strategies that can lower barriers for disabled students in OWI. In his chapter "Physical and Learning Disabilities in OWI," Sushil Oswal (2015) writes that LMSs, which are the main learning environments for many OWI courses, have not been developed to be usable or accessible for students and educators with disabilities, putting even more pressure of OWI teachers to "become aware of their students' needs as learners and to begin to address the access problems of an LMS that fails the students" (p. 266). While it could be argued that the technology companies themselves are building more accessibility features into their LMSs, the fact remains that, lacking institutional policies and professional development in accessible instructional design, it remains difficult for educators to do this additional (and, most often, uncompensated) work alone even when they are interested and willing to do so. Cynthia Pengilly offers one approach for the individual assessment of accessibility and usability in course content in her (2021) chapter "Confronting Ableist Texts: Teaching Usability and Accessibility in the Online Technical Writing Classroom." Pengilly takes usability, a common framework taught in technical writing, and applies it to course design and content to both model and explicitly instruct OWI students to be accessible creators of text. While Pengilly offers an important pathway for OWI educators to individually practice their commitments to accessibility, an inability to act at the program and course level forces even more onus onto overworked educators and disabled students to self-identify, advocate, and request additional rushed retrofitting to OWI materials.

Finally, we recognize that as a field, we are learning, too. As we continue to strive to make writing studies more inclusive for all students, we cannot forget that marginalization based on sexuality, gender, disability, race, and culture intersects with issues of online learning. Online learning is not acontextual or devoid of the larger social issues that affect students' health, wellbeing, and access. In moving towards finding solutions for OWI, intersectional inclusivity must be centered. Further, we must question the technologies that support OWI. Technologies, including academic ones, are typically built by a small number of White engineers and built within capitalist structures, which have shaped the systems we exist in (Noble, 2018). Safiya Umoja Noble's argument about algorithmic systems and critical questions we might ask of them are especially important when considering LMS design and virtual conferencing platforms: who creates these systems, by whom are they intended to be used, how are they intended to be used, and in what ways do those imagined expectations conflict with the lived experiences of the students learning in online writing courses?

Precarious Labor and Status in OWI

Staffed largely by non-tenure track (NTT) and contingent faculty, online writing courses have historically relied on the labor of under-supported educators with inconsistent preparation in writing studies and online learning. During a given semester, online writing educators might teach multiple course preparations, or "preps," across multiple institutions, navigating complex ecologies of institutional bureaucracies without the security of long-term employment, let alone tenure (Murray, 2019). Many times, these instructors are not the ones who have chosen the curriculum, nor designed the online experience. The challenges of teaching online can be immense, even for instructors with the opportunity for continuing appointments or, for an even more fortunate few, the promise of tenure. Before the COVID-19 pandemic, a 2017 Educause survey of 13,541 faculty found that only 9 percent of respondents preferred to work in an online environment (p. 25). Working from 2016 data from the Bureau of Labor Statistics, Darrin S. Murray (2019) estimates there are nearly one million contingent faculty with no available data for how many of those contingent faculty teach online courses.

OWI educators include a diverse array of professionals who hold vastly different positions in their institutional communities. For instance, take NTT colleagues who might have once been described as "freeway fliers," and who now remotely teach online for several institutions; while they have access to professional development specialists, they likely cannot attend most formal on-campus real-time training and rely on a network of supervisors and peers for professional development and course design. Another example is a visiting assistant professor who is on an annual contract with a writing program where the online course curriculum is set with limited opportunities to make adjustments in learning technologies and weekly activities. Still another example is a full-time, NTT professor given a teaching assignment and learning outcomes, but no additional curriculum guidelines or materials. They must design their course to their best ability using resources for online learning on campus. The OWI community encompasses all of these individuals and more with limited access and support for professional development that fits their situation and needs. In living these professionally precarious lives as a new generation of online writing instructors, the experiences of these NTT and contingent writing faculty are underrepresented in writing studies literature—even though they serve a significant number of students each year.

The professional precarity we identify is not specific to online educational labor and extends to contract workers in all fields; still, online educators can be most impacted by inequitable working conditions related to their rank or status, teaching load, class size, and student level. Because they may not live locally to where they work, OWI educators are more likely to experience isolation and restricted access to community resources generally provided to support teaching and learning (e.g., access to Centers for Teaching and Learning). They are further limited in their teaching autonomy by master syllabi, required assignments, and course shells, which they may or may not have had a voice in designing. Finally, they are often tasked with navigating multiple modalities within the same course prep. Yet, despite their footing as practitioners in the OWI community, they may not have the time and support to conduct research, publish, and access professional organizations in writing studies or OWI.

The professional conditions for online writing educators directly relate to the labor and time needed to develop technology-based pedagogies and online instruction. Griffin and Minter (2012) write that instructors need "high-quality training" in "technological tools" and "in the teaching of writing in digital spaces" (p. 151.)—an argument that has been made by a number of professional organizations, like the American Association of University Professors (AAUP), CCCC, and GSOLE. In their principles statement, GSOLE describes effective OWI professional development as including compensation for local, discipline-specific training in addition to being supported to join OWI professional organizations, participate in OWI instructor networks, attend conferences, and engage in research and publication related to OWI (2019). Designing such professional development can be challenging, particularly for departments that lack experts in online writing instruction. To mitigate the under-preparation and lack of support of online writing educators, writing program administrators and institutional stakeholders must fight for online writing educator professionalization: adequate compensation, appropriate rank and status, access to professional development resources, and the ability to engage with a professional community of other online writing educators.

The Effects of Emergency Remote Teaching during the COVID-19 Pandemic

In addition to this professional insecurity, online writing courses are also pedagogically precarious. While classrooms are always subject to everchanging social, political, and cultural contexts, higher education and its relation to online learning has never been as unstable (Hall et al., 2020; Murgatroyd, 2021). In 2020, the COVID-19 pandemic drove 1.37 billion students and 60 million educators to emergency remote instruction (UNESCO, 2020). Without much support or preparation, every writing educator in the United States became a de facto online writing educator though, in contrast to well-designed online learning, this condition has been described in many ways, including the term "emergency remote teaching" (Hodges et al., 2020). A previously existing need to professionalize online writing educators (CCCC, 2013; GSOLE, 2019; Hewett & Ehmann, 2004) quickly became a crisis. Despite the existence of a decades-old field of online writing instruction (for a full history, see Kentnor, 2015), many institutions sought immediate, short-term solutions, investing in LMS support, platforms that could host online real-time learning (e.g., Zoom), and online surveillance testing technologies, all without sufficiently preparing educators to consider how to leverage the affordances of online learning to effectively teach within their disciplines. Put another way, although professionalization in OWI has been an ongoing conversation in scholarship for over two decades, the pandemic led to an unprecedented number of educators needing explicit support and guidance in online instruction that was discipline-specific to writing studies.

Charles Hodges and colleagues (2020) note that misinterpreting emergency online education with well-prepared online education thus perpetuated unsupported assumptions that online learning was of lower quality than face-to-face learning. In fact, as they go on to stipulate, the qualities of effective online learning as articulated by online instructional designers were largely absent in the rush to remote: namely the careful design, planning, and delivery of course content that was tailored to fit the online learning environment. Without support, many new-to-online educators struggled to recreate—or, more importantly, reimagine—their practices from face-to-face writing classrooms in online spaces. For writing teachers, especially, the lack of discipline-specific support led to frustration as they tried to move their pedagogical practices to, in some cases, online real-time learning and, in other cases, online any time learning environments with minimal adaptation.

Since the pandemic, emergency remote learning has given rise to new online and hybrid modalities, like "hyflex" learning (Beatty, 2019), and educators have been forced to translate their courses across these multiple modalities—sometimes even transforming course materials from face-to-face to online to hybrid and then back to online, all within a given semester. Some taught in completely online any time contexts, with institutions disallowing real-time meetings so that online learning happened at a time that worked for students' individual schedules and lives. Others went hybrid, teaching on campus some days and online others so that social distancing and other safety precautions could be maintained. Moreover, the introduction of video conferencing tools means that "dual delivery," "concurrent," or "hybrid flexible" formats also became a part of new expectations for teaching writing to both the "roomies" and the "Zoomies" at the same time. These modal shifts were not consistent as new variants pushed institutions temporarily online again with little advance notice to educators (Gluckman, 2021; Jaschik, 2021). Despite the longstanding need to increase professional and instructional support for online writing educators, the precarity of online writing instruction and online writing educators persisted and heightened with the COVID-19 pandemic and continued into the endemic era.

Instructional modes that heighten educator labor continue to flourish in the endemic era, creating a new landscape of learning modalities. As mentioned above, while this collection identifies four learning modalities, the pandemic has caused an explosion of learning modes to proliferate without consistency across the field in how we use the terminology for these different learning modalities. For example, the Center for Distributed Learning website at the University of Central Florida identifies five modalities with courses offered across two fully online modalities (**web-based** and **video**), two partially online modalities: **mixed mode,** which is defined as a blended format where "in-person classroom activities are more than 20% of the instructional time," and **limited attendance,** which is defined as a blended format where "in-person classroom activities may use up to 20% of the instructional time" (n.d.). Finally, of course, the traditional **in-person** learning modality remains an option. These modalities offer students flexibility and personalization. A Division of Digital Learning offers professional development, coursework on online learning, as well as personnel and web resources for designing an online course. This non-discipline-specific infrastructure does not take up pedagogies specific to writing or literacy instruction.

Despite the decades long history in OWI and the possibilities that were afforded during the COVID-19 pandemic, there is still a problem that we face in the present moment. Now more than ever before, we need to explicitly name what we do in online and hybrid writing instruction. Moreover, we need to examine—and expand a vision for—how we prepare educators to enter these literacy learning environments. Even with a field of scholarship related to online writing instruction, our current context demands closer attention to the kinds of pedagogies that can improve student writing, no matter the course modality, all with a greater focus on how we prepare and professionalize online writing educators.

With this set of concerns about modalities—as well as the other five themes identified in the literature review—the work that went into building this collection was designed to meet this moment. More than simply issuing a call for proposals, the entire process of planning for, supporting authors during the process of, and reflecting upon our "better practices" for OWI has been an interactive, sustained effort, one of which we, Amy and Troy, are humbled to have been given the opportunity to lead and describe in more detail in the section below.

THE PROCESS FOR BUILDING *BETTER PRACTICES*

This collection shares discipline-specific practices from online writing educators from diverse institutional contexts. Contributors hold a range of professional ranks, including full, tenured professors and program administrators, tenure-track and non-tenure-track faculty, contingent faculty, graduate teaching assistants, and staff administrative positions. Chapters have been designed so that readers can reflect on and apply practices in their contexts with advice from authors on moving practices across learning modalities. TILT (Transparency in Learning and Teaching)[8] assignment directions are provided in each chapter (Winklemes, et al, 2016). The TILT framework, created by Mary-Ann Winkelmes and the Transparency in Learning and Teaching in Higher Education project out of University of Illinois, Urbana-Champaign in 2009–2010, has been publicly supported by the Association of American Colleges & Universities (AAC&U), the National Institute for Learning Outcomes Assessment (NILOA), and the Association of College and University Educators (ACUE) because it helps teachers better emphasize the purpose, context, and criteria for an assignment as they communicate that assignment with students.

More than just meeting a call for proposals with a general focus, these chapters on better practices provide resources for professional learning and graduate education and capture this unique moment in the field of composition's history. Specifically, the work of building this collection had three goals:

1. to bring together diverse online writing educators to make their teaching practices more explicit,
2. to feature a set of replicable "better" practices that show ideas articulated by professional organizations in national statements in-action,
3. to validate online teacher-scholars and make their intellectual contributions to writing studies more visible.

And, while similar goals might be described for any edited collection, our process for arriving at this final publication took a very different approach.

---

[8] Learn more about the TILT framework for assignment design at https://tilthighered.com/

In the spring of 2021, Amy and Troy were collaborating as instructor-mentors in a GSOLE certification course, a course that engages new-to-online writing educators of all ranks in acquiring foundational knowledge of OWI research and practice. They noted how difficult it was to distill explicit practices from OWI research, which often discussed the theory or data collected from a practice at the 30,000-foot level. Participants in the course wanted to know more about what practices looked like on the ground so that as they moved these evidence-based practices into their courses, they knew how to deliver them.

For instance, when using alternative forms of assessment with students, we wondered: how did online educators initially explain the new assessment structure to students who were learning online any time, how did they adjust the LMS gradebook so that students were not receiving inaccurate representations of their standing in the course, and finally when and how did they intervene with students who were at risk of failing the course? While participants could easily read about and agree with the importance of a given practice, they were less sure how exactly to move that practice into their local contexts. These concerns echoed many of the needs Amy and Troy heard in faculty development workshops and meetings of writing program administration. What was needed was more pedagogical scholarship that delved into the nitty-gritty details of OWI—what the day-to-day work of teaching writing online looked like.

To develop such a collection, we knew that dialogue and engagement in a community of practice would be necessary. More than just submitting a chapter proposal and then going off to compose a draft, we wanted to intentionally design learning experiences during the second year of pandemic teaching (2021–22) that could, in and of itself, serve as a kind of professional learning and mentorship.

To that end, as part of their initial proposal process, contributors invited to attend community of practice meetings throughout the Fall 2021 semester. Across eight weeks, we as editors held two optional synchronous meetings, on Monday and Tuesday afternoons. Meetings were recorded and shared in a Google Drive folder with contributors who could not attend live. A shared document also summarized notes and important takeaways from each meeting. The series of meetings subsequently walked contributors through parts of the chapter layout document and placed them in breakout rooms where they could share drafted or outlined initial attempts of each section or could simply talk through their prewriting ideas with other contributors. During the final week, contributors exchanged full chapter drafts and discussed feedback. They had additional opportunities to participate in an asynchronous peer review process, which offered more flexible timing during the month of December.

The community of practice conversations were quite generative in that contributors were sharing ideas and offering feedback to one another at a level that is unconventional for an edited collection in writing studies. As a result, chapters reflect the cohesiveness of our shared conversations. As authors provided feedback to others through breakout room conversations, a series of serendipitous connections, lesson strategies, and, of course, "better practices" emerged. As one co-author from the collection shared with us when submitting their draft chapter, "This has been the most collaborative work I've ever undertaken, and I believe it is significantly better because of it. Our project changed pretty dramatically over the course of the last few months, and we're pleased with the product—we hope you both will be as well!" Another said, "The equity, inclusion and transparency of the process that you set up for us definitely stands out to me."

In sum, the community of practice that was developed over the entire fall semester was crucial, as the collaborations between chapter co-authors were then extended through deliberative dialogue amongst all who could attend. For instance, two of our contributors, Ingrid Bowman and Briana Westmacott, write about their experience in their (2022) article, "Empowering Teachers to Write: An Innovative Online Framework for a Community of Practice." Bowman and Westmacott described the process as "appealing and motivating" because it "enabled individuals at all career stages to feel included and equally valued" (2022, p. 191). We agree and note that as co-editors we equally felt enriched by the community of practice experience and feel more connected to a new community of online and hybrid educators.

As noted above, each chapter is co-authored by two online writing educators: one experienced with the practice being explained throughout the chapter; the other reflecting on their experience implementing the practice for the first time. The clear line that is drawn from theory to practice in each chapter helps readers grasp the hidden pedagogical knowledge that is often unarticulated in more traditional journal articles and chapters, including the teachers' lived experiences in enacting the practice, their rationale for why they use the practice, and the exact materials they use to deliver the practice in their local contexts. Aside from sharing materials that readers will need to recreate the teaching practice, the authors collectively reflect on the practice's merits and limitations, connect the practice to theory and research, and offer advice for adapting the practice under different teaching contexts (higher teaching loads, different learning modalities, etc.). By featuring a range of "better practices," this collection offers online writing educators and writing program administrators who professionalize and support online writing educators a number of theoretically grounded, student-centered practices from teacher-scholars in online writing.

Although chapters are designed to be accessible to both new-to-online and new teachers, veteran online teachers can also review chapters to learn new strategies for OWI. In offering chapters detailing a range of approaches to OWI, readers will:

- Gain a sense of which approaches and practices are possible in online and hybrid writing classrooms with those possibilities representing innovative theoretical trends in writing studies scholarship and position statements;
- Access sets of materials that can be immediately adapted for local contexts, giving them a starting place to enact better practices in OWI; and
- Acquire a set of sample materials that can be shared with online writing instructors in their program as professional development and used to develop programmatic curricular resources.

THEMES THROUGHOUT THE COLLECTION

Six themes offer readers an approach to engaging with these chapters: exploring a particular topic in OWI by identifying chapters tagged with particular themes in their abstracts. These themes emerged in our conversations with co-authors throughout the fall and from our reading of their drafts. It is no surprise, then, that these themes include a number of topics that we have already noted above related to the history of OWI and existing pedagogies:

- **Theme 1:** Chapters tagged as **"Better Practices" in Accessibility and Inclusivity** demonstrate how educators can meet technical standards for accessibility while also, and perhaps more importantly, offering instructional scaffolding that builds welcoming online communities for diverse students. Moreover, contributors help students become mindful of accessibility standards and inclusive practices as they create their writing.
- **Theme 2:** Chapters tagged as **"Better Practices" in Multimodal Learning** offer a range of composing practices that build on the rich history of multimodality in composition. Chapters include practices exploring social media, audio and video composing, and data storytelling, all the while encouraging students to produce texts for wider audiences and, in some cases, use multimodal compositions to promote social justice.
- **Theme 3:** Chapters tagged as **"Better Practices" in Motion Across Teaching and Learning Modalities** discuss how they have designed practices that can move across different modalities and explain how the affordances of different modalities can be leveraged to provide more options for students and educators.
- **Theme 4:** Chapters tagged as **"Better Practices" Adapted from Classic Composition Strategies** return us to our pedagogical roots, taking

traditional pedagogical activities from writing classrooms and adapting them to meet the unique needs of online learning. Practices examine annotation, discussion, peer response, and revision. These adaptations remind us that, when intentionally designed to leverage the affordances of online and hybrid learning, our pedagogical values can transfer.
- **Theme 5:** Chapters tagged as **"Better Practices" in Assessment** include insights on trends related to rethinking evaluation, a theme that has been pushed further in the past few years with approaches like ungrading, labor-based contracts, and alternative forms of assessment. Contributors in these chapters examine how these unique assessment opportunities can play out in online instruction.
- **Theme 6:** Chapters tagged as **"Better Practices" in Professional Learning for Online Teachers** turn the focus from students to our colleagues and look at ways in which we can better prepare online teachers. Contributors share professional development related to creating teacher presence, communicating with students, scaffolding online instruction, and embracing alternative assessments in the context of collegial dialogue.

CONCLUSION: TOWARD BETTER PRACTICES IN OWI

As a collection, *Better Practices* is a response to the persisting precarity of OWI and the need to more explicitly name what we do in online writing courses. These concerns are articulated by the voices of OWI practitioners from a variety of teaching contexts, all of whom were building mentoring relationships along the way. By offering explicit conversations and pedagogical materials about teaching online writing well, we hope to assist faculty and administrators in implementing "better" practices in their courses and programs that intentionally enact theoretically informed practices from CCCC, GSOLE, PARS, and NCTE. Chapters clearly identify the primary modality(ies) associated with each practice while offering suggestions for adapting these practices across modalities. The TILT framework for assignment design offers clear and explicit moves instructors want their students to make and details a step-by-step guide for implementing the practice.

As we close this introduction and move into the collection itself, we pause for a moment to appreciate an anecdote from one of our authors in the final stages of revision. As Ana Contreras, a co-author with Troy, was putting the final revisions on the TILT section of her chapter—and thinking about how she would use the assignment in the current semester that she was about to begin teaching—she lamented, "You made me think more about every move in this one lesson than I had thought about in almost all of my lessons last semester!" Far from seeing this as a criticism, we are heartened by this revelation, and heard echoes of this refrain from other authors.

Teaching and learning online, in general and for writing teachers in particular, continues to create new spaces for us to talk about both what we do as well as why we do it. Through our community of practice meetings, consistent feedback from knowledgeable peers, and a clear focus on making our teaching practices explicit, we (both Amy and Troy, as well as all the authors in the collection) can take comfort in the fact that—while it is a difficult task to articulate what we do as teachers and exactly why we do it—the results in these chapters shows that a reflective, intentional approach can lead to better teaching in OWI, across modalities, time frames, and institutional expectations.

Rather than rest in the precarious situations in which we often find ourselves, we invite you to move toward "better practices" in your teaching of OWI, learning with and from 43 of your colleagues in the chapters ahead.

REFERENCES

Beatty, B. J. (2019). Beginnings. In *Hybrid-flexible course design*. EdTech Books. https://edtechbooks.org/hyflex/book_intro.

Beavers, M. (2021). Administrative rhetorical mindfulness: A professional development framework for administrators in higher education. *Academic Labor: Research and Artistry, 5*(1). https://digitalcommons.humboldt.edu/alra/vol5/iss1/9.

Blair, K. & Monske, E. (2003). Cui bono?: Revisiting the promises and perils of online learning. *Computers and Composition, 20*(4), 441–453. https://doi.org/10.1016/j.compcom.2003.08.016.

Borgman, J. (2019). Dissipating hesitation: Why online instructors fear multimodal assignments and how to overcome the fear. In S. Khadka & J. C. Lee (Eds.), *Bridging the multimodal gap: From theory to practice* (pp. 43–67). Utah State University Press. https://doi.org/10.7330/9781607327974.c005.

Borgman, J. & McArdle, C. (2019). *Personal, accessible, responsive, strategic: Resources and strategies for online writing instructors*. The WAC Clearinghouse; University Press of Colorado. https://doi.org/10.37514/PRA-B.2019.0322.

Borgman, J. & McArdle, C. (Eds.). (2021). *PARS in practice: More resources and strategies for online writing instructors*. The WAC Clearinghouse; University Press of Colorado. https://doi.org/10.37514/PRA-B.2021.1145.

Borgman, J. & McArdle, C. (Eds.). (2023). *PARS in charge: Resources and strategies for online writing program leaders*. The WAC Clearinghouse; University Press of Colorado. https://doi.org/10.37514/PRA-B.2023.1985.

Bowman, I. & Westmacott, B. (2022). Empowering teachers to write: An innovative online framework for a community of practice. *The Chronicle of Mentoring & Coaching, 15*(6), 186–192.

Brass, J. (2014). English, literacy and neoliberal policies: Mapping a contested moment in the United States. *English Teaching: Practice and Critique, 13*(1), 112–133.

CCCC Online Writing Instruction Standing Group. (2021). *The 2021 state of the art of OWI report. Conference on College Composition and Communication.* https://sites.google.com/view/owistandinggroup/state-of-the-art-of-owi-2021.

Cicchino, A., DePew, K., Warnock, S. & Snart, J. (2021). Course design: Online writing instruction, professional development, GSOLE. *Composition Studies, 49*(3), 101–117.

Conference on College Composition and Communication. (2013, March 13). *A position statement of principles and example effective practices for Online Writing Instruction (OWI). National Council of Teachers of English.* https://cdn.ncte.org/nctefiles/groups/cccc/owiprinciples.pdf.

Conference on College Composition and Communication. (2015). *Principles for the postsecondary teaching of writing. National Council of Teachers of English.* NCTE. https://cccc.ncte.org/cccc/resources/positions/postsecondarywriting.

Council of Writing Program Administrators, National Council of Teachers of English & National Writing Project. (2011, January). *Framework for success in postsecondary writing.* https://wpacouncil.org/aws/CWPA/pt/sd/news_article/242845/_PARENT/layout_details/false.

Cuban, L. (2010, February 3). The sham of "best practices." Larry Cuban on School Reform and Classroom Practice. *Wordpress.* https://larrycuban.wordpress.com/2010/02/03/the-sham-of-best-practices/.

Edge, J. & Richards, K. (1998). Why best practice is not good enough. *TESOL Quarterly, 32*(3), 569–576.

Educause. (2017, Mar.). *Training and certifications.* https://www.educause.edu/focus-areas-and-initiatives/policy-and-security/cybersecurity-program/resources/information-security-guide/career-and-workforce-development/training-and-certifications.

Global Society of Online Literacy Educators (GSOLE). (2021). Certification courses. https://gsole.org/certification.

GSOLE Executive Board. (2019, June 13). *Online literacy instruction principles and tenets.* Global Society of Online Literacy Educators. https://gsole.org/oliresources/oliprinciples.

Gluckman, N. (2021, December 15). More campuses go remote amid rising cases and evidence of omicron. *The Chronicle of Higher Education.* https://www.chronicle.com/blogs/live-coronavirus-updates/more-campuses-go-remote-amid-rising-cases-and-evidence-of-omicron.

Griffin, J. & Minter, D. (2013). The rise of the online writing classroom: Reflecting on the material conditions of college composition teaching. *College Composition and Communication, 65*(1), 140–161.

Hall, T., Connolly, C., Ó Grádaigh, S., Burden, K., Kearney, M., Schuck, S., Bottema, J., Cazemier, G., Hustinx, W., Evens, M., Koenraad, T., Makridou, E. & Kosmas, P. (2020). Education in precarious times: a comparative study across six countries to identify design priorities for mobile learning in a pandemic. *Information and*

Learning Sciences, 121(5/6), 433–442. https://doi.org/10.1108/ILS-04-2020-0089.

Hewett, B. L. & DePew, K. E. (2015). *Foundational practices of online writing instruction*. The WAC Clearinghouse; Parlor Press. https://doi.org/10.37514/PER-B.2015.0650.

Hewett, B. L. & Ehmann, C. (2004). *Preparing educators for online writing instruction: Principles and processes*. National Council of Teachers of English.

Hewett, B. L., Minter, D., Gibson, K., Meloncon, L., Oswal, S., Olsen, L., Warnock, S., Ehmann Powers, C., Newbold, W. W., Drew, J., Kevin Eric De Pew, K. E. (2011). *Initial report of the CCCC committee for best practices in online writing instruction (OWI)*. CCCC Committee for Best Practices in Online Writing Instruction. https://www.owicommunity.org/uploads/5/2/3/5/52350423/owi_state-of-art_report_april_2011.pdf.

Hodges, C., Moore, S., Lockee, B., Trust, R. & Bond, A. (2020, Mar. 27). The difference between emergency remote teaching and online learning. *Educause Review*. https://er.educause.edu/articles/2020/3/the-difference-between-emergency-remote-teaching-and-online-learning.

Jaschik, S. (2021, December 20). *COVID-19 changes plans for next semester*. Inside Higher Ed. https://www.insidehighered.com/news/2021/12/20/colleges-adjust-plans-because-covid-19.

Kentnor, H. E. (2015). Distance education and the evolution of online learning in the United States. *Curriculum and Teaching Dialogue, 17*, 21–35.

Laflen, A. & Sims, M. (2021). Designing a more equitable scorecard: Grading contracts and online writing instruction. In J. Borgman & C. McArdle (Eds.), *PARS in practice: More resources and strategies for online writing instructors* (pp. 119–139). The WAC Clearinghouse; University Press of Colorado. https://doi.org/10.37514/PRA-B.2021.1145.2.07.

Meloncon, L., England, P. & Ilyasova, A. (2016). A portrait of non-tenure-track faculty in technical and professional communication: Results of a pilot study. *Journal of Technical Writing and Communication, 46*(2), 206–235. https://doi.org/10.1177/0047281616633601.

Muilenburg, L. Y. & Berge, Z. L. (2005). Student barriers to online learning: A factor analytic study. *Distance Education, 26*(1), 29–48. https://doi.org/10.1080/01587910500081269.

Murgatroyd, S. (2021). The precarious futures for online learning. *Revista Paraguaya de Educación a Distancia, 2*(2), 5–19.

Murray, D. S. (2019). The precarious new faculty majority: Communication and instruction research and contingent labor in higher education. *Communication Education, 68*(2), 235–245. https://doi.org/10.1080/03634523.2019.1568512.

Noble, S. U. (2022). *Algorithms of oppression*. NYU Press.

Oswal, S. (2015). Physical and learning disabilities in OWI. In B. Hewett & K. DePew (Eds.), *Foundational practices of online writing instruction* (pp. 259–295). The WAC Clearinghouse; Parlor Press. https://doi.org/10.37514/PER-B.2015.0650.2.08.

Pengilly, C. (2021). Confronting ableist texts: Teaching usability and accessibility in the online technical writing classroom. In J. Borgman & C. McArdle (Eds.), *PARS in practice: More resources and strategies for online writing instructors* (pp. 153–166). The WAC Clearinghouse; University Press of Colorado. https://doi.org/10.37514/PRA-B.2021.1145.2.09.

Pomerantz, J. & Brooks, D. C. (2017). ECAR study of faculty and information technology, Research report. *EDUCAUSE Center for Analysis and Research, 43*. https://library.educause.edu/-/media/files/library/2017/10/facultyitstudy2017.pdf.

National Center for Education Statistics. (2019). The NCES fast facts: Distance learning. https://nces.ed.gov/fastfacts/display.asp?id=80.

National Council of Teachers of English. (2016). Professional knowledge for the teaching of writing. National Council of Teachers of English. https://ncte.org/statement/teaching-writing/.

Niyozov, S. & Tarc, P. (Eds.). (2014, April 25). *Working with, against and despite global "best practices": Educational conversations around the globe* [Symposium compendium]. Western Education and the University of Toronto OISE, Ontario Institute for Studies in Education, Toronto, Canada. https://www.oise.utoronto.ca/oldcidec/UserFiles/File/Website/Compendium_GBP_Final_Jan_2016.pdf.

Ruiz, R. & Sun, J. (2021, February 17). Distance education in college: What do we know from IPEDS. *NCES Blog*. https://nces.ed.gov/blogs/nces/post/distance-education-in-college-what-do-we-know-from-ipeds.

Snart, J. A. (2010). *Hybrid learning: The perils and promise of blending online and face-to-face instruction in higher education*. Praeger.

TILT Higher Ed. (n.d.). *Transparency in learning & teaching*. Retrieved January 2, 2024, from https://tilthighered.com/.

Winklemes, M. A., Bernacki, M., Butler, J., Zochowski, M., Golanics, J. & Harriss Weavil, K. (2016). A teaching intervention that increases underserved college students' success. *Peer Review*, Winter/Spring, 31–36.

United Nations Educational, Scientific and Cultural Organization (UNESCO). (2020, March 24). *1.37 billion students now home as COVID-19 school closures expand, ministers scale up multimedia approaches to ensure learning continuity* [Press release]. https://www.unesco.org/en/articles/137-billion-students-now-home-covid-19-school-closures-expand-ministers-scale-multimedia-approaches.

University of Central Florida. (n.d.). Webcourses@UCF support. *Center for Distributed Learning (UCF)*. Retrieved September 23, 2023, from https://www.ucf.edu/online/student-resources/webcoursesucf-support/.

CHAPTER 1.

USING PUSH NOTIFICATIONS TO ESTABLISH TEACHER PRESENCE IN HYBRID/ONLINE COURSES

Theresa (Tess) Evans and A.J. Rivera
Miami University (Ohio)

*In this chapter, the authors describe **push notifications** used in online, real-time learning; online, any time learning; and hybrid learning. Specifically, the authors offer guidance for using announcements in the LMS as push notifications, which are messages forwarded to mobile devices that encourage users to tap into the course app, as a practice to promote social, cognitive, and teacher presence in online learning. In describing their "better practice," this chapter addresses the themes of Accessibility and Inclusivity and Professional Learning for Online Teachers.*

FRAMEWORKS AND PRINCIPLES IN THIS CHAPTER

- **Global Society of Online Literacy Educators (GSOLE) Principle 1.2:** Use of technology should support stated course objectives, thereby not presenting an undue burden for instructors and students.
- **Jessie Borgman and Casey McArdle's PARS framework:** Instruction is grounded in user experience to ensure that it is **personal, accessible, responsive, and strategic.** All four PARS terms are discussed in this chapter.
- **Council of Writing Program Administrators (CWPA), National Council of Teachers of English (NCTE), and National Writing Project (NWP) Framework for Success in Postsecondary Writing:** Instruction encourages *persistence*, "the ability to sustain interest in, and attention to, short- and long-term projects."

GUIDING QUESTIONS BEFORE YOU BEGIN READING

- How can a strategic push notification program improve course design and help scaffold students through the work of the semester?

- How can push notifications help students persist in completing course assignments?
- Why should instructors carefully consider the timing and frequency of push notifications?
- How can instructors ensure their push notification program aligns with the PARS approach, which values being personable, accessible, responsive, and strategic?

INTRODUCTION

We are bombarded constantly with push notifications. Emergency notifications from our institutions. Weather alerts. Calendar reminders about upcoming meetings. Social media notifications about who just posted or what news is trending. Resisting the urge to click into those notifications depends largely on how compelling the message is and how important the information is to us in that moment.

And, whether we realize it or not, many of us are already using push notifications when we send out messages from our LMS.

One morning on the way to campus, Tess got stuck in a traffic jam due to an accident and realized she would not make it on time to her first class of the day. After initially panicking, she remembered she had the power to immediately alert her students. She got on the mobile app for the LMS and sent an announcement to students with the subject line: "Class canceled: Stuck in traffic." When she arrived at the classroom 15 minutes late, she was relieved that not one student had shown up for class or sent an email asking where she was. Everyone had received the message.

While that example shows the advantage of push notifications for late-breaking news, we can also use push notifications to create a better practice for online instruction, one that would more effectively establish teacher presence and improve student engagement.

STUMBLING UPON THE USE OF PUSH NOTIFICATIONS FOR A FAST-PACED ONLINE COURSE

In January of 2019, Tess began teaching a 21-day online version of a required advanced communication course for business students offered during a mini-semester just prior to the start of spring semester. An obvious downside of such a short time frame is the intense workload for both students and instructor. Aside from a couple of synchronous small group meetings for team projects, the course was mostly asynchronous, which created communication challenges.

Course materials were set up on the institution's Canvas LMS prior to the start of the course, so much of the day-to-day work for the instructor focused on feedback, grading, and responding to many student emails throughout the day. Tess quickly discovered that she was spending too much time either following up on missed assignments or answering emails from students who were asking about information that was already provided. Students seemed to be going directly into the Canvas calendar or "To Do" list to get to assignment forums, bypassing the supporting resources in the modules.

Tess realized that students were not always on their laptops, but they did tend to have immediate access to their mobile devices. She began to wonder if sending daily reminders that went directly to their mobile devices would be a pre-emptive move to reduce confusion about tasks. This assumption that students might download and use the app soon became a core part of the course design.

When she taught the course again in the summer of 2019, Tess set up a series of delayed-release Canvas Announcements that provided links to the assignments due each day and a link to the module. She added a statement directing students to go to the module for additional resources related to those assignments. Creating this series of messages ahead of time forced Tess to continually revisit the schedule, which helped her to recognize and adjust points of assignment overload or inadequate lead times for drafts.

Once the course began, reminders were automatically pushed out daily at 8:00 a.m. That semester Tess noticed fewer questions about where to find information and fewer missed assignments. Students received consistent, transparent communication and a daily reminder that they were taking a course with an instructor who was present. The reminders also provided support to students who struggled with time management or struggled to manage the rapid pace of a mini-semester course.

Tess had downloaded the instructor version of the mobile Canvas app, which notified her of student submissions and the release of announcements. One benefit of delayed-release announcements that Tess had not expected was experiencing, first-hand, her own enhanced teacher presence in the course. As she sipped her morning coffee, in a kind of out-of-body experience, Tess received the same alert on her mobile device that students received, which was herself reminding everyone about the tasks for the day. She began to look forward to the messages "past Tess" set up once she was immersed in the day-to-day tasks of running the course. She found it helpful to be reminded of what to expect students to be working on, especially when focused on responding to drafts or grading assignments already completed.

Fast forward to Fall 2020. Our state university, which is a mostly residential campus, had moved courses online for the first five weeks of fall semester, with students choosing to live on campus or complete the semester fully remote. The semester had unique challenges because, in addition to teaching four sections of technical writing, Tess was mentoring graduate assistants teaching the course for the first time—who were also teaching online for the first time. To accommodate university requirements in Fall 2020 that synchronous sessions be offered at least in some manner, they met with their students in small groups for weekly sessions of about 30 minutes. With the less-frantic pace of a 15-week semester and the weekly class meetings, Tess did not immediately think to use the system of delayed-release announcements.

Neither the undergraduate students nor the graduate teaching assistants had signed up for an online experience, which resulted in confusion, discomfort, and some resistance.

Tess noticed that students still needed an extra nudge to help them find the information and do the work—whether readings for discussion or assignments they needed to post. She returned to the practice of using delayed-release announcements, which proved valuable throughout a semester of shifting circumstances from online, to partially face to face, and back again to online as COVID-19 cases rose. Despite all the confusion, students could count on her presence through those push notifications.

STUMBLING THROUGH ONLINE INSTRUCTION FOR THE FIRST TIME DURING COVID-19

For the Fall 2020 semester, A.J. was one of the doctoral students[1] teaching online for the first time. Prior to 2020, his lack of online teaching experience had not been much of a concern. While he had taught many courses at different colleges before that semester, A.J. had never needed to teach an online course.

To complicate matters, that fall was the first semester A.J. taught technical writing. Part of the stress of teaching this new course in this new context was alleviated by the existence of a master course for the online version of technical writing, which Tess designed the previous summer. Although this master template was intended for the six-week online version of the course, it was easily adapted for the full semester, and it did provide support on two levels: should an instructor have become sick, another could take over their class without much hardship or adjustment needed; also, major assignment descriptions, as well as suggested daily activities, were included. Even with this fairly well-organized course template, though, students had trouble remembering where to look for activities or guidelines they would need.

---

1 Update: A.J. completed his PhD in Composition and Rhetoric in 2023.

As these types of problems emerged or issues needed to be addressed, A.J. would communicate with students. For A.J., this communication took the form of announcements sent out through Canvas to explain whatever the problem was. A student had a question about an assignment? Other students might have the same question, so send an announcement. A due date needed to be changed for whatever reason? Send an announcement. A link in the course page was broken or a page was unpublished? Send an announcement. Some of these messages would end up being fairly long, and, particularly as the semester went on, A.J. would end up sending announcements multiple times a week, if not daily, with no real strategy or planning behind these messages. The lack of organization and the erratic timing of his messaging resulted in confusion for both students and instructor.

Changing Practices to Address Changing Habits of Interaction

The experiences of Tess and A.J. led them to reconsider how students were accessing and engaging with course content and to think more strategically about how to communicate with students in digital forums. Not only did they want to increase student engagement and success, but they also wanted to focus their time and energies more productively.

With increased student engagement as a goal, and increased teacher presence as a strategy to achieve that goal, our chapter provides guidance for strategically communicating with students through regular, consistent messaging designed to keep students on track to successfully complete the course. Instructors can plan and set up messages ahead of time, saving themselves time and stress once the course gets underway. If those pre-scheduled messages can be edited right up to the release time (as they can in Canvas), then instructors are also in a better position to respond flexibly to needed adjustments in the course.

SCHOLARSHIP, THEORIES, AND PRINCIPLES THAT GUIDE OUR APPROACH

The theory informing our practice is the **Community of Inquiry Framework,** developed by D. Randy Garrison and colleagues (2000), which considers how **social presence, cognitive presence,** and **teacher presence** intersect to create the educational experience in online any time text-based environments.

Garrison et al. (2000) noted that, from the collaborative constructionist point of view, "Collaboration is seen as an essential aspect of cognitive development since cognition cannot be separated from the social context" (p. 92). The social presence and cognitive presence within a course depend on how effectively teacher presence is established (Garrison et al., 2000). The crucial role of teacher presence has evolved over time, as technology has advanced from asynchronous, text-only capabilities to more synchronous interactions through text messaging, real-time collaborative document editing, and videoconferencing. The strategies we use to communicate with our students must also evolve to keep up with the changing ways in which they interact with course materials.

Instructor-created push notifications promote **social presence** by emphasizing that teachers—and students—are real persons in a collaborative working relationship with one another, a fact that can be forgotten in the asynchronous online classroom. Push notifications promote **cognitive presence** by reminding students about assignments and directing them to information that can be accessed from their mobile devices. Push notifications can establish **teacher presence** if messages are clearly written by the instructor, even if that instructor is teaching from a course template designed by someone else.

Our practice also follows Jessie Borgman and Casey McArdle's (2019) PARS framework of Personal, Accessible, Responsive, and Strategic course design and teaching practices. The PARS framework suggests that instructors have a duty to be personal and personable, accessible to students, responsive to student requests for help, and strategic in their pedagogy, course design, and administration. The practice of strategic messaging—whether through push notifications or some other means—is aligned with the PARS framework in notable and important ways. Strategic course design is just the beginning of teacher presence: publishing a course with assignments mapped out and activities and readings already accessible allows for the instructor to focus on being personable and responsive—but only if students are proactively engaging with the course. Proactively establishing teacher presence through push notifications helps ensure that messaging stays focused more on encouragement and course progression than on frustrated or missing students.

The Global Society of Online Literacy Educators' (GSOLE) *Online Literacy Instruction Principles and Tenets* (2019) also work in tandem with the PARS framework. Principle 1 states that "Online literacy instruction should be universally accessible and inclusive," and under this larger umbrella exists the tenet that the "Use of technology should support stated course objectives, thereby not presenting an undue burden for instructors and students." The use of push notifications requires careful consideration of timing and frequency to ensure they are a help, not a burden.

A system of strategic messaging also aligns with *persistence*, from the *Framework for Success in Postsecondary Writing*; in particular, push notifications can encourage students "to follow through, over time, to complete tasks, processes, or projects" (Council of Writing Program Administrators et al., 2011). While some could consider these constant reminders enabling, we instead look at them as a gentle reminder for our students who are often juggling multiple courses, jobs, volunteerism, and other commitments, providing them with the ability to remain persistent in their work.

COURSE CONTEXT AND LESSON

Both Tess and A.J. teach in the department of English at a midsize state university in the midwestern United States. The campus is primarily residential. The courses we have recently taught are designed to satisfy the advanced writing requirement for majors such as engineering, computer science, business, statistics, and data analytics.

At our institution, three-week online courses are offered during the winter session and four- or six-week online courses are offered during the eight-week summer session. Only occasionally are online courses offered during regular semesters at the main campus. For instance, in the Fall 2021 semester, the department offered seven sections of technical writing (the course that A.J. was teaching). Two of those sections were offered as online courses; both were asynchronous and taught by an adjunct instructor. Tess has occasionally taught technical writing online or in a hybrid format during the regular semester to accommodate a long student waitlist or the constraints of limited classroom space.

Our institution uses Canvas as its LMS for all courses. Canvas offers a number of features, including the Canvas mobile app that is available for students and faculty, along with the push notifications that can be sent via this app. Push notifications can be a useful tool in addressing one of the biggest challenges for online instructors: maintaining presence in a course with limited or nonexistent synchronous interactions. Even web-enhanced in-person courses today require strategies for maintaining presence for those students who miss class meetings, particularly in an era of less stringent policies on attendance and a movement towards more flexibility in attendance requirements.

As previously mentioned, push notifications have become a fairly common medium for communication. The teacher version of the Canvas mobile app automatically sends push notifications to alert instructors of student submissions, and it allows instructors to create push notifications through the Announcements function. Announcements are automatically sent to a student's email, and they are also sent out as push notifications to the student's mobile devices, provided the student has downloaded the Canvas app. This direct messaging can go a long way to help students remember important assignments and deadlines, as well as direct them to useful course materials that are already available to them.

With our past experiences in mind, we were curious as to how many students were using the Canvas mobile app. An informal raise-of-hands survey of our Fall

2021 students at the beginning of the semester seemed to indicate that most students had downloaded the Canvas app and relied on their mobile devices, at least periodically, for accessing and receiving information about their courses. We conducted an IRB-exempted survey of our students at midterm to find out where students were going to find out about upcoming assignments and how they rated the helpfulness of our push notifications about upcoming assignments and due dates.

We had 20 respondents out of the 97 students who received the survey (23 students in the in-person technical writing course section taught by A.J. and 74 students in four hybrid business communication course sections taught by Tess). Out of those 20 respondents, 18 reported using the Canvas App; 16 rated Canvas Announcements as "very helpful" or "helpful"; and two rated the announcements as "neither helpful nor unhelpful" (n=20). None of the respondents rated Canvas Announcements as "somewhat unhelpful" or "very unhelpful."

The survey also asked students to identify all the places they go to find out what assignments are due. The results seem to confirm our suspicion that students often bypass the Canvas course site and go directly to the Canvas To Do list, which appears on the Canvas dashboard and shows students what is due for all their courses.

- The To Do list came in first, with notifications through the Canvas mobile app coming in second. Canvas email notifications and the Canvas calendar tied as the third most accessed. Of interest to us is that the To Do list and the Canvas calendar require a student to proactively seek out the information those forums provide. Notifications through the Canvas mobile app or through student email are passive sources of information.
- The Canvas Announcements forum itself ranked a distant fourth as a place to find out what assignments were due (all announcements are saved in a forum on the Canvas site; students can also access the forum from their mobile device).
- The last place students looked for course information was the Canvas Course Summary, which lists all published assignments in order of due date (published assignments also populate the To Do list and the Canvas Calendar). This result was surprising to Tess because, during the initial years following the university switch to Canvas in 2015, direct student feedback consistently showed a strong reliance on the Course Summary. Perhaps preferences have shifted as students have shifted to using the mobile app.
- The Canvas To Do list shows up on the Canvas Dashboard and within the Canvas course; however, students are more likely to go to the Canvas

Dashboard version of the To Do list, where they can find upcoming due dates for every class they are taking, not just ours. We believe that push notifications can provide the "nudge" students need to successfully complete assignments for our course. The messages can direct students into the course site and help students understand that their teacher is a human being who is present for them and accessible to them.

Our experience—and our survey—suggested that a strong reason for considering the use of push notifications is that the way students access information today may be changing. They may have been conditioned to wait for reminders or may be contending with information overload. Perhaps future studies will confirm a change in the cognitive processes of students, which will help instructors to understand why students seem to have difficulty finding information on course sites, even when the organizational pattern is explained to them. In the meantime, students are using their mobile devices more than ever to access course materials and even to complete assignments—and that is true for all delivery platforms, including web-enhanced in-person courses.

Establishing the Purpose of Push Notifications

In order to demonstrate the usefulness of push notifications, we can apply the Transparency in Learning and Teaching (TILT) framework to describe the purpose of this practice, the tasks involved in the practice itself, and the criteria that would make this practice successful. As mentioned earlier, the theory informing our practice is the community of inquiry framework, developed by Garrison et al. (2000), which considers how social presence, cognitive presence, and teacher presence intersect to create the educational experience in asynchronous online environments. Research on push notifications in online instruction is limited, but existing studies do point to possibilities that would serve our purpose: to enhance student engagement, increase student perception of teacher presence, improve course accessibility, and help online teachers better manage their workload. Among these studies, the following themes emerge:

Accessibility of Course Design Helps to Ensure Push Notifications are Effective.

The best way to achieve presence in an online course is through frequent announcements that remind students of the importance of reading instructor-provided resources, while ensuring that assignment instructions are clear and provided in both written and audio format (Fendler, 2021). For us, this means designing our Canvas pages for optimal use with screen readers and providing short, captioned video introductions for each module.

Even in a web-enhanced in-person course, oral announcements in class are sometimes followed by reminders sent digitally, so instructors must consider how students are accessing and experiencing digital messages. A user-centered design "places the student experience at the heart of the course" (Greer & Skurat Harris, 2018, p. 22). The multiple ways students access course content also suggests that "digital" and "device" must be considered together and separately:

- **User-centered design for digital environments**: Whether designing assignment prompts, syllabi, or course calendars, instructors need to be wary of simply replicating the kinds of documents and distribution practices used in the in-person classroom. Jessie Borgman and Jason Dockter (2018) have argued that, in online spaces, how course materials are created, included, and accessed within a course is just as important as the content of those materials. Abdulsalam Alhazmi and colleagues (2021) noted that student engagement is often improved by integrating updated text, audio, and video features in the LMS, making it important to consider what adjustments or updates may be needed to our course sites.
- **User-centered design specific to mobile devices**: A survey of 64,536 students at 130 higher education institutions found that 95 percent of students had smartphones (Galanek et al., 2018). Similarly, Pew Research Center (2021) reported that 96 percent of Americans ages 18–29 own smartphones. Given that some students rely mostly on their mobile devices, instructors should design a course that welcomes all students, no matter how they access course materials (Baldwin & Ching, 2020). That requires going into the mobile app to find out how announcements look on a smaller screen and how students can interact with the course site and its materials. For example, tables tend to get cut off in the mobile app, but a vertical listing format works well on both large and small screens.

The appearance and functionality of a Canvas Announcement can shift, depending on the digital platform from which it is accessed and on the type of device used by the viewer, e.g., a laptop computer or mobile device. Figures 1.1, 1.2, and 1.3 show how a message with embedded video is displayed differently when viewed on a laptop screen through the Canvas Announcements forum, on a laptop via Gmail message, and on a mobile device via push notification on the Canvas App. In the Canvas Announcement forum, the video is immediately visible and ready to play by clicking on the start arrow (Figure 1.1). In the Gmail message, the video link disappears: Students must click "View Announcement," which takes them into the Canvas Announcement forum (Figure 1.2). In the Canvas mobile app, the video is accessed by clicking on the "Launch External Tool" button (Figure 1.3).

Using Push Notifications to Establish Teacher Presence

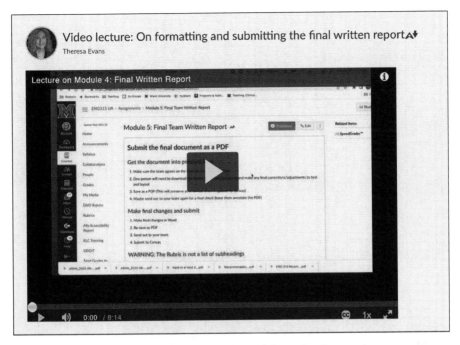

Figure 1.1. How a message looks when viewed from the Canvas Announcements forum on a laptop.

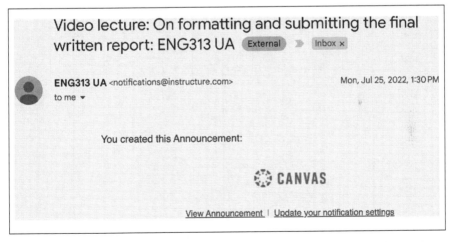

Figure 1.2. How the same message in Figure 1.1 appears in a Gmail message on a laptop. Note: The message appears to come from the system rather than the instructor; students click the "View Announcement" link to get to the Canvas Announcement that hosts the video.

Figure 1.3. How the same message from Figures 1.1 and 1.2 is viewed on a mobile device via push notification from the Canvas App. Note: Students click on the "Launch External Tool" button to get to the video player.

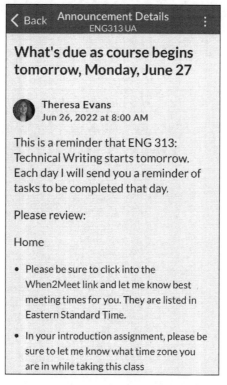

Figure 1.4. Push notifications can increase the perception of teacher presence in the course.

A study conducted by Cathy Stone and Matthew Springer (2019) found that course design and instructor presence are the top two criteria students use to rate the quality of online instruction. Themes emerging from a study by Logan Rath and colleagues (2019) also suggested that students want effective communication from the online instructor and clear course organization.

Kathleen Sitzman and Debra Woodard Leners (2006) have argued that announcements can do more than provide information: They can express empathy for students, demonstrate the teacher's expertise, and encourage students in their efforts. Students sometimes confuse automated notifications from the LMS (grades released, for example) with instructor-created notifications, so messages should be written in such a way that they are clearly coming from the teacher, rather than a system.

Broader research on the use of push notifications has led to insights that can assist teachers in developing a system of consistent messaging:

- **The subject line of a push notification should grab attention and compel students to tap into the message.** A study by Atilla Wohllebe and colleagues (2021) found that compelling subject lines positively correlate with users tapping into messages, which suggests that subject lines should clearly indicate need-to-know information.
- **Optimal timing and frequency of push notifications may be an art in itself.** Xuan-Lam Pham and colleagues (2016) have argued that engagement increases with the use of push notifications; however, too frequent notifications can have the opposite effect. Decisions about frequency may depend on the length of the course and the particular student cohort. It is worth noting, again, that Tess's push notifications went out regularly at 8:00 a.m. each morning, with only sparing use of notifications otherwise.
- **Push notifications can help ease instructor workload.** In a study on faculty perceptions of workload and the value of efficiency, Lori J. Cooper and colleagues (2019) reported that both adjunct and full-time faculty agreed that push notifications to students beyond the online classroom were helpful in improving student engagement and managing instructor workload. A planned communication strategy takes some up-front labor, but it does save time during the run of the course.

Outlining Tasks and Criteria for Strategic Communication

What follows are tasks and criteria for strategic communication using the Canvas LMS platform, based on our own practice (see Figures 1.1, 1.2, 1.3, and 1.4). While our own practice is based on the Announcements function in Canvas, which, in turn, syncs with the function of push notifications in the mobile app, we can also envision other technologies that might offer similar affordances. For example, instructors may be able to send push notifications through a GroupMe chat, a blog, or a closed social media group. If the platform does not offer the ability to schedule posts, the instructor can copy-and-paste from pre-written messages, on an as-needed basis.

Establish a Communication Schedule

Our first task is to work out the schedule for the course and set due times/dates for assignments. Next, we take a look at the Course Summary: The assignment links populate that list once the due dates and times are added and the assignment is published (see Figure 1.5). We make sure all assignments are published and show up on the Course Summary before messages are pushed out—otherwise, students will not be able to access the assignments through any links we embed.

Published Canvas Assignments are pushed out automatically to student To Do lists each day, along with the assignments for every other course a student is taking. This may help explain why students tend to actively engage most often through the To Do list: They are looking at all the tasks for the day, not just those for our class.

Course Summary:

Date	Details	Due
Mon Jun 27, 2022	Introduce yourself to your classmates	due by 1pm
	TC Ch 14: Corresponding in Print and Online	due by 1pm
Tue Jun 28, 2022	Resume Draft (Peer Response due 11:59pm)	due by 1pm
	TC Ch 1: Intro to Tech Comm & Ch 15: Applying for a Job	due by 1pm
	LinkedIn Profile Analysis	due by 5pm
Wed Jun 29, 2022	Cover Letter Draft	due by 1pm
	TC Ch 3: Writing Technical Documents	due by 1pm
Thu Jun 30, 2022	TC Ch 10: Writing Correct and Effective Sentences	due by 1pm

Figure 1.5. Published assignments as shown in Canvas Course Summary. Note: Course Summary shows published assignments, which also populate the Canvas Calendar the Canvas To Do.

This also explains why students may miss resources they need to do their work: If links to the module do not appear within the assignment, some students may not think to seek out those resources. We now embed links to relevant Canvas pages and other resources within each Canvas Assignment, which also helps streamline the effort to create push notifications.

Some might wonder why we go to all this effort; however, we believe it is crucial to create and schedule messages to establish our personal presence in the course.

After working out the course schedule and publishing assignments, we consider the following tasks as we schedule push notifications:

- **Deciding how many messages per week are needed.** For a regular semester course, we encourage students to vote for the best days and times for releasing push notifications. For courses with a shorter time frame, we let students know ahead of time how often and at what times they can expect to receive notifications (see Figure 1.3).
- **Using a combination of scheduled and unscheduled push notifications.** A mix of spontaneous and scheduled messages can increase our presence in the course from the perspective of students. These messages can also continually remind students that they are indeed taking a course and have tasks to complete.
- **Informing students that we may need to send additional notifications.** They should not be surprised to receive notifications when the schedule changes at the last minute or if other urgent information needs to be sent out.
- **Avoiding information overload by avoiding constant notifications.** We try to make each message count so students will pay attention. If we need to announce additional information, we consider whether that information could simply be added to an existing delayed-release notification. As A.J. discovered, noticeable confusion and frustration about assignments may be a sign that too many notifications are going out or that the timing is erratic, causing students to either ignore or miss the messages.

Encourage Students to Use the Canvas Announcements Forum as the Course News Feed

The Announcements forum on Canvas is on the main course menu and students can click in to find any messages they might have missed or want to revisit; the forum is also available through the mobile app. We make clear that students are responsible for reading all messages, even if they have ignored the notification or edited settings to keep the LMS from sending notifications to their email or mobile device. An example announcement is shown in Figure 1.6.

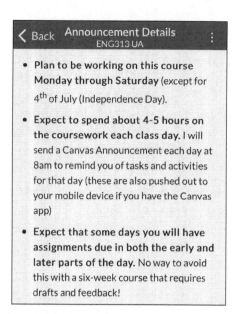

Figure 1.6. Announcement of plan for scheduled course reminders and due times for assignments. Note: The use of "I" clearly signals this is the instructor's notification, rather than an automated notification from Canvas.

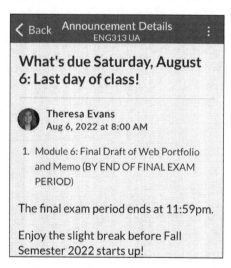

Figure 1.7. How a Canvas Announcement appears on the screen of a mobile device.

Consider the Tone and Style of the Message

Informational content of the message is just a starting point for consideration: We like to aim for a positive—or neutral—tone and style (see Figure 1.4). We also aim for brief and concise messages, often just a sentence or two to introduce a list of tasks or to announce late-breaking news. Messages should reflect the instructor's personality, expertise, and care for the students. We consider the following:

- **Being mindful of language use.** We want our "presence" perceived as helpful and friendly, not annoying or intimidating. We may "feel" the attitude—positive or negative—once we also start receiving the messages, so we adjust as needed. This adjustment could be as simple as rephrasing an accusatory "You must post your peer response by 11:59 p.m. or you will NOT receive credit" to a more neutral "Peer responses must be posted by 11:59 p.m. to receive credit" or even polite, "Please post your peer response by 11:59 so you receive credit."
- **Keeping messages as short as possible.** We do this by embedding direct links to published items in Canvas, where students can find more details. If this is not possible with an institution's LMS, then the instructor should clearly state where students can find the information. Using links does keep messages more concise. The less text in the message, the more likely the message will be read. It's best to focus on what students need to know at that moment.
- **Reviewing each message at some point prior to release to make sure it is still the message we want to send.** This is also the time to add new information, so that we do not overload students with too many notification alerts.

An example message is shared in Figure 1.7.

Maximize the Affordances of the Technology Platform

When setting up messages, we consider how our specific technology works and take advantage of its affordances, while working around the constraints:

- **Setting release date and time before composing the message.** Imagine students receiving a semester's worth of push notifications in one day! On a published Canvas course, a saved message is a sent message—unless the message is first set for delayed release. To avoid this embarrassing scenario, we set up the delayed-release date and time before writing the message. Otherwise, the message will be released to all our students immediately as soon as we hit "save." To eliminate that risk, we can leave the Canvas course unpublished until we have completed the scheduled messages, but there's a catch: If we forget to add the release dates or accidentally set release dates that occur before the course is actually published, those message will not be pushed out to students at all. The

messages would be available in the Announcements forum, but they would show up in the forum all at once, which is also not ideal.
- **Using consistent subject lines for scheduled messages.** For simplicity's sake, we use a generic heading such as "What's due today" for a fast-paced online course or "What's due this week" for a regular semester course. Adding a specific day and date is also especially helpful, so that messages are distinguishable from one another in the Canvas Announcements forum (see Figure 1.8). A consistent subject line allows students to immediately recognize the type of message they are receiving; however, a long list of messages with the same subject line will frustrate students who need to quickly locate a particular message.
- **Considering how many links are necessary.** One purpose of push notifications is to get students into the LMS module, not to help them avoid or minimize their presence in the course site. We have tried several ways to get students into the Canvas modules. One method is to place a link to the entire module, with a reminder that students need to access additional resources. Another option, one that also ensures push notifications are consistent with items on the To Do list, is to embed the necessary Module links within each Canvas Assignment or Discussion. This practice reduces the number of links required in our message and leaves us more space to be present as the instructor. The fewer the links, the fewer the links we need to test. Another advantage is that we can update information within Module pages without worrying about updating information in the assignment.
- **Considering how the message will show up on laptop screens and on mobile devices.** The message may look slightly different depending on where the Canvas Announcement is accessed. We check the message before it goes out, but also review it again on a laptop and mobile device after it is released.
- **Proofreading the text and testing all links.** Once we have set up the message—and every time we make changes to the message—we save the message, reread, and test all the links.

Enhance Communication with Additional Technologies

We take advantage of whatever technologies are available to enhance our communication practices, focusing on technologies students are already using whenever possible. Sometimes we need to check for any restrictions our institution may have placed on use of particular technologies, due to security concerns or privacy issues. We also must consider whether additional technologies will help or hinder students.

Using Push Notifications to Establish Teacher Presence

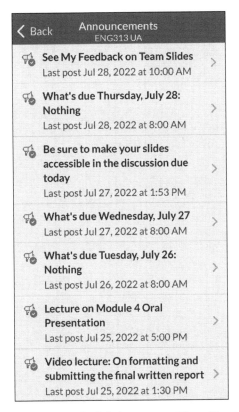

Figure 1.8. Subject lines for scheduled messages. Note: Consistent subject line "What's due today" helps students recognize the type of message, while the added date helps them locate the message later. Delayed notifications appear on the instructor version of the Announcements page, but not the student version.

Our institution uses Gmail, so we can use Google Calendar to schedule Zoom meetings, which sends out its own push notifications to students. When inviting the entire class to a Zoom meeting, we can use Canvas Announcements to send the link. If the meeting is required, we can also post it as an Assignment in Canvas so that it shows up on the Course Summary, the Canvas Site Calendar, and the Student To Do List. These features allow us to provide greater clarity as to where and how meetings may take place, what is due, and when it is to be turned in.

When sending messages to individual students, particularly about missed classes or assignments, we use the Canvas mail system so that messages are kept within each course and not mixed in with other messages in our Gmail accounts. This practice makes those messages easier to track when necessary. If students contact us via our Gmail accounts, we can add labels to those messages with the name of the course for easier retrieval later.

REFLECTION ON PRACTICE

Push notifications can be scheduled in advance, yet they can still feel very present—and even urgently present—the moment they are received. They can also feel very personal, as push notifications seem directed specifically to each individual recipient.

Affordances of the Practice to Promote a Community of Inquiry

Key benefits of this practice include the ability to alert students to upcoming assignments, wherever those students are, as long as they have their mobile devices with them. This practice increases opportunities for students to be regularly reminded about assignments, which they can also access right from their mobile devices. If students benefit from push notifications, then instructors benefit, too, because they will spend less time fielding questions and following up on missing assignments.

Challenges We Can Foresee When Using This Practice

As mentioned earlier, students can use the To Do list to go directly to assignments and simply follow whatever prompt is in the assignment forum. If our push notifications merely provide links from the To Do list, students could still miss the information they need to successfully complete their work.

The results of our survey raised more questions about how students perceive push notifications. Comments provided by respondents suggest that some students confuse announcements created by instructors with automatic notifications sent out by the LMS. This point of confusion makes it important to add more personality to messages to ensure students recognize the message as coming from their instructor.

We are not certain how many automatic notifications students receive from the LMS and whether that number depends on an institution's particular contract with Canvas or the particular implementation of Canvas. We do know our students can opt out of some or all automatic notifications. We also know that our students can opt out of having Canvas Announcements forwarded to them, and we try to make them aware that we use this feature, encouraging them to leave it turned on.

A major challenge we have already experienced and foresee will continue is that technology is always changing; platforms are updated or new platforms replace or enhance existing platforms. We have our vantage as the instructor rather than as the student, both in terms of how we conceive the arc of the course and how we see things in the LMS itself. Some instructors may lack experience using the LMS, which can lead to disorganization and confusion. Instructors may not be notified about updates to the LMS—or notified in time to adjust the course design.

Students—and instructors—are increasingly overloaded with information. This overload plays out beyond any updates in course objectives and outcomes: technology creates considerable information overload through the need to constantly fix bugs and update technologies. Changes in technology lead to shifts in how students engage with course sites, which further mandates an update in pedagogical practices. The lag time between each of these phases creates its own problems, including how quickly instructors migrate and adapt to new technologies, how much time passes before students shift to new ways of engaging with the technologies, and how much more time passes before instructors become aware of changes in student engagement to even determine what has changed and why.

Refining Tasks and Criteria to Ensure Student Success

Over time, as we continue to gain experience as instructors and as users of this LMS, we have refined our approaches to using the technologies available to us. The following is not a comprehensive list, but it does sum up major areas where we have identified room for improvement:

- **We Sought Out Student Input on the Timing and Frequency of Notifications.** Student input is not a foolproof strategy, as some students will be unhappy with whatever choice the group makes or will discover later the push notification schedule does not work for them. Seeking student input on the schedule is also not useful for shorter courses that require daily reminders. Finally, going forward, we need to become more aware of how often the Canvas system is sending students automated notifications to ensure we do not overload students with notifications to the point where they ignore our messages.
- **We Worked on Making Messages More Personable.** Students are more likely to communicate with instructors who present themselves as approachable. Style choices in subject headings and body text can help to immediately identify the message as coming from a real person, who has content expertise and empathy for students. For example, we might reference a discussion from a recent synchronous

session, say something about the weather or current events, or embed a video of ourselves providing whole-class feedback on a recent class activity. As we become more comfortable with this practice, we are starting to share more humor in our messages, such as a meme or video related to course content.

- **We Worked on Making Messages More Concise.** Our goal is to reduce the number of links required in a message, which would save labor and reduce the need to test so many links. Broken links are likely to cause students to focus on the instructor's failure to provide a live link rather than their responsibility to keep up with assigned tasks. At the same time, we recognized the need to direct students into the module so that they see all the resources available to them. We have come to realize that assignments themselves should include links to necessary module pages. That way, through one link to an assignment, students can find resources easily, whether they actively access assignments from the To Do list or passively retrieve them through push notifications. We continue to consider how to better leverage the relationship between the published assignments that populate the To Do list and the push notifications we send out through Canvas Announcements. More careful consideration of the text and links to include in assignment prompts may allow us to minimize links in the push notifications and ensure consistency of messaging.
- **We Began to Use Push Notifications for In-Person Web-Enhanced Courses.** We recognized that some students really do depend on their mobile devices. This observation was supplemented by a show of hands during an early in-person synchronous class session that showed how virtually all students in our classes were using the mobile app. Given this change in the manner that students interact with their courses, we cannot emphasize enough the point that even web-enhanced in-person courses are becoming less fully reliant on in-person interactions. Also, the need to be accessible to and stay in touch with students who are absent seems to make scheduled notifications a logical way to do this, while maintaining boundaries on instructor time and labor.

CONCLUSION

Planning out course announcements as push notifications can help instructors, both new and experienced, to become more organized. When teaching from a course template in particular, setting up messages ahead of time can also serve to reinforce the instructor's familiarity with the course structure and timeline. Having reminders set up ahead of time can alleviate stress once the semester gets busy because the instructor no longer has to remember to send them or take time to create them.

Additionally, planning out a course's communication strategy in advance provides a foundation for successful interactions with students; however, this practice also demands flexibility. Instructors must be willing to adjust the approach, based on direct student feedback and evidence of student learning. For example, the instructor should review upcoming messages to ensure the information is still relevant and useful as the course progresses and revise them accordingly if the need arises.

The goal of this practice is to benefit both students and instructors. However, a significant potential drawback is the creation of new expectations for teachers, making them responsible for actively reminding students about upcoming due dates. Instructors benefit from this practice only if they are able to spend more time on course concepts and less time on administrative tasks, such as following up on missing assignments—and missing students.

To summarize, push notifications are one part of a user-centered design, which must consider the use of mobile devices to access and interact with course materials. Push notifications need to be more than informational; they need to reflect the instructor's personality, expertise, and care for the students. Push notifications must also emphasize the importance of tapping into and reading the instructor-provided resources, which is especially critical for students who rarely or never click into the online course modules or who rarely or never interact with the course on a desktop or laptop screen. Finally, the frequency of push notifications and the subject lines of push notifications must be carefully considered to ensure that students respond to them, rather than ignore them. Ultimately, we believe this to be a worthwhile practice for instructors to use and adapt for the benefit of both students and themselves.

MOVING BETTER PRACTICES ACROSS MODALITIES

- **In-Person, Real-Time Learning:** A push-notification program can be created—with input from students about timing and frequency—to send personable instructor messages that remind students about tasks due for class meetings.
- **Online, Real-Time Learning:** A push-notification program can remind students of tasks to complete prior to each class meeting, and each message can also include the link to the scheduled video call.

- **Online, Any time Learning:** A push-notification program can establish and strengthen a sense of teacher presence in a course without real-time meetings while also scaffolding the assignments and reminding students of day-to-day tasks they need to complete.
- **Hybrid Learning:** A push-notification program can help reduce confusion by reminding students of the scheduled learning modalities for each week, in addition to reminding them about assignments to complete prior to real-time meetings.

REFERENCES

Alhazmi, A. K., Imtiaz, A., Al-Hammadi, F. & Kaed, E. (2021). Success and failure aspects of LMS in e-learning systems. *International Journal of Interactive Mobile Technologies, 15*(11), 133–147. https://doi-org.proxy.lib.miamioh.edu/10.3991/ijim.v15i11.20805.

Baldwin, S. J. & Ching, Y. H. (2020). Guidelines for designing online courses for mobile devices. *TechTrends, 64*, 413–422. https://doi.org/10.1007/s11528-019-00463-6.

Borgman, J. & Dockter, J. (2018). Considerations of access and design in the online writing classroom. *Computers and Composition, 49*, 94–105. https://doi.org/10.1016/j.compcom.2018.05.001.

Borgman, J. & McArdle, C. (2019). *Personal, accessible, responsive, strategic: Resources and strategies for online writing instructors.* The WAC Clearinghouse; University Press of Colorado. https://doi.org/10.37514/PRA-B.2019.0322.

Cooper, L. J., Laster-Loftus, A. & Mandernach, B. J. (2019). Efficient online instruction: Maximum impact in minimal time. *Online Journal of Distance Learning Administration, 22*(3), 1–9. University of West Georgia, Distance Education Center. https://ojdla.com/archive/fall223/cooper_lasterloftus_mandernach223.pdf.

Council of Writing Program Administrators, National Council of Teachers of English & National Writing Project. (2011, January). *Framework for success in postsecondary writing.* https://wpacouncil.org/aws/CWPA/pt/sd/news_article/242845/_PARENT/layout_details/false.

Fendler, R. J. (2021). Improving the "other" side to teacher presence in online education. *Online Journal of Distance Learning Administration, 24*(1), 1–16. https://ojdla.com/authors/richard-j-fendler.

Galanek, J. D., Gierdowski, D. C. & Brooks, D. C. (2018). *ECAR study of undergraduate students and information technology.* Educause Center for Analysis and Research. https://tacc.org/sites/default/files/documents/2018-11/studentitstudy2018_0.pdf.

Garrison, D. R., Anderson, T. & Archer, W. (2000). Critical inquiry in a text-based environment: Computer conferencing in higher education. *The Internet and Higher Education 2*(2–3), 87–105. https://doi.org/10.1016/S1096-7516(00)00016-6.

GSOLE Executive Board. (2019, June 13). *Online literacy instruction principles and tenets.* Global Society of Online Literacy Educators. https://gsole.org/oliresources/oliprinciples.

Greer, M. & Harris, H. S. (2018). User-centered design as a foundation for effective online writing instruction. *Computers and Composition, 49,* 14–24. https://doi.org/10.1016/j.compcom.2018.05.006.

Pew Research Center (2021). Mobile fact sheet. *Pew Research Center.* https://www.pewresearch.org/internet/fact-sheet/mobile/.

Pham, X.-L., Nguyen, T.-H., Hwang, W.-Y. & Chen, G.-D. (2016, July 25–28). *Effects of push notifications on learner engagement in a mobile learning app* [Conference session]. 2016 IEEE (Institute of Electrical and Electronics Engineers)16th International Conference on Advanced Learning Technologies (ICALT), Austin, Texas, United States. https://doi.org/10.1109/ICALT.2016.50.

Rath, L, Olmstead, K., Zhang, J. & Beach, P. (2019). Hearing students' voices: Understanding student perspectives of online learning. *Online Journal of Distance Learning Administration, 22*(4), https://ojdla.com/archive/winter224/rathbeacholmsteadzhang224.pdf.

Sitzman, K. & Leners, D. W. (2006). Student perceptions of caring in online baccalaureate education. *Nursing Education Perspectives, 27*(5), 254–259.

Stone, C. & Springer, M. (2019). Interactivity, connectedness and "teacher-presence": Engaging and retaining students online. *Australian Journal of Adult Learning, 59*(2), 146–169. https://files.eric.ed.gov/fulltext/EJ1235966.pdf.

Wohllebe, A., Adler, M. R. & Podruzsik, S. (2021). Influence of design elements of mobile push notifications on mobile app user interactions. *International Journal of Interactive Mobile Technologies, 15*(15), 35–46. https://doi.org/10.3991/ijim.v15i15.23897.

CHAPTER 2.

USING STRUCTURAL EXAMPLES TO PROMOTE CREATIVITY AND ENGAGEMENT

Brielle Campos and Candie Moonshower
Middle State Tennessee University

In this chapter, the authors describe **structural examples, or templates,** *used in online, any time learning and in-person, real-time learning. In describing their "better practice," the authors innovate on how writing templates can be reimagined to prompt student engagement and creativity. In describing their "better practice," this chapter addresses the themes of Accessibility and Inclusivity and Practices Adapted from Classic Composition Strategies.*

FRAMEWORKS AND PRINCIPLES IN THIS CHAPTER

- **CCCC Principles for the Postsecondary Teaching of Writing, 3**: Recognizes writing as a social act.
- **CCCC Principles for the Postsecondary Teaching of Writing, 5**: Recognizes writing processes as iterative and complex.
- **CCCC Principles for the Postsecondary Teaching of Writing, 6**: Depends upon frequent, timely, and context-specific feedback from an experienced postsecondary instructor.
- **PARS Online Writing Instruction**, Personal: Building community and fostering connections.
- **PARS Online Writing Instruction**, Accessible: Content needs to be accessible to students.
- **PARS Online Writing Instruction**, Responsive: Instructors should be responsive and anticipate students' queries, needs, and requests.

GUIDING QUESTIONS BEFORE YOU BEGIN READING

- What are some of your own, already-developed resources which can be further refined into templates for student learning?

DOI: https://doi.org/10.37514/PER-B.2024.2241.2.02

- Which content from your class do you feel needs examples to help supplement further discussion or expand student understanding?
- If teaching in an online setting, what are some tools you can use to distribute templates to the class?
- Why might templates be an accessible learning tool in both an in-person and online settings?

INTRODUCTION

CANDIE MOONSHOWER

Unlike many adjuncts or GTAs, I never taught college under the watchful eye of a mentor. The college hired me, they gave me books, they gave me sample syllabi, and off I went. The syllabi were helpful for planning a schedule but figuring out how to teach specific writing skills and rhetorical moves involved a lot of research and practice on my part. I asked kind colleagues a lot of questions. I kept wishing there were concrete examples I could learn from.

Early on in my first semester of teaching, I received my first set of essays from students. Many of them began the same way. It wasn't plagiarism—just a basic similarity between structures and rhetorical moves. I asked several of my students about their introductions. They admitted—separately—that they'd Googled "How to Write an Introduction." They'd been looking for examples.

My first instinct? "If they want examples, I'd rather they learn from *my* examples." Thus began my teaching with templates. Since many students bewailed the fact that getting started is the hardest part, introductions were first on my list.

First, I used the project we were working on, an advertising analysis paper, for which I had already devised guidelines, and I wrote the essay I was assigning. This changed how I saw my assignment, so I rewrote the guidelines so that they made more sense to the non-academic writer—the first-year student whom I'd asked to write the project.

Second, I wrote the "how to" aspect of wrting a good introduction, meaning the step-by-step directions explaining the moving parts: what a hook does and the types of hooks; how to then transition from the general hook to the thesis and what information might be necessary in that transition; and the thesis, stating their claim or stance. I did the same for body paragraphs and topic sentences (taken from the thesis points). Finally, I wrote instructions for how to conclude a short paper without simply regurgitating the thesis with different types of conclusions they could attempt, such as calls to action or a statement of the subject's broader implications.

I used my own essay as a template for my students. I color-coded each section of the essay and, using the "track changes" feature, added comment boxes in the margins explaining what I was doing—the rhetorical moves I'd made. "This will do the trick!" I told myself. And it did, to a certain extent. The students followed my templates in much the same way they had followed the instructions when they'd Googled "How to Write an Introduction." This was a good start, but I knew that the next step would be encouraging students to try different rhetorical moves to get beyond the template as a formula for their writing.

This prompted me to redevelop my methods for teaching rhetorical moves. Guidelines and templates are great, but I needed to show how to take the template examples and help students make them their own. The process of teaching each new skill became a deeper, more immersive activity. Students' writing projects showed that learning each new skill had become a deeper, more immersive activity for them as well. Group activities and full-class workshops during which students helped each other (with my guidance) take their individual topics and think up appropriate hooks, for example, moved us from following instructions and examples to making the ideas our own.

Not only did students find this new approach helpful, but they were also more animated in class, more invested in the projects, and expressed that they felt the writing was now their own—instead of simply creating something they thought the teacher might want.

When I began designing completely online courses in my two courses in the first-year sequence in Middle Tennessee State University's English department, expository writing first and then research and argumentation, I realized that the use of the templates for teaching writing skills transferred well to the online, any time classroom. The templates serve as meta-lectures for the students, telling them what their options are, as per different assignments, and how they can easily get started, but still provide every student room for creativity and voice.

BRIE CAMPOS

My entry into education came in a unique way. Before my master's degree, before I started college, I was a martial arts instructor. The benefit of teaching martial arts was that I came in contact with a wide variety of people, from all different age groups. While the children's classes were easiest and most fun, it was the adult classes which pushed me as an instructor. Unlike children, who rarely ask why we move a certain way or how a particular movement is executed, adults wanted to know every detail of my motion, from start to finish. At first this was frustrating; I had always learned things quickly, having great control over my body and mind. It wasn't until I started teaching my mother, who wasn't as agile as I was, that I started to see the need for the how's and why's. Since her body couldn't do what mine could, she had to understand why I was moving in a certain way so she could find a way to adapt that to her capability.

When I started teaching college, I found a similar need in my students; many of the students I taught at Youngstown State University (YSU) were coming in from lower income communities and had not been taught to write the way I had. Whereas it made sense to me, and I didn't question the need for thesis statements or citations, many students I encountered didn't even know what a thesis statement was nor why citations mattered. I found myself searching for a way to explain what to me was natural (or, at the very least, what I had internalized from years of playing the game of school).

Another experience which helped with this was my work in the reading and study skills department at YSU, a lower division university studies course. There I learned of a few different techniques made to improve reading and comprehension skills, but I immediately found other uses for them. By making a few modifications, I found myself finally having a vocabulary to discuss key elements of writing with my students. For example, in the R&SSC we taught a method of reading called SQ4R (Survey, Question, Read, Record, Recite, Review) (Becker, 2013). When teaching research, I would teach this same method, but would adapt parts of it. When students were in the surveying mode, they would look over the authors' works cited as well to check for interesting resources. After recording their notes, they would "recite" or review their notes often to see what could be used in their final papers. Through these efforts, we were able to create a common ground to discuss writing, and I was able to use these techniques on class readings or example texts to demonstrate their effectiveness.

I have never felt it beneficial to allow students to copy a prescribed template, and even found myself scoffing at things like the five-paragraph essay for its limiting nature. What I have come to realize in teaching is that there is a place for providing bones, a starting line for students, so they can develop not only their critical thinking skills, but also their writer's vocabulary and creative style. This may be looked at as a template, but I strive to make sure students understand how fluid these structures are based on their tone, purpose, and audience. It is for this reason, coupled with her extensive experience teaching online courses—which due to the pandemic I was now scheduled to teach—I gravitated to Candie and her teaching style, which also uses detailed meta-examples (or templates) to demonstrate key writing concepts in the online classroom.

SCHOLARSHIP, THEORIES, AND PRINCIPLES THAT GUIDE OUR APPROACH

Templates often get a bad rap. People see them as easy shortcuts and a way to avoid thinking creatively. However, a carefully crafted template can allay students' fears of starting the writing process, and students have often told us that templates spur their creativity by freeing them to think less about the requirements of an essay or project and more about what they want to say. This was something I learned while teaching with Gerald Graff and colleagues' (2012) textbook, *They Say, I Say: The Moves that Matter in Academic Writing*. While other composition instructors may use terms like "guide" (Lunsford & Ruszkiewicz, 2019), we will continue to use the term "template" for our process in this essay, with the understanding that what we mean is a set of meta-examples and activities which encourage exploration and creativity.

PARS

One of the current better practices in online writing instruction is the Personal, Accessible, Responsive, Strategic (PARS) framework, created by Jessie Borgman and Casey McArdle (2019). While we believe these principles relate to all classroom instruction, it is clear that especially in an online setting these are vital to strong course design and delivery. When employed by online writing instructors in strategic ways, these principles—Personal, Accessible, Responsive, and Strategic—help students feel connected to their peers and to us as instructors. Our templating method relates to the first three aspects of the PARS method, Personal, Accessible, and Responsive.

Each student is unique and comes from a personal writing background (**Personal**). These templates create a level playing field; for those who do not know what a thesis statement is, for instance, we can introduce the concept and provide chances to develop strong writing skills. In contrast, a student who already knows about thesis statements will be asked to identify what makes a strong statement and will be pushed to demonstrate improved skills. Because we offer the templates for students as opportunities, instead of demanding them in assignment expectations, we are able to personalize instruction, as well as share our experiences and make ourselves as instructors more personal to students.

These templates make learning more **accessible**, as they provide alternative ways of comprehending difficult concepts, and can be distributed as PDFs, videos, or other types of accessible media in the digital classroom environment (**Accessible**). Templating also makes us more accessible to students. We both teach templates to students as examples of how we learned about writing generally, and academic writing specifically, using these experiences as chances to connect with writers lacking confidence. Our templates serve this dual purpose; they first make writing less of a nebulous talent and more of an acquirable skill, and the second it makes us as instructors seem less like gatekeepers and more like relatable guides.

These templates give us material to **respond** to when used in low-stakes assignments, and they create a clear dialogue with students about their work in longer projects (**Responsive**). We invest a large chunk of time both in and out of class providing feedback to students. We want them to know that we value their work, and that our main objective is to help them communicate their ideas to others. By providing constant and consistent feedback, we can make sure that students understand concepts, are using templates correctly, and we have a chance to either compliment their efforts at experimentation; as an added benefit, employing the templates is an effective manner to help them avoid plagiarism.

While the PARS methodology has been developed for the online classroom, we believe that PARS is not limited to the online classroom—instructors should still be accessible to their students and build personal relationships with the class—but we do find that our teaching style in an online setting is well suited to the PARS methodology. Considering the lack of personal, face-to-face interaction in online classes, where students can take cues from our body language and tone, and where teaching—and learning—can sometimes be derailed, our template structures give us a chance to be extra responsive to students while they learn. We have the ability to teach them rhetorical choices, and then respond to their efforts asynchronously. Our templates, in conjunction with the PARS method, allow instructors to help students develop a universal classroom jargon (Accessible) about writing and teaches them how to scaffold their own writing projects (Strategic). Our templates cut through the noise of a traditional classroom environment, so the students experience the feeling of one-on-one instruction even in asynchronous classrooms (Personal and Responsive).

CCCC's Principles for the Postsecondary Teaching of Writing (2018)

The second set of best practices for online writing instruction is CCCC's *Principles for the Postsecondary Teaching of Writing* (2015). Specifically, there are three areas we see aligning with our work: having students recognize writing as a social act, recognizing the writing process as iterative and complex, and to understand that writing depends upon frequent, timely, and context-specific feedback from an experienced post-secondary instructor.

First, we align our structures with recognizing how iterative and complex writing can be. Writing these templates is not just a way to ensure that students, in turn, follow proper composition structures; it is also a chance to demonstrate, in real time, the writing process. We both use these templates as a chance to show students how complex the writing process is by making sudden changes or decisions while using the template in class. The templates become a foundation, a starting point so that students can easily identify what we are doing in the writing process, and then we demonstrate how our writing might change. Students see how important it is that being flexible with their writing will lead to generating an effective piece.

Second, we both feel that these templates improve our communication skills with students. While introducing a template, we develop a vocabulary with students, giving them clear direction, for instance, about what a thesis statement is and does. Once the template is introduced, students immediately move into low-stakes assignments where they put that template to use. We grade both the content and attempted use of the structure, or, as is often the case, successful deviation from the structure when seeking to improve the appeal of the argument.

For example, in a research and argumentation class, we might introduce a template for introductions where students create a hook, a transitioning sentence, and finish with a thesis statement. As a first assignment, Candie teaches them a summary and response essay, where she allows freedom with the hook but the transition must introduce the author, title, and thesis of the article they are responding to, and the thesis must state their explicit agreement or disagreement with the author's stance. In contrast, when writing their final argumentative papers, students have control over all three aspects of the introduction, since they have by the end of the semester mastered using hooks, transitions, and theses to convey their intended topics. Templates give us a shared vocabulary that we can use with students to improve their writing skills, terms we can reference when providing feedback, and immediate low stakes writing assignments we can have students engage in and then receive feedback on.

Beyond the communication between students and instructors that our templates generate, they also provide vocabulary and context for virtual peer review sessions. Traditionally, students tend not to trust peers when engaging in peer review because of a fear that peers may know and understand the process better than they do and that they will have nothing to contribute. However, with these templates, they have the ability to communicate in a way which develops a writing community. We have found that because of the work we have done teaching vocabulary and scaffolding, students approach the peer review on equal footing without the worry of having a reviewer who is significantly above or below their editorial abilities. Students also feel they have something to comment about on their peers' work; they can use their knowledge of the templates to provide useful feedback. Students feel empowered to critique peers' work with constructive criticism. Writers feel encouraged to listen to peer advice. Even in virtual spaces where students do not often meet face-to-face, they at least feel a sense that peers are willing to help their writing grow, and they engage in more communication.

As instructors, we believe in empowering students by teaching them methods of self-discovery. We value communication and understand the importance of things like rhetorical appeals, citation styles, and kairos. Since these are important to us as instructors, we seek to impart their importance to students by focusing on methods of creation, which, in turn, ask students to determine how best to use rhetoric to their advantage in communication. That being said, we also value a student's voice, their unique perspective on the world, and how they best learn material. It would be in conflict with this value if we taught students to only generate essays in a certain way, or to only use one rhetorical technique. Our template strategy walks the line between imparting the wisdom of essay construction, on the one hand, with encouraging student participation and autonomy, on the other. These templates demonstrate how a well-constructed thesis statement guides readers and makes clear the purpose of the work, but we never expect students to create the thesis statement they believe we would for their essay—our goal is to encourage them to state their own claims. Every time we use a template to teach a concept, we are not asking students to simply copy an existing paragraph or generate something that aligns with our verbiage; we are asking them to critically analyze the works of others and then learn how to generate their own work from it. We would liken this to the process of drawing, another challenging skill to learn.

In particular, there has always been some tension in art communities, especially so in recent years, about budding artists who trace masters works for learning purposes. This is not the same as plagiarizing an artist's work; young artists do not do this to make a profit. They copy another's work to learn brush strokes, to learn construction and layout. Practice pieces such as this are meant to help them learn technique, and learn they do, as budding artists learn how to break down shapes, shade in a particular way, or how to choose colors. Despite the contentions in the art community, the practice remains in pedagogical play, as we are all likely to have walked through a museum and to see a single student, or an entire group, sitting in front of a painting with their sketchbooks open, pencils in motion.

Our templates for writing work in the same way. For instance, Candie often asks students to identify thesis statements or hooks from established authors and their writings. This is not so that students will copy these writers as if they were simply plagiarizing, but so they can identify the building blocks and then try their own hand at them. How much or little a student relates their work to that of the example will depend on their own rhetorical choices and how they wish to convey meaning. The subject matter of the works of the "masters" is never fully related to the students; we may select an author who is writing an opinion piece on a restaurant, while students will be asked to write a movie review. Just like art students, writing students are being asked to practice copying the fundamentals, practice learning through doing, before creating their own original compositions with the knowledge they have gained. This practice, in general, reflects good composition practice, but can also easily translate to the online writing classroom, where we use best online writing practices.

COURSE CONTEXT AND LESSON

In our experience teaching first-year composition (FYC), we feel that students most fear the act of starting their essays. Even when they have researched and feel confident about their purpose and the information they wish to share, getting started is often a stumbling block that results in essays that are, eventually, written on the fly and at the last moment. Sharing templates and encouraging drafting based on the templates give students something to work with—a place to start. Drafting and redrafting increases confidence and the willingness to try different rhetorical techniques. You can tell a student multiple times how to write an effective introduction, orally and via written guidelines, and it still might not "click." Show them an example, and you're a step closer. Show them a template—a student example with the parts broken down—and your student can see how another student has done it. Allow the student to play with the template using their own topic and words. Provide feedback to the student and allow them to practice again. Provide feedback again—as is necessary—until there is mastery of the skill. This process is a bit like a written version of a YouTube tutorial video, but the student can refer to it more quickly and easily, selecting the elements of the process that they need, and more often, because it is posted in your LMS shell.

INTRODUCTION BREAKDOWN

An effective way for students to think of introductions is to break an introduction into parts:

- **Hook:** Using one of the many possible rhetorical moves, or combinations of moves, to engage the reader, such as rhetorical questions, anecdotes, "setting the scene," appropriate quotes, or humor.
- **Transition:** Moving from the general hook to the more specific thesis by introducing the topic or the literature the student is working with specific transitional words or phrases.
- **Thesis:** A statement of the student's argument that is debatable and defensible.

This kind of breakdown works no matter the topic—an expository or argumentative essay, or a literary analysis.

Lesson

For the purposes of illustrating the use of templates, we will use an essay, the Advertising Analysis, that we teach in the first semester of the first-year college writing sequence, expository writing. While these courses are delivered fully online in an any time format, in hybrid classes (both face-to-face and online), and in the on-campus real-time classroom and we use the templates in all modalities, we are focusing here on the courses taught online in an any time format. The following is our guidelines for the assignment.

Advertising Analysis Assignment Overview

Most of us are very familiar with advertising, but we tend to view advertisements from our position as consumers. In this project, you will step out of the role of consumer and provide a close analysis of two advertisements for the same product, from two different decades, by noting some of the rhetorical techniques and subliminal appeals the ads use to influence consumers. In the essay "Advertising's Fifteen Basic Appeals," Jib Fowles (1982) defines some of the common emotional/psychological appeals employed by advertisers in their efforts to sell products. This essay is the research you will use for your own analysis. You will provide a close comparison of your two advertisements by noting and analyzing some of these ads' emotional appeals, at least two or three emotional appeals per ad. You will use the Fowles' article and what he says as evidence for your own analysis and interpretation of the ads you choose.

Purpose

During this assignment, students will learn to critically look at both text and art and how they work together to deliver a message. Students will understand how ethos, pathos, and logos work both explicitly and subliminally. Students will engage in texts in more than a superficial fashion, learning to think deep about the messages they receive daily.

Tasks

1. Read Jib Fowles' "Advertising's Fifteen Basic Appeals" (1982).
2. Discuss through the LMS's forum. Activities will include working in online groups with ads, via the discussion board function, to identify appeals and practice describing how those appeals work, as well as

Using Structural Examples

choosing ads you like and dislike and explaining to the class why. You will have 24 to 48 hours to respond to discussion board activities.

3. The instructor will schedule the posting of an online lesson with the embedded librarian, so that students can learn about how to use the Periodicals Room, as well as the differences between commercially sold magazines and scholarly journals. After you complete the online library instruction, please take the quiz posted under Quizzes in your LMS. (An embedded librarian at MTSU is a librarian instructors can request to join the online course, giving students immediate access to them when needed for research purposes. The LMS provides students an email address, which the librarian responds to.)

4. Using commercial magazines, choose two ads of the same product (e.g., Maybelline mascara) or the same type of product (e.g., Maybelline mascara from 1930 and Cover Girl mascara from 1970) from two different decades. Scan or photograph and save your ads in color as you will be required to upload the ads in with your final draft. Choose advertisements that are complex and that you clearly understand. You must be able to identify some emotional appeals that are being targeted (as defined in "Advertising's Fifteen Basic Appeals," by Jib Fowles). Take your time in choosing these ads. A successful essay begins with the right advertisements.

5. Describe the ads in your own words. In this initial step, don't worry about perfect grammar and mechanics. Focus on describing the images and the textual messages in the ads into your own writing. A person who hasn't seen the ads before should be able to picture them. It might be easiest to begin with the thing/image that dominates the page. You'll need to use directional words to help guide your readers: above, below, behind, to the right, and so forth. Use your descriptive writing skills.

6. Fill out the Advertisement Analysis Worksheet on each ad and then carefully review all your answers. Start trying to figure out what you want to say about these ads in your essay. Make sure you know what the ads are trying to do and who they're trying to reach. You won't use every element of the Worksheet in your essay, but this process should help you focus your analysis. Try to find appeals that are similar and different. (Instructors might consider using the Center for Media Literacy's 5 Key Questions[1] as part of this step; we have our own questions we pose for students.)

---

1 Download a copy of CML's 5 key questions at https://www.medialit.org/five-key-questions-can-change-world

7. Now try to write your introduction. Start with an interesting hook. Then introduce the topic of advertising, broadly, and figure out a way to catch your readers' interest as it relates to the specific product you are exploring. Mention the Fowles article and summarize the ideas in it that are important to your essay. State a clear thesis. Your thesis should explicitly state the appeals in each ad that you will analyze and discuss. Upload your intro for instructor feedback.
8. Describe some of the emotional appeals that Fowles defines to the ad you have chosen. Analyze the advertisement's use of these appeals to entice and influence consumers.
9. Determine how to organize the description and analysis. You can present the body of the essay in two parts: description of the ad, 2) analysis of the ad. However, you might choose to analyze the ad as you describe it.
10. Decide how to organize the essay as a whole: Subject by subject (ad by ad) or point by point (appeal by appeal).

Success Criteria

These are the success criteria the student is given with the assignment sheet, but students will also receive a rubric, which further details the point values based on these criteria and other writing elements (grammar, punctuation, completion, etc.). The rubric is available from the beginning of the assignment on the LMS.

1. The student will learn to use the Periodicals Room and understand the difference between types of periodicals.
2. The student will learn to recognize and articulate how rhetorical appeals are used in text and graphics.
3. The student will learn to recognize and articulate how subliminal appeals, as described by Jib Fowles, are used in advertising.
4. The student will learn how to use descriptive language to write about graphics.
5. The student will learn how to organize a compare and contrast essay.

Use of Instructor and Student Templates

For the Advertisement Analysis project, templates are used to illustrate how to think about introductions. Once we are ready for step 7 (above) of the tasks, we share two ads we've chosen and the introduction we've written. We share our own introduction first, broken down into the parts (hook, transition, and thesis), then an example of a student-written introduction, also broken down into parts.

Instructor Template

Here's my HOOK: I set the scene about our love for cars and how our car needs change over time, and advertisers' responses to those changing needs. These templates are also provided in the format of an annotated PDF at https://bit.ly/CamposMoonshowerTemplates.

> Since the first Ford Model-T rolled off the production line in 1908, Americans have been obsessed with cars. We love to drive. When we're young, we want speedy, sexy cars. After we marry, we want more sensible vehicles, but still somewhat young and sexy. After the children arrive, safety is the watchword. But with all the car companies, makes and models out there, how do we decide? Advertisers want to help us—and automobile advertisements abound in magazines as diverse as Better Homes & Gardens and Motor Trend.

I then TRANSITION: I move from the general discussion of car ads to talk about my two particular ads.

> Interestingly, the more ads have changed, the more they have remained the same. In examining two automobile ads from 1938 and 1960, there are some subtle commonalities and some vivid differences. But both advertisements use "sub-rational" appeals, as described by Jib Fowles in his article "Advertising's Fifteen Basic Appeals," (1982) to establish their marketing message and sell their products.

And finally, I write my THESIS: I lay out what is similar (aesthetics and autonomy), and then I lay out what is different about each ad (1938: curiosity and nurture, and 1960: sex and escape). These are the points I will discuss in my paper.

> Despite the passage of 22 years between the two automobile advertisements, the advertisers continue to use the appeals to the need for aesthetics and autonomy in their ads. Different, however, are the audiences; thus, the 1938 ad appeals to the customer's need to satisfy curiosity and the need to nurture, and the 1960 ad appeals to the customer's need for sex and the need to escape.

Student Application of Template

Even though the student is discussing an entirely different product—a philanthropic clothing line produced by a television star—she can use the template to make a start. This student example is also displayed in the format of an annotated PDF at https://bit.ly/CamposMoonshowerExample. Here's her HOOK:

> In 1985, the word "period" was finally uttered in a Tampax commercial for the first time in television history. This was a new and shocking departure from euphemisms such as "Aunt Flo" and "that time of the month." But it was well past time to stop tiptoeing around the subject, and Tampax led the charge. From their founding in 1936 to today, the Tampax Tampons company has helped reach many such milestones in the fight to destigmatize menstruation.

She then TRANSITIONS by introducing Fowles:

> One approach they took to do so was advertising, specifically using various appeals to draw in audiences to sell and educate about the use of tampons. In Jib Fowles' article "Advertising's Fifteen Basic Appeals," he explains the different ways in which advertisers use emotional appeals to convince customers into buying their products. Now nearly 100 years old, Tampax continues to use our need for achievement and autonomy to prove why their product is essential to improving the lives of those who have periods. However, as times have changed, so too have their methods.

Finally, she lays out her THESIS:

> While a Tampax ad from 1967 primarily uses the appeals to the customer's need for curiosity and guidance, an advertisement from 2014 instead uses appeals directed more towards the need for autonomy and to satisfy our need for aesthetic sensations.

Other Applications

These templates are not confined to simply teaching introductions. We use them for drafting conclusions, teaching proper quoting techniques, and teaching how to develop topic sentences from a thesis. Key to this theory is that the materials used as examples should not be the same materials or readings as the students are using in their projects. We provide templates with examples we have written—or that other students have written and allowed us to use—and always using different readings that the current students are assigned. This helps keep the possibilities for plagiarizing low and brings some variety to our teaching each semester. In addition, we teach students how to draft their own templates for skills such as citations.

To draft their own templates for citations, students work in online groups with their source materials and their handbooks to come up with examples for various source types (i.e., books, essays, articles from databases, and digital resources). They divide the labor and then share their templates with each other through the Discussions widget. We offer a few appendices at the end of this chapter that show this and other skills, the templates, and how to use them in the classroom.

REFLECTION ON PRACTICE: PARS

In our summary and response assignment, PARS guides our pedagogical practice. First, in the assignment design and assessment, students are being asked to take an argument, summarize it, and then agree or disagree with it. While teaching summary, Candie also teaches interesting hook ideas to draw readers into the work. First, students are given the choice to select an article which reflects their personal interest. At the same time, Candie has selected a text to use as an example which is reflective of her own interest. Students are told they will be judged on their summary, but also on all aspects of writing which have led up to this assignment.

Since Candie is teaching them interesting hooks, students can expect that Candie's response to their work will involve some discussion of the hook they use for this paper. This makes the assignment more accessible; students have access to the assignment, the grading criteria, the lessons, as well as practice assignments before being judged. Candie has several smaller assignments which are low stakes for the students to get feedback with, as well as a peer review session. For online peer review, Candie assigns them peer review partners, they share their work via email, and they are given a set amount of time to respond and submit their reviews both to their peer through email and through the Dropbox widget in our LMS.

CONCLUSION

We argue that using templates applies good PARS practices and does not stifle student creativity. Through our examples, we've demonstrated that students take our instruction and examples and apply them to the development of their own rhetorical situations. Students fill their writing tool boxes with rhetorical moves they can use again and again, not only in composition or English classes, but across the curriculum. These practices transcend the classroom and work extremely well in online spaces, where lecturing is minimized or non-existent.

We have formulated this process using the CCCC's *Principles for the Postsecondary Teaching of Writing* (2015):

> *Recognizing writing as a social act:*
> We share our knowledge and processes and encourage students to share their work with us and each other as they learn and practice new skills.
>
> *Recognizing writing processes as iterative and complex:*
> We create the templates, show them the process as we and other students have practiced it, then allow them to practice again and again until they master the skills.
>
> *Depends upon frequent, timely, and context-specific feedback from an experienced post-secondary instructor:*
> We provide feedback on all drafts, as well as encouraging and facilitating peer feedback, until then students develop confidence to use the templates to practice the skills on their own.

At this point we feel it is necessary to respond to possible questions about this practice: the labor which is involved with developing these templates and the material ability to transfer between instructional modalities. There is inevitably some labor which is involved with creating new course materials. These template practices do not have to be implemented all at once, or generally across an entire course.

To generate our examples for these templates, we first completed our own projects as we expected them to be assigned. This gave us some insight into any potential problems students might face and any templates students might need. When grading our assignments, we ask students whose writing is either exemplary or shows growth in the process if we could use their work as examples for future classes (respecting student privacy along the way). In this way, we build a repository of materials to use. Once this repository is created, the materials in it can constantly be used or added to each semester (our LMS system allows us access to previous courses and student submissions, which we can use if we need to prepare or amend student examples).

In terms of the modality, these template assignments work in all learning spaces, though they will have to be adjusted based on whether the class is synchronous or asynchronous. As we have discussed here, the online class relies heavily on discussion boards, cloud sharing, emails, and other asynchronous spaces for students to engage, while a synchronous class or the traditional classroom can handle these activities in real time. Students in class may be asked to swap papers, use their textbooks and cell phones, or have discussions.

Regardless of their age, education, status as English Language Learners, or level of writing skills, examples such as our templates are useful to the learning process. We have developed these templates as a way of demonstrating good writing practices, especially for ease of learning in an online environment. We are pleased with how enthusiastically our online students respond to this method of instruction and benefit from these practices. Rather than boxing us into a corner, we find that templates open up the writing process for our students, and they continue to be a vital part of our teaching.

MOVING BETTER PRACTICES ACROSS MODALITIES

- **In-Person, Real-Time Learning:** Instructors can supply handouts with worksheets or direct students to the documents already uploaded on their particular LMS platforms.
- **Online, Real-Time Learning:** Instructors can use a combination of breakout rooms, screen-sharing, and file-sharing.
- **Online, Any Time Learning:** Instructors supply handouts and worksheets through their particular LMS platforms, and they supply links to important information via the Discussion, Dropbox, or News Flash apps.
- **Hybrid Learning:** Instructors should provide examples and instructions ahead of time, through the apps on the LMS platforms, and when meeting synchronously instruct students to perform the activities in real time.

REFERENCES

Becker K. *The art and science of quality learning* (3rd ed.). Van-Griner Publishing.

Borgman, J. & McArdle, C. (2019). *Personal, accessible, responsive, strategic: Resources and strategies for online writing instructors*. The WAC Clearinghouse; University Press of Colorado. https://doi.org/10.37514/PRA-B.2019.0322.

Graff G., Birkenstein C. & Durst R. (2012). *They say I say: The moves that matter in academic writing* (2nd ed.). W. W. Norton & Co.

Fowles J. (1982). Advertising's fifteen basic appeals. *ETC: A review of general semantics, 39*(3), 273–290. https://www.jstor.org/stable/42575622.

Lunsford A. & Ruszkiewicz J. (2019). *Everything's an argument* (8th ed.). Bedford/St. Martin's.

National Council of Teachers of English. (2015). *CCCC's principles for the postsecondary teaching of writing*. https://cccc.ncte.org/cccc/resources/positions/postsecondarywriting#principle1.

CHAPTER 3.

PEER REVIEW IN ONLINE, REAL-TIME LEARNING ENVIRONMENTS

Meghalee Das and Michael J. Faris
Texas Tech University

In this chapter, the authors describe peer review practices using synchronous tools for students to practice giving feedback: evaluating and providing peer feedback, evaluating feedback they receive, and using feedback in revision in online, real-time learning. In particular, the authors detail peer feedback activities that can promote flexible writing practices, metacognition, and engagement. In describing their "better practices," this chapter addresses the themes of practices in motion across teaching and learning modalities and practices adapted from classic composition strategies.

FRAMEWORKS AND PRINCIPLES IN THIS CHAPTER

- **Framework for Success in Postsecondary Writing, Engagement**: A sense of investment and involvement in learning.
- **Framework for Success in Postsecondary Writing, Flexibility**: The ability to adapt to situations, expectations, or demands.
- **Framework for Success in Postsecondary Writing, Metacognition**: The ability to reflect on one's own thinking as well as on the individual and cultural processes used to structure knowledge.
- **GSOLE Principle 3.4**: Instructors and tutors should migrate and/or adapt appropriate reading, alphabetic writing, and multimodal composition theories from traditional instructional settings to their OLI environment(s).

GUIDING QUESTIONS BEFORE YOU BEGIN READING

- How can online writing instructors design peer feedback activities drawing on the unique features of online, real-time instructional environments in ways that encourage flexible and meaningful writing processes for students?

DOI: https://doi.org/10.37514/PER-B.2024.2241.2.03

- What does successful learning look like for peer feedback activities?
- How can online writing instructors design peer feedback activities to provide space and time for reflection on those activities while also promoting metacognition?
- How can online writing instructors design activities in ways that provide space and time for productively practicing with peer feedback technologies without resorting to simply teaching tools?

INTRODUCTION

In spring 2020, I (Meghalee) taught a second semester first-year writing (FYW) class focused on inquiry and research that was delivered in an inperson, real-time learning environment. Through a series of scaffolded assignments like formal essays, discussion board posts, class activities, and peer reviews, students researched an issue of public interest that they were personally connected to. As an international first-year doctoral student teaching rhetoric-focused composition classes, I found that students and I had a lot in common with each other in the ways we were trying to navigate academic expectations, college writing, work-life balance, and the desire to form a sense of community with peers. The lively discussions that took place in class gave us an opportunity to engage with each other and with civic issues, and motivated students to ask questions, analyze audiences, evaluate the credibility of sources, discuss ethical implications, and look at people, discourse, texts, and topics beyond binaries to compose effective and purposeful texts in a variety of genres.

However, when our lives were disrupted by the COVID-19 pandemic with the sudden move to an online course delivery format, students were unsure of how to complete assignments, peer reviews, and activities, and I, with no background in online teaching, was anxious about recreating the same community in an online class. However, students expressed relief to be able to interact with their classmates over Zoom, and I was determined to find ways to research, learn, and apply online pedagogical strategies that would make classes fulfilling and engaging for students. My goal was not to find perfect online teaching solutions but instead to be adaptable to the rapid changes happening around us and to incorporate teaching techniques, video conferencing, writing and collaboration tools, and peer engagement strategies to meet the needs of students and facilitate a meaningful learning experience. I was preparing "better" practices, building on my experiences as a teacher and feedback from students, focusing on inclusive learning, student-centered instructional design, and dynamic online peer engagement strategies, among others.

In fall 2021, when I was assigned to teach the same FYW class again in an online, real-time learning format, I recalled how in the in-person version of the class, I put students in groups for peer reviews, and they gave each other feedback by making comments and annotations on printed drafts. I moved among these groups to answer questions, and, depending on how much time was left in the class period, we held a general discussion on the feedback session. In previous online, any time learning versions of the course, I used online peer review tools like FeedbackFruits[1] and discussion boards for peer reviews. I have more experience with online teaching now, but I was still concerned about designing effective online, real-time learning peer reviews, which are not only a crucial part of a writing class but also an indicator of what students are learning or how they are contributing. In digital environments, attention can be fragmented, engagement can be inconsistent, and the informal conversations that aid in building community and trust among students are often limited unless intentional online group activities are initiated by the instructor, as students don't share a collective physical space. I chose to embrace the technological features afforded by a video conferencing platform like Zoom, where the class was taking place, and to use an online word processor like Google Docs that has editing features to digitally reconstruct the peer review experience. But I wanted to go beyond mirroring in-person, real-time teaching strategies in the online environment by focusing not just on the tools but also on cultivating cognitive skills in students that help them engage with texts, provide feedback, and collaborate better. I also hoped that implementing an online, real-time learning peer review would facilitate interaction among students and develop their sense of agency and accountability in learning.

As Michael and I discussed the benefits and challenges associated with an online teaching modality and planned the peer reviews for this course, he advised me to include a practice and preparation session for peer feedback to help students understand the importance of peer reviews in the writing process, develop the skills of a peer reviewer, and become more comfortable with online peer review tools. This chapter, thus, was born out of functionality and a goal to create meaningful online, real-time learning peer review sessions, along with critical and iterative reflection on my part to improve the experience as we moved through the semester.

Our approach to peer review in this chapter is driven by three principles or values in the field. First, our approach is informed by the belief in the field that "All Writers Have More to Learn," one of the five threshold concepts for writing studies provided in Linda Adler-Kassner and Elizabeth Wardle's (2015) *Naming What We Know: Threshold Concepts of Writing Studies*. As contributors to the discussion

---

1   Learn more about FeedbackFruits at https://feedbackfruits.com/get-started-now/educators

of this threshold concept observed, writers need to learn flexible strategies through a variety of practices (Rose, 2015; Yancey, 2015); writers who are most effective can externalize their writing "into an independent artifact that can be examined, revised, or otherwise worked on by the writer, collaborators, or other people" (Bazerman & Tinberg, 2015, p. 61); and learning to write effectively means new and different types of practice and revision (Downs, 2015; Yancey, 2015). Throughout the semester, we created opportunities for students to give feedback on each other's drafts in real time and at various stages of the projects, learn from each other, and be flexible in feedback formats, such as in small breakout room groups, in whole-class discussions, and through comments on Google Docs.

This principle—that all writers have more to learn—is echoed in a second set of principles that guided our choices for designing peer feedback sessions in Meghalee's course: that students should "develop flexible [writing] processes," from the *Framework for Success in Postsecondary Writing* (Council of Writing Program Administrators [CWPA] et al., 2011, p. 8). Since writing is not a linear process, students need opportunities to practice different aspects of writing like "research, drafting, sharing with others, revising in response to reviews, and editing," and these practices can be facilitated by fostering eight habits of mind or ways of approaching learning, namely, curiosity, openness, engagement, creativity, persistence, responsibility, flexibility, and metacognition (CWPA et al., 2011, p. 8). Through online, real-time peer reviews, we draw particular attention to the following:

- **Engagement**: Students are encouraged to make connections between their own and their classmates' drafts, discover new meanings and ideas, and incorporate the feedback they receive through peer reviews to revise their ideas and projects.
- **Flexibility**: Students are given opportunities to approach assignments in different ways, encouraged to give verbal feedback or textual feedback to their peers, and make choices based on context, purpose, and audience.
- **Metacognition**: Students are encouraged to not just evaluate others' work but also reflect on their own writing process, goals, and choices, and use what they learn from reflections on one assignment to improve writing on following projects.

The third principle informing our approach is from the Global Society of Online Literacy Educators' (GSOLE, 2019) Principle 3.4, which states, "Instructors and tutors should migrate and/or adapt appropriate reading, alphabetic writing, and multimodal composition theories from traditional instructional settings to their OLI environment(s)." Setting up effective peer reviews requires making intentional choices that align with the course and assignment goals and can be particularly difficult to replicate in online classes, especially in terms of engagement, organic interaction, access, and technological proficiency. Moreover, most online writing instruction scholarship on evidence-based practices focus on online, any time learning classes, where instructors can enable peer review features like discussion forums or use peer review tools like FeedbackFruits in the learning management systems. There has been an increasing focus on online real-time teaching, particularly since the COVID-19 pandemic, and this delivery format continues to be adopted in many programs across institutions. Through practice and reflection, we have explored the benefits, opportunities, challenges, and solutions to barriers in online real-time peer reviews to recommend practices which can be replicated in similar class settings.

Our main driving question in this chapter is: How can online writing instructors design peer feedback activities drawing on the unique features of online, real-time instructional environments in ways that encourage flexible and meaningful writing processes for students? We also explore: What does successful learning look like for peer feedback activities? To encourage students to evaluate each other's writing, provide useful feedback to peers, evaluate the feedback they receive, plan and implement revision, and promote engagement, flexibility, and metacognition, we use the Transparent Assignment Design (TAD) format. Based on the Transparency in Learning and Teaching in Higher Education (TILT) framework, whose goal is to "make learning processes explicit and equitably accessible for all students" (Winkelmes et al., 2019, p. 1), the TAD prompt format gives clear instructions on the activity's purpose, task, and completion criteria.

COURSE CONTEXT AND LESSON

As mentioned in the introduction, in fall 2021, I (Meghalee) taught an online, real-time FYW class called Advanced College Rhetoric, which focused on conducting research on an issue that students choose for the semester, analyzing the various stakeholders associated with the issue, finding and evaluating sources, mapping out the conversations around the issue, and incorporating source material in their final project. The course was divided into three units, with the following major assignments:

- Unit I: Developing Interest and Inquiry: A low-stakes exploratory essay called the "I-Search Essay."
- Unit II: Mapping the Conversations: An Annotated Bibliography and an essay that synthesizes and analyzes research called the "Mapping the Conversations Essay."
- Unit III: Entering the Conversation: A Final Project that makes an argument and enters the conversation, with options for media, genre, and format.

Throughout the course, students conducted multiple peer reviews of drafts and scaffolded assignments related to these major projects. I aimed to learn from each peer review session and improve the prompt with each iteration. Some improvements I made, which I discuss below, included increasing the activity time, using technical features like commenting or suggesting, assigning meeting roles in breakout rooms, and adding a reflection task after the peer review activity.

In this chapter, we focus on three peer review sessions, one from each unit, to show the evolution of our plans and their implementation, students' experience with the exercises, and the modifications we made in the prompts and our approach as we progressed throughout the semester. We begin by explaining how we prepared students for online peer reviews in Unit I by setting up a practice peer review with a sample student essay and then a peer review session of students' drafts using the Describe–Evaluate–Suggest (DES) heuristic by Bill Hart-Davidson (Eli Review, 2016).[2] Next, we focus on peer feedback for one scaffolding assignment in Unit II for the Mapping the Conversations Essay. Lastly, we describe a peer review activity from Unit III for the Final Project, which also includes a reflection and revision element. For each example, we outline the plan and materials for scaffolding activities, including the peer review assignment prompt based on the TILT/TAD model (Winkelmes et al., 2019). The chapter also includes a reflection on these peer review activities and description of students' experiences and challenges, as they used various tools like Google Docs and Zoom for online peer reviews. Throughout our narrative, we have included excerpts from students' comments (shared with permission) during and after the activity to help readers understand our activity plans and student responses.

Practicing Peer Reviews

Research on peer review workshops indicates that teachers need to prepare students on how they can give effective feedback instead of assuming they know how to do so, and that such preparation, demonstration, and practice can lead students to giving more specific and numerous comments to their classmates (Atwell, 2014; Min, 2005). To prepare students for effective peer reviews, I assigned a sample I-Search Essay for students to read before class and uploaded the sample essay to a Google folder as a Google document. (While I used Google Drive for this activity, teachers could use a different file sharing space, such as Microsoft OneDrive.) On the day of the practice peer review session, I began preparing students by first discussing textbook readings on feedback and revision and the value of peer reviews in the writing process. The class also watched

---

2 Learn more about Eli Review at https://elireview.com/.

a video on giving helpful feedback using the DES heuristic by Hart-Davidson (Eli Review, 2016), which aligns with our approach that learning occurs through peer learning and collaborating.

The DES heuristic encourages students to describe or say what they see as a reader, evaluate or explain how a text meets (or doesn't meet) the assignment criteria, and suggest or offer concrete advice for improvement. It is one way to encourage novice writers to practice giving feedback that provides specific suggestions for revisions, thereby promoting metacognition and critical thinking. As we reviewed examples of comments that followed the DES format, some students said such a format was useful in planning how to give substantial feedback. During these discussions, students also shared their concerns about technology and inexperience with giving feedback, such as unfamiliarity with the tools, an unstable internet connection, and a general awkwardness about conducting peer review over Zoom with classmates they barely knew in the second week of class.

After the discussion, I shared the link for the Google Drive folder and the sample I-Search Essay in the chat. I had also posted the link on the course learning management system so that students could access the document from multiple places after we closed the Zoom room. I shared my Zoom screen and gave a brief tutorial on basic features of Google Docs, like the editing and suggesting features and the commenting tool. A few students said they had worked on Google Docs before, but most hadn't. In fact, many teachers assume that students are technologically proficient and familiar with a variety of new media tools. However, research shows that younger generations have a wide variety of experiences, access, and skill levels when it comes to new technologies (Hargittai, 2010). And so, writing teachers need to explicitly teach functional, critical, and rhetorical literacies around new technologies (Selber, 2004). I encouraged students to explore the editing, commenting, and suggesting features, and I observed how the more experienced students helped novice Google Docs users employ these features by speaking or commenting in the chat. I realized how important it was to allot enough time for online peer review preparation, as the technological and cognitive overload, exacerbated by the unfamiliarity of using online collaborative tools, can weigh on the minds of students and must be considered when planning peer reviews.

For this practice session, I shared a simple prompt with students, which was divided into two parts:

- **Part 1**: Using the "suggesting" and "commenting" features in Google Docs, give your feedback on the assigned sample essay based on the requirements of the I-Search Essay assignment prompt using

the Describe–Evaluate–Suggest method. Give at least one comment on what the writer is doing well and one suggestion or area of improvement.
- **Part II**: Now read the comments that everyone has posted on the sample essay. Which comments do you like the best, which are the most effective, and why? Share with the class by replying to the comment directly on the Google document, by writing a note in the Zoom chat, or by unmuting yourself and speaking to the class.

Using a sample for practice helped students to be frank and more comfortable than giving feedback to a classmate's draft for the first time. We discussed which comments were effective and why. It was important for us to use the practice session as an opportunity to learn how to give effective feedback and not just a demonstration of tools. Students remembered the earlier discussion on the DES heuristic and incorporated that into their review. For example, the sample essay contained the following sentence, referring to research questions: "The first I developed was simple." A student commented, "The first what? More clarification would make the sentence sound better." Another student suggested that their classmate's comment was effective because, rather than just pointing out a problem with the text, the peer reviewer offered a specific solution for the writer. A couple of students agreed with the comment and mentioned how they appreciated receiving specific comments with suggestions that helped them improve their drafts rather than vague compliments like "this sentence is effective."

Unit I: Peer Review of I-Search Essay

After the warm-up with the practice session, students were ready to begin reviewing each other's drafts for the I-Search Essay. I first asked students to upload their I-Search Essay drafts to a Google Drive folder and assigned students into breakout rooms in groups of two or three. Part of planning effective peer reviews consists of giving students clear instructions on what they are expected to do in the workshop. I shared with students an online activity handout based on the TAD format, and they began reading and reviewing their partner's drafts from the folder. Most of them were using suggesting and commenting functions to provide feedback in real time, although I reminded them that they could download these documents from the folder or refer to them again later. Although I had initially allotted 15 minutes for the peer review activity plus another 10 minutes for discussion, I had to leave out and postpone the discussion time because the practice session took longer than I had anticipated, and I did not want students to feel rushed. Nevertheless, some breakout rooms were less engaged than others, while some gave detailed feedback to each other, including mentioning the I-Search

Essay assignment evaluation criteria to support their feedback. This was the peer review prompt for the final draft of the I-Search Essay based on the TAD model:

Peer Review: I-Search Essay

Breakout Room Activity Time: 15 minutes | Main Room Discussion: 10 minutes

Purpose
- To recognize specific rhetorical choices in the drafts of other writers.
- To provide feedback on your classmate's I-Search Essay draft.
- To assess the strengths and weaknesses of your own writing.

The assignment is designed to help you reach the following goals and learning outcomes:

Writing Processes and Craft:
- Develop a writing project through multiple drafts.
- Develop flexible strategies for reading, drafting, reviewing, collaborating, revising, rewriting, rereading, and editing.
- Evaluate the work of others, give useful feedback to others on their writing, and evaluate and incorporate feedback from others in their own writing.

Teamwork: To include the ability to consider different points of view and to work effectively with others to support a shared purpose or goal.

Task
1. Get into breakout rooms on Zoom.
2. Click on your partner's essay in the Google Drive folder. The link to the Google Drive folder is provided in the chat.
3. Using the "suggesting" and "commenting" features of Google Docs, give your feedback on your partner's I-Search Essay draft. Review requirements in the I-Search Essay prompt and refer to the Describe-Evaluate-Suggest method to give at least two comments on what they are doing well and two suggestions or areas of improvement.
4. Come back to the main room, where we will discuss the comments and feedback as a class.

Criteria for Success
1. You have provided at least two comments on what your classmate is doing well in the draft and two suggestions or areas for improvement.
2. You've had a chance to briefly discuss your feedback with each other.

In the next class, I held a discussion about what worked and what needed to be changed for the next peer review session. It was important for me to gauge students' perceptions of this activity and make modifications based on their responses. Students, in general, said they found the exercise useful and interesting, although it took some time to get used to the technical aspects. For example, one student said they would like to do this again, while another accepted that their unfamiliarity with the tools along with the time constraints of the activity caused some anxiety (mostly because they were not sure if they would finish reviewing the document). A couple of students mentioned that they had done peer reviews in a previous online, any time learning FYW class using a tool called FeedbackFruits. So, I asked the class to share if they found online, real-time learning peer reviews different from online, any time learning, and if so, in what ways. Students said that they liked that in a real-time format they could ask their partner questions to have a more organic discussion on the drafts. My biggest takeaway from the activity and the follow-up discussion was that I needed to ensure that ample time be allotted for peer feedback preparation because we cannot assume students will be familiar with online feedback tools, which can lead to some anxiety, along with the pressure of performing well in front of classmates they barely know yet. Having a discussion with students post-peer review was also important and helped me to understand their needs and modify the approach or process accordingly.

UNIT II: PEER REVIEW OF MAPPING THE CONVERSATIONS ESSAY

In Unit I, my goal was to familiarize students with the process of online peer reviews and how to give effective feedback. In Unit II, students started to feel more comfortable with the peer review process and document editing tools. Even when there were technical difficulties—like when some students got disconnected due to an unstable internet connection, their audio stopped working during discussions, or they had trouble opening the Google document—they let me know what the problem was and promptly improvised. For example, they gave comments in the Zoom chat or LMS discussion board if their audio or the commenting feature in Google Docs did not work, and seamlessly continued the discussion on their phone if they got disconnected on their computers. As they participated in more breakout room activities, a sense of camaraderie had also developed among the students by Unit II, and so I encouraged them to engage in in-depth discussions with each other and invest in more complex analysis of the drafts than giving sentence-level stylistic comments. (I had noticed in previous peer reviews that students tended to focus on local, stylistic issues and not comment on larger, more global issues.) One way I tried to involve students in more productive discussions was by giving them the opportunity to choose meeting roles for themselves during the peer review activity. I discuss the roles in more detail later in this section, but the main idea was to encourage students to be accountable and time efficient by choosing roles like notetaker, facilitator, and timekeeper during the activity that allowed them to take responsibility for reviewing the prompt and meeting the assignment goals.

As mentioned earlier, Unit II had two main projects, the Annotated Bibliography and the Mapping the Conversations Essay. This essay builds on the sources that students collected in the Annotated Bibliography (including additional sources) and synthesizes the conversations happening around their issue. Through scaffolding assignments, students analyze and connect the perspectives of various stakeholders, or the people affected by the issue. In this section, we highlight one of the peer review sessions for a portion of the Mapping the Conversations Essay. In this session, students reviewed their classmates' write-ups on the values and perspectives of one of the stakeholders associated with the issue they were researching. Since the essay is a significantly longer assignment, students posted drafts of smaller chunks of the essay on the LMS discussion boards so they could receive early feedback and revise smaller portions of the essay rather than trying to tackle the entire essay at once. In the example below, students had posted their drafts to a discussion board in the LMS before our class meeting so that their drafts were available to each other for online, real-time peer review during class.

The prompt below outlines the task and includes instructions of how to select meeting roles. Before the activity started, I explained to the students the meaning of the different roles:

- **the notetaker**, to take notes of what is discussed in the breakout room,
- **the facilitator/presenter**, to facilitate the discussions according to the activity prompt and later present key points in the main Zoom room, and
- **the timekeeper**, to keep track of time and ensure all the tasks are completed on time.

I have used assigned roles in many online discussion sessions in other classes, and I found this practice translates well to discussion-based real-time peer review activities in writing classes too. Assigning these roles helps keep groups accountable, and each group has something substantial to share in the main room after the peer review session.

Peer Feedback Discussion of One Stakeholder

Breakout Room Activity Time: 20 minutes | Main Room Discussion: 10 minutes

Purpose
- To provide feedback on your classmate's choice of one stakeholder and their analysis of the stakeholder's perspective and arguments.
- To reflect on the strengths and weaknesses of your analysis of your own stakeholder.

The assignment is to help you reach the following goals and learning outcomes:
Writing Processes and Craft:
- Develop a writing project through multiple drafts.
- Develop flexible strategies for reading, drafting, reviewing, collaborating, revising, rewriting, rereading, and editing.
- Evaluate the work of others, give useful feedback to others on their writing, and evaluate and incorporate feedback from others in their own writing.

Teamwork: To include the ability to consider different points of view and to work effectively with others to support a shared purpose or goal.

Task
1. Enter the assigned breakout room.
2. Assign roles to each other:
   a. Facilitator/Presenter: Will facilitate activity and present key points in main room.
   b. Timekeeper: Will keep track of time.
   c. Notetaker: Will take notes of discussions.
3. Find your partners' discussion board posts on one of the stakeholders for the Mapping the Conversations Essay. In either verbal responses or by replying to the discussion board post, provide at least two comments on how they might better explain and analyze the stakeholder and their perspective. You might refer to these identification traits to help guide your comments:
   a. The draft is clear about who this stakeholder is.
   b. The draft is clear about the stakeholder's relationship to the issue.
   c. The draft is clear about what the stakeholder argues and their reasoning for that argument.
   d. The draft discusses the values that are informing the stakeholder's perspectives.
   e. The draft applies stasis theory to better understand the nature of this stakeholder's perspectives and why and where they disagree with other stakeholders.

f. The draft appears to be using complex enough and reliable sources.
   g. Sources are properly cited.
   h. The draft shows complexity and understanding of the stakeholder's perspectives, moving beyond mere description to analysis of why and how the stakeholder holds these positions.
   i. The draft is well organized.
4. You might, then, ask yourself: Are there places where the writer could explain the perspective with more clarity, specificity, or complexity? Do they need more analysis to explain the stakeholder's relationship to the issue and how and why they disagree with others (using stasis theory)? Do you have suggestions for the sources that the writer is using? Try using the Describe–Evaluate–Suggest model.
5. Join the main room and present the observations.

Criteria for Success

- You have provided at least two suggestions to each group member's posts either verbally or in comments.
- You've had a chance to briefly discuss your feedback with each other.
- You have noted key discussion points to be presented in the main room.

Once students came back from the breakout room, they enthusiastically presented their discussions according to their selected roles. However, since the activity prompt said they could share their feedback either verbally or as a reply in the discussion post, almost no one wrote down their comments. We still had an engaging discussion, but it is easy to forget these feedback points after class. So, for the next peer review, which I describe in the next section, I included not only written feedback but also a reflection task in which students briefly wrote about how they planned to implement the feedback they received. For the rest of the unit, there were more such scaffolding activities, where students posted on the discussion board and then had peer reviews in class. Such discussions involved analyzing more stakeholders, the background and context of the issue, and looking at sample essays.

UNIT III: PEER REVIEW OF FINAL PROJECT

In Unit III, students worked on the Final Project, where they made an argument on their chosen issue and persuaded a particular stakeholder to change their mind or to influence their actions on the issue. In this section, we share a peer review activity in which students provided feedback on statements of purpose for the Final Project—an early planning activity in which students designed three potential plans for their projects. At this stage of the semester, students also showed considerable improvement in the quality and usefulness of the feedback they gave to each other. For example, instead of superficial comments and only assessing whether drafts met the minimum requirements of the prompt, students also gave feedback in terms of audience analysis, specificity and clarity of purpose, and coherent organization of ideas, and they made suggestions on which medium would be most appropriate and realistically manageable for their final project.

Additionally, as mentioned in the prompt below, I added a reflection element in this peer review, during which students reflected on the comments they received on their drafts by writing a short reflection. I included the reflection task as a response to the peer review mentioned in the previous section: Students had participated in engaging discussions but did not write many comments or reflect on the comments beyond the class discussions. With the cognitive load from multiple classes that students take, it was unlikely they would remember every important point discussed during peer reviews unless they took notes or reflected on the effectiveness and relevance of the feedback received. This reflection of about 150 words required them to outline their plan on implementing the comments they received, thus making the peer review activity more productive. The prompt below outlines the whole peer review activity, with the reflection added as the third task in the session.

Peer Feedback Discussion of Statements of Purpose for Final Project

Breakout Room Discussion Time: 20 minutes | Main Room Writing Time: 10 minutes

Purpose
- To give and receive feedback on drafts of three potential statements of purpose for final project.
- To choose one statement of purpose for your project based on feedback received from others.
- To reflect on the feedback received on the chosen statement of purpose and write how you plan to implement the comments.

The activity will help you reach the following learning outcomes:
- Develop flexible strategies for reading, drafting, reviewing, collaborating, revising, rewriting, rereading, and editing.
- Evaluate the work of others, give useful feedback to others on their writing, and evaluate and incorporate feedback from others in their own writing.

- Assess accurately the strengths and weaknesses of their own writing and develop individual plans for revision and improvement.
- Enact revision as substantive change.

Task

1. Enter your assigned breakout room.
2. Find your partners' discussion board posts on three possible statements of purpose for your final project. By replying to the discussion board posts of each partner, provide at least two suggestions for continuing forward. Try using the Describe–Evaluate–Suggest model. Consider the following questions:
    a. Do the statements clearly state the rhetorical purpose, audience, and medium or context of the final project?
    b. Does one of these ideas stand out as the most interesting and useful to approach? Why?
    c. Do you have concerns about the audience (it could be more specific, or they don't seem to be considering a constraint or audience belief or value)?
    d. Can the purpose be more clearly stated or be more precise?
    e. Does one of these projects seem too extreme, unmanageable, or impossible (like the audience likely isn't persuadable)?
3. Join the main room when breakout rooms close. Reflect on the feedback you received on your own three potential statements of purpose and choose one statement/idea for your final project based on the feedback. Write a short reflection of 150 words as a reply to yourself in your original discussion forum post, where you will describe your final approach and how you plan to implement the feedback received or any revisions you want to incorporate.

Criteria for Success

- You have evaluated the draft statements of purpose of your partners based on the requirements of the activity prompt.
- You have given at least two suggestions to each partner by replying to their discussion board post.
- You have written your reflection and revision plan as a reply to yourself in your original discussion forum post (or as a new post if you do not have an original post).

Adding the reflection step reinforced learning as students both engaged with each other as well as exercised metacognition by being aware of their own thought processes. While some students shared their plans regarding the steps they planned to take next in terms of the content in the Final Project or the medium they planned to use, others used the feedback to assess the strengths of the drafts or to add any missing requirements. For example, one student's post reads,

> One of the suggestions I received was to keep the audience engaged and I think with a podcast I can implement this by using a variety of sound effects as well as including multiple types of content in the podcast such as research, interviews, commentary, etc.

In their reflection, another student wrote,

> I will probably use this feedback as a sign to work on the video statement of purpose, as I will find it the most interesting, and it seems to be the most effective way of showing my point. Since everyone watches videos nowadays. I will use statistics and appeal to a group of younger people to make the video more targeted.

One takeaway I had from these student comments was that the low-stakes reflection activity allowed them to pause, take in the feedback, learn the reader's perspective, review their choices, and build or modify their roadmap for the rest of the assignment. This action in reflection is a crucial part of the writing and revising process and can help make a peer review activity more meaningful.

As I developed these peer feedback strategies, I wanted to emphasize the dynamic nature of online learning modalities and how it was important to be flexible and responsive to students' developing needs and the environment. As an online writing instructor, I frequently updated activity prompts, sought feedback from students, and modified peer feedback activities according to the type of assignment reviewed. The strategies that I found most effective were preparing students on how to give meaningful peer feedback using the DES heuristic; giving clear instructions on the tasks, goals, time, and criteria in the TAD format; assigning enough time to comprehend and complete the task; and including a reflection task that allowed students to create a plan of action based on the feedback received. These practices encourage flexibility, engagement, and metacognition, the habits of mind which I tried to develop in students in this course.

REFLECTION ON PRACTICE

Many assume that the measure of success of an online class depends on its ability to replicate in-person, real-time learning pedagogies, which are more familiar to teachers and therefore seen as ideal; however, effective online teaching strategies can inform in-person, real-time writing instruction, too (Neal et al., 2021). While I, too, was initially trying to recreate aspects of an in-class peer review experience, I wanted to go beyond migrating in-person teaching strategies to the online environment. According to Michael Neal and colleagues (2021), an effective online workshop must make it possible for "the class to collectively come together to receive direction" and facilitate "peer-to-peer interaction that allows for sharing and responding to students' writing" (p. 193). As a facilitator of online peer review workshops, I reimagined the activity by embracing the affordances of online platforms, acknowledging the challenges of online collaborative writing and reviewing, and hoped to provide students with an authentic interactive experience rather than just a recreation of an in-class peer review session. Because online formats are different from in-person, real-time learning formats—and because online courses can vary widely in how they're delivered and structured—I hoped to build on my experience with in-person classes but not limit myself to in-person pedagogies or make assumptions that the same strategies can work in all formats.

I used the guiding principles discussed in the introduction to direct the planning, design, implementation, and modifications of the peer review activities to encourage flexible and meaningful writing processes for students. Writers learn flexible strategies through a variety of practices (Rose, 2015; Yancey, 2015), and it is this flexibility that allows us to implement new and different types of practice and revision (Downs, 2015; Yancey, 2015). Effective peer reviews can provide opportunities for writers to approach learning collaboratively through engagement with each other and help them to develop habits of mind like flexibility and metacognition, which can improve awareness of one's own writing (CWPA et al., 2011). This self-awareness was reflected in the comments students gave to each other, which gradually moved from surface-level comments to more substantive ones, and later in their own reflection and revision plans based on the feedback they received. As the semester ended, students wrote self-assessment essays in which they reflected on their experiences with the online, real-time peer reviews and how they used the feedback to improve their drafts. For example, one student reflected:

> The small groups were a way to get a different perspective on your writing and allow classmates to make friendly criticisms on ways to improve your writing or catch some mistake that

> you may have missed. This allowed for room for improvement with each draft progressing in a way that was more effective than before. Each time we were in small groups I was thankfully always helped by my classmates on improvements I could make on each assignment but mainly the annotated bibliography, the I-Search Essay, and the mapping the conversations essay. Each assignment required the submission of multiple drafts with hopes that with each draft, improvements were made and for me specifically they were. With each draft that was created, improvements were made on grammar, information selection, stakeholder credibility and effectively conveying the information gathered in a way that followed each assignment's criteria.

Another student also reflected on the peer review experience and wrote how he "evaluated the work of others, gave useful feedback to others on their writing, and evaluated and incorporated that feedback from others in his own writing." He added,

> I was fortunate enough to do this [peer reviews] on every draft we submitted. I was given the opportunity to give my feedback on three possible ideas my classmates had for their final project. It was useful to them because it aided them in narrowing down their thought processes. They could also incorporate my opinions and feedback from other classmates into their project. For example, with the Mapping the Conversations Essay we had a 20-minute peer reviewing group activity. We read through everyone's drafts and got to talk about some errors and some ideas that our peers would change or give kudos to the parts we enjoyed about their drafts.

Our third guiding principle was to develop appropriate composition teaching strategies for the unique features of the online instructional environment (GSOLE, 2019). We made use of the affordances of technology to try flexible approaches to both prevent monotony in the peer review activities and show students the multiple ways in which they can respond to each other and experience the advantages and the challenges associated with it. The goal was not to create a perfect peer review activity, but a realistic one, which can be messy, whether in-person or online. Rather, I wanted to cultivate habits of mind where students made connections between their own and others' ideas, acted on feedback, and discovered new meaning in their writing as a result of the guided interactions they had with each other in the form of scaffolded activities. I also wanted students to use tools as facilitators helping to reach those writing goals. Using Zoom breakout rooms, the chat function, Google Docs commenting and suggesting, and LMS discussion board posts, students engaged with their classmates in different ways that kept the peer review discussions lively. Even when faced with barriers like technical difficulties, students used their creativity to give comments verbally in the Zoom classroom or in the LMS and reflect upon their plans based on the feedback.

However, I noted any barriers so that I could avoid them in the future and proposed some better practices that could help other teachers create peer reviews for their online, real-time learning classes. For example, allotting enough time for peer reviews is important, especially in online classes, as students need some time to become familiar with the technical tools besides reading and comprehending the drafts to be able to give useful feedback. I felt I rushed a bit in the first few peer reviews, and after talking to my students, I realized they, too, would have liked more time. I tried to put myself in their shoes and did the activity myself, which also included allotting time to read the prompt and one or more drafts and was able to create a more realistic timeframe for the activity.

Another important takeaway was the importance of preparing students for peer reviews; I not only explained to them the rationale behind these activities but also gave them ample time to practice, review what is considered effective feedback, and become comfortable with each other. For example, I used a sample essay for the practice session so that students would not feel hesitant to comment honestly, and I developed an exercise during which students analyzed which comments were effective so that they could model their comments based on the DES heuristic. Being very clear with the instructions was also important.

The TAD prompt format allowed me to focus on the purpose of the activity, learning outcomes, the steps of the task, and the criteria for success, which communicated to students what steps they had to take to complete the peer review activity and how they knew if they were successful. Adding the meeting roles—notetaker, facilitator, and timekeeper—in the assignment prompt encouraged students to be time efficient during breakout room discussions and to take responsibility for meeting the activity's goals. Finally, including the reflection task at the end of peer reviews helped students to meaningfully engage in metacognition: to consider the comments they received and plan a roadmap of the next steps they would take to incorporate the feedback in their projects.

CONCLUSION

One of our guiding principles in this chapter was "that all writers have more to learn" (Adler-Kassner & Wardle, 2015), and while polishing online, real-time peer review strategies and writing this chapter as a community of practice, I was reminded again that all instructors and instructional designers also have more to learn. Instructors need to be flexible and responsive because our aim is to facilitate an environment where learning outcomes can be met, and students can practice habits of mind. GSOLE's (2019) Principle 3.4 says, "Instructors and tutors should migrate and/or adapt appropriate reading, alphabetic writing, and multimodal composition theories from traditional instructional settings to their OLI environment(s)." This chapter provides insight on a particular approach taken by us, which consisted of using a file sharing, editing, and commenting platform and real-time audiovisual feedback on a video conferencing site. We also used the TAD assignment format, created small group discussions, and added individual reflection tasks for students based on our observation and student responses mentioned earlier.

As an online writing instructor aiming to develop composition, feedback, and reflection skills in students, I have found peer reviews to be an excellent tool that engages students and allows them to be responsible for their learning. New online teachers may feel overwhelmed by the number of options available to choose from for peer reviews or may have experience in only teaching in-person, real-time classes. We end the chapter with a few takeaways and observations from our experience conducting these online, real-time peer reviews:

- Plan a class during which you discuss with students the importance of peer reviews, model and practice how to provide effective and substantive feedback using a heuristic like the DES, and demonstrate peer review tools and technologies.
- Allot ample time for students to familiarize themselves with peer review, word processing, and video-conferencing tools, especially in the beginning of the semester.
- Keep in mind the goals for the peer review to narrow the learning outcomes and tasks of the peer review activity, and choose tools that are compatible with these outcomes and tasks.
- Break down assignments and peer review of assignments into smaller, scaffolded activities.
- Be flexible so that you can make modifications based on students' responses and respond to any unexpected technical challenges.
- Use clear instructions for the peer review prompts (such as the TAD format) to explain the goals, tasks, and completion criteria.
- Instruct students to assign meeting roles in breakout rooms such as notetaker, facilitator, and timekeeper to make the discussions more productive and time efficient.

- Include a reflection task with each peer review for students to reflect upon the feedback and how to apply useful comments in their drafts to make the peer review activity meaningful.

MOVING BETTER PRACTICES ACROSS MODALITIES

- **In-Person, Real-Time Learning:** The peer review strategies that we described in this chapter can be replicated in in-person, real-time learning environments. For in-person, real-time classes in which some students are joining via hyflex video call, we encourage asking onsite students to bring their own devices and headphones and to join the class's Zoom session. This way, onsite and online students can work with each other in peer review sessions in breakout rooms and develop community across modalities. The same peer review activity prompts can be used in this modality because once everyone is on Zoom, there is better engagement among students as their interaction is not limited by modality, and those attending in person can also receive feedback from those attending through video call.

- **Online, Any Time Learning:** The peer review strategies we mentioned were tailored for our course's online, real-time learning environment, but these practices can move across modalities and be adapted to an online, any time learning environment, too. Scaffolding assignments, giving clear directions in activity prompts, using peer feedback tools like FeedbackFruits embedded in the LMS or posting on discussion boards, and asking students to give feedback and reflect on a Google document can also lead to a meaningful peer review activity. Such an approach can foster habits of mind like flexibility, engagement, and metacognition, which facilitate practicing research, drafting, revising in response to feedback, and editing.

- **Hybrid Learning:** As we adapt these activities in a hybrid format, we should consider which activities would benefit students more by being present in an in-person, real-time learning environment, where they get feedback from their peers and the instructor, and which would be better for an online format, either real-time or any time. It might be a good idea to have in-person peer reviews and scaffolding activities earlier in the semester, as students get to know each other. As students gain more practice and become more familiar with the activities and with each other, these activities can be facilitated in online formats later in the semester.

REFERENCES

Adler-Kassner, L. & Wardle, E. (Eds.). (2015). *Naming what we know: Threshold concepts of writing studies.* Utah State University Press. https://doi.org/10.7330/9780874219906.c000a.

Atwell, N. (2014). *In the middle: A lifetime of learning about writing, reading, and adolescents* (3rd ed.). Heinemann.

Bazerman, C. & Tinberg, H. (2015). Text is an object outside of oneself that can be improved and developed. In L. Adler-Kassner & E. Wardle (Eds.), *Naming what we know: Threshold concepts of writing studies* (pp. 61–62). Utah State University Press.

Council of Writing Program Administrators, National Council of Teachers of English & National Writing Project. (2011, January). *Framework for success in postsecondary writing.* https://wpacouncil.org/aws/CWPA/pt/sd/news_article/242845/_PARENT/layout_details/false.

Downs, D. (2015). Revision is central to developing writing. In L. Adler-Kassner & E. Wardle (Eds.), *Naming what we know: Threshold concepts of writing studies* (pp. 66–67). Utah State University Press.

Eli Review. (2016, August 3). Describe–evaluate–suggest: Helpful writing feedback. *The Eli Review Blog.* https://elireview.com/2016/08/03/describe-evaluate-suggest/.

FeedbackFruits. (n.d.). Retrieved January 2, 2023, from https://feedbackfruits.com/.

GSOLE Executive Board. (2019, June 13). *Online literacy instruction principles and tenets.* Global Society of Online Literacy Educators. https://gsole.org/oliresources/oliprinciples.

Hargittai, E. (2010). Digital na(t)ives? Variations in internet skills and uses among members of the "net generation." *Sociological Inquiry, 80*(1), 92–113. https://doi.org/10.1111/j.1475-682X.2009.00317.x.

Min, H.-T. (2005). Training students to become successful peer reviewers. *System, 33*(2), 293–308. https://doi.org/10.1016/j.system.2004.11.003.

Neal, M., Cicchino, A. & Stark, K. (2021). More than replication: Online pedagogy informing face-to-face writing instruction. In W. P. Banks & S. Spangler (Eds.), *English studies online: Programs, practices, possibilities* (pp. 182–200). Parlor Press.

Rose, S. (2015). All writers have more to learn. In L. Adler-Kassner & E. Wardle (Eds.), *Naming what we know: Threshold concepts of writing studies* (pp. 59–61). Utah State University Press.

Selber, S. A. (2004). *Multiliteracies for a digital age.* Southern Illinois University Press.

Winkelmes, M.-A., Boye, A. & Tapp, S. (2019). *Transparent design in higher education teaching and leadership: A guide to implementing the Transparency Framework Institution-wide to improve learning and retention.* Stylus Publishing.

Yancey, K. B. (2015). Learning to write effectively requires different kinds of practice, time, and effort. In L. Adler-Kassner & E. Wardle (Eds.), *Naming what we know: Threshold concepts of writing studies* (pp. 64–65). Utah State University Press.

CHAPTER 4.

SCAFFOLDING FOR COLLABORATION AND MULTIMODAL ASSIGNMENTS

Ashleah Wimberly, Amanda Ayers, Amory Orchard, and Michael Neal
Florida State University

In this chapter, the authors describe **activities that support collaboration** *used in online, real-time learning. Specifically, the authors suggest that students can learn best when their ability to interact and collaborate with others is deliberately supported through in-class activities. In describing this "better practice," the authors address themes of accessibility and inclusivity and professional learning for online teachers.*

FRAMEWORKS AND PRINCIPLES IN THIS CHAPTER

- **GSOLE Principle 1.2:** Use of technology should support stated course objectives, thereby not presenting an undue burden for instructors and students.
- **GSOLE Principle 1.3:** Multimodal composition and alphabetic writing may require different technologies; therefore, those involved should be appropriately prepared to use them.
- **GSOLE Principle 3.4:** Instructors and tutors should migrate and/or adapt appropriate reading, alphabetic writing, and multimodal composition theories from traditional instructional settings to their OLI environment(s).
- **GSOLE Principle 3.5:** Instructors and tutors should research, develop, theorize, and apply appropriate reading, alphabetic writing, and multimodal composition theories to their OLI environment(s).

GUIDING QUESTIONS BEFORE YOU BEGIN READING

- How can online writing instructors best teach and support collaborative writing projects?

DOI: https://doi.org/10.37514/PER-B.2024.2241.2.04

- What kinds of assignment sequencing and scaffolding would provide the structure and accountability for successful collaboration in online writing classes?
- What kinds of assessment and feedback would best encourage healthy, shared collaboration in online writing classes?

INTRODUCTION

"One of the things that Nicolleti's chapter suggests is that monuments may not remember events as much as bury them beneath layers of national myth and explanation—what are some obvious examples of this?"

Michael looks out expectantly at the Zoom room. Most of the participant boxes are black, with only a handful of disinterested students choosing to leave their cameras on.

After a slight pause, he goes on: "We're raised to respect and trust the rhetoric of monuments and to embrace their stories as our own, but what happens if a monument doesn't remember an event so much as it portrays a biased narrative of an event?"

A disembodied voice comes out from one of the black boxes: "So, monuments could be persuasive the same way that other images are . . . but since they're monuments we trust them more and question them less." Soon, another voice chimes in, but ultimately the discussion is a bit strained.

After the conversation pauses, the other two instructors, Amanda and Ashleah, explain the task of today: to start work on the final assignment in the course, the Monument/Memorial (Re)Design Project—a collaborative project where students select an existing monument or memorial, present a photo array of the current design, analyze the rhetoric of the current design, develop a model of a new design, and provide a rationale for their choices.

When the three of us (Ashleah, Amanda & Michael) worked together designing this course, we were worried about the logistics of assigning a large-scale project in an online environment, especially given the challenges that collaboration can often present regardless of the course modality. Since we were teaching in a real-time online environment, we knew that including a collaborative project at the end of the semester would be difficult due to the distance and different access needs of students. However, we didn't want to just toss out the project because it represents a culmination of several key themes in the course, such as rhetorically informed visual production, argument, analysis, and design. It also meets many of our course's goals, and students have historically enjoyed the project and done excellent work on it. Thus, we decided that the best way forward was to weave collaboration into the fabric of the course, allowing students to work together in small groups over the entire semester so that they would have the opportunity to learn and work through the course content together.

This chapter will detail some of the practices that we engaged in before and during the semester as we worked strategically to make our course and this assignment more accessible and engaging for online students. In the brief narrative above, we offered a small glimpse into the class session where we first introduced the Monument/Memorial (Re)Design Project. We wanted to demonstrate what our classroom was often like when we held discussions as a large group—the image of darkened screens and disembodied voices is one that many instructors who teach online real-time learning have experience with. This interaction, however, is a stark contrast to what happened once the assignment was redesigned to more intentionally scaffold online collaboration. One component of this scaffolding was small student groups.

As instructors who have experience in both online and face-to-face environments, we have become increasingly aware of the differences between classes delivered in various modalities. One of the most significant questions we faced while co-teaching was whether our assignments—three large multimodal projects, one of which (described above) was collaborative—were still feasible in an online environment. Our teaching team was committed to multimodal composition as a foundational element of our curriculum and pedagogies, but we were also mindful of the challenges students face in online classes and the various access challenges that they may face such as financial constraints, job and family responsibilities, unpredictable schedules, health issues, etc.

However, as we articulated in our other chapter in this collection, Chapter 12: "Open-Media Assignment Design to Address Access and Accessibility in Online Multimodal Composition," we saw multimodal composition as a way to make our course more inclusive because students could respond to the assignments using more than traditional text-based compositions. We were also conscious of warnings to keep writing central to online classes, such as those offered by the authors of CCCCs *A Position Statement of Principles and Example Effective Practices for Online Writing Instruction (OWI)* (2013). Bearing this in mind, we decided to make all of our assignments multimodal and open platform, meaning students could compose their multimodal assignments using whatever tools they chose, including non-digital ones. Since our assignments were multimodal and open-platform, students had the agency to choose the genre, modality, and tools they would use to compose their assignments and could base those decisions on their individual skills, comfort levels, and access needs.

Once we determined how to approach multimodal assignments in the course, we were faced with the challenge of whether to include, exclude, or revise the final project in the course, the collaborative Monument/Memorial (Re)Design.

Collaborative projects can be challenging in any modality, but especially so in a digital distance environments like an online course. In our experiences, students tend to embrace multimodal projects but are ambivalent at best regarding online collaboration. We determined that the best way to get students engaged with the course content and each other was to create opportunities for them to work together in small groups throughout the semester.

Facilitating meaningful collaboration, especially in online environments, is a struggle that many instructors face. Our biggest advantage in this regard was the synchronous online environment where students met with us via Zoom for approximately three hours a week over a sixteen-week semester. This advantage meant that we could set aside time inside the course for groups to meet, plan, and compose together while we circulated between breakout rooms offering guidance where needed. We also knew that even with the ability to facilitate group activities during class, we would likely still encounter some hurdles as the semester progressed. Therefore, we entered our course redesign open to change, acknowledging that we would have to be flexible with some aspects of the course to make the class accessible and engaging for students. In response, the "better practices" we offer in this chapter are scaffolding strategies developed to support students' collaboration and multimodal composing in a synchronous online class. Most notably, we'll focus on two areas: 1) creating opportunities for students to participate in supportive learning communities, and 2) scaffolding sequences of readings, activities, assignments.

SCHOLARSHIP, THEORIES, AND PRINCIPLES THAT GUIDE OUR APPROACH

The support structures we created to guide collaboration and multimodal composition are informed by the Global Society of Online Literacy Educators' (GSOLE) *Online Literacy Instruction Principles and Tenets* (2019). The first principle of online literacy instruction (OLI) is that it should be universally accessible and inclusive, a goal that is easier to espouse than implement. While universal accessibility and inclusivity aren't fully attainable, they are a "north star," so to speak, a direction rather than a destination, and one that we plan to continue pursuing as long as we teach. The tenets under this expansive first principle—specifically two and three—are relevant to our scaffolding strategies:

TENET 2: USE OF TECHNOLOGY SHOULD SUPPORT STATED COURSE OBJECTIVES, THEREBY NOT PRESENTING AN UNDUE BURDEN FOR INSTRUCTORS AND STUDENTS.

This common warning challenged us to consider if our commitments to collaboration and multimodality were central or peripheral to our curriculum and pedagogy. The stated course objectives (see below) include the production of—and not just the consumption and/or analysis of—multimodal artifacts. Collaboration, while not specified in the course objectives, is foundational to our understanding of literacy learning. The difficulty in this tenet is determining what constitutes an "undue burden for instructors and students." Our position is that the support provided through the scaffolding strategies in this chapter make the technology use more accessible to students in addition to streamlining our workload as instructors.

Tenet 3: Multimodal composition and alphabetic writing may require different technologies; therefore, those involved should be appropriately prepared to use them.

As with the last tenet, the scaffolding we provide for students is designed to help students develop competencies in various production technologies. Both group work and in-class instruction work toward this goal, though we acknowledge that some students need to avail themselves of available resources outside of class. In addition to online help, our institution provides support through an in-person and online Digital Studio to assist students working with various composing technologies (McElroy et al., 2015). And as our other chapter in this volume details, another commitment we have is to allow students to make choices on composing technologies, so they can determine which technologies best meet their particular circumstances.

Much like the OLI Principle 1, we found that two tenets of OLI Principle 3—which states that instructors should regularly reevaluate online courses to support best practices—were particularly applicable to our better practice of providing scaffolding in online courses.

Tenet 4: Instructors and tutors should migrate and/or adapt appropriate reading, alphabetic writing, and multimodal composition theories from traditional instructional settings to their OLI environment(s).

As we've stated previously, we don't assume that course content and pedagogy need to remain identical in face-to-face and online classes. While the course descriptions and objectives may remain consistent, how we teach in different environments should reflect the affordances and constraints of the setting. Therefore, we advocate for instructors to consistently evaluate what is and isn't working within the class with an eye toward student learning and performance. We should be open to revising our approaches to teaching when necessary. For example, if collaboration and multimodal composing don't work for our students, we should look for ways to incorporate more resources for students into the course to support their learning. If there isn't a way to build more support for students into the course, then we should be open to eliminating collaboration and multimodal composing entirely and replacing them with something that will better suit our needs. We shouldn't hold any assignment or activity as more important than student learning and success. In our case, we would rather try keeping collaboration and multimodal composition in place with scaffolding for student support before we cut them from our curriculum.

TENET 5: INSTRUCTORS AND TUTORS SHOULD RESEARCH, DEVELOP, THEORIZE, AND APPLY APPROPRIATE READING, ALPHABETIC WRITING, AND MULTIMODAL COMPOSITION THEORIES TO THEIR OLI ENVIRONMENT(S).

Similarly, we commit to continually investigating and exploring new ways to teach and learn in online environments. In addition to the growing body of publications on OWI, we're grateful to communities such as GSOLE, the National Council of Teachers of English (NCTE), the Conference on College Composition and Communication (CCCC), and others that provide forums and platforms for practicing online literacy instructors to meet and share ideas about online education.

Though this level of reflection on our courses might seem like a lot of labor, many changes we made as a result ended up decreasing our workload because we were able to streamline and prioritize content and delivery.

COURSE CONTEXT AND LESSON

While the course and assignment we describe are from an upper-level college class, we believe that the better practices could apply to many online courses where students engage in collaboration and/or multimodal composing. While our upper-level students are in a program focused on editing, writing, and media—which has given them more experience in producing multimedia and multimodal projects—digital composing skills are becoming more common for students at all educational levels. The principles of scaffolding we advocate for in this chapter remain relevant despite the class level or institution.

Additionally, certain local events preceding the shift to online teaching during COVID-19 provided us the unique opportunity to build a teaching team. The graduate students (Amanda, Amory, and Ashleah) were selected to co-teach with Michael because of their teaching excellence and our graduate program's commitment to mentoring. This teaching collaboration generated reflective teaching conversations that lead, for instance, to writing these chapters together. However, on a more local level, it provided us weekly opportunities to talk together about the process, students, assignments, online components, and more. This is a rare treat for instructors, and we acknowledge the privilege of this collaboration.

As we also detail in Chapter 12 of this collection, Amory and Michael were teaching the class face-to-face in the spring of 2020 until the sudden shift online for the second half of the semester with no time to prepare and few resources for support. In our institutional context, emergency online teaching meant synchronous delivery that still met on the same days and times that we met face-to-face before the shift online. Our institution had recently invested in a professional site license for Zoom, which allowed us to use it for class delivery, small group work, discussion, and screen sharing. Canvas is our university's learning management system and our central "hub" for the course. We used Canvas to distribute online materials such as readings and resources, to organize students' collaboration and communication, and as a place for them to submit completed assignments for us to grade and respond to. We also used software such as Google Docs for workshops, collaborative activities, and class notes. By the time Amanda, Ashleah, and Michael taught the next semester together in the fall of 2020, we knew that the course would be delivered online and had time to prepare for it.

Course Goals

Our syllabus states:

> Visual Rhetoric is designed to give students an introduction to rhetorical thinking and analysis, an introduction into visual thinking and analysis, and hands-on experience creating and manipulating images for a variety of audiences, purposes, and situations. By the end of the term, students should be able to . . .
> - Apply rhetorical principles to a variety of linguistic and non-linguistic texts in a way that communicates their ability to provide insight about the texts;

- Use visuals to find and communicate meaning;
- Find, manipulate, and produce a variety of visual texts that communicate to targeted audiences;
- Use a variety of digital platforms to deliver visual media via the internet; and
- Create thoughtful, academic projects in a variety of media for different audiences.

As noted, the outcomes for the course define the need for multimodal production. While collaboration doesn't appear in the outcomes, it's central to our teaching philosophies and pedagogy.

Assignment Sequence

The course consists of three multimodal projects: 1) the Investigative Photo Essay, 2) the Visual Identities Project, and 3) the Monument/Memorial (Re)Design. The first project highlights how visuals communicate, the relationship between images and texts, and the ideological nature of images. The second project explores visual representations of an individual or collective subject position (e.g., race, ethnicity, nationality, social class, gender, sexuality, disability, religion). Finally, our Monument/Memorial (Re)Design Project is the culminating assignment for the course. This project allows students to synthesize what they have learned in the class to produce the four components:

1. the selection and visual representation of a monument or memorial,
2. an analysis of the original design,
3. a redesign of the monument/memorial, and
4. a rhetorical rationale for the redesign.

While this chapter will briefly touch on the reflective work that surfaced in students' rhetorical rationale reflection document, reflective practice is an important better practice of learning regardless of modality. Christopher Etheridge and Heidi Skurat Harris further unpack the link between reflection and metacognition Chapter 14 of this collection on data literacy, highlighting reflection's ability to connect students' past experiences and knowledge with new knowledge.

While working on this project, students read about public, collective memory; the constructed nature of history that is reinforced through monuments/memorials; and several case studies of monuments such as the Vietnam Veterans' Memorial, the Montgomery Civil Rights Memorial, the Joe Louis Monuments, and the 9/11 Memorial. Students choose the media for the redesigns and have used digital technologies such as video, websites, Photoshop, and Prezi as well as analogue technologies such as Legos, popsicle sticks, clay, drawings, paintings, and sketching. The project is described this way to students on an assignment sheet.

Monument/Memorial (Re)Design Project

Purpose
The purpose of this assignment is to explore how monuments and memorials reflect values and interpret history. You will also practice collaboratively investigating a visual representation of public memory that constructs and is constructed by (Fleckenstein) various and contested histories (Rogoff), and you will practice applying the visual rhetorical design principles we have learned throughout the semester.

Tasks

1. Select a current monument or memorial and provide original images from numerous perspectives of the selected site.
2. Write a visual analysis of the current monument or memorial (approximately 1000–1500 words). This analysis should include:
    a. the history of the event or site associated with the monument/memorial,
    b. an analysis of the original design's rhetorical choice and impact, and
    c. references to secondary sources and/or visual rhetorical principles.
3. Create a visual representation (e.g., models, drawings, scripts, performances, etc.) of a rhetorically-informed redesign for a new monument or memorial using visual design principles from the class. Your group can determine the media and technology used for the visual representation of the redesign.
4. Write an explanation of the rhetorical choices made in the redesign and how it is meant to be experienced by various viewing publics (approximately 1000–1500 words).
5. Submit your group's complete Monument/Memorial (Re)Design.
6. Write and submit an individual Self-Reflection Cover Letter, which will explain your experience, your contribution, and your learning on this project. You might answer the following questions:
    a. What have you learned about yourself as a learner and as a team player?
    b. How can you apply what you learned in this activity to new situations?
    c. Describe your most successful or least successful interaction with your peers.

    d. How did this experience challenge your assumptions and stereotypes?
    e. What was the best/worst/most challenging thing that happened?
    f. How would you do this next time?

Criteria

Though the individual criteria of the project will be evaluated on a four-point scale, the final project itself will receive a holistic score that includes a consideration of all components of the project in relation to one another, as shown in Table 4.1.

Table 4.1. Grading rubric for Monument/Memorial (Re)Design Project

Criteria	Comments	Points Received	Points Possible
Insightfulness of the original design photos			4
Thorough analysis of the original design using relevant sources			4
Thoughtfulness and creativity of the re-design			4
Strength, unity, and depth of rhetorical explanation of the redesign			4
Comments			
Overall Grade			

BETTER PRACTICE 1: BUILD INTERACTIVE SUPPORT GROUPS

Despite the challenges of collaboration in online environments, we wanted to provide students with opportunities to engage with each other and the course materials. From experience, we know these multimodal assignments are meaningful to students because they often result in showcase artifacts for their professional portfolios. Yet, without strategic scaffolding, or intentional opportunities for students to engage with each other over the course of the semester, we don't believe these communities are likely to form on their own, especially in online classes.

Strategy 1: Create Opportunities for Student Collaboration

The scaffolding of collaborative work was conceptualized early in our teaching team's conversations about the course, and we designed it to begin immediately in the semester even though the major collaborative project wasn't due until the end of the term. We were committed to developing an online learning community in which students knew one another: their names, their working styles, and their ideas. In our own preparation for online teaching, we read the warning that online instruction can easily become one-on-one interactions between the instructor with each student, which is not sustainable, and that it is more challenging to foster a community in online classes where students interact with one another in meaningful ways (Bourelle et al., 2015). We knew the challenge that students would face when collaborating online, but we also knew that introducing a project that demanded high levels of collaboration later in the semester could set students up for frustration if we didn't foster those relationships early on. Building a learning community was a necessary and natural component for success in the course.

The first aspect of community scaffolding for us was to foster what we call Inquiry Groups, which would be intentional from the outset of the class and remain consistent throughout the semester. We were initially worried about the risks of creating these groups early in the semester, such as students dropping out of the course or anticipating social conflicts. In our case, we were fortunate that neither of these happened; however, we were prepared to shift people around in the first few weeks of class as needed, which would still provide plenty of time for the groups to work together.

We began by developing weekly, low-stakes tasks asking students to work together on course material. These small assignments allowed us to see how students engaged with each other and to work on establishing healthy group dynamics. We embedded interactions for the Inquiry Groups into all aspects of the class since we were leaning on them to provide an intentional community where students would benefit from the stability of a few close relationships throughout the semester. Their Inquiry Groups became the place that they could turn to if they were struggling, if they missed course content, or when they needed a sounding board for their ideas.

Our first scaffolded collaboration was on the first day of class where students introduced themselves to one another—without the use of any written or spoken words. In a face-to-face class, we would have asked students to form random groups. However, this was a bit harder to facilitate in a Zoom room, so we used Zoom's "break out" room feature to place students into random groups instead. Next, we gave them six to eight minutes to develop a slide or make a drawing that they would show their group members. Then, the hardest part: they were to remain silent as their group members spoke aloud what they thought was being communicated by the images. Only after a time did we let them affirm, correct, or complicate the interpretations. This activity introduced students to the peers who would likely form their Inquiry Group, but by the time they reach the Monument/Memorial (Re)Design collaboration, they will have worked together consistently to establish relationships, build rapport, and learn each other's strengths and weaknesses.

An example of this rapport can be seen with one of our groups that chose to redesign "Christ of the Abyss," an underwater statue designed by Italian sculptor Guido Galletti that was placed in the Mediterranean Sea in 1954. The students proposed a redesign that would move the statue to a new location in a museum exhibit, making it more accessible to the public. These students had been working together throughout the semester on discussion boards. They had also been regularly talking in breakout rooms during in-class discussions. By the time this high-stakes project came around, they were familiar with each other and their working styles. In their initial draft, they created a website that housed elaborate designs of the museum layout, including a 3D video tour of the exhibit. Yet, their effectiveness as a group was fully demonstrated when they made a late-stage decision to overhaul their project's delivery after receiving peer feedback on the limitations of their media platform. The week the project was due, we planned an in-class peer review day in which each group submitted a full draft of their project. Then, the groups were divided to review other groups' work, using a Google Doc to house their review and feedback. After spending the semester responding to and reflecting on each other's choices in these digital spaces through discussion board posts, students were primed and ready to provide in-depth feedback on their peers' projects. The "Christ of the Abyss" group received feedback about the need for more context about both the original monument and their redesign. Each group wrote a reflection on the feedback they received, and the "Christ of the Abyss" group can be seen processing the responses of their peers:

> We plan to use all the feedback we received because it was really helpful! Some of the feedback we hope to apply is:
>
> Transferring over to Wix so we can have a better design.
>
> Expanding on our analysis so we can [have] more information from the readings and why we went with this monument design.
>
> We also want to add more pictures and other visual items to add to the quality of our website design.

> We want to make sure we will have a good balance of information and visuals on the website.

The group went on to transfer their project to a new host site, accomplishing their goals by including extensive written explanations of the original monument, their proposed redesign, and several visual design examples. Without the scaffolding provided in the ongoing Inquiry Groups, we believe this group could not have managed such a comprehensive revision in an online class. However, since they knew each other well and had developed a working rapport, they were able to successfully bring this new vision to their project.

Strategy 2: Re-Vision Teaching Practices with Students

In addition to the regular working relationships student form in Inquiry Groups, we have revised other components of the class to scaffold active, supportive communities. Since we are mindful of the cognitive overload for students and instructors working in online environments (Mayer & Moreno, 2003), we also re-visioned our use of discussion boards. In the face-to-face class, discussion boards had been used primarily for students to demonstrate some engagement with assigned readings through a series of questions. These discussion boards were largely non-interactive between students; yet, as instructors, we read them to get a better sense of what content from the readings students connected with, where they had challenges, and if they could apply the abstract ideas to concrete examples. In the face-to-face setting, the discussion boards, despite their name, weren't used to foster interaction, which would happen more within the classroom setting.

Our first attempt at more meaningful dialogue on discussion boards was to break the assignment into two posts a week. Since we still met synchronously, we matched the posts up with the two class days in this way:

> **Week 1 Discussion Board Post**
>
> **Description:** Each week, you will complete two Canvas discussion board posts. The first post is due Tuesday by 8 a.m. and will usually ask you to engage with the course reading, viewing, and activities. Your second post will be due by 8 a.m. on Thursday and will respond to your inquiry group members on how these class materials apply to the larger project on which you are working.
>
> Breakdown:
>
> Tuesday: What concepts from the readings/viewings from this week were most meaningful to you? What resonated? What

did not? What aspects of the material are most confusing? How do you think these ideas could or should be used/considered in your larger project?

Thursday: Read through what your Inquiry Group members wrote in their discussion board posts for Tuesday. Respond to the posts, especially the question about how the materials from this week might relate to the larger projects on which you are currently working. We'll give you time at the end of class to discuss these projects and how you might be applying these principles.

Evaluation: These posts are graded as complete/incomplete. Each week the discussion board posts are worth a possible 100 points total:

Tuesday post complete: 50 points

Thursday post complete: 50 points

At the start of the third week of class, we checked in with students and asked them for feedback on the way that the discussion boards were designed and realized our students weren't as excited about the design of this assignment as we were. Thanks to their thoughtful feedback, we realized that Thursday's response was a struggle for many students because of the quicker turn-around for reading and response. Many students would need to read far in advance to keep up because of external factors such as jobs or childcare; several would only have access to technology or the internet at certain times in the week.

As Asao Inoue succinctly puts it in *Antiracist Writing Assessment Ecologies*, "Creating healthier, fairer, more sustainable assessment ecologies in the classroom is not always about the classroom" (2015, pp. 294). We quickly saw our students' point. Based on their feedback, we determined that it would be better to shift back to students choosing one prompt to respond to each week and that they could use the second post to connect to the larger assignment. After listening to the students, three major revisions were made to the discussion boards to make them more accessible:

1. students only needed to make one original post a week and could choose which day to respond,
2. responses to their group members focused on applications to the major assignment, and
3. the evaluation was altered to a modified complete/incomplete scale.

Here is a sample of a revised discussion board assignment:

Discussion Board Post (Peer Response Format)

Description: This week we will conduct peer review of Major Assignment 1: Visual Representations of Identity project, which is due on Thursday October 8th. To give you more time to read and respond to each other's drafts, the due dates for this week's posts are different from what you're used to, so be sure to mark your calendars!

Tuesday's Task: By 8 a.m. on Tuesday, October 6th, post a working draft* of your project to the Discussion Board. You'll upload a link to your website, your presentation file, your video, etc. We will give you time during class to meet with your groups to discuss your working drafts and any context or specific issues you'd like your group members to keep in mind.

*Note: a working draft is a full version of your project that is ready for substantive feedback.

Thursday's Task: By 8 a.m. on Thursday, October 8th, view your Inquiry Group members' drafts and post a brief reply to each group member (this means you'll make roughly two to three posts, depending on your group's size*). Remember, when engaging in peer review, you should position yourselves as an audience member. Think about your experience viewing, exploring, or listening to their project. Your replies should include:

A **quote** from their project that stood out to you. This could be a bit of audio from a video, text from a presentation/website, etc.

A **comment** that answers two questions: 1) What is working? 2) If this was your project, what would you do differently?

A **question** that critically engages with their project. These questions could be practical about a choice they made in their design or production OR they could be more theoretical about their argument or positionality. Remember, stay curious and ask critical questions.

*Note: We do not have a required reading for class on Thursday to give you more time to respond to each other's drafts. Like Tuesday, we will set aside time in class on Tuesday for your Inquiry Groups to meet and discuss feedback on each other's projects.

Evaluation: Total 100 points

100/100 points: draft and peer review comments posted on time.

75/100 points: draft OR peer review comments posted late.

50/100 points: draft AND peer review comments late.

50/100 points: draft OR peer review comments missing.

BETTER PRACTICE 2: SEQUENCE READINGS, ACTIVITIES, AND ASSIGNMENTS

In addition to scaffolding the active, supportive community, we also considered how we might intentionally scaffold the readings, activities, and minor assignments in the online class to help support students in a class that required both collaboration and multimodal composing. While our examples above were to illustrate building scaffolded communities, they also begin to demonstrate what we mean by scaffolded assignments. Note, for example, where we described how the discussion board posts pointed students toward applying the class readings and viewings to the production project on which they were working at the time. As a teaching team, we agreed early on to combat the cognitive overload students face in an online class by scaffolding assignments in three ways:

1. clarifying connections between the readings, activities, and minor assignment and the major projects,
2. cutting out extraneous readings, activities, and minor assignments that did not relate directly one of the three major projects, and
3. creating checkpoints along the way to provide accountability to provide opportunities for formative feedback on the major projects.

Strategy 1: Build Connections Between Assignments

In addition to the readings and viewings we listed in the assignment description for the Monument and Memorial (Re)Design Project, we had students participate in two minor assignments during this unit that we designed to help them generate ideas and practice applying concepts in ways that modeled the work they would need to complete on the larger project. The two minor assignments were on vernacular memorials (makeshift memorials created by individuals rather than institutions, or individual expressions such as tattoos or car decals) and ideographs. The vernacular memorial assignment challenged students to expand their view of monuments and memorials to include local, personal sites of remembrance. This assignment was meant to be a relatively small exercise that would let them practice "noticing" monuments and memorials around us that we often overlook. Our description of this minor assignment is as follows:

Vernacular Memorials Project

Purpose

The purpose of this assignment is to practice identifying vernacular memorials, analyzing memorials as visual artifacts, and bringing into view memory spaces that may have become invisible to us because they are so common. All these skills will help prepare you for the monumental memorial project, which will ask you to identify, analyze, and redesign a monument or memorial as a group. In this assignment, you will . . .

- Select a vernacular memorial.
- Identify its function(s) and purpose(s).
- Explore its relationship to traditional public memorials.
- Reflect on how it engages with audiences and collective memory.

Tasks

- Create a Google Slides presentation.
- Find an example of a vernacular memorial and place one or more images of it on Slide 1 along with its title or a brief description.
- On Slide 2, write down your thoughts on the following questions:
    - How does the memorial function?
    - What might you assume about the person/people who created it?
    - How does it represent memory?
    - What purposes might it serve for various audiences?
- On Slide 3, cite or attribute any materials used in creating your presentation, such as images or texts.
- Post your Google Slides on your Inquiry Group's discussion board.
- Review your peers' posts and reflect on the posts as a whole, using the following questions as a guide:
    - What similarities or differences do you see across your memorials?
    - To what extent are these memorials more personal than a traditional public memorial?

Criteria

100 Points Possible:

- Completed Google Slides: 75 points.
- Completed Responses: 25 points.

This project, which would take only an hour or two to complete, was designed to facilitate invention and to get students to become more aware of public memory spaces in their everyday lives.

Another minor assignment that we decided to keep in the online course is an ideographic mix. In response to a challenging reading called "Representative Form and the Visual Ideograph" by Janis Edwards and Carol Winkler (1997), students were asked to create an ideographic remix of a popular monument or memorial. As Edwards and Winkler describe, an ideographic remix happens when an artist or composer appropriates a well-known image and remixes usually to make a political statement by associating the value of the original image to the remixed image, challenging the value of the original, or both. The example they use in the article is the famous photo-turned-monument of the U.S. soldiers raising the flag at Iwo Jima (featured as Figure 4.1). To understand ideographic remix, students must first identify the context, values, and message of the original and determine the rhetorical effects of remixes that trouble the original. Like the vernacular memorials project, the ideograph project contained ways of thinking and composing that we thought were helpful steppingstones towards the larger monument and memorial project.

Figure 4.1. The famous photo-turned-monument of the U.S. soldiers raising the flag at Iwo Jima (available in the public domain).

Figure 4.2. Emily's reimaged ideograph.

For example, in Figure 4.2, Emily used her ideographs project to analyze and reimagine Alfred Eisenstaedt's iconic photo "V-J Day in Times Square" and Lt. Charles Levy's "Atomic Cloud Rises Over Nagasaki, Japan." In this remix, Emily layers the colorized version of the people kissing over the original atomic cloud photo with the words "Make Love Not War" (shown as Figure 4.2). Emily's remix demonstrates her understanding of context, values, and messages of the originals. The background image of the atomic cloud standing in for the devastation of war, while the two people kissing represents pure relief and hope at the end of WWII. Emily's reflection also noted that the positive feelings she attributed to the two people in Eisenstaedt's photo came at the cost of the devastation represented by Levy's photo of the atomic cloud, further establishing her full consideration of the contexts of the two images, which were taken a mere five days apart in 1945.

While designing this image, Emily intentionally chose to highlight the two people in color for aesthetic design and heightened visibility. She also wanted the contrast to represent her own understanding of the original images and her chosen quote: the two people in the photo are colorized because they represent hope for the future. While creating this image, Emily learned a good deal about how to combine and manipulate images, which was a skill that she later used when working with her group on their Monument/Memorial (Re)Design

111

to create images for their project. This minor assignment gave Emily a deeper understanding of a key concept in the course, practical knowledge for how to approach analyzing and remixing images, and an opportunity to experiment with different platforms and technical skills in order to create a deliverable product.

Ideographs Project

Purpose

The purpose of this assignment is to practice identifying ideographs, visually analyzing images using the principles we've learned in class and designing visuals with an argument in mind.

Tasks

1. Create a Google Slides presentation.
2. Find an ideographic image and two to three remixes of it. Put those photos on slide 1.
3. On slide 2, write down your thoughts about these two questions:
   a. What is the original context and meaning of the image?
   b. What is the current context and meaning of the remix?
4. Make your own remix on slide 3. Take the ideographic image you analyzed and remix it to make a new argument. On the same slide, write a short (two to three sentences) explanation of the new meaning.
5. On Slide 4, cite or attribute any materials used in creating your presentation, such as images or texts.
6. Post your Google Slides on your Inquiry Group's discussion board.
7. Review your peers' remixes and share your thoughts on their work.

Criteria

100 Points Possible:

- Completed Google Slides: 75 points.
- Completed Responses: 25 points.

Because students often choose to engage in cultural critique within the Monument and Memorial (Re)Design, we thought this assignment would prime them for the clever creative work they might engage in since many students select public memories that have flattened historical figures or events such as depictions of the Civil War, Civil Rights, American Independence, the Holocaust, etc. We kept both projects in the online version of the class because they offered students the opportunity to explore core concepts in depth that would likely be helpful to generate and focus on ideas for the larger project. We also intentionally mirrored the task and criteria of the assignments, which helped limit confusion while also streamlining our assessment of them.

STRATEGY 2: DEVELOP REGULAR CHECKPOINTS FOR MAJOR PROJECTS

Finally, we created scaffolded readings, activities, and minor assignments through developing a regular and intentional pattern of feedback that consisted of checkpoints, workshops, and conferencing. One of our concerns about education more generally but also specifically about online education is that coursework might be getting reduced and simplified in ways that undermine some of the experiences in relation to brick-and-mortar education. Of course, we need to be vigilant about accessibility and mindful of the busy lives of our students. At the same time, we don't want to lessen or otherwise devalue the online experience. While it's a hypothetical case, imagine if our face-to-face classes had collaboration, interactions, and multimodal composition while our online class contained only self-paced modules with multiple choice quizzes and tests for assessment? If online education isn't as rich and productive an experience as in-person education, we undermine the value of the online educational experience. Therefore, in our commitment to a robust course that includes collaboration, interaction, and multimodal composing. Moreover, we know that students need accountability and formative feedback in order to stay focused on the larger assignments throughout the full time-period we have allotted for the project. Part of the value of these larger, creative multimodal projects is that they can't be completed the night before the assignment is due. They have components that require time to think, develop, consider feedback, revise, and edit if they want to have the type of showcase pieces they'll want to include in their professional portfolios.

In response, we developed checkpoints and other graded activities that would ensure that students would begin working right away, have opportunities for formative feedback from our teaching team and their classmates, and develop their work over time. We scheduled these at minimum every other week, but many times, we had something due weekly. To make this manageable for us as instructors, the checkpoints and assignments had to be relatively quick and easy to evaluate and provide feedback. A first checkpoint for an assignment might be for students to identify the topic for or site of the first project in just a sentence or two; this initial idea could come in the form of writing, video, or brief conference even within a class period using a breakout room. By creating expectations and rewarding students for their efforts, we nudge them along to ensure they have early momentum on the projects and receive the feedback and technical support along the way to expect and reward them to work throughout the project.

In face-to-face instruction, but even more so in online education, providing scaffolding like checkpoints assists students in managing these larger projects and gives instructors the opportunity to see along the way which students are making good progress and which are struggling with anything from ideas to production to time management. These short check-in times don't take long, but they provide us with a wealth of information to help support students as they develop the knowledge and skills to participate in these more ambitious projects. While not all online classes need to be this ambitious all the time, we hope at least some are, especially when students get into classes that are closely related to their personal and professional goals. Otherwise, we run the risk of minimizing students' educational experiences and undermining the value of accessible education.

REFLECTION ON PRACTICE AND CONCLUSION

One of the most difficult tasks we faced while working on the design of our course was finding ways to cut down and revise content in a way that would still allow us to meet the course goals and outcomes that we wanted and finding creative ways to build community and support that wouldn't put an onerous burden on ourselves or our students. We were starting to "think holistically about what classroom writing assessment is or could be for teachers and students" and "seeing classroom writing assessment in its entirety, not just parts of it" (Inoue, 2015, p. 9). Thanks to Michael and Amory's experiences in the spring, we knew that we would have to do quite a lot of revision to the course to make it align with the best practices for teaching online. Even with careful planning and the best intentions, things still went awry, as tends to be the case in any given semester. If something was broken, we listened to students before determining a course of action together, and this act served to strengthen discussions and lessons in the larger class.

The overarching frame of our course is interconnected, relying on strategic scaffolding throughout all aspects of the course. For example, we were very intentional when choosing readings and revising low-stakes projects for the course, ensuring that both always contributed directly to each other. The strategic scaffolding with minor projects and readings, components were designed to build on one another as we progressed through the semester. We also used the major projects to help us frame the units of our classes to create a tangible, specific vision for everything we did in class or online. If we could make a recommendation to other instructors hoping to implement collaborative and non-traditional projects in their online courses, we would urge them to be

Scaffolding for Collaboration and Multimodal Assignments

flexible in course design, responsive to students' needs, and intentional with each assignment and reading.

We owed many of our successes to the advantages we had as a three-person team who had both time and experience on our side as we planned. Some of the practices we used here may not be feasible for an individual instructor to attempt, and the agency that we had over our course content and design was a privilege that many instructors may not share. Even so, our chapter offers a snapshot of one approach to building meaningful learning moments and communities in digital environments and many of our practices are adaptable across contexts and modalities. In an in-person, real-time learning course, soliciting regular updates or feedback on the course throughout the semester could help instructors identify and address problems early, function as a form of accountability for students, or some combination of both. Another example is creating long-term small groups to foster community in larger classrooms, regardless of modality.

The most important thing for determining the value and usability of these practices is the instructor's individual and institutional context. There's no one-size-fits-all solution to scaffolding a writing course. Taking the time to articulate what we wanted our students to learn and how we wanted to help our students to learn is what inspired our re-visioning of this course. The ongoing reflection and discussions we had amongst ourselves and with students helped us make decisions that centered student experiences, scaffolded their learning, and fostered collaboration—all in the interest of building a sense of community and support in a distanced environment.

MOVING BETTER PRACTICES ACROSS MODALITIES

- **In-Person, Real-Time Learning:** feedback on the course can be collected by providing time in class for students to discuss assignments or expectations in small groups before discussing it as a larger class.
- **Online, Real-Time Learning:** feedback on the course can be collected by providing time in class for small group discussions in breakout rooms or through anonymized quizzes or surveys. In both options, discussing the concerns that students bring up can help instructors make helpful adjustments or clarifications to the course schedule or assignments.
- **Online, Any Time Learning:** incorporate conferences or email "check ins" with individual students to discuss their progress in the course or set up an anonymized quiz or survey to collect feedback from students. A third option might be to have students respond to smaller, group discussion boards rather than a large class-wide one.

Checking in with students enrolled in online, any time courses and creating opportunities for them to engage with each other in smaller settings can help the class to feel less impersonal and more like a learning community.
- **Hybrid Learning:** any combination of the above suggestions could work for this modality. For instance, instructors could use the times that they meet face-to-face with students as an opportunity to check in with them regarding their progress or they could do the opposite and allow students to check in via a survey or quiz as one of their online assigned tasks.

REFERENCES

Bourelle, T. Bourelle, A., Spong, S., Knutson, A., Howland-Davis, E. & Kubasek, N. (2015). Reflections in online writing instruction: Pathways to professional development. *Kairos: A Journal of Rhetoric, Technology, and Pedagogy, 20*(1). https://kairos.technorhetoric.net/20.1/praxis/bourelle-et-al/scholarlyfoundation.html.

Conference on College Composition and Communication. (2013, March 13). *A position statement of principles and example effective practices for Online Writing Instruction (OWI)*. National Council of Teachers of English. https://cdn.ncte.org/nctefiles/groups/cccc/owiprinciples.pdf.

GSOLE Executive Board. (2019, June 13). *Online literacy instruction principles and tenets*. Global Society of Online Literacy Educators. https://gsole.org/oliresources/oliprinciples.

Inoue, A. B. (2015). *Antiracist writing assessment ecologies: Teaching and assessing writing for a socially just future*. The WAC Clearinghouse; Parlor Press. https://doi.org/10.37514/PER-B.2015.0698.

Mayer, R. & Moreno, R. (2003). Nine ways to reduce cognitive load in multimedia learning. *Educational Psychologist 38*(1). https://www.uky.edu/~gmswan3/544/9_ways_to_reduce_CL.pdf.

McElroy, S. J., Wells, J., Burgess, A., Naftzinger, J., Lee, R., Mehler, J., Custer, J., Jones, A. & Cirio, J. (2015). A space defined: Four years in the life of the FSU digital studios. *Sustainable learning spaces: Design, infrastructure, and technology*. https://ccdigitalpress.org/book/sustainable/s1/fsu/index.html.

COURSE MATERIALS REFERENCED

Blair, C. & Michel, N. (2000). Reproducing civil rights tactics: The rhetorical performances of the Civil Rights Memorial. *Rhetoric Society Quarterly, 30*(2), 31–55.

Edwards, J. L. & Winkler, C. K. (1997). Representative form and the visual ideograph: The Iwo Jima image in editorial cartoons. *Quarterly Journal of Speech, 83*(3), 289–310.

Eisenstaedt, A. (1945). *V-J day in Times Square*. [Photograph]. Wikipedia. https://en.wikipedia.org/wiki/V-J_Day_in_Times_Square

Fleckenstein, K. S. (2004). Words made flesh: Fusing imagery and language in a polymorphic literacy. *College English, 66*(6), 612–630.

Gallagher, V. J. & LaWare, M. R. (2010). Sparring with public memory. In G. Dickinson, C. Blair & B. L. Ott (Eds.), *Places of public memory: The rhetoric of museums and memorials* (pp. 87–112). University of Alabama Press.

Galletti, G. (1954). *Cristo degli abissi (Christ of the abyss)*. [Photograph]. Wikipedia. https://en.wikipedia.org/wiki/Christ_of_the_Abyss .

Hariman, R. & Lucaites, J. L. (2003). Public identity and collective memory in US iconic photography: The image of "Accidental Napalm." *Critical Studies in Media Communication, 20*(1), 35–66. https://doi.org/10.1080/0739318032000067074.

Levy, C. (1945). *Atomic cloud rises over Nagasaki, Japan*. [Photograph]. Wikipedia. https://scn.wikipedia.org/wiki/File:Nagasakibomb.jpg.

Mix, D. (2015). In loving memory: Vernacular memorials and engaged writing. In J. Greer & L. Grobman (Eds.), *Pedagogies of public memory: Teaching writing and rhetoric at museums, memorials, and archives* (pp. 172–182). Routledge.

Morris, A. (2019, March 12). Take 'em down 901: The kairos of progressive activism during a national rise of racist rhetoric. *Spark: A 4C4Equality Journal*. https://sparkactivism.com/volume-1-intro/take-em-down-901-the-kairos-of-progressive-activism-during-a-national-rise-of-racist-rhetoric/.

Nicoletti, L. J. (2008). Mediated memory: The language of memorial spaces. In C. David & A. R. Richards (Eds.), *Writing the visual: A practical guide for teachers of composition and communication* (pp. 51–69). Parlor Press.

Rogoff, I. (1998). Studying visual culture. In N. Mirzoeff (Ed.), *The visual culture reader*. (pp. 24–36). Routledge.

Sturken, M. (1991). The wall, the screen, and the image: The Vietnam Veterans Memorial. *Representations, 35*, 118–142.

U.S.M.C. Archives. (2012, June 14). Flag raising on Iwo Jima, 23 February 1945. *Flickr*. https://www.flickr.com/photos/60868061@N04/7371568006.

CHAPTER 5.

ANNOTATION AND RHETORICAL ANALYSIS WITH DISCUSSIONS HOSTED IN FLIP

Ana Contreras
Harper College

Troy Hicks
Central Michigan University

In this chapter, the authors describe **an annotation practice** *used online, any time learning. Specifically, the authors share annotation activities that create deliberate scaffolding as students move from their initial annotations of a text to ongoing class discussion and, finally, to the draft of an essay using the learning technology Flip. In describing their "better practice," this chapter addresses the themes of accessibility and inclusivity and practices in motion across teaching and learning modalities.*

FRAMEWORKS AND PRINCIPLES IN THIS CHAPTER

- **GSOLE Principle 1.4:** The student-user experience should be prioritized when designing online courses, which includes mobile-friendly content, interaction affordances, and economic needs.
- **GSOLE Principle 4.2:** Educators and researchers should insist that various OLI delivery models (including alternative, self-paced, and experimental) comply with the principles of sound pedagogy, quality instructor/designer preparation, and appropriate oversight detailed in this document.
- **Framework for Success in Postsecondary Writing, Persistence:** Consistently take advantage of in-class (peer and instructor responses) and out-of-class (writing or learning center support) opportunities to improve and refine their work.
- **Framework for Success in Postsecondary Writing, Engagement:** A sense of investment and involvement in learning.

- **Framework for Success in Postsecondary Writing, Flexibility:** The ability to adapt to situations, expectations, or demands.
- **Framework for Success in Postsecondary Writing, Metacognition:** The ability to reflect on one's own thinking as well as on the individual and cultural processes used to structure knowledge.

GUIDING QUESTIONS BEFORE YOU BEGIN READING

- How do we encourage and support writers through intentional response to one another's work?
- How do we guide students in using textual evidence to support their ideas?
- How can we utilize technology to enhance and support students in online learning environments, especially in asynchronous interactions?

INTRODUCTION

Two weeks into the fall semester of our online, asynchronous composition I course, my student, Julieta, and I were in our second WebEx meeting. Like many students, she had enrolled in this online course after a semester of emergency remote learning due to COVID shutdowns yet had never experienced an asynchronous course.

As we talked, she hesitated through pauses and glanced away from the camera. I tried to listen even more intently. The assignment for the week was to view the TED Talk by Chimamanda Adichie, "The Danger of a Single Story," and to add "substantive annotations" on the transcript (Adichie, 2009). The Ted Talk's written transcript was copied into a Google Doc, so it was then easy to highlight and comment upon. Students could explore the content in multiple ways (watching and reading).

Julieta was catching up on assignments, and this activity was the first we discussed in our meeting. I shared the assignment with her again, restating the goal that students were supposed to be creating annotations that made connections, asked questions, or summarized main ideas.

Then, I tried to move into a discussion about the assignment, and the text itself. "So, I understand that you are still a bit confused by the assignment, so let's start from the text first. Can you summarize some of the ideas you heard in Adichie's TED Talk?"

"Well," Julieta began, "I remember her talking about Nigeria and some aspects of their culture. And, stereotyping. She talked a lot about stereotypes."

Nodding, I encouraged her. "Tell me a bit more. What kinds of stereotypes?"

"So, she said how her roommate kind of thought of Nigeria as being one thing, yet she didn't really think of Nigeria that way. It was like Adichie didn't, you know, fit the image."

"That's interesting," I said. "So, what did Adichie say about that? Where can you point to a moment in the transcript where she said or hinted at that idea?"

Julieta paused, and I could tell, even through the webcam, that she was looking at the transcript as her eyes moved back and forth. The pause turned to silence.

My mind flooded with questions that, suddenly, I couldn't answer. For Julieta herself, I wondered if she had watched the TED Talk yet was unable to understand the main idea. Then, there was the scolding teacher part of me, wondering if she had, indeed, even watched the TED Talk at all.

I started to question my instructions for students, moving from my own hurt ego toward empathy. Was the assignment unclear? Did I need to rephrase things? Was I unintentionally placing pressure on her to "perform" and "deliver" at that moment? Was she embarrassed and struggling to find the "right answer"? How could I help her navigate this new space of online—and almost completely asynchronous—learning?

My mind spun further. I began to wonder about my institution and about online learning in higher education more broadly. How do we create online learning environments that take the best of in-person real-time instruction and integrate technology in a meaningful way? How do we as educators ensure that our teaching, both to the entire class and through individual coaching, is effective? Moreover, how do we insert ourselves into students' homes, working assertively to connect with them without being overly intrusive? I, as the guide, felt helpless and searching for my own answers.

Maybe the way that we reach students through a screen instead of face-to-face is through connection—if we can suspend our beliefs about what "should be" and be more mindful of the moments we have with students. I needed to listen and support the needs of the student in front me so that we could work together. This meeting was an opportunity for me to make this student feel welcome. It gave me an opportunity to listen to what she needed. I took a breath and brought myself back to the WebEx room.

I must have been silent for a long time. Julieta, leaning toward her webcam, looked quizzically at me. With that, I decided to ask a different question.

"So, Julieta, did Adichie talk about *someone* specific? Is there a spot in the text that you can point to?" I was again trying to encourage Julieta to refer to the text, to confirm her answer and support her claim. However, she remained silent.

I paused, hoping to find just the right question to ask in order to move her forward.

From there, I began thinking about a number of other ideas, especially about equity and access in online learning. Had I prepared Julieta enough for this task?

What kinds of assumptions did I make in the design of this assignment? Would she be able to use the smartphone and laptop that she had to effectively engage in these annotations and, soon, our video-based discussion using the Flip website and app?

Here I was, in a moment that brought many values as an instructor into sharp focus, as well as my need to be more explicit about those values in my teaching. Three professional texts, in particular, had been formative in my approach for designing the course: *Principles for the Postsecondary Teaching of Writing* (2015), especially its focus on invested learning, adaptability, and reflection, composed by the Conference on College Composition and Communication (CCCC); the *Online Literacy Instruction Principles and Tenets* (2019), especially the need to develop mobile-friendly, sound instructional design, composed by Global Society of Online Literacy Educators (GSOLE); and the "habits of mind" from the Council of Writing Program Administrators (CWPA), the National Council of Teachers of English (NCTE), and the National Writing Project's (NWP) *Framework for Success in Postsecondary Writing* (2011), hereafter cited as CWPA.

In my design of the course and assignment, I wanted to show that writing is social and that we must engage students in a scaffolded process to make connections between their ideas and their peers. I had included a structured activity with guides to help students with creating annotations. I had built on that activity asking them to use those annotations to support their ideas in a Flip video discussion post. I had asked them to reflect on the posts of their classmates to reply and engage in a conversation about Adichie's TED talk. In many ways, I thought I'd provided layers where students utilized specific skills that they continued to build upon to improve their understanding of the text and improve their ability to craft their thoughts. All of these elements, I had thought, were incorporated in the design of my assignment. Yet, were they?

The tension remained. Here I was, in dialogue with Julieta, who was likely sharing concerns that other classmates would have as well. Something wasn't working. As a result of that interaction with Julieta—and in later dialogues with my coauthor and other contributors in this collection—the revised, articulated lesson shared below is my attempt to take what I learned and rethink the assignment through an equity-oriented lens of transparent assignment design. I realized that I could create a slow and steady progression for students, and this lesson prompts more productive and engaging conversations about the text amongst my students. Like many of our colleagues, I'm rethinking, learning, and continually improving so that I can be a better teacher and writer.

Before getting to that lesson, I provide a bit more background on some of those foundational documents noted above and then consider how my experience with Julieta helped me reimagine that lesson for future sections of my class.

SCHOLARSHIP, THEORIES, AND PRINCIPLES THAT GUIDE OUR APPROACH

These conferences with Julieta emphasized the importance of guiding students through the process of academic reading and writing, with their many associated (and often invisible) skills. As an undergraduate, I would usually be given a sheet of paper with the parameters of an essay and then be asked to submit my work a few weeks later. These assignments assumed that I understood how to closely read, annotate, and engage in discursive conversations using academic language, let alone employ conventions like proper grammar and citations. Sadly, I realized that I was making some of those same assumptions with my students, and the asynchronous demands of our course had only exacerbated the problem. As I spoke with Julieta, I articulated each of those steps and scaffolded a process of learning so that she could practice and build the skills included in the writing process.

First, I share a brief description of the assignment in relation to the theoretical frameworks that underpin the assignment's design. I originally designed a three-part assignment that asked students to use the video discussion platform Flip to engage in a discussion about Adichie's talk, "The Danger of a Single Story." Students used a Google Doc with the transcript to make annotations and read aloud a passage as they recorded a video reflection in Flip. Then, they replied to a classmate who had posted a question, using an excerpt from Adichie to support their ideas. In this post, students would continue the conversation by also including a question of their own. The asynchronous discussion was supposed to last about a week. Finally, at the end of the week, I offered the students an opportunity to gather as a class in an optional WebEx meeting to reflect on the asynchronous conversations we had in Flip.

Not accounting for the final video conference call in WebEx, this lesson incorporated the use of two primary technologies, Google Docs (with which readers are likely to be familiar) and the web-based, video sharing program Flip. Briefly, Flip (formerly Flipgrid, see Novet, 2018) can be described as a cross between an online discussion forum and a social media site with video upload options. Flip describes itself as a fun, interactive space for all learners, regardless of age, to share their voices. While video-based conversations may not traditionally be considered a space where one builds on skills related to composition, the use of multimedia allows students a way to practice being in conversation with a text, a key element in the design of this particular lesson.

The choice of these technological tools was intentional. The use of Flip can be used across the different kinds of technology that students have available, including phones, computers, laptops, or tablets. Students can access it with a link or a QR code. Flip also includes accessibility options and multiple ways that students can engage with captions, timestamps, and the use of Microsoft's Immersive Reader.

While GSOLE's principle 1.4 does not reference a comprehensive request to address all obstacles involving equity, the intention is clear: instructors must design tasks and choose technology tools that include affordances that will meet the needs of their students. The design of the assignment, with Flip as a key component, both meets standard 1.4 and speaks to specific instructional moves, in addition to the technology, also meant to address the needs of students, many of whom, like Julieta, were new to online learning.

Or, so I had thought . . . until I brought my mind back to the conversation at hand with Julieta, and began to consider how her classmates might be experiencing similar challenges.

COURSE CONTEXT AND LESSON

As noted earlier, this lesson is part of a three-week assignment series that focuses on annotation, close reading, and discussion. This assignment exists within an ENG 101 English composition course provided online with any time and real-time learning components at a community college in a suburb west of Chicago. The student population is diverse with about half identifying as Black and Latinx and includes individuals from varied ethnicities, cultural backgrounds, home languages, abilities, and experiences. Students need varying levels of academic support and the assignments in ENG 101 are, ideally, structured to provide all students that support. Also of note, most of my sections for ENG 101 are completely online and asynchronous. Students are invited and encouraged to set up additional, one-to-one meetings with the professor via Webex.

The course content, broadly, is focused on multicultural identity and builds on the scholarship of Iris Ruiz, who encourages the inclusion of culture, identity, and community (Ruiz, 2016). It was developed by a group of ENG 101 professors, primarily adjuncts, in a community of practice. We all customize our courses a bit, yet there are four major assignments in the course: a narrative essay, a synthesis essay, a rhetorical analysis essay, and a digital story. The better practices featured in this chapter relates to the second assignment, the synthesis essay.

This lesson involving Flip, then, serves a few purposes at this moment in the overall arc of ENG 101 course. It helps students to engage in:

- Close reading, annotation, and finding evidence to begin crafting an argument,
- Multimodal discussion that allows for multiple ways of expression, and
- Thinking about how they, as writers, will soon make similar rhetorical moves in an essay.

Flip, as a tool for expression, is important as it gives students an opportunity to share their ideas in the way that they prefer: via video, audio-only, or with written text. As long as students are meeting the objectives of the assignment, they can fulfill those requirements in multiple ways without adding to their own labor or the labor of their instructor. Flip serves my students well, yet it is not the only technology tool that could be used in this lesson. Other platforms that facilitate video discussion can work equally as well if an educator does not have access to—or choose not to use—Flip. In considering other tools like GoReact, VoiceThread, or similar platforms, educators should ask:

- Will the tool allow students to engage in an online discussion using multimedia (video, audio, and text) recording?
- Can students connect to that platform easily with a weblink or another accessible link?
- Will students be able to work with the tool across multiple devices (smartphones, tablets, laptops)?
- Does the tool have a space where the instructor can provide students with clear, transparent directions and support materials like tutorials?
- Does the tool allow for full accessibility for all students, regardless of ability?

While the tools we use are important as a component of developing lessons and activities, they should not be restrictive. Often, we can explore other tools or reimagine a lesson to be specific to our context in our communities. Here, based on my rethinking of the task with Julieta and other students in mind, is my more transparent version of the assignment, one that I would share with them directly.

Assignment Sheet: Flip Discussion of Adiche's TED Talk, "The Danger of a Single Story"

By the end of Week 3, you will:

- Make an initial post to Flip, due on Wednesday by midnight,
- Be prepared to discuss your initial ideas during our real-time class meeting on Thursday, and
- Reply to two classmates' posts due on Sunday by midnight.

Purpose

As we move more deeply into our work together this semester, let's begin with a conversation that moves us from simply sharing our opinions and, instead, encourages us to focus on a specific text. To support this conversation, we will use a video-based discussion board, Flip, to look at Chimamanda Ngozi Adichie's 2009 TED Talk "The Danger of a Single Story." In her talk, Adichie makes the case that our perceptions regarding the identity of other folks are often incomplete, allowing each of us an opportunity to learn more about other identities, communities, and cultures.

Skills

The purpose of this assignment is to help you practice the following skills that are essential to your success in this course and as a way to develop ideas for writing in future college courses and professional contexts. Specifically, you will . . .

- Identify main ideas in a mentor text, using substantive annotations and note taking,
- Enhance your comprehension of a text and draw connections to other texts and real-world experiences through the practice of close reading,
- Support your interpretations of a text using quotations from the author as evidence, and
- Summarize and synthesize your ideas about a text to open the dialogue with others who have also viewed/read the text.

Knowledge

For this particular lesson, let's think about the disciplinary thinking that good writers use to form arguments. You don't need to master specific content. There is no quiz, no right or wrong answers. Yet, there are some ways that we need you to think about what Adichie is discussing in her TED Talk.

Key Vocabulary Terms:

- **Intersectionality:** Developed by Dr. Kimberlé Crenshaw (1989) as a way to consider how various forms of identity (e.g., race, class, gender) sometimes overlap and create unique challenges and opportunities (in particular, from Crenshaw's earliest writing, African American women). According to the Oxford English Dictionary (2021), intersectionality is "[t]he interconnected nature of social categorizations such as race, class, and gender, regarded as creating overlapping and interdependent systems of discrimination or disadvantage; a theoretical approach based on such a premise."
- **Discourse:** As defined by the Oxford Learner's Dictionaries, discourse is "the body of statements, analysis, opinions, etc., relating to a particular domain of intellectual or social activity, esp. as characterized by recurring themes, concepts, or values; (also) the set of shared beliefs, values, etc., implied or expressed by this" (2021). To speak more

plainly, discourse is the term we use to describe ongoing conversations that occur in academic fields where experts exchange ideas about their field of expertise. When we read academic journals and use these as evidence in our writing, we are engaging in that conversation.
- **Mentor Text:** When writing teachers want to provide students with a high-quality example of writing, they will find a model or example text that students can use as a guide. These mentor texts can also describe course content texts that students are to read or review in their course.

Key Questions to think about as academic writers:
- How do you contribute your own ideas, questions, and opinions to an ongoing conversation?
- How do you write about and analyze a text, focusing on how the author was making key choices about content, language, and evidence used?
- How do you read and analyze multimodal texts composed in different tones, styles, and levels of formality?
- How do you use technology strategically and with a clear purpose in order to enhance your writing for an audience?
- For more information, you could look at the "habits of mind" from the *Framework for Success in Postsecondary Writing* (2011), especially the ideas of persistence, engagement, flexibility, and metacognition.

The Task for the Week
1. Begin your post to Flip by choosing one of the annotations you highlighted as you were reviewing the TED Talk transcript. As you record your video, read the passage you are annotating aloud. Note the annotation you are using from your Google Doc, and then describe the connection between the text and your annotation. If you are not comfortable having your image on the screen, you can record just audio at this stage. If you are uncomfortable with speaking and/or recording, you can reach out to me for other options.
2. To help you create this post, I've provided a few resources below to review:
    a. Review the slides from last week's class session (on Blackboard).
    b. Review my example posts in the Blackboard discussion (on Blackboard).
    c. Review these resources from the University of North Carolina Learning Center for tips on higher-order thinking and reading comprehension:

i. https://learningcenter.unc.edu/tips-and-tools/higher-order-thinking/.
ii. https://learningcenter.unc.edu/tips-and-tools/reading-comprehension-tips/.

3. Create your initial post by Wednesday by midnight to allow members of the class an opportunity to review your contributions to the discussion throughout the week. At the end of your post, ask an open-ended question that will invite your classmates to respond to your initial ideas.
   a. For instance, "In what ways do you think Adiche ___" or "To what extent do you agree with Adiche that ___" are both the beginnings of good open-ended questions.
4. As you prepare for our synchronous class on Thursday, please review the initial posts and be prepared to discuss these questions.
   a. Are there common themes that emerge in the discussion?
   b. Are the passages that our classmates are citing from Adichie's talk in their initial posts the same, or are there many different selections?
   c. Is there a particular classmate's post in the discussion that sticks out to you?
5. Finally, as the week comes to a close, draft a response or a reply to a classmate in the Flip discussion by Sunday at midnight. If the classmate already has a response to their Flip video, please choose someone who has not yet received a response.
   a. Respond by indicating how their thoughts and ideas contributed to your understanding of the text and then ask a question that moves the conversation forward. You can use one of the Conversation Stems (https://bit.ly/ConversationStems) we discussed in class. Again, you can review my example response post in the Flip Discussion.

Criteria for Success

While this is a "pass/fail" assignment—and is meant to encourage you to participate—there are some elements that must be completed. The rubric has three criteria for the "labor-based" logistical aspect of participating, as well as three criteria for the quality of your intellectual contributions.

"Labor-Based" Criteria (Credit or No Credit based on meeting deadlines and minimal requirements):

- By Wednesday, create your initial post to the Flip Discussion Board, 0/5 points.

- By Thursday, review the posts in the Flip Discussion and be prepared to review your thoughts in class, 0/5 points.
- Sunday, create your reply to the Flip Discussion, 0/5 points.

"Quality of Intellectual Contribution" Criteria (Credit or No Credit based on quality; may be revised and resubmitted):

- Annotations show the depth of thinking by incorporating evidence from the text through reading aloud and reflection on the connection between the annotation and text, 0/2/3 points.
- Responses show active listening and response empathy that reflect on comments made by our classmates in their initial post. Responses also incorporate a reflective question intended to move the conversation forward, 0/2/3 points.

Table 7.1. Assignment Rubric

Criterion	Y/N (full or no credit)	Points Earned
Labor-based Criteria (Work must be completed on time; no make-ups)		
Initial post by Tuesday	Y/N	0/5
Participate on Thursday	Y/N	0/5
Responses by Sunday	Y/N	0/5
Quality of Contribution Criteria Y/N (with comments)		
Initial annotations on GDoc transcript show depth of thinking by commenting on specific evidence from Adichie's text	Y/N	0/2/3
Initial Flip response poses at least one substantive question, based on annotations, for others to respond.	Y/N	0/2/3
Response to a peer in Flip shows evidence of active listening by "saying back" what was heard and engaging with ideas presented.	Y/N	0/2/3

FULL LESSON DETAILS OUTLINE

Though no single lesson can capture all the principles we hope to teach, directly or indirectly, this particular lesson has been designed to address the CCCC's principle that "Writing can also be developed socially if writers are expected to collaborate with one another in stages, from drafting to revision to publication," as well as GSOLE's "OLI 1.4: The student-user experience should be prioritized when designing online courses, which includes mobile-friendly content, interaction affordances, and economic needs." In doing so, I examine the lesson in more detail in four major phases, each tied to one element of the CWPA framework including . . .

- **Persistence:** "consistently take advantage of in-class (peer and instructor responses) and out-of-class (writing or learning center support) opportunities to improve and refine their work."
- **Engagement:** "make connections between their own ideas and those of others."
- **Flexibility:** "approach writing assignments in multiple ways, depending on the task and the writer's purpose and audience."
- **Metacognition:** "use what they learn from reflections on one writing project to improve writing on subsequent projects."

In what follows are brief sections where we explain the practice in greater detail and explicitly connect them to persistence, engagement, flexibility, and metacognition to illustrate to readers how these ideals can transform into better practice.

Flip, Support, and Persistence

During the first week of class, students complete a self-introduction in Flip. In this initial assignment, I provide students with my own introduction to use as a guide. In the Flip discussion forum, instructions for the assignment are also provided to students in addition to Flip video tutorials. The intention is to build community by having students converse with one another through video posts. This assignment can be a basic introduction that includes a name and a brief statement regarding what students want to learn in the course. Inspired by the work of Kimberly Crenshaw, students could create an introduction that shares aspects of their identity and experiences with their classmates to find commonality and connection. From a technological standpoint, this introductory exercise also includes the benefit of allowing students to become acquainted with Flip and experiment with the features or options in the creation of their posts.

This lesson focuses on the CWPA element of "persistence"—the ability to sustain interest in short and long-term projects—in that it elicits students' thinking to engage them in conversation that essentially stays with them the entire semester. Students begin their discursive work at the beginning of the semester with an introduction to Flip and a low-stakes task described above. They continue to engage with Flip in a more complex task posting their ideas about Adichie's TED talk and they become more familiar with the tool.

Close Reading, Scaffolding, and Engagement

As students move into the second week of class, they begin to engage with Chimamanda Adichie's TED Talk, "The Danger of a Single Story." Students begin the lesson by reviewing the module in Blackboard. I provide them with a six- to eight-minute video that emphasizes the importance of close reading and annotation when understanding a text. In the video, I demonstrate each annotation connection, questioning, and summary using a transcript from Adiche's TED Talk.

Students use this example as a guide to help them with their assignments for the week as they annotate the transcript of Adichie's TED Talk in a Google Doc. Students highlight passages in the transcript and use the comment feature to add notes to the text. At a minimum, students should use each kind of annotation (connection, question, and summary) three or four times. However, I emphasize with students that they can use each of these annotations as much as they like. A Google Doc allows me to easily add feedback that nudges students to extend their ideas or acknowledges the strengths in their work. Students have a week to complete this assignment. The CWPA element of "engagement" occurs throughout this lesson starting with the text itself. Students perform a close reading and listening to Adichie's TED Talk. Later, students will add ideas to a Flip discussion with the intention of leaving their viewers with a question. Afterward, they will review posts and reply to their classmates, again asking a question. Through Flip, they engage and share with one another.

Flip and Flexibility

The next week, students are reintroduced to Flip. To give students a guide and show the differences in this round of conversation, I provide students with an example video as the first post on the Flip discussion board, in which I review these slides (https://bit.ly/FlipDiscussSlides), which walks students through why we are doing this activity, how to prepare and complete the activity by preparing and recording their video, and modeling with embedded examples of Flip videos.

Students are given a week to create their second post in the Flip discussion. The following week, students are asked to craft a reply to their classmates in the Flip in a similar way as they had in the previous round. Students review classmates' posts and choose a post they find compelling and reply. At the end of their reply posts, students again ask a question that encourages continued conversation. I also provide my own reply in the first post to the discussion so that students have a model to work from.

The CWPA element of "flexibility" applies not only in the options that students use to encounter the text but in how students reply to the TED Talk itself. Students have access to both the recording and the transcript of Adichie's TED Talk. Flip also provides students with a number of options in terms of accessibility. The platform allows students to choose the manner in which they will participate in the discussion by creating video, audio, or screenshare recording that includes a text-based document. That being said, Flip also includes editable captions for each video that is shared as well as timestamps and screen reader capability, among other features.

CONCLUDING THE LESSON AND METACOGNITION

At the end of the week, when the discussion is concluded, I ask students to reflect on their experiences. This period of reflection also includes an optional synchronous class meeting where I help students make the connection between our Flip discussion and writing. Prior to the meeting, I request that students review posts in the Flip discussion board one more time and take notes about what they observe. What ideas were shared most frequently? What did you find interesting? What would you have liked to see the class post about more? In giving students a reflective assignment like this one, we will already have a starting point for our discussion as students gather thoughts to share in our class meeting. For those who aren't able to attend, I provide a recording they can view afterward.

I begin the meeting with a "mixtape" video of our Flip discussion. The mixtape is a feature recently added to the Flip platform and gives the moderator/instructor the ability to combine a series of posts from a Flip discussion into a single video. For this synchronous meeting, I would collect a handful, probably no more than three, of student posts that serve as good examples and add them to the mixtape. The advantage of using the mixtape is that, when the video plays, students see each of the posts sequentially; in this sense, the video seems more like a conversation between the participants as opposed to a disjointed series of comments placed on the discussion board.

After playing the mixtape, I encourage students to freewrite briefly using the "I like, I wish, I wonder" protocol. When I introduce the prompt, I mention that we will all be sharing. As they review the posts, they take notes on what they "like" and why. Students will then move to "wish" as they think beyond the discussion taking notes about what might have been missing from our conversation. Finally, they will end with the "wonder," taking notes about questions that arose during the conversation. This allows students to write and gives them a moment to collect their thoughts and review what they plan to share in class. As the freewriting time passes, I participate with students and include my thoughts; I share a thought, word, or idea from my writing and go around the room asking students to share the same. This freedom to share as little or as much as students feel comfortable is a strategy I adopted from a colleague, Andy Schoenborn. Acknowledging Schoenborn's ideas of "invitation" that he shares with students (Hicks & Schoneborn, 2020), we know that sharing writing with classmates can be intimidating. However, asking students to share something as small as a word allows students the freedom to participate when they might not feel comfortable reading lengthy passages.

This discussion might also include ideas from students that include the following.

- Students will say something like "I like what Student A said . . . " or "I can see a connection from Adiche to Text B."
- Or, they might try to validate what another person has said in a more generic way.
- Or, because I knew what I was going to say to my classmate and professor, I tried to . . .
  - Ask them: how does this relate more broadly to what we are trying to do with teaching writing? How are we imagining that other teachers/authors might talk about this?

After students share ideas from their writing, I summarize and then transition into discussing the ideas and skills that they utilized in the Flip. I elaborate on how each of the skills we used in the Flip can be applied to writing an essay.

- Close reading to understand a text more thoroughly,
- Annotating to take notes and point to main ideas in a text,
- Citing text as evidence for an idea,
- Summarizing to convey an understanding of an idea, and
- Synthesizing texts to critically observe, understand and challenge an idea.

This discussion prefaces a larger, reflective essay which integrates ideas resulting from our synchronous meeting. Students submit a reflective journal entry at the end of this assignment, thinking about what they learned from engaging in this Flip conversation and our class discussion. Students might share what they liked about the Flip discussion or Adichie's "Danger of a Single Story." Students might share frequent themes that appeared in Flip. They might make connections to their writing and the skills that we practiced in this lesson including annotation and close reading. Most importantly, they may reveal that they didn't realize writing a paper was like a conversation.

The CWPA element of "metacognition" applies to this portion of the exercise in that students spend time reflecting on the activity after it concludes. They are thinking about the posts they shared, as well as reflecting on the Flip discussion overall. I begin the activity series by asking students to verbally speak as they pull ideas from Adichie's text when preparing to record their Flip post. The task also encourages students to deepen their thinking in the construction of their post. They perform similar exercises when they create reply posts, this time considering the ideas of their classmates. Finally, at the conclusion of the discussion, they reflect on new ideas offered in the Flip. When we come back together in the synchronous meeting, students make connections between the work we are doing and the iterative nature of the writing process.

While we often think of online learning as disconnected and solitary, this particular lesson utilizes the discussion platform provided by Flip as a space to build community with the voices, text, video of student contributions. Having conversations about difficult topics can be challenging because it requires us to reveal our own ideas and show some vulnerability. Students are encouraged to use the text as a basis for reflection and then share a thought or idea about a difficult topic through video or audio. In doing so, they see others including their instructor put forward that vulnerability, too. With clear discussion guidelines set before class, students have the safety to share their ideas and respond to the ideas of others. Our community is built as we ponder and relate our thoughts of this particular text together. This metacognitive task is enhanced when we meet and hear the mixtape video then reflect on what we've learned and how we will use those lessons going forward.

Looking ahead, the next step would include the process of students composing a one-page paper synthesizing Adichie and connecting to another mentor narrative text. While it is beyond the scope of this chapter to provide details about that second assignment here. I would use a prompt similar to the one below as the kernel of the task.

> Prompt: Choose one idea that Adichie and one idea that the <mentor text author name> both discuss. Compose a one-page synthesis essay that explores this idea as it is presented in both mentor texts.

As an instructor, there are multiple points in this week-long series to offer feedback, though I don't offer feedback on all of those points to each student every time (as that would be excessively time-consuming). Instead, I use the rubric noted above to focus feedback on a student's strengths and where they might need support and offer students thoughts on how they might build upon the skills they already have.

When I think of the connection to better practices, I see it as a consistent thread. Connecting with students, both individually and collectively, is at the heart of our teaching, regardless of modality. The connections made are not accidental, they are intentional moves that come from a genuine commitment to supporting students. The chapter began with a student, Julieta, who I connected with to offer support. The better practice shares an approach for guiding connections as well: connections with text, with peers, and with a classroom community. The hopeful result of having completed this lesson is that our community will be more encouraged to engage in difficult discussions and support one another as writers as we progress through the semester.

REFLECTION ON PRACTICE

Technological tools can empower learners and build confidence. Technological tools can also be used to enhance equity and access to learning with features that promote community, critical thinking, and perception. However, those same technological tools can be prohibitive, limiting access and increasing inequity in the classroom.

In this case, Flip as a tool did not create a more equitable classroom, in and of itself. This aligns with the OLI principle 4.2 which emphasizes sound pedagogy and quality instruction regardless of the online delivery model or technology. While it is true that the functions available within Flip made a more equitable approach possible, I needed to design an assignment that would capitalize on features of this tool to provide students with multiple ways of fulfilling the assignment requirements, all while being given the opportunity to express their ideas in the manner they preferred.

Equity in online environments begins first with the instructors and their perceptions of the learners in their classes as well as what "learning" itself really means. After considering one's role and disposition as the instructor, one should consider the context in which the learning is occurring; this includes the communities where we are teaching and learning and the life experience of the students in front of us. Additionally, lifting up the work of Tia Brown McNair and colleagues (2020), the data that comes from our classrooms—both quantitative and qualitative—can share another perspective of what is happening in our classroom:

> Indeed making the equity gaps visible can be disquieting—this is, in large part, the point. Seeing race-based equity gaps is intended to "create an 'indeterminate situation'" by which practitioners realize that their practices are not working as intended and are "moved to a mode of deliberation or reflection that prompts them to ask 'Why do unequal outcomes exist' What can we do?"

Teachers who understand the classrooms, students, and communities in which they are teaching can better design learning experiences and address the needs of the learners before them. Utilizing better practices, the instructor needs to consider the educational objectives that are required of students in their class, reflecting on if these objectives also meet the needs of the students in their courses. Perhaps using a framework for integrating technology, one can consider the tools at their disposal that would meet the objectives, provide equitable access, and support the needs of students. Educators can consider how the tools could be used to allow students to demonstrate their understanding of the material with flexibility, too. It is only after this preparation and reflection that one can begin designing assignments that serve students well. While each of these elements could require a much longer explanation, I mention them here to emphasize the fact that the design of this particular activity and the consideration of equity in this exercise comes from a deeper exploration of the educational context and the students in my classroom in addition to considerations of content and design.

Having an awareness of all of these things, even if not a full understanding, provides us with a perspective that we can then use to ask the same question we've always asked ourselves as teachers—What can I do in my classroom to support my students in their success? To do this, we need an equity-orientated lens.

As I reflect on the lesson described above, and continue to refine it, what becomes most clear to me is the importance of *intentionality* in the way that we craft our teaching. Teaching is a crafted profession, full of choices that lead to the opportunities we offer our students to learn. The threads come together to create beautiful experiences in the hopes that someone else will learn or appreciate its form. Tying together each of the elements of the lesson, the writing skills (annotating, reading aloud, textual evidence), the technology, community building, and finally the reflection are all parts of the lesson that provide a space for students to make connections with one another while learning with and from their instructor. While the full picture might not be evident at the start, as each of my choices came together the art of the learning revealed itself.

At the end of the day, I believe that I am learning with and from a group of learners who are in front of me. We contribute to learning in the ways that we engage with one another. We do so through the connections we forge by sharing our ideas, asking for support, providing guidance, and opening ourselves to the opportunities to understand the world from a different perspective.

CONCLUSION

When Julieta and I met for the fourth and final time during our six-week abbreviated semester, she brought her printout—with annotations—of Gloria Anzaldúa's "How to Tame a Wild Tongue" (1987). The conversation began with some quick pleasantries, and then we jumped right in. Right away, Julieta noted key points about Anzaldúa's article: it was written in three languages and this emulated what the author was aiming to do in a discussion of border spaces. Julieta shared her annotations, and she initiated new stages in our conversation from the many items she had noted. More importantly, at one point, she even pushed back on my interpretation of Anzaldúa's text, again citing a place in the text where she was able to draw in additional evidence. In short, Julieta had grown as a reader, thinker, and writer.

In this last meeting, she gained confidence in the way that she presented her ideas, asserting her role as a scholar. I didn't hear the pauses in her voice or the uncertainty that I recalled from our first meeting. She was assured and comfortable in the way she responded to my inquiries. Julieta wasn't searching or looking for me to provide answers because she was using the skills she'd adopted to share her ideas. I asked her what she thought of the in-class discussion we'd had about Flip.

"I liked listening to the ideas of other students. I realized that even though I didn't agree with everyone's views, I learned from listening to what they said."

"That's good," I replied. "I also learned a lot from reviewing everyone's responses and reflections on Adichie. We all come to the class with different perspectives, experiences, and world views. That's why I brought us back together in that class meeting."

Her eyes drifted a bit from the screen as she shifted to that final reflection paper. "Yeah, the classmate I spoke to gave me good ideas for my reflection. And I used some of those ideas in my one-page synthesis paper."

I smiled. We spoke for a few more minutes before we ended the call. While it seemed like the meetings were there to support her learning, they taught me about my strengths and weaknesses as an instructor, too. In our conversations, I took the time to ask how she was doing before we began and listened. I also took away lessons that applied to all students in the course. I considered where I might need to build in more support and where I could do with less guidance as we moved through the lesson. She had a guide in me, yes, but I also was being guided by Julieta.

MOVING BETTER PRACTICES ACROSS MODALITIES

- **In-Person, Real-Time Learning:** Students can still make annotations in a Google Doc before coming to class with opportunities to engage in discussion in-person instead of using Flip.
- **Online, Any Time Learning:** While the asynchronous components of this lesson could remain the same, students could reflect on what they learned by contributing to a final Flip discussion instead of meeting synchronously to discuss those final takeaways.
- **Hybrid Learning:** This better practice could largely remain the same in hybrid learning environments, with synchronous online conversations occurring during in-person meetings and asynchronous activities still completed online by students between in-person sessions.

REFERENCES

Adichie, C. N. (2009). The danger of a single story. *Ted Conferences.* https://www.ted.com/talks/chimamanda_ngozi_adichie_the_danger_of_a_single_story.

Anzaldúa, G. (1987). How to tame a wild tongue. In *Borderlands: The New Mestiza—La Frontera.* Aunt Lute Book Company.

Brown McNair, T., Bensimon, E. M. & Malcom-Piqueux, L. (2020). *From equity talk to equity walk: Expanding practitioner knowledge for racial justice in higher education.* John Wiley & Sons.

Council of Writing Program Administrators, National Council of Teachers of English & National Writing Project. (2011, January). *Framework for success in postsecondary writing.* http://tinyurl.com/9t7ejehm.

Crenshaw, K. W. (1989). Demarginalization the intersection of race and sex: A Black feminist critique of antidiscrimination doctrine, feminist theory, and anti-racist politics. *University of Chicago Legal Forum, 14,* 538–554.

GSOLE Executive Board. (2019, June 13). *Online literacy instruction principles and tenets.* Global Society of Online Literacy Educators. https://gsole.org/oliresources/oliprinciples.

Hicks, T. & Schoenborn, A. (2020). *Creating confident writers for high school, college, and life* (1st ed.). W. W. Norton & Company.

The Learning Center. (n.d.). *Higher-order thinking: Bloom's taxonomy.* The University of North Carolina at Chapel Hill. Retrieved January 2, 2023, from https://learningcenter.unc.edu/tips-and-tools/higher-order-thinking/.

The Learning Center. (n.d.). *Reading comprehension tips.* The University of North Carolina at Chapel Hill. Retrieved January 2, 2023, from https://learningcenter.unc.edu/tips-and-tools/reading-comprehension-tips.

National Council of Teachers of English's Conference on College Composition and Communication. (2019). *CCCC's principles for the postsecondary teaching of writing.* https://cccc.ncte.org/cccc/resources/positions/postsecondarywriting#principle1.

Novet, J. (2018, June 18). Microsoft acquires education start-up Flipgrid in latest challenge to Google. *CNBC.* https://www.cnbc.com/2018/06/18/microsoft-acquires-education-start-up-flipgrid.htm.

Oxford University Press. (2021). *Oxford English dictionary.* Oxford University Press.

Oxford University Press. (2021). *Oxford Learner's Dictionaries.* https://www.oxfordlearnersdictionaries.com/us/definition/american_english/discourse_1.

Ruiz, I. D. (2016). *Reclaiming composition for Chicano/as and other ethnic minorities: A critical history and pedagogy.* Palgrave Macmillan.

CHAPTER 6.

TEACHING TEXTUAL ANALYSIS THROUGH COLLABORATIVE, ONLINE ANNOTATION

Valeria Tsygankova and Vanessa Guida Mesina
Columbia University

This chapter demonstrates a practice of collaborative, online annotation that helps students expand their abilities to analyze complex texts. The authors describe a series of assignments, in which students read and re-read a published essay for homework over three class sessions, each time making public annotations on a communal, digital copy of the text. At each reading, students receive new prompts to elicit engagement with specific aspects of the assigned text. Each layer of annotation involves more conversation among students and deeper analysis. Students learn to use annotation as an exploratory, early-stage writing tool that helps generate ideas, and as a strategy for building up and refining ideas over time. Moreover, students practice taking part in a community of inquiry, working with other readers and writers to create new knowledge. The assignments described are easily used across teaching modalities (in-person, real-time; online, real-time; online, any time; hybrid). This chapter addresses the themes of accessibility and inclusivity and assignments adapted from classic composition strategies.

FRAMEWORKS AND PRINCIPLES IN THIS CHAPTER

- **GSOLE Principle 1.2:** Use of technology should support stated course objectives, thereby not presenting an undue burden for instructors and students.
- **GSOLE Principle 1.4:** The student-user experience should be prioritized when designing online courses, which includes mobile-friendly content, interaction affordances, and economic needs.
- **Framework for Success in Postsecondary Writing, Curiosity:** The desire to know more about the world.
- **Framework for Success in Postsecondary Writing, Openness:** The willingness to consider new ways of being and thinking in the world.

- **Framework for Success in Postsecondary Writing, Engagement:** A sense of investment and involvement in learning.
- **Framework for Success in Postsecondary Writing, Flexibility:** The ability to adapt to situations, expectations, or demands.
- **Framework for Success in Postsecondary Writing, Critical Thinking:** The ability to analyze a situation or text and make thoughtful decisions based on that analysis, through writing, reading, and research.

GUIDING QUESTIONS BEFORE YOU BEGIN READING

- How can instructors make student reading practices more visible in order to make them a site of learning?
- In what ways can online annotation facilitate student collaboration and classroom community?
- How can online annotation be used to teach an iterative approach to reading, writing, and textual analysis?

INTRODUCTION

It was Vanessa's first one-on-one meeting with Hae, and the kind of meeting she had become accustomed to. It tended to happen soon after the initial session of Vanessa's first-year writing (FYW) class: a student would show up to office hours, eyes wide with panic. "I just . . . I just . . . I don't think I belong here. I don't understand the reading. At all."

Our college campus is filled with bright, ambitious, overachieving students from all over the world and all walks of life. According to Columbia's International Students & Scholars Office (2023), over 19,000 of our campus' students and scholars identify as "international," and our School of General Studies specifically serves returning, older students beginning their undergraduate education after time off from an educational setting. There is no one single type of Columbia University student. Yet every semester, a number of our students start their undergraduate journey feeling overwhelmed and out of place. What if they hadn't read the right books, or had been out of school for too long? How would they ever keep up?

Vanessa had no doubt that Hae did, in fact, "belong" in her FYW course. She told Hae she thought the essay that the class was reading, Zadie Smith's "Speaking in Tongues" (2009), was a tricky one, and asked Hae to talk about a place in the text where she felt confused. Hae directed Vanessa to the second page; "I don't understand," she said. "It's a personal essay—nonfiction, no? So, why is she using a character from a play as evidence?"

"That's interesting," Vanessa said. "Why would you expect her not to?"

As Hae began to explain her thinking, it immediately became clear that her struggle with Smith's text was not one of comprehension but rather of confidence. Hae was working to articulate a tension of sorts that she had found in the reading—one that relied on nuanced understandings of genre, evidence, and reader expectations. But, when she was sitting alone in her bedroom trying to get through her homework, having questions felt like failure; if something about the text was confusing, she must be missing something obvious. Hae feared her confusion meant she didn't belong at the university, but Vanessa saw Hae's struggle with the text as a productive starting point—a way into the kind of inquiry-based thinking and writing practiced by a university discourse community (Swales, 1990, 2016). Vanessa knew it was her job to show Hae that scholarship begins from articulating confusion, a foundational scholarly practice that the college writing textbook *How Scholars Write* (2021) puts this way:

> When scholars analyze a text—a novel, a building, a journal article, a film, a performance, an event—they're mining for problems. They search for tensions or dissonances: things that don't quite fit together in expected ways. Scholars then work to make sense of the tensions or dissonances. (p. 6)

Vanessa asked Hae if she had started the annotation assignment. That semester, both of us (Vanessa and Valeria) were debuting an annotation assignment in our FYW classes, which we hoped would help students not only effectively mine for problems, but also see themselves as members of a community of inquiry that works toward a shared goal—making sense of complex texts.

We were asking students to use the annotation program Perusall—a free tool designed for "[s]tudents [to] help each other learn by collectively annotating readings in threads, responding to each other's comments, and interacting" (Perusall.com). The platform allows instructors to create "courses" that students can join using an email address and a unique course code. By uploading PDFs, linking to web pages, or searching for texts on Perusall's own digital library, instructors provide students with digital copies of course readings; once enrolled, students can read and annotate the texts using the Perusall interface. Highlighting a passage on the digital copy automatically opens a new "Conversation," where users can add notes, which other users can then reply to. Annotations in conversation threads can incorporate a hashtag (#) to create an instantly searchable key term (e.g., #question) or mention other members of the course using the @ feature. Students can "second" questions posed by their peers with a click of the "?" button on any given annotation, and instructors can "upvote" comments as especially useful for others. Figures

6.1 to 6.2 show sample Perusall threads featuring hashtags, mentions, and instructor upvoting.

While we had both previously given quick lessons on annotation in our FYW courses, we had never read and commented on student annotations, or even checked that students were completing them. But the semester that we were debuting the annotation assignment was also one of our first semesters teaching entirely online (in real-time), due to the COVID-19 pandemic, and, while we found ourselves no longer able to see and teach annotations as we had in the past, we also felt that we had been presented with an opportunity to investigate the affordances of collaborative, online annotation.

There were immediate practical advantages. Most students didn't have access to printers at home and were doing their reading digitally. Perusall offered a free way to interact much more thoroughly with the readings than was offered by more common free platforms for digital reading. Perusall was also built for educational use (not for harvesting student data). For all these reasons, it accorded with GSOLE OLI Principle 1.4: "that student-user experience should be prioritized when designing online courses, which includes . . . economic needs" (GSOLE, 2019).

Other advantages having to do with our stated goals (to deepen student engagement with texts through inquiry, to help students try on the practices of a university discourse community, and to increase their sense of belonging) soon became apparent. As Hae and Vanessa started looking through the annotations that some of Hae's peers had added, it became evident that Hae was not the only one with questions. Sure, she was the only one questioning Smith's use of Eliza Doolittle as evidence (at that point in the assignment, at least). But her peers had *many* questions, some of which Hae actually felt she had answers to. Vanessa suggested that Hae could highlight the passage on the second page that they had talked about and pose her question in an annotation. Hae did, pausing at the end before typing, "What do you think?" and hitting return. By posing her first question, Hae was acknowledging that, yes, she had questions about the text, as well as starting to actively seek out answers from her fellow readers.

Our approach to this assignment was informed by three major claims made by researchers studying writing pedagogy and reading practices in the last two decades. First, researchers have argued that, to make reading a site of learning, teachers must find ways to make reading visible. As Robert Scholes wrote in 2002, in a passage often quoted in later studies:

> We normally acknowledge . . . that writing must be taught and continue to be taught from high school to college and perhaps beyond . . . because we can see writing. . . . But we

> do not see reading. We see some writing about reading, to be sure, but we do not see reading. (p. 166, as cited in Carillo "Engaging" (2016), in Carillo "Creating" (2016), and in Lockhart & Soliday, 2016)

As Scholes and the scholars who have followed him have noted, assessing, intervening in, and promoting reflection around student reading presents difficulties for writing instructors because reading practices are, by default, hidden; not being able to see reading happen means not being able to address it. "We must find ways to make reading as visible as writing," Ellen C. Carillo has argued, "so we can work as deliberately on reading as we do on writing" (2016, "Creating," p. 18). In online learning—be it "real-time" or "any time"—student reading practices are potentially even less visible than in the traditional classroom. After all, in a traditional classroom, we might still see some incidental evidence of how students are reading: a book full of Post-it notes, or a highlighted printout on the seminar table.

Second, research has suggested (as we detail later in this chapter) that explicitly teaching annotation as a reading-to-write strategy is a productive way to make reading into a site of learning. And third, while online teaching may initially look like an obstacle for teaching annotation, it may—in certain, significant ways—actually be an advantage. As Carillo (2019) has pointed out: "Annotation makes the process of reading visible, and therefore, makes reading easier to address in the classroom . . . Digital platforms such as *hypothes.is, Diigo,* and *iAnnotate* have made this practice that much easier" (n.p.).

Tara Lockhart and Mary Soliday's (2016) research provides compelling evidence for annotation assignments' efficacy in teaching concrete, nuanced engagement with texts. Lockhart and Soliday interviewed 76 undergraduates from 20 majors after these students had taken a writing class that integrated the teaching of reading and writing. Students in the study tended to report that "annotation practices helped them better understand and engage what they read and helped to prepare them for later writing or reading tasks" (Lockhart & Soliday, 2016, p. 28). Even better, many students in Lockhart and Soliday's study went on to adapt the annotation practices they learned in the writing class to other courses and contexts, especially the use of annotation for the brainstorming and invention stages of their writing (2016, pp. 28–30). Finally, students also reported that leaving traces of their thinking on the page during a particular period of reading created an opportunity for them to "compare previous knowledge with new knowledge" when they returned to a text (Lockhart & Soliday, 2016, p. 30). If we wanted to teach students to pay close attention to texts and to build up and refine their ideas over time, annotation would be a key practice to teach.

Existing research supports the efficacy not only of individual annotation practices, but also of collaborative ones, especially for helping students identify problems, tensions, and complexities in a given text. A lesson study conducted by Nancy Chick and colleagues (2009), for instance, has suggested that collaborative annotation is an especially effective vehicle for teaching students to articulate and respond to tension in a literary text. Chick and her co-authors oversaw an in-person, real-time lesson in collaborative annotation, devised with the goal of teaching students to read "for contradictions [and] paradoxes that do not fit a single, coherent interpretation" (2009, p. 404). During the lesson, student groups annotated patterns and pattern breaks in a poem on a transparency film, linking each pattern and each break "to the concrete language of the poem." Students then saw all of the groups' transparencies overlaid and projected via an overhead projector, "as a visual representation of the poem's layers of meaning and complexity," and wrote "about how they [saw] the patterns relating to each other, how it is possible for these patterns to coexist in one poem, and how they explain the elements that do not seem to fit the patterns" (Chick, et al., 2009, p. 405). After class, students reflected in writing on how the method of reading that they were taught affected their overall interpretation of the poem.

For us, this study from Chick and her co-authors has some particularly exciting results: the authors noticed that, in a sample of 65, students on the whole moved from the "flat" and "reductive" readings (2009, p. 400) evident in their pre-class writing to more nuanced readings that could acknowledge and reflect on multiplicity. Chick et al. speculated that there were two main reasons for the lesson's success:

1. students were being specifically directed to identify patterns and seeming discrepancies, using an annotation method that could make those patterns and tensions visible, and
2. students were encountering the observations and interpretations of their peers, which in itself raised productive dissonance and made multiplicity apparent.

As we designed our lesson, we were especially excited by this last thought—that seeing each other's observations might help students develop more nuanced and interesting interpretations.

In designing our online annotation assignment, we aimed to take advantage of the individual benefits described by Lockhart and Soliday, as well as the benefits of collaborative annotation described by Chick and her co-authors. By explicitly asking students to look for seeming discrepancies and ambiguities in a text, and by asking them, through rereading, to complicate their initial impressions, our assignment teaches students a transferable habit: noticing and responding to complexity in their objects of analysis (be they texts, or images, or organisms, or data sets). In this way, this early assignment acts as a touchstone for our entire semester and offers our students a generalizable approach to scholarly engagement with, and response to, complex material. We hoped, also, that annotating collaboratively would promote students' awareness of being part of a scholarly community. And, in an online course, students annotating together would be able to experience writing as a social practice, even without sharing a classroom space.

Our use of Perusall to accomplish these goals is informed by GSOLE provision 1.2, that "use of technology should support stated course objectives, thereby not presenting an undue burden for instructors and students." Our assignment sequence using Perusall is designed to teach a number of moves and habits central to our pedagogy—including careful attention to the particulars of an object of analysis, rereading to sharpen and complicate thinking, and the articulation of tensions and questions.

These objectives, in turn, are informed by the *Framework for Success in Postsecondary Writing* (2011), which encourages instructors to foster the habits of mind of curiosity (students "use inquiry as a process to develop questions . . ."), openness (students "examine their own perspectives to find connections with the perspectives of others; listen to and reflect on the ideas and responses of others . . ."), and engagement (students "make connections between their own ideas and those of others; find meanings new to them or build on existing meanings as a result of new connections; act upon the new knowledge that they have discovered") (para. 5).

In addition, this lesson helps students develop what the Framework calls critical thinking, since it asks students to "write about texts for multiple purposes including (but not limited to) interpretation, synthesis, response, summary, critique, and analysis" and to "generate questions to guide research." It also encourages students to "develop flexible writing processes," to see that these processes are "not linear," to "move back and forth through different stages of writing," and to practice several generative moves for the "invention" stage of writing. The annotation lesson that we designed helps students see that flexible, exploratory writing at the start of a project can help them develop compelling lines of inquiry for the project's middle and later stages. Using an online platform for collaborative annotation, students are able to draw on each other's observations as they develop and refine their questions about the text.

COURSE CONTEXT AND LESSON

We teach a one-semester FYW seminar, capped at 14 students, that meets twice per week for 75-minute sessions. Over the course of the semester, our class moves through four units, or "progressions," each progression building up—through low-stakes, ungraded pre-drafting and drafting exercises—toward a final essay that students turn in for a grade. The essays written during the first three progressions steadily increase in length and complexity, and the fourth and final progression asks students to write a shorter essay, an op-ed, for an audience beyond the university.

The first essay assignment, a single-text analysis essay, tasks students with identifying a compelling question or tension that arises for them in a text, and to use that question to motivate a close-reading and analysis of the text. The first essay assignment is similar to typical close-reading assignments in literature and composition classes that ask students to choose a passage in a text "and then 'unpack' the passage, paying close attention to the textual elements including the passage's language, tone, and construction [and to] connect this passage to the rest of the work" (Carillo "Engaging," n.p.). However, our first essay assignment also adds an emphasis on identifying a compelling question that motivates this analysis and "unpacking," in order to encourage student writers to practice scholarly inquiry and to think rhetorically about engaging their readers. If readers can see that an essay begins from a pressing inquiry, they are more likely to be interested in reading on and discovering the essay's findings.

Thus, the aim of the first essay assignment is to teach not only transferable analysis skills like close-reading, citation, and quotation, but also in a larger sense to teach concepts and habits generalizable beyond literary studies. Writ large, the objective of the first assignment is to introduce students to a set of fundamental moves of inquiry-based, scholarly writing—i.e., beginning by naming something difficult to understand or poorly understood, developing a plan or project for examining it, and, through analysis, coming up with claims that help illuminate what was initially unclear.

The first essay assignment provides a robust scaffolding for the second essay assignment in our FYW sequence, which asks students to choose some object of analysis (a text, a film, an event, a performance, etc.) that raises an interpretive problem for them, and to draw on ideas and concepts from several other writers, whose work circulates in a related scholarly conversation, as they examine their object of analysis and respond to their problem. If the chosen object of analysis fulfills the role of what Joseph Bizup (2008) has called an "exhibit" source, the other sources that students must engage in conversation (chosen by the instructor during this unit) play the roles of "argument sources" and "method sources." The third essay assignment in the course is a research essay that asks students to choose their own objects of analysis and to find most of the other sources that they will draw upon as they develop their arguments. This third unit includes instruction in locating and managing multiple sources. Finally, the fourth essay assignment is an op-ed written for a target publication selected by each individual student, giving students a chance to write for an audience beyond the university. At all of these stages, students use annotation to generate ideas.

Lesson Design and Rationale

The following assignment sequence unfolds over three class sessions at the start of the semester, in the early days of the first progression, as students begin working toward their first essay. As our class meets synchronously, in real time, a fair amount of scaffolding for using the Perusall platform occurs during class meeting time. In Class 1, students register for Perusall, join the class Perusall "course," and read the first page of the class text together. As students read, they generate observations and questions, which are added as Perusall conversation threads (first by the instructor as a model, then by students themselves).

In Class 2, we introduce the term "interpretive problem" or "scholarly problem," building on the definition in Aaron Ritzenberg and Sue Mendelsohn's *How Scholars Write* (2021): "By 'problem,' we don't mean mistake or fault. We mean an intellectual tension that merits resolving" (p. 6). Referring to some of the examples of problems in *How Scholars Write*, we review in class some of the annotated questions and confusions that students have posted in Perusall—first as a large group, then in pairs—to discuss whether or not these questions might stem from (or lead to) problems ripe for analysis and interpretation.

In Class 3, we work together on a model interpretive problem as a class, looking for textual evidence that could help us stage this problem for a reader, as well as evidence that might offer some clues towards its analysis and/or resolution. Students also use class time to select an interpretive problem they think they would like to work on in their own essays and generate a list of keyword hashtags associated with that problem.

This assignment arc reflects three features we believe are essential in "better practices" for online writing instruction (and in writing instruction more broadly). First, students are afforded ample opportunities to see and experience reading and writing as inherently social acts. In this assignment arc, students' annotation is necessarily collaborative, as students not only add their own observations and questions, but also respond to lines of inquiry opened up by their peers. Students are not reading (or, in turn, writing) in a vacuum, but rather as part of a larger intellectual community. Second, students have the opportunity to encounter texts and learning strategies multiple times. By returning to the same text (with the same technology) repeatedly and with decreasing amounts of instructor support, students become more comfortable using the technology and, crucially, develop a more comprehensive and complex grasp of the text. Third, instructor expectations are transparent and supported via clear models and ample examples. Perusall has the potential to make reading more visible to both us and our students, but only if they are confident enough to use it and understand annotation as a process, as opposed to a final product to be assessed. Modeling early reactions to the text as annotations on a shared document allows instructors to validate initial responses as essential first steps in comprehension and analysis. Continued incorporation of annotations in lesson plans allows instructors to point out sites of progressing comprehension and complexity.

Reading to Write: Perusall Collaborative Annotations

Due dates: Classes 2, 3, and 4

Purpose

The purpose of this assignment is to help you practice the critical reading skills that are necessary to not only *understand* difficult texts, but also to *analyze* them and thereby offer your own scholarly interpretation of their content and form. This assignment is also designed to help you identify the interpretive problem that will form the basis for your first essay project, and to generate a collection of possible textual evidence that you can use in that essay.

Skills

Upon completion of this assignment, you will be able to . . .

- *Pose* questions that can effectively motivate analysis of complex texts.
- *Analyze* specific parts of a text to find new meanings and interpretations of the text as a whole.
- *Evaluate* and *select* strong textual evidence that will allow you to present a persuasive interpretation to your readers.
- *Use annotation* as a tool that makes it easier to identify evidence, develop rich questions, and generate interpretations.

Knowledge

This assignment will also help you become familiar with the following important content knowledge in the discipline of academic writing . . .

- Nuanced analysis usually requires multiple readings of a single text.
- Academic writing identifies and incorporates concrete examples as evidence.

- Academic essays often center on problems that merit interpretation, originating from a place of questioning, rather than a place of *knowing*. Remember, in this case, confusion can be productive . . . if we put it to good use!
- Academic writing is written for an audience of other readers and interpreters.

Task

For Class 2: Reading to Understand

Part 1: By 12:00 p.m. (noon) the day before class, please finish reading our class text, "Speaking in Tongues," by Zadie Smith on Perusall. As you read, select any sections of text (anything from a word to an entire paragraph) that raise questions for you and/or confuse you in some way. In the conversation thread that opens, explain what questions you have or what confuses you. You may post as many comments or questions as you like, but you must start *at least* two threads on questions or confusions. Please be sure to label each post with a hashtag: #question #confusion

When writing your comments, try to be as specific as possible: for example, instead of just telling us "this is confusing!" explain why you were confused. Did Smith do something unexpected? You might write, "Smith's coldness towards the character of Joyce confused me because she doesn't seem so hard toward anyone else."

Part 2: By the start of class, please look through the Perusall threads started by your classmates and reply to *at least* two threads. Your responses can take the form of agreement, respectful disagreement, complication, or answering a question. For example, you might comment that you, too, were surprised by a passage and explain why. Or, you might explain why you *don't* think a passage is so confusing after all. You might complicate an observation by a peer by pointing out some conflicting evidence in the text. Or, you might offer an insight into a peer's question about the text. All of these are useful contributions to the conversation threads.

For Class 3: Reading to Interpret

Part 1: By 12:00 p.m. (noon) the day before class, please *reread* Smith's text on Perusall. This time, we are reading for *interpretive problems*. As you read this text a second time, try to identify tensions within the text that you believe are rich interpretive problems—that is, not flaws in the text, but cruxes that can be better understood and/or resolved via analysis and interpretation. You might find that some of your original confusions or questions from your earlier annotations are, in fact, interpretive problems. That's great! If so, add on to your original conversation thread, and explain two things: 1) What two elements are in tension? That is, what expectation did Smith create, and where did you see her deviate from it? And 2) Why do you believe the question or confusion merits interpretation? That is, how do you think making sense of this one might help us illuminate something important about "Speaking in Tongues"?

If none of your original confusions or questions seem like interpretive problems, that's fine! Try to identify an interpretive problem with this second reading. Keep in mind that interpretive problems have two parts—an expectation and something unexpected; two elements that appear contradictory or in tension; etc. Therefore, you might actually need to highlight and annotate two places in the text in order to identify one interpretive problem.

You are welcome to annotate as many interpretive problems as you like, but you should identify at least two for class. Please label your posts with the hashtag #IP.

Part 2: By the start of class, please read through the interpretive problems identified by your peers. You can easily do this by filtering for the #IP hashtag on the left-hand side of Perusall. Reply to at least two of your peers (prioritizing annotations that do not yet have a response). Do you agree that this annotation identifies an interpretive problem? Why or why not? For this portion of the assignment, consider the questions that we addressed in class that can help you assess the effectiveness of an interpretive problem:

- Is it identifying a seeming flaw or mistake in the text, or does it ask a question that motivates interpretation?
- Does it capture a tension or ambiguity, which, if resolved, could help us better understand the text as a whole?
- Does it capture something confusing, not only to you, but potentially to other readers?
- Is it a question that requires analysis, or a question whose answer is already out there somewhere and can simply be looked up?
- Can we try to make sense of it with more reading and thinking about the text? Or would it require outside research?

You are also welcome and encouraged (but not required) to suggest other places in the text that you think might be relevant to an analysis of this problem.

For Class 4: Reading for Evidence

Part 1: By 12:00 p.m. (noon) the day before class, reread Smith's text once more, this time with an eye towards finding textual evidence that might help you interpret or resolve your chosen problem. Are there places in the text that might help you figure out *why* your tension exists in the text, or to say something about how it affects the meaning of the text as a whole? Specifically, you might look for:

- Patterns related to your interpretive problem that appear throughout the text.
- Parts of the text that seem newly relevant to you, now that you've been thinking about your interpretive problem.
- Parts of the text that change your initial understanding of the author's aim. Has studying your interpretive problem brought you to a more complex understanding of the author's project?

As you annotate, hashtag each comment with one of the project keywords that you identified in class. For example, if you were writing an essay on the interpretive problem of Joyce ("why does Smith express opposition toward Joyce's self-identification as 'multiracial' if Smith herself advocates for 'multiplicity'?"), you might want to label your evidence with #Joyce or #multiplicity.

You should aim to identify and label *as many* pieces of relevant evidence as possible; you might not use it all in your essay! As a minimum, however, you should aim to find three pieces of evidence that you believe could help you *interpret* your problem (as opposed to seeking out evidence that simply *exemplifies* the problem, which you began to do for Class 3).

Remember: You can filter comments on Perusall to see all annotations, just your annotations, or no annotations. Pick whatever view is easiest for you as you look for evidence.

Part 2: By the start of class, return to the interpretive problems identified by your peers. Remember, you can easily do this by filtering for the #IP on the left-hand side of Perusall. Assist at least one of your peers (prioritizing posts that do not yet have a response) with a suggested piece of evidence that they might use in their analysis. Rather than replying directly to your peer's IP, highlight the text you think might serve as evidence and mention your peer in your annotation using the @. Explain why you believe the evidence is relevant to the problem, as your colleague explained it. For example, you might write, "@Valeria I think this relates to your Joyce IP because here, Smith discusses 'pride and shame'—terms she also uses when writing about Joyce."

Criteria for Success

Successful completion of these assignments will result in at least seven original annotations (2, 2, and 3, respectively, in the order of assignments noted above) on Smith's text that will help you identify and develop your textual analysis essay. You will also generate at least five annotations (2, 2, and 1, respectively) in response to your colleagues' ideas and comments, offering them feedback on the viability of their projects and suggesting specific places they might look in the text for deeper analysis.

While your annotations are graded as complete/incomplete, they are an essential part of your reading and writing process for this progression and will be factored into your overall participation grade for the progression. Additionally, the quality of your annotations will necessarily impact the quality of your final essay—the more closely you work with the text, the more advanced your thinking will be in your final essay.

Exemplary annotations will:

- Identify concrete examples of specific language in the text (e.g., "Here Smith claims her voice 'deserted' her, which makes it sound like something was done *to* her—like she was a #victim").
- Demonstrate an awareness of the text as a whole (e.g., "I don't understand why Smith critiques Joyce for wanting to avoid the '#singular' when Smith's whole essay seems to advocate for #multiplicity.")
- Offer concrete suggestions to peers in the forms of evidence to look at (e.g., "@Vanessa, check out this quote for more on whether Smith thinks #multiplicity is a #choice or a #gift)."
- Draw connections between specific textual moments. (e.g., "This is surprising because at other places in the text, she suggests that she could have kept her original voice if she had tried harder; in other words, she suggests it was a #choice, in her control.")
- Reflect an evolving awareness of both the text itself and the writer's interpretive problem (e.g., "This seems like useful evidence because while I used to think Smith was being mean about Joyce, after rereading it, I think Smith actually relates to her in some way . . .")

REFLECTION ON PRACTICE

One of the most immediate observations we made when first implementing these lessons was the impressive degree to which students interacted with one another's annotations, building a virtual conversation about the text and beginning to negotiate meaning together before our class meetings. Simply receiving affirmation of confusion via a "seconded" question, or having an observation marked as useful by a peer seemed to encourage students to share more observations, questions, and complications. Students especially gravitated toward the use of hashtags to label their annotations, introducing their own keywords (such as #observation) without being prompted. The keyword labels allowed students to associate passages to other passages, and annotations to other annotations, and to implicitly call on each other to work on possible interpretations together in the comments. This willingness to embrace inquiry and to approach it collectively was an exciting step forward for our goal of promoting curiosity and critical thinking.

Discussing their lesson study on "reading literature for complexity," Chick et al. note that, "[f]or many, this prompt may be their first encounter with the idea that a text may contradict itself or have pieces that 'do not fit' by design" (2009, p. 409). In our teaching context, too, we often find it to be true that students have not previously been asked to read in this way. While novelty and the inherent challenge of complexity itself make the assignment no easy feat, the recursive and interactive nature of the Perusall annotation assignments seemed to position the challenge as worthwhile and workable, and complexity as something to be sought out, speculated about, and interpreted.

The iterative approach in Perusall provided our students with a concrete method that they could use for developing a rich interpretive problem, a strategy for beginning to generate ideas and take notes toward the essay in tandem with reading, and a way to use their colleagues to deepen their engagement with the text. In the example in Figure 6.1, for example, we see a student ("CL") pose a question as part of the first exercise, "Reading to Understand." This annotation points to a seeming contradiction in Smith's text but is labeled with the hashtag #question; on the first reading of Smith's essay, CL understood this as an issue with their own comprehension, not as a site of potential textual analysis. At the bottom of the same conversation thread, however, we see "CL" return to the same place in the text five days later as part of the second assignment, "Reading to Interpret." Here, CL adds an #observation: this contradiction may not, in fact, reflect a failure of comprehension on CL's part, but rather might be an interpretive problem (IP) that merits analysis. Further, CL cites a conversation started by another student (Diya) as a source of potential insight. This evolution of CL's thinking suggests that students did return to places they had annotated on their first reading in subsequent readings, and that rereading allowed them to find opportunities for analysis they may not have initially seen. It is these principles–annotating to generate rich ideas, rereading, engaging with the ideas of others–that we hope students will take with them into other reading and writing contexts outside of FYW.

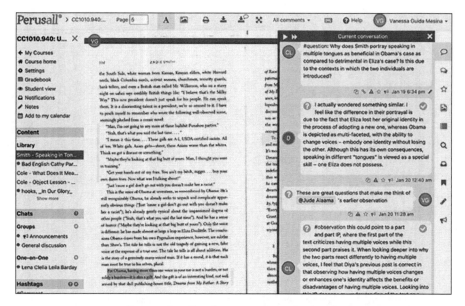

Figure 6.1. Reading to interpret example.

While we have found Perusall to be a valuable tool in helping students develop and practice these critical skills, we don't mean to suggest that simply moving annotations online and into a "public" space will inherently translate to collaboration, critical inquiry, and analysis. Chick et al. noticed that a potential pitfall of collaborative annotation exercises is interpretive relativism: seeing peers' observations and interpretations of the text can lead students to believe that "all interpretations are correct . . . instead of seeing that the text itself contains multiple meanings, [students can focus] on their classmates as the sources of the multiple responses" (2009, 415). While the authors are clear that this isn't where they want their students to stop, they note "this relativism may serve as a developmental way station" (2009, 415).

With such unintended byproducts in mind, we found it vital to model the kinds of annotations students might add to the texts on the assignments themselves. As can be seen in Figure 6.2, initial annotations on Perusall can be made by the instructor—either based on their own impressions of the text, or based on contributions of students during real-time instruction. In a real-time class discussion, for example, Vanessa elicited observations about the text that could be added as model annotations. The initial comment in Figure 6.2's conversation thread was a comment made verbally by a student that Vanessa typed up to model the functionality of Perusall and attributed to the student (Francesca) via the @ mentioning function. While this was a model annotation intended to help students better understand how and when to use the conversation feature, this

Teaching Textual Analysis

conversation was continued by classmates during the initial annotation assignment, with one student (Jose) making a personal connection to the content of the text, and another ("SP") posing a subsequent question about the text's meaning in turn. This conversation thread also provided an opportunity for Vanessa to "upvote" a potentially fruitful line of inquiry regarding the definition of a key term ("voice") in Smith's text.

By both modeling annotations and participating in the conversations as fellow readers, we were able to facilitate conversations about potential misunderstandings about the text, as well as to help students practice distinguishing between interpretive and research problems, identifying persuasive textual evidence, etc. This also allowed us to frame annotations not as an end in and of themselves, but as a means to enhance class discussion and student drafting; in other words, we were also able to more fully integrate the Perusall technology into our larger curricular design. Figure 6.3 features a conversation thread that began with straightforward praise of the writer's style and message. Such observations are, of course, valuable insofar as they allow students to identify writing that they admire and begin to reflect on why they admire it. Here, however, we see the annotations quickly progress from students praising the text as *readers* to students critically examining the text as *writers* and *interpreters*.

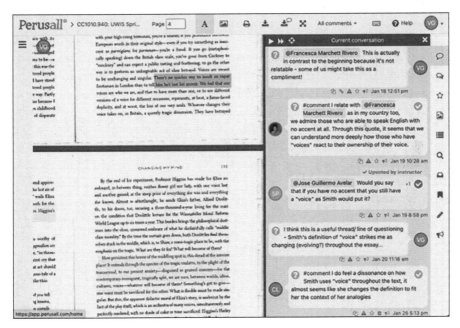

Figure 6.2. Instructor annotation example.

155

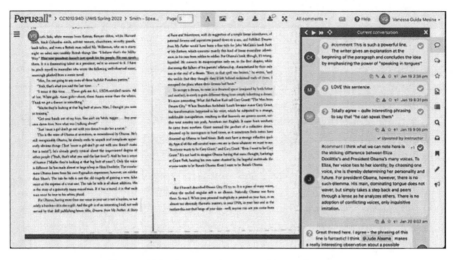

Figure 6.3. Annotating as readers and writers.

In the fourth comment in the conversation thread, a student ("J") shifts from praise to a detailed consideration of how this passage differs from a previous one on a similar subject. In doing so, "J" shifts the conversation from evaluative of the sentence-level prose to analytical about the text as a whole. An instructor "upvote" signals to fellow readers that this is an especially helpful progression of this thread.

Teachers interested in incorporating collaborative annotation into their curricula would thus benefit from first considering how much time they have to devote to "onboarding" their students to a new technology and scaffolding the use of that technology in practical terms. In our teaching, it became immediately clear that some students would catch on to the annotation technology faster than others, resulting in uneven contributions. We found it helpful to first introduce students to Perusall during real-time instruction to ensure students were comfortable registering for Perusall, joining their Perusall course with the class code, highlighting text, and starting conversation threads. Building in this preparation allowed us not only to demonstrate how to use the program, but also to scaffold annotation practices more broadly by modeling sample annotations and discussing student annotations during class.

Alternatively, turning to a simpler, but more familiar, technology (such as Google Docs) might allow students to contribute fully with less labor upfront from instructors. While programs like Perusall are built for educational use and offer advanced functionality (not to mention seamless integration of PDFs), the benefits of "visible" reading practices and interactive annotation can be gained through simpler options as well, some of which allow for enhanced accessibility options such as the integration of screen readers and talk-to-text technology. Regardless of the particular interface, however, online annotation in general promotes access and inclusivity in the sense that moving beyond analog, pen-to-paper annotations acknowledges the very real financial concerns of our students; in addition to doing away with the need for expensive printing and printer supplies, digital annotation offers a practical solution to students reluctant to annotate their assigned texts because they anticipate reselling their books at the end of semester (Carillo, 2019, n.p.).

CONCLUSION

In our teaching context, collaborative annotation with Perusall served as a way to teach better textual analysis because it helped instructors and students break down the process of interpreting a text into concrete, repeatable moves, and it dramatized the advantages of rereading and rethinking. The assignment also demonstrated that academic writing is an inherently social practice, as it required students to work together in a community of inquiry. And, finally, at its most basic level, the assignment rendered more visible the often-invisible act of reading.

For instructors, the benefit of such visibility is clear; the opportunity for assessment and pedagogical intervention grows exponentially when we have insight into how our students are engaging with their readings—the kinds of questions they ask, and the ways in which they go about answering them. For students, online annotation platforms offer the opportunity to track their own thinking over time, and also to develop the habits of mind central to the Council of Writing Program Administrators, National Council of Teachers of English, and National Writing Project's *Framework for Success in Postsecondary Writing* (2011); by engaging with their colleagues' annotations, they both gain the confidence in performing inquiry in the exploratory stages of writing and learn to develop their ideas in relation to the ideas of others.

We see opportunities for expanding on this annotation practice, especially by incorporating more active student reflection on its affordances and challenges. Carillo's work (2016, "Creating"), which builds on existing research into learning transfer, points to reflection's effectiveness in promoting a more deliberate, and therefore a more flexible and adaptable, reading practice. Students who learn to reflect on the choices they make while reading, Carillo suggests, will be better able to adapt the reading strategies they know to new contexts outside of their initial learning environment; students exposed to multiple reading approaches, who are then asked to reflect on which approach works for them in which context, may more readily "mov[e] among reading approaches in deliberate and mindful ways" in new contexts outside of class (2016, p. 12). We suspect that deliberate instruction in reading techniques throughout the semester, as well as deliberate prompts for student reflection on the affordances of each approach, can help students become more mindful and flexible readers.

MOVING BETTER PRACTICES ACROSS MODALITIES

We originally designed these lesson plans for an online, real-time class format, but we have since used them primarily for in-person, real-time teaching. With proper scaffolding, collaborative annotation assignments can promote student engagement and learning across teaching modalities: in-person, real-time instruction with technology-enhanced assignments in class and at home; online, real-time instruction; online, any time instruction; and hybrid instruction.

- **Online, Real-Time Learning:** These lesson plans can be implemented "as is"; the focus on digital texts and online annotation is especially well-suited to the online or hyflex classroom.
- **Online, Any Time Learning:** For any time instruction, we suggest using screen-cast videos to introduce students to Perusall, to introduce the idea of Interpretive Problems, and to model good annotations. Following along with a screencast orientation to Perusall could be an initial assignment, serving the function of "Class 1" above. Teachers might also include an initial "pre-assignment" task to ensure that all students are able to leave comments on the document before embarking on the three-assignment arc. Notably, the teacher's role as facilitator serves a special purpose in the any time learning modality. As students may never see each other or interact in real time, teachers can look for moments of connection in the student annotations, and make note of these in their responses, even tagging classmates to help students see their annotations as contributions to a larger conversation (see Figure 6.3 for an example). In so doing, instructors can help foster a sense of community and collaboration, with or without real-time interaction.
- **Hybrid Learning:** Instructors teaching in a hybrid environment will likely find it beneficial to introduce the Perusall platform during in-person, real-time sessions as this will minimize the chances of the technology becoming a barrier to engagement early on, supplemented by short, on-demand instructional videos. As the occasional in-person meetings of the hybrid learning modality offer more opportunities for student engagement with each other, teachers might allot some class time to student discussion about the annotations they've made and

read to keep the conversation going in real-time. For example, students might be placed in groups corresponding to themes or hashtags appearing in their annotations.

REFERENCES

Bizup, J. (2008). BEAM: A rhetorical vocabulary for teaching research-based writing. *Rhetoric Review, 27*(1), 72–86. https://doi.org/10.1080/07350190701738858.

Carillo, E. C. (2016). Creating mindful readers in first-year composition courses: A strategy to facilitate transfer. *Pedagogy 16*(1), 9–22. https://doi.org/10.1215/15314200-3158573.

Carillo, E. C. (2016). Engaging sources through reading-writing connections across the disciplines. *Across the Disciplines, 13*(1). https://doi.org/10.37514/ATD-J.2016.13.2.06.

Carillo, E. C. (2019). Beyond the research institution: Preparing graduate students to teach in various contexts. *Profession*. https://profession.mla.org/beyond-the-research-institution-preparing-graduate-students-to-teach-in-various-contexts/.

Chick, N. L., Hassel, H. & Haynie, A. (2009). "Pressing an ear against the hive": Reading literature for complexity. *Pedagogy, 9*(3), 399–422. https://doi.org/10.1215/15314200-2009-003.

Columbia University International Students & Scholars Office (ISSO). (2023, June). *Statistics*. Columbia ISSO international students & scholars office. https://isso.columbia.edu/content/statistics.

Council of Writing Program Administrators, National Council of Teachers of English & National Writing Project. (2011, January). *Framework for success in postsecondary writing*. https://wpacouncil.org/aws/CWPA/pt/sd/news_article/242845/_PARENT/layout_details/false.

GSOLE Executive Board. (2019, June 13). *Online literacy instruction principles and tenets*. Global Society of Online Literacy Educators. https://gsole.org/oliresources/oliprinciples.

Lockhart, T. & Soliday, M. (2016). The critical place of reading in writing transfer (and beyond): A report of student experiences. *Pedagogy, 16*(1), 23–37. https://doi.org/10.1215/15314200-3158589.

Perusall. (n.d.). Retrieved January 2, 2023, from https://www.perusall.com/.

Ritzenberg, A. & S. Mendelsohn. (2021). *How scholars write*. Oxford University Press.

Scholes, R. J. (2002). The transition to college reading. *Pedagogy, 2*(2), 162–172.

Smith, Z. (2009). Speaking in tongues. In *Changing my mind: Occasional essays* (pp. 132–148). Penguin.

Swales, J. (1990). *Genre analysis: English in academic and research settings*. Cambridge University Press.

Swales, J. (2016). Reflections on the Concept of Discourse Community. *ASp: La Revue du GERAS (Groupe d'Étude et de Recherche en Anglais de Spécialité), 69*, 1–12. https://doi.org/10.4000/asp.4774.

CHAPTER 7.

#WRITETEACHCHAT: SOCIAL MEDIA FOR WRITING TO LEARN AND LEARNING TO WRITE

Jessica Eagle, Michelle Falter, and Caitlin Donovan
North Carolina State University

In this chapter, the authors describe **#WriteTeachChat,** *a practice used in both in-person and online learning modalities. Specifically, the authors engage students in social media conversation and enact dialogic theories of language and learning. In describing their "better practice," this chapter addresses the themes of multimodal learning and practices in motion across teaching and learning modalities.*

FRAMEWORKS AND PRINCIPLES IN THIS CHAPTER

- **CCCC Principles for the Postsecondary Teaching of Writing, 2**: Considers the needs of real audiences.
- **CCCC Principles for the Postsecondary Teaching of Writing, 3**: Recognizes writing as a social act.
- **CCCC Principles for the Postsecondary Teaching of Writing, 4**: Enables students to analyze and practice with a variety of genres.
- **CCCC Principles for the Postsecondary Teaching of Writing, 7**: Emphasizes relationships between writing and technologies.
- **CCCC Principles for the Postsecondary Teaching of Writing, 8**: Supports learning, engagement, and critical thinking in courses across the curriculum.

GUIDING QUESTIONS BEFORE YOU BEGIN READING

- How can writing instructors leverage social media to facilitate multimodal writing?
- What are the ways teachers and students engage in authentic dialogue and inquiry to improve professional writing skills using online communities?
- What are the affordances and limitations of certain online platforms or applications for both writing to learn and learning to write?

DOI: https://doi.org/10.37514/PER-B.2024.2241.2.07

INTRODUCTION

> The best writing teachers are writers themselves. Why? Because we know the writing process inside out, we can support our students' work in authentic ways. . . .
>
> – Cindy O'Donnell-Allen, English Education Professor, Scholar, Writer

The first question appeared on our X (formerly called Twitter) feeds. Attractively designed, the font popped with a reserved floral border: "Do you think attendance and classroom behavior should be included in a student's final grade?" It asked, prompting students to respond with the hashtag #WriteTeachChat.

We—instructors with breath baited and fingers hovering over the refresh button—waited patiently. The students in our course, undergraduate teacher candidates in a course on teaching writing, were not in front of us. They were, instead, participating in online, real-time learning, waiting to practice their writing to a specific task and audience while demonstrating their thoughtful reflection on the week's readings. Using X, they would share their knowledge and engage in professional discourse with one another and the authentic audience of their future teaching colleagues.

"No, behavior and attendance should not count as a grade," the first response noted, citing experiences in their volunteer setting with sixth graders and behavior management.

"I support classroom behavior being part of a student's final grade within a participation context," another student shared, questioning how else to motivate students who were more grade focused.

"Will you consider verbalizing a part of the participation grade? In what contexts?" We responded, prompting the second student to reflect and respond, but not before other students typed their responses.

"What qualifies as participation? Not all students are going to want to raise their hand."

"Classroom behavior is too subjective to grade fairly."

"Exactly! Measuring behavior can be affected by personal biases, resulting in an unfair grade?"

"This all boils down to the question of 'How do any of these things reflect academic achievement . . .'"

"Student attendance at this age is beyond their control . . ."

"Even while being a non-academic factor, [attendance] still plays a part in determining students' academic success."

Quickly, our students began not only responding to us and the question, but also proactively engaging with each other. Students began to question the relationship between attendance or behavior with learning and growth as well as the nuance of how participation in a discussion should be graded, in theory, and could be graded, in practicality.

The posts (formerly called tweets) came in quickly, peppered not only with references to course readings and their prior experience volunteering in local classrooms, but also with the standardized rhetorical context of X in 2020: additional hashtags, callouts, and emojis punctuated the posts, as did links to multimedia, gifs, and memes that expressed the ethos of the statements. Empty professional X profiles, created and abandoned as one-off activities in previous courses, came alive and became relevant, blossoming with conversations on pedagogy, ethics, and equity.

Over the course of this project, we sought to engage our pre-service teachers' sense of curiosity and flexibility, to engage them as writers, and to position them as professionals. As we think about all the elements that are part of both writing and professional expression, we are giving our students opportunities to see that writing is a tool for thinking, processing, and connecting. Even though social media is not regarded as a traditional type of discourse valued by schools and institutions, it is a valuable type of talk that permeates at-home, school, and professional knowledge, and it is the center of this chapter's practice. Both the writing knowledge and the professional dispositions facilitated by this practice grew our pre-service teachers' understanding of writing, literacy, and professional community in a multimodal, online, social setting.

SCHOLARSHIP, THEORIES, AND PRINCIPLES THAT GUIDE OUR APPROACH

The National Council of Teachers of English's (NCTE) *Professional Knowledge for the Teaching of Writing* (2016) frames our practice in terms of positioning composition as a "suite of activities in varied modalities" facilitated by digital tools. Our students used their phones and computers to participate in nuanced discussions on an online platform; their multimodal responses made use of unique text features to the online space as they incorporated hashtags, hyperlinks, and video clips into their written responses. These thoughts also tie into the Conference on College Composition and Communication's (CCCC) *Principles for the Postsecondary Teaching of Writing* (2015), which guides our expectations of students' success in developing writing for various audiences, contexts, and purposes. Specifically, we draw on principles 2, 3, 4, 7, and 8 to view writing practices in terms of authenticity (e.g., real audience), social activities, multigenre productions, technology contexts, and opportunities to think critically.

Additionally, we recognize that that writing is generative (i.e., an "act of discovery") and positions our students as authors who compose to explore and negotiate ideas in authentic spaces. What had been dubbed as "Teacher Twitter" (circa 2023) was a wellspring of ideas, both practical and theoretical. Pre-service teachers can connect with others and explore resources while on a platform most already use. Further, X's emphasis on dialogue and use by the academic community made it an excellent space for the generation of writing. As per the Council of Writing Program Administrators' (CWPA) *Framework for Success in Postsecondary Writing* (2011), we assert that writing is a conduit for students to engage in dialogue regarding assumptions held by different audiences and thus think critically about various ideas, problems, and issues. Furthermore, additional guidelines within this framework support our belief that internet technologies necessitate students' ability to develop informed criteria to analyze best compositional practices for electronic-mediated contexts. The aim of these "better practices" was also to model and practice multimodal and new literacies while also quite literally writing to learn with a wider audience than just their classmates.

As instructors of Teaching Writing Across the Curriculum, a writing methods course for pre-service English and social studies teachers, we are always invested in ways to help students see the role of writing across contexts, particularly those that they value and use in their day-to-day lives. When questioned about their understandings regarding the role of writing and the writing process in classroom instruction, our students generally imagined instructional end-goals as the end-of-quarter essay or document-based question response. Through this approach, we wanted to shift student understanding of what "counts" as writing in school (e.g., literary analysis essays and research papers) and the types of writing society generally values (e.g., emails, memos, and reports). We wanted students to see writing as relevant to their daily lives and a way to thoughtfully respond to others.

The platforms we chose for these writing better practices involved the two of our students' favorites: Twitter (now called X[1]) and Instagram. We chose these platforms due to their popularity, ease of use, lack of fees, and relative level of information security (though we recognize that individual's willingness to provide personal data to any company, including a social media company, is a nuanced decision). Although the nature of our students' posts meant that they were less likely to go "viral" as compared to popular culture posts, we advertised our slow-chat hashtag with persons within our professional networks to invite

---

1   When we began this writing exercise with students, the platform was called "Twitter." In April 2023, it was renamed "X." In this transition, some things have changed in terms of the platform's use and capabilities. As such, we use "Twitter" for most of our discussion to indicate that this is the version of the platform we used within our classes at the time. When we use the new name, "X," it is to demonstrate how people might currently or in the future use this social media platform.

their participation. By doing so, we increased the odds that our students would have the opportunity to engage with an audience beyond their classmates. For this reason, Twitter and Instagram became authentic conduits for dialogue in contrast to tools more often used for reading reflections such as online learning platform discussion boards. Thus, these practices allow students to think of social media platforms not only as methods for connection and networking, but also as tools for deepening engagement with writing.

Furthermore, effective use of social media requires specific writing abilities, like being both succinct and analytical within a professional context. Social media messages are short, snappy, and concise. At the time of student use, platforms like Twitter had a strict character limit for messages, while more image-focused platforms like Instagram emphasized visual composition to communicate messages neatly. Education professionals are increasingly turning to social media platforms for professional networking and expression. Having preservice teachers practice using these platforms as part of their professional learning thus scaffolded both the skills of effective communication as well as helping them to develop a more mature understanding of how these tools are used professionally. These practices exhibited the authenticity of the works for the pre-service teachers and their future students and may be used within other professional learning contexts and courses for these reasons.

Finally, as teacher-educators, we view our pedagogical charge as one that adheres to instructional "best practices"—those that meet current socially and culturally-driven student needs as well as those that align with relevant organizational guidelines and theoretical constructs put forth by trusted experts in the field of education. The International Society for Technology in Education (ISTE, 2021, https://iste.org/standards/educators) defines an educator as a professional who helps students become empowered learners. The ISTE standards serve as a useful framework for creating, adapting, and utilizing digital age tools and learning environments. Through the implementation of the semester-long Twitter and Instagram activities, we as educators have modeled several of the ISTE standards for our own pre-service teachers by designing and implementing authentic, learning driven, and technologically influenced assignments. Specifically, these assignments meet the following 2021 ISTE standards:

- "Use collaborative tools to expand students' authentic, real-world learning experiences by engaging virtually with experts, teams and students, locally and globally" (2.4c).
- "Use technology to create, adapt and personalize learning experiences that foster independent learning and accommodate learner differences and needs" (2.5a).

- "Model and nurture creativity and creative expression to communicate ideas, knowledge or connections" (2.6d).

Additionally, the creation and implementation of the assignments were informed by the following frameworks:

- **Dialogic Language Theory:** We use Mikhail Bakhtin's theory of dialogic language to view language as a semiotic system that creates, and is influenced by, social context (1981). Thus, we regard language itself as a social practice and dialogic act amongst the self, idea, text, and audience. As an active and responsive process involving the self and others, communication, and therefore learning, is facilitated through the confluence of past experiences and their present reinterpretations.
- **New Literacies:** We used Brian Street's the New Literacies theory (2003) as our broader conceptual approach. This theory also views social practice as central to literacy learning, specifically. In this light, we draw upon New Literacies theory to focus on students' skill acquisition but also to situate writing as a "literacy practice" that takes place within the broader cultural conceptions of the ways people think about and enact writing in technology-based cultural contexts (i.e., social media platforms).
- **Participatory Culture:** Guided by the work of Henry Jenkins (2014), we purport that social media platforms have allowed a new generation of technology to transform and influence the masses. Thus, we view composition via social media as an opportunity for political and civic engagement and thus, collective action.
- **Writing to Learn:** Lastly, we use Kathy Knipper and Timothy Duggan's (2006) definition of "writing to learn" as students' exploration of particular information by way of recall, clarification, and questioning processes. Writing to learn allows students to engage in exploration and reflect on disciplinary content, class discussions, and related readings (Knipper & Duggan, 2006).

COURSE CONTEXT AND LESSON

Our classes are in a well-established college of education at a large, research-intensive, public land grant university in the southeastern United States. Our students in both years from which we are documenting this assignment were undergraduate juniors enrolled in Teaching Writing Across the Curriculum, a course for pre-service middle grades English and social studies teachers to learn practical strategies for teaching writing that instill the power and beauty of words as well as how to utilize writing as a learning tool.

In line with the words of Stephen King, who essentializes the core-being of those who embark on writing in his famous book, *On Writing: A Memoir of the Craft*: "You can, you should, and if you're brave enough to start, you will" (2002, p. 275). The course is designed to teach new teachers that we can, we should, and we will become writers within the discipline of education, and more broadly as well. In this course, students are taught that teachers can be academic readers and writers who foster critical thinking, reading, writing, and speaking and thus providers of immense pedagogical possibilities for their students. The course was designed to convey the principle that, to teach students to read and write within the discipline, educators must be readers and writers first.

Specifically, our students focus on general writing, writing instruction, and technology. In this class, students are encouraged to examine writing practices from both socio-cultural and critical perspectives, with an emphasis on culturally responsive writing pedagogies. Another key focus is on students developing their own writing identities and self-efficacy so that they, like their future students, can move beyond the conception of all writing as an essay. To these ends, we use a variety of pedagogical strategies such as lectures, group activities, discussion, demonstration, written responses, reflection, conferencing, dialogic communication, online technologies, mock teaching assignments, and virtual field work with middle school students.

The effective use of technology to increase writing efficacy as well as for the process of multimodal composition has always been a significant component of the course but was intensified when the first cohort of students' in-person classes were moved online due to the COVID-19 pandemic. The second cohort met completely online in the semester of 2021, using real-time learning on Zoom with any time learning happening through some assignments. In these online iterations, we used digital platforms like the university's course management system, Zoom, Google Suite, and the platforms for these writing better practices, Twitter and Instagram.

Our relevant course objectives were:

1. Define, identify, and develop practical and applicable writing skills as teachers as writers and teachers of writers.
2. Analyze, produce, model, and teach different genres of writing.
3. Explore and analyze the use of technology in the teaching of writing.
4. Teach writing as a means for learning, inquiry, and social change.

Lesson

Year One: Twitter Assignment Description

In year one (2020), from January to May, students in the initial face-to-face context reflected on the course's writing methods content using the social media platform Twitter due to its potential for authentic audience participation without prior planning and real-time response. In our assignment, students took turns acting as moderators of "slow Twitter chats" while the rest of the class would participate in the slow Twitter chat discussions the day before our class met face-to-face. This allowed students to simultaneously learn a new genre of writing (tweets/posts) and associated language tools (e.g., @ & #) while also providing us with an inside look at how students construct arguments and personally connect to ideas in course readings prior to our whole class oral discussions.

The chat took place between 5:00 p.m. and 11:59 p.m. the evening before class to allow students to think about the course material and extend their ideas in dialogue with one another. In doing so, students were held accountable for the readings and prepared to engage more fully with the material in the upcoming class. As instructors, we therefore came prepared to only briefly summarize the material and approached the following class with the expectation that students were equipped to engage more deeply with the course content because of their recent engagement via Twitter.

Because Twitter was a free public social media platform, students were able to engage in this work while simultaneously undertaking the opportunity to engage with the public and other teachers and education stakeholders in the field. The assignment served as a supplement and extension for in-class discussion. This helped students understand that the course material holds relevance not only "for class" but for their future careers as writing instructors and educators. During the following in-person class section, we would often mention content our students wrote or writing content that was generated by "outsiders who joined the chat." Our students engaged with several teachers and/or teacher-educators each week. We imagined that, in following iterations of the assignment, former students who had previously engaged in this work could be invited to join the conversation. The activity provided students opportunities to demonstrate their knowledge in a new way for and with their peers using their authentic voice. To see examples of what students created you can check out our course hashtag #WriteTeachChat on both X (formerly Twitter; https://twitter.com) and Instagram (https://www.instagram.com).

To introduce the assignment, students were presented with a brief overview of the meaning of "slow Twitter chats." Slow chats can be described as a back-and-forth conversation that takes place between two or more participants

#WriteTeachChat

without the element of instantaneity. Relevant hashtags are either generated or used to add a sense of cohesiveness and for ease of accessibility. Additionally, these chats often rely on the "Q1/A1" format—the host/moderators will label the discussion questions with "Q1" (Question 1), and participants will respond and chat accordingly by starting with "A1" (Answer 1). For this assignment, our students used these logistics for organization.

For the assignment's debut during the first week, we began by tweeting/posting invitations and reminders to both our students and outside-participants for the slow chat (see Instructor Advertisement examples in Figures 7.2–7.4).

Figure 7.1. Sample promotion for #WriteTeachChat.

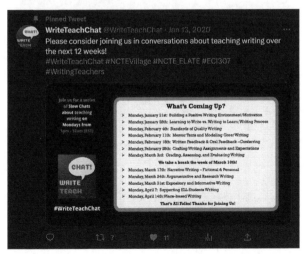

Figure 7.2. Sample promotion for #WriteTeachChat.

169

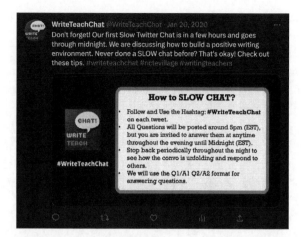

Figure 7.3. Sample promotion for #WriteTeachChat.

Figure 7.4. Instructor modeling Moderator #WriteTeachChat opening.

We also modeled the process of moderating and responding to one another using that week's course content. We then engaged in a back-and-forth conversation using the constraints of Twitter to model both professional and substantive responses. Our models are presented in *Figures 7.5–7.8*, and these tweets/posts are also documented under the hashtag #WriteTeachChat via X (formerly Twitter) (https://bit.ly/TeachWriteChat).

After the first week of having all students engaging with the instructor-as-moderator posts, two students each week were then tasked with moderating the slow chat as partners. The responsibilities of the weekly moderators included generating three to four relevant and discussion-enriching questions, as well as monitoring the chat during the hours it was running, while also responding to classmates and other participants. Our assignment tasked moderators with creating and communicating their discussion questions before 5:00 p.m. the evening prior to class. Moderators were told to capture big ideas, address all the readings, and elicit dialogue. Additionally, students who took on the moderator role engaged in the chat in order to further the class's discussion by either posting additional questions, connecting participants' ideas, and/or ensuring the dialogue maintained content integrity. Thus, moderators were required to individually respond with at least three of their own tweets/posts that maintained participants' conversation between 5:00 p.m. and 11:59 p.m. the evening before class, a timeframe that was suitable for our university-aged students but may be shifted earlier for younger learners.

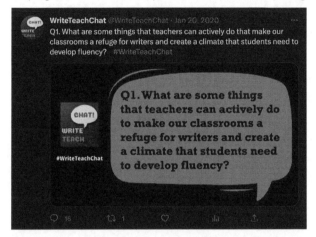

Figure 7.5. Instructor models asking questions for #WriteTeachChat.

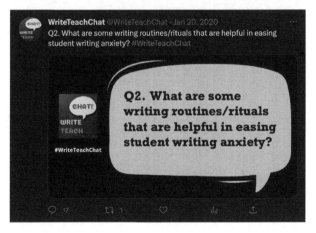

Figure 7.6. Instructor models asking questions for #WriteTeachChat.

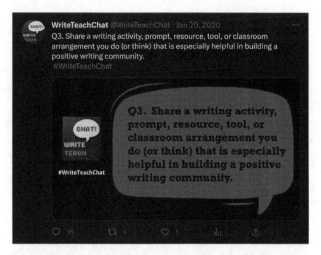

Figure 7.7. Instructor models asking questions for #WriteTeachChat.

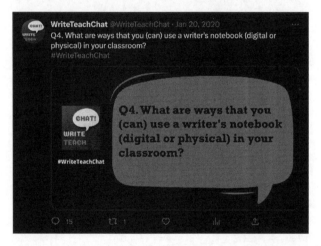

Figure 7.8. Instructor models asking questions for #WriteTeachChat.

Our students who did not take on the role of moderators engaged in the activity as slow-chat participants. Between 5:00 p.m., with the questions already posted, and 11:59 p.m. in the evening prior to class, these students were tasked with responding to the moderator's discussion questions using textual evidence and connections to relevant personal school or field experiences. Although we could have requested students respond using either textual evidence or personal experience, we felt that to achieve the goal of ensuring our students were engaged with the readings, students must be able to cite the readings, in context, accordingly.

Those who were participating were required to respond to at least five other classmates (or other outside participants who joined the discussion) by directly tagging them in the replies. Participant content included the selection and dissemination of memes, links to sources, questions for one another, and writing that expressed agreement and/or disagreement with previous tweets/posts. Our students were pushed to provide nuance to points that were made and to pose questions from an inquiry stance, thus facilitating their engagement in low-stakes argumentation of ideas. Many students used personal anecdotes to exemplify ideas, after drawing evidence from the texts. Moreover, the Twitter platform allowed students to creatively write using genres that best suited the needs of their communication and audience; thus, they produced many distinct types of writing which included persuasive, narrative, and informative all within the chats.

Year Two Instagram Assignment Description

In year two (2021), from January to May, spanning the duration of the Teaching Writing Across the Curriculum course for pre-service middle grades English and social studies teachers, students reflected on the course's writing methods content using the social media platform, Instagram. Rather than students moderating a slow-chat on Instagram, as was protocol for the Twitter assignment, students were asked to make use of Instagram for writing in order to, as Joseph Harris argues, "come to terms" with course materials and to define how readers and writers "strive to represent the work of another, to translate the language and ideas of a text into words of your own . . . to give a text its due and to show what uses you want to make of it" (Harris, 2017, p. 16). In addition to the increased text limit that Instagram posts afford as compared to Twitter at the time, we chose to use Harris' (2017) ideas for academic argument as a framework for the year two assignment to help students better understand what it means to take an in-depth exploration of the course content and produce written content that demonstrates critical reflection of the content.

Due to the University's response to COVID-19, in year two, the course was completely conducted online, with both real-time and any time learning. This caused us to consider how a different social media platform might more successfully facilitate more in-depth student engagement with the course texts and content. We felt that although the utility of Twitter was mainly realized through its facilitation of back-and-forth exchange, the character limits (280 characters) often limited the depth to which our students wrote. We wanted to mitigate this limitation as well as create an assignment that served as a tool for exploring multimodal expression—Instagram is adept at facilitating the sharing of memes, images, and videos. As in year one, students needed to write and respond to others, but this assignment was structured differently. In lieu of acting as moderators, the Instagram assignment gave every student equal and individualized options for how to "come to terms" with the methods of writing and teaching of writing we were learning about in class. We still used the #WriteTeachChat hashtag as a standardized means of connecting with each other. We also continued to invite others who were not in the course into our conversations, as this platform served as a public engagement forum in this regard.

Coming to Terms with our Course Content:

Weekly Posts via Instagram Assignment

Student Directions

1. Create a Professional Instagram Account (a separate one from any personal one you have).
2. Capture how you are "Coming to Terms" with what you have read for the week through either one single image or a series of images that you will post. This image or images can be created, found, or your own photography. Consider: How will you represent your learning for the week through the image(s)?
    a. Create a caption for your post that meets the following criteria:
    b. A summation of your personal learning.
    c. At least one quote (including author last name & page number).
    d. Evidence of critical assessment either by using one of Harris' frames: "forwarding, illustrating, authorizing, borrowing, extending, or countering."
    e. A word count of ~150–350 words.
3. Use the course hashtag #WriteTeachChat and any other hashtag you deem relevant.
4. After you post, search #WriteTeachChat, read, and comment on at least two of your peers' posts.
5. Your comments should show evidence of in-depth engagement.
6. Responses such as "I agree. "and "I like that" do not fulfill the assignment requirements.
7. Your initial posts are due by 9:00 AM on the day of class. Your comments to your peers are due by class time: 1:30 PM.

To receive full credit for the points-based assignment, students had to follow the assignment directions and meet the relevant criteria (as shown above). Additionally, in order to ensure that students' engagement would facilitate critical synthesis, reflection, and dialogue about the course material, assessment of their work also included the extent to which students demonstrated the following: understanding of the course material and ability to synthesize the readings, thoughtful evaluation of and a "coming to terms" with the reading, creative representation of the material through multimodal presentation, and a clarity of writing in terms of their organization of ideas.

The students' goal in participating in the assignment was not to "simply *re*-present a text, but incorporate it into your own project as a writer" (Harris, 2017, p. 16). Thus, for this assignment, students were asked to represent, translate, make use of, and synthesize the readings into their own ideas and images. Based on the work of Harris (2017), students were provided with the following three guidelines to help them "come to terms" with the texts written by someone else in their posts:

Define the project of the writer in your own terms. Think about: What is a writer trying to achieve? What position does he or she want to argue? What issues or problems does he or she explore? This week's readings ask me to think about or to do xyz . . .

Assess the uses and limits of the writer's ideas. This does not necessarily mean that you are critical (in the negative way). It can mean any of the following:

- **Forwarding the ideas of the writer:** When you "takes terms and concepts from one text and applies them to a reading of other texts or situations" (Harris, 2017, p. 5);
- **Illustrating:** "When you look to other texts for examples of a point you want to make" (Harris, 2017, p. 40);
- **Authorizing:** "When you invoke the expertise or status of another writer to support your thinking" (Harris, 2017, p. 40);
- **Borrowing:** "When you draw on terms or ideas from other writers to use in thinking through your subject" (Harris, 2017, p. 40);
- **Extending:** "When you put your own spin on the terms or concepts that you take from other texts" (Harris, 2017, p. 40);
- **Countering:** When you "aim not to refute what has been said before, to bring the discussion to an end, but to respond to prior views in ways that move the conversation in new directions" (Harris, 2017, p. 57) through arguing the other side, pointing out bias, providing new counter examples.

Note keywords and passages in the text. In deciding what to quote, the question to ask is not: What is the writer of this text trying to say, but what aspects of this text stand out for me as a reader? Quote to illustrate your view of a text, to single out terms or passages that strike you in some way as interesting, troubling, ambiguous, or suggestive. You can see quotations as flashpoints in a text, moments given a special intensity, made to stand for key concepts or issues.

Our advice was to imagine themselves as rewriting—as drawing from, commenting on, adding to—the work of the authors we were reading in this course. Some students added video clips they found and repurposed to represent their ideas (although they were encouraged to create their own as well); some loved using repurposed memes. Others were more literal in their choice of image as they used direct representations of their content in image form. Students also engaged in dialogic exchange as they were tasked with responding to each other's Instagram posts. See Figures 7.9 and 7.10 for examples of students' work illustrating their engagement with dialogic exchange and remixing of popular memes, repurposed for representing course content.

In sum, like what was offered through Twitter, students made use of Instagram to learn a new genre of writing for social media and the multimedia functionality that the social media platform offered. Student writing for Twitter was shorter, more concise, and revealed tendencies to summarize and pose questions, whereas student-authored text on Instagram focused on explanations of conceptual media representations and offered increased analysis and evaluation. The extended-assignment this year, just as the year before, provided the instructor insights into students' abilities to synthesize and extend the readings through writing before our online classes.

Figure 7.9. An example student post from #WriteTeachChat (Matin Maani, 2021).

#WriteTeachChat

Figure 7.10. An example student post from #WriteTeachChat. (Timothy Sellers, 2021).

REFLECTION ON PRACTICE

We will now discuss how each of the assignments functioned as a support for twenty-first century learning and communication (i.e., technologically-driven), the affordances and challenges we experienced throughout the implementation process, and some of the benefits our students gained through their experiences engaging with the assignments as developing professional teachers of writing. We will later conclude the chapter with brief remarks concerning how we imagine the assignments may be implemented and adapted to meet needs that differ from those within our course context.

The Role of Technology

Because technological advances have permeated our lives, the ways in which we view and engage with literacy and literacy practices (e.g., writing) have shifted. New media and social media platforms have shifted the production, communication, and interpretation of information and provide a wide range of opportunities for reading, writing, and communication. Schools across the US are also gradually requiring the use of social media as part of daily disciplinary instruction. Moreover, modern technology and global events such as the COVID-19 pandemic have played a large role in shifting communication from offline to on-the-screen, so teachers are called to explore the transformative implications for their instruction and learning environments.

Developing comfort and self-efficacy utilizing various technological tools and platforms is of the utmost importance for teachers as students' college and career readiness is increasingly established through technological proficiency. According to the Framework for 21st Century Learning (Battelle for Kids, 2019):

> People in the 21st century live in a technology and media-driven environment, marked by various characteristics, including 1) access to an abundance of information, 2) rapid changes in technology tools, and 3) the ability to collaborate and make individual contributions on an unprecedented scale. Effective citizens and workers of the 21st century must be able to exhibit a range of functional and critical thinking skills related to information, media, and technology. (p. 5)

Along these lines, the Common Core State Standards Initiative (CCSS) (National Governors Association, 2010), positions modern students as learners who are proficient users of digital environments (though critics of the standards would likely suggest that they are not agentive at all). Furthermore, social-media discussion-based assignments provided opportunities to practice good digital citizenship and to record their work so that they could later model the process of scholarly discussion and inquiry for their students in the future. For these reasons, it was important to us that we challenged our students, as pre-service teachers, to make use of popular technologies to reflect on their writing course content, develop their own skills as writers within the constraints that the platforms held, and prepare them to help their future students accomplish the same goals as part of their pedagogical actions.

While our chapter takes up the multimodal expression that is possible on social media, Syndee Wood and Mary Stewart share a TedTalk and Cajita video practice that asks students to remix the findings of their research in Chapter 11 of this collection. In both instances, challenging students to critically think about the types of communication that becomes possible in digital environments and helping them leverage those affordances leads to a richer understanding of writing.

Assignment Affordances

Both sustained assignments provide quite a few affordances in terms of student engagement with learning the course content as well as creating opportunities for these pre-service teachers to generate authentic writing. Each of the assignments were introduced on the first day of class to generate a sense of community and routine that would unfurl over the entire semester while also opening an opportunity for students to document both their growth as writers and the evidence of their comfort with the technology platforms over time. In each of the years, we anticipated and noticed that the quality (writing technique and criticality of content) and amount of writing within their posts both increased.

Moreover, in both years, as instructors, we were able to ensure that our students were attuned to both local features (e.g., spelling, punctuation) and global features (e.g., content, organization) of the writing task. Because of the everyday nature of social-media in our society, each of the platforms offered a more relaxed atmosphere in which to produce writing for real-audience as opposed to traditional eLearning platforms (e.g., Moodle or Canvas) discussion boards or essay-based reflection papers. This has implications for English language learners, too. As social media environments reflect the everydayness of communication outside of school, they thus provide ELL students opportunities in academic contexts for "genuine, meaningful communication" in the target language (Brown, 2018, p. 54). Social media platforms do not necessarily require communication that adheres to the traditional and more formal demands of language usage as required by other writing genres. Thus, these types of assignments for ELLs may support increased confidence with their command of the target language and allow them to experience a transfer of this confidence to the disciplinary literacy practices within other academic content-areas (Yuan et al., 2019). Despite social media's support for common language use, both platforms also offer all students the opportunity to make considerations for how and what ends language manipulations and contextual rhetorical moves (e.g., strategic hashtag use or turn of phrase) can inspire dialogue. Furthermore, we noted that all students enjoyed the "quick-write" nature of the assignments as they were less lengthy than more traditional discussion-board type reflection posts in academic settings. Nevertheless, being succinct, yet analytical, is important for these multimodal communications.

Each platform's support for multimodal communication opened the possibility for our students to affirm their writing for different purposes, audiences, and genres. Although some may be justly concerned with the use of social media in school contexts (due to increased risks of cyberbullying and communication of inappropriate content), the parameters of the two assignments were bounded by our course content and the higher education context. For a middle or high school classroom, we maintain the importance of allowing students to use digital technologies to function as consumers of available information and producers of their own writing. Readers may keep in mind that by structuring the assignments as a supplement to in-class discussion around instructor-selected readings, we decreased the likelihood that our students would produce and share content unacceptable for the course context. Other benefits of using social media to write about and discuss course content included our ability to confirm that students were prepared for class by not only having read the assigned texts but also equipped with reflective thoughts based on the texts and the dialogic conversations they held with their peers.

The assignments also created circumstances favorable for instantaneous instructor-student communication (we participated by posting comments on students' posts to further discussion) and feedback outside of the class. Social-media notifications reached students' devices directly and thus increased our students' awareness of feedback and likelihood of reactive engagement on an individual or group basis. Learning management systems, on the other hand, typically notify students of instructor feedback via email, and those notifications are often only sent to students who are considered authors on initial posts.

For the Twitter assignment, we chose to provide additional feedback in-class by presenting to the class each week one student post that stood out as reflective and thought-provoking. The author of the outstanding post was given a "Sweet Tweet" award certificate during class. Figures 7.11–7.14 provide examples of our students' work using Instagram in which they made use of multimodal text as a support for their discussion. To illustrate their reflective points on the course readings, the student posted a video-clip from a popular movie scene in the first example. In the first example, the student included a metaphorical image, and in the last two-examples, the students incorporated popular teacher-memes. Each of the examples illustrates the creativity involved in the assignment and demonstrates one of the "real-world" aspects that writing via social media elicits. These posts are also documented under the hashtag #WriteTeachChat via Instagram.

Figure 7.12. Example student post. (Rachel Dureaux Clark, 2021).

#WriteTeachChat

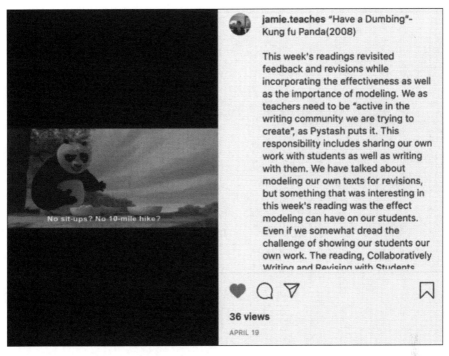

Figure 7.11. Example student post.

Figure 7.13. Example student post. (Kristin Mares, 2021).

Figure 7.14. Example student post (Yasmine Jallal, 2021).

ASSIGNMENT CHALLENGES

There were few challenges associated with this assignment, although we do feel that there are several key points in this regard that are worth mentioning for readers who wish to implement and/or adapt this assignment for their own pedagogical purposes.

First, this assignment is labor intensive on behalf of the instructor. Specifically, we were tasked with reviewing both types of posts (Twitter and Instagram) before class. For Twitter, this was particularly necessary to select a winner for the "Sweet Tweet" award which we also considered as a basis for jumpstarting in-class discussion on the weekly readings and course material. We reviewed student posts on both platforms to make determinations about students' understandings and thus how we would structure the subsequent class conversation to address confusion and/or include our students' voices.

Additional instructor labor included grading. We strived to provide students rubric/point-based feedback in a timely manner each week. This meant that we had to review and assess hundreds of posts and replies per week as part of the requirements were that students had to respond to other participants multiple times. Although locating initial posts is relatively straightforward (made possible by searching for the hashtag and/or specific user accounts), locating and keeping track of individual student comments required us to be more strategic with our recordkeeping. We overcame this challenge, in part, by asking our students to use "A1/A2" denotation with Twitter then later realized this format would work on Instagram replies with "C1/C2" to denote first and second comments. Submissions of individual written reading reflections or learning platform discussion posts do not require the same labor of searching for user activity amidst a collection of posts. And more generally, between the two years, assessing the Instagram assignment was less intensive as students did not have the specific, one-night constraints that the slow chat held, thus not requiring us to be logged-in and responding during a particular time frame. Nevertheless, we consider both assignments as time consuming on behalf of the instructor.

Other challenges to this work readers may face include issues of accessibility given that not every student in other learning contexts may have access to the necessary technology resources. Students' familiarity with online digital technologies and social media platforms may also influence their initial success with the assignments. One way we addressed privacy issues by some of our students was that we allowed them to create a private Twitter and/or Instagram account, but then had to follow and allow friend requests from each of the members of the course. This allowed for their participation with cohort members, but did not allow for wider participation beyond our class. Sometimes compromises like this must be made. Additionally, we required that our students make professional accounts separate from their personal social media accounts. Challenges may arise in this regard when students are less than willing to create and keep track of multiple accounts and for those who—of their own accord or, for younger students, might have a parent who may on their behalf—reject the idea of creating social media accounts altogether. In these instances, individual students may need special support or be provided with individualized conditions that promote participation. We therefore suggest that these assignment types will be more easily used with high school and university students as compared to younger writers.

Potential Implementations and Adaptations

These two assignments were implemented in a teacher-education context; however, we feel that the benefits of the assignments may lend themselves to their use in other content-area domains and writing classrooms. Some of the ways we see that these assignments may be adapted include the use of current events circulated on X feeds or Instagram from trustworthy news sources to facilitate open student-led discussion or the implementation of a "closed section" for either platform by having students create private accounts that only follow each other. This places limitations on engaging with others outside of the classroom but decreases the likelihood of undesirable interactions (if this is a concern). Teachers may also consider contacting and enlisting specific and relevant professionals as agreed-upon participants in the discussions to ensure students are writing for authentic audiences beyond the classroom.

CONCLUSION

Much of the discussion surrounding teaching writing online emphasizes the struggle of making in-person methods work via technological tools, but digital and hybrid spaces foster the potential for engaging writing curriculum that utilizes the benefits of online platforms to their true potential. Using Twitter (in 2020) and Instagram (in 2021), our students reflected on and crafted content while simultaneously connecting with their peers online in a relevant way. Based on the frameworks of dialogic language theories and new literacies, these social media moves illustrate how participatory culture can be used as an effective tool for writing to learn (Jenkins, 2014). Leveraging the participatory elements of an authentic audience inherent in social media allows instructors and students to practice writing in a new way, proving its power as a better writing practice in hybrid and online spaces.

With the ever-increasing push towards digital, hybrid, and online learning there is a large learning curve for the teachers and professors implementing lesson plans and creating engaging online and digital spaces for students. Not only are teachers and professors adapting to this new model of teaching, but many students are as well, especially those who are not current users of social-media platforms such as X and Instagram. These platforms have a wide range of content presented through them that branches out to many different fields including information that may be explored for science, history, and English language arts learning. With a plethora of content constantly streaming, students could use these platforms to engage in many written discussions surrounding instructor- or student-selected topics to garner a strong interest for the class subject matter while simultaneously branching out with the generation and communication of new ideas. In a traditional classroom setting, some students may be afraid to share or voice their knowledge and opinions. But, the distance involved in digital communication tends to encourage students' feelings of safety, greater inclusion, and encourages vocality while reducing the fear of being ostracized, which may more widely occur in the oral-based traditional classroom atmosphere. As in our experience, we note that social-media platforms also foster an online any time learning atmosphere given that students can use these tools to access and relay information simply and quickly.

In line with Harris (2017), we believe that the job of an intellectual is to push at and question what has been said before, to rethink and reinterpret the texts he or she is dealing with. Having student moderators for discussion in the year one study of Twitter certainly helped engage students in fostering inquiry for themselves and their peers, thus promoting their experience in taking on a leadership role. By putting students in the role of moderators, we as teachers create the space to remove ourselves from directing class conversations, thus providing students the opportunity to have open and honest discussions through the creation of thoughtful and meaningful questions surrounding the subject matter. While the year two use of Instagram was not based on a back-and-forth exchange, it still allowed students to post more in-depth responses to the readings and share a variety of other exchanges of ideas through multimodal texts.

Altogether, our two assignments represent an acknowledgement of the advancement and potential for digital learning. The use of these assignments lend to a future in which students and teachers alike can engage in a creative and inclusive space to facilitate writing practices that consider socio-cultural and critical practices of digital text. The implementation of the two assignments have shown foresight into the possibilities and limitations that social media platforms hold for the future of education. We thus assert that teachers of writers can develop both their and their students' writing capabilities through applying the #WriteTeachChat philosophy to their courses.

MOVING BETTER PRACTICES ACROSS MODALITIES

- **In-Person, Real-Time Learning**: One way to adapt these practices to an in-person, real-time learning experience is having a silent written discussion in class using a social media platform of the students' choosing. Students can notice with whom they communicate and to return to their points at the end of the semester by looking back at their posts to note any changes or patterns.
- **Hybrid Learning**: Adapting these practices to a hybrid space facilitates students engaging in professional dialogue with members of the community not involved in the course, for example, professionals from another country or in another time zone.

REFERENCES

Bakhtin, M. (1981). *The dialogic imagination*. (C. Emerson & M. Holquist, Trans.). University of Texas Press.

Battelle for Kids. (2019). Framework for 21st century learning. *Partnership For 21st Century Learning*. http://www.battelleforkids.org/networks/p21/frameworks-resources.

Brown, M. (2018). Mind the gap: A critical guide to digital literacies. In G. Ubachs & L. Konings (Eds.), *The envisioning report for empowering universities* (2nd ed.) (pp. 52–55). EADTU.

Committee, CCCCE. (1989). Statement of principles and standards for the postsecondary teaching of writing. *College Composition and Communication, 40*(3), 329. https://doi.org/10.2307/357777.
Council of Writing Program Administrators, National Council of Teachers of English & National Writing Project. (2011, January). *Framework for success in postsecondary writing*. https://wpacouncil.org/aws/CWPA/pt/sd/news_article/242845/_PARENT/layout_details/false.
Dureaux Clark, R. [@dureauxteaches]. (2021, April 6). For this week's set of readings, we read about the different views people hold on grading and on assessment as [Photograph]. Instagram. https://www.instagram.com/p/CNU0fK9pQMq/.
Jenkins, H. (2014). Participatory culture: From co-creating brand meaning to changing the world. *GfK Marketing Intelligence Review, 6*(2), 34–39. https://doi.org/10.2478/gfkmir-2014-0096.
Harris, J. (2017). *Rewriting, second edition: How to do things with texts.* University Press of Colorado; Utah State University Press. https://doi.org/10.7330/9781607326878.
International Society for Technology in Education. (2021). *ISTE: Standards for educators.* https://www.iste.org/standards/iste-standards-for-teachers.
Jallal, Y. [@yasmineasateacher]. (2021, February 27). In Amanda's podcast, she mentions that the third step of creating her mini-lesson process is to model in front of [Photograph]. Instagram. https://www.instagram.com/yasmineasateacher.
King. S. (2002). *On writing: A memoir of the craft.* Simon and Schuster.
Knipper, K. J. & Duggan, T. J. (2006). Writing to learn across the curriculum: Tools for comprehension in content area classes. *The Reading Teacher, 59*(5), 462–470. https://doi.org/10.1598/RT.59.5.5.
Maani, M. [@matin.tries.teaching]. (2021). I think it's safe to say that the act, the art, the idea of writing transcends the common environment of [Photograph]. Instagram. https://www.instagram.com/matin.tries.teaching/.
Mares, K. [@mares.in.the.middle]. (2021, February 15). This week's readings were really interesting and helpful. Of the two readings, I tended to gravitate towards Bunn's "How To [Photograph]." Instagram. https://www.instagram.com/mares.in.the.middle.
National Council of Teachers of English. (2016). *Professional knowledge for the teaching of writing.* http://www.ncte.org/positions/statements/teaching-writing.
National Governors Association. (2010). Common core state standards. *Washington, DC.*
Sellers, T. [@teachingwithtimothy]. (2021, January 25). When it comes to teaching writing, a one size fits all approach simply isn't the best approach to take. Educators [Photograph]. Instagram. https://www.instagram.com/teachingwithtimothy.
Street, B. (2003). What's "new" in New Literacy Studies?: Critical approaches to literacy in theory and practice. *Current Issues in Comparative Education, 5*(2), 77–91.
Yuan, C., Wang, L. & Eagle, J. (2019). Empowering English language learners through digital literacies: Research, complexities, and implications. *Media and Communication, 7*(2). 128–136. https://doi.org/10.17645/mac.v7i2.1912.

CHAPTER 8.

FISHING FOR ONLINE ENGAGEMENT

Ingrid K. Bowman and Briana Westmacott
University of California, Santa Barbara

In this chapter, the authors describe the **Fishbowl Technique** *used in online, real-time learning; online, any time learning; and hybrid learning. Specifically, an online "fishbowl technique" builds community while preparing students with academic skills such as comprehension, summarizing, critical thinking, text or grammar analysis for undergraduate writing tasks. In describing their "better practice," this chapter addresses the themes of practices in motion across teaching and learning modalities and practices adapted from classic composition strategies.*

FRAMEWORKS AND PRINCIPLES IN THIS CHAPTER

- **Framework for Success in Postsecondary Writing, Critical Thinking:** The ability to analyze a situation or text and make thoughtful decisions based on that analysis, through writing, reading, and research.
- **Framework for Success in Postsecondary Writing, Rhetorical Knowledge**: The ability to analyze and act on understandings of audiences, purposes, and contexts in creating and comprehending texts.
- **Framework for Success in Postsecondary Writing, Writing Processes:** Multiple strategies to approach and undertake writing and research.
- **Framework for Success in Postsecondary Writing, Knowledge of Conventions:** The formal and informal guidelines that define what is considered to be correct and appropriate, or incorrect and inappropriate, in a piece of writing.
- **PARS Online Writing Instruction,** Personal: Building community and fostering connections.
- **PARS Online Writing Instruction, Strategic:** Focusing on the student experience and plan for what students will need to be successful in achieving the learning outcomes.

- **GSOLE Principle 3.4**: Instructors and tutors should migrate and/or adapt appropriate reading, alphabetic writing, and multimodal composition theories from traditional instructional settings to their OLI environments.

GUIDING QUESTIONS BEFORE YOU BEGIN READING

- Are you seeking new, interactive teaching practices for your curriculum?
- How is it possible for students to conduct their own meaningful, online discussions based on reading texts?
- Will implementing a new hybrid practice into a course create more work for me?

INTRODUCTION

I could feel my heart racing as the whole class looked at me. My eyes darted around the room connecting with a handful of students as I held a wedding-like grin on my face that I hoped conveyed some sense of reassurance; nobody said a word. We all sat in complete, uncomfortable silence. The clock continued to tick and, still, nothing was uttered from anyone. *Do I continue to let the air hang thick with the quiet or do I interject my two cents?* This was one of my first struggles with the fishbowl activity (an adaptation of the Socratic method of discussion), allowing the awkward, silent reflection time for students to organize their thoughts before sharing in the class discussion. I remember telling my colleague Ingrid about this struggle and she gave me some simple, yet powerful advice, "I don't make eye contact with the class. If I look down at my papers on my desk, they don't look to me to break the silence."

Amazingly, the next time I assigned a fishbowl lesson in class this strategy worked wonders. By looking down, I was removed from the focus of the class and the students took more ownership of the discussion. Their ideas began to ping-pong around the group. The topic of the discussion began to branch off; students were debating access to education and how much financial wealth plays a role in an avenue to higher education. They were expressing their own personal experiences and opinions based on the concepts presented in the reading. These were the components that would be the backbone for their writing assignment. But what would it look like without me present? Could the students conduct a self-guided asynchronous discussion online? Would they be able to conduct Socratic seminar-styled groups from behind a computer screen? How would the student discussions flow if they are all in a Zoom meeting and not seated next

Fishing for Online Engagement

to one another? How could I take this **in-person, real-time learning** lesson and make it **hybrid**?

What is the Fishbowl Technique?

The classic structure of a fishbowl for engaging in class readings in the **in-person** classroom begins by dividing the class into observers and speakers (see Figure 8.1) who then swap roles. The observers build on the first discussion they witnessed once they become the speakers. After both discussions, the observers all complete a follow-up written task which creates a bridge to writing. The follow-up task (also known as the audience task) is assessed on either completion, organization, clarity, or correct grammar. For instance, students might be asked to summarize the main idea or three new insights they gained from a fishbowl discussion they witnessed from the outer circle, while taking notes as an audience member.

Figure 8.1. In traditional classrooms, an inner and outer circle form the fishbowl and observers. Instructors sit in the inner circle.

As we, Ingrid and Briana, began teaching the hybrid class, we renamed the fishbowl practice peer *discussion groups* and set up a consistent 10-week asynchronous process for an **online, any time** class with members rotating into different groups. A key challenge was finding a way to maintain a text-driven conversation and accountability despite the shift to student-led fishbowls. As students led their own text-based discussions in our **online, any time** learning adaptation, with the usual written follow-up tasks, each group was invited to participate in one of their Zoom discussions (preferably early in the quarter) and to record their other discussions for credit. By watching these recordings, the instructors listen to students' analyses and create subsequent writing prompts directly built from the discussions. While attending one meeting per group, Ingrid was also able to model a text-driven conversation with deeper questioning and listening techniques during the fishbowl discussions that she participated in. Interestingly, in the **online, any time** format, Ingrid began experimenting with a much wider variety of audience tasks since we did not have the traditional outer and inner circles on Zoom.

For the new audience tasks, similar to classic literature circles in reading instruction, each individual in a group was assigned a different written follow-up task. These tasks rotated after each fishbowl. For example, a five-person peer discussion group each completed one of the following tasks: (1) a **content summarizer** of the discussion;(2) a **vocabulary-recorder** detailing key words that were central to the discussion; (3) a **question poser** who posts three unresolved group questions to an online class forum;(4) an **opinion writer** who explains personal responses to the text discussed; (5) a **logistical reporter** who offers insight into participation, leadership or time management in the group. Each person completed all of the different roles at least once over the course of the 10 weeks.

From our **online, any time** writing instruction, a new **hybrid learning** modality has evolved. After teaching the fishbowl in-person for many years, Briana fully shifted from **online, any time learning** to a **hybrid** course. She began our practice in her hybrid courses, where group meetings or break-out groups on Zoom mimic a classic in-person or online style of the fishbowl. Students choose convenient Zoom meeting times for their small groups, resulting in excellent participation. In the University of California, Santa Barbara (UCSB) hybrid course design, Briana began meeting the students once a week in a campus classroom and once a week asynchronously. This modality invited an interesting challenge for the fishbowl Technique to exist between fully **in-person, real-time** learning or completely **online, any time** learning formats, opening opportunities for community-building and critical conversations about the readings in virtual settings.

One thing that is different in this hybrid version of the practice is that students receive instructor-prepared slides to independently guide their peer discussions. Leaning on their annotated, assigned reading texts, each person must speak in their own words to respond to probing questions using text evidence.

However, just as in the traditional fishbowl Technique, it is still preferable not to provide the fishbowl discussion questions too far in advance, but only shortly before the students meet in order to encourage a more spontaneous discussion and to prevent students from pre-writing and reading their answers.

Silence or uneven participation were common challenges for some student-led groups, just like when an instructor is present, coincidentally. That hallmark "discomfort" of the fishbowl Technique reemerged in its online, any time learning forms. This is the beauty of being an educator—we are, in fact, innovators, continually working to solve problems. All good innovators require tools and the fishbowl Technique is an accessible teaching tool for critical engagement with texts as a basis for writing that emphasizes comprehension, vocabulary or grammar exploration, student interaction, inquiry, and community. The **hybrid** learning modality influenced our classroom community, interaction levels, and writing outcomes in new ways. This chapter will focus on **online, any time** and **hybrid** learning deliveries of the fishbowl practice.

SCHOLARSHIP, THEORIES, AND PRINCIPLES THAT GUIDE OUR APPROACH

As an English for multilingual students (EMS) program at a large public university where our department offers multiple sections of the same course in live or hybrid modalities, we recognize how classic, consistent teaching techniques which are readily adaptable to all modalities serve as an anchor in the curriculum. When we re-examine our variations of the fishbowl technique, we are grounded in four characteristics of sound online writing instruction: personal, accessible, responsive and strategic (PARS), as illustrated by Jessie Borgman and Casey McArdle in pages 4–5 of their introduction to the *PARS in Practice* collection. A particular focus on the concepts of personal and strategic are detailed in two extended lesson plan charts (see Appendix).

A multilingual reader's personal experience of interacting deeply with reading texts cannot be taken for granted. The Socratic Method[1] and the framework of activity theory in L. S. Vygotsky's sociocultural theory (1978) have both been readily applied to language learning to pinpoint how learners' motives and social mediation of meaning contribute to their learning process. In second language acquisition, Vygotsky's "zone of proximal development" has been a major subject of interest to examine "how learning is formed through learning from the more experienced peers (teacher-learner or learner-learner) for more scaffolded

---

1   If you are unfamiliar with the Socratic Method, you can learn more about it at https://tilt.colostate.edu/the-socratic-method/

collaborations" (Kung, 2017, p. 4). Both of these theories point a lens on the fishbowl technique, particularly for online writing instruction grounded in the concept of "scholarship as conversation" (Kung, 2017, p. 4). This principle, articulated in the Association of College and Research Libraries' (ACRL) Framework for Information Literacy for Higher Education (2016) emphasizes how information literacy emerges by genuinely engaging students in interested reader conversations much like the members of a book club would do (https://www.ala.org/acrl/standards/ilframework). At the heart of writing instruction, we contend, lie discussions that are intentionally layered to tease out not only comprehension, but also grammar or vocabulary inspiration, brainstorming and genre awareness, or the dissection of rhetorical devices such as tone, style, or flow. The fishbowl technique is also aligned with the Writing Program Administrators, National Council of Teachers of English, and National Writing Project's *Framework for Success in Post-Secondary Writing* (2011) definition of Developing Critical Thinking through Writing, Reading and Research in which students:

- Read texts from multiple points of view
- Identify and draft texts for multiple purposes
- Craft discipline-specific responses and build genre awareness
- Analyze and synthesize quality of sources
- Create informed written texts for various audiences
- Generate questions to guide research

Even with these principles in mind, we struggle to consider adaptations across modalities. Can consistent and effective peer-directed reader conversations emerge in online modalities? Do such online conversations support students in the writing process? To explore these questions, we referred to the Global Society for Online Literacy Education's (GSOLE) definition of an online literacy course (OLC) which states that "OLC educators make use of core literacies to promote skill and/or knowledge development. OLCs promote critical thinking and communicative expression of that thinking; many such courses are writing-centric and may be called online writing courses (OWCs)" (*Online Literacy Instruction Principles and Tenets*, 2019). We realized the broad pedagogical potential of applying the fishbowl technique in this hybrid learning setting demonstrated our commitment to critical thinking in our online writing instruction.

COURSE CONTEXT AND LESSON

The English for Multilingual Students (EMS) program is in the linguistics department at UCSB. The EMS program includes four levels of undergraduate writing courses focused on teaching English for academic purposes with multilingual students. These required writing classes provide instruction and practice in academic reading, writing, and oral skills needed for university-level work. Three of the four levels in this program are pre-entry level writing classes in which students are placed based on the results of a written exam. These first three levels emphasize academic writing, grammatical and lexical approaches. However, the fourth level focuses more on rhetorical strategies and genre-based writing.

The new hybrid courses have 18 international students and are offered for 10 weeks. The class meets in person for one hour and 50 minutes, once each week, with asynchronous material posted online in a module as support (live classes meet twice each week). The fishbowl technique will be introduced live in class only for the first time—to teach the format and strategies for conducting a productive discussion. After that, fishbowl discussions will be student-led and conducted online.

Incorporating the fishbowl technique aligned our classroom practice with several guiding principles of effective online writing instruction as defined in key online writing instruction guidelines and theories. By using these lesson plans, Briana streamlined preparation of a hybrid writing course. Lessons such as these resulted in a regular structure for critical thinking and writing preparation that students became increasingly more autonomous with and invested in as the quarter progressed.

In the following section, we unpack two lesson plans for the **hybrid** course. At the beginning of the course, students practiced one fishbowl during an **in-person, real-time learning** class with a traditional written follow-up task due immediately (Lesson Plan 1). This type of lesson plan only needed to be conducted once as an introduction to the process. One week later, students began their own hybrid fishbowl experiences online using an alternative format which would be repeated throughout the course (Lesson Plan 2). Two extended lesson plans, with a teaching rationale for each step of the lessons, are available in the Appendix.

Lesson Plan 1: Introduction to the Fishbowl Practice (live)

Purpose

By the end of this fishbowl lesson, you will have a better understanding of how to write a literary, narrative, non-fictional paper. You will also gather new vocabulary and grammar structures to use in your upcoming paper. In addition, you will become more familiar with the genre of memoir writing and how to conduct a seminar-style discussion.

PowerPoint Slide 1: Fishbowl Arrangement

Slide text: We will arrange desks to create an "inner circle" and "outer circle" for the discussion. Follow this diagram and rearrange your desks.

Skills

When you are in the fishbowl discussion, the specific skills you will practice include:

1. Interpersonal communication skills
2. Identifying the main idea of the text
3. Genre understanding
4. Posing and answering critical thinking questions
5. Active listening
6. Synthesizing
7. Summarizing
8. Vocabulary-building

Knowledge

The fishbowl is a method of discussion that helps you to improve reading comprehension, develop both oral and written summarizing skills, utilize critical thinking, and practice grammar and genre analysis. Students will be expected to include descriptive prose, first-person narrative, and figurative language in their papers.

Task

Preparation: For this live fishbowl discussion (slides available at https://bit.ly/FishbowlDiscussionSlides) you will read and annotate *this excerpt from Educated*[2] prior to our class meeting. Utilize active annotation strategies to formulate your own opinions and responses to the author's perspective about education. Post the following response on the online class forum:

- What are the different forms of figurative language Tara Westover uses at the beginning of her excerpt from the book *Educated*?
- Do you feel this is a powerful use of the language or was it confusing to you and why?

PowerPoint Slide 2: Fishbowl Discussion Questions

Slide text: Address these questions in your group:

- How does the author give you the sensation of being in the setting of her childhood?

---

2   Excerpt is available for reading or listening from WBUR at https://www.wbur.org/hereandnow/2018/12/31/educated-tara-westover

- What types of figurative language does she use? Give an example.
- What might you infer about the author's father?
- Do you agree with the author's viewpoint about education being a privilege?
- "I do think that whatever life we have becomes normalized to us, because it is the only one we have."—Westover

What is an example of something that you have lived through that became normalized to you?

Guidelines:

1. During the discussion, be sure to honor the person who is speaking by never interrupting them.
2. You can add your own personal experiences or comments to any of the guiding questions. You do not need to respond to the guiding questions in any specific order; the questions are there to guide your discussion topics.
3. Some topics may lead you to discuss ideas in your native language. Be sure your whole group can participate in this language shift and switch back to English when the questions are specific to English vocabulary and language structure.
4. Remember, silence is golden; this is when the thinking is occurring.

Follow Up

While you are not actively participating in the discussion group, you will be assigned an audience task that asks you to summarize the key components that were addressed in the fishbowl. This will be completed while you are listening to the discussion group.

PowerPoint Slide 3: Audience Task

Slide text: Listen to the fishbowl discussion. Focus on how your partner contributes to the conversation. Answer these questions on a separate piece of paper. Hand them in today for credit.

- Paraphrase when your partner used a vocabulary term or phrase from the instructor's questions in the discussion.
- Summarize the main ideas that come from the fishbowl discussion.
- Write one opinion that you had after listening to the discussion. Did you agree or disagree with your partner's perspective?

Criteria for Success

Your success in the fishbowl practice will be assessed on four criteria:

1. Discussion preparation in the form of effective text annotations and specific questions or notes
2. Active participation in response to all questions
3. Written audience task
4. Self-assessment of your participation based on the teacher-provided checklist

Extended Lesson Plans 1 and 2

Our teaching practice is based on an established theoretical rationale, outlined above. To move our fishbowl technique from **in-person, real-time learning** instruction, through **online, any time learning** modalities, and into the new **hybrid** modality, we included two extended lesson plans and the guiding principles which underlie each teaching step.

This first extended lesson plan in Briana's **in-person, real-time** class served as essential preparation for the subsequent, student-led online discussions. It is important to note that it only happened once (live) at the beginning of the quarter, so it was a key moment of instructional scaffolding (see Appendix).

LESSON PLAN 2: HYBRID FISHBOWL (ONLINE)

Briana has set up a collaboration with the editors of the UCSB student newspaper *The Daily Nexus*. Student work is considered for print publication in the opinion section of the newspaper after this essay assignment (https://bit.ly/HybridFishbowlAssignment) has been completed. Students have the choice to submit their Mock Nexus Paper to be considered for publishing.

Purpose

This fishbowl session will take place virtually. You will meet with your group via Zoom to discuss the published work from former Linguistics 12 students in *The Daily Nexus*[3] campus newspaper (https://dailynexus.com/2021–06–29/international-students-reflect-on-a-year-of-online-education/). Your Mock Nexus Paper that you will begin drafting will use a similar genre of writing aimed at the same audience as these articles. Be sure to look at how these authors provided evidence to support their written position.

---

3   We use *The Daily Nexus* because it is our campus newspaper. Learn more at https://dailynexus.com/

Here is a brief slide presentation for one of these student-led discussions (https://bit.ly/HybridFishbowlSlides):.

Slide text: Follow these steps:

1. Complete reading and tasks before your meeting.
2. Arrange a group meeting date. Each person chooses one of the roles.
3. Have a synchronous discussion using Zoom, Facetime, WeChat or another live option. Spend 40–50 minutes on tasks. Take notes.
4. Go deep into ideas, language and questions that you noticed.

Skills

When you are in the fishbowl discussion, the specific discussion, reading, and writing skills you will practice include:

Discussion:

- Interpersonal communication skills
- Posing and answering critical thinking questions
- Active listening

Reading:

- Annotation strategies
- Synthesizing

Writing:

- Genre analysis
- Summarizing
- Vocabulary-building
- Analysis of evidence to support an opinion/position
- Writing for a particular audience

Knowledge

A main goal for your fishbowl session focuses on rhetorical knowledge—to analyze and write for appropriate audiences, purposes, and contexts. While the subject of your Mock Nexus paper may be different from those you are reading, the tone, choice of academic vocabulary, use of authoritative evidence, writing genre, and structure will be similar.

Tasks

Preparation: Please read and annotate the published submissions from former students in the UCSB newspaper *The Daily Nexus*. Review the specific job that you will be taking on for the group discussion in the slide below. If you are the questioner, you will need to prepare your questions prior to the group meeting. Procedure: Your group will hold your meeting at a specific time online. Have one member record the session to submit to your teacher with all of your individual work. Be sure to take notes while you are participating in your discussion.

The focus for discussion:

- Summarize the position that each author presents in their article.
- How do the authors target this specific audience?
- What is the overall tone of each author?
- How do they use academic vocabulary in their writing?
- Is their article concisely written?
- Do the authors successfully provide evidence to support their position?
- Share your personal opinions about the different topics these authors have covered.

Slide text: 3. In the first discussion, each person chooses a role. Switch roles in the subsequent discussions.

Role 1 (Summarizer): Write a summary of what happened in your group.

Role 2 (Questioner): Post three group questions to the forum. Your questions should be specific to the tasks assigned.

Role 3 (Vocabulary profiler): Choose five key phrases or words from the article that are important. Define each one. Write an original sentence with each in the context of the article's topic.

Each student must invite the instructor to ONE group discussion for a grade this quarter. You choose when. We will have four to five group discussions.

During that observation, I will be grading your contribution and participation, not the correctness of your answers.

Schedule your date in advance by email. Do not wait until late in the quarter, otherwise there may not be enough time.

Follow up: Gather all of your materials in one GoogleDoc to share with your instructor prior to our next class session. Be sure to include the recording of your meeting.

Criteria for Success

- Your group will make one Google document to share with your instructor.
- Provide your individual roles and a link for the recording of the discussion.
- Your contributions must be written in complete sentences and paragraphs.

- The summary must contain a thesis statement and topic sentences for any supporting paragraphs.
- Check your notes and work for grammar and spelling.
- The questioner must submit to the class forum posted on the LMS.

Extended Lesson Plan 2

A second extended lesson plan chart continued to aid us in aligning established theories with the practice as Briana shifted the fishbowl technique into the hybrid learning modality (see Appendix B).

REFLECTION ON PRACTICE

OVERALL EXPERIENCE

As Briana looked back on the fishbowl lessons from her **hybrid** course, it became clear that this technique bettered her writing instruction. By using the technique in a **hybrid** course design, she got the best of both worlds. She was able to introduce and model the practice **in-person** and then scaffold the lessons online in weekly **hybrid** models. Students voted to keep their fishbowl groups consistent throughout the quarter and this allowed many of them to establish new friendships from the class. They would meet online for their weekly fishbowl practice, and some even went on to meet for dinners and gatherings. In course feedback, students used words like "fun," "collaborating," "interesting," and "friendships" when reflecting on their fishbowl experiences. Writing, and the preparation for the writing process, became a social activity for the students. By removing the instructor from being present in the discussion process, students became independent, and the social dynamic shifted in their groups. In some groups, they were able to establish a stronger connection with their peers that continued to thrive outside of the walls of the classroom. What an outcome for any teacher to have from their class!

In mid-quarter feedback, many students said that the fishbowl was one of the highlights of the course. They stated that it helped them to develop their vocabulary and speaking skills: "I felt that the fishbowl meetings really helped me to understand the readings and I could ask my friends questions," was a statement from one undergraduate student. Some also expressed that it assisted them in idea construction, outlines, crafting a position or thesis statement. They reflected on the ideas they had shared from the fishbowl discussion and said that they felt clearer in developing their writing.

Students also expressed how the fishbowl clarified certain concepts in the readings and enabled them to use authors' ideas as evidence in their own writing pieces. By following guided instructions for the process that were distributed to students in the lesson plans, they were able to run their seminar-like groups for forty-five minutes to an hour . . . completely on their own. They talked about purpose and audience, genre, tone, vocabulary, and evidence. They each took their role within the group very seriously and most groups were successful. Of course, there was one group that had some struggles, yet the vast majority of students reported their Zoom-based fishbowl conversations were quite successful.

Labor

For a visual overview of the instructor's preparation and labor cycle throughout the quarter, please see Figure 8.2.

For each discussion, Briana posted a five- to ten-minute lesson plan with instructions for the in-person session. More preparation time is needed in week 0 for reading selections, writing prompts and lesson plan drafting, but it evened out once Briana was comfortable with the format. Providing students with clear expectations and fishbowl practice guidelines is imperative.

Much of the labor and preparation for this activity takes place in week 0 and subsequently weeks 4, 6, and 8 when Briana had to preview and score each groups' Google Document content. A helpful suggestion to teachers using this practice is to skim through the Zoom meeting videos. By using double speed and visually skimming through the videos, you can get used to scanning students' Zoom sessions and save time in the grading process.

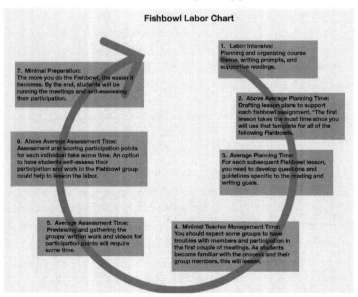

Figure 8.2. This visual overview depicts the stages of instructor preparation for an overview of the labor cycle during one 10-week quarter.

Group Dynamics

One student struggled with attendance, only meeting with her group a couple of times during the quarter. However, Briana made adaptations to their fishbowl assignments. This was also very easy to track when Briana was calculating participation points for the fishbowl meeting because students were recording their sessions and sharing links to those recordings in a Google Document. That group did experience frustration and stress due to the irregular attendance of one member, yet, this is a specific situation that cannot truly be fixed in the future. It is an unforeseen element of any group assignment. In this case, at least, Briana did lessen the load of the members of this group that were participating and she believes this helped them to feel better about the situation.

The fact that some of the group discussions turned to arguments of sorts isn't surprising, considering the nature of the readings that were assigned for this specific fishbowl. The reading content was based on current campus topics and therefore it elicited impassioned, strong debates. This was aligned to a position paper writing assignment, so students were learning the art of formulating an opinion and crafting a thesis based on this position. The Mock Nexus paper allowed students to choose a topic to research and report on for the editorial section of the UCSB newspaper. This paper produces a wide variety of topics since students have choices in their writing topics.

Further Reflections

We truly believe that a hybrid section is a perfect place to use the fishbowl Technique. By introducing the process in class, Briana could address questions in person before they completed their tasks and meetings. Sharing the lesson plan and all the logistics for the practice allowed students to ask questions such as, "Who is in charge of the talking? How do we turn in all of our work? What will be graded?" These questions could be clarified before students departed to run fishbowls on their own, choosing a time that would work best to gather in Zoom and to use the accountability structures that were in place.

The other personal piece of this practice in **hybrid** courses is that we could have a follow-up debriefing discussion in person when a teacher could address any concerns. Students had some problems with recording their meetings in the first round of the fishbowl. Others asked about the question forum that was posted on our course module. In one of the follow-up debriefings during class, Briana used some of the questions that were posted on her class forum to guide a whole-class discussion. This only took 10–15 minutes of unstructured discussion time at the beginning of class and Briana could check in on their overall comprehension of the materials they had read and discussed. At the beginning of the quarter, there were more questions and concerns about the logistics for the fishbowl; as Briana reached the end of the quarter, students were so familiar with the fishbowl they did not have any questions about the process of the work. In short, their online engagement through the fishbowl technique became a routine.

There are some things that she would do differently with the fishbowl in the future. First, the assessment for the fishbowl was tricky; she had to have students share a Google Doc to view their Zoom meetings and this overloaded her email box. Next time, it would be more productive to create a class Google file from the start where they would all post their fishbowl meetings and materials.

On that same note, assigning grades or participation points for the activity was a task. Since it was Briana's first time teaching a hybrid course, she gave the students participation points for the fishbowl. It was grouped into the participation category that is weighted 10 percent for the course. Next time, she might experiment with defining participation assessment criteria to establish A-level versus C-level participation. Ingrid has done this with criteria such as (a) Natural speaking with no direct reading from notes; (b) At least one bit of text evidence is referenced in the comments; (c) Complete sentences and some academic vocabulary from the text were used. Next time, Briana would like to increase the weight of participation to 15 percent and add a self-assessment task for each student to complete after they finish the fishbowls.

On one final note, many students shared that they felt more comfortable talking and discussing in small groups over Zoom than they did in a whole-class format. When Briana compared the discussions she had observed in week 1 compared to week 10, she could see stronger discussions and deeper reflections from these students. This supports our goal of responsive teaching. The fishbowl added an element of live peer discussion that had not been present in many of their prior online modules. The **hybrid** fishbowl helped to build a community of learners in the sections, something that is unique and oftentimes challenging to foster in **online, any time** writing instruction.

CONCLUSION

The benefits of connecting speaking and writing have been extensively documented, particularly to overcome writing barriers and reach new levels of proficiency. The fishbowl Technique offers countless options to modify discussions from the live classroom into both asynchronous and hybrid teaching modalities. Utilizing fishbowl dialogues in our online writing instruction forced our students to interact more directly online while they deciphered linguistic devices and other elements that drive the composing process.

A compelling reason to include this Socratic-style fishbowl technique is that hybrid modalities offered us wiggle room to introduce necessary student-to-student interaction with texts, mutual interpretations of evidence, and collaborative editing of their language for academic writing. The beauty of being an educator is that we are, in fact, innovators. All good innovators require tools and the fishbowl technique is a versatile teaching tool for critical engagement with texts as a basis for writing that emphasizes comprehension, vocabulary or grammar exploration, student interaction, inquiry, and community. And we were also pleasantly surprised at how effectively the fishbowl technique reinforces strong online writing instruction.

For example, our program requires extensive written feedback on students' work. In online writing instruction, student-to-student discourse can parallel and complement formal written assignments and conventional, ongoing written feedback that is offered through rubrics, margin, and end comments. In the case of limited face-to-face interaction, we as instructors can squeeze into either asynchronous or hybrid landscapes, and peer discussion groups effectively pull together several elements of the hybrid course.

One beautiful element of the fishbowl practice is that—once you get it established—it begins to run itself. Students gain confidence and control of the discussion sessions. Their writing began to be sprinkled with evidence from their fishbowl meetings. Students expressed how it became easier to build their outlines for the longer writing pieces after completing fishbowl meetings. They said that their fishbowl meetings were a great way to gather information for the writing prompts. It is also noteworthy to mention that this practice was successfully completed in a 10-week **hybrid** course; it would be even more beneficial to establish this practice in a longer semester structure.

Why would you want to try the fishbowl in your **hybrid** or **online, any time** writing course? Our answer would be, why wouldn't you? As educators, we strive to provide motivating content, dynamic lessons, and an opportunity to build community in online sections. The fishbowl technique facilitates these objectives because whether the instructor is fishing for more critical textual engagement, or students are casting their own nets, the aim of online engagement is being met. It empowers the students as they run their discussion groups and facilitate their online engagement, so their confidence grows. The instructor scaffolds student learning outcomes that drive the lesson, but the actual learning is led by the students themselves.

MOVING BETTER PRACTICES ACROSS MODALITIES

- **In-Person, Real-Time Learning:** Traditional fishbowl discussions are conducted in class with Instructor participation. Each group may incorporate some students via "hyflex" video call.

- **Online, Real-Time Learning:** Simultaneous fishbowl discussions conducted through breakout rooms with a general debriefing session at the end.
- **Online, Any Time Learning:** Assigned peer discussion groups meet at scheduled times outside of class. A prescribed discussion process is established. Each student submits a reflective discussion report afterwards.
- **Hybrid Learning:** Fishbowl technique is practiced once in the live meeting. Then, assigned peer discussion groups meet at scheduled times outside of class. Class debriefings about the process occur in the following live meeting.

REFERENCES

Borgman, J. & McArdle, C. (Eds.). (2021). *PARS in practice: More resources and strategies for online writing instructors*. The WAC Clearinghouse; University Press of Colorado. https://doi.org/10.37514/PRA-B.2021.1145.

Conference on College Composition and Communication (CCCC). (2015). *Principles for the postsecondary teaching of writing*. https://cccc.ncte.org/cccc/resources/positions/postsecondarywriting.

Council of Writing Program Administrators, National Council of Teachers of English & National Writing Project. (2011, January). *Framework for success in postsecondary writing*. https://wpacouncil.org/aws/CWPA/pt/sd/news_article/242845/_PARENT/layout_details/false.

Dean, C. & Patterson, K. (Eds.). (2020). *Starting lines: An anthology of student writing*. UCSB Writing Program, Hayden-McNeil/Macmillan Learning. http://www.startinglinesmagazine.com/.

Felton, P. & Lambert, L. M. (2020). *Relationship-rich education: How human connections drive success in college*. John Hopkins University Press. https://doi.org/10.1353/book.78561.

Framework for Information Literacy for Higher Education. (2016). *Association of College and Research Libraries (ACRL)*. https://www.ala.org/acrl/standards/ilframework apps#usefaculty.

The Institute for Learning and Teaching. (2023). *The Socratic method. Fostering CRITICAL THINKING*. Colorado State University. https://tilt.colostate.edu/the-socratic-method/.

Kung, F. (2017). Teaching and learning English as a foreign language in Taiwan: A socio-cultural analysis. *TESL-EJ The Electronic Journal for English as a Second Language, 21*(2).

GSOLE Executive Board. (2019, June 13). *Online literacy instruction principles and tenets*. Global Society of Online Literacy Educators. https://gsole.org/oliresources/oliprinciples.

Paul, R. & Elder, L. (2008). Critical thinking: The art of Socratic questioning, Part III. *Journal of Developmental Education, 31*(3), 34–35.

Paul, R. & Elder, L. (2006). The thinker's guide to the art of Socratic questioning. The Foundation for Critical Thinking. https://www.criticalthinking.org/TGS_files/SocraticQuestioning2006.pdf.

Vygotsky, L. S. (1978). *Mind in society: The development of higher psychological processes.* Harvard University Press.

APPENDIX A: EXTENDED LESSON PLAN 1

Step 1: Preparation

Read the assigned text. Apply active annotation strategies in the margins.

Teaching Rationale: Socratic-style questioning in the fishbowl technique challenges students to identify and explore "threshold concepts" in source readings in order to feel equipped to complete their writing assignments. Information literacy is one building block for our academic writing curriculum, as outlined in the ACRL *Framework for Information Literacy for Higher Education* (2016), so we also teach or review effective annotation techniques.

Step 2: Reflection

Post a response to the reading question in the online class forum.

Teaching Rationale: Reflective tasks, encouraging students to bring their own questions to a fishbowl discussion, acknowledge "information creation as a process" and encourage "research as inquiry" (ACRL *Framework for Information Literacy for Higher Education* (2016)). These two principles are central to our technique.

Requiring short written response assignments elicits a connection between the assigned academic reading texts and future writing tasks. The online forum response serves as a simple jumping-off point with which students begin a reflection online, briefly read or interact with peer responses in the online discussion, and then move into the remotely-conducted fishbowl discussions.

Step 3: Slides 1 and 2:

In small groups, conduct your first 15-minute fishbowl discussion using your text annotations and the questions posted on the slides.

Slide 3: Students sitting in the outer circle must complete an audience-listening task while witnessing the fishbowl discussion.

Then all of the inner circle swaps places with students in the outer circle.

Teaching Rationale: In the hybrid modality, this is the only chance for students to conduct a fishbowl discussion live since future discussions will all be held on

Zoom (or other platforms). Staging one fishbowl discussion in the classroom is a chance to establish a safe group dynamic, but this step can also be done very effectively online, if necessary.

The basic live structure of the fishbowl creates speakers (like goldfish in a bowl) and observers (just watching and listening) who then swap roles. The observers then build on the discussion that they just witnessed when they move into the fishbowl.

The instructor provides guiding questions or topics for the discussion groups to address in their speaking sessions. English language learner research shows that scaffolded lesson plans are an important component of writing preparation. So, we aim to balance students' need for structure with enough flexibility for groups to engage in their own process of inquiry. For example, slide 2 shows five questions about: rhetorical devices, vocabulary, comprehension, reader response, and application of ideas. Other possible guiding points might be genre-based comparisons, topic-specific vocabulary use, parts of speech or grammar concepts to note from the reading.

The observers are given a set of "audience tasks" to complete during their listening session. How to effectively write a summary of the discussion is a common written audience task assignment since summaries are an important genre of academic writing. However, the tasks should be varied, so they might include comparisons, opinions, or vocabulary development, too.

Both students' annotations and the quality of the suggested teacher questions determine the effectiveness of each fishbowl discussion. Probing with the right questions at the appropriate time is an art in which the questioner intentionally strives to vary the "moves" used throughout the discussion. According to Paul & Elder, some of the sample spontaneous Socratic questioning "moves" that instructors should typically use include:

- Ask for an example of a point a student has made or of a point you have made.
- Ask for evidence or reasons for a position.
- Propose a counter-example or two.
- Ask the group whether they agree. (e.g., Does everyone agree with this point? Is there anyone who does not agree?)
- Suggest parallel or similar examples.
- Provide an analogy that illuminates a particular position.
- Paraphrase an opposing view.
- Rephrase student responses clearly and accurately.

Paul and Elder's (2006) "moves" support academic essay writing preparation because they can target elements of the prompt which students are expected to write about, such as supporting evidence (point 2 above), formulate similar or hypothetical examples based on their own understanding (point 4 above), paraphrase (point 7), or rephrase (point 8) authors' ideas (Paul & Elder, 2006, p. 34). However, the crucial difference between instructor-led fishbowl discussions, as envisioned by Paul and Elder, and our hybrid fishbowl technique is the online learning component through which students develop ownership over these moves. The hybrid modality promotes a practice of relationship-rich education through this loose learning community in which academic interactions between peers not only build confidence of expression yet supply the writers with concrete ideas and language as they create meaning together.

In the subsequent hybrid discussions, we rely on students to continue with the (often uncomfortable) process of inquiry with increasingly less instructor guidance. For example, future discussions may or may not have specific instructor questions to guide the discussion. Sometimes a focus on vocabulary, themes, grammar structures, or other areas are chosen in student-designed discussions as they become more proficient in mining every text.

Step 4: Review Discussion Guidelines

Listen carefully to each speaker- don't interrupt.

Address the guiding questions in any order.

Add relevant personal experiences or comments to any of the guiding questions.

If topics lead to discussion in your native language, ensure that the entire group can participate. Then switch back into English.

Thinking pauses are normal. Silence is golden, so embrace it.

Teaching Rationale: This review of the guidelines is intended to establish a ritual or fishbowl format that students can lean on once they are facilitating hybrid discussions on their own.

Using the Socratic Method, a curious instructor does not impart information directly to the students, yet models and guides each discussion into deeper understandings through a series of spontaneous, exploratory, or critical questions, along with intense listening and written follow-up tasks. As Paul & Elder explained, "The key to success here is entering or adopting the Socratic spirit; this occurs when one becomes genuinely curious, truly wondering what students are and are not thinking. . . The Socratic spirit wants them to become concerned with intellectual standards, with whether or not what they think is true or false, logical or illogical, reasonable or unreasonable" (Paul & Elder, 2008, p. 34).

To assist in adopting this Socratic spirit, Paul and Elder developed a helpful checklist of discussion "moves" ("The Art of Socratic Questioning Checklist") to guide the direction a discussion takes. For example, if a language barrier arises, an instructor asks, "What is the main idea you are putting forth? Could you explain it differently?" (Paul & Elder, 2006, pp. 4–5).

APPENDIX B: EXTENDED LESSON PLAN 2
Ingrid's Hybrid Extended Lesson Plan

Lesson plan 2 details a student-led hybrid fishbowl discussion once the students have been introduced to the process, and is aligned with the GSOLE principle #3.4 that "Instructors and tutors should migrate and/or adapt appropriate reading, alphabetic writing, and multimodal composition theories from traditional instructional settings to their OLI environment(s)" (Global Society of Online Literacy Educators OLI Principle 3.4).

Step 1: Slides 4 & 5

Deepening the discussion practice

Teaching Rationale: The hybrid discussion format is outlined and explained to students. As fishbowl sessions take place virtually, the guided process of read + annotate + reflect + discuss + write + edit continues in the instructor's effort to address the complex dynamics of course design and instruction by offering students a personal and strategic approach (Borgman and McArdle, 2020) to composing.

The objectives of this lesson include posing and answering critical questions, active listening, summarizing, vocabulary building, and more. Continuing the discussions online frees up the limited number of classroom meetings we had for other writing preparation. This is also aligned with GSOLE Principle 3.4 (see above).

Our multilingual students regularly express frustration if group work is inadequately structured or guided, such as during some peer review or self-assessment tasks. Yet, student-generated questions preparing for written tasks do, at times, run the risk of merely including lower-order questions according to Bloom's Taxonomy—knowledge, comprehension, and application. Therefore, it is crucial to balance the need for structure and spontaneity while ensuring that higher-order questions, such as analysis, evaluation, and synthesis, are also prompted. As confidence in the fishbowl Technique and their peer group grows, students reflect on the autonomy to listen to and respect each other's diversity of ideas and benefit from some time to polish their written follow-up tasks. This lays the foundation for a community of writers—a personal approach to writing (Borgman and McArdle, 2020).

Step 2: Bridge to writing instruction

Step 3: Specific audience follow-up written task options

Teaching Rationale: Our varied written follow-up assignments are one bridge to written work. Students rotate and complete a different role after each discussion. The role titles might be: a) Summarizer; b) Vocabulary Profiler; c) Logistical report; d) Questioner.

Mentor texts: Analysis of student-written essays and mentor texts (i.e., Starting Lines, Nexus articles) encourages a level of discussion that is one step closer to the students' final written assignments. because using these models allows students to compare work timed writing tasks, peer response tasks, or simple revision of their drafts. According to the WPA, NCTE, and NWP *Framework for Success in Postsecondary Writing* (2011), this establishes "rhetorical and twenty-first-century skills as well as habits of mind and experiences that are critical for college success." More specifically, these skills and habits are:

- Rhetorical knowledge: the ability to analyze and act on understandings of audiences, purposes, and contexts in creating and comprehending texts;
- Critical thinking: the ability to analyze a situation or text and make thoughtful decisions based on that analysis, through writing, reading, and research;
- Writing processes: multiple strategies to approach and undertake writing and research;
- Knowledge of conventions: the formal and informal guidelines that define what is considered to be correct and appropriate, or incorrect and inappropriate, in a piece of writing;
- Abilities to compose in multiple environments: from using traditional pen and paper to electronic technologies.

APPENDIX C: ONE SAMPLE FISHBOWL SUMMARIES WRITTEN BY STUDENTS

Graduate Class Student Zhencheng Wang (Ling 3G) Winter 2021(asynchronous); three-person group.
Discussion Summary 1

Dorde Nikolic, Xin Jiang and me (Zhencheng Wang) had a discussion on Zoom from 8:15 to 9:20 p.m. on Tuesday (Jan 12). During the discussion, we went through Tasks 1–7 in Unit 2 in AWGS together. We took turns to read our own responses to other group members, who gave comments or asked questions afterwards. Overall, this discussion proceeded smoothly, with some small disagreements among us that Xin posted as questions.

During the discussion, there are several points that we found useful or important. First and foremost, by reading the texts and finishing the tasks, we had some concrete feelings on how to write a General-Specific passage. Useful openings include general statements, statistics and definitions. Secondly, audience is important. For example, for Task 1 on Page 56, three of us found the text hard to read and understand, especially for part A. One possible reason is that this text might be aimed for people who have some knowledge in TV programs. Another example is that, in Task 4 on Page 64, Xin showed a deeper understanding than Dorde and me since she majors in (economics. Additionally, we agreed on the point that the flow of information is important, for example the Task 1 and 4 mentioned above. Repeating some key words is useful for this flow.

Several fun things that we learned from each other include: 1) Language usage is different among disciplines. For instance, when we talked about using statistics as openings, I pointed out that in physics this is seldomly used. 2) We do have some similarities. In Task 7 on Page 70, we shared our screens to show the definitions in the journal papers. We found that we have similar ways to define notions, although the definitions seem to appear in different parts of an article. 3) Dorde and Xin are excellent partners to work with. We had a great discussion.

APPENDIX D: INGRID'S FISHBOWL INTRODUCTION

Sample video clip of Ingrid's brief, informal, course introduction of peer discussion groups (aka fishbowl discussion) in an asynchronous course (https://bit.ly/FishbowlIntroduction). Note: AWGS stands for our textbook, Academic Writing for Graduate Students by John M. Swales & Cristine B. Feak.

APPENDIX E: THREE STUDENT ESSAYS PUBLISHED IN UCSB CAMPUS NEWSPAPER, THE DAILY NEXUS, AS A RESULT OF BRIANA'S CLASS:

1. International Students Reflect on Remote Learning, Nexus, June 2021. https://dailynexus.com/2021-06-29/international-students-reflect-on-a-year-of-online-education/
2. International Students Speak Out, Nexus, February 2020. https://dailynexus.com/2020-02-20/students-speak-out-on-coronavirus/
3. International Students on the Transition to Remote Learning, Nexus, June 2020. https://dailynexus.com/2020-06-30/international-students-on-the-transition-to-remote-learning/

CHAPTER 9.

CRIPPING WRITING PROCESSES: COMPOSING (NEURO)DIVERGENTLY

Ada Hubrig
Sam Houston State University

Anna Barritt
University of Oklahoma

In this chapter, the authors describe **works-in-progress** *as a pedagogical intervention used in online, any time learning and hybrid learning. Specifically, the authors respond to ableist assumptions about the writing process by encouraging writing process practices that more suitably accommodate diverse learners in sustained thinking about a topic, and more advantageously meet the demands of online learning. In describing their "better practice," this chapter addresses the themes of accessibility and inclusivity and practices adapted from classic composition strategies.*

FRAMEWORKS AND PRINCIPLES IN THIS CHAPTER

- **GSOLE Principle 1.1:** All stakeholders and students should be aware of and be able to engage the unique literacy features of communicating, teaching, and learning in a primarily digital environment.

GUIDING QUESTIONS BEFORE YOU BEGIN READING

- What might all writing instructors need to know about the theory and practice of "cripping," as a framework that foregrounds social justice and resilience for marginalized students who are disabled and neurodivergent?
- How might we recognize, appreciate, and honor neurodivergent learners' thought processes in our classroom contexts and spaces?
- What assumptions does your own writing pedagogy make about your students and their learning?

- How can the writing process respect students' agency, ownership, and ways of thinking about who they are as writers?

INTRODUCTION

> I want us to examine how we—as WPAs, teachers, and colleagues—operationalize and reinforce ableism in the very design of our programs.
>
> – Remi Yergeau (2016, p. 156)

A Glimpse into Ada's Experience

In an informal, interdisciplinary mentorship group of undergraduate and graduate neurodivergent students, Ada (they/them) commiserated with others about sites of struggle we experienced in our education as autistic and otherwise neurodivergent students. A frequent topic of dismay in our group was this thing called "the writing process." As something of the de facto organizer of our group and the writing studies person, I listened patiently as one of my compatriots expressed her frustrations: "I don't think they get that I don't write that way! I end up writing my whole paper first, and then go back to jump through all the extra hoops they ask for."

Being asked to move through formal stages of brainstorming and outlining, then making a rough draft, revisions, and a final draft was often anxiety inducing for neurodivergent students, who would frequently describe it as "jumping through extra hoops" to please their neurotypical professors, rather than the productive, useful exercises they were meant to be. One student would draft her essay weeks ahead of time, only to reverse engineer documents for the brainstorming and outlining assignments. As a neurodivergent person, I (Ada) identified with these students' struggles. Throughout my education, the more stream-of-consciousness rough drafts I would first create were clearly unacceptable to my teachers, who believed I was not putting in the required effort to meet their demands, despite the fact that I was often spending much more time drafting than seemed to be normal. My rough drafts were often incomprehensible to instructors, so it would appear to them that I had made more or less complete essays; I, too, would then engage in this reverse engineering of "products" that I could use to meet drafting requirements throughout my educational career. Could I make an outline first? No. But I'd draft a more completed form of my essay and go back and produce required artifacts like an outline. I noted that in contexts outside of classes, I was rarely required to do this. Noting this disconnect between how we were expecting students to write and how we are expected to "perform" the writing process in composition, I wondered how else we could frame the writing process.

A Glimpse into Anna's Experience

~~I, Anna, (she/her) am neurotypical (I think). But I am also a lifelong procrastinator who needs the pressure and chaos of an imminent deadline to perform.~~ I, Anna, (she/her) began writing this chapter thinking I was neurotypical. Shortly before the final editing stage, I was formally diagnosed with ADHD, confirming my lifelong suspicion that I was neurodivergent. There have been many instances throughout my undergraduate and graduate education in which professors required a fully developed rough draft before the final deadline. I acquiesced and met their demands, but I was never satisfied with my project when this process was imposed upon me, and it was reflected in my grade. Despite my own negative experiences, I found myself prescribing a linear writing process to my own composition students. Shoehorning students' writing processes into a presentable draft that instructors can assess is just what we do, right? I always believed that my own chaotic prewriting and revision process was an exception to the rule, and that I should exert the same kind of teacherly control that past writing instructors had done with me. However, I was struck by a student evaluation I came across during my time as an assistant writing program administrator. It was this comment that helped me begin to see that perhaps I am not an outlier, and that there is a need to make space in composition pedagogy for the many ways students engage with the writing process. The student in our program (but not in my class) wrote:

> [This class] sucked. I think the course is tailored to a specific writing/research method that is especially uncommon in students with ADHD or autism. When I write a paper I write it from start to finish as it is going to be written. This means that it takes a lot more time for me to finish a paper, but it takes a lot less time for me to edit it. Requiring a rough draft a week before the paper is due only benefits students who write faster and sloppier papers and edit details later. Frankly, this expectation for a specific work style in a gen ed course is a bit unrealistic and ableist.

I found the comment jarring. I have always felt that my own chaotic writing process, which does not follow the standard procedure of rough draft, revision, final draft, was an anomaly. Suddenly I saw my own feelings reflected back at me, except the complaint was in a way lodged at me as administrator who oversees the requirements of first-year composition (FYC) courses.

Towards (Neuro)Divergent Writing Processes

We share these stories about autistic/neurodivergent experiences with a degree of hesitation, knowing too-well how anecdotal evidence of disabled peoples' experiences are often narrativized in institutional settings and used against us/them (Dolmage, 2017; Hubrig, 2020; Kerschbaum, 2015). We approach this work considering carefully anecdotal evidence about neurodiversity, and echo Margaret Price (2011) who argues, "[w]e must resist facile conclusions about our students based upon their diagnosed, self-identified, or suspected neuroatypicalities, and focus instead on ways that their writing and ways of knowing might change and inform our practices" (p. 56). Together, we (Anna and Ada) work to better respect and honor students' ways of knowing, their ways of engaging in the writing process.

Centering neurodivergent experiences, then, we ask: Is it possible that drafting requirements are doing harm? We are not suggesting that we abandon the rough draft or a composing process; rather, we challenge writing instructors to question why we require a rough draft, and to question what counts as evidence of student effort, especially within the context of online writing courses. We propose a more open drafting system we call "works-in-progress," coupled with any time online workshops that allow for more divergent drafting processes.

SCHOLARSHIP, THEORIES, AND PRINCIPLES THAT GUIDE OUR APPROACH

We come to this work as writing scholars interested in cultivating what Elizabeth Brewer calls "a culture of access" (Brewer et al., 2014) that centers disabled positionalities and experiences to transform pedagogical approaches. We echo Allison Harper Hitt (2021), who argues that issues of disability and neurodivergence are often positioned in writing studies as an obstacle that can be overcome. Hitt establishes how this orientation toward "overcoming" disability is often deployed with the expectation that disabled students alter their practices, rather than writing instructors confronting the ableism of our own pedagogy and practices. We echo disability scholars in writing studies in reorienting the field's understanding of disability, as Tara Wood and colleagues (2014) argue, "Disability's presence, like the presence of students with race, class, or gender differences, is not a 'problem' but rather an opportunity to rethink our practices in teaching writing" (p. 148). That is, rather than seeing disability and neurodivergence as an issue needing to be solved in the writing classroom—and in an attempt to respect neurodivergent writers' processes—we imagine how we can center disabled ways of knowing in our pedagogy.

We begin this work by imagining how we might become more receptive and more inclusive to (neuro)divergent composing processes. To that end, we turn to the National Council of Teachers of English's professed commitments to students' rights to their own language. We turn to the Conference on College Composition and Communication's *Students' Right to Their Own Language*. We truncate the long history of this document: originally drafted in 1971–1972, the *Students' Right to Their Own Language* statement was printed in *College Composition and Communication* in 1974, reaffirmed in 2003, an annotated bibliography was added to the document in 2006, and it was again reaffirmed in 2014. We imagine how individual instructors might take up *Students' Right to their Own Language* in regard to neurodiversity.

Throughout the statement's long history, the document emphasizes variance and variety of *spoken* language, though it also explores the importance for variances with written language. The statement discusses "dialects" of the English language, and insists that variants of the English language each follow their own rules of correctness. We push back against the framing of Black Englishes as "dialects," understanding that many of the examples in the statement refer to Black Englishes, which we recognize to be full languages in their own right and point to the *This Ain't Another Statement! This is a DEMAND for Black Linguistic Justice!* document created by the 2020 CCCC Special Committee on Composing a CCCC Statement on Anti-Black Racism and Black Linguistic Justice, Or, Why We Can't Breathe. While we highlight this reference to "dialects" as one shortcoming of the *Students' Right to Their Own Language* statement, we also point out that in the *Students' Right to Their Own Language* statement the central argument that a teacher's role in language learning should be to assist students in further developing their own language skills—"in short, to do what they are already doing, better."

As we reflect on the purpose of the *Students' Right to Their Own Language* statement, we appreciate the main focus on honoring students' language practices. But we also feel the ways the statement has been taken up—usually in terms of students' word choice, grammar, syntax, and other features of writing—are admirable, but ultimately too limited in that these articulations do not do enough to honor the students' language *processes*. We extend this line of thinking from language practices to include not only the words that are spoken or written on the page, but the processes students employ to *write words* on the page. We believe that a student's right to their own language must also include student's rights to their own language *processes*. We seek to better understand the nuances and differences writers exercise in their writing process, including differences in the composing processes of neurodivergent writers.

Let's consider the words of neurodivergent scholar Amy Gaeta (2020), who describes their own writing process and critiques of that process as something akin to stream of consciousness, recording what they think. They describe how this is received poorly by their instructors:

> Multiple professors told me this was my problem—I didn't know how to write. But, there is no other way that I can write. One thing that is misunderstood about neurodivergent people is this: it is not our preference to think and process differently, it isn't just more comfortable for us. We cannot think and process any other way. (Gaeta, 2020)

In Gaeta's account of their experience, we read a lack of respect for neurodivergent processes, and we see this failure to respect neurodivergent processes as "anti-autistic ableism" (Osorio, 2020). In response, we seek another way of framing writing processes, one that might support writers like Gaeta, respecting not only their own language in terms of word choice, but their language in terms of process. In other words, we extend the mandate that teachers should support learners in what they are doing, better, to the writing, drafting, and workshopping process. We believe this extension of the central argument from the *Students' Right to Their Own Language* statement has important repercussions for language instruction for neurodivergent learners and disabled learners more broadly, honoring not only their *words* but their *processes,* recognizing process is a part of language.

Interconnected and inextricable to our concerns about neurodivergent writing processes are the ways writing is racialized in our classrooms. As Asao Inoue (2015) argues, "As judges of English in college writing classrooms we cannot avoid this racializing of language when we judge writing, nor can we avoid the influence of race in how we read and value the words and ideas of others" (p. 33). We understand that the ways in which we read and evaluate language cannot be separated from the racializing of language: the embodied experiences of neurodivergence and disability cannot be separated from embodied experiences of race and ethnicity. We also strive to better respect students' writing processes as an issue of justice more broadly. As Christina Cedillo (2018) establishes in their account as a Chicanx, disabled, neurodivergent professor of writing and rhetoric, the ways race, ethnicity, and disability shape how the embodied process of writing is received are inseparable from one another. Cedillo writes:

> Writing, which was once all I ever wanted to do for a living, now feels oppressive, mentally and physically painful every time I have to do it. I often spiral and shut down, driven to bed to avoid facing my failure. Years later, I am a teacher of writing and I can't even follow my own advice to get things done. I'm a charlatan just trying to make it from one day to the next. I don't think this profession is really for me. (2018)

We read, throughout Cedillo's account—both the glimpse of their story we've offered here and the larger context of their article—a centering of White, neurotypical, nondisabled ways of knowing and writing, as well as a privileging of White, neurotypical, nondisabled process in writing instruction. We move to respect a wider range of writing processes in the classroom to decenter not only nondisabled ways of composing, but to decenter Whiteness as well.

A space that is uniquely poised to embrace students' rights to their own processes of language, especially neurodivergent students' processes, is the online classroom—more specifically, the any time classroom. Online Literacy Instruction Principle #1, established by the Global Society of Online Literacy Educators, foregrounds universal accessibility and inclusivity, including the ability of "all stakeholders and students [to] be aware of and be able to engage the unique literacy features of communicating, teaching, and learning in a primary digital environment." As we work to expand the work of CCCC's *Students' Right to Their Own Language* statement, we also work to extend the OLI Principle #1, pushing this principle's commitment to accessibility and inclusivity in online literacy instruction to also respect neurodivergent students' ability to engage in their own writing processes, not just one typically valued in the "brainstorm, outline, draft, revise, copyedit" steps that dominate most college writing classrooms. As we will discuss later in this chapter, the affordances of asynchronicity position instructors to "crip"—intentionally centering the embodied experiences of disabled people to challenge ablenormative understandings, imagining new possibilities beyond existing systems, and creating more just spaces (McRuer, 2006, p. 32)—many of the intrinsically ableist features of the traditional classroom in favor of more inclusive pedagogy, including how we teach and assess the writing process.

COURSE CONTEXT AND LESSON

Anna teaches FYC at the University of Oklahoma, a large public research institution in the Midwest. Students are typically highly prepared and represent the highest test scores in the state. The writing program curriculum is based on rhetorical education, enacted through the teaching of key concepts such as rhetorical listening, critical inquiry, and the questioning protocol of stasis theory in order to exercise deliberation and participate in public life. In the first course of the two-course sequence (Comp I), students practice "slowing down" argumentation and focus on excavating the values, beliefs, and worldviews that motivate individuals and groups. Building on this groundwork, the second course of the sequence (Comp II) asks students to select a public controversy to investigate throughout the semester, beginning with an analysis of the issue's history, context, and stakeholders. Using stasis theory to identify what is at stake for different individuals and groups, students then work to discover the heart of disagreement in a public controversy and identify what kinds of arguments—i.e., what stasis category—stakeholders are making about the issue (arguments of fact, definition, quality, or policy). Eventually, students craft an argument to an indifferent or resistant stakeholder with the goal of persuading them to change their mind or actions. Throughout the course sequence, students are expected to produce drafts of each major essay project that receives feedback both from peers and the instructor.

In the spring of 2021, Anna taught Comp I in a hybrid blended format, with one day in-person, one day on Zoom, and the equivalent of one day of any time learning. Though there was some wiggle room as to what day was designated for which modality, Anna was required to hold at least two synchronous class sessions due to mandates imposed by upper administration. Anna was then assigned to teach Comp II in the summer of 2021, though to do so fully asynchronously. The nature of summer session courses meant that many students had returned home and were in different time zones, were working full time, and were juggling family obligations. The deadlines for drafts and final projects were also in rapid succession due the condensed schedule (eight weeks). We see these constraints as access barriers, where students were ultimately assessed by their compliance rather than their writing. And we believe that they make the affordances of asynchronicity all the more important.

In the fall of 2020, Ada began teaching composition classes at Sam Houston State University. SHSU is a regional research state university with over 20,000 students and has recently been designated a Hispanic Serving Institution. Moving to a new city and beginning teaching in a new context, mid-pandemic, proved to be a difficult transition, and Ada's students were also (quite understandably) struggling to make progress in their online classes during this difficult time. Because of various pandemic-related struggles, Ada chose to structure their Composition I and Composition II online classes as any time learning, but also found—through informal surveys to the class—that they really wanted a deeper sense of connection to the class itself and to one another. Ada began to imagine what it would mean to crip this class in this any time learning context.

Partly because of the newly asynchronous nature of our online composition courses, we both found ourselves thinking carefully about constraints of time. We echo the disability studies concept of *crip time* introduced by Allison Kafer (2013) and expanded on by Ellen Samuels (2017). In short, crip time establishes that time is not experienced in a standard way, but that disabled people experience time (and constraints of time) quite differently. Kafer (2013) explains that "rather than bend disabled bodies and minds to meet the clock, crip time bends the clock to meet disabled bodies and minds" (p. 27). Wood (2017) has explored crip time in the writing studies classroom, arguing that "we must pay attention to how we construct time; otherwise, we may enforce normative time frames upon students whose experiences and processes exist in contradiction to such compulsory measures of time" (pp. 260–261). We write alongside Wood as we think more critically about how our course expectations draw on ableist norms and expectations of how students experience time and labor. For instance, as our own vignettes as well as Gaeta's experiences demonstrate, the drafting process may take more time and look altogether different than their nondisabled peers. As another example, in contrast to the typical stage of brainstorming in the writing process that is expected to happen in the beginning of the process, the perspective of crip time invites us to reconsider this stage entirely, as the student in Anna's program suggests by stating that they write a paper "from start to finish as it is going to be written." In short, typical composition classrooms do not acknowledge the needs—and timing considerations—of neurodivergent people.

Returning to Wood's point about constructing time, then, this reorientation towards disability also caused us to carefully reimagine the drafting process and peer response workshops—a staple of our synchronous, in-person writing classrooms—and how we might reinvent both drafting and writing workshops as an asynchronous, more neurodivergent-friendly process. We noted the difficulty many students had expressed with the drafting process and workshops. As we worked to create our any time, online composition classes, we sought ways to better respect the languaging and drafting processes of neurodivergent writers in our classes.

As part of this reflection on the drafting process in terms of crip time and neurodivergence, we asked ourselves, *what if instead of focusing our efforts on convincing students of the value of the rough draft, we rethink how we define process and revision?* We turned to other neurodivergent writers and disability scholars for answers. We considered, for example, Shawn Patrick Doyle, author of the blog Good Writer Bad Writer (https://goodwriterbadwriter.com), who often documents his experience writing with and through ADHD. Despite years of negative associations with writing, Doyle has found that for him, the key to unlocking the generative potential of ADHD relies on "planning for the storm," as he puts it. Doyle writes,

> The brain works much faster than the fingers can type. Ideas do not occur linearly in the order that is best for the reader to understand them. Writers need to manage this storm of ideas, capture the best points, and order them on the page. . . . I find that the key to managing this storm is to know it

will come and put a plan in place to capture as many of these thoughts without having to worry about the order and structure of ideas. (2014)

In similar language, Griffin Keedy and Amy Vidali have coined the term "productive chaos"—a term that invokes "both mess and motion, an intentional juxtaposition pointing to the normative nature of the writing process and embracing the creative and threatening value of chaos and disability" (2016, pp. 25–26). Keedy and Vidali show us the discomfort writing instructors may feel when working with students who have very different thinking and/or writing processes, perhaps due to neurodivergence. If instructors can resist the impulse to "correct" what might present as disorganization or procrastination, we might begin to see the potential.

Keedy and Vidali further describe this concept:

> Productive chaos means allowing and even anticipating writing not as a formulaic process but as a highly personal and productive, if sometimes painful, creative act . . . Embracing disability in supporting writers and writing is a many-layered intervention that sometimes comes together into an engaging work of art and always challenges our common definitions of the writing process. (2016, p. 26)

What we want to emphasize from blogger Doyle and scholar-teachers Keedy and Vidali is that *process still matters*. A disability-centered approach to drafting does not mean we have to abandon the spirit of process and revision. What we do think it means is that we should *expand our definitions of process,* embracing the similar, yet subtly different term "progress." We can move away from shaming students for procrastinating or allegedly maintaining poor time management skills, and lean into "the storm" or the "productive chaos," to better honor neurodivergent ways of composing. To this end, we shifted our focus to "works-in-progress" (rather than "rough drafts") as well as created space for any time discussions of "works-in-progress" to better account for neurodivergences and crip time in our online writing classes. And, as we know from our understanding of students' rights to their own language, even a subtle shift from "process" to "progress"—ignoring our own student process could make a substantive difference for our writers.

Better Practice

Our suggestion for a more inclusive writing process begins with a "Works-in-Progress" (WIP) rather than a full rough draft, and moves toward an any time writing workshop that makes more affordance for crip time, specifically relying on the asynchronicity of our courses, in the drafting process. In this section, we share our experiences with assigning the WIP in our courses and running any time writing workshops with the assignment. We will also offer generalized TILT assignment sheets—first for the "Works-in-Progress" assignment and second for the any time workshop that accompanies the WIP—that may be integrated into any writing course with room to customize for a specific essay project.

RE-FRAMING THE WRITING PROCESS: "WORKS-IN-PROGRESS" RATHER THAN "ROUGH DRAFTS"

How do we allow for multiple writing processes in our writing classrooms that respect a variety of languaging processes while also honoring the progress that individual writers are making? Our interests and experiences with neurodivergent writers (and, in Ada's case, being a neurodivergent student and scholar) has led us to question conventionally held wisdom about the singular, capital "W" "Writing Process." We echo Jimmy Butts (2017), who argues that writing processes vary, not only across context, purpose, and audience, but also across individual writers. Butts points to the origins of our current process of crafting a full rough draft as a byproduct of the typewriter, where making revisions to a complete text at a time—rather than a more recursive revision process afforded by modern word processors—was an imperative set by technological limits (2017, pp. 109–112).

In moving away from this norm of "beleaguered revision" (Butts, 2017, p. 109), we instead imagine how we might thoughtfully engage students in their own emergent drafting processes, as unique and varied as our students are. While we can certainly share strategies that they might use in the writing process, we want to move away from the belief that there are concrete, universal steps in the writing process. This is why we ask students to submit a "work-in-progress" (WIP). While this means some students might turn in a traditional rough draft, this also allows for Keedy and Vidali's "productive chaos" in a conscious attempt to create space to honor the writing processes of neurodivergent writers. While WIPs do have certain labor-based guidelines (see "Rationale for the Works-in-Progress," below), they are also explicitly left more open-ended, and invite this "chaos" of composing. We are happy to receive stream-of-consciousness writing, bulleted lists or outlines, writing that more closely resembles a journal entry, diagrams or maps, a video discussion of their idea, or any other form that students are comfortable composing, enabling their own unique writing process.

The Work-in-Progress (WIP) draft functions as a practice that we recommend adopting in the composition classroom, rather than a specific lesson.

WIPs are thus highly context-specific; they can and should be adapted for the nuances of an instructor's particular essay assignment. For example, if we were focusing on the use of sources in the essay, we might ask to see an attempt at that task in some form so we can offer feedback on that particular task. For the first WIP due for Anna's summer Comp II course, for instance, she included a brief overview of why she was asking for a non-traditional draft (since students had already taken Comp I where more traditional rough drafts were assigned), an overview of how students might go about creating their WIP, and a list of minimum criteria, as demonstrated in Anna's artifact below.

Rationale for the Work-in-Progress

Everyone's writing process is unique. Personally, I struggle with the concept of writing a full "rough draft" that undergoes many rounds of revision before I submit a "final draft," which tends to be the writing process teachers and professors expected of me when I was in college. My brain works a bit more chaotically. I prefer to gather a lot of ideas, quotes, and concepts, and roughly organize them in the general structure I imagine for the paper. Then, I spend several hours "binge-writing" and voila! There's an essay! However, this does not mean that I don't value revision or that I don't believe writing can't be improved beyond the first draft—quite the contrary. What it does mean is that I value all forms of writing and thinking. I ask us to draft "works-in-progress" rather than "rough drafts" to respect our unique writing processes.

Purpose

For every major project, you will submit a "work-in-progress" draft that you will receive feedback on from your peers and from me. These drafts should demonstrate the project objectives in whatever form that may take for you. For some, that may mean writing a **cohesive draft** from start to finish, complete with an introduction, body paragraphs, transitions, etc. For others, it may mean a **detailed outline**, plugging in quotes and short commentary that helps you imagine the essay in its entirety before you write cohesive sentences and paragraphs. Or, you may be a visual thinker, so creating some sort of **diagram**, **map**, or **matrix** may help you imagine connections between your ideas that you can then translate to a cohesive, written essay.

If you are not in tune with your own writing process, I encourage you to use this first work-in-progress draft to explore. However, please keep in mind that your classmates and I will be giving you feedback. Your draft should be substantive (as outlined in the criteria below) so that we can help further your thinking and give you as much constructive feedback as possible.

If you have any questions about the work-in-progress draft, don't hesitate to reach out. Remember, you are more than welcome to write a conventional rough draft of the essay. The loose guidelines of this work-in-progress draft are meant to be helpful, not a hindrance. That being said . . .

- You should include a minimum of 1,200 words (of the 2,500- to 3,000-word final essay) in some form throughout the draft (or equivalent in another modality).
- The four key stakeholders/stakeholder groups you have found to be invested in and/or affected by the issue should be identified.
- It should be clear that you are applying stasis theory to the issue's debate, including key arguments and stakeholder positions.
- You must include a Works Cited page that lists the sources you intend to include in the final draft (eight sources minimum), with each entry correctly formatted in MLA.
- (Optional) If you have any questions or concerns you would like your peer reviewers to keep in mind, please include those either on the draft itself or as a comment on your assignment submission.

For the first WIP, most students submitted a traditional rough draft, though a few took advantage of the open-ended nature of the assignment and created outlines. As the semester progressed, Anna kept the WIP assignment description relatively the same apart from making changes to criteria that matched the needs of the current essay project. More and more students began to embrace the affordances of the WIP. One student uploaded several pictures of their hand-drawn notes of how they envisioned structuring the essay and an accompanying Word document with potential quotes to include in the final draft. Another student created what they called a "rough draft table," complete with topic sentences for each paragraph of the essay, direct quotes and a summary of the source material, and commentary that mapped out the student's goal for every paragraph. This process for assembling their thoughts was so different from anything Anna had seen before. Outlines are common, but the way in which the student segmented their thinking into categories with proposed ideas for how to analyze and synthesize sources painted a picture of a mind at work in an exciting and innovative way. In a survey of the WIP assignment at the end of the course, this student expressed the following,

> I loved how I had the freedom to organize my paper how I wanted. In regards to my writing process I thought it really helped me figure out how I wanted to write paper. Putting all my ideas and information onto a paper really helped me see the end result.

The student's drafting process certainly looked like "productive chaos" to her, but she and the student's peers were still able to offer constructive feedback that helps the student connect the dots, resulting in an excellent final essay.

In Ada's classes, changing expectations for drafts led to a reverse of what had become a pandemic trend. Since the pandemic began, more and more students were not turning in their rough drafts. But after changing to the WIP model, nearly every student turned in their WIP. In a mid-semester check-in that followed Boston University's "start / stop / continue" (https://www.bu.edu/ctl/teaching-resources/start-stop-continue/) model for midterm feedback, many students remarked that they appreciated the greater degree of flexibility this offered them (Boston University Center for Teaching and Learning, 2023). Students' remarks touched on how this flexibility not only helped disabled students, but students managing family life, work outside of school, and many other aspects of students' lives.

In office hours, one student who had chosen to disclose her neurodivergent status to Ada shared that she was especially appreciative of the WIP model, commenting that this feedback early on helped her better understand the goals of the assignment. She pointed to how she often felt instructors had *secret* objectives for their assignments, but having feedback on a draft early on helped her feel she was better meeting the goals/criteria for each essay.

In both of our experiences, the freedom and flexibility of the Work-in-Progress was generally well-regarded by most students, as they found it to be beneficial for their thinking and writing process. Some students still chose to submit a traditional rough draft, which was acceptable and fell within the criteria of the WIP assignment. And, as we evaluated these WIPs and provided feedback, we appreciated how this approach to drafting allowed for neurodivergent composing processes, which we will elaborate on in the final sections of this chapter.

Work-in-Progress TILT Assignment Sheet

Purpose

For the Work-in-Progress assignment, you will make a good-faith effort to meet the objectives of the project in whatever form that may take for you. For some, that may mean writing a cohesive draft from start to finish, complete with an introduction, body paragraphs, transitions, etc. For others, it may mean a detailed outline where you plug in quotes and short commentary that helps you imagine the essay in its entirety before you write cohesive sentences and paragraphs. Or, you may be a visual thinker, so creating some sort of diagram, map, or matrix may help you imagine connections between your ideas that you can then translate to a cohesive, written essay.

The purpose of this assignment is to help you explore and develop a writing process that works for your own learning needs and preferences, which is essential to your success in this composition course and future college and professional contexts. Specifically, you will:

- Understand writing as a process of exploration.
- Develop a flexible and effective strategy for composing.

In completing a WIP draft, you will practice important skills of a successful writer, including planning, drafting, and revising, though the ways in which you go about practicing these skills (and the form they take) will depend on your own writing process.

Task

1. Begin by reviewing the essay assignment description, including the minimum requirements.
   - Develop a Work-in-Progress draft that demonstrates your ideas, plans, and/or attempts at the essay project.

Criteria for Success

Though the WIP is an open-ended assignment that may be completed according to your drafting preferences, there are some requirements.

- You have submitted a WIP assignment.
- You have included author's notes.

ASYNCHRONOUS WORKS-IN-PROGRESS WORKSHOPS

As we continue to reflect on crip time and how we might better respect the language and composing practices of neurodivergent students, we turn our attention to asynchronous writing workshops as a key element of our "works-in-progress" practice.

Echoing our consideration of crip time earlier in this chapter, we are interested in the "works-in-progress" practice as part of an any time online classroom because of the affordances it might make for accessibility. In the GSOLE Webinar, "Accessible Affordances of Asynchronicity: Cripping Online Instruction," Leslie R. Anglesey and Molly E. Ubbesen (2021) reflect on their own access needs as instructors as well as those of their students, especially as they were impacted by the 2020 shift to online learning. This resulted in a rich discussion of the affordances of the any time classroom and the ways in which asynchronicity counters much of the embedded ableism stemming from normative assumptions about what "time" and "engagement" often look like in the synchronous classroom. Anglesey and Ubbesen (2021) argue that the synchronous classroom, whether in-person or digitally mediated, often comes with narrow views of presence, creating a narrative in which "students' bodies, behaviors, and dispositions represent their engagement in the course," which can become problematic when engagement is assessed for a grade. The any time classroom, on the other hand, offers students more control over their learning experience in ways that align with their needs and preferences. Asynchronicity allows instructors to crip attendance and to crip engagement—students may choose when, where, and how to engage with class content. While the freedom and flexibility afforded by any time classrooms may benefit a number of students who may struggle in a synchronous classroom for a variety of reasons, we argue from our experiences that it is especially beneficial for neurodivergent students, particularly in the drafting process.

Version 1: Running Asynchronous Writing Workshops through Canvas LMS

For Anna's Comp II summer course, she relied on features of the Canvas Learning Management System (LMS). As Ada will explain in the next section, though, asynchronous writing workshops can be facilitated successfully through other platforms outside of an LMS. Students received completion grades for fulfilling all steps of the workshop.

First, students were asked to submit their WIP drafts as .docx files to the assignment dropbox. When creating the assignment in Canvas, the "Automatically Assign Peer Reviews" feature was enabled. As long as students submitted by the deadline, they would automatically and randomly be assigned two drafts to review that would appear on their dashboard. It is also possible to manually assign peer reviews, which can be useful for research-based projects that the instructor would like to group thematically, but can be very time-consuming. Enabling "Anonymous Peer Reviews" is not recommended. In her experience, students are more likely to leave inappropriate feedback when anonymous, and this feature also prevents students from using the annotation tools in Canvas. Each WIP assignment (four total) had criteria specific to the essay project, but typically asked for a minimum word count, a Works Cited page, and optional author's notes included with the submission. In the future, she will require author's notes, as WIPs that included author's notes received more substantial feedback in the workshop. Requiring the notes ensures that students are thinking critically about what they have accomplished and what kinds of input might help them move forward. It also ensures deeper engagement from peers.

To receive full credit for the writing workshop, students were asked to answer several peer review questions specific to the essay project, offer one compliment about a specific strength of the draft, make at least one concrete suggestion for revision, and respond to any author's notes. Students were encouraged to use the annotation tools available through Canvas DocViewer (automatically available through the Canvas Peer Review function as long as peer review is not anonymous) or leave their feedback in a summative comment. Because the course took place over an eight-week summer semester, students had only 48 hours to leave feedback. This short turn-around certainly contrasts with Anna's goals to enact crip time, but at the time felt necessary due to the truncated summer session. After the student deadline for leaving feedback, Anna read through the drafts, leaving each student a summative comment that focused on ways to develop the draft more fully or potential areas for focused revision.

After receiving instructor and peer feedback, students were asked to submit a full draft of the essay project by a particular date (note: Anna usually offered a full week). Some students had only minor revision goals to attend to if they submitted a more complete draft for the Work-in-Progress. Other students' final drafts differed greatly from the WIP submission. In either case, the writer had comments from two peers and the instructor to refer back to, as compared to a reliance on their own notes and memory of a traditional, synchronous, and talk-dominated peer review session.

Version 2: Running Asynchronous Writing Workshops through Google Docs and Flip

For Ada's 1301 and 1302 courses, students worked outside the LMS using free educational technology (including the video-based discussion tool, Flip, and Google Docs). Though unfortunately neither Google Docs nor Flip are integrated into Blackboard (the LMS at Ada's university), these two free-to-use programs allowed for a relatively smooth asynchronous writing workshop experience. Students received points for completing each step of the process.

First, students would be asked to share their "works-in-progress" drafts as a shared Google Doc in an established Google Drive folder, with their last name as the title (this made it much easier for peers to search for each other's work). Importantly, each of these documents were set so that anyone who accessed the folder had in-app permissions to comment on each other's work.

After sharing their files with their peers, students would record their own author's note video in Flip. In these videos (usually three to five minutes), students would be able to describe the feedback they would like to receive on the draft. While they were encouraged to ask about the specific features we were working on developing for that individual assignment (such as using sources in writing, using narrative to support a claim, etc.), students would share a range of questions about their writing. Among the most common requests for feedback were concerns about "flow" (something of a nebulous idea that we worked together, through these videos, to define as a class), organization of the essay, and clarity of the main idea.

For our asynchronous workshop, students would be given usually a week (though sometimes more for larger projects) to read and respond to three to five of their peers' WIP assignments (the number was dependent on the course, the project, and the time we had to respond). For the first half of the semester, these were randomized (Ada randomized the groups in a spreadsheet), but students formed their own groups in the second half of the semester. Students would be asked to leave four to five comments in the Google Doc (that responded to the questions asked in the author's note video), as well as respond to their peers' Flip author's note. In student's video responses to the author's note, they would recap the comments and feedback they left for the author. These would usually be about one-to-two-minute videos that offered quick summaries of their feedback. Oftentimes, students would follow up asynchronously with questions for their reviewers, though this was not a required stage of the workshop process. Ada—as their instructor—was also able to give students feedback directly in response to their author's note on Flip.

Based on the feedback each author received, they would then be tasked with completing their essays. Because of the nature of the WIP, that meant some students were already working from full drafts, while others were working from an outline or a couple paragraphs. Ada would ask students to post their essay on Blackboard (because of external institutional pressures to have artifacts for course assessment). Students would use the comment box alongside their submission to also post the three most important insights they used in the final drafting process from the feedback they received, and how their completed essay responded to those insights as a way to give Ada a framework for responding to their work.

Through both of our experiences, we are encouraged by the mostly positive reception to the WIP and workshop, and we've found it's helpful to:

- tailor the WIP instructions to the writing assignment, to be sure it still highlights the writing task(s) central to the goals for the assignment (see the Assignment Sheet below)
- include author's notes to help guide students through the workshop process, ensuring feedback that is more relevant and useful to the student and
- articulate the usefulness of reflection in asking students to retrace what they learned about writing through the WIP process.

WIP Writing Workshop TILT Assignment Sheet

Purpose

Now that you have explored your own writing process in the Work-in-Progress draft, it is time to workshop your draft with your peers and instructor. Receiving feedback not only helps you imagine new paths for your own writing, but engaging with your peers' WIP drafts exposes you to other ways of composing.

The purpose of this assignment is to help you to continue to develop and refine your writing while learning about others' unique writing processes, which is essential to your success in this composition course and future college and professional contexts. Specifically, you will:

- Improve synthesis of your ideas.
- Clarify your claims.
- Develop methods for evaluating others' writing.

By participating in the WIP writing workshop, you will practice important skills of a successful writer, including giving and receiving feedback.

Task

1. Read the WIP drafts assigned to you, paying careful attention to the author's notes.
2. Using the platform (ex. Canvas DocViewer, Google Docs, Flip), give feedback on your peer's draft.

Criteria for Success

- You have left four to five comments on a peer's draft that responds to their author's notes.
- You have asked one to two generative questions that will further your peer's thinking and drafting.

REFLECTION ON PRACTICE

As we reflect on our emerging works-in-progress workshop, we focus on challenges we've encountered with WIPs, mostly related to the ideas that, first, some students who struggle with the degree of choice they are given and, second, the ways that WIPs reshape peer review and writing feedback. We note that some students did not respond well to the freedom of the WIP; the degree of freedom was overwhelming and some simply asked us as instructors, "but what do you want me to do?" To meet this challenge, we've tried to continually emphasize that writing a more formal, complete rough draft is still always an option. At the same time, we believe this freedom to be a useful challenge, asking students to contemplate their own writing processes.

Closely related to some students struggling with a greater degree of freedom for the WIP assignment was the point that students similarly struggled to give peer feedback. As one student described,

> I was not really a big fan of reading other people's work in progresses because everyone has their own style in which they did the work in progress . . . read[ing] one which described what he was going to do rather than just writing what he was going to write [was challenging].

While the WIP workshop is a learning curve for us as instructors, as well, we are encouraged by the progress we've made so far. One measure that helped a great deal with the challenges of the WIP workshop was to ask students to craft author's notes; as a preface for their own feedback, these notes gave their peers helpful guidance on what kind of feedback the author was hoping for or what aspects of the assignment they may still have felt uncertain about. Some of the kinds of feedback students asked for in author's notes included:

- Being vulnerable in admitting they were still trying to find their main idea or argument, and asking for further discussion about the ideas they were communicating to help them find a focus.
- Asking readers if specific ideas in their WIPs were clear/unclear, including asking readers to say in their response what the reader thought the author was saying in the reader's own words.
- Asking where they might expand on ideas or add details.
- Pointing out places in their WIPs where they felt "stuck" and asking for suggestions on how they might proceed.

For students who had written more than the minimum, asking if there was writing they should consider cutting or sections/ideas that were unhelpful.

These author notes allowed students to ask thoughtful questions that helped them develop their writing, regardless of what stage of development their WIP was in.

Despite the challenges of using WIPs as compared to "rough drafts" or "outlines" of the past, we are committed to more fully explore WIPs as a better, more inclusive practice that centers the needs of neurodivergent learners. We believe it's a practice that moves us toward a classroom where neurodivergent students' writing and thinking processes are proactively integrated into the structure of the course. This is the "centering" of disability that we argue for. So often disabled students are only "accommodated" or "tolerated."

Though not all students love the WIP assignment at first, we think exposing students to this way of thinking is beneficial, on top of the obvious win for neurodivergent students. In addition to WIPs complementing the writing process for written assignments, they could similarly be used in multimodal assignments, such as the open-media assignment described by Orchard et al. in this collection (Chapter 12). Aside from the continuing benefit to neurodivergent learners, WIPs used in this context provide the flexibility necessary for multimodal composers working across different composing platforms.

CONCLUSION: MOVING BETTER PRACTICES ACROSS MODALITIES

Though we have focused this chapter on the affordances of the any time classroom for cripping the writing process, the WIP and any time feedback can be integrated into any writing classroom—be it synchronous, asynchronous, or hybrid. Synchronous classrooms most often require peer review activities to be completed during scheduled class time, asking students to read a draft, compose a written response, and then verbally discuss their feedback. Such strictures often provoke anxiety in students who may read, write, or speak at non-normative paces, but also have the potential to limit how deeply students can engage with their peers' work. Synchronous classrooms can easily forgo in-class peer review in favor of the any time workshop, regardless of the type of drafting process required.

Of course, we encourage synchronous instructors to adopt the work-in-progress model as well. The WIP is also easily adaptable to any installment of FYC. Ada and Anna both introduced the assignment in a Composition II course, where students typically have already had experience writing rough drafts. Assigning the WIP to students with an existing knowledge of what works and doesn't work for their own writing process allows them to experiment with new ways of composing and revising; however, introducing the WIP in a Composition I would certainly benefit students as well, particularly neurodivergent students.

Our ultimate wish is for writing instructors of all modalities to become more attuned to the generative potential of centering disability in our pedagogy—remembering that it's not instructors doing disabled students a favor when we make our classroom accessible, but rather that disabled students do us a favor when they demonstrate to us the ways in which are classroom spaces have foreclosed access (Hubrig, 2021), challenging us to develop better, more inclusive practices. While our practice is something of a Work-In-Progress itself, we have found initial success in making the drafting process more accessible by experimenting with the Work-in-Progress assignment and subsequent asynchronous writing workshops. To return to Yergeau's insight which opened our article, we see this process as working to examine the ableism of our practices that center nondisabled experiences—like Anna's anonymous student who highlighted that ableism for us.

Our "better practice" is by no means the only way to make the online writing classroom more inclusive, but we believe that honoring students' right to their own writing process is one step toward cripping the composition classroom.

- **In-Person and Online, Real-Time Learning:** Synchronous classrooms can easily forgo in-class peer review in favor of the any time workshop, regardless of the type of drafting process required.
- **Online, Any Time Learning:** This practice is intentionally designed to leverage the affordances of any time learning, because real-time peer review can provoke anxiety in students who may read, write, or speak at non-normative paces, but also have the potential to limit how deeply students can engage with their peers' work.
- **Hybrid Learning:** For hybrid courses, this practice works best between real-time, in-person meetings, leveraging the affordances of the online, asynchronous periods of learning time.

REFERENCES

Anglesey, L. & Ubbesen M. (2021) *Accessible affordances of asynchronicity: Cripping online instruction* [Webinar]. Global Society of Online Literacy Educators. https://gsole.org/webinars/2021-2022-series.

Boston University Center for Teaching and Learning. (2023). *Getting feedback from students*. Boston University. https://www.bu.edu/ctl/teaching-resources/start-stop-continue/.

Brewer, E., Selfe, C. L. & Yergeau, R. (2014). Creating a culture of access in composition studies. *Composition Studies, 42*(2), 151–154.

Butts, J. (2017). The more writing process, the better. In C. E. Ball & D. M. Loewe (Eds.), *Bad Ideas about Writing* (pp. 109–116). West Virginia University Libraries. https://textbooks.lib.wvu.edu/badideas/badideasaboutwriting-book.pdf.

CCCC Special Committee on Composing a CCCC Statement on Anti-Black Racism and Black Linguistic Justice. (2020). This Ain't Another Statement! This is a DEMAND for Black Linguistic Justice! *Conference on College Composition and Communication*. https://cccc.ncte.org/cccc/demand-for-black-linguistic-justice.

Cedillo, C. (2018). What does it mean to move? race, disability, and critical embodiment pedagogy. *Composition Forum, 39*. https://www.compositionforum.com/issue/39/to-move.php.

Conference on College Composition and Communication. (2003). Students' right to their own language. https://cccc.ncte.org/cccc/resources/positions/srtolsummary.

Dolmage, J. T. (2017). *Academic ableism: Disability and higher education.* University of Michigan Press. https://doi.org/10.3998/mpub.9708722.

Doyle, S. P. (2014) Writing with ADD. *Good Writer Bad Writer.* https://goodwriter badwriter.com/2014/07/08/writing-with-a-d-d/.

Gaeta, A. (2020) Writing and resisting: Owning your neurodivergent process. *AntiAbleist Composition, 1*(1). https://antiableistcomposition.wordpress.com/2020/03/05/561/.

GSOLE Executive Board. (2019, June 13). *Online literacy instruction principles and tenets.* Global Society of Online Literacy Educators. https://gsole.org/oliresources/oliprinciples.

Hitt, A. H. (2021). *Rhetorics of overcoming: Rewriting narratives of disability and accessibility in writing studies.* National Council of Teachers of English.

Hubrig, A. (2020). Narrativizing dis/ability: Deconstructing institutional uses of disability narratives. In A. R. Carr & L. R. Micciche (Eds.), *Failure pedagogies: Learning and unlearning what it means to fail* (pp. 223–237). Peter Lang.

Hubrig, A. (2021, April 19). Access from/as the start: On writing studies and "accessibility." *FEN Blog.* https://compstudiesjournal.com/2021/04/19/access-from-as-the-start-on-writing-studies-and-accessibility/.

Inoue, A. B. (2015). *Antiracist writing assessment ecologies: Teaching and assessing writing for a socially just future.* The WAC Clearinghouse; Parlor Press. https://doi.org/10.37514/PER-B.2015.0698.

Kafer, A. (2013). *Feminist, queer, crip.* Indiana University Press.

Keedy, G. & Vidali, A. (2016). Productive chaos: Disability, advising, and the writing process. *Praxis: A Writing Center Journal, 14*(2).

Kerschbaum, S. (2015). Anecdotal relations: On orienting to disability in the composition classroom. *Composition Forum, 32*(1).

McRuer, R. & Berube, M. (2006). *Crip theory: Cultural signs of queerness and disability.* New York University Press.

Osorio, R. (2020). I am #ActuallyAutistic, hear me tweet: The autist-topoi of autistic activists on Twitter. *Enculturation: A Journal of Rhetoric, Writing, and Culture.* http://enculturation.net/I_Am_ActuallyAutistic.

Price, M. (2011). *Mad at school: Rhetorics of mental disability and academic life* (Illustrated ed.). University of Michigan Press. https://doi.org/10.3998/mpub.1612837.

Samuels, E. (2017). Six ways of looking at crip time. *Disability Studies Quarterly, 37*(3).

Wood, T. (2017). Cripping time in the college composition classroom. *College Composition and Communication, 69*(2), 260–286.

Wood, T., Dolmage, J., Price, M. & Lewiecki-Wilson, C. (2014). Moving beyond disability 2.0 in composition studies. *Composition Studies, 42*(2), 147–150.

Yergeau, R. (2016). Saturday plenary address: Creating a culture of access in writing program administration. *Writing Program Administration, 40*(1), 155–165.

CHAPTER 10.

CREATING CULTURAL AWARENESS, BUILDING COMMUNITY: ENCOURAGING STUDENT WRITER IDENTITY THROUGH PURPOSEFUL ASSIGNMENT DESIGN

Jennifer Burke Reifman
University of California at Davis

Jessie Borgman
Arizona State University

In this chapter, the authors describe **culturally sustaining blog and discussion boards** *used in online, any time learning, focusing on a three-week assignment sequence aimed at helping students to break away from focusing on homogeneous community practices that tend to value singular ways of knowing, writing, and reading to instead allow students to explore multimodal composing while appealing to a diverse audience of peers and other readers. Specifically, the authors mention that using these modes of writing help raise awareness of the global nature of writing among student writers. In describing their "better practice," this chapter addresses the themes of accessibility and inclusivity and practices adapted from classic composition strategies.*

FRAMEWORKS AND PRINCIPLES IN THIS CHAPTER

- **PARS Online Writing Instruction,** Personal: Building community and fostering connections.
- **PARS Online Writing Instruction,** Accessible: Taking advantage of the affordances of a digital learning environment.

- **GSOLE Principle 1.1**: "All stakeholders and students should be aware of and be able to engage the unique literacy features of communicating, teaching, and learning in a primarily digital environment."
- **GSOLE Principle 3.5:** "Instructors and tutors should research, develop, theorize, and apply appropriate reading, alphabetic writing, and multimodal composition theories to their OLI environment(s)."
- **Framework for Success in Postsecondary Writing, Openness**: the willingness to consider new ways of being and thinking in the world.
- **Framework for Success in Postsecondary Writing, Engagement**: a sense of investment and involvement in learning.
- **Framework for Success in Postsecondary Writing, Creativity**: the ability to use novel approaches for generating, investigating, and representing ideas.
- **Framework for Success in Postsecondary Writing, Metacognition**: the ability to reflect on one's own thinking as well as on the individual and cultural processes used to structure knowledge.
- **Framework for Success in Postsecondary Writing, Knowledge of Conventions:** the formal and informal guidelines that define what is considered to be correct and appropriate, or incorrect and inappropriate, in a piece of writing.

GUIDING QUESTIONS BEFORE YOU BEGIN READING

- What is the benefit of exploring community and heritage practices with students in writing classes?
- What transferable skills do working in multimodal texts and the blogging genre teach students as writers?
- How can instructors encourage students to write about topics they are interested in while inviting more ownership over and connection to their own writing?

INTRODUCTION

When we first decided to write this chapter, we met to talk about our own teaching contexts and student demographics. We found that we had shared struggles as writing teachers that were aligned in some specific areas, despite our different contexts. We both experienced challenges with students accessing course content and with getting our students to view themselves as writers who could be empowered with choices. Our combined experience told us that students are often fed a number of myths from high school, popular discourse, previous learning experience, and beyond about college writing before we ever see them in our classrooms. Some have been told that writing is always strict and formal, based on rigid templates or essay structures. Or, they believe that writing is assessed solely based on grammar and correctness. What we found exceptionally troubling is that many come to us believing that their personal experiences and lives are not relevant topics or sources of information. They're sure no one cares what they think or experience in their lives—not really anyway.

We wanted to tackle this challenge of writerly identity and belonging a bit more directly, and one success Jennifer had previously had students write about a family or community practice on personal blogs. When students hear that they should write about themselves and their heritages, use their experiences and observations as sources of evidence, and put these experiences in conversation with scholarly texts, there's a solid amount of skepticism on their parts. "Shouldn't I argue against global warming?" they ask. "Won't it be too informal to talk about my family?" they worry. Their questions highlight the difficulty our students experience in exploring a line of inquiry born of personal experience, rather than starting with a thesis they attempt to prove. It also conveys how hard it is for them to see their lives as foci of academic inquiry, despite the ways in which we see their breadth of identities as valuable and necessary components of the classroom. This disconnect is also exasperated by the distance between student and instructor inherent in online writing instruction.

We wanted our students to connect with each other, to gain more confidence in their ability to make choices as the authors of their texts, to have more practice writing outside of a rigid structure (i.e., the five-paragraph essay), and to see more chances to value their identities/communities in academic spaces. By the end of our conversation, we aimed to craft an assignment sequence to break some of these student writing cycles and to build an identity-sustaining, community-building practice in our online courses. To do this, we started with Jennifer's blog assignment and began crafting a three-week assignment sequence that focused on inclusivity.

Because we both knew of our diverse student audiences—for Jennifer, 65 percent of student arrives with a high school GPA of 4.0, 55 percent of students are STEM majors, 17 percent come from international contexts, and 28 percent are from under-represented minoritized identities, and, for Jessie, at an institution where 67 percent are over age 20 (non-traditional age college students), and 36 percent of students are from under-represented minoritized identities—we felt we could create an assignment sequence to meet their needs but also to encourage them to use their own voices and make their own choices in their writing.

While this collection utilizes shared language for online course modalities and defines asynchronous online courses under this term, we aim to be clear and reiterate to our readers that our courses only somewhat fall into the definition of "online, any time learning" as defined by this collection. For us, this definition is somewhat limiting because both of our courses do have expectations for interaction and attendance and are not self-paced; both of us interact with our students frequently and provide instruction through the announcements, emails, and discussion areas. That said, we do not meet in real time with a whole class via web conferencing software like Zoom, so our particular better practice is focused on an "online, any time" learning; however, we do feel that readers who teach primarily face-to-face or hybrid/blended could replicate this practice with some minor adjustments.

WHAT THEORIES, SCHOLARSHIP, AND PRINCIPLES INFORM THIS APPROACH TO OLI?

Getting students to view themselves as active writers who don't simply need to replicate dominant language and writing practices they have previously experienced at school is, in short, a challenge. The challenge of helping them establish a writerly identity is exacerbated when taking into account the nature of online courses and the diverse backgrounds of our online students. Online courses, which offer flexible access to students, often host diverse student cohorts from varying cultural and linguistic backgrounds; in turn, they prove even more challenging for meeting needs of community, connection, and writer autonomy. In order to meet calls to develop linguistically and culturally inclusive pedagogies in online writing instruction (OWI) contexts (Miller-Cochran, 2015; St.Amant & Rice, 2017) and maintain universal accessibility and inclusion (CCCC Position Statement on Globalization, 2017), this chapter will offer online writing instructors a specific approach to developing personal writing through dialogic discussion boards and blog assignments. Specifically, this chapter's better practice includes a series of sequenced discussions that work with the blog assignment to accomplish two goals:

1. to break away from homogeneous community and heritage practices that tend to value singular ways of knowing, writing, and reading and
2. to allow students to explore multimodal composing while appealing to diverse reading audiences.

Particularly, our chapter provides strategies and assignments that can be used over a variety of institutional contexts to meet the needs of shifting student demographics and help instructors to provide online writing instruction that is inclusive, and follows the best practices outlined by Jessie Borgman and Casey McArdle's (2019) PARS (personal, accessible, responsive, strategic) approach to online writing instruction. Additionally, we feel that the teaching practices outlined here may aid students in learning about and valuing the home and heritage practices. Finally, while students in online courses don't typically get to know much about each other's personal lives, this practice also provides students an opportunity to learn about each other and from each other, creating a stronger community in the online course.

For the purposes of our chapter and because we wanted to explore the option of a "better practice" using discussions, we chose to use an assignment that Jennifer had used previously in her hybrid course, an ongoing personal blog assignment aided by a series of discussion posts and responses. We used this assignment in our online, any time learning classes in the fall of 2021. In this chapter, we wanted to illustrate that:

- Participating in discussions can be effective at building community for online courses
- Engaging in discussions and blogging can contribute to the students' growth as writers
- Blogs and discussion boards can act as places where students can explore their familial and community backgrounds or discover new ones

This blog/discussion assignment sequence asks students to explore a community or family tradition or practice through their diverse social contexts and identities. In crafting our assignment to work for both courses, we worked to make it accessible to a variety of student demographics. We wanted the assignment to not only be accessible in its content and direction, but also in its use. Because of this, we extended access to consider language barriers (specifically including non-native English speakers), technology barriers (specifically for those who are unfamiliar with technology), and writing barriers (specifically personal writing as a way to access more academic genres). Because we were asking students to expand their ideas of audience and consider some of their own community practices, we looked to the Accessible component of the PARS framework (Borgman & McArdle, 2019; 2021; 2023) to ground our best practice.

Additionally, our best practice was also grounded in one element of the Frameworks for Success in Postsecondary Writing: "Knowledge of conventions—the formal and informal guidelines that define what is considered to be correct and appropriate, or incorrect and inappropriate," in a piece of writing, focusing the assignments on understanding writing for a blog and broad audience versus the technological components of the blog. Blogs are fairly easy to set up and don't take a lot of technological prowess to navigate, so we felt the blog as a technology would work well, especially for students who are not as comfortable with technology in general; the blogs, as a genre, then acted as space for students to explore personal topics, address public audiences, and experiment with multimodal practices as a means of communication while learning the informal conventions often practiced by other bloggers.

Keeping access in mind, we also wanted to foreground culturally inclusive pedagogical practices. Building off of Gloria Ladson-Billings' (1995) work on culturally relevant pedagogies, Django Paris (2012) furthers an asset-oriented approach to literacy instruction by suggesting a culturally sustaining pedagogy. This approach rejects deficit-oriented pedagogical practices that only ask students to conform to dominant language practices and instead asks teachers to build classroom practices that sustain "the cultural and linguistic competence of their (student) communities while simultaneously offering access to dominant cultural competence" (Paris, 2012, p. 95). Particularly, we orient the series of activities presented in this chapter around Paris and Samy Alim's (2014) terms of "community" and "heritage practices"; these terms work to avoid essentializing language practices as cultural practices and instead acknowledge the ever-shifting language and cultural practices of our students. In doing so, we seek to counter dominant narratives about language and cultural "appropriateness" (Rosa & Flores, 2015) that asks students to assimilate to largely White language and cultural practices. Instead, we pull in the concept of "Global Audiences" through Kirk St.Amant's (2020) student-facing text to begin exploring concepts of community and heritage practices where he notes that, "Globalized rhetoric involves understanding: The culture of the audience for which you are writing [and] the genre you are writing in when sharing information with that cultural audience" (p. 148). By asking students to draw on their community and heritage practices as a valuable line of inquiry, we hope to value the myriad of identities present in our classes, which we feel extends accessibility and inclusivity.

In the shared assignment sequence, students were asked to develop a personal blog topic and craft three different blog entries over the course of three weeks. For Jennifer's course, this assignment was part of an expanded series of blogs that students create throughout the class which lead to a larger research assignment. For Jessie's course, the students completed the personal blog assignment in isolation and focused on other patterns of writing as they worked up to a research assignment based on their degree of study.

What Needs Does This Practice Meet?

We believe that the assignments described here address a particular need in OWI: the intersection of asset-based pedagogies, community building practices, and digital literacy instruction. While there has been a great deal of work on connecting students in online courses, despite their physical distance, our inclusion of culturally sustaining pedagogies highlights the need to build community among students from a variety of backgrounds and experiences. Students, by focusing on their heritage or community practices—as both topics of conversation and as lines of inquiry—are using the online space to explore their identities and learn about differing perspectives.

Our better practice for constructing blogs helps meet the needs of more diverse learners because it acknowledges that students come from a variety of home and heritage practices and they may benefit from participating in multimodal compositing practices using genres of writing (discussions/blogs) that focus more on personal writing, a form that is more accessible to developing writers; put another way, usually it's easier to write about yourself and we encourage them to do so. Additionally, we see this practice as one that is responding to critiques of discussion boards used in online writing instruction as one-dimensional forums for communication, as discussed by Beth Hewett (2015); instead, the discussion boards in our practice ask students to engage with each other recursively, further emphasizing personal connection between students. In general, students tend to be more engaged and connected because the topics are more personal and not typically associated with academic writing (e.g., The Elf on the Shelf, KPop Fandoms, Phillippinx Communities, etc.) as these topics can help to build community in online courses.

We feel the discussion and blog assignment that we explore here illustrates one way to build community through the medium of online instruction. Since both courses fall under the collection term "online, any time learning," where synchronous interaction occurred online in the learning management system, Canvas, building community in digital space was even more important because the students rarely got the chance to interact in real time. Sharing these interests and practices through discussion and blog entries allowed students to learn more about each other and to explore diverse interests.

WHAT DOES SUCCESSFUL LEARNING LOOK LIKE?

A goal of any assignment is to both develop and improve students' abilities to think critically *and* metacognition in order to convey exactly how they think critically. We felt students would be successful in this assignment by sharing what they learned. Therefore, success for us was demonstrated in the blog entries and the progression of the students' topics, as this showed they were thinking about their topics while, at the same time, they were thinking about the rhetorical situation for their posts. In implementing these sequenced blogs and discussion boards, we also intended to pay special attention to the heightened literacy load of online writing courses (Sibo, 2021) by including multimodal elements and asking students to consider composing/designing in alternate formats/modalities such as blogging, screencasting, and visual analysis (Parrish & Linder-VanBerschot, 2010). Discussion assignments often pose challenges for students and instructors alike (de Lima, et al., 2019; Lieberman, 2019; Mintz, 2020). Some of the challenges include:

- Participation: Should instructors set participation requirements? If so, through a set number of posts? Or, through a more general requirement, such as "converse with your peers"?
- Forced/Transactional Interaction: Do students actually read the posts? Or do they cherry pick, responding to just the required number of posts/students? Does the instructor respond or does the instructor set a discussion moderator?
- Busy Work: Due to the above items—and often gleaned from their previous experience—some students don't see the value in discussions and view them as busy work.

How Does This Represent a Best Practice in OLI?

Our assignment sequence illustrates one way to encourage students to think about heritage and home practices as well as approaches to different audiences. We also feel this assignment sequence encourages students to write in different genres (discussion posts/blog entries) and incorporate multimodal elements into their writing. For this project, the blog entries utilized student-selected topics combined with multimodal components of the student's choice for a broad audience, while the discussion boards leveraged the academic community of the class for students to process ideas, strategies, topics, and so on. While this assignment sequence certainly touches on other principles and practices identified for successful OWI, we feel the ones below are the most pertinent:

Borgman and McArdle's PARS framework (2015): specifically, letters (P) Personal (building community and fostering connections) and (A) Accessible (taking advantage of the affordances of a digital learning environment), though our better practice does align with the entire PARS framework.

GSOLE Principles:

- Online literacy instruction should be universally accessible and inclusive (GSOLE Principle 1).
- Instructors and tutors should commit to regular, iterative processes of course and instructional material design, development, assessment, and revision to ensure that online literacy instruction and student support reflect current effective practices (GSOLE Principle 3).

COURSE CONTEXT

Jessie and Jennifer teach at different schools on different sides of the country. Jessie teaches online, any time learning courses at a community college. The course described in this chapter was an English 102 course (the second course in a two-course sequence). Jennifer teaches at a large four-year public research university in California. The course for this assignment was the university's first-year composition (FYC) course. Both teach at schools where there are diverse student populations.

Despite the differing contexts, both of us used Canvas for housing course materials and discussion boards, and both utilized WordPress as our blogging platform because it is free and easy to use; however, other blog technologies (such as Blogger) could work, too. These shared tools allowed for specific shared instructions that for the most part were identical with one exception, Jessie's course used this discussion/blog unit as a single assignment while Jennifer's course used this discussion/blog unit as a connected longer course assignment that asks students to research a discourse community related to their blog topic.

Lesson

We began by sketching out the assignment and the accompanying discussions, identifying why we wanted the students to complete certain steps and how these steps contributed to their learning in the larger project. For this assignment sequence, students wrote three blog entries and participated in three discussions that facilitated the blog assignments. Our initial brainstorming sketch for the series of assignments is explained in Table 10.1.

Table 10.1. Sequence of Activities for the Discussion Board and Blog Entry Assignments

Assignment	Activity	Goals
Discussion Board 1	Students will . . . Use different academic texts & student-produced blog examples to explore the genre of blogging. Begin responding to: What is blogging?; What does it look like? What are the characteristics of a blog entry?	Students . . . Explore the blog genre. Begin to understand conventions. Practice describing the writing process.

Assignment	Activity	Goals
Blog Entry 1	Students will . . . Identify a community/heritage practice that they are interested in or currently engage in. Find a blog example discussing that community/heritage practice. Write about the community/heritage practice they identified and the blog example they found.	Students . . . Start to think about their own traditions or cultural practices. Search online for blog examples and identify model texts. Practice & develop awareness around the blog genre.
Discussion 2	Students will . . . Brainstorm 3 possible topics to blog. Begin researching these possible topics.	Students . . . Think about topics & consider why they are interested in writing/blogging about specific topics. Garner peer feedback about these topics
Blog Entry 2	Students will . . . Select one of the three topics they proposed. Write/blog on that topic including multimodal elements such as hyperlinks and images.	Students . . . Narrow to one topic. Explore blog writing and working with multimodal elements.
Discussion 3	Students will . . . Find two blogs written by authors outside the classroom that present different perspectives. Create a screen capture comparing/contrasting these blogs and author perspectives in light of global audiences.	Students . . . Practice creating a multimodal response. Explore different perspectives from authors writing on a similar topic. Consider writing for global audiences.
Blog Entry 3	Students will . . . Write/blog in depth about the topic they wrote about in Blog Entry 2.	Students . . . Write/practice blogging more in depth about their blog topic. Get more practice incorporating multimodal elements.

After we had a clear picture of what we wanted the students to do and why, we crafted the assignment instructions for the blog assignment. The discussion prompts can be found in Appendix C.

Student-Facing Assignment Instructions (Blog Assignment):

See Appendix A and Appendix B of both the blog and discussion assignments. Also, please see the weekly units for both Jessie and Jennifer's classes in the next section.

Weekly Units

Below are our weekly lessons for the three-week cycle. Due to differing schedules (Jennifer is on the quarters system/Jessie on a traditional 16-week semester system), Jennifer's assignment was the first assignment that students completed in her course. Jessie's assignment was the second major writing project and third assignment they completed for her course (the students complete a Start of Course Reflection as their first assignment in the course). The charts shown in Tables 10.2 and 10.3 detail the work we both did to scaffold and manage the labor of this assignment.

Table 10.2. Jennifer's Weekly Calendar

Week 1 Overview	**Tasks for Week 1**
	As a major assignment this quarter, you will choose a topic to blog about and investigate a discourse community around this topic. To build our project over the quarter, you'll be writing three different blog assignments (one per week) over the next three weeks. You will also be completing three different discussion assignments (one per week) that are crafted to help you develop your blog topic. These blog and discussion assignments are connected and encourage you to think about your community and practices or traditions.
	Build your blog on WordPress:
	Review our resources page for links.
	Review Blogging & Publish your first blog entry:
	First, review what you know about blogging in this discussion board: Blogging
	Next, read "Why Blog" (Reid, 2011) and "Writing in Global Contexts: Composing Usable Texts for Audiences from Different Cultures" (St.Amant, 2020).
	Then, post your first blog entry here: Blog Entry #1: Exploring Blogging
	Tips for submitting your first blog entry:
	Make sure your blog is active and publicly available, and make sure your blog entry is published, not just in draft form.
	Make sure the direct link to the individual post you are submitting is accessible to those not signed into your account. This usually means you have to click on "Preview" then "Visit Site" and then copy and paste the link from there. You can use Google Incognito to double check if this link works.

Week 2 Overview	Tasks for Week 2
	Learn about the concept of Discourse Communities (DC) and discuss.
	First, Read "Understanding Discourse Communities" by Dan Melzer (https://wac.colostate.edu/docs/books/writingspaces3/melzer.pdf)
	Then, listen to "This American Life" episode (https://www.thisamericanlife.org/573/status-update) that provides a different way of understanding Discourse Communities
	Finally, discuss your Understanding of Discourse Communities with your peers in this discussion board: Discourse Communities
	Propose a Blog Topic!
	Review this graphic based on your Blogging Discussion.
	Before you begin your blog topic proposal post, you are also more than welcome to email me your blog topic idea and we can discuss it, but you are also going to discuss your ideas with your classmates in this discussion board: Blog Topic Ideas
	Then, finalize your topic in our second blog entry: Blog Entry #2: Blog Topic Proposal
Week 3 Overview	Tasks for Week 3
	Get to know each other's blogs and topics and keep blogging about your topic.
	Now that you have begun your journey into your topic, you should see what your peers might be talking about via this discussion post: Blog Commenting, Round 1
	Dig deeper into your proposed blog topic in a new post: Blog Entry #3: Explore Blog Topic
	Keep blogging and start thinking through the Discourse Community (DC) that you might investigate.
	First, review/solidify the concept of a DC and see examples of DCs in this video.
	Then, propose a Discourse Community that is related to your topic that you might want to analyze for your paper in our next blog entry: Blog Entry #4: D.C. In-Depth

Table 10.3. Jessie's Weekly Calendar

Module Overview	In this module, you'll focus on Writing Assignment 2. In Writing Assignment 2 you'll be asked to create a blog and post three blog entries on it. This module is three weeks long and in each week you will participate in a discussion and write a blog entry. At the end of the three weeks, you will submit the link to your blog with the three blog entries on it for grading. The discussions will be graded separately from your blog during each of the three weeks.
	You'll also complete readings, activities, and grammar lessons in each week of the module:

Week 4 Readings and Tasks	Reading: What is a blog?: https://firstsiteguide.com/what-is-blog/. Why Blog?: Reid's Text Tasks: Read the Writing Assignment 2 instructions completely. Note: This is a three-week project, and you will submit your completed at the end of it in week 6 Use WordPress (https://wordpress.com) to create a free blog How to setup a blog: Video: https://www.youtube.com/watch?v=mta6Y0o7yJk. Text Instructions: https://wordpress.com/support/five-step-blog-setup/. Personalize your blog! Write your first blog entry by following the Blog Entry 1 Instructions Note: you will not submit any of your blog entries in Canvas until week 6, but you should complete them as they are assigned in weeks 4, 5, and 6 Discussion Week: Answer the posted question by Wednesday by 11:59 p.m. EST Week 4 DQ Participation: respond to at least two of your peers or two of the instructor follow up questions, or one peer and one instructor follow up question by Saturday by 11:59 p.m. EST See the syllabus for more information on discussion participation and posting.
Week 5 Readings and Tasks	Reading: "Writing in Global Contexts: Composing Usable Texts for Audiences from Different Cultures" by Kirk St.Amant Tasks: Write your second blog entry by following the Blog Entry 2 Instructions Note: you will not submit any of your blog entries in Canvas until week 6, but you should complete them as they are assigned in weeks 4, 5, and 6 Discussion Week: Answer the posted question by Wednesday by 11:59 p.m. EST Week 5 DQ Participation: respond to at least two of your peers or two of the instructor follow up questions, or one peer and one instructor follow up question by Saturday by 11:59 p.m. EST See the syllabus for more information on discussion participation and posting.

Week 6 Readings and Tasks	Reading:
	No readings this week
	Tasks:
	Write your third blog entry by following the Blog Entry 3 Instructions
	Read through your blog and revise and edit as needed. Ensure you have links, images, and references (for any sources used).
	Submit the link to your blog by Saturday by 11:59 p.m. ET using the submission link in Writing Assignment 2
	Discussion Week:
	Answer the posted question by Wednesday by 11:59 p.m. EST Week 6 DQ
	Participation: respond to at least two of your peers or two of the instructor follow up questions, or one peer and one instructor follow up question by Saturday by 11:59 p.m. EST
	See the syllabus for more information on discussion participation and posting.

As a reminder, the specific assignment prompts for each of the blogs and the specific discussion prompts for each of the discussions can be found in the appendices.

Assessment

Teaching in the quarter system, Jennifer has ten weeks to get students through a major project. She uses blogs to help students develop a traditional introduction, methods, results, and discussion (IMRaD) style research paper that details some aspect of an online discourse community connected to their blog topic. Throughout the class, she also uses a labor-based grading contract to assess work using specific benchmarks for each assignment. These benchmarks are designed to de-emphasize the subjective grading students are used to with the exception of "Consider Blog Form and Genre," which is a set of standards around blogging that the students create that are usually lists of defining blog features (images, hyperlinks, etc.). Students create this list of typical blog features from their analysis of the genre. Each assignment is marked as complete or incomplete, depending on how well they meet the guidelines. Students who receive an incomplete can revise throughout the quarter for a complete.

As mentioned previously, Jessie's series of blog entries and discussions functioned as one major writing assignment in her course, Writing Assignment 2. Therefore, she had students submit all three blog entries at the end of the three-week cycle. The three blog entries were connected to the discussion activities so students were encouraged to complete one blog entry per week and couldn't wait until the last minute to put the whole blog together. The three blog entries were assessed separately on a points scale of how well the student followed the instructions for the individual post. The use of multimodal elements was its own grading category (multimodal elements were required in each blog). External sources was an individual category, as was spelling/grammar/mechanics as shown in Table 10.5 in the grading criteria table.

Table 10.4. Jennifer's Assessment Plan

Blog Entry 1	Contract Grading Guidelines. For Full credit your blog entry should:
	Be over 400 words
	Include at least three hyperlinks
	How to Add Hyperlinks (https://www.authormedia.com/how-to-add-a-hyperlink-to-wordpress/).
	Why add hyperlinks? (https://michellerafter.com/2011/05/18/8-essential-reasons-to-put-links-in-blog-posts/).
	Include at least two images
	How to Add Images (https://wordpress.com/support/classic-editor-guide/)
	How to give credit for images (https://wordpress.com/go/digital-marketing/sharing-is-caring-how-to-give-photo-credit-the-right-way/).
	Consider the blog genre based on our class discussion
Blog Entry 2	Contract Grading Guidelines:
	Must be over 600 words
	Must include at least five hyperlinks
	Must include at least four images
	Must consider form and blog set up based on our class discussion
Blog Entry 3	Contract Grading Guidelines:
	Must be over 500 words
	Must include at least five hyperlinks
	Must include at least four images
	Must consider form and blog set up based on our class discussion

Table 10.5. Jessie's Assessment Plan

Blog Entry 1	Instructions for Blog Entry 1 are followed. All requirements are met.
Blog Entry 2	Instructions for Blog Entry 2 are followed. All requirements are met.
Blog Entry 3	Instructions for Blog Entry 3 are followed. All requirements are met.

Incorporation of Multimodal Elements (links, images, external sources, etc.)	Incorporation of multimodal elements is purposeful and adds visual interest and depth to the blog entr(y/ies).
Style/ Grammar/ Mechanics	Sentences are clear and varied in pattern, from simple to complex, with excellent use of punctuation. Strong use of grammar, spelling, syntax and punctuation.

The grading practices shown here reflect the ways in which this series of assignments can be assessed differently, depending on instructor choice. We hope readers will notice how different grading philosophies can both facilitate a culturally-sustaining practice and encourage community in the online writing classrooms as is evident in the variety of topics students chose and their engagement in the topics we reflect on later. Success for this assignment sequence will look very different for everyone pending your students' demographics and institutional context. We encourage instructors attempting to use this sequence to outline what they think success would look like for their students to cater to their specific contexts.

REFLECTION ON PRACTICE
Jennifer's Reflection on Practice

The inspiration for this combination of discussion boards and blogs comes from years of Jennifer's own experimentation with a large-scale blogging project in her FYC classes. Through its development, the project has emphasized student choice regarding their blog topic and how this leads into a more formal research paper. In previous iterations, students had an open choice of the topic they selected, which was both fun and challenging, as some topics did not lend to the final project and analyzing a related discourse community as well as others. This specific version of the assignment allowed students a more structured and thoughtful process for picking a topic, which helped to avoid issues from previous iterations. Specifically, this version was more scaffolded to help students develop a thoughtful, personal topic.

The emphasis on community, heritage practices, and traditions also served to preemptively answer a recurring question from students in Jennifer's past experience with this assignment: can I talk about myself? In this version of the assignment, students were led to a topic that naturally tied to their identity, they saw their identity as a valuable source and topic in academic writing, and they were given the opportunity to privilege this often-unseen part of themselves, while still connecting to formal writing tasks and research. Previously, students would arrive at topics like this on their own, but in this version, it was abundantly clear to students that they could—and should—write about their lives and their families.

In previous versions of this assignment, instructor labor traditionally peaked around the time that students were selecting topics, which was typically managed through routine check-ins with students. This was not the case in this version. Instead, the labor seemed to peak when students were asked to consider more multimodal aspects in their blogging and needed assistance in understanding technology and the purpose of this kind of writing. In response, Jennifer typically adds more built-in resources for students in the assignments. This has resulted in a FAQ page on her Canvas site and list of applicable links and videos to help students navigate technology. In general, because the assignment so intentionally centered on heritage and communal practices, there were far fewer individual topic-related questions than before; this allowed for more time devoted to providing feedback on blog entries.

Jessie Reflection on Practice

In the early part of this chapter, we discussed how the discussion assignment in online courses can be fraught with issues, but that by creating more interactive prompts we can help alleviate some of the traditional challenges of discussions and encourage students to engage more. For example, requiring students to use multimodal elements or create a video screencast encourages them to be more creative than posting a text-based response to a discussion prompt. As noted above, we asked them to create a screencast as their response to Discussion 3. Jessie saw an increase in engagement firsthand in her courses because the students were learning something by reading each other's blog entries, they were personally interested in the content of their blogs, and they enjoyed the alternate way of presenting information in the discussion (screencast vs. text). In the three discussions, many students participated more than was required, which she assumed was due to the fact they were interested in each other's topics.

The design of this assignment facilitated a stacked, scaffolded learning, too. Students were building on the blog project in each week, in each discussion, and through each blog entry. Because of this stacked learning approach, the students were able to see the value of the project as a whole; they were able to see how it all worked together to create their final blog. Because the instructions for each blog were very clear and the requirements outlined, Jessie didn't have many questions on the assignment. The students knew what to do and what was required of them, which in turn made assessing the project a lot easier. Jessie didn't participate in the discussion forums, but she did read through them to ensure that the students were understanding and completing the tasks appropriately. Because she read through all of the discussion responses each week, she became more familiar with the students' topics; the layered discussions also allowed Jessie to see the students' projects progress and develop, which made assessing their final blogs easier.

Additionally, we discussed earlier how examining a community tradition or family practice would aid in creating global awareness; that often we're writing for more diverse audiences and some audiences that are from other communities and heritage practices. Framing the idea of global awareness with St.Amant's (2020) article encouraged students to think more critically about audience in relation to the blogs they were viewing and the blogs they were creating. The influence of St.Amant's text and the heightened awareness of their reading audience showed in the students' work; they illustrated a stronger awareness of a global audience. Their blog entries provided contextualization for the community traditions or practices they were writing about. They introduced their topics, provided background information, and explored how the tradition or practice manifested in other countries/communities. Even the students who chose to write about very personal and specific family traditions were able to draw connections to other more known or popular traditions used in other communities.

This was Jessie's first time teaching this assignment, but it was not her first time using multimodal discussion posts and having her students compose in digital mediums. In reflecting on the assignment sequence after it was completed, Jessie was very excited by the quality of the student submissions and has continued to refine and use this assignment in her courses. The students really got into the assignment and were very creative with their topics (from Elf on a Shelf, to The Christmas Pickle, to the Dia De Los Muertos).

Because the students at Jessie's school tend to struggle with using technology and with access to technology, she was worried about the skill level, technical prowess, and available resources required to complete this assignment sequence (not all students have money for a computer or internet access at home). However, only four students out of the two sections had technical issues with properly submitting their blog URLs; this was easily remedied with a quick reiteration of guidance about how to publish a blog entry and make it publicly available.

As general guidance for the challenges that come with this assignment, Jessie advises readers to have some examples ready to share with students. Having the examples of mentor texts from one of Jennifer's previous iterations of this assignment really helped Jessie's students. Additionally, having a list of topics ready to share with students is valuable. Some of Jessie's students initially struggled to come up with a topic, so she encouraged them to consider something they were interested in learning more about (and that was not necessarily something that their family practiced). Lastly, readers who want to replicate this assignment should anticipate a few technology challenges from the students. Creating videos and sharing the official WordPress tutorials will help cut down on technology woes from students.

Joint Reflection on Practice

We believe the above assignment is especially engaging and useful for diverse student populations across institutions. Jessie and Jennifer shared similar successes regarding their students' interests and engagement in the project. Both saw diverse and thoughtful topics from students and heard positive feedback from students on the ability to discuss and learn more about their community and heritage practices. Overall, students remained engaged and thoughtful throughout the series of assignments and, for Jennifer's course, this engagement carried through to the research paper.

However, the assignment was not completed without a few hiccups. Particularly, some of the students in both of our classes did not pick up on the fact that all three blog entries were supposed to be on the same community or heritage practice. Both of us had a handful of students who wrote on three different traditions or practices (one for each blog entry) instead. There also seemed to be some confusion in both of our classes about how to narrow their topic from Blog Entry 1 to Blog Entry 2; some simply wrote same thing in a more general way from Blog Entry 1 to Blog Entry 2 instead of narrowing focus and writing on something more detailed (on the same topic) in Blog Entry 2. In general, the process of narrowing scope is difficult for students, and we saw this assignment as a mostly effective means helping them, even though some more nuanced language in prompts might help them to delineate the different activities and purposes of these blogs more.

Additionally, we both had a few students that struggled with the blogging technology, WordPress, despite the tutorials that were offered. Each of us had two to three students that were not able to get their blogs posted and/or published and ended up having to submit their blog entries in an alternate format (a PDF or Word Doc.). While we found this challenging, we also learned that there is room for improvement in the tutorials; perhaps a short assignment or discussion where they practice publishing their blog earlier in the process would be useful and allow us as the instructors to step in and help prior to the full assignment being due.

Finally, we realize this series of assignments is only one step toward culturally sustaining practices in online learning environments. While we encouraged students to consider home and heritage practices while publishing for global audiences in broad and dynamic ways, it was difficult to get students to leave their perceptions of what was appropriate for school and, in turn, to truly explore the many topics at hand. This invitation to explore new ideas and genres beyond the typical essay was not as clearly received by some as others. Additionally, we recognize that we need to pay more attention to home languages and non-dominant language practices; this is something that could be developed further in this thread of assignments in future iterations.

CONCLUSION

There are many meaningful ways to do personal writing in an online course and many ways to raise awareness of nondominant perspectives and experiences and global audiences. As St.Amant (2020) says "Writing in greater global contexts can be complex. It involves understanding the rhetorical expectations of other cultures—and of groups within those cultures—to craft messages they can use to achieve an objective" (p. 158). While our students may not have a full grasp on this concept just yet, we feel this assignment sequence begins to raise awareness about audiences and global communities.

By allowing students to pick a meaningful topic and by scaffolding the work that students are doing, instructors can better engage students in their writing. Our better practice illustrates a way to build community, too, as this assignment sequence could be done earlier in a course to help students get to know one another and their community and familial practices and traditions. As we invite students from different backgrounds to participate, share their heritage practices, and acknowledge that writing is a global act, we continue to bring humanity to online learning and to support more relevant writing practices.

MOVING BETTER PRACTICES ACROSS MODALITIES

- **In-Person, Real-Time Learning**: In practice, the discussion boards can become in-class discussions. If students have computers in front of them, we would suggest employing reflective writing and conversation to elicit understandings of blogging and for inventing topics. Additionally, blogs could be shared and discussed in person. Instructors could review and discuss the St.Amant article and additional global community resources, asking students to share blogs they found and discuss them in class.
- **Online, Real-Time Learning:** Similarly, discussions about the blog genre and readings could be had in a Zoom room using the chat function for writing-to-think moments. Additionally, blogs from both students and others could be shared and discussed in breakout rooms. Instructors could also use Google Docs to create shared understandings around readings (e.g., St.Amant & Rice, 2015) in synchronous class meetings or otherwise.
- **Hybrid Learning:** Hybrid learning could combine strategies from all of the above, depending on the balance of in-person and online

instruction. We would suggest that discussions would still be held asynchronously in the learning management system, while analyzing blogs, discussions about audience, and discussion readings (e.g., St.Amant) could be done in face-to-face spaces.

REFERENCES

Borgman, J. & McArdle, C. (2015). PARS framework. https://www.owicommunity.org/pars.html.

Borgman, J. & McArdle, C. (2019). *Personal, accessible, responsive, strategic: Resources and strategies for online writing instructors.* The WAC Clearinghouse; University Press of Colorado. https://doi.org/10.37514/PRA-B.2019.0322.

Borgman, J. & McArdle, C. (Eds.). (2021). *PARS in practice: More resources and strategies for online writing instructors.* The WAC Clearinghouse; University Press of Colorado. https://doi.org/10.37514/PRA-B.2021.1145.

Borgman, J. & McArdle, C. (Eds.). (2023). *PARS in charge: Resources and strategies for online writing program leaders.* The WAC Clearinghouse; University Press of Colorado. https://doi.org/10.37514/PRA-B.2023.1985.

Conference on College Composition and Communication. (2017). *Statement on globalization in writing studies pedagogy and research.* http://tinyurl.com/mueh7dht.

de Lima, D. P., Gerosa, M. A., Conte, T. U. & de M Netto, J. F. (2019). What to expect, and how to improve online discussion forums: the instructors' perspective. *Journal of Internet Services and Applications, 10*(1), 1–15. https://doi.org/10.1186/s13174-019-0120-0.

Glass, I. (2015). Status Updates. [Audio podcast]. National Public Radio. https://www.thisamericanlife.org/573/status-update

GSOLE Executive Board. (2019, June 13). *Online literacy instruction principles and tenets.* Global Society of Online Literacy Educators. https://gsole.org/oliresources/oliprinciples.

Hewett, B. L. (2015). *Reading to learn and writing to teach: Literacy strategies for online writing instruction.* Bedford/St. Martin's Press.

Ladson-Billings, G. (1995). Toward a theory of culturally relevant pedagogy. *American Educational Research Journal, 32*(3), 465–491.

Lieberman, M. (2019). Discussion boards: Valuable? Overused? Discuss. *Inside Higher Ed.* https://www.insidehighered.com/digital-learning/article/2019/03/27/new-approaches-discussion-boards-aim-dynamic-online-learning.

Melzer, D. (2020). Understanding discourse communities. *Writing Spaces: Readings on Writing, 3*, 100–15.

Miller-Cochran, S. (2015). Multilingual writers and OWI. In B. Hewett & K. DePew (Eds.), *Foundational practices of online writing instruction* (pp. 291–307). The WAC Clearinghouse; Parlor Press. https://doi.org/10.37514/PER-B.2015.0650.2.09.

Mintz, S. (2020). Beyond the discussion board. *Inside Higher Ed.* https://www.insidehighered.com/blogs/higher-ed-gamma/beyond-discussion-board.

Paris, D. (2012). Culturally sustaining pedagogy: A needed change in stance, terminology, and practice. *Educational Researcher, 41*(3), 93–97. https://doi.org/10.3102/0013189X12441244.

Paris, D. & Alim, H. S. (2017). What is culturally sustaining pedagogy and why does it matter? In D. Paris & H. S. Alim (Eds.), *Culturally sustaining pedagogies: Teaching and learning for justice in a changing world* (pp. 1–21). Teachers College Press. https://doi.org/10.22329/JTL.V11I1.4987.

Parrish, P. & Linder-VanBerschot, J. (2010). Cultural dimensions of learning: Addressing the challenges of multicultural instruction. *International Review of Research in Open and Distance Learning, 11*(2), 1–19.

Rosa, J. & Flores, N. (2017). Unsettling race and language: Toward a raciolinguistic perspective. *Language in Society, 46*(5), 621–647. https://doi.org/10.1017/S0047404517000562.

Sibo, A. (2021). The literacy load is too damn high! A PARS approach to cohort-based discussions. In J. Borgman & C. McArdle (Eds.), *PARS in practice: More resources and strategies for online writing instructors* (pp. 71–81). The WAC Clearinghouse; University Press of Colorado. https://doi.org/10.37514/PRA-B.2021.1145.2.04.

St.Amant, K. (2020). Writing in global contexts: Composing usable texts for audiences from different cultures. *Writing Spaces: Readings on Writing, Volume 3*. WrtingSpaces.org; Parlor Press; The WAC Clearinghouse. https://wac.colostate.edu/books/writingspaces/writingspaces3/.

St.Amant, K. & Rice, R. (2017). *Composing locally: Rethinking online writing in the age of the global internet.* Utah State University Press. https://doi.org/10.7330/9781607326649.

St.Amant, K. & Rice, R. (2015). Online writing in global contexts: Rethinking the nature of connections and communication in the age of international online media. *Computers and Composition, 38*(B), v–x. http://doi.org/10.1016/S8755-4615(15)00104-8.

APPENDIX A, CULTURALLY SUSTAINING BLOG PROJECT

This assignment design is based on the TILT model, which you can learn more about at https://tilthighered.com.

PURPOSE

In this project, we are using blogs, a multimodal genre of writing, to investigate a community practice or family tradition that you are interested in learning about.

SKILLS

The purpose of this assignment is to help you practice the following skills that are essential to your success in this course / in school / in this field / in professional life beyond school:

- Understanding expectations in different writing genres.
- Delivering content in a variety of modalities.
- Synthesizing and evaluating sources and evidence to discuss a topic.
- Operationalizing personal experience and community connections in research.

Knowledge

This assignment will also help you to become familiar with the following important content knowledge in this discipline:

- How writing practices shift depending on genre and audience.
- The use of sources to support and explore lines of inquiry.

Task

1. You should read over the prompt and devise a plan.
2. Before writing, I suggest you do some preliminary research, collecting credible sources where authors are entering a conversation about a topic by citing/hyperlinking to other people that you can include your blog (see class resources for more information on finding credible sources/primary vs. secondary research).
3. As you draft your blog, you should consider how you can include 1) images, 2) hyperlinks, and 3) other multimedia elements.
4. You should also consider a strong title that will catch the reader's attention and organize your text in headers, subheadings, and so on that will aid in their understanding of your post.
5. Once you have a draft, you should revise, considering your audience and prompt.
6. Finally, you should edit your post for clarity and post your blog.

Criteria for Success:

While a successful blog will meet the stated criteria in terms of word count and multimodal components, a good blog is much more than these criteria. Particularly, a successful blog works to engage and address a defined audience in your topic of choice through your tone, style/word choice, and use of multimodal elements. In general, blogs tend to be more informal pieces of writing than typical academic work. Excellent work in this genre will capture a tone that is appropriate for the topic and audience you are addressing and be thoughtful about organization and presentation of text, images, and hyperlinks.

APPENDIX B, DISCUSSION BOARDS

This assignment design is based on the TILT model.

Purpose

As a way to inform our blogging, we will use discussion boards throughout this project to workshop ideas and strategize our blog entries.

Skills

The purpose of this assignment is to help you practice the following skills that are essential to your success in this course/in school/in this field/in professional life beyond school:

- Engage in pre-writing and collaborative writing practices.
- Provide constructive feedback to your classmates and peers.
- Vet sources and ideas.

Knowledge

This assignment will also help you to become familiar with the following important content knowledge in this discipline: How writing practices shift depending on genre and audience.

Task

1. Read over the discussion board prompt.
2. Before writing, I suggest you do some preliminary research, collecting reliable sources that you can include your blog.
3. As you draft your blog, you should consider how you can include 1) images, 2) hyperlinks, and 3) other multimedia elements.
4. You should also consider a strong title that will catch the reader's attention and organize your text in headers, subheadings, and so on that will aid in their understanding of your post.
5. Once you have a draft, you should revise, considering your audience and prompt.
6. Finally, you should edit your post for clarity and post your blog.

Criteria for Success

A successful discussion board interaction will meet the stated criteria in terms of word count and multimodal components; however, a successful discussion board post thoughtfully engages with your peers in a conversation by responding to the question prompts. Excellent work in discussion boards will thoughtfully respond to the questions prompted and engage with the peers in your class.

CHAPTER 11.

PROMOTING SOCIAL JUSTICE THROUGH MULTIMODAL COMPOSITION IN THE HYBRID WRITING CLASSROOM

Syndee Wood and Mary K. Stewart
California State University, San Marcos

In this chapter, the authors describe **multimodal assignments** *used in online, any time learning, and hybrid learning. Specifically, the authors offer guidance on designing multimodal online learning assignments to promote social justice. In describing their "better practice," this chapter addresses the themes of multimodal learning and practices in motion across teaching and learning modalities.*

FRAMEWORKS AND PRINCIPLES IN THIS CHAPTER

- **GSOLE Principle 1.3:** Multimodal composition and alphabetic writing may require different technologies; therefore, those involved should be appropriately prepared to use them.

GUIDING QUESTIONS BEFORE YOU BEGIN READING

- In what ways do you currently ask students to draw on their diverse linguistic resources to communicate with both community and academic audiences?
- In what ways does composing in non-alphabetic modes impact student confidence?
- When adopting practices from research literature and connecting theory to practice, what does it mean to "succeed"? For students as well as instructors?

INTRODUCTION

It was the end of the Spring 2020 semester. In the midst of pandemic chaos and fear, and when paired with forced asynchronous remote learning, what was already a difficult class (a first-year writing course in which the learning goals feel mountainous) had become exponentially more difficult in an unexpected era of unrest and uncertainty. Estrella had started the semester of our in-person, real-time learning class quiet yet attentive.[1] She was reluctant to volunteer to share in classroom discussions, but, if called on, would contribute effectively. After we moved to emergency remote learning during the global pandemic, Estrella's writing began to demonstrate a deeper connection with self, and a feeling of importance and ownership. It was exciting to read her work.

Then, in the final reflection of our semester, Estrella described her experiences in finding self-empowerment through writing and the sharing of stories, all in the context of our research project. She explained that the primary text for our project was, although more difficult a text to read and conceptualize than she had previously experienced, a text to which she had connected on a deeper level. Once she'd read the text—"Mapping the Margins: Intersectionality, Identity Politics, and Violence Against Women of Color," by Kimberlé Crenshaw (1991)—Estrella spent her isolation learning about the experiences shared by women of color who've been sexually assaulted, a group to which she belongs. She began writing every day, sharing her stories in online forums, encouraging other victims to share their own stories. She wrote an article that was shared on a website dedicated to sexual assault awareness. In her reflection for our class, Estrella expressed her dedication to sharing her story and encouraging others to share theirs. In her final sentences, Estrella explained that our course research assignment had given her the push she needed to find the person she "was meant to become."

Estrella embodies the power of writing and the importance of sharing stories. As a non-traditional, first-generation student myself, I (Syndee) use my class to expose and challenge existing inequalities, inviting students to use their writing to find and value their own academic voice, and to find their own unique position in academia.

The Intersections of Me research assignment that prompted Estrella's reflection (and that is the focus of this chapter) is one that I use in all of my 100-level composition classes, which I teach in courses across three colleges—two community colleges and a four-year state university. The project was born out of my desire to help students find validity and empowerment in their research and their writing. It is an invitation for students to find out about themselves and to identify their intersectionality by researching people like them. Students learn about the experiences faced by people with their particular intersections and identities—race, class, gender, sexuality, body type, education, health, ability,

---

1   We did not seek IRB approval for this project. Instead, Syndee received permission from the student via email to share this vignette in a publication.

etc.—then write an argument about themselves through that lens. It's a tough assignment, but one that students invest in.

In what my pre-pandemic self thought of as a "normal" semester—one in which we gather together once, twice, or three times a week, in a space we call a classroom, for the purposes of learning—the Intersections of Me research project concludes with an academic-style conference. Originally, this final activity of the semester had one purpose: to give students experience in speaking in front of a group, an important skill I had wished I'd had more time to practice. I simply wanted to give students a safe space in front of their class community to share their thesis, quotes from sources, and the overall findings of their research. Over time, I had noticed that it was the effort spent preparing to speak to their peers that gave students the motivation to make their writing something that mattered to them. That last step in their research—presenting their findings to others—was an intrinsic motivator as well as an outward exhibition of learning. Our conference became a low-stakes, yet still serious, activity in which students celebrate their learning by sharing with their writing community. In short, it's amazing.

And, that semester, COVID-19 stole that celebratory experience away from my students.

With no synchronous meetings and too many students who had ineffective, unreliable technology (not to mention an instructor with no idea how to translate the activity to something viable and valuable in an online setting), the conference had been canceled for the Spring 2020 semester. But when I read Estrella's reflection, I knew I had to find a way to introduce the conference in a way that worked in our new, now remote setting.

It was a comment from a colleague in a faculty learning community that brought in the next piece of the puzzle.

"What if," she said, "students did a TED Talk or something?"

Boom. There it was.

A TED Talk-styled video—in which students would share their research findings—was the perfect new modality for the conference presentation.

At the same time, having been introduced to the idea of Cajitas, or sacred boxes, in a professional development workshop—and subsequently discovering Alberto López Pulido's (2002) "The Living Color of Student's Lives: Bringing Cajitas into the Classroom"—I decided to bring in an option for a Cajita-style video into my course. In a face-to-face format, students would present their own Cajita into which they'd placed artifacts that connect their research with their own personal lives. By giving students a choice of a TED Talk or Cajita-style video, I hoped to help them practice making rhetorical decisions about which genre best fit their story and their research (see the Better Practice Lesson section for more details).

In the first iteration of this project, I was teaching online, real-time classes and the video project became a means to an end, a workaround for an unplanned (and, dare I say, unwanted) course delivery format. I simply wanted students to be able to articulate and share the results of their research in the same way they had been able to in person. I wanted them to be able to experience the pride and share the joy in their hard work and new knowledge. I wanted to give them something, anything, that felt normal.

Over time, I came to see the specific benefits of multimodal composition in online writing courses, which are detailed in the literature that I hadn't yet read. As the latter half of this chapter argues, designing multimodal compositions increases students' confidence in expressing themselves, which Laura Gonzales and Janine Butler (2020) maintain is because they have to draw on diverse linguistic resources to communicate with both community and academic audiences. On our Fall 2020 video presentation day, students voiced their excitement at sharing their videos with their classmates, most of whom had never even seen each other, and few of whose voices had even been heard. By the time fall of 2021 had come 'round, I had iterated this activity twice, and I was in three different class modalities. Class participants watched their peers' videos through the Zoom call (in "online, real-time" classes) or on the discussion forum (in "online, anything" classes) or in the classroom together (in "hybrid" classes)[2] understanding what it meant to be part of an academic audience, engaged in a sustained dialogue. I watched them recognize the rhetorical strategies they were employing in both their alphabetic writing and their digital design, while simultaneously finding value in their unique academic voice. The result was increased engagement and a sense of belonging in academic conversations. So, while this experience started in the pandemic, emergency remote learning was merely the catalyst that informed how I approach online writing instruction today.

To that end, this chapter will put my experiences and impressions in conversation with "best practices" related to multimodality in Composition Studies, particularly focusing on the recommendations posed by Gonzales and Butler (2020). It will also explore the relationship between theory and practice, illustrating how my anecdotal experiences gave me an understanding of the practice before I had the vocabulary from the literature to discuss it. At the same time, my practice directly impacted how my co-author (Mary) and I (Syndee) responded to the emerging research literature while drafting this chapter.

In the following pages, we first offer an overview of the theory of multimodality in composition studies and describe our teaching context. Then, we

---

2   Our institution defines "online, real-time" as 50 percent video conference call-based engagement and 50 percent asynchronous activities; "online, any time" as 100 percent asynchronous activities, and "hybrid" as 50 percent in person and 50 percent asynchronous activities.

describe the Intersections of Me assignment in more detail and include the assignment sheet. Finally, we build upon Gonzales and Butler's (2020) work on multimodality, multilingualism, and accessibility to analyze the ways in which my practice relates to or departs from the recommended practices.

SCHOLARSHIP, THEORIES, AND PRINCIPLES THAT GUIDE OUR APPROACH

In her 2002 *College Composition and Communication* article, Diana George offers a robust history of visual communication in the teaching of writing. She demonstrates that, as early as the 1940s, visuals were a common component of writing instruction. Typically, however, these visuals were prompts for writing, such that students would analyze the visual in their writing, or the visual would jumpstart the invention stage of the writing process; it was also the case that visuals were regarded as a lower or lesser form of communication than alphabetic writing. George argues that a key shift towards seeing visuals as part of the composing process occurred in 1987, with David Bartholomae and Anthony Petrosky's *Ways of Reading*. Bartholomae and Petrosky challenged the barriers between "high culture" (art history) and "low culture" (advertising), which, George explains, illustrated that "not only was meaning no longer restricted to the verbal, the visual was also not used as a gentle step into the 'more serious' world of the verbal" (2002, p. 23). The argument that visuals "counted" as serious and complex conveyors of meaning laid the groundwork for arguments that multimodal composition "counted" as an important skill for first-year writing students to study and practice.

It was not until the late 1990s that this concept came to fruition because, up until then, George explains, writing instructors did not have the tools to produce non-alphabetic composition. Computers and the internet made the production and, eventually, the distribution of multimodal composition accessible to both students and teachers. Implementing the theory in practice was thus possible, but not yet widely recommended or adopted.

In the decade following George's article, composition scholars like Kathleen Yancey (2004), Richard Selfe and Cindy Selfe (2008), Elizabeth Clark (2010), Cheryl Ball and James Kalmbach (2010), and David Sheridan and James Inman (2010) drew on the theories put forward by multiliteracy experts (e.g., Kress, 2003; New London Group, 1996; Selber, 2004) to effectively illustrate the value of multimodal composition in first-year composition (FYC). Today, composition studies has come to accept multimodal composition as an uncontroversial (though still sometimes under-taught) component of FYC, as evidenced in textbooks like *Understanding Rhetoric* by Elizabeth Losh et al. (2021), which is designed like a graphic novel. Specific to OWI, scholars have detailed the unique advantages of multimodal composition in online contexts, especially as it relates to facilitating digital literacy (Bourelle et al., 2016). Accordingly, the *Online Literacy Instruction Principles and Tenets* (GSOLE, 2019) names multimodal composition as one of the key components of an online writing course: "Instructors and tutors should research, develop, theorize, and apply appropriate reading, alphabetic writing, and multimodal composition theories to their OLI environment(s)." The GSOLE principle of Accessibility also recognizes that instructors and students should be "appropriately prepared" to use the technologies required for multimodal composition.

Despite the scholarly commitment to multimodal composition, this "best practice" is not necessarily employed by first-year writing instructors, and at some institutions the question of whether multimodal composition "counts" as writing is still hotly debated in department meetings (Pandey & Khadka, 2021). Many instructors additionally hesitate to teach multimodal composition because they worry about the logistics, about making the project too complicated, about confusing students, and about implementing a pedagogical practice that is not understood or valued (Borgman, 2019). All of this—the department debates and the instructor hesitation—was the reality at our institution; consequently, it was not until the shift to emergency remote instruction in response to the COVID-19 pandemic that Syndee began to experiment with digital, multimodal composition.

In this chapter, we hope to demonstrate a "better practice" of multimodal composition in online FYC by building on the work of Gonzales and Butler (2020), who synthesize research on multilingualism and disability studies to introduce "composition pedagogies that embrace multilingualism, multimodality, and accessibility simultaneously." We are particularly drawn to Gonzales and Butler because they advocate for an understanding of multimodal composition that promotes social justice instead of building on research that argues for the value of multimodal composition only as an enhanced form of communication. This theory resonates with Syndee as a teacher and aligns with our department's commitment to social justice. As our program mission statement explains (Program Information, n.d.), we are first and foremost aiming to teach students that "writing (re)produces particular social constructions and power relations." Syndee's Intersections of Me assignment addresses our program goals by asking students to reflect on their own intersectional identities and view their diverse linguistic resources as assets that help them contribute meaningfully to academic conversations. The addition of a multimodal component to that research project enhanced Syndee's goal of promoting social justice in unanticipated ways.

Consequently, our "better practice" is neither theory-into-practice or practice-into-theory; it is instead an attempt to understand where theory and practice organically meet—the theory from Gonzales and Butler of multilingualism, multimodality, and accessibility gives us language to describe Syndee's practice, and the practice gives us concrete examples that enhance our understanding of the theory. In taking this approach, we hope to invite readers to reflect on their own practices and identify moments where they are already enacting the recommendations from the scholarship. Our goal is to offer an alternative to the understanding of "best practices" as something that we take from the literature and apply in our classrooms; the "better practice" we advocate for involves identifying overlaps between theory and practice and then using the language from the literature to better understand and subsequently revise our practice of inviting students to compose multimodal texts that explore intersectional identities.

More specifically, this chapter will discuss the relationship between Syndee's practice and the four recommendations at the conclusion of Gonzales and Butler's article:

1. "Enrich students' possibilities for strengthening their communication skill through multiple languages and modes, such as through video assignments" (2020, para. 48);
2. "Support students' access to intersectional understandings of accessibility and multimodality in collaboration with academic and community audiences" (2020, para. 49);
3. "Position students as social justice designers who not only witness technological oppression, but who also intervene in opposition through their own compositions" (2020, para. 50); and
4. "Promote intersectional accessibility as a social justice issue relevant to writers and designers" (2020, para. 51).

At the end of this chapter, we use those recommendations to organize our reflection on the multimodal project Syndee facilitated in Fall 2021. But first, we describe our teaching context and Syndee's Intersections of Me assignment.

COURSE CONTEXT AND LESSON

The authors of this chapter—Syndee and Mary—both teach at a four-year, public university on the west coast; 47 percent of the student population is Latinx and 53 percent of graduates are first-generation college students. Syndee's eleven years as an instructor at this institution began when she was an MA student in the department that delivers the writing program. Syndee also teaches FYC at two different community colleges in the area. Both of those colleges serve student populations that are between 42–46 percent Latinx; one college reported

28 percent first-gen students and the other did not have this information available. At the time of this writing, Mary was new to the four-year institution where she met Syndee, having joined the department as the writing program administrator in Fall 2020. She has 15 years of online teaching experience at for-profit and public, four-year institutions, and maintains a scholarly interest in multimodal composition and online writing instruction. This chapter is the result of many conversations, with Syndee discussing her plans for Fall 2021 or reflecting on her experiences in the classroom, and with Mary contributing with commentary on the connections she sees between Syndee's practice and OWI research, as well as reflections on how Syndee's practice is similar to or different from her own. Throughout those conversations, we each influenced how the other understood both the theory and the practice of multimodal composition.

In what follows, we offer a composite reflection on Syndee's experience teaching six sections of hybrid and online, real-time FYW across her institutions in Fall 2021. Our shared institution defines "hybrid" as one to two hours per week in person plus asynchronous activities and "online, real-time" as one to two hours per week on Zoom plus asynchronous activities. We begin with a detailed explanation of the Intersections of Me project and then put that practice in conversation with Gonzales and Butler's theory of multimodal composition.

BETTER PRACTICE LESSON—SYNDEE'S INTERSECTIONS OF ME PROJECT

At all three institutions, the second half of Syndee's first-year writing semester is spent deep diving into a research project in which students look at themselves through the lens of intersectionality. In the final step of this Intersections of Me project, students take the most important parts of their seven-page (approximately 1750 words) argument paper and present those parts in a brief video, approximately four to five minutes, choosing the video style (TED v. Cajita) that best suits their purpose and message. Leading up to this stage of the semester, students have practiced:

1. **Academic reading:** Crenshaw's "Mapping the Margins: Intersectionality, Identity Politics, and Violence Against Women of Color" (https://www.jstor.org/stable/1229039) is the primary text. All assignments for this project center around Crenshaw's arguments and ideas.
2. **Summary:** Students write a five or more paragraph summary of Crenshaw's text. The summary must include an overall synopsis of the text and its main ideas, as well as an outline of some of the evidence Crenshaw uses as support.

3. **Application:** A worksheet and discussion guides students to apply Crenshaw's concepts to their own experiences, reflecting on how their experiences are shaped by visible and invisible intersections.
4. **Synthesis:** Students complete a research proposal and an annotated bibliography, which helps them integrate sources in support of an argument about their intersectional self.
5. **Multimodal Composition:** Students complete multimodal activities and assignments such as weekly presentations and asynchronous discussions. They also engage in synchronous discussion about the rhetorical strategies used for the different modes, purposes, and audiences.

After students have submitted the final draft of their written project, Syndee facilitates a class-wide conversation that consists of two synchronous sessions and an asynchronous conversation about how to use the most important parts of their composition as a script for their video, which will be presented to their academic and community audiences, in the form of a TED Talk or Cajita video. The formal assignment instructions that Syndee shares with her students is featured below.

STEP SIX: TED TALK OR CAJITA VIDEO

Four to five minutes

- **Ted Talk Video:** The purpose of your video is to teach your viewers about people like you. What do people with your unique intersections experience? Where/when are people with your intersections considered "normal" in our society? In what ways do people like you receive help, get the benefit of the doubt, blend in with the crowd, or get "a pass"? What discrimination do you—and others who share similar intersectional identities—face?
- **Cajita Video:** Share a Cajita that is a representation of you. In this sacred box will be artifacts that represent who you are and the experiences you have had as someone with your intersections. Tie your artifacts to your sources, explaining the significance of each item, including the box itself. You have absolute creative freedom for this box, including whether or not it is an actual box, or some other physical or virtual container.

Purpose

This final piece of our Intersections of Me project is where your research becomes relevant beyond the virtual walls of this class and, more importantly, beyond the imagined walls of academia. With this assignment, the skills you've practiced all semester become critical in a new way, for a broader audience. Your unique voice brings validity to the information you share. This final assignment invites you to find your own unique voice in your writing, and to share the importance of your research with a broader audience. This project contributes to Student Learning Outcome #1.

Task

Once you have submitted your research paper, read it out loud and select the parts of your paper that feel like the heart of your argument. Consider which parts of your paper are the most important overall and which parts your new audience might find the most interesting. Using these most important parts of your paper, create either a TED Talk video or a Cajita Video. Your video will be four to five minutes long.

Skills

This assignment gives practice in the writing skills we employ in the real world. Since this is a video, your message will come through in more than just your words. Combine all of the unique qualities of you—your voice, presence, tone, and gestures—with the images and/or physical artifacts you will share in your video. In the process of moving your argument from the written page to a video, you will:

1. Practice making rhetorical choices and decisions for your argument.
2. Consider the ways that your unique message comes through in a new mode of communication.
3. Judge and evaluate the usefulness of your sources in this new mode and text.
4. Synthesize multiple perspectives as you integrate sources and quotes into your video.

Knowledge

As you design your video and make decisions about which information and sources to include, consider the knowledge you have gained this semester. Your video will display your knowledge of:

1. The concept of intersectionality and differing experiences individuals face.
2. Rhetorical decision making and strategies for your writing in a new mode of communication.

Important Information to Consider

1. You will be on camera for your video, and you will include some sort of visual in your video. (TED Talk = shared PPT, doc, and/or images. Cajita video = share your Cajita and its contents).

2. Include integration of two sources, two quotes, and a 2021 MLA style Works Cited page/slide.
3. Use the technology that works for you, whether that be the program used for your video production, or the programs you use in your video. This video is about your argument, not about your knowledge of technology or your ability to make a great video.

Video Presentation Reflection

Complete this assignment after you have completed your video and it has been uploaded to the discussion assignment. Write a cohesive paragraph that responds to the following questions.

1. Which video genre (TED Talk or Cajita video) did you choose? Why?
2. What points from your paper did you include in your video? Why?
3. In what way did your time in this class help you make decisions for making this video?

Students complete this project in the latter half of the semester, which, depending on the college, is anywhere from four to eight weeks. The project, from start to finish, is challenging in both subject and skill: they read a 60-page article published in the *Stanford Law Review* written in 1991 by Crenshaw on the topic of intersectionality. Then, they are asked to take this concept—which they've just begun to understand—and apply it to their own lives. Next, they conduct academic research and locate scholarly sources and then write in unfamiliar genres such as the research proposal and annotated bibliography. Throughout, they are daunted by the knowledge that they ultimately have to produce a seven-page paper that integrates sources in meaningful ways.

For most students, the struggle persists until they reach the "ah-ha" moment of what Syndee calls the "this-is-why-it-matters," which typically occurs as they are designing their multimodal compositions. The one thing they are not daunted by is making a video. Because these first-year students are a part of a culture of social media videos, they understand the purpose and the potential of using videos to reach both intended and unintended audiences. The process of creating this video helps them see that same potential for their alphabetic writing.

In the fall of 2021, to assess the Intersections of Me project, Syndee used a labor-based grading contract. In order to receive a "high pass," the students needed to revise their work in response to instructor feedback and to submit a paragraph that reflected on the rhetorical choices they'd made throughout the composing process. This project continues to evolve. At the time of this writing

(Spring 2023), Syndee's labor-based grading contract asks students to create a "video process reflection letter" directed to Syndee in which they explain and reflect on their rhetorical strategies in translating essay to video with an audience of peers and a more global audience of video viewers in mind. Additionally, in this final piece of writing for the semester, students must reflect on the learning they've done over the course of the class, and what they will continue to work on. It is in this letter that students show the work they've put into their writing over the course of the class, and articulate their purposeful process for their video, focusing on course objectives such as audience, process, and purpose, and where they inevitably describe themselves as members of different communities who are navigating between those communities, making choices about how to present to each.

REFLECTION ON PRACTICE

In this section, we put Syndee's experience with this assignment in Fall 2021 in conversation with the four recommendations that Gonzales and Butler offer at the conclusion of their article. Throughout, we reflect on the relationship between "best practices" in the literature and actual practices in the classroom.

RECOMMENDATION 1: STRENGTHEN COMMUNICATION CONFIDENCE THROUGH MULTIMODALITY

Gonzales and Butler's first recommendation is to "enrich students' possibilities for strengthening their communication skills through multiple languages and modes, such as through video assignments." They further explain that multimodal assignments "encourage students to recognize the communication skills that they already possess and correspondingly to develop confidence expressing themselves through written English and other languages and modes" (2020, para. 48).

Butler offers an example of this in her Video Reflection on Multiple Differences in Communication Practices assignment. She asks her students to conduct an interview about a person's intersectional communication practices. For example, Butler explains, they might "interview a Deaf person who comes from a Spanish-speaking family and communicates through American Sign Language, español, and English" (2020, para. 33) Then, in their video, they build on what they learned from the interview to create a "multimodal and multilingual text" that persuades a target audience "to recognize the significance of multiple and different communication practices." In Butler's example, the video might feature a person signing directly at the camera with written English captions that occasionally include palabras en español. This assignment requires students to draw on their own communicative expertise and lived experience, as well as on the expertise of their interviewee, while making rhetorical decisions about how to best combine and synthesize multiple modes and languages to effectively reach an audience. These overlapping practices underscore the intersectional nature of all communication in a way that celebrates linguistic diversity and embodied difference.

Syndee's students similarly make decisions about what alphabetic, visual, and aural elements to incorporate into their videos, and they deliberately base those decisions on an analysis of what will persuade their target audience of the importance of their message. In Syndee's case, the emphasis is on developing an academic identity; the goal is for students to develop a sense that they have something valuable to say and to contribute in academic conversations. The video assignment also requires them to leverage multiple communicative strategies to reach an audience they have identified. Their success in this effort enhances their confidence that they belong in the academic arena because it highlights the many different language varieties and languages and communicative modes involved in constructing academic knowledge, many of which these students already have experience with.

While Syndee's assignment looks quite different from Butler's, it nevertheless achieves the recommended goal of encouraging students to "recognize the communication skills that they already possess and correspondingly to develop confidence expressing themselves." Syndee did not design the assignment with the intention of enacting Gonzales and Butler's recommendation, but reading the scholarship informed the way we thought and talked about the project in the course of drafting this chapter.

Recommendation 2: Understand Accessibility and Multimodality in Collaboration with Academic and Community Audiences

Gonzales and Butler's second recommendation is to "support students' access to intersectional understandings of accessibility and multimodality in collaboration with academic and community audiences" (2020, para. 49). Engaging with public audiences "puts multimodality and multilingualism in action, in spaces where these practices are already connected" (para. 49). Additionally, the opportunity for community engagement "encourages students from historically marginalized communities to stay connected to their communities and incorporate community knowledge into their work as writers and designers" (2020, para. 49).

Gonzales offers an example of an assignment that employs service learning to connect students with public audiences. Her students "collaborate on a digital book making project with an Indigenous rights advocacy organization" (2020, para. 27). The project taught students about the "history of Indigenous language translation and interpretation" (2020, para. 27) and facilitated conversations about "the connections between race, culture, disability, and access" (2020, para. 28). It also led students to create "digital materials (i.e., videos) that were multilingual and accessible" (2020, para. 29). Most importantly, "social justice was centralized in this course through the course readings, through student projects, and through the overall impact that students' assignments were positioned to have outside of our classroom" (220, para. 29).

In Fall 2021, Syndee's course did not employ service learning or emphasize technical or digital accessibility, but it did leverage multimodality to help students engage with community and academic audiences. By creating TED Talks or Cajita videos, students addressed their peers as an academic audience and also imagined the public audiences who might see their videos online, should students choose to post them. Students also had to decide whether a TED Talk or a Cajita video was more appropriate for their intended audience and purpose. Creating videos that could be circulated on social media networks—and making intentional decisions about what modes, languages, and language varieties to integrate into those videos—further prompted students to reflect on the ways that multimodality and multilingualism pervade digital public spaces.

The juxtaposition of the video and the alphabetic research project additionally facilitated reflection on the role of multimodality and multilingualism in academic spaces. Ultimately, the students' efforts to reach a public or community audience pushed them to figure out the "this-is-why-it-matters." By the time they submitted their TED Talk or Cajita video, students had a much clearer sense of what they were trying to achieve in the written research paper for an academic audience. They also had concrete examples of how to draw on and combine their linguistic resources in a way that appeals to particular audiences.

When they finally shared their videos with peers, they discovered that some classmates are members of both their intended academic and community audiences. Consequently, Syndee's assignment not only helped students understand "multimodality in collaboration with academic and community audiences" (Gonzales & Butler, 2020, para. 49), but also helped them navigate between those audiences and showed them that they already possess the communicative skills to contribute to academic conversations (for more on how multimodal composition creates rhetorically rich communicative contexts, see Jessica Eagle, Michelle Falter, and Caitlin Donovan's work, Chapter 7 of this collection). Furthermore, because the project is about the students' personal intersections, their imagined online audiences are likely members of their own communities, thus somewhat achieving Gonzales and Butler's goal of encouraging "students from historically marginalized communities to stay connected with their communities and incorporate community knowledge into their work" (2020, para. 49). This is particularly evident when students recognize their peers as members of their community audience. They've shared about themselves, breaking down perceived barriers. They're connecting in more ways than just being part of the same first-year writing class, and they feel the connection.

Recommendations 3 & 4: Intersectional Accessibility

Gonzales and Butler's third and fourth recommendations focus on the relationship between social justice and technological accessibility. Recommendation three asks instructors to "position students as social justice designers who not only witness technological oppression, but who also intervene in oppression through their own compositions" (Gonzales & Butler, 2020, para. 50). The idea is for students to analyze the accessibility of particular technologies, and then create their own multimodal compositions that intentionally counter the technological oppression they've observed. Recommendation four requires us to first acknowledge that "separating language from race, class, and disability does not provide a clear picture of how real individuals engage with writing or with technologies," and to then advance "intersectional approaches to writing, access, and technology" by positioning "intersectional accessibility as a social justice issue relevant to writers and designers" (Gonzales & Butler, 2020, para. 51).

Gonzales provides an example of these recommendations in her Designing for Intersectional Accessibility assignment. She asks students to reflect on the ways "technologies are inherently imbued with cultural ideologies" and then "create multimodal projects where they practice highlighting the ideological and cultural values embedded in particular interfaces" (2020, para. 23). The project emphasizes intersectionality by asking students to consider more than one access point. For example, students might analyze a school website for an audience of multilingual parents as well as an audience of students with disabilities. The goal is to help students design projects that "are accessible on multiple levels," and to acknowledge "language diversity, race and power, and disability as factors that guide design decisions" (Gonzales & Butler, 2020, para. 25).

Syndee's assignment has the potential to enact these recommendations—students could analyze the accessibility of the TED Talks or Cajita videos that they produce, as well as the accessibility of the platforms they use to distribute those videos. However, this was not the focus of Syndee's courses. These recommendations from Gonzales and Butler have shown her a potential next direction for the project, and they've raised both of our awareness of the role of technical accessibility in multimodal composing.

BEYOND THE RECOMMENDATIONS

As we drafted this chapter, we talked about what it meant to "successfully" enact the recommendations from the research literature and principle and framework documents. In our early conversations, we concluded that Syndee's class achieved recommendations 1 and 2 from Gonzales and Butler and did not achieve recommendations 3 and 4. One conclusion to this chapter, then, could be that a next step for us and our readers is to help students analyze the intersectional accessibility of the tools they use to create and distribute their multimodal compositions. But as we continued to talk, we worried that such a conclusion implied that Syndee had "failed" to achieve or facilitate recommendations 3 and 4, and we especially worried that such an implication would contribute to narratives that teachers always need to do better and be better. This narrative is particularly problematic in the context of OWI, where so many faculty are contingent (Mechenbeir, 2015; Philbrook et al., 2019) and where institutional resources, such as compensation for professional development and training, are scarce (Breuch, 2015; Kahn, 2020).

These conversations also led us to notice that most "best practices" articles tell a positive story. In short, these kinds of articles suggest that the authors' pedagogical goals and intentions were met and the students experienced valuable learning as a result. In our own examination of Fall 2021, we found a much more complicated reality. There were, of course, some wonderful things that came out of this assignment. In their final reflections, Syndee's students demonstrated a clear understanding of the diverse communicative strategies required to reach both academic and community audiences. They remarked on how enjoyable the video assignment was and reported that it made them feel more confident and capable as writers/designers. But it was also the case that several students who demonstrated positive and successful learning in response to the video did not pass the class. In most cases (and this is something we are seeing with more and more regularity at our institution), the students failed because they simply didn't finish, meaning they didn't submit the final project or they didn't follow through on opportunities to make up work missed earlier in the semester. In a few instances, students completed the video assignment even though they knew that they were not going to be able to pass the class.

Issues with retention and persistence have been part of the story of online education for a long time (Boston et al., 2009), and the pandemic has exacerbated both drop rates and equity gaps (Gordon, 2021). While composition studies scholars have offered recommendations for how program directors and institutional decision-makers can improve retention in first-year composition (Ruecker, 2021), issues like retention are often absent from calls for faculty to enact best practices. Nevertheless, there is often an implication that if we faculty would employ the best practices, then things like retention would improve. Instead of agreeing or disagreeing with that statement, we want to call attention to the unproductive pressure of the implication.

Thus, as a conclusion to our "better practice" chapter, we invite readers to reflect on what it means to adopt practices from the research literature and principal documents (and thus actively participate in connecting theory to practice), as well as on the consequences of expecting those kinds of "best" practices to result in "success" for both the students and the teacher.

CONCLUSION

Engaging with best practices in the teaching of writing—reading the literature, talking with colleagues, collaborating on projects like this one—highlights the ways that teaching is an ongoing and iterative process. Our practice evolves as we gain experience and exposure to new strategies for facilitating learning. In Syndee's case, the pandemic prompted her to first cancel in-class presentations and then reimagine them as multimodal compositions; that reimagining was facilitated by conversations with colleagues about how to manage the pivot to online, and by her past experience in faculty learning communities and engagement with Pulido's scholarship on Cajita videos. What began as a reaction to emergency remote instruction has now evolved into a pedagogical strategy that Syndee consistently employs across the modalities in which she teaches.

At first, the assignment instructions were simply to "use four to five minutes" of their papers to make the video, much like their in-class conference-style presentation had been. The goal was for students to translate their seven- to nine-page papers into a four- to five-minute video. After a few semesters, the prompt evolved, more directly instructing students to include what they feel are the "most interesting parts," and the parts that "feel like the heart of their argument." Next semester, Syndee is changing it up once again: she's going to move the video assignment so that the "this-is-why-it-matters" occurs earlier in the semester and hopefully helps more students complete the final project. She's also going to put more emphasis on the reflections, which should help her assessment scheme better account for the positive "ah-ha" moment that students experience during the video project.

Because of conversations during the co-authoring of this chapter, Syndee and Mary have both changed the way they talk about multimodal composition.

We sensed that creating videos made students more confident in expressing themselves, and we felt that some of the success was related to students making intentional decisions about how to address both academic and community audiences. We also felt that multimodal composition was in line with our writing program's commitment to social justice. But we didn't have the language to explain why. Gonzales and Butler gave us that vocabulary. Their work has changed how we talk about these ideas with each other and with our department, and it's helped us more precisely explain the intended goals of multimodal composition to our students.

Looking further into the future, we'll both be thinking about intersectional accessibility; while we can't totally see how we'll revise our courses to adapt that recommended practice right now, it's on our radars and will become part of our continued conversations. Most likely, in a couple more semesters, we'll find that what started as a theoretical conversation has woven its way into our classroom practice. This is the goal of "best practices" scholarship. Teaching, by nature, pushes us to revise and reconsider our practice; reading articles about teaching similarly inspires us. These resources—and the scholars who have created them—don't show us how we've failed; they give us the language to talk about what we are already doing, and encourage us to acknowledge the existing strengths in our practice. They also challenge us to consider how we might do things differently, in a way that feels authentic to us and our students.

MOVING BETTER PRACTICES ACROSS MODALITIES

Syndee teaches this assignment in all of the below modalities. In what follows, she offers tips for each.

- **In-Person, Real-Time Learning:** Reserve class time for discussion of how to translate an essay into a video. Have students work in groups to create scripts, and allow them to work together to create the videos. Watch the videos together, perhaps on final exam day, and have students reflect on their decisions for their videos, especially where audience and language is concerned.
- **Online, Real-Time Learning:** Similar to the in-person class, videos are played synchronously. Students put questions in the chat for every video author, which should focus on decisions made with audience and language in mind, and then the author answers two or three questions from the chat.
- **Online, Any Time Learning:** Students post their video at the beginning of the week on a discussion forum. Throughout the week, they

leave comments in the forum about their peers' videos.
- **Hybrid Learning:** At our university, the hybrid version of this activity works identically to the in-person, real-time version. Another option is to have students post their video at the beginning of the week, have students watch all the videos before the final class meeting, then spend that last day discussing and celebrating rhetorical strategies.

REFERENCES

Ball, C. & Kalmbach, J. (2010). *RAW: Reading and writing new media.* Hampton Press.

Bartholomae, D. & Petrosky, A. (1987). *Ways of reading.* St. Martin's.

Borgman, J. (2019). Dissipating hesitation: Why online instructors fear multimodal assignments and how to overcome the fear. In Khadka, S. & Lee, J. C. (Eds.), *Bridging the multimodal gap: From theory to practice* (pp. 43–67). Utah State University Press. https://doi.org/10.7330/9781607327974.c005.

Boston, W., Díaz, S. R., Gibson, A. M., Ice, P., Richardson, J. & Swan, K. (2009). An exploration of the relationship between indicators of the community of inquiry framework and retention in online programs. *Journal of Asynchronous Learning Networks, 13*(3), 67–83.

Bourelle, A., Bourelle, T., Knutson, A. V. & Spong, S. (2016). Sites of multimodal literacy: Comparing student learning in online and face-to-face environments. *Computers and Composition, 39*(1), 55–70.

Breuch, L. K. (2015). Faculty preparation for OWI. In B. Hewett & K. E. DePew (Eds.), *Foundational practices of online writing instruction* (pp. 349–388). The WAC Clearinghouse; Parlor Press. https://doi.org/10.37514/PER-B.2015.0650.2.11.

Clark, J. E. (2010). The digital imperative: Making the case for a 21st-century pedagogy. *Computers and Composition, 27*(1), 27–35.

Crenshaw, K. (1991). Mapping the margins: Intersectionality, identity politics, and violence against Women of Color. *Stanford Law Review, 43*(6), 1241–1299.

George, D. (2002). From analysis to design: Visual communication in the teaching of writing. *College Composition and Communication, 54*(1), 11–39.

Gonzales, L. & Butler, J. (2020). Working toward social justice through multilingualism, multimodality, and accessibility in writing classrooms. *Composition Forum, 44.* https://compositionforum.com/issue/44/multilingualism.php.

Gordon, L. (2021, August 20). Cal State students failing, withdrawing from many required classes at a high rate. *Los Angeles Times.* https://www.latimes.com/california/story/2021-08-20/csu-students-failing-withdrawing-from-many-required-classes-at-a-high-rate.

GSOLE Executive Board. (2019, June 13). *Online literacy instruction principles and tenets.* Global Society of Online Literacy Educators. https://gsole.org/oliresources/oliprinciples.

Kahn, S. (2020). We value teaching too much to keep devaluing it. *College English, 82*(6), 591–611.

Kress, G. (2003). *Literacy in the new media age*. Routledge.
Losh, E., Alexander, J., Cannon, K. & Cannon, Z. (2021). *Understanding rhetoric: A graphic guide to writing* (3rd ed.). Bedford/St. Martin's.
López Pulido, A. (2002), The living color of student's lives: Bringing cajitas into the classroom. *Religion & Education, 29*(2), 69–77.
Mechenbeir, M. (2015). Contingent faculty and OWI. In B. L. Hewett & K. E. Depew (Eds.), *Foundational practices of online writing instruction* (pp. 227–249). The WAC Clearinghouse; Parlor Press. https://doi.org/10.37514/PER-B.2015.0650.2.07.
New London Group. (1996). A pedagogy of multiliteracies: Designing social futures. *Harvard Educational Review, 66*, 60–92.
Pandey, S. B. & Khadka, S. (Eds.). (2021). *Multimodal composition: Faculty development programs and institutional change*. Taylor & Francis Group.
Philbrook, J., Borgman, J., McClure, C. I., Mechenbier, M. & Warnock, S. (2019). Forum: Issues about part time and contingent faculty. *College Composition and Communication, 23*(1), A1–A16.
Program information. (n.d.) *General Education Writing, CSUSM*. Retrieved April 18, 2023, from https://www.csusm.edu/gew/program_information/index.html.
Ruecker, T. (2021). Retention and persistence in writing programs: A survey of students repeating first-year writing. *Composition Forum, 46*. https://compositionforum.com/issue/46/retention.php.
Selber, S. A. (2004). *Multiliteracies for a digital age*. Southern Illinois University Press.
Selfe, R. J. & Selfe, C. L. (2008). "Convince me!" Valuing multimodal literacies and composing public service announcements. *Theory Into Practice, 47*, 83–92.
Sheridan, D. M. & Inman, J. A. (Eds.). (2010). *Multiliteracy centers: Writing center work, new media, and multimodal rhetoric*. Hampton Press.
Yancey, K. B. (2004). Made not only in words: Composition in a new key. *College Composition and Communication, 56*(2), 297–328.

CHAPTER 12.

OPEN-MEDIA ASSIGNMENT DESIGN TO ADDRESS ACCESS AND ACCESSIBILITY IN ONLINE MULTIMODAL COMPOSITION

Amory Orchard, Michael Neal, Ashleah Wimberly, and Amanda Ayers
Florida State University

In this chapter, the authors describe **open media assignments** *used in online, real-time learning. Specifically, the authors offer guidance for applying the principles of Universal Design for Learning and as well as considerations for technological access when designing online multimedia assignments. In describing their "better practice," this chapter addresses the themes of accessibility and inclusivity and multimodal learning.*

FRAMEWORKS AND PRINCIPLES IN THIS CHAPTER

- **GSOLE Principle 3.4:** Instructors and tutors should migrate and/or adapt appropriate reading, alphabetic writing, and multimodal composition theories from traditional instructional settings to their OLI environment(s).
- **Framework for Success in Postsecondary Writing, Creativity:** The ability to use novel approaches for generating, investigating, and representing ideas.
- **Framework for Success in Postsecondary Writing, Flexibility:** The ability to adapt to situations, expectations, or demands.
- **Framework for Success in Postsecondary Writing, Metacognition:** The ability to reflect on one's own thinking as well as on the individual and cultural processes used to structure knowledge.

GUIDING QUESTIONS BEFORE YOU BEGIN READING

- To what degree is it ethically responsible for online instructors to assign multimodal projects to students who likely have disproportionate access to composing technologies?
- What support structures do online students need to successfully complete complex, long-term multimodal projects?
- How can students exercise agency in making decisions not only about project topics but also the *media* in which they compose these projects?

INTRODUCTION

Multimodal composition projects such as webtexts, videos, podcasts, and other texts that use various combinations of written, visual, audio, and spatial modes of communication are often seen as challenging to teach, especially when the class is online (i.e., real-time, any time, or hybrid). Assigning multimodal projects in online courses may result in problems due to disproportionate access to expensive machines and programs; the differing abilities, skills, and experiences students and instructors bring to the task; and the limited access online students might have to multimodal composing support networks (e.g., a writing center that provides consulting services). In short, online writing instructors must consider how the challenges with online education might be exacerbated for students composing multimodal texts.

Moreover, some students prefer online (any time or real-time) education because of work or family responsibilities, unpredictable schedules, or health issues, which might make the time needed for composing multimodal projects more daunting. Others might prefer online courses because of learning styles or disabilities, which also might make managing large, multi-faceted projects more difficult. If not avoid them altogether, a "safer" route might be to minimize their complexity or make lockstep assignments with detailed and often prescriptive instructions that undermine learning. As such, it may be tempting for online instructors to avoid multimodal composition assignments, an issue Jessie Borgman (2019) addresses in "Disrupting Hesitation: Why Online Instructors Fear Multimodal Assignments and How to Overcome the Fear."

In this chapter, we explore two obstacles for students working with multimodal composition in online courses—access and accessibility—and suggest using open media platform assignments as our "better practice" to help students mitigate some of the challenges. We define "access" in this chapter as students owning or having convenient availability to technologies such as computers, software, and the internet. A student who owns a high-end laptop with programs such as iMovie, Photoshop, and InDesign has more privileged access than students who might use a computer in a school lab or public library or those students who might be composing with tablets or their smartphones. Even those who have computers might not have equitable access if their machine doesn't have expensive programs on it or the necessary processing speed or memory for rendering large multimodal productions. "Access" can also mean availability of the support structures to help use the technologies, be they online or in person. Since multimodal projects take both technological and human resources, inequitable access places some students at an advantage over others. When we use the term "accessibility," we mean people with various physical, cognitive, mental, and/or emotional abilities can equitably participate and succeed in the activities, assignments, and interactions in the class. Since multimodal projects use various communication modes that may exclude some students, accessibility should always remain a central concern. In addition to disabilities such as sight or hearing loss, accessibility also includes less apparent disabilities such as cognitive differences that might make it harder for some students to navigate procedural tasks or to multitask. As instructors, we don't wish to create more access and accessibility barriers for our students, so it's easy to see why many online instructors shy away from complex multimodal composition assignments.

In this chapter we ask: what might happen if online instructors don't back away from multimodal composition assignments but instead give students the freedom to choose the modalities and media platforms—be they comprised of particular devices, software, and/or online applications—to compose and share their projects? This way they can make informed choices based on their unique access, abilities, and goals rather than avoiding multimodal composition altogether.

The following vignettes are examples of students selecting the modes and media on multimodal assignments in an undergraduate visual rhetoric course:

Wilson

Wilson was a football player at our university during seasons that resulted in multiple bowl games victories and even a national championship. Since he was in an in-person class, at 6 foot, 5 inches and 335 pounds of muscle, Wilson was easily recognizable as a world-class athlete. One of the friendliest and most outgoing students in the class, Wilson would occasionally come up to the front of the class "to teach" and would imitate the instructor, much to the delight of the other students. His peers loved him for his winsome personality and because he enjoyed celebrity status at a school that prides itself on its competitive athletic programs. For the class in which Wilson was enrolled, students were asked to compose a "slice of life" open media project, a multimodal representation of an aspect of their college lives.

Wilson's video starts with a media montage taken from television broadcasts that highlight his performance on the football field. On several occasions the announcers point to exceptional plays by the offensive line and even call out Wilson's name, praising his performance. After over a minute of video footage of him and the team with high-energy music pulsing in the background, the video freezes and goes silent until we hear a voiceover as Wilson introduces himself. In the next segment of the thirteen-minute video, Wilson interviews expert and non-expert sources, asking them about what they understand about the role of the offensive line in football. He starts with students, who have a more difficult time answering the question before shifting to experts including then head coach Jimbo Fisher, other players such as star running back Dalvin Cook, and "the voice of FSU football" Gene Deckerhoff. After the series of interviews, the last segment of the video shows Wilson walking the viewer through a day-in-the-life of an offensive lineman with video footage of the athletic facilities and reflections of how he understands himself as a student, an athlete, and as a father. At the time we're writing this chapter, Wilson's video has been viewed over 93,000 times on YouTube (Bell, 2016).

SAMANTHA

Samantha also chose to compose a video project entitled "Being Hispanic at FSU," where she argues that it's difficult to be Hispanic in north Florida away from her south Florida home community that has a more extensive and diverse Latinx population and culture. However, as she explains, in the process of interviewing her friends, she is surprised to learn that they have different experiences based on their own backgrounds and expectations. She begins her video with video footage of these two friends sitting on a bed talking about their experiences at college with other Hispanic students, especially those from south Florida. Since these two friends grew up in predominantly White communities in the American southeast, they explain how unprepared they were for the practices and interactions with other Latinx students from south Florida (e.g., kissing cheeks, food, music, dancing), which contrast with Samantha's experiences and expectations.

The interviews continue and are woven together with Samantha's experiences and reflections. She doesn't use any voiceover or advanced video editing techniques until about halfway through the project when she includes some general footage of campus, which at first has little to do with the content of the video. However, toward the end of the video, she includes a short clip of a university

Latinx dance club and a quick scan of the "Hispanic food section" at an in-town Walmart to show the lack of food diversity in local grocery stores. The footage of both of these scenes complements and extends the argument she is making at the time in her video. Samantha's video still exists on YouTube, and at the time we're writing the chapter it has had 540 views (Samantha, 2018). While of course lower in number than Wilson's video, given his role as an athlete, the viewership exceeds the circulation of most school-based projects.

SHERIDAN AND SUZANNE

Sheridan and Suzanne responded to a prompt about digital identities, which most students complete by drawing on personal experiences negotiating their own subjectivities. Sheridan and Suzanne chose to develop websites on a similar theme: gendered stereotypes and expectations within online gaming communities.

Sheridan was the president of a campus organization for online gaming. In addition, she was the social media manager for the campus' eSports team. One of the few women in that student organization, Sheridan was hyper-aware of her positionality in relation to "the guys" in the club. She was also well-versed in feminist arguments about sexist and heteronormative representations of gender and sexuality in video games. Her website articulates the differences between "girl gamers" and "gamer girls." According to Sheridan, a "girl gamer" welcomes and encourages the attention she receives as a woman-identifying player, often playing up her sexuality to draw attention to herself and "flirt" in the largely male-dominated space. Conversely, "gamer girls" are "serious" about their gaming. They don't draw attention to themselves and may even represent their avatars as male or androgynous, so they don't have to deal with unwanted attention. Sheridan explores stereotypical depictions of women in video games as she recounts some of her experiences as a gamer girl. Her website is constructed from a Wix template and includes combinations of visual and written texts. The design isn't as important as the argument and the narrative of her experiences, which is the evidence to support her claims. At the time she completed this project, Sheridan was planning an undergraduate thesis project, an interview-based study of an online writing group. Her personal and professional interests connected more to writing-based communities than to visuals and design, which is reflected in the final draft of her website.

Suzanne, while completing a Wix-based website on a similar topic, took a different approach. Her project on the increased inclusivity of the online Dungeons and Dragons (D&D) gaming community is noticeably more aesthetically neat and appealing. She has a drop-down menu navigation bar, and she has images for all six of what she calls "chapters" for this project. Suzanne draws attention to the strategies used by this gaming community to move away from the more male-dominated landscape to a "sandbox world" that allows storylines and characters that explore contemporary issues and are inclusive of underrepresented populations in mainstream media. Suzanne points to the fourth edition of D&D introduced in 2008 where that shift was first enacted, and she provides research and commentary on the varied response to those changes within the gaming community. She also points to "Critical Role," a weekly broadcast of voice actors playing campaigns that encourage women's participation and non-standard game play.

Suzanne, who at the time was also preparing for an undergraduate thesis, planned to continue her education in information technology. She saw herself as a creative programmer. In fact, her honors thesis is an experimental hybrid text between a creative and critical project in which she is writing and designing a webcomic that reflects her interests in non-binary character interactions within webcomics. Suzanne's professional goals and skill set are represented in this project through her design. Even so, she notes her hesitation to use a design template when she has the skills to have created her own webpages.

These student examples represent a range of multimodal projects that students often complete in all classes, but they can be more challenging for online students because of access and accessibility. In the process of adapting our course from in-person learning to online, real-time delivery, we asked ourselves: are the access and accessibility issues too great to continue having students compose multimodal projects? Or, might we be able to implement strategies and better practices that would mitigate those potential inequities?

SCHOLARSHIP, THEORIES, AND PRINCIPLES THAT GUIDE OUR APPROACH

We draw on the various versions of a multimodal project on negotiating identities to demonstrate how we believe an open-media platform assignment may address both access and accessibility issues that might prevent instructors from including multimodal assignment in an online class. We use the term "**open-media platform**" **to mean that students decide which modalities and media to use based on their own technological access, expertise, abilities, and personal/professional goals, rather than these decisions being predetermined by the instructor and the same for all students (e.g., assigning a video or podcast project).** We reject the idea that equity and fairness means that all students need to do the same things in the same ways. Instead, an equitable assignment can allow students to make choices and work in ways that meet their individual needs and circumstances. The instructor's job, then, is not to create and oversee prescribed media assignments, but rather to create project parameters and goals as well as provide guidance and support for students working in various software platforms, media, and modes.

In creating a sample assignment sheet, we take inspiration from GSOLE's Online Literacy Instruction (OLI) Principle 1, which emphasizes that online teaching should be universally accessible and inclusive, as well as Principle 3, which challenges teachers to revise online course materials and support to ensure that it is most effective in that environment. Moreover, we have found that open-media platform assignments are more than just equal opportunities for students with accessibility issues; they also align with three Habits of Mind from the WPA-NCTE *Framework for Success in Postsecondary Writing* (2011): flexibility, creativity, and metacognition. Although students might not be accustomed to making their own choices on this level, their enthusiasm and engagement on these assignments show to us how eager they are to take ownership and make these decisions. If online courses are to include open-media platform assignments, they must be designed to respond to concerns about the workload of these assignments for students with differing access to and abilities. Otherwise, the inclusion of open media platform assignments will work against the inclusive and equitable goals of online learning.

COURSE CONTEXT AND LESSON

The assignment we highlight comes from a visual rhetoric class in a major called Editing, Writing, and Media (EWM), which has become a catch-all within our English department. Since our institution doesn't have a journalism program, many see EWM as meeting that demand. Most students see it as a professional degree program for their interests in writing and publishing, and many students pair it with another professional degree such as marketing or public relations. With the exception of about 10 percent of students applying for law school, only a small number of EWM students are preparing for graduate education. Therefore, our students tend to be open to "practical" (or, perhaps more accurately, "practice-based") learning that they get from multimodal assignments like ours since they see the value in developing showcase artifacts for their ePortfolios.

Within the major, we offer three core courses that all students must take: Rhetoric, a historical survey of rhetorical theory; Writing and Editing in Print and Online (WEPO), a production-based class that explores composing practices in various media and modalities; and the History of Text Technologies (HoTT), a historically-based study of textual production with an emphasis on the history of the print technologies. In addition to the core classes, we offer a range of courses that allow students to customize their major. They can take a course on media and/or critical theory, a range of editing and textual production courses, rhetoric classes, and applied writing courses. In part because of the wide range of possibilities within the major, students don't all have the same interests in learning a variety of media production technologies or producing polished media projects. Like any group of students, they enter our classes with significantly different access to and expertise with premium computer programs like Photoshop, InDesign, Illustrator, Premiere Pro, or Final Cut Pro. However, nowhere in the description of the major are technology-based learning outcomes. Despite this, many students want to gain proficiency in software to enhance their professional profiles. Thus, our students often want to complete media production projects that include audio projects such as podcasts, web design, photo editing, and video production.

The major was designed to be taught by faculty and graduate students across the English department. While advanced doctoral students teach the gateway courses, most don't get the opportunity to teach upper-level electives. Our authorial team's collaboration began when graduate students Amory, Amanda, and Ashleah were assigned as co-teachers in a mentoring relationship with Michael in two different sections of an elective called "Visual Rhetoric in the Digital World." As fate would have it, the two semesters we taught together were also the two most drastically affected by COVID-19. In the spring of 2020, Amory and Michael were teaching an in-person section when the global pandemic caused a sudden shift to real-time online learning for the second half of the semester. By the fall of 2021 when Ashleah, Amanda, and Michael taught another section of the class, we knew it would be offered in real-time online and had the summer to plan for it.

In our case, the courses met for seventy-five minutes twice a week. Our institution has a professional site license for Zoom, which we used for full-class presentations and discussion; small group work and discussion; and screen and link/file sharing. We use the Canvas course management system to distribute online materials such as reading materials, for submitting assignments, and for grading and response. We also used third-party software such as Google Docs for workshops and collective class notes. Both courses used the same basic reading and assignment structure, but the pedagogy changed in response to the online, real-time delivery.

Course Goals

This course is designed to give students an introduction to rhetorical thinking and analysis as well as visual analysis and production. By the end of the term, students should be able to:

1. Apply rhetorical principles to a variety of linguistic and non-linguistic texts in a way that communicates their ability to provide insight about the texts;
2. Use visuals to find and communicate meaning;
3. Find, manipulate, and produce a variety of visual texts that communicate to targeted audiences;
4. Use a variety of digital platforms to deliver visual media via the internet; and
5. Create thoughtful, academic projects in a variety of media for different audiences.

Key here is the balance between theory and practice, as well as analysis and production. Much like other outcomes within the broader writing community, we note that multiplicity is highlighted in such phrases as "a **variety** of linguistic and non-linguistic texts," "a **variety** of visual texts," "a **variety** of digital platforms," and "a **variety** of media for **different** audiences." This repetition signals that a single strategy, medium, modality, or approach will not be sufficient for this class. Teaching toward flexibility and a range of possibilities is often more challenging, but the payoff for students is great as a result if they learn to navigate various contexts, audiences, and media.

Assignment Sequence

We assigned three, major multimodal projects, each of which spans four to five weeks of a 16-week semester. The first project is an "Investigative Photo Essay" in which students capture, edit, arrange, and caption a set of their own images to make and support an argument about a topic of their choosing. During this assignment, students read and explore ways in which images make meaning (Arnheim, 1969; Barthes, 1977; Foss, 2004; McCloud, 1994), how they are ideological (Rogoff, 1999; Sturken & Cartwright, 2001), and how they function socially (Adichie, 2009; Carter, 2008; hooks, 1994; Simon, 2009).

The second multimodal project, which we explore in this chapter, is called "Negotiating Identities" in which students create a multimodal production that explores visual representations of an individual or collective subject position. These identities can include everything from conventional categories (e.g., race, ethnicity, nationality, social class, gender, sexuality, disability, religion) or other ways people construct identity (e.g., work, clothing, tattoos, social organizations, athletics, music).

The final multimodal assignment is our "Monument/Memorial (Re)Design Project," which we detail in Chapter 4 within this collection. This assignment asks students to visually represent a current monument or memorial, analyze the original design, redesign it, and provide a rhetorical rationale for the redesign. While working on this project, students read about collective memory; the constructed nature of history through public monuments/memorials; and several case studies of monuments such as the Vietnam Veterans' Memorial, the Montgomery Civil Rights Memorial, the Joe Louis Monuments, and the 9/11 Memorial (Blair & Michel, 2000; Gallagher & LaWare, 2010; Hariman & Lucaites, 2003; Mix, 2015; Nicoletti, 2008; Sturken, 1991). Like the other multimodal assignments, students choose the media and modes, which have included Legos, popsicle sticks, clay, drawings/paintings/sketching, Photoshop, digital video, etc.

In this chapter, we will focus on the identity negotiation project that combines theory in identity politics and issues of social justice with a multimodal composition. As we will detail in the assignment sheet and sequence below, we progress through a range of identity-related issues to which students readily connect and have much to contribute from their lived experiences. The biggest challenge that they often face is finding a clear focus since they have many ideas they want to develop.

"Negotiating Identities" Assignment Sheet

Purpose

For this second project, you will create a multimodal production that explores visual identities of an individual or collective group. These identities include everything from conventional categories (e.g., race, ethnicity, nationality, social class, gender, sexuality, disability, religion) or any other areas that in part construct—and are constructed through—identity (e.g., work, clothing, tattoos, social organizations, athletics, music).

This project can be historical or contemporary, personal or about others. Importantly, this project must go beyond description to articulating and supporting a position on the topic. Note that some of the most interesting work in identity today lies in the overlap between identity positions. For instance, if you are exploring representations that include gender, race, and sexuality, you must grapple with the inability to isolate those subject positions from one another and instead decide how they function collectively. Since identity is not fixed and absolute, you must think of ways to represent it as fluid, constructed, and negotiated.

This is an open media platform project. In other words, all media platforms are acceptable as long as they allow you to integrate the range of modalities you need to make and support your positions to your target audience. Former students have composed their projects in a range of multimodal platforms:

digital video, slide shows, Prezi presentations, webtexts, image-embedded documents, and more.

Skills

Students will . . .

- **Identify** a topic of interest related to visual rhetoric and identities.
- **Investigate** the topic through primary and/or secondary research.
- **Determine** an angle and position to take on the subject.
- **Support** the position through argument and examples.
- **Design and assemble** a multimodal production that considers the affordances (what the technology allows for or does easily) and constraints (what challenges or difficulties will result from its use) of the chosen platform to effectively convey your argument.

Knowledge

Identities will be explored and explained as . . .

- multiple, contested, fluid, shifting,
- both seen and unseen,
- integral to how we understand ourselves in relationship with others,
- negotiated as we communicate with others,
- never neutral,
- central to the hierarchies that exist within our communication practices and, in turn, our society, and
- framed through images circulated within various communities.

Task

1. Select an issue related to visual rhetoric and identity that you want to explore for this project. In class we will explore everything from more traditional representations of identity (e.g., race, class, gender, sexuality, nationality, ethnicity, religion, disability) to other aspects of identity that might not be relevant to students (e.g., majors, jobs, clubs, families, stereotypes, clothing, body art).
2. Once you select a topic, complete some preliminary research, looking at ways that this topic is represented. Also think about how this identity issue overlaps with other identity issues and to what effect. You might also consider how this identity issue is fluid, how it changes, and/or how it is negotiated by individuals. Research might include finding traditional academic sources, and/or it might include primary research such

as capturing your own photographs, interviewing or surveying relevant subjects, collecting images and video online.
3. As you investigate the topic, look for an angle to develop a position on the subject. You need to do more than merely describe this identity position.
4. Once you have your sources and your ideas for the project, determine what media platform is best to create what you've collected for the audience you envision.
5. Conference with the instructor(s) to discuss available options and your composing plan.
6. Begin composing your multimodal project.
7. We'll have checkpoints along the way so you'll receive feedback from the instructors and your peers.
8. Consider the feedback you've received as you develop the final version of the project.
9. Complete the following reflective questions about your project:
    - How/why did you come up with your topic?
    - What primary and/or secondary research did you complete for this project? Why?
    - How did you come up with the angle and argument for this project?
    - What media platform did you select? Why?
    - What did you do in response to the feedback you received from your instructors and peers?

Criteria for Success

For this project, we will provide comments and evaluate it based on the following criteria:

- Identify and describe an issue related to visual identities.
- Develop a position about the topic.
- Provide commentary on the images.
- Organize the visual and linguistic texts.
- Edit the multimodal texts.

Overview of Unit and Activities

The following readings and activities are all part of a large scaffolding in which we hope to prepare students for the work they will need to do on their larger projects. While Unit and Project Two focus explicitly on visual identities, that theme is introduced earlier in the semester and is a thread that runs throughout the course. Irit Rogoff (1999) provides a framework to understand the work of visual culture:

Open-Media Assignment Design

1. Images are claimed by various and often contested histories,
2. Viewing apparatuses guided by cultural models (e.g., technology or narratives), and
3. Subjectivities of identification from which we view and by which we inform what we view (p. 18).

This third aspect, then, becomes the focus of our unit on negotiating identities. As Rogoff points out, visuals can never be objective or neutral, and the work of visual culture becomes responding to how cultural, ideological, political, and historical contexts shape how and what we see.

Even before we start into the unit on negotiating identities, we've already begun to explore how people view images from particular subject positions. One of our lessons has students watch Chimamanda Ngozi Adichie's (2009) "Danger of a Single Story," which many students will have seen before in middle or high school (https://www.ted.com/talks/chimamanda_ngozi_adichie_the_danger_of_a_single_story?language=en). In this TED Talk, Adichie argues that repeated narratives about someone or a group of people can become "single story" stereotypes. She describes her experiences coming to the US for college and realizing what Americans believe about Africa (and thus her) were based on singular narratives of poverty, war, disease, and starvation from the news, books, and media. Since the focus of our class is visual, we apply Adichie's concepts to the circulation of images through advertisements, movies, and other media that are so common that they create "single stories," flattening the diversity and experiences of individuals or groups. Once we've introduced this concept, we ask students to present and then complicate "single story" images, which they readily tackle by identifying visual narratives of racial or ethnic groups, student athletes, clubs and organizations, religious groups, occupations, and more.

Another way we introduce viewing subjectivities is through bell hooks' (1994) "In Our Glory: Photography and Black Life" in which she writes about Black people choosing self- representation through the photographs they display at home. The article opens with a black and white photo of hooks' father as a young man in a pool hall. He's posing in a white t-shirt, smiling for the camera. While one of hooks' sisters is mortified by the informality and "scandalous" nature of the pool hall photo, another sister is indifferent to it, but bell loves it because in it she sees something in her father that she never knew. We ask students to consider how they might view images in different ways than others and how people make different meanings of photos based on their positionality, beliefs, and assumptions. Later in the article, hooks discusses losing a picture of herself in a cowgirl Halloween costume, which devastates her because it represents what she calls "proof that there was a me of me" (1994, p. 57), something foundational to how she sees and understands herself. The lost picture is a loss of the happier moments of her childhood. Always looking to engage students in active applications of the readings, we ask students to locate pictures of themselves that they might consider a "me of me." In sharing these photos, they explore and attempt to explain how and why certain images carry deeper significance regarding their identities.

While we have other early readings and assignments on identities, these two demonstrate the kinds of activities we use to introduce the idea and to get them to apply their learning in low-stakes, media production. Thus, by the time we get to the unit on negotiating identities, students have already thought about subject positions and identities, which will help them move into their larger project. After introducing the assignment and viewing models from previous semesters, we dive into invention activities that encourage them to consider a wide range of identity-based issues.

While a difficult read for many students, Sue Hum's (2007) article on the racial gaze is a class favorite in part because she uses the original Disney cartoon *Mulan* to argue that racial representations are trivialized and erased through the processes of authenticity and universality in visual culture. Hum argues that authenticity (realism), which seems positive at first glance, reduces race to stereotypes located in images of culturally specific clothes, plants, animals, or objects that ultimately denies deeper differences as it simulates realism for the viewer. Similarly, universality (sameness) erases racial identity or makes differences seem inconsequential by simulating naturalism for the viewer.

After grappling with Hum's analysis of *Mulan*, students are eager to point to other media with the same problem, often starting with other Disney princess movies but then moving out to other films and visuals in our culture. A local connection we make to our institution is our school mascot, which remains a Seminole despite decades of protest and recent moves within college and professional sports to replace racist mascots. When college athletics first challenged our appropriation of Chief Osceola, an important historical figure who fought against European colonization, the conversation turned to authenticity, which reframed the debate away from minoritized people groups being mascots to one centered on the inauthenticity of Chief Osceola's costume. The offense wasn't the mascot himself, but rather the inauthentic, stereotypical costume. Once the problem of inauthenticity was identified, the logical solution was to provide a more historically accurate costume. Even though Hum's article is already relatable because she uses a popular Disney example, applying her ideas to another localized situation helps students see applications beyond film.

A similar lesson is based on Jay Dolmage's (2014) "Framing Disability, Developing Race: Photography as Eugenic Technology," which chronicles photographic representations of disability at the turn of the twentieth century on Ellis Island. Under the auspices of creating an objective catalog of immigrants, the photographs reinforced the "ideal immigrant" through comparisons of everything from skin color to height to the size, shape, and proximity of facial features. Thus, in one "snapshot evaluation," border officials determined the desirability and even supposed mental health and capability of the immigrant. We also read Chris Carter's (2004) "Writing with Light," that makes a similar case that the photography of Jacob Riis—who was largely understood as a progressive philanthropist—only reinforced divisions and provided a safe form of border crossing in which middle- and upper class-people could "experience" the plight of immigrants (p. 139). In response to readings such as these, students create a continuum of racial representations that purport to be progressive but instead flatten or otherwise diminish the values they supposedly espouse.

With a thread of accessibility running throughout the class and its emphasis within this second project, our goal is for students to become more aware of themselves as viewing subjects and how their viewing then shapes—and is shaped by—their identities. As such, students have developed thoughtful and engaged media projects on a range of topics—views of mental health, images of LGTBQ+ in popular Netflix shows, Catholic iconography, strong women characters in science fiction, and the list goes on and on—that investigate and explore visual representations.

REFLECTION ON PRACTICE

As we defined in the introduction, we considered access and accessibility to cover two related but distinct areas: 1) access: ownership or availability to use technologies and support for them, and 2) accessibility: the assurance that people with various (dis)abilities can equally participate in the activities, assignments, and interactions in the class. In this section, we refer to GSOLE's Online Literacy Instruction (OLI) Principles 1 and 3 as our framework for technological access/accessibility. Designing open-medium platform assignments with access in mind also opens up opportunities that align with three of CWPA, NCTE, and NWP's Habits of Mind—flexibility, creativity, and metacognition—for all students, not just those who might otherwise struggle with the assignment based on access issues (*Framework for Success in Postsecondary Writing*, 2011).

TECHNOLOGICAL OWNERSHIP AND/OR AVAILABLE USE

Online Literacy Instruction (OLI) Principle 1 states "online literacy instruction should be universally accessible and inclusive," while its tenets on accessibility and inclusivity elaborate that:

- Multimodal composition and alphabetic writing may require different technologies; therefore, those involved should be appropriately prepared to use them (Accessibility and Inclusivity Tenet #3).
- The student-user experience should be prioritized when designing online courses, which includes mobile-friendly content, interaction affordances, and economic needs (Accessibility and Inclusivity Tenet #4).

Since our real-time online students may not have had access to on-campus resources (e.g., libraries, digital studios, writing centers), we had to consider the additional constraints they might encounter with multimodal assignments. Take, for example, Wilson's and Samantha's videos from earlier in our chapter. Wilson had privileged technological access because, as an athlete, he had the equipment and video support resources in the form of a media specialist to assist him, which is reflected in the quality of his video project. Receiving technological help was explicitly allowed for this assignment as long as the students were engaged, learning, and the ultimate decision-makers in the composing process, much like we expect if they receive help from the writing center. Because of his privileged access, Wilson's final project has many bells and whistles such as spliced television footage, layered audio, and smooth cuts for transitions, not to mention access to our head football coach and other collegiate players.

Samantha's video, meanwhile, thoughtfully presents an argument that demonstrates an evolution in her thinking about identity and how her experiences might differ from others who she assumed would have shared experiences based on ethnicity. She effectively conducted primary research, and she provided observations and evidence to support her claims. The video meets all the expectations of the assignment criteria, yet Samantha's video lacked some of the splashiness of a polished video. She almost certainly used her phone to capture the audio and video, which meant the sound and picture quality were limited. The video editing software—and her expertise with it—were more rudimentary as well. Cameras, tripods, microphones, and editing software are all expensive. Likewise, Samantha had no professional goals that included video editing, so it was not in her interest to spend the time and money to acquire the software and expertise to develop a more professional video. Nonetheless, Samantha created a successful multimodal project within the constraints of her own abilities, needs, and goals, which is a primary goal of the open-media platform assignments.

Not all students have an equal need or desire to learn certain multimodal production technologies, so we lean heavily on self-motivation and personal/professional goals to drive students' choice of when they need to invest in and learn these technologies. While we provide some limited support in and out of class, our strategy is to point students to resources that will enable them to set their own expectations and meet their own goals. This is especially important because, as English instructors, we often don't have the knowledge or skills that some of our students have or might need to complete these projects. Something we regularly tell ourselves is that we don't want our own lack of expertise to limit their projects. The best way we have found to address these inequities is to allow students to make their own choices and not to penalize students who, to their credit, do thoughtful projects that may not have engaged in the same level of technological expertise.

Flexibility to Accommodate Various (Dis)Abilities

In addition to students having access to computer technologies and the support to use them to develop their multimodal projects, the "better practice" of open-media platform assignments is also mindful of the various (dis)abilities that students embody, be they physical, mental, and/or emotional abilities. The principles of Universal Design for Learning (Brueggemann, et al., 2001; Vie, 2018; Womack, 2017) encourage educators to make assignments with built-in flexibility so that disabled students do not have to self-identify or provide diagnostic evidence that might trigger an accommodation, usually in the form of more time on a project or an alternative assignment. If assignments include built-in flexibility for all students, they can proceed in ways that best fit their abilities, goals, and skills. When students are allowed to make modalities and media decisions for themselves, disabled and neurodiverse students can complete the assignment under the same description and parameters as all students. We are not the only authors to theorize the power individualization can have on creating more accessible OLI. In Chapter 9 of this collection, Ada Hubrig and Anna Barritt similarly encourage online educators to embrace a more flexible approach to drafting and revision with their "Works-in-progress" practice, giving students choice in how they illustrate their learning.

The open-media platform assignment model also corresponds closely with OLI Principle 3:

> Instructors and tutors should commit to regular, iterative processes of course and instructional material design, development, assessment, and revision to ensure that online literacy instruction and student support reflect current effective practices.

In particular, OLI Principle 3's fourth tenet is pertinent: OLI Design and Pedagogy specifies the role of the instructor is to "migrate and/or adapt appropriate reading, alphabetic writing, and multimodal composition theories from traditional instructional settings to their OLI environment(s)." We also interpret this principle as an exercise in flexibility—the ability to adapt to situations, expectations, or demands—for both instructors and students alike.

We believe it would be a shame if multimodal composition did not migrate to online classes since they are central to student engagement, creativity, and investment in writing for public audiences outside of the academy. Earlier sets of online writing principles such as *A Position Statement of Principles and Example Effective Practices for Online Writing Instruction (OWI)* (CCCC, 2013) suggested that online courses should focus exclusively on writing and not multimodality: "OWI Principle 2: An online writing course should focus on writing and not on technology orientation or teaching students how to use learning and other technologies." As online instructors, we understand this impulse. Teaching online is challenging, and certain aspects of the course need to be simplified and streamlined (see our other work, Chapter 4 in this collection, about scaffolded assignments); however, multimodal composition is not a peripheral component of the class that we'd be willing to cut to streamline the course. At the same time, we understand the various technological challenges that accompany this type of the assignment, which is why we believe it's important for students to make their own decisions about what media platforms they will use for the multimodal projects, which they can base in part on their own access and accessibility.

Habits of Mind

With an open-media platform assignment, students should be given the opportunity to reflect on their work, which helps foster three different "habits of mind": flexibility, creativity, and metacognition. The "habits of mind" refer to "ways of approaching learning that are both intellectual and practical and that will support students' success in a variety of fields and disciplines" (Council of Writing Program Administrators, 2011, p. 5).

Building flexibility into an assignment allows students to, as *Framework for Success in Postsecondary Writing* (2011), states, "approach writing assignments in multiple ways, depending on the task and the writer's purpose and audience" (Council of Writing Program Administrators, 2011, p. 9). While COVID-19 was the exigence for our course revision, it provided us with opportunity to re-conceptualize better practices as we adapted the course for online delivery. The shift to online—first in the emergency scenario of the pandemic but then in a more intentionally-crafted online course design—allowed us to reconceptualize the class for better access and support while remaining committed to multimodal composing. While we had experimented with open platform assignments before shifting online, this flexibility became essential for the way we thought about multimodal assignments in online environments in order to address our concerns about access and accessibility. For these multimodal assignments, students took full advantage of the freedom to choose.

- what identity issues to explore (e.g., race, sexuality, disability, gender, stereotypes, anxiety/depression);
- which parts of their lives to represent (e.g., family/home life, college jobs, future careers, campus organizations, extra-curricular activities, and personal hobbies);
- what media platform to use (e.g., videos, podcasts, Prezis, webtexts, photo essays); and
- what modalities to compose in (e.g., audio, visual, spatial, gestural, written, multimodal).

For Wilson, because football was such an important aspect of his personal and professional identity, his project was a slice of life on what it meant for him to be an offensive lineman on the university football team. For Samantha, her personal experiences and expectations (as well as those of her friends) were central to her argument and her representations of culture, language, food, music, and more. For Suzanne and Sheridan, their gendered interests in digital gaming communities drove the content and delivery of their webtexts. When students have the freedom to develop their own interests in digital spaces that have the possibility of reaching authentic audiences on topics they care about, their investments tend to be deeper and more meaningful.

Creativity is central to the design of this assignment as well. As educational spaces—including writing classes—are becoming more standardized and subject to top-down administration, multimodal composing itself emphasizes creativity in various forms while potentially still fulfilling more traditional objectives of the class, such as making and supporting an argument, conducting primary and secondary research, organizing or arranging materials, and even learning and using mechanics through editing. Even with those more traditional goals, multimodal composing allows for combining linguistic and non-linguistic texts, building/making a composition using a range of materials and tools, and distributing that composition broadly to academic and non-academic publics. Students, many of whom are bored or disenfranchised from years of traditional education, are often energized and engaged in multimodal composition in surprising ways. It's not uncommon for students to report that they work harder and longer on these types of "creative" projects than anything else in their college careers. Plus, they provide opportunities for students to showcase their creative prowess to potential employers, friends, and families.

As the course objectives for the visual rhetoric class hold a commitment to multimodal composing, we ask students to consider their own socially and educationally informed choices about the technologies they use to compose multimodal projects. Therefore, assigning the "Rhetorical Questions" our students write at the end of the project is necessary, as it asks them to reflect on the creative choices they made and the challenges that might have emerged when they chose a certain platform and modes to present their argument. Writing about why and how they composed something also gives them the chance both to defend their creative choices as well as to think about what they would do differently next time—such as when Suzanne noted her ambivalence of using a template when she could create her own design.

CONCLUSION

As online and hybrid classes are becoming more of the norm rather than an exception, we're excited to see the affordances they provide both teachers and students. Involuntarily shifting to online instruction and then teaching the redesigned class in a more intentional manner as an online, real-time delivery provided an interesting opportunity for us as co-instructors to consider the adjustments that we'd need to make for ourselves and the sake of our students. One point of tension for us was that we wanted to keep our dynamic, creative multimodal projects—which have long been central to the engagement and investment of students in the class—while also being mindful of access and accessibility issues of these projects as well as students' differing personal and professional goals. Therefore, we leaned heavily on our "better practice," the open media platform assignment, to address our two primary concerns regarding access and accessibility.

By allowing students to select the media platform for their multimodal projects, they had the opportunity to think about their own access to technologies, their own goals, and their own abilities, they could decide for themselves how to approach the modalities and media required of the projects. For some, it would make sense to invest in a computer, software, or the time to develop the expertise to use a particular program. For other students, that cost would not be worth the financial or personal investment. These students could still complete smart, engaging projects that fulfilled all the criteria for the assignment.

In making choices about the media platforms, students could also consider their own accessibility needs. If they had more or less aptitude or ability to work in certain media, they could make the choice about what modalities of communication (text, image, audio, or video) might be emphasized in the various programs. Students in the class were taught to make all their media projects accessible through alt-texts on images and closed captioning on videos, yet the open media platform project moved beyond that baseline to allow a more universal design appropriate flexibility in the ways students could engage with, complete, and circulate their media projects. As students consider their own strengths and limitations, they choose media platforms in modalities that best accommodate their needs and goals.

Our desire is that multimodal projects will continue to play a central role in the production assignments in our classes, regardless of the mode of course delivery. Students who take online classes should have the same access to engaging, creative course content and composition projects as students in face-to-face classes. Just because technological access and student abilities might present challenges in online instruction, we still believe that one step toward better accessibility practices include student agency in selecting the media platforms they will use to complete these assignments. In doing so, they can consider their own unique access, needs, and abilities as they determine how to develop the projects and share their voices.

MOVING BETTER PRACTICES ACROSS MODALITIES

- **In-Person, Real-Time Learning:** class sessions can be used to discuss the benefits and limitations of various media platforms they might use to complete the project task. Instructors might lead the class in an exercise where students generate a list of media platforms (e.g., Canva, Wix, iMovie). Students may use their own devices to test one platform in small groups before reporting back on their experiences to the rest of the class. In another class period, students might show each other examples of their work in formal or informal peer reviews.
- **Online, Real-Time Learning:** platforms such as Zoom have breakout rooms where students could work in smaller groups to share their screens as they plan, test, and otherwise reflect on their progress. This will allow them to discuss options and choices they are making on their open-media platform assignments and troubleshoot technical issues.
- **Online, Any Time Learning:** students could post project ideas or outlines to discussion boards or shared documents (e.g., Google Docs) where they could view and make comments on the possibilities of different media platforms.
- **Hybrid Learning:** since students are likely working in different settings and times, providing a discussion board platform or shared document might help organize the feedback regardless of when/how it's complete.

REFERENCES

Adichie, C. N. (2009, July). *The danger of a single story* [Video]. TED Conferences. http://tinyurl.com/73tzwtnw.

Arnheim, R. (1969). *Visual thinking*. University of California Press.

Barthes, R. (1977). The rhetoric of the image. In S. Heath (Ed., Trans.), *Image, music, text* (pp. 32–51). Fontana Press.

Bell, W. (2016, December 4). *A slice of life- The offensive line (FSU)* [Video]. YouTube. https://www.youtube.com/watch?v=HAPIAJcqjDY.

Blair, C. & Michel, N. (2000). Reproducing civil rights tactics: The rhetorical performances of the civil rights memorial. *Rhetoric Society Quarterly, 30*(2), 31–55. https://doi.org/10.1080/02773940009391174.

Borgman, J. (2019). Dissipating hesitation: Why online instructors fear multimodal assignments and how to overcome the fear. In S. Khadka & J. C. Lee (Eds.), *Bridging the multimodal gap: From theory to practice* (pp. 43–67). Utah State University Press. https://doi.org/10.7330/9781607327974.c005.

Brueggemann, B. J., Feldmeier White, L., Dunn, P. A., Heifferon, B. A. & Cheu, J. (2001). Becoming visible: Lessons in disability. *College Composition and Communication, 52*(3), 368–398. https://doi.org/10.2307/358624.

Carter, C. (2008). Writing with light: Jacob Riis's ambivalent exposures. *College English, 71*(2), 117–141. https://www.jstor.org/stable/25472312.

Conference on College Composition and Communication. (2013, March 13). *A position statement of principles and example effective practices for Online Writing Instruction (OWI)*. National Council of Teachers of English. https://cdn.ncte.org/nctefiles/groups/cccc/owiprinciples.pdf.

Council of Writing Program Administrators, National Council of Teachers of English & National Writing Project. (2011, January). *Framework for success in postsecondary writing*. https://wpacouncil.org/aws/CWPA/pt/sd/news_article/242845/_PARENT/layout_details/false.

Dolmage, J. (2014, March 11). Framing disability, developing race: Photography as eugenic technology. *Enculturation: Journal of Writing, Rhetoric, and Culture, 17*. http://enculturation.net/framingdisability.

Foss, S. (2004). Theory of visual rhetoric. In K. Smith, S. Moriarty, G. Barbatsis & K. Kenny (Eds.), *Handbook of visual communication* (pp. 163–174). Routledge. https://doi.org/10.4324/9781410611581.

Gallagher, V. J. & LaWare, R. M. (2010). Sparring with public memory. In G. Dickinson, C. Blair & B. L. Ott (Eds.), *Places of public memory: The rhetoric of museums and memorials* (pp. 87–112). University of Alabama Press.

GSOLE Executive Board. (2019, June 13). Online literacy instruction principles and tenets. *Global Society of Online Literacy Educators*. https://gsole.org/oliresources/oliprinciples.

Hariman, R. & Lucaites, J. L. (2003). Public identity and collective memory in U.S. iconic photography: The image of accidental napalm. *Critical Studies in Media Communication, 20*(1), 35–66. https://doi.org/10.1080/0739318032000067074.

hooks, b. (1994). In our glory: Photography and black life. In D. Willis (Ed.), *Picturing us: African American identity in photography* (pp. 54–64). The New Press.

Hum, S. (2007). The racialized gaze: Authenticity and universality in Disney's *Mulan*. In K. Fleckenstein, S. Hum & L. Calendrillo (Eds.), *Ways of seeing, ways of speaking: The integration of rhetoric and vision in constructing the real* (pp. 107–130). Parlor Press.

McCloud, S. (1994). *Understanding comics: The invisible art*. Harper Perennial.

Mix, D. (2015). In loving memory: Vernacular memorials and engaged writing. In J. Greer & L. Grobman (Eds.), *Pedagogies of public memory* (pp. 172–182). Routledge.

Nicoletti, L. J. (2008). Mediated memory: The language of memorial spaces. In C. David & A. R. Richards (Eds.), *Writing the visual: A practical guide for teachers of composition and communication* (pp. 51–69). Parlor Press.

Rogoff, I. (1999). *Visual culture reader*. Routledge.

Samantha. (2018, April 29). *Being Hispanic at FSU* [Video]. YouTube. https://www.youtube.com/watch?v=h3gX-lGQmp8.

Simon, T. (2009, July). *Photographs of secret sites* [Video]. TED Conferences. https://www.ted.com/talks/taryn_simon_photographs_of_secret_sites.

Sturken, M. (1991). The wall, the screen, and the image: The Vietnam Veterans Memorial. *Representations, 35*, 118–142. https://doi.org/10.2307/2928719.

Sturken, M. & Cartwright, L. (2001). *Practices of looking: An introduction to visual culture*. Oxford University Press.

Vie, S. (2018). Effective social media use in online writing classes through universal design for learning (UDL) principles. *Computers and Composition, 49*(1), 61–70. https://doi.org/10.1016/j.compcom.2018.05.005.

Womack, A. M. (2017). Teaching as accommodation: Universally designing composition classrooms and syllabi. *College Composition and Communication, 68*(3), 494–525. https://www.jstor.org/stable/44783578.

CHAPTER 13.
ACCESSIBLE MULTIMODAL SOCIAL MEDIA PROJECTS

Alex Wulff, Christina Branson, and Cecilia Ragland Perry
Maryville University

In this chapter, the authors describe **accessibility activities** *used across modalities: in-person, real-time learning; online, any time learning; and online, real-time learning. The activities were designed for and first utilized in an online, any time classroom. They were then adapted for in–person real-time learning and online, real-time learning. Specifically, the authors offer guidance for teaching students to learn and practice accessibility in digital multimodal writing assignments. In describing their "better practice," this chapter addresses the themes of accessibility and inclusivity and multimodal learning.*

FRAMEWORKS AND PRINCIPLES IN THIS CHAPTER

- **GSOLE Principle 1:** Online literacy instruction should be universally accessible and inclusive.
    - **1.1:** All stakeholders and students should be aware of and be able to engage the unique literacy features of communicating, teaching, and learning in a primarily digital environment.
    - **1.3:** Multimodal composition and alphabetic writing may require different technologies; therefore, those involved should be appropriately prepared to use them.
- **PARS Online Writing Instruction, Accessible**: Thinking beyond ADA compliance.
- **CCCC Principles for the Postsecondary Teaching of Writing, 2:** Considers the needs of real audiences.

GUIDING QUESTIONS BEFORE YOU BEGIN READING

- What do your students already know about accessibility, both in terms of ADA compliance and broader conceptions about why accessibility is important?

- What kinds of texts could your students design and create that would be accessible?
- What strategies can students use to make a project or text accessible?
- What can your students gain from creating a project or text that is accessible?
- Why is it important for students to learn about accessibility?

INTRODUCTION

"I do all my posts so that my friend who doesn't see well can read them. Is it ok if I caption everything?"

As soon as our student said those words, we should have realized that the social media project we were assigning our students needed to be designed with the creation of accessible content at the forefront of the project. We wish that had been our reaction.

Instead, we said something like, "Of course! Sure! That sounds great!" and it was another year before we realized that we were missing out on an opportunity to teach the importance of accessibility to our students.

While our initial "Sure!" was about answering a specific student question in a specific moment, the one-year delay speaks to a lack in our own professional development and our own thinking about access and accessibility. At this point, the educational lens we used for thinking about accessibility was focused on providing materials to our students. In their introduction to their 2013 special issue of *Kairos*, "Multimodality in Motion: Disability and Kairotic Spaces," Cynthia L. Selfe and Franny Howes point to the "need to pay attention to the teaching of composition through the lens of disability studies to remind ourselves of just how much our profession has to learn, and just how much we have been content to ignore" (para. 2).

We have a lot to learn, but we believe the changes we have made to our social media assignment have helped our program ignore less and think more about the difference between accessibility as something we produce for students and accessibility as "expression and engagement," to use Jay Dolmage's phrasing from *Academic Ableism: Disability and Higher Education* (2017, p. 145). Dolmage is looking to capture the need to see access as an action, and an ongoing one at that. To overly emphasize accessibility as a product, or a "checklist" according to Tara Wood, Dolmage, Margaret Price, and Cynthia Lewiecki-Wilson in "Moving Beyond Disability 2.0" (2014), risks turning accessibility into accommodation "we" make to "others" rather than an understanding that "disability is us" (p. 148). Instead, the authors "emphasize a dynamic, recursive, and continual approach to inclusion" (2014, p. 148).

Without such an approach, we were missing an obvious chance to show our students the importance of access, both from a legal and technical perspective that was codified in the Americans with Disabilities Act as well as an imperative for multimodal authors who are aiming to reach a wide audience. We were also missing out on the ways that having students create work that was inaccessible to some of their classmates undercut the other accessibility efforts we had been making such as using proper heading structures in our student-facing documents and adding alt text to images that we build into the course materials. We were thinking of our courses as content to be made accessible, rather than opportunities to engage our students in a broader understanding of the need for accessibility to be created, produced, distributed, and engaged with on a consistent basis. We were making accessibility a checklist rather than a receptiveness to access. In short, we had not done enough in terms of critically reflecting on the choices we were giving to our students.

We have come to believe that it is not enough to create course materials that are accessible or have environments that are accessible. Instructors in higher education need to design opportunities for students to create work that is accessible to and for each other. One of our major takeaways in committing our entire program to just this task is that our students are ready. Sometimes good pedagogy means leading students away from where they have been and what they are comfortable with. At the same time, the three of us are also familiar with having our students lead us into new pedagogical directions. This is one of those times. Our students are ready, and we need to be as well.

We certainly support the need to educate instructors on accessibility. There is work to be done in that vein, and we know we need to be vigilant there as well. At the same time, it is important that our students learn to produce accessible texts. Real-world, multimodal genres are an excellent place to do this. It can be difficult for students to see or value the rules behind APA formatting, for instance. We can help them by showing how those rules can be used to support access. For example, students might see rules about headers as overbearing or overly complicated, but we can show students how consistent heading structures can help with accessibility.

Once we realized that we needed to make a change, we got to work designing and planning implementation. Christina and Alex worked together to design the course and project updates while Cecilia piloted the first iteration of the project with her students. We knew we wanted to pilot the materials outside the designers' classrooms before we launched the changes to this assignment as a program. Because a majority of our courses are offered exclusively as online, any time learning (and because the level of technical design required can be so much higher for online courses), the pilot would be in an online, any time learning course. We wanted to make sure that our pilot met our highest design standards. Technical design elements in the online, any time learning courses include not only disability awareness, but also instructional videos, images, and integration of support services. From there, we exported the design elements to our in-person real-time course shells and into our online real-time learning course shells as well.

With our desire to impact as broad an audience as possible, we share our better practice for teaching students accessible design through a social media project from our online course, ENGL 104: Writing Across Disciplines. In this chapter, we outline our experiences with implementing a better practice for teaching students features of accessible design. We have tried to balance the need for students to have a "checklist" of sorts, without overly emphasizing accessibility as a mere product that one generates. We used considerations about audience to drive discussions and opportunities to think about accessibility as an ongoing act of engagement and inclusion.

For instance, we point out to students that even if some members of their audience consider themselves "able" rather than "disabled," they are only so temporarily. "Disability" is far closer to a norm than an exception once we consider the full life cycle of a human being. This is not a new idea in scholarship (Selfe & Howes, 2013), but it is a meaningful example for getting students to think about accessibility and their audience. While our better practice was designed for an asynchronous online course, we built the materials so that they could be used in our face-to-face and hybrid courses as well. Our initial test of the materials was in the online environment, but we are using them, with adaptations, in face-to-face and hybrid courses with great success.

It is our hope that our better practice helps students learn why accessibility matters in social media posts and how to create accessible social media posts in their online projects. We believe this practice is a way to expand and emphasize the "accessible" in Jessie Borgman and Casey McArdle's (2019) Personal, Accessible, Responsive, Strategic framework for online writing instruction. Students learn strategies for increasing accessibility, yes, and, in so doing, we hope to instill an ethos of awareness and responsibility. We want our students to see the value of creating accessible content in their future coursework and beyond. Our final accessibility goal with the social media project is to help students envision themselves as responsible for, and capable of, meeting their own accessibility needs, the needs of their peers, and the needs of individuals in their future communities.

INSTITUTIONAL AND PROGRAMMATIC CONTEXT

Access had been considered programmatically when the course, ENGL 104: Writing Across Disciplines, was redesigned by Christina and Alex to have a focus on multimodal composition. Most of our courses are taught in an online eight-week format, and the course shells are vigorously maintained and reviewed at the program level so that individual instructors do not have to retrofit materials on the fly. The institution we teach at has seen steady and consistent growth, specifically among online enrollment. Currently, the student population is 11,000 students, of which 4,000 are traditional undergraduates and over 7,000 are online, non-traditional students. Our online composition program consists of a two-course sequence: an introductory ENGL 101 course and a research-driven ENGL 104 course. Although the majority of students enrolled in these courses are adult-nontraditional learners, no parameters prevent traditional students from enrolling in online courses. This is a major consideration in the development and evolution of both courses. We believe it also means that the materials and practices we describe here can be utilized across a wide variety of institutional contexts. For 104, the cornerstone project is the research-based multimodal social media project. This project is an opportunity for students to learn and practice information and media literacy skills. Additionally, there is a focus on writing for a real and specific audience.

As a program without a firewall between our in-person real-time students and online any time student populations, all of our student populations can take our online courses. Because of this we had long ago created shells in our LMS for all instructors who taught in our composition program that meet Web Content Accessibility Guidelines (WCAG)[1] for our online and in-person students. These courses were carefully curated and audited to meet internal and external accessibility standards (like WCAG). Learning designers and faculty alike were involved in auditing the content in these courses. Our program has focused on this understanding of accessibility for a number of years, with our course shells designed to be accessible for students.

For example, we ensure that all Word documents are created with accessible heading structure and styles. We also create our materials to have color contrast and build in alternative text for images. When our university introduced *Blackboard Ally* as an automated means of scoring the accessibility of course shells, we were able to see that our shells were 95 percent accessible. We were able to hunt down the remaining 5 percent of problems and confirm that it was caused by documents being offered in multiple forms, with some options being deemed less accessible by *Blackboard Ally*.

In fact, one of the reasons we began to provide pre-made shells for all instructors was to impact the design of the content provided. It was simply too much to expect individual adjunct instructors to design the kind of robust environment

---

1 Learn more about WCAG guidelines at https://www.w3.org/standards/

we wanted students to experience in our LMS, while simultaneously creating and maintaining content that was accessible to all students. When instructors did add new content, we encouraged them to keep accessibility at the forefront of their planning and design.

In previous versions of the course, the social media project in ENGL 104 was an opportunity for students to publish their research findings in a multimodal format. In thinking about accessibility, we realized that the project had the potential to do more. We were already selecting and researching a relevant audience, but with the updated project, we could now focus on ensuring students were considering inclusion issues. For instance, we want them to consider that some members of their audience cannot see images.

In the first week of ENGL 104, students are introduced to the social media project and decide on a research topic. The role of the instructor at this stage is to guide students through the process of constructing an open-ended question that is a viable research topic so that they can explore and present it through the entirety of the course. A common challenge for students at this stage is taking a topic of interest, formulating a question that lends itself well to the project, and identifying a target audience. When providing feedback to students on potential research questions, we advise them to consider the importance of identifying a target audience. When generating ideas for research questions, we guide students in drafting both open and closed questions. Through this process, students are guided to consider the audience they will want to reach. For instance, a student might be thinking about addressing PTSD research. What segment of the population with PTSD does that student want to examine? What type of research might that population be interested in? What does the audience already know? Answering these kinds of questions can help a student direct their research.

One other benefit of focusing on a real audience so early in the course is that students are asked to think about who they want to talk to before they completely nail down what they want to talk about. The "Who" in this construction is more important than the "What." We want them to know that content always depends on the audience. We are making this for people, and those people have needs, wants, desires, goals, and habits.

Because students are asked to consider who they want to address, we have a chance to get students to see the importance of accessibility. If a student selects college students in the United States as their audience, we ask, "Do you want to reach college students or only college students who can easily access information in certain formats?" We found that students understand the overt implications of this kind of ableism. They want their project to reach all college students. Instructors can even use this opportunity to show students information about disability in an audience. For example, 19.4 percent of post-secondary students report having a disability (National Center for Education Statistics, 2018).

In week two, students begin working on their audience analysis assignment. The importance of this assignment to the scaffolding process of the social media project cannot be overstated. Students identify and analyze the strengths, weaknesses, threats, and opportunities of their target audience, which is crucial to formulating a plan for their research and the social media platform they choose. For instance, someone looking at college students as an audience might focus on how many hours the average college student works. Then, they would have to decide if this kind of information is a strength or weakness of their audience. Later in the project, they could use this information to craft an appeal to their audience.

Students' ability to craft a good research question and comprehension of the audience analysis is predictive of their successful completion of the project, and thus the course. The accessible and targeted version of these learning outcomes helps students better understand the importance of all abilities in their target audience. Considering the needs of an audience is a foundational element in this project where students can more clearly imagine an audience beyond their instructor. Writing for a real audience lines up with *Principles for the Postsecondary Teaching of Writing* (2015) outlined by CCCC: "Sound writing instruction considers the needs of real audiences." This also has implications for instructors who need their students to produce more accessible texts.

Our experience teaching this project—with a focus on accessibility—proved mostly positive for students. Students invested themselves into the idea of creating accessible documents quite quickly. There was no resistance in student communication, discussion boards, or conferences. When Alex taught the project with this focus for the first time, he openly lamented that it had taken him this long to figure out that this was, indeed, the way the project needed to be taught, and his students simply agreed. In all of our classes, many students produced documents that provided only passing evidence of having considered that making documents accessible involves rhetorical choices. Yet, each of us had experience with students asking wonderful questions about accessibility.

Of course, students always have questions navigating assignments, especially when those assignments are scaffolded (too many directions, perhaps, yields even more questions) and high stakes (as a summative assessment worth a good deal of points in the course). The students in Cecilia's section had never designed texts with accessibility in mind prior to this experience. However, the questions received during this term were more targeted and focused than those that speak simply to a student's lack of understanding of the assignment and thus missed previous module learning outcomes (i.e., weeks one through five). For example, a student using Facebook to address the importance of mental health services for children during the COVID-19 pandemic regularly attended office hours to work through drafting various posts and discussing how to make them accessible.

Our Field's Complicated Relationship with Multimodal Pedagogy

Outside of our own institution, the word "multimodal" is not without its controversies. While all textual interactions are multimodal (Norris, 2004), multimodal pedagogy is a flash point in composition studies. Because no discipline can lay claim to fully understanding something like Facebook, and because the pace of multimodal growth seems to move faster than any single discipline is up for the chase, the place of multimodal pedagogy within our own discipline has been fraught with conflict.

We acknowledge this conflict. Multimodal pedagogy is not a solution so much as a challenging field experiencing growth. This is why we focus on the OLI principle that "Online literacy instruction should be universally accessible and inclusive" to the point where we extend this to students' writing, let alone our own course materials (*Online Literacy Instruction Principles and Tenets*, 2019). We want students to focus on preparing accessible, multimodal texts. We believe this helps emphasize the importance of audience, and of writing clearly, writing inclusively, and making intelligent rhetorical choices writ large.

For some scholars, composition scholarship about multimodal communication is valuable, but pedagogical approaches to helping students understand how to compose multimodal projects may actually get in the way of scholarly pursuits (Dobrin, 1997). In defiance of this position, Jonathan Alexander and Jacqueline Rhodes (2014) argue that we must embrace the multimodal writing tools our students already use by reasserting the place of the student in our formulations of what we teach. We echo Alexander and Rhodes and hope that multimodal pedagogy can amplify the relevance of what we teach for students.

We think multimodal pedagogical advancements are all the more important because our students are reading and compositing in rich, multimodal environments, whether we feel ready as a discipline for them to do so or not. As Ryan Shephard (2018) has argued, "Students may not perceive their digital and multimodal writing as connected to classroom practice. Because of this, they may have a challenging time using writing knowledge learned in digital spaces to help with their academic writing" (p. 103). We want to help our students make this type of transfer.

Accessibility is usually introduced as a concern for instructors only: and, indeed, instructors' courses should be accessible. In fact, as stated, the first OLI principle outlined by GSOLE in their *Online Literacy Instruction Principles and Tenets* (2019) is that "online literacy instruction should be universally accessible and inclusive." Furthermore, the NCTE's "Definition of Literacy in a Digital Age" (2019) states that our students should be able to "explore and engage critically, thoughtfully, and across a wide variety of inclusive texts and tools/modalities" (para.2). . This is an important first step, as we have argued above, yet it is not enough.

As Douglas Eyman and colleagues point out in "Access/ibility: Access and Usability for Digital Publishing" (2016):

> As creators of content, students need to be aware of access/ibility concerns. With this knowledge, students can make better rhetorical decisions and create texts that increase the potential for all readers to make meaning from those texts (Teaching Access/ibility section, para. 2).

Having students create accessible documents—like those using images or videos that require captioning in order to be accessible—is a chance to emphasize to our students that captioning, like all writing, involves choices.

As Sean Zdenek has pointed out in *Reading Sounds: Closed-Captioned Media and Popular Culture* (2015), captions are interpretive acts. They are never the same as the sounds they turn into text. Student projects vary and the importance of choice in captioning can vary with those choices. Sometimes students include images in their projects more as an aftereffect rather than something integral to the project. The use of a picture that appears more "decorative" than integral can make it difficult for the student to see the choice involved in captioning. When captioning an image, students are indicating the purpose or the intent behind the choice of image. If an image is purely decorative, the caption may reflect the limitations of the student's choice. Our instructors can use this as an opportunity for discussion, but we also know that we are introducing the concepts. We are not expecting mastery.

In sum, having students share work where choice is more apparent can help students see the importance of choice, even as their own work may not point in this direction. It may be that in a context outside of an introductory course, instructors would want to grade students on the creating context that makes choice more apparent. For us, we are more concerned that a student's introduction to accessibility is not punitive and, instead, opens generative conversations about how to design for all users.

COURSE CONTEXT AND LESSON

ENGL 104: Writing Across Disciplines is the second of our university's two-course composition sequence. In ENGL 104, students commit to a research question and identify the needs of an audience early in the course. They then invest heavily in finding and evaluating multiple sources. Students use those sources to analyze their audience, develop a proposal for completing a social media project to address their research question, and then work towards publishing the social media project. The research and writing projects that students have completed up to the midpoint in the semester build to the social media project described below.

Teaching Outline for the Accessible Social Media Project

Purpose

The social media multimodal project is a culmination of the research completed for the previous writing assignments in the course (audience analysis and proposal). Students use the research they have completed in addressing the research question through a social media platform.

For the social media posts, students summarize, analyze, and synthesize the information from their research to demonstrate a conversation with the sources. We emphasize that students should be aware of their chosen audience, making decisions about their writing based on this group they have in mind as an intended audience. This conversation teaches students how to also build accessibility features into their social media posts to be more inclusive.

Skills

Students' work on the accessible social media project connects with various skills:

- Write an engaging—that is, an informative, argumentative, evaluative, and coherent—research project based on finding, reading, interpreting, analyzing, critiquing, and synthesizing sources.
- Produce research-based writings using library sources and evaluate additional sources from outside the library.
- Use quotations, paraphrases, and summaries correctly and appropriately.
- Build accessibility features into social media posts.

Knowledge

This project will also help students to become familiar with content knowledge related to composition:

- Understand that writing is a social process.
- Read, and be prepared to read, texts in diverse genres and disciplines in order to prepare them for a world increasingly complex, digital, and elusory in its textual representations.
- Develop skills in academic literacy, including critical reading, writing, summary, audience analysis, textual analysis, synthesis, and argument.
- Develop skills in digital literacy, including gathering and vetting sources, the evaluation of visual media and data, and the creation of digital arguments.
- Apply knowledge of rhetorical concepts and situations by tailoring writing to audiences and genres that are academic, professional, and public.
- Take a project-based-learning approach to learning and use key rhetorical concepts for addressing a specific, public audience.

Teaching and Learning Tasks

Introduction to Project

For the social media multimodal project, students summarize, analyze, and synthesize sources to create an informed argument that addresses their research question.

Posts will be customized to appeal to students' chosen audience. Discussing the needs of an audience leads to teaching students how to build accessibility features into their social media posts to be more inclusive with audience connections.

Using Images

Each post that students publish on their social media project is accompanied by an image. We direct students to use Pexels (https://www.pexels.com/) and/or Unsplash (https://unsplash.com/) for relevant images.

Example Instagram Project

Before getting too far into the project, we guide students in examples of posts that we have created on a model Instagram project. This video walks through sample posts from our Instagram.

Project Recipe

The social media project should consist of at least 16 social media posts:

- Eight summary posts—posts should include a summary of the source in your own words,
- Four analysis threads—posts should include your original evaluation of one source,

- Three synthesis threads—posts should create a dialogue between multiple sources, and
- One accessible infographic (with the option to create a second infographic in the place of the third synthesis post).

Social Media Prewriting—Part 1

The first step of the social media project that students complete is the Social Media Prewriting—Part 1 assignment. This prewriting assignment is a chart that students use to make a plan for using the sources they have gathered throughout the course. The chart is an organizational tool to provide structure and direction for the project.

Social Media Multimodal Project Prewriting Chart

Directions: Complete the prewriting chart for your social media project (shown below). You will be using the chart to organize your sources. Add the names of your sources in the boxes. Each numbered box represents one post in your social media project.

Infographic	Synthesis	Analysis	Summary
What sources can you use for your infographic? You will want multiple sources because the infographic is a visual synthesis. Write the names of your sources below.	What sources can you use for your synthesis posts? You need at least two sources for each. Write the names of the sources.	What sources can you use for your analysis posts? Write the names of the sources in the boxes below.	What sources can you use for your summary posts? Write the names of the sources in the boxes below.
Infographic 1	Synthesis 1	Analysis 1	Summary 1
			Summary 2
		Analysis 2	Summary 3
	Synthesis 2		Summary 4
		Analysis 3	Summary 5
			Summary 6

Social Media Multimodal Project Prewriting Chart: Model

Directions: Complete the prewriting chart for your social media project. You will be using the chart to organize your sources. Add the names of your sources in the boxes. Each numbered box represents one post in your social media project.

Infographic	Synthesis	Analysis	Summary
What sources can you use for your infographic? You will want multiple sources because the infographic is a visual synthesis. Write the names of your sources below.	What sources can you use for your synthesis posts? You need at least two sources for each. Write the names of the sources.	What sources can you use for your analysis posts? Write the names of the sources in the boxes below.	What sources can you use for your summary posts? Write the names of the sources in the boxes below.
Infographic 1 "Women and Girls in STEM" "Closing the Gender Gap through STEM"	Synthesis 1 "How to Get More Girls Involved in STEM" "Girls Now Outnumber Boys in High School STEM" "Best Science Jobs" "Best Engineering Jobs"	Analysis 1 "Girls Now Outnumber Boys in High School STEM"	Summary 1 "How to Get More Girls Involved in STEM" Summary 2 "The Next Generation of Girls in STEM"

SOCIAL MEDIA PREWRITING—PART 2

Next, students move into the Social Media Prewriting—Part 2, which is a discussion board in the course LMS. In this discussion, students create their first post for their social media project, which is a synthesis post using two or more sources. In their responses, they provide feedback to two classmates. The purpose of this prewriting discussion is to get started on the writing for this project and get feedback before completing all of the posts.

Information on Accessibility in Writing Posts

We then present instructions on how to build accessibility features into the social media project along with a rationale for why this is important. As noted above, millions of people have a visual impairment. To increase inclusiveness and to reach more members of their audience, they need their social media posts to be accessible. While this better practice in developing alternative text has been tailored to a series of social media posts, asking students to develop accessible descriptions is a meaningful practice across all aspects of multimodal composition. Readers could easily pair this practice with other multimodal chapters, such as Wimberly and colleagues' Monument/Memorial (Re)Design Project (Chapter 4) or Wood and Stewart's TED Talk or Cajita video (Chapter 11). It can also be transferred to other social media driven instructional practices, like Eagle, Falter, and Donovan's #TeachWriteChat practice (Chapter 7).

Students watch a YouTube video showing a person with a visual impairment using Instagram (Rath, 2018). The video also walks through the steps to add alt text.

Accessibility Features for the Social Media Project.

1. Students can consider using hashtags at the end of each post to build engagement. Capitalizing each word in a hashtag instead of having all lower-case letters is better for accessibility. Example: #AccessibilityInSocialMedia
   a. Why? When people are using a screen reader, the reader will be able to distinguish between separate words. If words are all lower case, they can be jumbled.
2. Students can use emojis in their posts, but they should be strategic and use no more than two per post. Emojis should be placed at the end of posts.
   a. Why? Screen readers will read the emojis, which can be time-consuming and may interfere with your message. Example: "smiling face with sunglasses, winking face, thinking face" can, eventually, become distracting.
3. Each post should have an image. Students should add alternative text for image descriptions to describe the content of the image.

Why? Alt (alternative) text can be read by screen readers.

> Ok: Ice cream
>
> Good: Two chocolate ice cream cones
>
> Better: Image of two chocolate ice cream cones in waffle cones upside down in stainless steel metal tray of chocolate ice cream with a plain, white background

Adding alt text to images gives students training in adding accessibility features to their writing. Additional work in building accessibility features could contain opportunities to develop more nuanced work for alt text and captioning. For example, if students were to include an interview in their social media project, more detailed captioning would be appropriate. Our assignment scaffold is meant to start a dialogue that individual instructors can tailor to their courses and the projects students create within them.

Figure 13.1 provides an example that we offer to students.

Accessible Multimodal Social Media Projects

Figure 13.1. Example of alternative text generation (Unsplash, 2023).

Our instruction also includes a table for instructions for how to add alt text for their choice of social media platform. Please note that these instructions are a heuristic and were accurate as of early 2023; the interfaces of these platforms have changed in the past—and will change again in the future

Instagram:
1. Upload image
2. Choose Filter or Edit, if desired
3. Click Next
4. Click Advanced Settings
5. Click Write Alt Text
6. Write a description of the image. How would you describe it to someone who is visually impaired? Do not say "image of" or "photo of"
7. Click Done/Save

Facebook:
1. Choose image
2. Click Edit
3. Write a description of the image in the alt text box. How would you describe it to someone who is visually impaired? Do not say "image of" or "photo of"
4. Write a caption in the caption box. You can use the caption to add context.
5. Click Save

Note: Your caption will appear with the photo in your post. The alt text will not appear and will only be read by the screen reader.

Twitter/X:

1. Write your tweet
2. Click on Photo
3. Attach photo
4. Click Add Description (there might be a button on the photo with an +ALT)
5. Write a description of the image. How would you describe it to someone who is visually impaired? Do not say "image of" or "photo of"
6. Click Done

CREATING THE INFOGRAPHIC

As part of the social media project, students also create an infographic. The infographic also presents an opportunity to build accessibility features into the project.

To make the infographic more accessible, we encourage students to include a transcript or summary of their infographic in the caption/text of their post that can be read by a screen reader.

We also present an infographic from WebAIM (an organization that works to make web content more accessible) that captures features of accessible design (WebAIM, 2022; https://webaim.org/resources/designers/). Key elements from this infographic include:

- Students should plan for and use headings in their infographics.
- Students should be intentional with choosing colors that have higher levels of contrast.
- Students should use a font size that makes the text easier to read.

PROJECT GRADING CATEGORIES

To present students with a clear idea of how they will be assessed on the social media project, we include grading categories for the project.

- **Infographic (1):** The infographic is a visual way to present research and information. The infographic should be aesthetically appealing and easy to read. It should be easy for the reader to digest the information presented. The infographic should show evidence of careful and thoughtful planning in what information to present and how. The infographic should also show evidence of careful design choices. The caption for the infographic should include a detailed description of the information as well as images.

- **Summary (5):** The summary posts should clearly and accurately capture the main ideas from the original source. The summary should be written completely in the student's own words and be written in a way to encourage the reader to pursue the linked source.
- **Analysis (3):** Analysis posts/threads should include the student's original evaluation of one source, offering his/her summary and critique of the source. The analysis should be crafted in a way that would encourage a reader to click on the link of the analyzed source.
- **Synthesis (3):** A synthesis requires students to combine multiple sources, creating something new, with a clear argumentative purpose. The synthesis should encourage the reader to follow up on the linked sources.
- **Audience Awareness and Style Choices:** Audience awareness is a significant component of this project. Did you use the research and analysis of your audience to make choices when presenting your argument? Keep in mind the expectations of your audience, including their specific needs for accessibility. Your project should be accessible per WCAG standards. Did you build in accessibility features for each type of post and your infographic?
- **Habits of Mind, Process Management, Peer Review(s), and Revisions:** Habits of mind are patterns of behavior or attitudes and develop over time. Habits of mind include openness to interactive revision. Writing is a recursive process; therefore, it is expected that you engage in this process. You will participate in peer reviews, giving and receiving feedback to make updates.
- Creating multimodal products also includes **larger project management skills**, such as time management, as well as the ability to collaborate with others in diverse and interactive situations. How has your social media project improved consistently over time?

REFLECTION ON PRACTICE

While students creating accessible social media projects has been a recent development for our program (other than the instances where students were already doing this by themselves), it has largely been a welcome addition from students' perspectives. In part, in relation to all the assignments for the course, we accounted for the additional labor that it takes to make posts accessible and reduced the overall number of posts required for the project.

Many of our learning experiences within this project have come over a long period of time. The project has been a successful part of our program for four years. Still, students raise concerns, especially when using social media. For instance, some students express privacy concerns. This is an easy fix, as we can encourage students to make their accounts private. They are still fulfilling the outcomes of learning while maintaining their online privacy.

When teaching this practice for the first time, educators may see that students need help creating social media accounts. To support these students, we have found that providing links to online help guides and tutorial videos, as well as supporting students one-on-one have been the most successful strategies.

Some students remain wedded to more traditional research genres, and struggle to translate the findings of their research into social media posts. We have supported students in this challenge through multiple strategies. First, they get some experience with writing about their sources through a previous project in the course, the annotated bibliography. For the annotated bibliography project, they have already searched for, evaluated, and written about several of their sources. We encourage students to recycle (or, perhaps more accurately, "upcycle" and improve their use of) these sources, as well as to revisit their original notes, all as they prepare for their social media posts. We also break the "types" of posts into summary, analysis, and synthesis so that students can see a direct relationship between social media and some of their more traditional academic assignments.

Another strategy that has proven valuable is the use of templates. We have crafted a set of templates for the summary, analysis, and synthesis posts. Students rely on these templates to help them get started on some of their posts and build confidence. We want students to move away from these templates as they progress through the assignment, but taking away the blank page can help students get started. We have also had some success with having students generate their own templates as a prewriting exercise after initially using instructor generated templates. For example, after writing one synthesis post, we have asked students to collaborate to brainstorm templates for another synthesis post.
Composite student sample:

> One article, _____, provides an overview of _____. At the same time, it discusses _____ and _____.
>
> In fact, in another source, ___, the author presents ____. These points are meaningful because ___. Finally, ___ this leads to ___.
>
> For takeaways, both sources approach _____, which tells us _____. Based on the reading of these two sources, _____. Overall, I would suggest that _____.

There may be some topic choices that become problematic. For instance, a student researching middle eastern peace accords found it difficult to educate his audience without receiving hateful responses. To address these issues, we sometimes encourage students to select a topic that connects to their program or professional goals. Students can also make accounts private.

We have found what this assignment does well, and we have addressed many of the challenges outlined above. As an added benefit, we have found that students are able to transfer their research and writing skills directly into future coursework in their disciplines.

When students give feedback on the social media project, we hear about its relevance and meaning for them. Publishing their message through social media allows students the opportunity to communicate and connect with a real audience. We also believe that the project works well for teaching responsibility in publishing research and information.

CONCLUSION

The first principle outlined by GSOLE in their *Online Literacy Instruction Principles and Tenets* (2019) is that "online literacy instruction should be universally accessible and inclusive" and to leave students' own work out of that principle means we will always fall short of universal accessibility. That said, we do understand that universal accessibility is not an achievable goal. Accessibility needs are always shifting. Introducing students to creating accessible documents and content for their peers and specific audiences is a means of introducing them to accessibility concerns and sets them on the path of addressing it in their further academic work and careers. It is a start, but one we think is a best practice that is taking shape. Students are ready to do this kind of work. They are receptive to it. We already have the language we need in our guiding documents and principles.

Our own assignment is an example of a project that seemed to be waiting for this change. We know that other assignments may be more challenging to adapt. Yet, in many of those cases the adaptations may be quite small. If students are producing excel spreadsheets rather than social media posts, there are ways to make Excel spreadsheets more accessible. We have work to do as educators to keep educating ourselves on accessibility. We can help future educators by educating them as students.

MOVING BETTER PRACTICES ACROSS MODALITIES

- Hybrid Learning: While this practice began in our online, any time classes, we have now taken the practice into our in-person, real-time and online, real-time courses. The adaptations we make in both modalities could also be used in the hybrid learning environment. We take the opportunity of in-person class meetings to work collaboratively on accessibility features with real-time feedback from the instructor. Students can give peer feedback on accessibility in these environments, which can reinforce the practice. We believe similar engagement strategies would work in a hybrid environment.

REFERENCES

Alexander, J. & Rhodes, J. (2014). *On multimodality: New media in composition studies.* Conference on College Composition and Communication; National Council of Teachers of English.

Ball, C., Boggs, J., Booher, A., Burnside, E., DeWitt, S., Dockter, J., Dolmage, J., Eyman, D., Gardner, T., Georgi, S., Hinderliter, H., Ivey, S., Keller, M., Kelley, R., Kennedy, S., Kennison, R., McClanahan, P., Ries, A., Roberts, K. . . . Zdenek, S. (2016). Access/ibility: Access and usability for digital publishing. *Kairos: A Journal of Rhetoric, Technology and Pedagogy, 20*(2). https://kairos.technorhetoric.net/20.2/topoi/eyman-et-al/index.html.

Borgman, J. & McArdle, C. (2019). *Personal, accessible, responsive, strategic: Resources and strategies for online writing instructors.* The WAC Clearinghouse; University Press of Colorado. https://doi.org/10.37514/PRA-B.2019.0322.

Conference on College Composition and Communication. (2015). *Principles for the postsecondary teaching of writing.* National Council of Teachers of English. https://cccc.ncte.org/cccc/resources/positions/postsecondarywriting.

National Council of Teachers of English. (2019.) *Definition of Literacy in a Digital Age.* https://ncte.org/statement/nctes-definition-literacy-digital-age/.

Dobrin, S. I. (1997). *Constructing knowledges: The politics of theory-building and pedagogy in composition.* SUNY Press.

Dolmage, J. T. (2017). *Academic ableism: Disability and higher education.* University of Michigan Press.

GSOLE Executive Board. (2019, June 13). *Online literacy instruction principles and tenets.* Global Society of Online Literacy Educators. https://gsole.org/oliresources/oliprinciples.

National Center for Education Statistics. (2018*). Table 311.10. Number and percentage distribution of students enrolled in postsecondary institutions, by level, disability status, and selected student characteristics: 2015–16* [Data table]. U.S. Department of Education, Institute of Education Sciences. https://nces.ed.gov/programs/digest/d20/tables/dt20_311.10.asp.

Norris, S. (2004). *Analyzing multimodal interaction: A methodological framework.* Routledge. https://doi.org/10.4324/9780203379493.

Rath, J. (2018, November 29). *How blind people use Instagram!* YouTube. https://www.youtube.com/watch?v=767YJe7R-2Y&t=155s.

Shephard, R. (2018). Digital writing, multimodality, and learning transfer: Crafting connections between composition and online composing. *Computers and Composition, 84,* 104–113. https://doi.org/10.1016/j.compcom.2018.03.001.

Selfe, L. & Howes, F. (2013.) Over there: Disability studies and composition. *Kairos: A Journal of Rhetoric, Technology and Pedagogy, 18(*1). https://kairos.technorhetoric.net/18.1/coverweb/yergeau-et-al/pages/index.html.

Unsplash. (2023). *American heritage chocolate, chocolate ice cream* [Photograph]. Unsplash.com. https://unsplash.com/photos/DCRQC41u2U8.

WebAIM. (2022). *Web accessibility for designers.* https://webaim.org/resources/designers/.

Wood, T., Dolmage, J., Price, M. & Lewiecki-Wilson, C. (2014). Moving beyond disability 2.0 in composition studies. *Composition Studies, 42*(2), 147–150.

Zdenek, S. (2015). *Reading sounds: Closed-captioned media and popular culture.* The University of Chicago Press. https://readingsounds.net/.

CHAPTER 14.

REFLECTIVE LEARNING IN DATA STORYTELLING

Christopher E. Etheridge
University of Kansas

Heidi Skurat Harris
University of Arkansas at Little Rock

This chapter describes **reflective activities to strengthen data literacy** *in hybrid learning. Specifically, the authors consider the role of reflection to highlight how data knowledge can advance student progress toward professional or personal goals. The reflective activity is then used as a foundation to reinforce both conceptual and operational definitions of data. In describing the "better practice," this chapter addresses the themes of multimodal learning and practices in motion across teaching and learning.*

FRAMEWORKS AND PRINCIPLES IN THIS CHAPTER

- **PARS Online Writing Instruction, Strategic:** Focusing on the student user experience (UX). After all, students are our primary users!
- **PARS Online Writing Instruction, Personal: Showing** your students you are a human! Writing is personal and teaching is personal so make it that way in your OWC. Build community and foster instructor/student & student/student connections.
- **Framework for Success in Postsecondary Learning, Metacognition:** The ability to reflect on one's own thinking as well as on the individual and cultural processes used to structure knowledge.

GUIDING QUESTIONS BEFORE YOU BEGIN READING

- In what ways does having accurate and reliable data improve progress toward your personal or professional goals? Can you think of a personal example?

- What is the benefit to you of reflection? When you think about past experiences, how does the process of *reflection*, beyond *just recalling* those experiences, benefit you?
- How do you talk to your students about how they create evidence of learning? What are the ways that students demonstrate to you that they have learned?

INTRODUCTION: WARY STUDENTS AND THE REFLECTIVE PROCESS

Often, one of the first questions on the first day of class in a data analysis course for communicators in our mass communications program centers around how *difficult* the class might be. After all, the course is ostensibly about data and numbers and these students come to the program to be *writers*. They want to pursue the story, not the numbers. They are well aware of the trope that *writers don't do math*. Even *some* math might be problematic, so a class called "Data Storytelling" awakens the terror inside all of us.

Even readers not familiar with how to construct a data story have seen data storytelling in action. For instance, as police use of force has become increasingly scrutinized in the United States, *The Washington Post* has published a searchable database of police shooting incidents since 2015 (https://www.washingtonpost.com/graphics/investigations/police-shootings-database/). Each election cycle since 2008, FiveThirtyEight.com (ABC News, 2020, 2022) has attempted to forecast the winner of American elections—check out examples from 2020 and 2022 (https://projects.fivethirtyeight.com/). The attention this model received, especially for presidential elections, has spawned several other popular forecasts.[1] In public health communication, the Coronavirus Resource Center at Johns Hopkins University published and regularly updated the COVID-19 Dashboard for nearly two years during the Coronavirus Pandemic (https://coronavirus.jhu.edu/map.html). The dashboard became an essential tool for researchers and the public alike to understand the spread of the disease.

Data storytelling combines evidence in the form of data with compelling visuals and a narrative to communicate insights (Ojo & Heravi, 2018). Data literacy (characterized well by Javier Calzada Prado and Miguel Ángel Marzal,

---

1 These include *The Economist's* pre-election forecasts (https://projects.economist.com/us-2020-forecast/president), *Politico's* 2020 election forecast (https://www.politico.com/2020-election/race-forecasts-and-predictions/president/), CNN's 2020 Electoral College outlook (https://www.cnn.com/2020/11/02/politics/electoral-college-outlook/index.html), and CBS' Battleground Tracker (https://www.cbsnews.com/2022-us-battleground-tracker/).

2013) is in demand in the various communication fields. *The New York Times* has called data journalism an "essential part" and "an increasingly common" aspect of their news content (Baquet et al., 2022). So, even for our students who may not think that data storytelling is a compelling career choice will come to realize that data storytelling is all around them.

The instructors of this newly developed course at a large midwestern university in Fall 2021 were fully expecting students to be wary of the course material and concept. Data Storytelling had only recently been added to the mass communication curriculum and was designed from inception to be a hybrid learning course with both online, any time learning and in-person, real-time learning components. The online, any time learning components included short videos featuring professional communicators who use data in their jobs and videos produced by the instructors focused on specific components of what is termed "the Data Project Lifecycle" (Bobkowski & Etheridge, 2023).

This lifecycle argues that data literacy can be improved by instruction that builds first from collection of data to then cleaning and transforming data to, finally, analysis of data and communication of results. Students answered questions about the videos in the online, any time learning content for weekly course credit. In the in-person, real-time learning component, students practiced the data storytelling skills such as data collection, data cleaning, data analysis, or communicating using data to reinforce the online, any time learning material. Each semester, the instructor developed a single class-wide (across the multiple sections) shared dataset on a single topic to use for examples and for student projects. Previous shared datasets have included state-wide high school characteristics, traffic data near the university, college basketball teams and postseason tournaments, Titanic survivor records, or recent Olympics results.

Students who were accepted to the school—offering a single major with concentrations in journalism media arts, or marketing communications—were required to take this new course. Development of the class was motivated by internal research conducted on the school's curriculum and course offerings. Recent graduates had told a study group of faculty and staff reviewing the curriculum that they would have liked to have had more opportunities to improve skills in data storytelling as students. Likewise, professional communicators in positions to hire recent college graduates said they were looking for candidates with a demonstrated ability to incorporate data into their writing and production across platforms. As we established earlier in this chapter, data literacy and numeracy—the ability to tell stories that emerge from data—are skills in high demand in many communication fields. This increased focus on data in this mass communications program paralleled an initiative campus-wide, especially in the social sciences, to grow data literacy course offerings. Data storytelling was a part of an interdisciplinary data science certificate organized by faculty from the computer science and psychology departments.

The faculty and staff study group indicated that the skills developed in a data storytelling course were important in two key areas of professional communication. First, a comfort with writing with and about numbers has shifted from a useful to an essential skill. Surveys have shown that many communication programs—in social science-focused media studies as well as more humanities-focused writing studies and applied communication—lack a strong offering in contemporary data literacy practices (Bobkowski & Etheridge, 2023). To be sure, journalism and other writing programs long ago developed "computer-assisted" writing courses. There students learned that simply including numbers in content created without accurately reflecting the meaning behind those facts and figures (what is defined here as *literacy*), can give the audience a false sense of objectivity and misrepresent a true accounting. Mass communicators ply their trade on a foundation of trust. Viewers, readers, listeners, and audiences of all kinds must believe and understand that content creators have taken the time and effort to understand the context, climate, and environment in which a story unfolds. In a digital world this slate of course offerings needs to increase.

Second, those hiring managers queried by the curriculum study group said that professional writers in modern communication careers *were expected* to be able to read and interpret digital and social analytics data that help content creators understand what audiences want from that content. Courses on content creation do not consider the growing need for an understanding of digital audience metrics, engagement data, and analytics (Dunwoody & Griffith, 2013; Gotlieb et al., 2017; Martin, 2017; McLaughlin et al., 2020). Using data to support development of content can display the content creator's authority on a topic but only when used accurately and transparently. The sense of data-driven decision-making needs to be cultivated in our fields.

However, as noted above, instructors in Data Storytelling knew that students in the mass communication program were budding writers in part because of their passion for *the story*. Whether they were inspired by a love of communication or following a path into mass communication driven by an uncomfortableness with scientific information grounded in hard facts, the hard truth was that *data and statistics knowledge* was not found to be inspirational to budding scribes.

To achieve a level of confidence whereby students could write effectively both with and about numbers, instructors felt it was important to demonstrate the accessibility of numbers as support for the kinds of content they were used to creating in previous courses. To do this, they identified key moments in the course where students could demonstrate to themselves that they were learning the material through assignments that allowed students to reflect on their data literacy and demonstrate connections between the course content and their lived experience.

In this chapter, we discuss one example of how instructors seized on the feeling of reticence among students in the Data Storytelling course and used metacognitive approaches to ameliorate this fear, helping students build confidence in their learning, and demonstrate how identifying personal experiences and connecting them to skills and concepts students were learning could benefit them in their future careers or even personally. By providing opportunities for students to recognize moments where they have already encountered data, the assignment and discussion outlined below build students' self-confidence, which has a demonstrated ability to improve learning outcomes (Steele, 2011). To develop this better practice, we draw from The Conference on College Composition and Communication Committee for Best Practices in Online Writing Instruction's (2013) *Principles for the Postsecondary Teaching of Writing* as well as the *Framework for Success in Postsecondary Writing's* (Behm et al., 2017) adaption of Arthur Costa and Bena Kallick's *habits of mind* (2000).

DON'T CALL IT "REFLECTION"

We recognize that "reflection" can sometimes—especially among students—be identified as simply thinking about the process or thinking about the experience. Reflection can mean students writing about their thoughts and feelings throughout a course or activity. Students can keep a journal or record video entries about their experience throughout a course. Reflective components can additionally complement major projects. Ashleah Wimberly and colleagues (Chapter 4, this collection), for instance, highlight a reflective "rhetorical rationale" assignment that students complete alongside their memorial/monument redesign project. This component tasks students with reflecting on the choices they made and how those choices align to their rhetorical goals for the assignment. These kinds of activities are important to the learning process.

In practice, however, we have found that students do not always take reflective practices as seriously as they might other assignments. As college instructors, we have additionally found that assessment of these kinds of activities can be difficult. Students' pre-conceived notions of reflective practice can structure their responses to "reflection activities." Because of this, we are wary to call the types of activities we discuss in this chapter "reflection" in the assignment descriptions, framing our activities simply as "thinking about a time where data did or could have benefitted you." Students may then reflect on experiences without thinking about the activity as a performative "reflection assignment." In doing so, we hope that students will more easily see the connections we are trying to create—to make data, an often new and different concept, one that is more familiar and comfortable.

In this chapter, our *better practice* highlights activities that allow students to recognize what they *have* learned in the course *by connecting ideas in the material to personal experiences or goals*. Specifically, we want students to *know* that they can incorporate numbers—from demographic data to survey results to sports statistics to crime rates to social media analytics and more—into their communication approaches because these activities have already laid the groundwork to allow them to see where data literacy might benefit them. In this course, we used structured reflective learning activities to address students' discomfort with numbers, highlighting ways that numbers already exist in students' lives.

Writing studies—and communication studies more broadly—have a rich history of reflective writing both as a means of writing practice and an assessment tool (Huot, 1996; Irvin, 2020). Reflective learning practice in mass communication writing instruction has clear benefits to retention of knowledge, demonstration of learning, and reinforcement of the educational experience (Burns, 2004). Reflective thinking in some form has been advanced in professional and educational settings for nearly a century (Dewey, 1933; Rogers, 2001; Schön, 1983). Donald Schön (1983) identifies reflection as "the dialectical process by which we develop and achieve, first, specific goals for learning; second, strategies for reaching those goals; and third, means of determining whether or not we have met those goals or other goals" (p. 6). Likewise, the Conference on College Composition and Communication's Committee for Best Practices in Online Writing Instruction explicitly recommends the use of "the inherently archival nature of the online environment" to "encourage students to rhetorically and metacognitively analyze their own learning/writing processes and progress" (2013, p. 14).

Kathleen Blake Yancey (2016) defines reflection as "tightly focused on the mental activities of the composer in the process of composing" through three reflective practices: "reflection-in-action," "constructive reflection," and "reflection-in-presentation" (pp. 3–4). We draw from Yancey's rich characterization of reflection to demonstrate how students can connect to the course material through constructive reflection, or reflecting on how text is interrelated with identity, and reflection-in-action, or reflecting upon relationships between the writer and the text.

In doing so, we also recognize the important contribution of Jesse Borgman and Casey McArdle's (2019) Personal, Accessible, Responsive, and Strategic approach (PARS) to online writing instruction by focusing on the student experience as they work to understand the role of data in storytelling (*strategic*) and showing students the human aspects of learning by empathizing with their concerns and providing instructional scaffolding to support their learning (*personal*).

Additionally, the *Framework for Success in Postsecondary Writing* (Behm et al., 2017) advances the idea that *metacognition* can be achieved through prompting students to examine processes they use to think and write and connecting choices they have made in previous work to improve subsequent projects. These are all important learning approaches that have shown to improve outcomes.

Moreover, data literacy requires a rhetorical understanding of data communication, including 1) the audience, 2) the situation, 3) the available data, and 4) the medium. Reflective writing allows students to practice rhetorical analysis with data literacy, thus encouraging them to look beyond assumptions of objectivity in quantitative data. Numbers, just like words, can tell a story. The students' role is to interrogate that story to ensure the data used in storytelling is represented as accurately and completely as possible.

Cultivating the "Habits of Mind"

To provide a grounded framework for developing students' data literacy through reflective practices, we incorporate Costa and Kallick's (2000) *habits of mind*, what these scholars call "a disposition toward behaving intelligently when confronted with problems," to create practical and actionable tasks that achieve the stated goals of metacognitive, strategic, and personal learning. We present a scenario where students can demonstrate mastery of data literacy in both concept and operation. The habits of mind framework for solving problems include emotional responses such as finding humor in a situation (Habit #14) or more rational responses such as managing impulsivity (Habit #2).

Recognizing that students were coming into the course with high anxiety about the subject matter drew us to highlight how important students' disposition and individual problem solving would be in confronting the course material. For our purposes, we think of data literate habits of mind as responding mindfully and personally when asked to process and explain sets of data. Communicators are often tasked with addressing tasks with personal distance and objective thought. These practices are important. However, for students to internalize learning they must attach it to personal experiences, goals, feelings, or outcomes. This is where the habits of mind are advantageous.

Quite simply, this framework gives educators 16 mindsets for creating an environment where students can be confident they have learned. In the following sections, we highlight one example assignment that uses reflective practices to identify connections between habits of mind and data literacy. For important context, we also describe the class discussion that led into the assignment. Later, we describe how this lesson could be adapted to in-person, real-time; online, real-time; or fully online, any time learning.

COURSE CONTEXT AND LESSON

DATA LITERACY THROUGH OUR EXPERIENCES

To demonstrate how data literacy and reflective learning were interconnected in this data storytelling course, this section of the chapter discusses one key moment early in the course where students were given the opportunity to identify relationships between data and their personal experiences. This reflective moment centers around the conceptual and operational definitions of data, which are important ideas in the first several weeks of the course. After presenting the assignment, we will then describe what occurred in the classroom that led into the assignment, followed by additional context about the structure and design of the hybrid learning course.

This assignment was developed in part as a result of the instructor's observation of reticence among students early in the in-person, real-time learning component of the course. He quipped on that first day of class that a common sentiment among writers—both professional and amateur, across disciplines and fields—was that they *became* writers because there wouldn't be any math in their jobs. Heads nodded among the students. One student nervously asked how challenging the course was going to be for students who were uncomfortable with numbers. Another added that they were thinking about switching majors after seeing what this course was about. The instructor anticipated these types of questions. However, the connection between establishing a foundation of previous knowledge among the students and connecting that knowledge to the concepts in the course was not as apparent as it would become until an important opportunity to assuage their fears and make the learning more relevant arose.

He explained on that first day that data storytelling required a *comfort* with data but not an *expertise* in data. Data storytelling centered around *understanding* how and when numbers, facts, and figures improve a story and help the writer tell better stories. This was reinforced by professional communicators who were in a position to hire recent graduates. They wanted early career professionals with "spreadsheet wherewithal," (Bobkowski & Etheridge, 2023) not necessarily a cadre of coders and statisticians. Developing advanced knowledge of statistics and data manipulation would be an option for students who were interested in taking additional courses on the topic through an interdisciplinary data science program, but this course focused primarily on *data literacy*, or simply knowing when was a good time to use numbers, where to find them, and how to incorporate them seamlessly into a story.

A few days later, as a way to address these overlapping concerns, the instructors developed an assignment using the Transparency in Learning and Teaching (TILT) framework (Winkelmes, 2013; Winkelmes et al., 2016). This activity is scaffolded to position students to respond clearly and concisely with artifacts that allow them to demonstrate both conceptual and operational definitions of data. In development of this sample assignment, we focused specifically on question and problem posing (Habit #7), applying past knowledge to new situations (Habit #8), and gathering data through all senses (Habit #10) from Costa and Kallick's habits of mind (2000). More than simply "reflecting" on a past experience, this assignment asks students to explore how skills in the course could have benefitted them in the past and could benefit them in the future.

We provide students with a prompt we use to assess skills they should be bringing with them from previous coursework as well as new concepts we are introducing. We provide reminders about skills they have learned in previous courses (a story includes necessary context, such as who, what, where, when, and why) and ask them to demonstrate their ability to communicate with those skills. We use personal experience as a backdrop for asking students to explore new concepts in data literacy.

Assignment: Where Can Data Be Found in Your Life?

Purpose

One of the objectives of this course is to "Understand the essential role of data in journalism and strategic communication workflows." In previous courses, you have seen how generating topics for your news stories, news releases, videos, and audio projects from experiences and observations is an essential part of your future career. In this assignment, you should draw on a personal experience to show how data can enhance a story. Don't worry about newsworthiness or news value for this assignment. Just think about a time in your life where *more* data would have benefitted a personal situation and write about it. Include where you might get those data and what characteristics of those data would be necessary to tell a better story.

Skills

The purpose of this assignment is to help you practice identifying sources of data and to think critically about where valid data could be found to enhance your storytelling. For this assignment, you should demonstrate how datasets have *observations* (defined as the individual events that occur and are captured in the rows of the dataset) and *characteristics* (defined as the aspects of each case that are different). For example, your transcript shows all of the classes you have taken (cases) and their characteristics such as semester taken, class number, course title, and grade. Formatting your transcript as a dataset allows you to more easily calculate your grade-point average.

Knowledge

This assignment will also help you to become familiar with the following important data storytelling concepts:

- Identifying valuable narratives in mass communication
- Sourcing data (for example, kaggle.com or github.com)
- Cases and variables in data
- Using evidence to support narratives

Task

In this assignment, you should:

1. identify a story from your own life that might be expanded or improved by supporting data and write about that experience in as much detail as possible (about 200 words), and
2. in a separate paragraph (about 200 words), describe the data that might improve or support that story. Identify sources of these data. Describe why you think these data are valid. Then, describe the cases and characteristics of these data. Be sure to include what characteristics you might analyze to include in the story from your own life.

We have discussed how data should have cases (observations in rows) and variables (characteristics of those observations in columns). Another example: If you wanted to know what percentage of people in class wear glasses, you would need a list of the people in the class (cases) and whether they wear glasses or not (a variable). In what you submit for this assignment, highlight how many cases you think your data might have and what characteristics your data might have.

Example scenario: Let's say you tried to convince your parents over the summer to let you spend a semester studying abroad. First in this scenario, write a paragraph on where you wanted to go, when you wanted to do it, why you thought it would be a good experience, and what you said to your parents. Then, identify where you might find good data to support your argument. You might try a Google search for information about study abroad programs and learning outcomes. You might see if the KU International Affairs office has data showing why study abroad programs are beneficial. In that second paragraph, describe what the data might look like. You're not citing facts and figures about study abroad here; you're trying to imagine how someone might measure if students who study abroad do better in their future jobs or earn more or that they express a higher satisfaction in life.

Criteria for Success

This assignment will be assessed in three ways and is worth 15 points (5 points for each part; 5 = fully present down to 0 = not present).

- All three parts below will be assessed in part on professional use of grammar, punctuation, spelling, and tone.
- Part I: Did your experience include enough detail that someone who was not there could understand it fully? Make sure you include the Who, What, Where, When, Why, and How of the story.
- Part II: Do you identify possible data sources to support this experience? Do you discuss how you know the sources of data are valid and reliable?
- Part III: Do you identify the cases and characteristics of the data? Did you connect those variables to the experience you outlined in the first part?

BETTER PRACTICE IN ACTION

While a planned assignment such as this example is constructed with the ideal outcome in mind, as educators we know that meeting students where they are is a critical skill. In this section of the chapter, we highlight the experience of one instructor as he introduced the conceptual and operational definitions of "data" and then described this assignment to students.

In this vignette, the Week 2 in-person, real-time learning session of the course opened with a discussion of the terms that comprise the name of the course. The assignment above was then distributed and discussed. At the start of the class session, students were asked to define for themselves the terms "data" and "storytelling." They were given five minutes to write down a definition for each term. They were then told to share their definitions with someone sitting close to them in the classroom. After students thought about their definition and shared it with a partner, the instructor asked if students would like to share what they wrote with the entire class. Giving students time to think about a concept and then share it in a small group can help students build confidence in their responses (Azlina, 2010). This confidence can then help facilitate a more robust discussion as students grapple with ideas that are being introduced to them for the first time. The process is sometimes called "Think. Pair. Share."

The instructor returned the discussion to the entire class after the small-group period and opened the floor to volunteers who might describe their definition of "storytelling." In the activity outlined above, "storytelling" serves as a foundation upon which data sits and is a skill students should be more comfortable with. This can serve as a stronger starting point in the whole-class discussion. Students providing a clinical definition of storytelling itself was not as important as the activity of asking students to recall previous experiences with storytelling and then formulate what they know goes into a storytelling narrative.

In mass communication coursework, students are exposed to the idea that a good story must focus on the experiences of individual actors in the story. The anecdote drives the narrative. For journalists, the "rule of three," where three sources make a story, guides the foundation of reliability and veracity. For strategic communicators, the personal experience of an employee, a customer, a fan, or a member of an organization can be highlighted to support the organization's goals. Conceptually, data in mass communication builds on this idea of a "source" by recognizing that the aggregate experiences of hundreds or thousands of individual sources can serve to elaborate on the anecdotal experiences featured in a story. By having students define the term "storytelling," the instructor was giving students a launching pad to think about what they know of sources. Data storytelling is, in essence, the same kinds of sourcing practices they performed in previous classes, but with hundreds or thousands of sources, rather than one, two, or three.

When students were asked to share their definition of "storytelling," the classroom went silent. Silence is valuable to a discussion because it gives students time to collect their thoughts. Silence is also uncomfortable and eventually the discomfort will build to a point where a student jumps in to speak. (In the online, any time learning environment and to a certain extent in the online, real-time learning environment, the "silence" tool is not one available to the instructor. We offer some suggestions for how to address that issue later in this chapter.) After some prolonged silent awkwardness, one student said a story was an experience that a person wished to share with others. Another then said that storytelling was the act of communicating. A third added that she was not sure how to define it but offered to give an example. Early in the semester, students and the instructor were still getting to know each other, so supportive statements that facilitate discussion wherever it may go can be valuable.

"Examples are important ways to communicate definition," the instructor said. "So what's your example?" This student described a situation where she was nearly hit by a car earlier that day on campus, adding the location and time of the incident. This example was in-fact a clear story with contextual details that allow a writer to build a narrative. To drive the discussion toward "data storytelling," the instructor asked the class if that intersection was particularly dangerous. Students did not know. Then the instructor asked if students knew what the worst intersection was on campus. Students did not know. The opportunity to discuss the conceptual and operational definitions of data presented itself and so the instructor shifted to that line of thinking.

He told the class to hold on to what they have written about "data" and "storytelling." They were going to work with this student's example to explore possibilities of data storytelling. All stories need a source. Students were familiar with the idea of a source of information. In previous courses, they had discussed how to identify and scrutinize individual sources in news content. As stated above, conceptually, data can be thought of as the aggregation of many sources. The instructor told the class that the student's experience at the intersection that day was one source and a valuable story. Data to enhance this story could simply be the collection of many individual experiences at that intersection. When considering even broader scopes, the data could be the collective experiences of individuals at many intersections across campus, the city, the state, or the country.

The instructor then asked students, drawing on their personal experiences, to identify the variables that would be considered to evaluate the "worst" intersection on campus. The class brainstormed that car-to-car accidents, car-to-person accidents, car-to-bike accidents would have to be considered. Then the instructor prompted the students to consider the degree of severity in the evaluation. For instance, an accident causing a fatality would be worse than an accident-causing injury but not fatality, right? Of course. Then students were asked to identify where these data may be gathered. Students were given time in class to identify possible sources for these data. The goal of this activity was to demonstrate how narrative or storytelling ("I almost got hit by a car") could be an opportunity to explore how data or evidence ("How many people are hit at this intersection a year?") might help provide important context to that story.

This discussion builds from Habit #7 in Costa and Kallick's habits of mind (2000) model: question and problem posing. Students were asked to reflect on how they knew something to be true—the danger level of an intersection—and what evidence they needed to demonstrate that truth—how many people have been hit at the intersection or how many accidents there have been at the intersection. This behavior could most closely align with what Yancey (2016) termed "constructive reflection" or the act of "developing a cumulative . . . identity" (p. 14). As Yancey noted, constructive reflection and reflection-in-action are closely aligned. In this experience, we think about the role of reflection in classroom discussion as "constructing" the knowledge that will be demonstrated in the practice activity.

Through personal and strategic approaches to this discussion (Borgman & McArdle, 2019), the instructor was drawing students closer to an operational definition of data with this line of questioning. Data has two important components: cases and characteristics. The characteristics are often called variables and cases are sometimes called observations. In this course, students would be asked to functionally place the cases in the rows of a spreadsheet and characteristics of the cases in the columns to create a dataset. By the end of the course, students should be comfortable with the terms "cases," "observations," "variables," and "characteristics."

He asked students to think about how they would find out how many accidents occurred at an intersection. "Police reports," said one student, drawing from previous coursework about sourcing. The instructor nodded and asked "what if a car goes through an intersection but does not get into an accident. Could that be an important measure of the level of danger at the intersection?" The conversation continued, eventually establishing that "danger" might be designated as the number of *accidents per cars that go through the intersection*. In this scenario, cases would be the number of cars going through an intersection and the characteristics of each case would be to determine if the car gets into an accident or not. This was the first introduction in the class to "rates," which would be a valuable tool to compare differences in cases. In social media analytics, professional communicators want to know the volume of engagement with content as well as the rate at which people engage (reactions per number of followers). Thus, "rates" would also be a term with which students should be comfortable by the end of the course. "So both the number of accidents at an intersection as well as the number of accidents per cars going through the intersection are important," the instructor said, summarizing and concluding the discussion.

At this point, the instructor told students that repeating this activity they had done together in class would be one of their assignments for the week. They were to think of a story or experience in their lives that might be made better by data and then think about the cases and characteristics of that data. The instructor could then assess the degree to which students had a grasp on "data," both conceptually and operationally. As students reflected on their past experiences, they were expected to apply new knowledge to a past situation (an adaption of Habit #8). Additionally, they were prompted to pose questions (Habit #7) about where the data to support their story might originate and think about how they might gather data through all senses (Habit #10).

Whether they knew it or not—or welcomed it or not—they were becoming data storytellers.

EXAMPLES FROM STUDENTS

In this section, we summarize two strong examples that students submitted for this assignment. The first example is practical and applicable to the student's professional goal to be a social media manager. The second example is from a student who is a fan of college baseball and enjoys making predictions about games and the season as a whole.

The student who wanted to be a social media manager discussed an internship where she was a part of a team developing a strategy to build sales online. She wrote that the company analyzed their online traffic, but it appeared that most of the evidence used to determine where their efforts would be best applied was anecdotal or based on where other organizations in the industry were putting their attention. The student believed that this approach would not capture a new audience because much of the in-house discussion focused on the company's website. In the second section of the assignment, she discussed how the company had access to data such as "time spent" on the website as well as "clickthroughs" and "engagement" on social media, yet they were not considering what they could learn from this data. She wrote that cases could be "social media posts" or "time spent" on each page of the website.

The second student wrote a more personal narrative about being interested in college baseball from a young age. He learned about players on different teams and followed them as they went from college to professional leagues. He wrote that he would like to develop a dataset to determine what qualities made a college player a good "major leaguer." He proposed using baseball players who had played in college and were now in the major leagues as cases in the dataset. He proposed characteristics such as height, weight, position, and college statistics to include.

The feedback the instructor wrote on the first submission centered around the broadness of the scope of the idea. Social media users behave differently than website users. The student may want to consider how to differentiate between the two. By narrowing the scope of the analysis, the cases and characteristics needed to complete an analysis would become clear. The instructor's previous experience indicated that time spent narrowing students' scope on a topic early is valuable in the end. In the second example, the instructor wrote that the student should think more about the concept of a "good" baseball player. What statistics might be more illustrative of "goodness?" Further, what defines "good?" This could be different over time, but it could also be different by position. The student may want to consider analyzing data only of position players or pitchers. He may also want to consider differences over decades. Further, the instructor encouraged the student to avoid superlatives that reduced the analysis to a binary. Is a player "good" or "bad?" Well, there are many factors that go into it. Instead, reframe the question, such as: "Does high fielding percentage in college lead to high fielding percentage in the pros?"

COURSE DESIGN

As a component of a professionally focused mass communication program, the hybrid learning environment of this data storytelling class was designed to mimic what students might find in a technology-laden working world such as a newsroom or an advertising agency. The hybrid learning design of the course was structured to provide both online, any time and in-person, real-time learning situations, similar to what might exist in many of those workplaces.

The course was capped at 30 students and met in a classroom with mobile desks and chairs to allow for small groups to coalesce in different formations and sizes. Attendance was not recorded in the in-person, real-time learning sessions in an attempt to give students the maximum flexibility during and after the COVID-19 pandemic. However, students were still expected to demonstrate knowledge of the material delivered each week.

In this section of the chapter, we further explore the structure of the course, the learning outcomes and other assignments. The course was designed to be delivered in a hybrid learning format with one weekly in-person, real-time learning laboratory session for structured discussions of and elaboration on the online, any time learning course material made available through the course management system at the start of each week. Students watched a series of brief (five- to ten-minute) instructional videos each week on portions of the Data Project Lifecycle model (Bobkowski & Etheridge, 2023) as well as three- to five-minute practical-focused videos that featured an interview with alumni of the program who use data in their professions. After watching and taking notes on these videos, students responded to a prompt for a small amount of points (10–20 each week out of a total of 900).

Following the Data Project Lifecycle model, the first five weeks of the course examined the capabilities and uses of spreadsheeting software such as Microsoft Excel, including sorting and filtering data, using functions to transform data, and generating pivot tables for analysis of the data. Data manipulation skills in this course were limited primarily to data validation, generating ratios, creating tables for displaying data, and visualizing data. The course's narrow scope aligned with the argument that all professional communicators should be comfortable performing basic calculations using spreadsheets but would not be expected to write code unless it was expressly a part of the job for which they were hired.

The middle portion of the course explored visualization of data using self-guided instructional tutorials for the online, any time learning portion and deeper, more robust discussions about the purpose of visualizations such as The Pudding's Heat Records (https://pudding.cool/projects/heat-records/) and USA-Facts.org's analysis of rent increases during the Coronavirus pandemic (https://

usafacts.org/articles/where-are-rents-rising-post-covid-19/) were held in the in-person, real-time learning portion. The Financial Times' Visual Vocabulary (2021) is a useful tool to discuss effective ways to communicate data graphically (https://www.ft.com/content/c7bb24c9–964d-479f-ba24–03a2b2df6e85). The final third of the class was reserved for students to develop and produce their own data stories, including drafting, revising, and refining the content with regular feedback from the instructor.

Additional assignments after each of the first two thirds of the course were designed to provide opportunities for summative assessment. After the first five weeks, students were tasked with identifying a professionally written data story from one of a list of "data-driven" online outlets and write a "biography" of the data, assessing the degree to which the author of the piece transparently described the source and transformation of the data as well as the conclusions that came from that manipulation. This assignment was repeated at the end of the semester to allow students to demonstrate growth throughout the course. After 10 weeks of the course, students were to submit a demonstration of how they self-directly learned a visualization tool such as Flourish (https://flourish.studio/) or Tableau (https://www.tableau.com/) they identified as being beneficial to Data Storytelling. Self-directed learning was also highlighted by graduates and hiring managers as an important skill in professional communication.

As a final summative project in the course, students were expected to produce a data story by the end of the semester for inclusion in their professional portfolios. Course designers allowed students to develop summative projects that demonstrated data storytelling fitting their individual educational goals. In the course, students found a topic that interested them and either generated their own data or manipulated secondary data related to their subject to tell a compelling story. Students were encouraged to find a topic related to the shared dataset—on a topic selected by the instructor and data curated jointly by students in the class—but were not required to do so.

Some examples: Students who were working towards a career in sports communication could create final projects analyzing coaches' salaries across college sports in the semester where the shared dataset topic was college athletics. In the semester where a state-wide high school database was the topic of the shared dataset, students interested in teaching as a career could use it to identify post-graduate destinations. Outside of the shared dataset, a student interested in international studies could find and analyze data on military spending by country. A student interested in fashion could develop a dataset on features of different fashion house websites. The final project analysis might be delivered in the form of static or interactive infographics, timelines, maps, charts, or graphs, among other types of data visualization.

With a few adjustments, we believe the course content could be transitioned to fully in-person, real-time learning; online, real-time learning; or online, any time learning environments because of this project-based assignment model the instructors developed. For example, the online, any time learning videos produced by instructors could be converted to live lecture/discussion sessions for in-person, real-time learning or online, real-time learning. The in-person, real-time learning sessions of Data Storytelling could be converted to more scaffolded low-stakes practice activities guided by written or audio instruction for fully online any time learning. Additional suggestions for modality shifts are included at the end of this chapter.

REFLECTING ON REFLECTING IN DATA SCIENCE

Instructors in this data storytelling course anticipated the reticence writing students would express towards data science and designed reflective learning activities to help students connect with the material and see how data could enhance their writing skills. In this section of the chapter, we discuss why the assignment highlighted above was important to the goals of the course. Then we explore how the assignment might be adapted to other modalities. Finally, we consider how multimedia might be incorporated into this assignment.

By making the experience of learning personal (Borgman & McArdle, 2019), the assignment allowed students to reflect on how data could impact their lives, yet the assignment was not positioned to students as a "reflective learning" which could bias students to respond in a way they have been conditioned to think of as "reflection." Like Borgman and McArdle, we believe that it is important not simply to reflect on learning, but to do so with strategic purpose and a connection to the course goals and learning outcomes. We and the instructors of the Data Storytelling course, one of whom is an author of this chapter, understand that professional storytelling is often inspired by personal experience or observation. The assignment outlined in this chapter required students to perform an activity many of them will hopefully continue to do throughout their career—approaching an experience with wonderment (Habit #12, Costa & Kallick, 2000) to examine the extent to which it might be a broader trend or phenomenon. After deeper exploration, perhaps the student who was nearly hit by a car would find that the data indicate the intersection where that event occurred is relatively safe compared to others on campus. Perhaps that intersection is a death trap. With a strong understanding of numeracy and data literacy, students can use their senses (Habit #10) to apply past knowledge to new situations (Habit #8).

Reflective learning has been a significant tool used by teachers for more than 100 years (Dewey, 1933; Rogers, 2001; Schön, 1983). This featured assignment as well as others in this hybrid learning course demonstrate how reflection can build data literacy skills. With only one in-person, real-time learning session weekly, the hybridity of the course required structuring assignments and discussions that could be recalled after a full week of other classes, part-time jobs, club meetings, and other tasks. We believe that the personal experience aspect can help address that obstacle.

The assignment is adaptable to other modalities. For example, the in-person, real-time learning discussion detailed in this chapter could be conducted over video conferencing software in an online, real-time learning or through a discussion board in an online, any time learning course. In the any time environment, instructors could ask students to write a story in the first week of class they believe could be enhanced by data and other students could annotate their thoughts about how data might be applied to the scenario using digital tools in the following week to develop community in online environments. We appreciate that technology affords us the ability to use different interactive tools across modalities. The chat function of video conferencing software would be a useful tool in an online, real-time learning class but could even be used in a similar fashion in an in-person, real-time learning course to allow students to brainstorm without the pressure of performing in front of a class of peers.

As communication instructors, we also recognize that multimedia is a significant focus in professional programs such as ours. With that in mind, we propose that students could be asked to submit a video detailing their reflective activity or an audio file such as a voice memo recorded on a smartphone or computer. Alternatively, students could be asked to take pictures of a situation that could be enhanced by data and then write about what data could enhance the scene in the photo. These modifications to the assignment could reinforce that professional communicators use a variety of platforms and techniques to communicate.

CONCLUSION

Effective data storytelling demands that practitioners know the capabilities as well as limitations of data, understand the ethical issues and implications of data collection, and possess the logic skills to balance the limitations and issues with the capabilities and implications. Data literacy requires a knowledge of software tools available for collecting, transforming, and analyzing data. This chapter highlighted one opportunity in a course to draw on reflective learning practices in a hybrid learning environment to demonstrate the utility of data storytelling and data literacy to students, many of whom felt unprepared for the course material.

We see data literacy as crucial for future communication professionals and believe that data storytelling should be incorporated into any writing curriculum. Data literacy can contribute to skills in argumentation when data is used to support a point of view. It can also be beneficial in social science as scaling of sources from a handful to dozens, hundreds, or thousands can lead to a deeper understanding of social trends and behaviors. Further, programs that emphasize data provide students with skills to recognize how and when to respond to audience wants through analysis of digital analytics data, increasing reach, profitability, and effectiveness.

This is the way of the world now. Quantitative information processing is essential in "the increasingly mathematical complexity of our society" (Paulos, 1996, p. 3).

In this course, the instructors challenged the contention that writers are necessarily bad at math, while still recognizing that numeracy as a skill presents challenges that other forms of information gathering typical for writers in communications fields may not (Dragga & Voss, 2001). These lessons are translatable across modalities. We believe that students who reflect on their learning and the application of past knowledge to current situations can build confidence and eventually strong numeracy skills. We demonstrated how this can happen through a sample assignment and structured class discussion about the conceptual and operational definitions of "data" and "storytelling." This assignment and discussion are inspired by Costa and Kallick's (2000) framework for developing habits of mind in a life-long learner and draw from Borgman and McArdle's (2019) *personal* and *strategic* activities in online writing instruction. These practices are important to development of metacognitive skills, in which students can grow by analyzing their own work (Conference on College Composition and Communication Committee for Best Practices in Online Writing Instruction, 2013).

And while our students may still identify first as writers through words and second as data storytellers with numbers, we contend that the opportunities provided through this assignment (and course as a whole) will certainly get them to reflect on the role of data in the information they provide, the arguments they make, and the stories that they tell.

MOVING BETTER PRACTICES ACROSS MODALITIES

- **In-Person, Real-Time Learning:** Metacognition and learning through reflection occurs slowly over time. Yet, this assignment began first as

an in-person discussion and could be effective as simply that. Students can be prompted to write about their experiences for a brief period of time (five minutes) and then share those thoughts in small groups. Rather than students suggesting ways their own stories could be improved with data, the instruction could prompt students to suggest opportunities to other group members.
- **Online, Real-Time Learning:** Likewise, in real-time online environments, tools such as video conference breakout rooms can put students in small groups outside of the intimidating ear of the instructor. This gives students some free will to test ideas with their peers before stating it in a large group setting.
- **Online, Any Time Learning:** Students in writing programs benefit from repeated and frequent opportunities to write. In an asynchronous environment, students could be asked to submit work from a previous class or other experience and other students could then be tasked with using collaborative editing tools such as Google Docs or Microsoft Word Online to comment on opportunities to add data.
- **Hybrid Learning:** As currently structured, this better practice, originates from a real-time discussion where the class is able to openly exchange ideas and suggestions, critique their own work as well as others, and receive formative feedback live from the instructor. Yet, this activity has a crucial reflective element as highlighted in this chapter. Instructors should think about their goals when adapting this activity to their own classrooms. When the goal is to build camaraderie and collaboration, instructors may choose to emphasize the discussion. When the goal is to build metacognitive skills, instructors may choose to emphasize the written response. This activity works well when both are present, but these portions can function independently.

REFERENCES

ABC News. (2020, November 3) *2020 FiveThirtyEight Election Forecast*. FiveThirty Eight. https://projects.fivethirtyeight.com/2020-election-forecast/.

ABC News. (2022, November 8) *2022 FiveThirtyEight Election Forecast*. FiveThirty Eight. https://projects.fivethirtyeight.com/2022-election-forecast/.

Azlina, N. N. (2010). CETLs: Supporting collaborative activities among students and teachers through the use of think-pair-share techniques. *International Journal of Computer Science Issues, 7*(5), 18–29.

Baquet, D., Kahn, J. & Duenes, S. (2022, March 22). Expanding our data journalism ambitions. *The New York Times Company*. https://www.nytco.com/press/expanding-our-data-journalism-ambitions/.

Behm, N. N., Rankins-Robertson, S. & Roen, D. (Eds.). (2017). *The framework for success in postsecondary writing: Scholarship and applications*. Parlor Press.

Bobkowski, P. S. & Etheridge, C. E. (2023). Spreadsheets, software, storytelling, visualization, lifelong learning: Essential data skills for journalism and strategic communication students. *Science Communication, 45*(1), 95-116. https://doi.org/10.1177/10755470221147887.

Borgman, J. & McArdle, C. (2019). *Personal, accessible, responsive, strategic: Resources and strategies for online writing instructors*. The WAC Clearinghouse; University Press of Colorado. https://doi.org/10.37514/PRA-B.2019.0322.

Burns, L. S. (2004). A reflective approach to teaching journalism. *Art, Design & Communication in Higher Education, 3*(1), 5–16. https://doi.org/10.1386/adch.3.1.5/0.

CBS News. (2022, October 30). *2022 US Battleground Tracker*. CBS News and YouGov. https://www.cbsnews.com/2022-us-battleground-tracker/.

CNN. (2020, November 4). *Electoral College outlook: A remarkably stable race comes to an end*. CNN Politics. https://www.cnn.com/2020/11/02/politics/electoral-college-outlook/index.html.

Conference on College Composition and Communication. (2013, March 13). *A position statement of principles and example effective practices for Online Writing Instruction (OWI)*. National Council of Teachers of English. https://cdn.ncte.org/nctefiles/groups/cccc/owiprinciples.pdf.

Costa, A. L. & Kallick, B. (2000). *Discovering and exploring habits of mind*. Association for Supervision and Curriculum Development.

Dewey, J. (1933). *How we think: A restatement of the relation of reflective thinking to the educative process*. D. C. Heath.

Dragga, S. & Voss, D. (2001). Cruel pies: The inhumanity of technical illustrations. *Technical Communication, 48*(3), 265–274.

Dunwoody, S. & Griffin, R. J. (2013). Statistical reasoning in journalism education. *Science Communication, 35*(4), 528–538. https://doi.org/10.1177/1075547012475227.

The Economist. (2020, November 3). *Forecasting the US 2020 elections*. https://projects.economist.com/us-2020-forecast/president.

Financial Times. (2021, March 7). *Charts the work: FT visual vocabulary*. https://www.ft.com/content/c7bb24c9-964d-479f-ba24-03a2b2df6e85.

Flourish. (n.d.). *Data visualization & storytelling*. Retrieved January 2, 2024, from https://flourish.studio.

GitHub. (n.d.). *GitHub: Let's build from here*. Retrieved January 2, 2024, from https://github.com.

Gotlieb, M. R., McLaughlin, B. & Cummins, R. G. (2017). 2015 survey of journalism and mass communication enrollments: Challenges and opportunities for a changing and diversifying field. *Journalism & Mass Communication Educator, 72*(2), 139–153. https://doi.org/10.1177/1077695817698612.

Huot, B. (1996). Toward a new theory of writing assessment. *College Composition and Communication, 47*(4), 549–566. https://doi.org/10.2307/358601.

Irvin, L. (2020). *Reflection between the drafts*. Peter Lang Publishing.

Johns Hopkins University of Medicine, Coronavirus Resource Center. (2023, March 10). *COVID-19 map.* https://coronavirus.jhu.edu/map.html.

Kaggle. (n.d.). *Kaggle: Your machine learning and data science community.* Retrieved January 2, 2024, from https://kaggle.com.

Martin, J. D. (2017). A census of statistics requirements at U.S. journalism programs and a model for a "statistics for journalism" course. *Journalism & Mass Communication Educator, 72*(4), 461–479. https://doi.org/10.1177/1077695816679054.

McLaughlin, B., Gotlieb, M. R. & Cummins, R. G. (2020). 2018 survey of journalism & mass communication enrollments. *Journalism & Mass Communication Educator, 75*(1), 131–143. https://doi.org/10.1177/1077695819900724.

Ojo, A. & Heravi, B. (2018). Patterns in award winning data storytelling. *Digital Journalism, 6*(6), 693–718. https://doi.org/10.1080/21670811.2017.1403291.

Paulos, J. A. (1996). *A mathematician reads the newspaper.* Penguin.

Politico. (2020, November 2). *Who wins 2020? Presidential election predictions & key races.* https://www.politico.com/2020-election/race-forecasts-and-predictions/president/.

Prado, J. C. & Marzal, M. Á. (2013). Incorporating data literacy into information literacy programs: Core competencies and contents. *Libri, 63*(2), 123–134. https://doi.org/10.1515/libri-2013-0010.

The Pudding. (n.d.) *Tracking heat records in 400 U.S. cities.* Retrieved January 2, 2024, from https://pudding.cool/projects/heat-records/.

Rogers, R. R. (2001). Reflection in higher education: A concept analysis. *Innovative Higher Education, 26*(1), 37–57. https://doi.org/10.1023/A:1010986404527.

Schön, D. A. (1983). *The reflective practitioner: How professionals think in action.* Basic Books.

Steele, C. M. (2011). *Whistling Vivaldi: How stereotypes affect us and what we can do.* W. W. Norton & Company.

Tableau. (n.d.) *Business intelligence and analytics software.* Retrieved January 2, 2024, from https://tableau.com.

The Washington Post. (2023, July 22). *Police shootings database 2015–2023: Search by race, age, department.* https://www.washingtonpost.com/graphics/investigations/police-shootings-database/.

USA Facts. (2023, March 23). *Where are rents rising post COVID-19?* https://usafacts.org/articles/where-are-rents-rising-post-covid-19/.

Winkelmes, M. (2013) Transparency in teaching: Faculty share data and improve students' learning. *Liberal Education, 99*(2).

Winkelmes, M., Bernacki, M. L., Butler, J., Zochowski, M., Golanics, J., Weavil, K. H. (2016). A teaching intervention that increases underserved college students' success. *Peer Review, 18*(1/2).

Yancey, K. B. (2016). *A rhetoric of reflection.* Utah State University Press.

CHAPTER 15.
RETOOLING DECISION-MAKING IN A/SYNCHRONOUS ONLINE LITERACY INSTRUCTION

A. Chase Mitchell
East Tennessee State University

Rich Rice
Texas Tech University

In this chapter, the authors describe the intentional development of transferable asynchronous and synchronous professional skills used in both online real-time and any time learning. Specifically, the authors discuss the importance of highlighting student communication modality as part of design-making. In describing a "better practice," the chapter addresses the themes of practices in motion across teaching and learning modalities, and professional learning for online teachers.

FRAMEWORKS AND PRINCIPLES IN THIS CHAPTER

- **PARS Online Writing Instruction, Strategic:** Focusing on the student user experience (UX).
- OLI Principle 1.1: All stakeholders and students should be aware of and be able to engage the unique literacy features of communicating, teaching, and learning in a primarily digital environment (https://gsole.org/oliresources/oliprinciples).

GUIDING QUESTIONS

- Do you have asynchronous and synchronous tools that you prefer to use in your teaching?
- What are technological affordances and constraints of these asynchronous and synchronous tools?
- What are ways in which some students might benefit from the use of some tools, and other students benefit from other tools?

DOI: https://doi.org/10.37514/PER-B.2024.2241.2.15

- Can students achieve the same goals and objectives using different tools?
- What kinds of reflection can be helpful in getting students, themselves, to see the value of the use of different tools to engage specific users in specific content given specific situations and contexts?

INTRODUCTION: RETOOLING DECISION-MAKING IN A/SYNCHRONOUS ONLINE LITERACY INSTRUCTION

Yellow Zoom-hands light up the interface of an online media studies course. Engaged faces populate the screen, floating and bobbing with varied background messiness in each video feed. Initially, there's an awkward overlap of student voices speaking over one another. For those who can't get a word in, the chat box rapidly fills. But there are many points to reply to, affirming a diversity of voices coming through the speakers. Students discuss the course reading questions without too much prodding. The Zoom call with its chat is becoming a space where students feel comfortable contributing through audio, video, text, and emoting. For those who need more time, key points can be added to the discussion board later. They've overcome what some students and many teachers call "Zoom fatigue," because the students are truly engaged. There are many ways to communicate, and students are learning how to do so given the content and situation. They're learning that both the medium *and* the message is important in effective communication, delivering the right message in the right amount at the right time. A community-based, shared netiquette slowly emerges. As we look at this intensive moment of student engagement, we pause to consider: what's really happening here and what brought about this experience?

SCHOLARSHIP, THEORIES, AND PRINCIPLES THAT GUIDE OUR APPROACH

Flexibility and adaptability in asynchronous and synchronous online literacy instruction are critical to effective student-centered teaching, optimizing student-to-student, student-to-content, and student-to-teacher engaged interaction. We must prepare learners for diverse, task-driven communicative situations, sometimes onsite and sometimes online, sometimes live and sometimes not. But it can be difficult to design online courses that intellectually challenge each student, however, due to administrative or logistical requirements. For instance, courses are usually predetermined to be onsite, online, or blended for scheduling reasons; sometimes differentiated tuition rates are used; and instructors may not have much choice in the tools they can use. Pivoting to another modality after a course begins can disrupt expectations and may even be institutionally prohibited. And many students prefer asynchronous courses for scheduling or convenience reasons rather than pedagogical affordances, unwilling to engage in synchronous activities, even if optional.

What if we could, instead, design assignments and courses that give students greater choice in how they communicate with some combination of the asynchronous and synchronous? The hypertext of modality choice by design? For instance, we can encourage students to bounce ideas around in small groups synchronously before presenting ideas in class asynchronously via screencast recordings. Or we can encourage synchronous, collaborative review in addition to asynchronous discussion posts. Or we can use synchronous exchange to test the usability of artifacts produced. Student readiness to move from one modality to another to optimize progress on a task should be somewhat determined by the communication exchange need itself. Our better practice is this: designing variable entry points into communicative interactions and requiring students to select and reflect on what's most conducive given the rhetorical situation.

Workplaces commonly blend a/synchronous practices dynamically, pivoting when needed, especially in multicultural or global contexts. Obstacles abound, requiring communication platforms and approaches to pivot. A recent report from the Pew Research Center points out that even as workplaces reopen, teleworkers often choose to work from home due to the health necessity. Specifically, as of February 2022, 59 percent of U.S. workers work from home all or most of the time, and 83 percent of those working from home reported they were doing so before the omicron variant of the COVID-19 pandemic (Parker et al., 2022). As the pandemic, the economy, technological literacies, and the increasing ubiquity of communication tools continue to reshape work practices, it is critical we prepare students as both content experts and communication design decision-makers.

Teachers, too, must create such opportunities for students to make project management communication decisions because the process of deciding the best combination of modalities to prepare and convey content in the right way at the right time is a critical literacy skill. When so many workplace projects involve collaborative communication in timely ways to complete work effectively, close attention to dynamic communication processes—processes that span the devices they use and the modalities that include text, image, audio, and video—is critical to student professional development. Rather than choosing the easiest or most convenient approach, students must take ownership over how they meet project deadlines, maximize team member skill sets, integrate user feedback, and overcome obstacles. Otherwise, students might graduate from our schools underprepared.

At a time when increasing numbers of students are learning at a distance or in some blended format, it is crucial for teachers to train students in multiple ways to communicate with peers in educational contexts as well as with future fellow employees and employers in workplace contexts. The "distance" in distance learning has less to do with location and more to do with functional literacy. In this sense, "literacy" can be defined as fluency in something or the ability to transact an exchange through language or some facility with media or technology. Literacy is voice and conviction and confidence stepping into an ongoing conversation, using both oral and written communication modes. Nicholas Carr quotes from Walter Ong's (1982) *Orality and Literacy* to detail ways in which relying only on orality or the synchronous is limiting, and how the written word functions asynchronously to liberate knowledge from memory. According to Ong (1982, as cited in Carr, 2010), the ability to write is "utterly invaluable and indeed essential for the realization of fuller, interior, human potentials" (p. 57). Calling attention to what is often practiced in transparent ways, reflecting over the medium and the message is critical to effective communication. By design, teachers can use the oral and written together, in varying ways, through offering a/synchronous communication options to do so. As Stephen Kucer (2014) writes in *Dimensions of Literacy: A Conceptual Base for Teaching Reading and Writing in School Settings*, "limiting our understanding of literacy to the linguistic and cognitive dimensions . . . is to overlook the social dimension of written language" (p. 229).

Similarly, Jessie Borgman and Casey McArdle (2019) in *Personal, Accessible, Responsive, Strategic: Resources and Strategies for Online Writing Instructors* relate social dimensions and strategies to focus instructional design. Teachers must design courses with a user experience for students in mind, including what students might transfer to workplace writing situations. Soliciting student feedback, utilizing that feedback, presenting content in multiple ways, ensuring accessibility—these are all critical processes to effective teaching design and to model ways in which students should pay close attention to technological and communication needs of future workplace projects (Borgman & McArdle, 2019, p. 73). According to Borgman and McArdle, "We can't tell you how many meetings we've attended that could have been handled with an email or went 30 minutes too long" (2019, p. 78). No doubt many of us can concur. Knowing the best modality to use, given specific rhetorical situations, can be as significant as the content itself. Yet, such decision points are often understated in student preparation.

With digital tools, we can facilitate individualized instruction within ongoing collaborations, such as by combining the a/synchronous in designing and presenting information, using the a/synchronous to facilitate meaningful checkpoints, and teaching the value of the a/synchronous as an immediate feature of effective communication. Different combinations of a/synchronous can be used for different learners, just as location and modality must be considered alongside reader, writer, and text when meeting complex needs of varied audiences. As Erica Stone (2021) writes in "Aiming for the Sweet Spot: A User-Centered Approach to Migrating a Community-engaged Course Online" within Borgman and McArdle's (2021) *PARS in Practice*, translating what engages students in different modalities is valuable to produce writers more responsive to user needs. Stone traces changes in her teaching given specific shifts in modality, when "all too often, writing studies departments and writing program administrators will construct one predesigned version of a course for all . . . to teach instead of allowing instructors to incorporate their expertise and located ethos," paying close attention to varied workplace situations (2021, p. 322).

The Global Society of Online Literacy Educators (GSOLE) recognizes the importance of location and modality in pedagogical contexts, working to prepare teachers to be agile and flexible in their approaches as well. GSOLE lists four Online Literacy Instruction (OLI) principles and tenants that aid understanding and praxis. The first OLI principle, for example, is that such instruction should be universally accessible and inclusive. Its first accompanying tenet (1.1) reads: "All stakeholders and students should be aware of and be able to engage the unique literacy features of communicating, teaching, and learning in a primarily digital environment" (2020, para. 9). Outcomes in digital environments, that is, depend on the technological (il)literacies of both teachers and students, as well as their ability to navigate expanded rhetorical landscapes that are shaped by diverse technological, social, institutional, and cultural factors.

The expanded rhetorical triangle includes reader, writer, text, location, and modality, and a/synchronous communication options call attention to relationships between these points, giving students preparation to practice social dimensions of written language for different audience types. If a composition is to be read by a multinational audience (or not really read carefully at all), on different devices, while heading to a meeting with some urgency, consideration of audience and purpose changes. Increasingly, for instance, we tell students most audiences want to accomplish tasks rather than spend too much time reading what has been written (see Tebeaux & Dragga, 2021). Literacy instruction should be situated within the messy communication constructions of society, which are sometimes onsite and sometimes online, sometimes live and often not, and are often task-driven in most workplace situations. If our goal is to prepare students for global, technologically rich environments reliant on the co-existence of asynchronous and synchronous communication, a better practice is to model this in our classrooms.

COURSE CONTEXT AND LESSON

Assessing Functional Literacy

Given the rhetorical awareness and pedagogical dexterity required to cultivate this new kind of functional literacy, it is critical to gauge student knowledge regarding asynchronous and synchronous modalities. Such takeaways are designed for teachers as well as students. They can be easily adapted for different writing and technical communication classrooms. To do so, we administered a survey in an undergraduate online media studies class. The survey is not meant to be a prescriptive exercise, and we suggest administering a similar survey only as a way of assessing your students' understanding of the importance of analyzing audience and purpose carefully to select the right communication modalities. It is crucial to know the level of familiarity students have with various learning modalities to come up with student-centered teaching approaches, modules, and assignments that neither alienate students with inordinate expectations nor confirm the limited perception of synchronous as time intensive and asynchronous as time saving.

In our own case, because the course was originally designed to be entirely asynchronous, student contact usually took the form of asynchronous email exchange, posts and responses in an online discussion forum, weekly recorded video lectures, audio files, and reading materials for students to review at their own pace. However, because synchronous modalities "can provide a vehicle for meaningful student involvement" (Mick & Middlebrook, 2015, p. 146), and since obstacles like the pandemic have prevented effective synchronous interaction for many, we decided to integrate an optional synchronous component. Most weeks, students responded to posted content in 250–350 words. Early in the course, students were given the opportunity to join an hour-long synchronous meeting with the incentive that attendance would exempt them from the usual written response. Less than half took advantage, even though students were informed if scheduling prevented them from joining other times could be made available. The relatively lower number of students who attended may be due to many reasons, but what became clear is that students were not necessarily getting an opportunity to see the value in the difference between modalities. In this chapter, we offer insights into our survey design process—and outcomes—as a better practice for all instructors, in any modality, to think about as an initial way to garner their input and design communication processes that will be effective for all.

First, to gauge ways in which functional literacy changed and to better understand student goals and expectations, we asked the following questions (IRB #c0921.1e-ETSU):

1. Do you know what "asynchronous" means? Yes/No.
2. If yes, describe what asynchronous learning is.
3. Do you know what "synchronous" means? Yes/No.
4. If yes, describe what synchronous learning is.
5. Do you prefer asynchronous or synchronous learning, or some combination of both?
6. What do you like about asynchronous learning?
7. What do you like about synchronous learning?
8. What do you like about a combination of asynchronous and synchronous learning?
9. Describe one class and/or assignment that implemented your preferred method the best.

Of course, as we consider the way we designed this first version of the survey, sharing examples of different technologies or scenarios may make more sense to students than using the terms asynchronous or synchronous. And only one section of students responded to the survey. Nevertheless, the survey and reflective action research allows us to reinforce our teaching practice (offering flexible communication options to better prepare students to use communication tools effectively). Survey responses then informed our teaching practice.

All respondents answered "yes" to knowing what asynchronous and what synchronous means. But when asked to clarify, it became clear that our students' understanding of both is varied, incomplete, and often incorrect. One student, for example, wrote that asynchronous learning is "a class that is 100% online." What it means to interact online is unclear to the student. Other responses focused on negative elements of asynchronous learning (i.e., what asynchronous learning is not or does not facilitate), and not on beneficial communication affordances such as time for extended reflection. For instance, students defined asynchronous these ways:

- "Generally, online classes that do not have scheduled class-collective meeting times but set only work deadlines."
- "All learning objectives are being completed but not at the same time or in the same way, necessarily."
- "Learning entirely virtually, without in-person or Zoom meetings."

Students wrote or indicated asynchronous is "Learning mostly on your own," which implies student-to-teacher instructional interaction is not recognized. Only one response suggested the asynchronous gives unique opportunities for learning, that "online learning [is] on a student's schedule." Still, flexibility is for scheduling or logistical expediencies rather than for valuable communication attributes.

Our students articulated synchronous learning values more directly, but still demonstrated a lack of understanding. Some responses:

- "It's when a class has students attend lectures/class meetings at regular scheduled intervals throughout the semester."
- "Synchronous means real-time learning from different locations."
- "It's a class where you are virtually attending lectures with professors and other classmates."

Students struggled to relate clear understanding. One wrote, "Learning objective[s] are completed together, 'in sync,' and exactly the same way." Another did not seem to realize that synchronous communication in an online course usually indicates a type of online tool: "meeting in-person for class weekly." These and other responses indicate that our students were not entirely clear what asynchronous and synchronous refers to in educational learning. Beyond understanding the value of both communication modalities, students did not discuss using both together and playing an active role in deciding which combination of tools would be most effective.

Still, despite limited understanding or even misunderstandings among students, several insights were presented. Out of the three types of modalities—asynchronous, synchronous, and blended—our students preferred asynchronous. When asked what they like about asynchronous communication, students referenced their schedules and flexibility. "I have many constraints on my time, so I cannot carve out enough time for full-time, synchronous learning"; "It allows for more job flexibility and saves a lot of driving time"; and "I can access information any time I like without having to worry about budgeting time for lectures during my busy days." Students focused on how asynchronous opportunities allowed them to *not do* something such as be somewhere at a certain time, rather than relaying communication effectiveness benefits.

On the other hand, in our courses, as well for experiences we are preparing our students for beyond our courses, focusing on benefits to enhance communication in addition to convenience is important, even if the focus is to free additional time to focus on refining communication. When asked what students like about synchronous learning, answers included, "It provides a personable, tactile and sometimes entertaining college experience"; "More help"; "Benefits of face-to-face instruction"; "Being able to talk with my professors and other students"; and "More in-depth learning, and personal connection." Students identified personal and relational benefits. What is missing is reflection over the combination of the cognitive and the social, which reflecting over combinations of a/synchronous communication options can enable.

When asked directly about combining a/synchronous communication in learning environments, student answers were varied, from "I prefer one or the other, having a combination makes me feel scattered"; to "More help combined with working at my own pace"; to "It allows you to take classes you need more instruction with in-person, while taking subjects you feel more comfortable with on your own time." Responses suggested to us that according to students, teachers have not done a great job of strategically integrating the a/synchronous, or of reflecting on benefits and limitations. One response, though, which albeit could have been along the lines of *let me write what the teacher wants to hear*, supports our better practice directly. The student stated, "The implementation of optional synchronous opportunities creates variety and a more memorable human experience." The survey was valuable for our students to prioritize media tools we have access to use, to consider ways in which the medium and the message are both critical, and to think about how we have choice and must decide which communication tools are most effective given different rhetorical situations. The survey is valuable for teachers in that it can be administered at the beginning and toward the end of a course to see development of this important functional, critical literacy in action.

TILT'ing the Scales on Course Communication

Though it was a small sample, we were intrigued by what our students offered us. Because our survey results suggest that students are relatively unfamiliar with the differences between synchronous, asynchronous, and blended learning environments—and since they seem to focus primarily on the negative aspects of each modality without recognizing each one's unique positive affordances—we have devised a TILT assignment to address these issues. Originally developed by Mary-Ann Winkelmes (2023), the TILT model (Transparency in Learning and Teaching) is designed to help faculty implement transparent teaching practices. One of TILT's primary goals is to facilitate "workshops for both faculty and students that promote student's conscious understanding of how they learn" (Winkelmes, para. 1).

In the assignment outlined below, we provide an opportunity for students to research, reflect, and write about their understanding of the differences between learning environments; each modality's affordances and limitations, including technological and rhetorical considerations; and how they might navigate subsequent course assignments equipped with this new knowledge.

We recommend that faculty assign this project after administering the survey. Since each class will comprise students who have varying experiences with different types of course modalities, this lets faculty adjust the assignment parameters and questions according to gaps in student knowledge, class scheduling, and other course assignments. Whatever changes the teacher makes because of the survey, the goal should remain the same: to facilitate student reflection and ideation concerning different types of online learning environments.

ASSIGNMENT SHEET

Purpose

Student experiences are increasingly characterized by diverse modes of course delivery: synchronous, asynchronous, and/or blended. The purpose of this assignment is to gauge student experiences with—and understanding of—differences between these three kinds of learning environments, and to teach them how technological mediums affect (and are affected by) their experiences.

Skills

Upon completion of the assignment, students will be able to:

- Clearly define and articulate the differences between synchronous, asynchronous, and blended learning environments;
- Identify each modality's technological/logistical affordances and limitations (i.e., what unique opportunities does each provide, as well as obstacles);
- Rhetorically analyze how learning experiences affect (and are affected by) different modalities; and
- Reflect and write about how they might use this new knowledge to navigate this and future courses.

Knowledge

Upon completion of the assignment, students will be knowledgeable about:

- Differences between the three types of modalities;
- Each modality's technological/logistical affordances and limitations;
- Rhetorical context as it relates to learning experiences within and across modalities, and
- How to dexterously navigate course modalities in evolving educational landscapes.

Task

1. During week 1, administer the survey to establish student knowledge of modalities (subsequent tasks can be adjusted according to results).
2. During week 2, teach students about the expanded rhetorical triangle—reader, writer, text, location, and modality—with specific attention to

how a/synchronous communication options call attention to relationships between these points. Delivery mode can be synchronous, asynchronous, and/or blended.
3. During week 3, prompt students with the following:
    You're tasked with writing a 2500- to 3000-word essay that answers the questions below. To support your claims, you must cite at least 1 reputable source in your response to each question. (Some of these questions are like the ones that students respond to in the survey; the difference is that they'll be responding to these after discussing the expanded rhetorical triangle in week 2. They'll also be responsible for researching these topics to add to their existing knowledge, instead of just gauging existing knowledge like the survey does. Students are encouraged to research, including interview, instructional designers.)
    a. What are the primary differences between online synchronous, asynchronous, and blended learning?
    b. What are a few unique advantages to learning in an online synchronous environment?
    c. What are a few unique advantages to learning in an online asynchronous environment?
    d. What are a few unique advantages to learning in an online blended environment?
    e. What are a few unique challenges to learning in an online synchronous environment?
    f. What are a few unique challenges to learning in an online asynchronous environment?
    g. What are a few unique challenges to learning in an online blended environment?
    h. What are some rhetorical considerations—drawing on terms and concepts from the expanded rhetorical triangle—when considering which modality would be best suited to a given learning context? Give at least one example from your own experience to illustrate.
4. Equipped with your expanded knowledge about the unique advantages, challenges, and rhetorical considerations as they relate to different types of modalities, how might you adjust your learning approach in other courses?
5. Based on student responses to the questions, the instructor can adjust the delivery modalities according to student expectations, strengths, weaknesses, course content, and needed areas of improvement. In that way, the above assignment fosters multimodal competence in students, and at the same time provides valuable data to the instructor who can then construct the course in adaptive ways.

Criteria for Success

The project will be evaluated according to the following criteria:

- How well the student defines and articulates the differences between the three types of modalities.
- How accurately and clearly the student identifies each modality's technological/logistical affordances and limitations.
- The quality of the student's rhetorical analysis about how learning experiences affect (and are affected by) different modalities.
- The quality of the student's reflection about how they might use this new knowledge to navigate this and future courses.
- The quality of the student's writing.

In our undergraduate and graduate classes in composition, technical communication, and media studies, there is always a mixture of students with varied technology skillsets, facility with written and oral communication, understanding of media literacy, awareness of visual representation and data ethics, experience as a major or non-major, and vision for strategies to overcome obstacles. We emphasize these topics as needed by students in our courses. Further, procrastination, family emergencies, technological difficulties, health concerns, other deadlines that must be prioritized—our syllabi detail what students should do when such obstacles arise. Such advice and direction are required for good reason. However, we should also acknowledge obstacles are frequent in workplace environments, and students must know in advance how to make good decisions themselves to optimize quality of work. Obstacles to understanding are the norm, not the exception. Just as good teachers, through instructional design, prepare multiple avenues for instruction given directions students take conversations in, all communicators should be prepared to shift modalities, use different tools, and relate content in different ways by design. If students do not have opportunities to decide which combination of communication strategies should be used to overcome problems, which requires flexible a/synchronous online experiences by design, their preparation for agile communication workplace decision-making is limited.

Knowing how to best determine effective communication practices—as well as which critical literacies need strengthening—varies from student to student. Where one student may need the challenge of presenting information in front of a live audience to explore benefits and limitations, another student may learn by practicing and revising a recorded presentation. Further, this practice allows students the flexibility to make decisions for learning based on their strengths and needs as learners, which can be especially important when considering students with diverse educational backgrounds and accessibility needs. Where one student may shy away from the use of a specific technology due to apparent overuse, another student may value extensive experience as a foundational advantage. And where one student may be a non-native English speaker or a struggling writer who requires more time on task, another student may need a live audience to practice adjusting on-the-fly. What is clear is that every student in each class needs to be challenged in unique and flexible ways to prepare learners authentically for communication in workplaces.

Writing instructors can all relate to classroom examples where individual student strengths were not fully engaged. For instance, in our classes we routinely ask students to give a final, synchronous presentation over a significant project with time set aside for questions and answers. Communication literacy is a key component in our course goals and objectives, because if students can come up with great ideas but do not convey them well, messages miss their mark. Effective communication design is a form of functional literacy, in other words, and our students often must study good examples, refresh technology skills, and perform usability tests in addition to creating content to share ideas effectively. Combining the asynchronous (written) and synchronous (oral) is needed. In terms of practice, combining the a/synchronous addresses and helps mitigate the common obstacle of procrastination, which is often encountered with collaborative exercises or assignments.

For instance, one strategy we employ is breaking students into small groups, and the more tech savvy student might lead in design on small group discussion, with other group members then taking different responsibilities. The "divide and collaborate" approach, teaching individual students how to recognize which skill sets they have that can be combined to best solve problems, then prepares students, as purpose-driven meaning making collaborators, for workplaces. Groups struggle when one or more members do not complete their work in a timely manner. Breaking assignments down into components on a timeline can mitigate the impact of procrastination. Deciding who must accomplish what and by when, whether asynchronously or synchronously or some combination, is a very important workplace skill, employing communication strategies such as checkpoints. When teaching online, our practice must provide participants scaffolding to collaborate in guided, self-determined, meaningful ways that minimize procrastination but make allowances for contingencies.

Assignments leading to live presentations, though, even with many student checkpoints and ample teacher scaffolding, assume presenting synchronously is optimal to convey information or to demonstrate achievement. Can teachers offer more varied options? A second strategy we employ, as one example, recognizes that in many workplaces, presentations may be delivered at a distance where some audience members may be together onsite, and some may be online or prefer receiving the presentation at another time. Preparing a presentation for hybrid delivery requires dexterity in sequencing the a/synchronous. In our classes, students might practice their presentation several times before finalizing a recording, submit their presentation asynchronously, and stand by it synchronously to answer questions. Students record, review, and re-record several times, typically dedicating more time on task than if they prepared to present it live. The additional practice often helps students determine where design and content must be revised. Options can remove on-demand pressures that some students are not ready for, while giving others more time to give attention to different components. The presentation is delivered as if it is live, but it is presented the moment the audience is ready to receive it, which is common in workplace environments. Retooling the a/synchronous by shifting modes of interaction can be more conducive to learning.

A/Synchronous Online Learning instruction

We can better synthesize ways in which the asynchronous and the synchronous work together by providing students opportunities to reflect on decisions guiding their use. A common perception among students is that they spend less time learning asynchronously as they are saving on hours they might otherwise spend attending synchronously. Related to this is the view that asynchronous classes are less rigorous so that students believe they will also save time on learning and assignments. Students must understand that asynchronous modalities, for instance, are not just "less time" (Paull & Snart, 2016, p. 13). One method is to conceptualize ways to do so through assignment and course redesign—focusing on student-to-student, student-to-content, and student-to-teacher interaction—to give each student in every class flexible pathways toward demonstrating achievement. The practice is essential as higher education becomes more expensive and as companies require employees to retrain themselves by acquiring emerging functional literacy skills. Serving the needs of various kinds of learners, this "buffet style of learning" theory suggests using a variety of activities involving the visual, the auditory, and the kinesthetic supported by more individualized attention (Veal, 2016). What matters more than serving one type of lesson is letting learners decide which materials and approaches are needed to achieve learning goals and objectives.

Embracing the idea of combining the a/synchronous, imagine a shared file to write in—such as a GoogleDoc or a Word file on OneDrive—that is accessed by multiple small groups simultaneously. The shared document might serve as a checkpoint for each small group, with teacher prompts and questions provided as needed throughout the course, answered, updated, and revised by individuals and/or small groups asynchronously. During a synchronous class session, a small group chat enables the team to synchronously discuss and update their section of the asynchronous document. The teacher can move from small group chat to small group chat while reviewing each team's work simultaneously in the shared document. Students engage in the space through text, with voice, transacting with video, chat, hyperlinks, and whatever else is required or preferred to take ownership, to maximize skill sets, to integrate feedback, and to plan strategies to overcome obstacles. Students often continue working individually in the document asynchronously after the synchronous class session ends. The document becomes a sort of refined chat space, which is a form of secondary orality. Specifically, this interactive thinking space helps students work through ideas in our courses leading toward individual or small group project generation. The strategy foregrounds reflection over modality decisions made, teaching students skills that can transfer to a variety of interactive communication exchanges beyond the class.

As Steven D'Augustino (2012) points out in "Toward a Course Conversion Model for Distance Learning," effective online learning is facilitated by "high authenticity . . . high interactivity, and high collaboration" (p. 148). Using only one communication modality at a time, such as all asynchronous or synchronous exchange, will not likely achieve high authenticity, high interactivity, or high collaboration by each learner. Likewise, using a predetermined modality without giving students decision-making affordances does not prepare students for types of globalized workplaces impacted by time and distance (Talley, 2017). Whether a course is predetermined to be delivered onsite, online, or in a blended format using primarily asynchronous or primarily synchronous communication modalities, teachers must help students navigate the a/synchronous for meaningful communication purposes for changing educational and workplace environments. Our teaching practice must accommodate these changes to keep pace.

Communication strategies are meaningful to students if benefits can transfer beyond the course to other situations. Just as presentations recorded asynchronously prior to a synchronous delivery can help students better understand strategies to overcome obstacles, integrating synchronous communication as needed in predetermined asynchronous courses can be helpful. For instance, teachers can offer synchronous teacher-to-student conferences during office hours, even in an asynchronous course that usually relies on email exchanges, posts, responses, recorded video lectures, audio content, reading materials, or other largely self-paced work. Such synchronous interaction "can provide a vehicle for meaningful student involvement" (Mick & Middlebrook, 2015, p. 146). If needed, students can choose to meet with a teacher in one modality or another synchronously, at any appropriate checkpoint. However, when asynchronous communication is employed, it should be used intentionally. The choice to engage asynchronously should not solely be based on "it's easier" or "it fits my schedule better"; instead, teaching students to reflect over the value of communicating in one style or another can lead to a better practice where education is not just seen in terms of a grade or convenience. Instead, connecting the choice to transformations in higher education, workplace cultures, and the diversity of learners in terms of location, age, gender, race, occupation shifts the focus from convenience to optimizing communication situationally.

Connie Synder Mick and Geoffrey Middlebrook (2015) note in their chapter "Asynchronous and Synchronous Modalities," "the question . . . is not whether either the asynchronous or synchronous option is intrinsically better" (p. 136), but rather that students consider "when to reverse modalities or when to use both modalities in order to meet different learning styles and objectives" (p. 142). Generally, according to Mick and Middlebrook, the asynchronous modality affords flexibility, more time to increase cognitive participation, more time for processing information, multiple opportunities to read and write, and readily available archival records (2015, pp. 136–137); the synchronous modality affords interpersonal more so than cognitive exchange, helping mitigate miscommunication (2015, p. 137). Both types of communication are needed to limit the potential for misinformation when working with diverse student and workplace audiences. Beth L. Hewett and Kevin Eric DePew offer additional strategies for sequencing the a/synchronous in many teaching, learning, and administrative contexts in *Foundational Practices of Online Writing Instruction*, building on CCCC's *A Position Statement of Principles and Example Effective Practices for Online Writing Instruction (OWI)* (2013; 2016).

Distance learning scholarship on a/synchronous modalities is robust (see Skurat-Harris, 2019; *The Bedford Bibliography of Research in Online Writing Instruction*, 2019; see also Raes et al., 2020, on gaps in the literature). Mary Stewart's (2021) webtext "Student-Teacher Conferencing in Zoom," for instance, documents her shift to online teaching that resulted in enhancing both her online and onsite praxis. She offers two case studies of student-to-teacher conferences on Zoom, examining ways in which the use of the a/synchronous modalities impact what can be taught and learned. According to Stewart, real-time affordances might offer some momentum toward voice for some students and can motivate learners to move toward asynchronous deep reflection and focus. The interface creates a sense of distance that can be helpful for students, enabling them to feel as if they're on the same playing field, a distance that "seems productive for the type of trial-and-error digital literacy" that some students need (Stewart, 2021, "Discussion"). A common problem, though, is that students need to know that they're on track toward achieving course goals and objectives; however, they report that when teachers simply relay what is in a syllabus or assignment prompt, provide asynchronous comments, or give feedback on a scoring guide, teachers are not interactive enough. Students need transactional explanation to understand how the content is personally and professionally meaningful (see Newbold, 1999). Such transactional explanations are best offered when teachers are aware of the educational and workplace goals of their students, and this awareness necessitates asynchronous and synchronous interactions.

We can reconceptualize distance and time by offering students opportunities to design combinations of the a/synchronous. Paul Mihailidis (2019) underscores the idea that such access to valuable tools is a fundamental right, and that teaching students principles of digital media literacy with meaningful participation through a variety of platforms is critical, working toward a classroom of students "engaging in a diversity of voices" (p. 7). Access is a core principle and tenet to ensure stakeholders can engage and interact online (see GSOLE's OLI tenants). As online literacy includes digital reading, writing, and media skills, connecting the synchronous and asynchronous as a form of access may help our students understand they are producing and sharing ideas through meaningful transactional exchange in various communities, what Mihailidis and many media literacy theorists refer to as "civic intentionality" (2019, p. 13). We are co-authors stepping into ongoing conversations that take place a/synchronously in-person and at a distance, both in real-time and any time. Deciding on communication modalities is critical to functional media literacy. To be media literate is to be aware of the impact of bias and subjectivity, the merging of persuasive and informative rhetoric, and the uncovering of information that is reliable yet could remain invalid. Teaching students how to situate communication strategies strategically helps them develop literacy skills critical to effective communication (Newbold, 1999). By using both the asynchronous and synchronous modalities together as a better practice we teach students to embrace converging information flows, leading to engagement and empowerment, practicing empathy, and developing divergent perspectives to compose in an increasingly networked global society (Castells & Kumar, 2014; Robinson, 2009).

REFLECTION ON PRACTICE

To be clear, the survey we administered is action research, one way of gauging student understanding. Its specific value in this instance is that its results allow reflecting and rethinking on our practice of flexible teaching to accommodate students at various life and career stages, motivational levels, and global locations via asynchronous and synchronous means. Our survey's results suggest that most of our students do not value a/synchronous communication affordances for online learning problem-solving. In their responses to the survey, students suggest that the asynchronous modality is usually referred over synchronous modalities due to scheduling (a polite way of saying "procrastination," at least for many) benefits only. Students do not seem to recognize the unique affordances of synchronous learning, nor do they know how to wield them. As we reflected throughout the course on the ways in which choosing modalities or combinations thereof for specific reasons can increase communication effectiveness—project management, clarity of design, reaching multiple types of audiences, connecting the cognitive and the social, and reflecting over archived content for deeper revision through usability testing, for instance—our online learning environment and student success was strengthened.

By deploying the TILT assignment that we outline above in combination with a similar survey at the beginning of the course, instructors can practice data-driven, iterative course design that accounts for students' existing knowledge and skills. Having students research the different kinds of online modalities—and write about the unique traits of those modalities—increases their knowledge of the various affordances and challenges each one presents. Instead of thinking of online modalities in mere logistical or scheduling-related terms, this assignment will help students think critically about each environment's rhetorical context. It will also help them engage with course content, instructors, and classmates in more proactive ways.

Effective communication requires sustained engagement by designing appropriate communication strategies, through close attention to the ongoing conversation, and through weaving all the threads together to make meaning. Skills needed to use technology effectively to express self accurately and responsibly are challenging to teach in any learning environment, and navigating distance requires experience in conveying meaningful thought through virtual environments, practicing how to express voice and opinion empathically without dismissing others' perspectives. Facilitating positive experiences for students in online classes requires constant iteration, dexterity with multiple software technologies, and cultural sensitivity. We suggest here that integrating optional components (be they asynchronous or synchronous) can open doors to creative learning environments that are otherwise difficult to reproduce.

Simply diversifying delivery modalities and making one or more types optional, however, is not enough. We need to be strategic about how to mix modalities. While working with a peer response team on portfolios after some experience focusing on the benefits of both asynchronous and synchronous transactions, one of our students wrote:

> I prefer to just exchange portfolios and send an email with bulleted notes concerning what works and what could use some improvement on my peer's portfolio. However, I am

> open to other methods. Another method I thought of could be a video response. It might be more time consuming, but using video recordings of our portfolio and our feedback for specific areas on the portfolio could be a helpful alternative if live meetings are not an option. Again, I am open to other methods. The main thing is to offer quality feedback and get some quality feedback in return. (K. Goode, personal communication, October 25, 2021)

A well-considered combination is informative, and aids us in predicting potential obstacles, detailing benefits and limitations of different methods, and reflecting on our modalities in ways that benefit the work rather than simply seems easier. Such an approach allows students to remain flexible, makes them more receptive to (and even excited about) receiving quality feedback, and lends opportunities to develop and practice skills useful in workplace environments.

Because bridging distance between perspectives online requires some knowledge of audience awareness and facility with technological literacy, a value system and skillset that varies widely amongst students, time is needed to scaffold distance. Just as distance is more about functional literacy, "time" in online teaching and learning environments has less to do with the progress of events from past to present to future than it does offering students opportunities to work at their own pace with their own tools to arrive at a satisfactory level of understanding and achievement. What is important for teachers is that students achieve the goals and objectives of a lesson, unit, or course. How students go about doing that matters less, but each must be cognizant of options and decide to use media to deliver content purposefully. Students must reflect on the values of the a/synchronous in strategic ways, deploying tactics attuned to the expanded rhetorical triangle.

Students are, we contend, going to find themselves in a new kind of functional illiteracy if they graduate our English courses with skills in persuasion, with an understanding of grammar and style, with some attention to good research and audience, but without such media literacy skills across locations and environments. Students must be taught how to determine what is reliable and valid across many different media modalities and platforms, which in turn will help them reflect over the dangers of sharing information when some environments appear to be more informal than others. Such informed and situated literacy embraces an understanding of the expanded rhetorical triangle, including relationships between reader, writer, text, location, and modality. As we strengthen our teaching by embracing digital technologies in different ways, reimagining how distance and time can work in our classes, reflecting over how to combine asynchronous and synchronous strategies can give learners many and flexible opportunities for engaging with content, with other students, and with teachers; doing so underscores the idea that effective learning and communication steps into an ongoing conversation.

MOVING BETTER PRACTICES ACROSS MODALITIES

- *In-Person, Real-Time Learning:* prioritize a/synchronous modality decision-making processes, offering options for communication exchange in informal and formal composing processes, and introducing those options as early as possible while limiting them to just what is needed.
- *Online, Real-Time Learning:* offer a/synchronous opportunities for sustaining communication on projects for learners who have ideas to contribute immediately and for those who need more time.
- *Online, Any Time Learning:* provide flexible project management internal deadlines to offer team members opportunities to engage in projects using self-selected a/synchronous tools at their own pacing.
- *Hybrid Learning:* document transcripts and recordings of synchronous meetings to capture engaged thinking as "text" requiring further analysis as key contribution to projects, enabling students using different tools to contribute apart potential time and space restrictions.

REFERENCES

Conference on College Composition and Communication. (2013, March 13). *A position statement of principles and example effective practices for Online Writing Instruction (OWI)*. National Council of Teachers of English. https://cdn.ncte.org/nctefiles/groups/cccc/owiprinciples.pdf.

Borgman, J. & McArdle, C. (2019). *Personal, accessible, responsive, strategic: Resources and strategies for online writing instructors.* The WAC Clearinghouse; University Press of Colorado. https://doi.org/10.37514/PRA-B.2019.0322.

Carr, N. (2010). *The shallows: What the internet is doing to our brains.* Norton.

Castells, M. & Kumar, J. (2014). A conversation with Manuel Castells. *Berkeley Planning Journal, 27*(1). https://doi.org/10.5070/BP327124502.

Conference on College Composition and Communication. (2016). Committee for effective practices in online writing instruction. https://cccc.ncte.org/cccc/committees/owi.

D'Augustino, S. (2012). Toward a course conversion model for distance learning. *Journal of International Education in Business, 5*, 145–162.

GSOLE Executive Board. (2019, June 13). *Online literacy instruction principles and tenets.* Global Society of Online Literacy Educators. https://gsole.org/oliresources/oliprinciples.

Hewett, B. L. & DePew, K. E. (2015). *Foundational practices of online writing instruction*. The WAC Clearinghouse; Parlor Press. https://doi.org/10.37514/PER-B.2015.0650.

Kucer, S. B. (2014). *Dimensions of literacy: A conceptual base for teaching reading and writing in school settings* (4th ed.). Routledge.

Mick, C. S. & Middlebrook, G. (2015). Asynchronous and synchronous modalities. In B. Hewett & K. E. DePew (Eds.), *Foundational practices of online writing instruction* (pp. 129–148). The WAC Clearinghouse; Parlor Press. https://doi.org/10.37514/PER-B.2015.0650.2.03.

Mihailidis, P. (2019). *Civic media literacies: Re-imagining human connection in an age of digital abundance*. Routledge.

Newbold, W. W. (1999). Teaching on the internet: Transactional writing instruction on the world wide web. *Kairos: A Journal of Rhetoric, Technology, and Pedagogy, 4*(1). http://kairos.technorhetoric.net/4.1/features/newbold.

Parker, K., Menasce Horowitz, J. & Minkin, R. (2022). COVID-10 pandemic continues to reshape work in America. *Pew Research Center*. http://tinyurl.com/ywnm4cts.

Paull, J. N. & Snart, J. A. (2016). *Making hybrids work: An institutional framework for blending online and face-to-face instruction in higher education*. National Council of Teachers of English.

Raes, A., Detienne, L., Windey, I. & Depaepe, F. (2020). A systematic literature review on synchronous hybrid learning: Gaps identified. *Learning Environments Research, 23*, 269–290. https://doi.org/10.1007/s10984-019-09303-z.

Robinson, K. (2009). Why creativity now? A conversation with Sir Ken Robinson. *Educational Leadership, 67*(1), 22–26.

Skurat-Harris, H. (2019). *The Bedford bibliography of research in online writing instruction*. Macmillan Learning. http://tinyurl.com/ydsxvcmu

Stewart, M. (2021). Student-teacher conferencing in Zoom: Asymmetrical collaboration in a digital space/(nonplace). *Kairos: A Journal of Rhetoric, Technology, and Pedagogy, 25*(2). http://kairos.technorhetoric.net/25.2/praxis/stewart.

Stone, E. (2021). Aiming for the sweet spot: A user-centered approach to migrating a community-engaged online course. In J. Borgman & C. McArdle (Eds.), *PARS in practice: More resources and strategies for online writing instructors* (pp. 317–336). The WAC Clearinghouse; University Press of Colorado. https://doi.org/10.37514/PRA-B.2021.1145.2.19.

Talley, P. C. (2017). Preparing students for the globalized workforce: A mission statement for Taiwanese universities. *International Journal of Humanities and Social Science, 7*(3), 57–60.

Tebeaux, E. & Dragga, S. (2021). *The essentials of technical communication* (5th ed.). Oxford University Press.

Veal, P. (2016, March 9). Differentiation and accommodations: Buffet style learning. *The FLTMAG: ALLT's Free Language Technology Magazine*. https://fltmag.com/differentiation-accommodations-world-language-classroom.

Wilkelmes, M. (2023). TILT higher ed examples and resources. *TILT Higher Ed*. https://tilthighered.com/abouttilt.

CHAPTER 16.
ITERATIVE PROCESSES FOR ALL: REWARDS AND RISKS IN CONTRACT GRADING

Shawn Bowers and Jennifer Smith Daniel
Queens University of Charlotte

In this chapter, the authors describe **contract grading** *used in online, real-time learning. Specifically, the authors explain contract grading as a practice which can be adapted to asynchronous online learning and hybrid learning contexts with particular attention to honoring students' processes, engagement, and labor. In describing their "better practice," this chapter addresses the themes of accessibility and assessment.*

FRAMEWORKS AND PRINCIPLES IN THIS CHAPTER

- **Framework for Success in Postsecondary Writing, Engagement**: A sense of investment and involvement in learning.
- **Framework for Success in Postsecondary Writing, Creativity**: The ability to use novel approaches for generating, investigating, and representing ideas.
- **GSOLE 3.1**: Instructors should be familiar with online instructional delivery practices to ensure the same level and hours of instruction across all OLI settings.

GUIDING QUESTIONS BEFORE YOU BEGIN READING

- How would your pedagogy change if you cultivated a "beginner's mind" in regards to grading practices?
- Outside of institutional constraints, what additional concerns does ungrading bring up for you given your experience with grades as a student? As an instructor?
- What models of ungrading are you familiar with? What might a starting place be to implement ungrading in your curricular, instructional, and assessment practices?

DOI: https://doi.org/10.37514/PER-B.2024.2241.2.16

- What challenges do you think ungrading could solve? What challenges do you think it could create?

INTRODUCTION

Ideas have a habit of floating around and landing in opportune moments.

We first began to pay closer attention to inequities in grading with Dr. Asao Inoue's keynote address at the Conference on College Composition and Communication (CCCC) in Pittsburgh (2019). Well, we'd both been teaching for a decade and knew that grading was a flawed system, but something about the "call-ins" to dismantle racism in the classroom from Dr. Inoue's keynote and, again, from Dr. Vershawn Young's CCCC Chair's Speech (2021) lodged themselves into our consciousness.

Specifically, Young and Inoue's naming of our complicity—that is, complicity in a system built on White language supremacy—made us uncomfortable enough to check our own practices. To answer these "call-ins," we investigated ungrading as a way to address a curricular, instructional, and assessment ecosystem that sets students up to fail in many ways, especially given the hegemonic systems that privilege certain literacy practices over others.

Ungrading is an approach that shifts away from subjective summary judgment by removing traditional letter and numeric grades from assessment of the artifact to focus feedback on the process (Blum, 2020). Then came the pandemic, which drove us to triage our classes for the spring semester. It is important to note that the call-ins were the exigence for the shift, not the conditions brought on by emergency remote teaching during the pandemic. Fortuitously, we had both chosen to take advantage of a professional development opportunity through our institution in the summer of 2020 to reflect and to revise our course designs with intentionality; in particular, we began with some reflection in order to understand who our students were and what knowledge(s) they brought with them into the classroom. We can imagine that it seems obvious that as instructors we would start with what our students know. What we learned in our workshop was that we made a lot of assumptions about their previous classroom experiences. This workshop stopped us short, calling us back to the "beginner's mind" and inducing us to shed our preconceptions (Hartman, 2022). The concept of the beginner's mind draws on Buddhist philosophy which invites introspection from the perspective of the novice and not the expert. In short, the beginner's mind asks us to operate from the abundance of possibility. After a decade of teaching, we fell into the myth of what a first-year student would know about writing, even as they are new to the ecology of the college classroom. In typical academic fashion, it was another year before we were able to act on our ideas yet began to do so in the summer semester of 2021.

Moving from theory to practice was the biggest leap. At the level of theory, we had to get comfortable with this radical idea—that ungrading was a more equitable model of assessment, and that we needed to use it. At the level of practice, we simply had to carve out the time, space, and energy to revise our pedagogy. As the universe would have it, we had signed on to teach in a learning community together that next summer, 2021—two paired courses for the same students that would be delivered as online, any time learning. These were the ideal conditions to take our conversations from the drawing board to the classroom; that summer, we piloted a model of ungrading in two introductory level writing courses. We can admit that we didn't quite feel ready yet had that precise constellation of circumstances—the speeches echoing in our minds, the pandemic-induced remote teaching, the collaboration on our learning community courses—not presented itself, we likely would still be talking about ungrading instead of actually doing it. What we offer here is our thought process as we moved ungrading into online, any time classroom.

Thus, in the summer of 2021, we used a contract grading model and a portfolio model in lieu of traditional grading.

As noted above, our institution pairs courses, thematically, to form learning communities as the central delivery method of the general education program, which also houses the first-year composition (FYC) program. Because of the pandemic conditions at the time, these courses were delivered exclusively online in the summer of 2021; also, because we needed to anticipate challenges such as students in different time zones, we opted to deliver the courses as online, any time learning. The experience was rewarding, and it gave us some space to fully lean into this new way of supporting student writers that felt more equitable and pedagogically-driven instead of assessment-driven. Ungrading is pedagogically-driven because it centers ongoing formative feedback over summative grades; moreover, it is equitable as it accounts for a student's learning development. The arbitrary grading scale positions students to learn strategically and to minimize risk-taking. In courses that underscore the creative, recursive nature of writing, traditional grading methods discourage student engagement.

Additionally, we were fortunate enough to have low enrollment in our courses, so we were afforded the time and space to pay close attention to students' reactions (and our own) regarding this new way of assessing writing. We note that here to describe the context for our summer course, and understand that not all instructors—especially those who are contingent faculty—have such a luxury.

The modality of the learning community gave us an opportunity to test and develop this new-to-us grading system, which helped us explicitly signal to students that—as teachers of writing—what we value is a revision process informed by a student's curiosity about their ideas and their ability to use language to communicate those ideas. The specific ungrading practices described in this chapter—contract grading and portfolios—began first as an attempt to develop better practices for online teaching although we later adapted ungrading pedagogies beyond this modality. Because we were already committed to redesigning this course, we decided to "go for it" on ungrading, too, exploring the opportunity to collaboratively rethink our courses from all angles.

In this deliberate move away from traditional grading models, we hoped for a space where students would feel emboldened to write for themselves and not perform as a "good student" for a grade—a grade that is predicated on a constructed idea of what qualifies as good writing. Put differently, the evaluation of writing (whether it is formative or summative feedback) is subjective to the biases and perspectives of the grader, which is in turn informed by culture, social location, and the myriad identities we carry with us. Because many writing instructors hold privileged identities, we grade from our privileged habitus, as Inoue, Young, and others suggest. The concept of habitus we are using here is based on the ideas of the French sociologist, Pierre Bordieu. Habitus as theorized by Bordieu "is a 'system of dispositions' or acquired patterns of thought, behavior, and taste that correspond to social position" (Beare & Stenberg, 2020, p. 105). In other words, our own positionalities, which have been externally conditioned, inform how we show up in the classroom. Same for students.

Any time you move from "this is how we've always done it," there will be unease. Still, we find this approach a far better way to assess student learning because it shifts the emphasis from the grades to the students' engagement in the course. We do not claim this shift to be only embraced as a student-centered pedagogy. In fact, it is as much a teacher-centered move. We see this shift as akin to Christina Cedillo and Phil Bratta's (2019) assertions that "[t]here are times when centering the teacher's experience may contribute to a student-centered pedagogy" (p. 216). Logically, it seems to us that if instructors have negative feelings towards grading using the current model, those feelings are more apt to show up in the evaluation process.

Put another way, what makes a good student for one instructor may not always translate to other instructors, leaving students to strategically enact a performative stance for every course context. If a student matriculates as a multiply marginalized learner in a system not built to value their literacy practices, then they are at a disadvantage for navigating education in its current state. Simply put, it is unlikely they are aware of all the tacit rules that higher education has deemed "good writing" (i.e., using Standard American English). All of these factors reinforce the idea that ungrading is a "better practice" in the teaching of writing, especially in our online, any time context.

So, after two years of ungrading, we've adopted this approach in other courses and cannot imagine going back. Even on hard days, when we find a student expressing their intense discomfort with ungrading, we remember the same angsty feeling that other students expressed from our first iteration of ungrading; coincidentally, this is the same angsty feeling we had initially. We then rest in the knowledge that growth can often come from uncertainty. Writing has taught us that uncertainty leads to growth; now ungrading is teaching us again.

CONTRACT GRADING

Contract grading, as one specific practice of ungrading, shifts the focus from the evaluation of some unattainable standard to focus on and assess the ways students pursue deep learning. Other forms include the aforementioned portfolios, specs grading, self-assessment to name a few (Blum, 2020). Susan Blum (2020) states "Grading contracts convey expectations about what is required for each potential grade . . . Students work toward the grade they want to achieve, and goalposts don't unexpectedly shift" (p. 38). We patterned our own contract grading after Inoue's (2019) "kind of grading contract, one that calculates final course grades purely by the labor students complete, not by any judgments of the quality of their writing" (*Labor-Based Grading Contracts,* p. 3).

We see ungrading as an opportunity to ameliorate some of the ways students feel judged and, occasionally and unfortunately, shamed for their writing. These strong emotions hinder the ability for students to develop impressionistic thinking. Barbara Bird (2012), advancing the work of Charles Bereiter and Marlene Scardamalia, asserts that one criterion for developing deep thinking habits is through impressionistic thinking, defined as "an emotional commitment to what is being learned" (p. 2). Students who feel a sense of embarrassment about their writing are unlikely to commit to learning about writing or being a writer.

For our courses, we chose to use contract grading to invite students to see the value in an iterative process of drafting and revising their writing. By unhitching grades from writing feedback and assessment, we hoped to offer students an environment that honors their process of learning. In courses that center writing processes, contract grading asks students to claim some ownership of their work by taking risks, framing mistakes as learning outposts, and valuing students' efforts. That effort varies by student, and is informed by students' own learning goals such as using feedback more effectively. Moreover, it encourages students to develop metacognitive skills to consider how their writing choices influence the effectiveness of their writing and its purpose.

This approach matters to us because we believe that "to educate as the practice of freedom is a way of teaching that anyone can learn" (hooks, 1994, p.

13). Our university, a predominantly White institution, has seen record growth in Black, Indigenous, People of Color (BIPOC) and first-generation students, which reflects the national shift in student demographics in higher education (Hanson, 2021). Old practices that reinforce Paulo Freire's conception of the "banking model" (Freire, 2014) and the current bureaucracy of our educational system's myopic focus on assessment do not always account for the divergent literacies that are now part of our landscape. Contract grading, with its expressed focus on engagement and effort, can provide more access to more students to demonstrate learning.

Performance to Action: GSOLE & Framework for Success in Postsecondary Writing

This framing of education's purpose is our call to practice what we believe with intentional pedagogies that challenge us to move from ideation to action. Furthermore, intentionality is an essential consideration for teaching in any modality. One such resource that advises our work is GSOLE's *Online Literacy Instruction Principles and Tenets* (2019). The third tenet, which affirms "iterative processes of course and instructional material design, development, assessment, and revision" speaks to our approach (n.d., OLI Principle 3). These iterative processes are imperative for the sake of ethical course design.

The world is different; our students are different. As instructors, it is our duty to adapt our pedagogies to meet the students where they are and with the variety of knowledge that they bring to the learning space. Teaching online took us out of the "muscle memory" of in-person, real-time learning, such as our reliance on a well-timed student question for clarifying our instructions or reminding them of a deadline. Teaching this ungrading practice in an online, any time learning environment necessitated that we thoughtfully considered every aspect of the communications that we shared with the students. We had to repeatedly check in with ourselves, each other, and our students to ensure that we weren't just cramming old lessons into a new format. Ungrading provided the added benefit of keeping us anchored in these new (to us) ways of teaching without the crutch of verbal clarification. We approached this class with an intentional pedagogy informed particularly by GSOLE's third principle as it helped us attend to the rhetorical situation of the asynchronous online course; by necessity, such courses are mediated by written text, course materials, the learning management system (LMS), and students' prior experiences with writing courses. Having a beginner's mindset with both the practice of ungrading and the new course modality kept us accountable for being explicit in our teaching.

Both contract grading and the third tenet of GSOLE are infused with the practice of revision. Not only do the students need to revise to get their best work—we as instructors need to revise our practices, too. Contract grading offered students a tangible signal to invest in the revision process; the third tenet offered in GSOLE's framework gave us a tangible guide for teaching well in an online space that was newer to us. In order to ensure we didn't create more labor for students by having them decipher our tacit expectations, we had to be quite explicit about the purpose of the course, the assignments, and how we intended students to engage. For example, our assignment guidelines became lengthier as we articulated our expectations explicitly. While this tenet was written as a framework for online modalities, frankly, we find it to just be an ethical practice in any modality to commit to "iterative processes that develop, revise, and refine all aspects of teaching and tutoring to include pedagogy" (Global Society of Online Literacy Educators, 2019).

Furthermore, the GSOLE principle cultivates useful transferable skills that extend not just to other classes but to working environments as well and aligns nicely with the *Framework for Success in Postsecondary Writing* (2011) developed by National Council of Teachers of English (NCTE), Writing Program Administrators (WPA), and National Writing Project (NWP). This framework focuses on habits of mind that are paramount to a student's success in the collegiate landscape. Within the enumerated eight habits of mind, several can be enacted with contract grading. Chief among these are engagement and creativity. Ungrading affords the opportunity for students to buy into the revision process of writing for the sake of learning, highlighting the way that engagement can encourage "investment and involvement" and creativity can be a key part of "generating, investigating, and representing" ideas.

We've seen tangible outcomes of this revision investment as more students came to us with ideas for their drafts after receiving our formative feedback—often with more draft iterations than were assigned in the courses. This departure from earlier semesters displays a level of curiosity in their writing not previously seen by us. For instance, anecdotal evidence would suggest that students felt a greater sense of agency to make changes to their work beyond the scope of our feedback. While we are not making empirical, quantitatively-measured claims here about changes in students' levels of engagement, we do believe that most students saw the process of writing as more than aiming for a grade.

We also noticed demonstrable expressions of creativity. We have each received emails from students that show a clear desire to be more playful in their writing, which we interpret as a discrete ability to investigate and generate new ideas. This commitment to the possibilities of what the writing can do is represented in questions about a draft going in new directions. Take for example, this email from a student:

> However, I would like to ask . . . is there such a thing as "too much" of a change? I have started rearranging and reconstructing my poem. In doing so I have noticed that the main focal point and foundation of my poem is shifting. Shifting in a good way. Though I must say . . . it has evolved so much so that it looks like a completely different work. It bears little to no evidence of its previous version. (Student Email, personal communication, 2021)

Her response made us wonder whether she had ever considered such a question within typical assessment systems of grading prior to this class. Given her intersectional identities (cisgender, Creole, Haitian American), we also wondered if she perhaps didn't feel comfortable enough to ask her instructor about this given traditional models of assessment? As Lisa Delpit (1988) asserts, students learn within a "culture of power" (p. 282). Further, education as an institution "systematically domesticates our bodies; it incarcerates them in rows of wooden desks, robs them of spontaneity through rigid demarcations of time and space, and in fact devotes a great deal of energy to hiding the fact that we have bodies at all" (Pineau, 2002, p. 45). All students operate in an educational frame that, most often, hinders improvisation and choice. In a system where "passive students are indoctrinated into social mores as well as socioeconomic positions," multiply-marginalized students may internalize their "otherness" as something to hide in performance of "good student" (Pineau, 2002, p. 42). In short, our very classrooms and curriculum may deny our students freedom. Equity-informed course design promotes accessibility by removing the gatekeeping utility of grades. Students can choose their path to learning as opposed to simply editing to fulfill whatever proclivities a singular professor holds about what constitutes good writing.

It is important to address that one of the scholars we look to in this work, Inoue, critiqued the thinking that informed the *Framework for Success in Postsecondary Writing* (2011). In his CCCC address, Inoue (2019) challenges our field by saying:

> Do you think that White racial habitus, that the historical White language biases in our disciplines and lives, have affected these places, or the building of something like the *Framework for Success in Postsecondary Writing*? Or your own pedagogies? Or your own ways of judging student writing,

what you see, and can see, as clear, effective, and compelling?
Do you think you're special, immune to the biases?

Indeed, Inoue's critique is part of a larger conversation of how the White habitus influenced many of the central documents and professional organizations within the field of writing studies.

This might be a good place to share our own subject positionalities. I, Jennifer Daniel, am a cisgendered, neurodivergent, straight White woman. I've moved through some marginalized spaces related to class, gender, and ability that inform my desire to be an inclusive teacher and human in a flawed world. I, Shawn Bowers, was born in Costa Rica, am a bilingual, biracial cisgendered, straight woman and had to adopt a pen name that sounded more "Latina" to be taken seriously as a Latinx writer. In response to Inoue, we know we are not immune to biases, hidden and transparent alike. We respect and appreciate Inoue's critique. We acknowledge that the *Framework for Success in Postsecondary Writing* (2011) was most certainly influenced by the White habitus, yet it still offers us a place to start. What the Framework does offer, as suggested by Tristan Abbott (2020), is a "rhetorical neutrality" that operates "as a sort of distancing mechanism within the institutional systems that claim writing can be objectively assessed" (p. 177). Abbott reminds us that while we can never be objective, the Habits of Mind articulated in the *Framework for Success in Postsecondary Writing* (2011) can help us design assessment that values the process-oriented ethos of our classrooms instead of a product-oriented ethos.

Looking Inward: Teacher-Researcher Practice and Positionality

Any pedagogical choices we make as teachers ought to originate from intentional, ethical, and informed positions. Times of crises might limit our ability to build new practices out of reflective intention, but our responsibilities to our students require us to make our best efforts towards such a position, regardless of external factors. In concert with the GSOLE principle of iterative processes for course design, our experiences as teacher-researchers give us a practical and material path towards this liberatory educational stance. For the purposes of our chapter, we claim the position of teacher-researcher as instructors who "accept the close relationship between the writing process and the human growth process" and who are observer-participants who also learn and create knowledge within the classroom context (Mohr, 1980, para. 7). We learn alongside our students.

Our practices are also informed by several educational, compositional, and rhetorical theories, but originate in the critical pedagogies of Freire and his critique of education's banking model, "where teachers seek to make deposits or fill students up with all of the essential points and right answers" (Pappas & Zecker, 2001, p. 3). The grade is the marker for what a student has learned to do independently within an assessment system designed to confine knowledge to a narrow understanding that sustains the dominant systems of power and oppression. In contrast, reflective and critical teaching moves us to consider what our students already know and to leverage that knowledge. We also want to offer that critical pedagogy also calls us to a stance of "radical hope" understood by education scholar Darren Webb (2013) as the "profound confidence in the transformative capacities of human agency, a confidence that enables real subjects to insert themselves into history and commit themselves to confronting and overcoming the 'limit situations' that face them" (p. 410). As teachers, we have profound confidence in the transformative capacities of our students' human agency; we were just done with grades mediating the relationship we wanted to develop with them.

IN AND AROUND THE COURSE CONTEXT

In both the pilot sections and in our subsequent courses, we positioned ungrading as the primary mechanisms for our assessment system. Our grading contracts are informed by the work of Jesse Stommel, Blum, and, as noted above, Inoue. For instructors interested in this approach, we recommend starting with Stommel's "How to Ungrade" (2018), and Blum's (2020) text *Ungrading: Why Rating Students Undermines Learning (and what to do instead)*. While we studied Stommel to better understand contract grading—he contends that "[g]rading contracts convey expectations about what is required for each potential grade" and students are given the freedom to choose goals for themselves (2018, p. 2)—we also zeroed in on portfolios as another alternate approach to assessment. This focus led us to consider a combination for the pilot: we opted for grading contracts with a final portfolio of work that would be assessed as well. We see this move as a focus on the students' efforts and not the professors' predilection for particular writing styles.

OUR PURPOSE AND INTENTION FOR CONTRACT GRADING

Our primary purpose for using contract grading was to promote a writing-to-learn experience so that students saw the value of using writing to understand their intersectional identities and how those intersectional identities were shaped by a sense of place. We hoped that students would come to see writing as a tool for learning and not just a way of mimicking standardized models of writing.

Moving through multiple drafts—with steps including ideation, messy first attempts, and employing feedback—is a critical series of steps for creative thinking that is at the heart of addressing rhetorical situations and making meaning. We echo Hubrig and Barritt in Chapter 9 of this text, as we also recognize that this is not a codified, singular process. Ungrading allows students the flexibility to work through this process in their own manner.

Again, as writing teachers for over a decade, we each understood that this experience would be our students' first with ungrading; thus, we opted for a simple contract that primarily used narrative descriptions to scale expectations of the assignments and other important components of the courses. We share the example below to illustrate the language we used to explain the grading contract to students; in this sample, the "I" is Jennifer as the contract is from her FYC course at Queens University of Charlotte, our institution.

QEN 102: Contract Grading

Note: Our version of the contract is borrowed heavily from versions that Stommel has generously shared widely across multiple platforms including various academic talks and his professional website: https://www.jessestommel.com/. He graciously allowed us to use our adapted model in this chapter.

Purpose: What is contract grading exactly?

Contract grading is a way to honor your labor and give you space to take risks without fearing failure. Indeed, failure is one of the best learning tools we have. Often grading isn't really about learning. It's about assessment, which measures neither your work, nor your potential. There is quite a bit of research in both education and writing studies that indicates that grading negatively impacts students' actual learning as well as motivation for learning (Kohn, 2011). Ultimately, I want you to drive and own your learning and to set goals appropriate for that purpose. Below is the contract grading scale that YOU may select for this class. If you object to this, please let me know via email and we can set up a meeting to discuss a different way of grading that suits your academic needs. If this scale sounds like something you want to pursue, take some time to read through your options. Choose the one that feels best for you as a learner and your goals as a student in this class. Once you decide on a level of work, you will commit to it in Canvas.

Criteria for Success:

Please be sure to note that you will have the option to adjust up or down as the course proceeds. Here are the options:

1. Turn in all formal assignments on time with the assignment guidelines fulfilled.
2. Turn in all (full) drafts of formal assignments on time—except one may be late.
3. Turn in all Process Writings on time.
4. Complete 90% of all Free Writings at the satisfactory level.*
5. Complete 90% of all Practice Writings at the satisfactory level.*

1. Turn in all formal assignments on time with the assignment guidelines fulfilled.
2. Turn in all drafts of formal assignments on time—except two may be late.
3. Turn in all Process Writings on time.
4. Complete 85% of all Free Writings at the satisfactory level.*
5. Complete 85% of all Practice Writings at the satisfactory level.*

1. Turn in all formal assignments on time with the majority of the assignment guidelines fulfilled.
2. Turn in all drafts of formal assignments on time—except three may be late.
3. Turn in all Process Writings on time.
4. Complete 75% of all Free Writings at the satisfactory level.*
5. Complete 75% of all Practice Writings at the satisfactory level.*

* Satisfactory means that you met the minimum of the prompt guidelines. Example, for a free write, you will write a robust paragraph that's appx 300 words.

The professor reserves the right to award a grade of D or F to anyone who fails to meet a contractual obligation in a systematic way. A "D" grade denotes some minimal fulfillment of the contract. An "F" is absence of enough satisfactory work, as contracted, to warrant passing of the course. Both a "D" and "F" denote a breakdown of the contractual relationship implied by signing any of the contracts described above.

I also reserve the right to reward exceptional work throughout the semester using the full range of Queens' grading scale. If you contract for a "B," for instance, and submit particularly strong pieces to fulfill that contract, I may elect to raise your contracted grade to a "B+."

Likewise, if you consistently submit mediocre work in fulfillment of your contract, I reserve the right to adjust your grade one half-step down (e.g., from "A" to "A–") or even, in extreme cases, a full step.

Contract Adjustments

Periodically during the semester, I will ask you to evaluate your work thus far and compare it against what you agreed in your grade contract. In these moments, you can also take the opportunity to request an adjustment to your contract in either direction. If you find that you will be unable to meet the obligations of your contract, you may request to move to the next lowest grade and its requirements. Alternatively, if you find that you've been performing above the obligations of your contract, you may request to fulfill the requirements for the next higher grade.

Important Note: In order to effectively evaluate your own progress, you must keep track of your work including when/if items were late or not satisfactory.[1]

Final Notes

Professor Bowers and I wrote our grading contracts collaboratively, so they may have similar or the same language.

REFLECTION ON THE CONTRACT

In reviewing this contract, we wish to emphasize a few important details that are essential to this practice. After first providing an extended definition of contract grading, we lay out descriptions that both qualify and quantify process work into a three-tiered scale: strong (typically considered "A" work), satisfactory (typically considered "B" work), and developing (typically considered "C" work). We also included a brief narrative about "D" and "F" work. We chose to pair traditional letter grades with our contract grading descriptions as a bridge for students to scaffold from previous learning landscapes to this new one. Of course, at the end of the semester, the institution required a letter grade. While we cannot avoid all summative grading, we were able to delay a focus on grades until time to translate contract grades to the university's alphabetic grading system. In our classroom discussions introducing grading contracts, we were explicit in framing traditional letter grades as a subjective construct. What constitutes an A for one professor may be a B for a different professor. Performance then becomes a strategic endeavor to meet the quirks of the instructor.

By describing strong, satisfactory, and developing work in terms of quantity[2] (all drafts or some drafts being turned in, for example) and quality[3] (in refer-

---

1   Our LMS system is Canvas, which allows assignments to be marked as "Complete/Incomplete" in place of a letter or numeric grade. We and the students used this setting to track dates of submissions. Additionally, we provided the formative feedback directly within the LMS system both within the body of the assignments and the global comments function.
2   By quantity, we mean did the student complete all or the majority of the assignments of the class. We provided targets for page ranges, but not specific page or word count.
3   By quality, we gave descriptions for what we considered quality work. We understand quality is subjective. We attempted to mitigate the subjectivity through other tools in the course such as

ence to assignment guidelines), we attempted to give students explicit requirements. The expectations described the process and work, and not the student. In Jen's class, students indicated which level of work (and ultimately, grade) they wanted to strive for at the beginning of the semester. At any point in the course, students could change their minds. For Shawn, students were not required to specify the grade they were aspiring to. We both used language from the grading contracts (strong, satisfactory, developing) in our feedback to students, so they understood their standing in the course with each assignment. Also, each assignment's guidelines explicitly detailed what constituted strong, satisfactory, and developing work. We feel it important to note that while we used the same grading framework and intentionally aligned our contracts because of the learning community aspect, we did deviate from each other on occasion. The biggest deviation was that students in Jen's composition course chose which grade they were contracting to, whereas in Shawn's course, students did not articulate a specific grade. We point this out to underscore that this practice is not a one-size-fits-all and to encourage readers to adapt their contracts to best suit the needs of the learning environment and students they teach. In fact, we did the very same thing for ourselves.

Our summer enrollment was exceptionally low, and initially we worried about the process of piloting a new grading system with only three students in our learning community but continued with our plan given that contract grading doesn't necessitate a particular number of students to be successful. In fact, contract grading saved us from the tendency to compare students to one another within the course. In the fall term of 2021, as the university went back to mostly in-person, real-time learning, our courses saw healthier enrollment numbers, and we decided to again apply our ungrading practices in a new set of courses.

Of note, a significant distinction of the fall slate of classes is that they are not part of the general education program and therefore are not linked to other courses in learning communities. Instead, these writing-intensive courses are housed in the English department, serving all three of our major tracks: professional writing and rhetoric, literary studies, and creative writing. The language of the contracts shifted slightly to accommodate the specific writing assignments of each course and addressed issues of "engagement" differently to better reflect the course modality. For example, the peer review process in our respective courses had different aims and, therefore, required students engage differently with peers.

Also, because we had a larger sample size, we felt we could implement an anonymous midterm student evaluation to check in on students' perceptions towards

---

SLOs and explicitly repeated feedback that we were not prioritizing lower order concerns (i.e., grammar).

ungrading without risk of disclosure of identifying information. (Had we done this over the summer with our three participants, we feel we would have been able to ascertain students' identities based on the responses). The student feedback illuminated things we already suspected; it affirmed that ungrading is a pedagogical approach that—when paired with other antiracist and inclusive teaching practices such as self-evaluation, encouraging multilingualism, and creativity around genre artifacts—creates a less fraught, more inclusive environment that is conducive for deep learning (see Felicia Chavez, 2021; Hogan & Sathy, 2022).

As we reflect on how this distinct approach to assessment impacts our teaching, we see a great number of advantages to ungrading with the use of grading contracts. Chief among them is how it has changed the way we provide feedback to student writing. Our feedback has become more robust and conversational as we seek to guide students to self-discovery as it relates to topics, lines of argument, and rhetorical techniques. One example of this is how the feedback we offered stopped policing grammatical conventions. Free from having to "correct" a composition based on Standard American English, formative feedback was individualized, tailored to the students' goals expressed in the scaffolded pre-writing assignments. While we still give feedback on grammar and mechanics, it does not factor into our evaluations process.

At another level, this alternative assessment practice released us from grammar policing to ceding space for real conversations about themselves as writers. For example, Shawn noticed a pattern in her feedback to students where she responded to writing from two lenses: a human making personal connections to human experiences and then as an instructor offering advice about how to better engage an audience. Before ungrading, it felt odd to assign a grade to a personal narrative where trauma or abuse was disclosed. That is not to say that we ignore all conventions of academic writing but prioritize responding to the writer's choices using the language of rhetoric around audience, purpose, genre, and other more global features of their work. We offer a different focus that does not ask the student to eschew their literacy practices by codeswitching or imitating language born from the hegemonic educational systems in service of a grade (Young, 2021). Like other instructors who embrace contract grading, we believe that if the goal is meaning making, we must include students in the process of assigning value to their learning.

Reflection on Practice

First, we want to assert that contract grading is not a magic solution, and there are certainly challenges still present in adopting this method of assessment. Sherri Craig (2021) rightly contends in her recent essay from the summer 2021

WPA Journal's "Anti-Racist Classroom Practices" section, "Your Contract Grading Ain't It," "[contract grading] is low hanging fruit that does the most injustice to our Black students, to our Black faculty because it attempts to convince them that the university cares for their lives and their experiences" (p. 146). Principally, Craig reminds educators that inequity and racism is not eradicated by a singular teaching intervention in the face of systemic oppression. Moreover, she warns us that marginalized students still have to navigate within this system, so the practices must serve our students and not our guilt-laden egos. Craig's position is sharply pointed and certainly needed. We recognize the recent trend to use contract grading does not address the systemic issues in higher education related to writing and language—a system whose very DNA is imbued with White-supremacy using the tools of language and writing as its custodians as suggested by educators and scholars such as Delpit and Rosina Lippi-Green. Ungrading was just part of a larger suite of changes we made as we reflected on our teaching practices that also included revisions in attendance policies, minor shifts in flexibility of deadlines, and transparent assignment design.

In her extended essay, *The Hidden Inequities in Labor-Based Contract Grading*, Ellen Carillo (2021) extends this critique and elaborates on a couple considerations we have found true in our own practice. Namely, there is a clear risk of substituting one standard for another. Carillo (2021) warns, "This sort of substitution is especially dangerous because quantifiable information—the kind of information that is collected by students as they labor—gives the appearance of objectivity" (p. 18). Carillo troubles the antiracist claim championed by antiracist practice advocates, specifically about the ways that accounting for labor may create biased practices for students with disabilities. When we substitute labor for other grading criteria we need to be careful in how we define labor because it is not neutral. Ungrading practices that assess students based on time-on-task could disadvantage disabled individuals whose learning is supported by accessible pedagogies such as crip time defined as "a flexible approach to normative time frames" (Price, 2011, p. 62). If antiracist practices are about inclusivity, then they must be inclusive with relation to accessibility as well. In using Stommel's version, which provided descriptions that speak to both quantity and quality, we hoped that our grading contracts center student engagement over quantifiable labor, though we are still thinking through this issue each semester. As DePew and Matheson point out in their chapter on grading contracts in this collection, your contract should align with your pedagogical values and be intentionally designed to create the learning environment and behaviors that encourage student success (see Chapter 17, this collection).

Moreover, we would be remiss if we left readers thinking that the process was easy for both us and the students. In fact, we have both engaged in uncomfortable conversations with students who were deeply opposed to this new form of assessment. Interestingly, these resistant reactions came from students on a continuum of social locations: neurodivergent students, honors students, and BIPOC students are just three of our demographics that responded in negative ways. They expressed feelings of angst, asserting that while they understood our intentions, they were uneasy about not having the grades to validate themselves as good students, which is a fraught term that is not really even achievable as its definition is circumscribed by race, gender, class, ability.

Students continue to return often to check in, to ensure that they are on track with their work, and we have responded with affirming language. As teachers, and humans in an uncertain world, we see this as a chance to support them in learning to understand that they are valuable—not just as good students, but as people in the world. This can be difficult in online landscapes, where communication is usually expressed solely in writing. We found that by utilizing office hours, where we could meet students over video platforms (or, on occasion, in person) created an atmosphere that allowed for real-time dialogue so that we could respond to each concern. Their resistance begs the question: what are we doing as educators if our students need grades to know that they are valuable as human beings?

Reticence to adapt a new way of assessing might reflect the false narrative that grades are the only way to teach; however, the custom of grading as we know it is a nineteenth century invention. To continue embracing a single system that upholds grading as the only way to capture student learning is deeply problematic. Stommel (2020) posits that "[g]rading is so ingrained in our educational systems that small acts of pedagogical disobedience can't do enough to change the larger (and hostile) culture of grading and assessment" (para. 14). We acknowledge that this disobedience required much labor on our part to enact this practice, but it was a labor of love to make our teaching pedagogies match our teaching philosophies. Recalling the work of bell hooks, grades do not "create participatory spaces for the sharing of knowledge" because students have no input into the grading design (hooks, 1994, p. 15). In fact, students who have completed our courses come back and talk about their experiences returning to courses that use the traditional alphabetic grading system. They report a new awareness of just how much their attention was oriented towards the grade at the expense of their learning.

Strategic learners figure out the system, which is to say those who learn how to manage their professors and play the game of school, end up performing a show of knowledge and risk not making deeper connections in their learning. Our experience tells us that grades don't necessarily demonstrate deep learning. Take this instance of a student who openly admitted she knew how to write papers in response to texts she never read and earned high marks on the essays. For her midterm reflection in an ungraded course, where she was asked to make connections between the texts and her learning, she admitted the process was both freeing and more academically challenging. She was invited to learn for the sake of personal development and not an arbitrary GPA. The crux of the issue is that she knew how to write the paper without engaging the texts. Why? Because her social location meant that she had "the accouterments of the culture of power" (Delpit, 1988, p. 283.) In this course, she was afforded an opportunity to name how she's been able to game the system. Would she have taken that risk had she known she was performing for a grade? Without the freedom from the subjective grading, how would she have shared this pivotal learning moment? Would she even have had it?

If education is about freedom, grades can shackle a student's agency. Grades assess what a student knows at that particular moment. To be explicit and to use the parlance of assessment, grades indicate mastery, while ungrading turns the eye to a student's potential.[4] We want to challenge the system that accounts for what a student has already learned to do independently in favor of options that make visible to the student their potential development and growth. Using development and growth as an inducement for engagement in learning potentially shifts student motivation from extrinsic (grades) to intrinsic (potential growth). Prior to ungrading, we used feedback to justify the alpha grade. Once we stopped using the feedback to justify a grade, the nature of the communication with our students changed. We approached their work with bigger questions, rooted in the principles of the rhetorical situation. I (Shawn) found myself using the phrase, "I wonder if" to open space for broader ideation; I (Jen) found myself modeling specific connecting sentences to help students see pathways to develop ideas. Feedback became the most tangible way our students experienced us as teachers. We (Jen and Shawn) want to be teachers, not gatekeepers. Feedback was highly personalized, differentiated for each learner, and the goal line was different for each student. This practice was, of course, more work for us as teachers, but it was also more meaningful. Whatever discomfort we initially felt by throwing the old rulebook away was quickly replaced by joy. Reimaging assessment and feedback as collaborative dialogue with our students transformed the learning environment (regardless of modality) to a space of shared governance. Obviously, we can't erase grades from the institution, but we can redirect student focus to learning that serves them beyond the classroom. We stopped policing and started teaching.

---

4   We acknowledge the fraught nature of the word "mastery" both as a fixed goal that can ever be achieved for any academic standard, but also as a term that evokes the traumatic history of our country's enslavement of millions of Africans and indigenous peoples.

CONCLUSION: EMBRACING CHANGE

The COVID-19 pandemic compelled us to reconsider our priorities as teachers of writing in unexpected ways—ways that we didn't know at the time would be generative, positive, and energizing in a time when everything around us wasn't. Now, we carry back with us into the teaching landscape a heart for what really matters: agency (for students and faculty alike) and a reclamation of joy. We want to be architects of better learning spaces. Ungrading equips instructors with a different foundational starting point. Ultimately, design is what drives outcomes and realities. If we start from the point of design, we can dream of learning spaces meant for everyone . . . including us. Contract grading and other ungrading methods, when designed with the students in mind, can be employed in any educational modality. Stuckey and Wilson's chapter give examples of the contract in play in two different online, any time settings (Chapter 18, this collection). Since writing this chapter, we have each utilized grading contracts in in-person, real-time and hybrid learning environments. Across *all* modalities, contract grading has become an adaptable tool in our teaching practices; we can assess what we need for that course in order to align with our own teaching ethos.

We warn you, starting the work of dismantling our old grading systems had a snowballing effect. What started with contract grading has led to significant changes in feedback, assignment design, and engagement practices. While there is still a lot of research to be done in this space, contract grading does seem to be a stepping stone towards more inclusive pedagogies that underscore the importance of acknowledging students' many knowledges. Starting this process in the online, any time learning class provided the impetus to design and implement from the understanding that, throughout the course, we would need to revise and adjust our teaching practices to ensure that students felt supported. Inclusive practices—whether for antiracist stances or accessibility—should always inform our teaching in every modality. Moving to the online format afforded us a break from our face-to-face practices that had become comfortable; it gave us a beginner mindset. Ultimately, that discomfort motivated our curiosity for ungrading and invited us to enact our commitment to critical pedagogies that offer students experiences with education not as a place defined by correctness but by freedom.

MOVING BETTER PRACTICES ACROSS MODALITIES

- **In-Person, Real-Time Learning:** This modality offers dedicated space to engage in class conversations that recenter learning over grades and making visible the uneven expectations grades set up. Students can

share experiences around grades that might help alleviate the competition that grades encourage.
- **Online, Real-Time Learning:** Similar to in-person, real-time learning—instructors can use class time discussing student experiences with grading to recenter learning.
- **Online, Any Time Learning:** Ungrading practices offer a variety of assessment measures that support building a relationship between student and instructor that might otherwise be hindered in this modality as there is no real-time class.
- **Hybrid Learning:** As with online, any time learning, this modality reduces face time between student and instructor, so ungrading may feel more flexible for students.

REFERENCES

Abbott, T. (2020). The métis of reliability: Using the Framework for Success to aid the performance of neutrality within writing assessment. In D. P. Richards (Ed.), *On teacher neutrality: Politics, praxis, and performativity* (pp. 176–190). Utah State University Press.

Beare, Z. C. & Stenberg, S. J. (2020). "Everyone thinks it's just me": Exploring the emotional dimensions of seeking publication. *College English, 83*(2), 103–126.

Bird, B. (2012). Rethinking our view of learning. *The Writing Lab Newsletter, 36*(5–6), 1–6. https://wac.colostate.edu/wln/archive.

Blum, S. D. (2020). *Ungrading: Why rating students undermines learning (and what to do instead)*. West Virginia University Press.

Carillo, E. (2021). *The hidden inequities in labor-based contract grading*. Utah State University Press.

Cedillo, C. V. & Bratta, P. (2019). Relating our experiences: The practice of positionality stories in student-center pedagogy. *College Composition and Communication, 71*(2), 215–240.

Council of Writing Program Administrators, National Council of Teachers of English & National Writing Project. (2011, January). *Framework for success in postsecondary writing*. https://wpacouncil.org/aws/CWPA/pt/sd/news_article/242845/_PARENT/layout_details/false.

Craig, S. (2021). Your contract grading ain't it. *WPA: Writing Program Administrator, 44*(3), 145–146. https://wpacouncil.org/aws/CWPA/asset_manager/get_file/604397?ver=1.

Delpit, L. (1988). The silenced dialogue: Power and pedagogy in educating other people's children. *Harvard Educational Review, 58*(3), 280–298. https://doi.org/10.17763/haer.58.3.c43481778r528qw4.

Felicia Chavez, R. (2021). *The anti-racist writing workshop: How to decolonize the creative classroom*. Haymarket Books.

Freire, P. (2014). *Pedagogy of the oppressed: 30*th *anniversary edition*. The Continuum International Publishing Group.

GSOLE Executive Board. (2019, June 13). *Online literacy instruction principles and tenets*. Global Society of Online Literacy Educators. https://gsole.org/oliresources/oliprinciples.

Hanson, M. (2021). College enrollment & student demographic statistics. *EducationData.org*. https://educationdata.org/college-enrollment-statistics.

Hartman, Z. B. (2022, January 6). The Zen of not knowing. *Tricycle: The Buddhist Review*. https://tricycle.org/article/zen-not-knowing/.

Hogan, K. A. & Sathy, V. (2022). *Inclusive teaching: Strategies for promoting equity in the college classroom*. West Virginia University Press.

hooks, b. (1994). *Teaching to transgress: Education as the practice of freedom*. Routledge.

Inoue, A. (2019). How do we language so people stop killing each other, or what do we do about white language supremacy? *College Composition and Communication, 71*(2), 352–369.

Inoue, A. (2019). *Labor-Based grading contracts: Building equity and inclusion in the compassionate writing classroom*. The WAC Clearinghouse; University Press of Colorado. https://doi.org/10.37514/PER-B.2019.0216.0

Kohn, A. (2011). The case against grades. Educational Leadership, 69(3), 28–33.

Lippi-Green, R. (2011). *English with an Accent: Language, ideology and discrimination in the United States* (pp. 182–213). Taylor & Francis.

Mohr, M. M. (1980). The teacher as researcher. *The Quarterly, 3*(1). https://archive.nwp.org/cs/public/print/resource/1894.

Pappas, C. & Zecker, L. (2001). Urban teacher researchers' struggles in sharing powers with their students: Exploring changes in literacy curriculum genres. In C. Pappas & L. Zecker, Eds., *Transforming literacy curriculum genres: Working with teacher researchers in urban classrooms* (pp. 1–32). Taylor & Francis Group.

Pineau, E. L. (2002). Critical performative pedagogy: Fleshing out the politics of liberatory education. In N. Stucky & C. Wimmer (Eds.), *Teaching performance studies* (pp. 41–54). Southern Illinois University Press.

Price, M. (2011). *Mad at school: Rhetorics of mental disability and academic life*. University of Michigan Press.

Stommel, J. (2018, March 11). *How to ungrade*. Jesse Stommel. https://www.jessestommel.com/how-to-ungrade/.

Stommel, J. (2020, February 6). *Ungrading: An FAQ*. Jesse Stommel. https://www.jessestommel.com/ungrading-an-faq/.

Webb, D. (2013). Pedagogies of hope. *Studies in Philosophy and Education, 32*(4), 397–414. https://doi.org/10.1007/s11217-012-9336-1.

Young, V. A. (2021). 2020 CCCC Chair's Address. *College Composition and Communication, 72*(4), 623–639.

CHAPTER 17.

THE RADICAL EQUITY OF GRADING CONTRACTS IN ONLINE WRITING COURSES

Kevin E. DePew and Kole Matheson
Old Dominion University

In this chapter, the authors describe **contract grading** *used in online asynchronous learning; online, real-time learning; online, any time learning; and hybrid learning. Specifically, the authors help online writing teachers implement anti-racist assessment practices through the creation of grading contracts using two approaches: one that emphasizes consistent approach to all the labor in an online course with the other focusing on contracts that align to the labor of the individual assignments. In describing their "better practice," this chapter addresses the themes of accessibility and inclusivity, assessment, and professional learning for online teachers.*

FRAMEWORKS AND PRINCIPLES IN THIS CHAPTER

- **GSOLE Principle 1.4:** The student-user experience should be prioritized when designing online courses, which includes mobile-friendly content, interaction affordances, and economic needs.
- **CCCC Principles for the Postsecondary Teaching of Writing, 1:** [Writing instruction] emphasizes the rhetorical nature of writing.
- **CCCC Principles for the Postsecondary Teaching of Writing, 12:** [Writing instruction] is assessed through a collaborative effort that focuses on student learning within and beyond writing courses.

GUIDING QUESTIONS BEFORE YOU BEGIN READING

- What learning outcomes do your assessment practices measure? Do these metrics systematically benefit some students and/or disadvantage others?
- How might an anti-racist approach be useful in conversations with your students as it relates to grading contracts?

- How do you sell grading contracts to a student audience who have been indoctrinated by the ideologies of A–F assessment? How do you make these arguments through the digital technologies that mediate your online course?
- How do grading contracts make instructor and assignment expectations more transparent?
- How do you leverage the affordances of the digital technologies that mediate the online course to create a system of labor or engagement that fits organically into the course?

INTRODUCTION

I, Kole, observed my first composition course as a graduate student-teacher shadowing a composition instructor. At first unsure of how I would manage a composition teaching load, I was soon relieved when the teacher arrived and began instruction on the five-paragraph essay, a writing instruction approach I knew and could teach!

Later that semester, after the instructor delivered lessons grounded in current-traditional rhetorical philosophy, the students' first essay was due. Again, following the lead of the veteran teacher, I received my first stack of papers and began identifying, describing, and counting the number of errors I found in the students' essays. Each of these errors resulted in a point deduction from the essay grade, which dropped some students' grades as much as two letters, regardless of the quality of thought or insightfulness of the content.

Despite this assessment practice's prevalent precedence, something just didn't feel right. Here I was, demanding students (1) write five-paragraph essays, a form that does not clearly exist beyond placement testing and first-year composition (FYC) classes and (2) demonstrate "academic diction" proficiency—which I have come to believe echoes White language normativity. After teaching on my own for several years, I met Megan Weaver who invited me to participate in the research project that became her award-winning dissertation, "Critical Language Awareness Pedagogy in First-Year Composition: A Design-Based Research Study" (2020), an investigation into the strategies for developing critical language awareness in instructors and students alike. During this two-year process of reading groups, discussions with colleagues, and eventually class observations and teaching interventions and reflections, I experienced a realization in my pedagogy: my grading upheld biased, if institutional, and White normative understandings of writing.

My habits of assignment designing and grading might have been understood as a kind of linguistic segregation in which some White, academically sanctioned language habits were demanded in some places, while other language habits were forbidden. While this code-switching, or accepting "mother tongues" on early drafts while demanding Standard Academic English (SAE) on final drafts, has been common practice among progressive writing educators (Elbow, 1999), I began to realize that separate is not equal, especially in terms of our linguistic practices. To refuse non-standard language and genres on final submission was to announce to my students that these communicative forms were not legible in academic spaces. How could I reconcile a demand for linguistic justice (Baker-Bell, 2020) on one hand, while on the other hand demand that students code switch? Educators are either for White language supremacy or against it. Any middle ground is complicit racism—a racism that Kevin also acknowledges has characterized his own instructional practices and that we believe many in our audience will find familiar.

To understand and work to resist the racism in our own pedagogical practices, we had to understand the *habitus* that we privileged—a term grading contract advocate Asao Inoue (2019) borrows from Pierre Bourdieu (1990) to describe "linguistic, bodily, and performative dispositions" (2019, p. 5). To understand habitus, one should reflect on the ways that they appear, speak, act, and behave in contexts, like their homes, when they are with people who make them feel comfortable. Then reflect upon those ways of being in other contexts, especially professional contexts or contexts in which we are being judged. While most people alter their ways of being from one context to the next, the shifts that the White, middle- and upper-class populations of American society are asked to make are minimal compared to those in minoritized populations or at the intersection of multiple minoritized populations. For them the expectation is often to adopt the "linguistic, bodily, and performative dispositions" of their White, middle- and upper-class peers (Inoue, 2019). As Inoue (2019) argues, most educational decisions are designed to accommodate this privileged population, a practice that carries over to online instruction.

In writing studies, over the last 25 years, scholars (Ball, 1997; Haswell & Haswell, 1996; Yancey, 1999) have asserted that traditional practices of grading student writing are unreliable and invalid. Implicit biases and subjectivity inhibit a grader's ability to objectively assess student writing: what one instructor sees as an asset to writing can be viewed by another as a weakness. For example, when literacy instructors primarily access writing for its approximation to privileged habitus, they systematically disadvantage many student populations, including English language learners (CCCC *Statement on Second Language Writers and Writing*, 2020; Ortmeier-Hooper, 2013; Ruecker, 2015) and other students not immersed in this habitus.

Linguistic justice is an anti-racist response to the privileged habitus in literacy education. April Baker-Bell (2020) describes linguistic justice as an active corrective to "Anti-Black Linguistic Racism and White linguistic hegemony and supremacy" that pedagogically "places Black Language at the center of Black students' language education and experiences" by affording "Black students the same kind of linguistic liberties that are afforded to white students" (p. 7). In short, linguistic justice seeks to raise the Black habitus to the level of intellectual legibility as the established habitus. We believe that a linguistic justice approach to online writing instruction, via pedagogical tools like grading contracts, fulfills the letter of GSOLE's *Online Literacy Instruction Principles and Tenets* (2019) first principle: "Online literacy instruction should be universally accessible and inclusive (GSOLE, 2019). Yet this principle's tenets focus primarily on digital technologies as the obstacle to be overcome for our diverse student body. We argue that habitus, including language, is a technology, or manipulation of the human environment, that needs to be accounted for in conjunction with online instruction's digital environments. So when Tenet 1.4 states, "The student-user experience should be prioritized when designing online courses, which includes mobile-friendly content, interaction affordances, and economic needs" (GSOLE, 2019), we emphasize the presence of language—specifically language variation—among the interaction affordances.

OUR RATIONALE FOR GRADING CONTRACTS

Grading contracts have been part of pedagogical conversation for the last half-century (Avakian, 1974; Barlow, 1974; Hassencahl, 1979). Our chapter adds to the current conversations about grading contracts in OLI (Laflen, 2020; Laflen & Sims, 2021) by arguing that grading contracts adopted for the online literacy context need to leverage the affordances of the digital applications instructors use to mediate their classes.

During the last two years, we have separately adopted grading contracts because, as Inoue (2019) notes, they "focus on negotiated learning processes and outcomes or goals for individual projects and are individualized to each student" (p. 64). We believe we are lucky to be teaching at an institution with a relatively diverse student population. Our campus has traditionally been a commuter campus serving mostly the local region (i.e., southeast Virginia); however, over the past decade, like many institutions, it has built an infrastructure to serve more residential students. Many of these students are working class and military-related, and over half of the students in 2019 took courses either off-campus or took a combination of on-campus and off-campus courses. Of the 24,286 students enrolled in 2020, 48.6 percent could be classified as BIPOC with 28.9 percent being Black Americans, 8.6 percent being Latinx, and 2.5 percent being "non-resident aliens" or international students. While we would personally like to see the university's administration foster a more diverse campus, we, more importantly, believe that an emphasis should be placed on developing better strategies for teaching the diverse students we have, especially those online. Moreover, we are particularly responsive to the stories our diverse students tell us about previous K–12 teachers characterizing their English language use as "incorrect," "broken," and "ghetto." Therefore, the contracts that we have designed are our response to their lived experiences. Our assignments and grading contracts were designed to establish "outcomes and goals" for students to labor upon, correlating each student's labor with their grade. As all students are assessed based on their demonstrated quantity of labor, we try to ensure that no racial habitus, including linguistic practices, are privileged in our respective assessment designs. The logic of grading contracts, including our own, are illustrated in Figures 17.1 and 17.2.

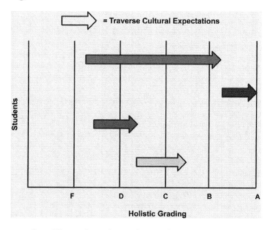

Figure 17.1. Example of how four hypothetical students are traditionally assessed.

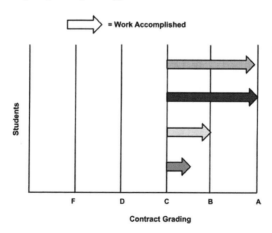

Figure 17.2. Example of how four hypothetical students are assessed based upon labor.

Figure 17.1 depicts how four hypothetical students' assessment moves through a holistically assessed course. Each arrow then represents a student's ability to learn—attempting to adopt the privileged habitus—and to move closer to many writing instructors and writing programs' expected ideals. To understand how grading contracts work, focus on the students represented by the purple (i.e., the top) and orange (i.e., the bottom) arrows. The purple arrow represents Student A who starts the semester with little background in the privileged habitus but over the course of the semester demonstrates both an ability to understand and appropriate the cultural expectations—such as language performance, Aristotelian logic. This student who arrives in our classes with knowledge and lived experience which the academy traditionally finds illegible must traverse more cultural ground, probably moving outside of their comfort zone or feeling culturally conflicted to reach an "A." Student B, the orange arrow, understands many of the privileged habitus, maybe because they are practiced at home, yet begins the semester struggling to demonstrate their proficiency in these practices. As this student understands the expectations of the academy, they tap into their knowledge of the White habitus and are able to raise their grade. As we look at all of them, we see that students do not come to our classes with the same understanding and ability to practice privileged cultural expectations, which systematically supports some students and disadvantages others. Thus, if we are trying to prioritize the student-user experience in our course designs, as advocated by GSOLE, then we need to acknowledge how the traditional assessment of writing perpetuates linguistic and cultural inequity.

Figure 17.2 depicts how contracted grades are earned for four hypothetical students. In this example, all students are guaranteed a base grade of C for demonstrating the minimum amount of effort and/or a demonstration of competency, as illustrated by all four arrows beginning on the same line. Being the same students from *Figure 17.1*, they come to class with different relationships to the privileged habitus, yet they all start the class with the same passing grade and the same opportunity to raise their grade; in many ways, very few are systematically disadvantaged. Again, Student A, the top purple arrow, starts the course with little background in the privileged habitus, yet, by doing the contracted extra labor, can earn an A without having to demonstrate conformity to the White supremist habitus. This does not mean that students do not fail; grades will be lowered when students fail to do the work or meet certain assignment criteria. Or Student B, the orange arrow (i.e., bottom), begins the course proficient in the privileged habitus but chooses to do little work beyond the minimum requirements; thus they earn a C. Student B may have struggled in the class because they had difficulty understanding the expectations or chose to put minimal effort into this course because of work, athletics, or a desire to focus on more major related classes. Rather than starting all students at a perfect grade and finding reasons to lower those grades, students start from an average or good grade and are given multiple opportunities to improve upon this assessment through extra labor, including revisions. Students' grades will only go down if they are not doing the work or if they are struggling to meet certain expectations. While some of these expectations can be objective (e.g., meeting a word length, demonstrating one has read the text), others are more subjective (e.g., sufficient explanation of the evidence) and, admittedly, pushes against the culturally sustaining nature of the practice.

Benefits of Contract Grading

The grading contracts we describe in detail is our step towards imagining new futures. We approach these grading contracts and our rationales for them with humility, understanding that students from socially and economically disadvantaged backgrounds have and will continue to succeed according to traditional assessment methods. But we also recognize that most writing instructors can imagine how grading contracts alleviate the psychological stress for students who have been told that they "write wrong"—a situation further exacerbated when the online instructor only knows you by an English that others have called "broken." Perhaps, this is a fundamental benefit which grading contracts have on teaching and learning from the student perspective, especially those previously demoralized ones. As Alan Blackstock and Virginia Exton (2014) have noted, "the use of grading contracts can provide those students with space to grow in confidence, skill, and perhaps even love of writing" (p. 278). As teachers who love writing, perhaps we can instill this same love in our students by means of our teaching and our assessment practices.

Challenges of Contract Grading

Most of the concern about grading contacts in online classes, up until this edited collection, has been about how learning management system (LMS) gradebooks can be adapted to accommodate them (Laflan, 2020). The emphasis is on how and whether the affordances of grading contracts mesh with the affordances of the course mediating technologies. Grading contracts are not a one-size fits all practice as some instructors design different contracts for different types of classes and others create universal contracts. In many ways it depends upon the instructor's negotiation of their pedagogical goals, their values, and the affordances of the technological application used to mediate the class.

For our online writing classes, we have grading contracts that have not only been designed to challenge the assessment paradigms that privilege students who have more experience with academic expectations, but their designs emphasize our respective values as writing instructors—such as effort, student agency, collaborative learning—and leverage the affordances of the applications we have adopted to mediate our courses' curriculum and communication (see Figure 17.3). Our assessment systems—our versions of the labor-based grading contracts—are a product of our reflection upon our pedagogical goals, our personal values, and the application's affordances. But both the compromises that we make and the strong justification are depicted in the ways reflection is recursive and moves both ways.

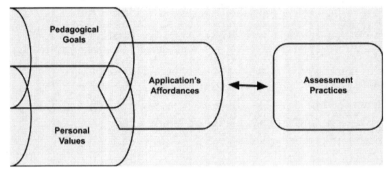

Figure 17.3. Instructor's assessment practices decision-making process within the online instructional context.

EXAMPLE CONTRACT APPROACHES

In this chapter, we will detail two approaches for online labor-based grading contracts, one that illustrates a single assessment approach that can be applied to all assignments in the online course and another that focuses more on contracts that are unique to the labor of the individual assignments. First, Kevin has designed a grading contract based upon an assessment approach he has coined as MICE which measures whether work submitted in Google Documents is missing, incomplete, complete, or extra. Second, Kole has developed a grading contract inspired by the Council of Writing Program Administrators' (WPA) Outcomes Statement for FYC in which students self-select how they might demonstrate each outcome—rhetorical knowledge, information literacy, processes, and conventions—in their writing. While we will reference the specific technologies that we have adopted to give the audience a point of reference for our practices, we understand that technologies come and go, change, and are not accessible at all campuses. Therefore, we will focus more on the affordances of the applications we use and encourage you to also consider using applications with similar features that you are comfortable using.

MICE: Kevin's Approach to Contract Grading

On the first day students are provided with the course website which includes both a page and a video that explain the MICE grading contract's method, summarized in the TILT handout.

Purpose

The MICE grading contract is probably different from any grading you have experienced before. It evaluates you on the completion of your work rather than on how well you have mastered the competencies the completion criteria are asking you to practice. In this asynchronous course, your work will consist of submitting weekly Entries—prompt-driven 350- to 500-word responses or assignment drafts—and an ePortfolio at the end of the semester. Because you are being evaluated on whether you attempted all criteria detailed in the Entry instructions, you do not have to be concerned with how your performance on each Entry differs from my ideal expectation (or 100%). This allows you to "step up to the plate and take a swing" and get credit towards a B grade even if you miss the ball. Furthermore, you are allowed to use a variation of English that is comfortable for you and take risks with thinking, grammar, or conventions (as discussed in the first module). You will still receive feedback based upon my expectations that is meant to be the beginning of a conversation between us rather than a justification for why you did not receive 100 percent credit. Engaging in this conversation with me and/or engaging your peers in conversations about their writing and your own writing will help you to hone your thinking, understand audiences' expectations, and work toward earning an A in the course.

Task

Every week read through each Entry's instructions using the Purdue OWL's page "Understanding Writing Assignments" (https://owl.purdue.edu/owl/general_writing/common_writing_assignments/understanding_writing_assignments.html) to help you identify the Entry's specific tasks to complete. Compose the Entry attempting to complete each criterion. There is no right answer for each criterion or right expression of language when composing these entries. If you are struggling to fulfill a criterion, try to explain what you think is being asked of you and why you are struggling to fulfill the criteria; this will also earn you complete credit. Again, it is useful to view each Entry as the beginning of a conversation between us.

Practice

The following marks are used to assess your work:

- M = Missing. The work is not submitted when the instructor finishes grading an Entry.
- I = Incomplete. You submit timely work, but you fail to perform one or more required criterion. You can revise this work for complete credit.
- C = Complete. You submit timely work and perform all required tasks.
- E = Extra. You respond to questions posed by the instructors or visibly converse with your peers.

Skills

- The ability to provide specific examples from the text or your own experiences to reach a minimum word count.
- The ability to apply a course concept to a personal experience and/or an assigned text.
- The ability to compare how writers of different document types apply the course concepts.
- The ability to find and explain relevant sections of a text to exemplify your point.
- The ability to use a recognized citation format.
- The ability to rethink your own writing.
- The ability to challenge the instructor's perception of a topic.
- The ability to explain a point in a way that your audience can imagine your perspective.
- The ability to make rhetorical decision about your writing.
- The ability to engage a peer in a productive discussion about each other's writing.

The Contract

Kevin's approach to contract grading—an approach he is calling MICE based upon the marks used—is designed to be adopted and adapted as the primary assessment strategy throughout the semester until A–F grades need to be assigned at the end. This example of contract grading, which is introduced at the beginning of the semester in writing, in a video, and during second week conferences, establishes the assessment practices for students' weekly entries—prompt-driven 350- to 500-word responses or assignment drafts—which are mostly based upon objective evaluations of whether their work meets (or attempts) certain competencies (e.g., meeting the word limit, defining a course concept, responding to the assigned readings). Because Kevin values students engaging with him and each other, he poses questions to his students about their writing and encourages students, assigned to small groups to interrogate each other's writing via technological affordances like the document comment function and email. Students earn extra work credit by responding to the instructor or each other.

How The Contract Works During the Semester

Students in Kevin's online writing class are assigned a personal Google Drive folder that is populated with two Module Workbooks (Google Documents),[1] an Extra Work Journal (Google Document), and a Module Documents folder that is itself populated with six blank documents with the title of each "major assignment." Each Module Workbook has the instructions for seven or eight entries that are a series of sequenced writing opportunities that build upon previous entries in that workbook or the previous workbook. Each week students, working asynchronously, compose 350–500 words, cite the readings to apply the course concept (e.g., audience, genre) to their own experiences, and compare how the course concepts are applied in some example texts (e.g., a review of *In the Heights*). If a student does all that labor, the student receives complete work credit with feedback describing the quality of that labor and what that student can work on to improve the quality of that labor. However, if the student does not write 350 words, does not cite the course reading, or does not make the required comparison, then the student will receive incomplete credit for the entry and will be given explicit instructions on how to revise the entry for complete credit—which they have until the end of the semester to do.[2]

Since the entries are sequenced and built toward the final entries of each Module Workbook, Kevin has students engage with him and/or each other to earn extra work credit. Students can earn extra work credit when they 1) respond to the questions he poses in the marginal comments, 2) respond to his end comments via email, 3) pose questions to their peers in their peer's workbook, or 4) respond to questions posed by their peers. Using any combination of these four methods, students must compose an extra 250 words a week and record it in the Extra Work Journal to earn extra work credit. Most of this extra engagement would be doing work that not only modeled expectations of academic writing but would be useful thinking that can be drawn upon later when composing

---

1   As readers will see later, these Module Workbooks are shared with other students in the class to allow them to pose questions to each other. To be compliant with FERPA regulations and not let peers see how the instructor was evaluating a student's work, the instructor sent summative comments and his evaluation to the students via email.

2   Kevin checks these documents every few weeks until the end of the semester.

future entries in that module. Furthermore, this method of feedback leverages one technological affordance of the word processing and email programs used.

Calculating the Final Grade

At the end of the semester, Kevin needs to shift students' grades from MICE to the traditional A–F grading scale (see Figure 17.4). Understanding that almost all students, at this modestly selective public university, bring communicative competence to their work in his class, he has set a B as the baseline grade that all students will receive entering the course. Since he needs to submit an A-F grade to each student, he uses the scale in Figure 17.4 to calculate a final course score based upon the number of missing entries, unresolved incomplete entries, complete entries, and completed extra work.

Overall Course Grade

At the end of the semester the instructor will keep track of your labor based upon how many of each mark (c, e, i, and m) you earn. Each mark has the following effect to the baseline "B" grade.

- m = -1 to the baseline
- i = every 2 i's is 1 m
- c = no change to your grade
- e = +1 to the baseline

With a "B" being equal to zero (0), I will count the amount of each type of mark to determine your deviation from the baseline. The following scale will determine your final grade in English 110C.

Extra Work	Base-line	Missing Work
A = 7 or more "e" A- = 5 or 6 "e" B+ = 3 or 4 "e"	B = 0 (equal to no e's or m's) 1 or 2 "e" 1 or 2 "m"	B- = 3 or 4 "m" C+ = 5 "m" C = 6 "m" C- = 7 "m" D+ = 8 "m" D = 9 "m" D- = 10 "m" F = 11 or more "m" OR any missing Module Documents

Figure 17.4. MICE to A–F scale.

This assessment practice only minimally penalizes students who experience setbacks during the semester—whether they are responsible for these instances or not. However, complete disengagement from the course results in failing the class. For each week students earn extra work credit, their final grade will gradually be raised from a B to a B+ to an A– to an A. Because Kevin does not use an LMS gradebook, Kevin has created a place on each module where students can record the marks on each entry and use the MICE A-F Scale (see Figure 17.4) to keep track of their grade. Or students can just email the instructor and ask.

Benefits and Challenges of this Contract Design

The MICE approach has benefits and challenges for both students and instructors. Because all students start the course with a B and know that this is the grade they will earn if they complete all their work, they do not have to be anxious that their diverse *habitus* will prevent them from passing the class. Likewise, the assessment system gives them some agency to weigh their time and effort more accurately against the final grade they want to earn (Inoue, 2019). The single parent who balances raising two kids and a 40-hour-a-week job with their college work can look at the syllabus and know how to earn their desired grade. They also know if life goes sideways once or twice during the semester, there are ways to compensate and still earn the desired grade. MICE also encourages students to predominantly focus on the writing itself at the level of ideas. Since students know their "score" when they begin writing, they can engage with cognitive tasks rather than worrying about the work's correctness. For example, one student who did extra work mentioned multiple times that they appreciated being allowed to express their academic ideas and respond to their peers in a "gooberish" way. By writing as a "goober," they use a comfortable *habitus* to articulate their evolving academic ideas without being penalized for violating the rules of Standard Academic English. MICE, however, is not without its challenges. Students need to buy into it without worrying about it being designed to sabotage their GPAs or humiliate them. This assessment practice works against twelve years of A–F assessment and the ideologies it has indoctrinated into students. Furthermore, MICE also problematically assumes that the labor of completing one's work does not disadvantage some students along socioeconomic and racial lines; students who can afford to "just be students" are better positioned to complete the labor for their classes than students who must pick and choose priorities. But by identifying students who are failing to start the work and those who struggle with the course's rhetorical tasks, the instructor can point students to institutional resources they need.

For the instructor, MICE creates two tasks: 1) look for the criteria to be accomplished and 2) review the rhetorical effectiveness of the students' composition. The former decides their grade if they complete the criteria; the latter, depending upon the assignment's purpose, becomes a teachable moment to raise questions about expectations and ask students to consider how various intended audiences might experience these tasks. The instructor's comments are almost exclusively formative, individually asynchronously teaching about future writings. These conversations, should students choose to engage in them, provide a relatively organic means to create instructor presence (Garrison et al., 1999) for students who want more one-to-one instruction. Moreover, the affordances of the technologies they are already using to do their work support these conversations. Although I can imagine how instructors can adopt the LMSs' affordances to support similar practices.

Because of the focus on the student's rhetorical decisions and the desire to engage them in conversations about them, this approach can be labor-intensive. Instructors need to decide which submissions will just be assigned a MICE mark and which ones will also receive comments. Trying to review and comment upon all submissions can become overwhelming, so some submissions should just be evaluated for completion based upon a criterion like how much a student wrote. Also Kevin still pedagogically struggles assigning completion marks to a longer entry that is really thoughtful and well-articulated and another entry that barely makes the word count and demonstrates minimal comprehension and proficiency at applying the course concepts. His long-standing immersion in a traditional grading system tells him that the former student should be rewarded for their acumen. And if the former student does not do extra work—and the latter student who does not qualitatively write as well does do it—then the "weaker writer" earns a better grade than the "stronger writer." While Kevin has questioned whether this is fair, he is also reminded that traditional meritocratic assessment practices are questionably fair too (Gibbs, 2020).

Choosing Practices: Kole's Approach to Contract Grading

Kole's approach to contract grading is described within the context of FYC. In this course, students are challenged to develop effective writing processes in accordance with various rhetorical situations. Students are presented with a general grading contract at the beginning of the semester which introduces the grading rationale and forecasts how each assignment sheet will contain its own unique criteria. As such, Kole's labor-based grading contracts are uniquely designed for each assignment to help students understand the writing competencies that he wants them to focus on for each assignment.

To develop a grading contract for a particular assignment, Kole first considers the WPA Outcomes Statement for FYC (2014) as a means of articulating the target competencies or goals of the writing assignment. These outcomes include rhetorical knowledge, information literacy, processes, and conventions, and students are challenged to demonstrate these outcomes in writing on all major assignments. After considering the WPA Outcomes Statement, Kole then develops his assignment-specific grading contracts by articulating specific ways students can demonstrate these outcomes in target practices of writing. In this way, every assignment sheet Kole delivers to students includes an assignment-specific collection of target practices of writing that students can select from. Importantly, a grading contract for a rhetorical analysis essay looks very different from a creative narrative, simply by virtue of the unique rhetorical knowledge(s) and processes that are inherent to these genres and assignments.

An example contract is featured below as a part of an assignment sheet for a rhetorical analysis essay. In this assignment sheet, Kole reminds students of the four WPA learning outcomes and explains general practices involved when conducting and writing a rhetorical analysis. After instructing students on the steps of completing the assignment in the Task section, Kole then presents the assignment's grading contract. Therein, students are met with a variety of target practices in writing from which they might select to earn a grade.

Composing a Rhetorical Analysis

Purpose

Demonstrate rhetorical knowledge, information literacy, process, and conventions by composing a rhetorical analysis essay.

Practices

This assignment will help you develop the following skills . . .

- Read for inquiry, learning, critical thinking, and communicating.
- Analyze a source for it rhetorical effect.
- Incorporate outside materials in your own writing through quotations, paraphrase, and summary, as well as interpretation, synthesis, and critique.
- Work through multiple drafts of an essay and recognizing the role of reflecting, revising, and editing.
- Practice genre conventions for structure and paragraphing.
- Understand the concepts of intellectual property that motivate documentation conventions through application of citation style.

Knowledge

This assignment will help you develop knowledge in rhetorical studies. Rhetorical studies explores what makes communication effective and persuasive. The study of rhetoric is attributed to Aristotle, who sought to explain effective processes and strategies for crafting great speeches that would influence events in Athenian democracy. Today, we think of rhetoric in many contexts to include politics, sales, and online writing contexts. Knowledge in rhetorical studies will help you better understand effective communication both as a listener and speaker.

Task

In completing this assignment, you should do the following:

- Locate a source (advertisement, social media post, etc.) from your everyday life.
- Examine a source for its topic and purpose.
- Analyze the source for rhetorical features, identifying how the source demonstrates logos, pathos, ethos, kairos, and/or telos as taught by readings and explored in previous low-stakes writing assignments.
- Argue for or against how effective the source is.
- Support your argument with evidence based on specific features of the source.

Grading Contract

For an A, complete eight of the following target practices. For a B, complete four. Late work is accepted for a C.

- Write at least 750 words.
- Draft a 100-word introduction paragraph to include background information, general to specific information, anecdote, or some other introductory strategy.
- Explain how the source does or does not demonstrate logos.
- Explain how the source does or does not demonstrate ethos.
- Explain how the source does or does not demonstrate pathos.
- Draft a 100-word conclusion which demonstrates summary, future contextualization, or a call to action.
- Produce a figure, graphic, or image to support your writing.
- Include a credible quote from an online source, with bibliographic statement, in your essay.
- Find a reputable source from the library website to support your writing.
- Submit an outline with your essay.
- Book a conference with the instructor to engage a "brainstorming session."

- Book a conference with the instructor to receive feedback on a completed draft.
- Email the instructor with an essay draft to receive feedback.
- Format the essay to MLA or another style (e.g., header/heading, spacing).
- Produce a full text citation of your source on the Works Cited page.
- Develop clear transition sentences between paragraphs.
- Write in Standard American English (SAE).
- Write in a language other than SAE.
- Propose an additional way the essay might be graded.

The assignment sheet and corresponding grading contract above is introduced to students after scaffolded course work is completed, explained below, which is designed to prepare students for writing the major essay. For example, one low-stakes assignment students encounter in Kole's asynchronous learning environment is a reading response assignment, in which students are introduced to a collection of genre-specific readings that relate to an upcoming essay assignment. Specifically, students encounter both instructional and model readings. In the unit on rhetorical analysis, for example, students complete readings that define rhetorical appeals—such as logos, pathos, and ethos—and that demonstrate rhetorical analysis in action. As per this assignment's instructions, students must not only read but also respond in writing. As such, students must not only read the words on the page, but also monitor their reading progress by focusing on main ideas and purposes presented by the author, taking notes on their observations. Simply put, students not only encounter the text but also leave the text having deduced at least one important point to share, respond to, or debate. After having completed the reading and note-taking process outlined in the reading response assignment sheet, students are then instructed—via the assignment sheet—to review the notes and produce a summary paragraph of the important points from the reading, offering a citation thereof, while concluding their reading responses with their personal reactions to the text.

After engaging multiple steps in completing their reading responses, students are tasked to join a class community forum in which they are challenged with situating their knowledge gained from reading within a broader class discussion. Generally, the prompts in the community Writing Forum, available via the course LMS, task students with extending the discussion that they began in their reading response. They can share their opinions on topics from readings or introduce a related topic to the forum, commenting on their peers' responses and responding to their peers in turn. Finally, after having joined and participated in the Writing Forum, students then encounter the essay assignment that encourages them to leverage their initial Reading, developed by the Writing Forum, as invention for a longer essay.

Importantly, Kole offers feedback—via synchronous video conferences and asynchronous comments embedded in student writing—on each of these assignments, which is designed to aid students in their learning process leading up to the Rhetorical Analysis Essay. Instructor feedback relates to accurate uptake of concepts relevant to the rhetorical analysis unit. Feedback on the reading response, for example, might comment on the accurate summarization—and uptake—of concepts foundational to the assigned readings and rhetorical analysis unit. Feedback, importantly, is both constructive and complementary.

With preliminary assignments complete with instructor feedback, students are prepared to continue their learning in essay form. This is when students encounter the essay's grading contract, which is included at the end of the assignment sheet for their Rhetorical Analysis essay. Within this assignment sheet, students are encouraged to review the necessary practices and knowledge required in completing a rhetorical analysis. Furthermore, a writing process is explained as the task of the assignment. With an understanding of the assignment, students then consider the assignment's grading contract. As the assignment sheet and corresponding grading contract states, there are more than a dozen target practices that constitute success on this assignment, each of which is reflective of a WPA learning outcome. Importantly, students are in control of shaping their writing according to the disciplinary standards articulated in the grading contract. In this way, teaching and assessment become complementary if not simultaneous. These target practices, which have been the focus of low-stakes assignments and instructor feedback, shape the grading contract for the rhetorical analysis essay. Crucially, these practices correlate with a guaranteed grade. This practice can also alleviate some of the grading workload for the teacher once assignments are submitted. As assessment is embedded in the instructional process, teachers have already encountered, and by consequence "graded," student work within the aforementioned assignment scaffold.

In the Rhetorical Analysis Essay grading contract, for a "B," students are challenged to demonstrate in writing at least four of the grading contract items. More labor is required, however, for an "A." Accordingly, Kole asks students to meet eight items on the grading contract to earn the highest possible grade. For example, one student who wants to earn a "B" on the Rhetorical Analysis Essay might draft a 100-word introduction for the essay to include a description of the chosen source; explain how that source demonstrates ethos and pathos; and draft a 100-word conclusion which demonstrates summary, future contextualization, or a call to action. This will earn a "B" for completing four items on the grading contract. Another student might earn an "A" by completing the aforementioned four items of the grading contract—for example, booking a conference with the instructor, finding a reputable source on Google to support their writing, developing a multimodal graphic, and formatting the essay to MLA for a total of eight grading contract items. Once students meet the contracted practices in their own writing, the essay grade, as promised, is posted to the course LMS.

Importantly, Kole's approach to contract grading accounts for the quality, relevance, and punctuality of student writing. To be eligible for these grades, students must meet assignment expectations and submit their essays on or before the due date. Nevertheless, Kole also accounts for students who do not successfully meet assignment expectations or deadlines in that late work is accepted for a C. Writing that does not meet assignment expectations is not accepted. For example, if instead of submitting a rhetorical analysis, the student submits an opinion piece on an unassigned topic, Kole returns the writing for revision and resubmission. At this point in time, the assignment is considered late and is then only eligible to earn a C if successfully resubmitted. In short, students cannot submit just anything and receive credit. Their writing must meet the contracted expectations. However, Kole has never had to return an essay to a student that did not meet expectations, provided that students completed the preliminary reading and writing assignments listed above. Rather, he has only had to return essays to students who were not present for the various and scaffolded lessons and assignments that prepared students to meet the expectations of a respective grading contract.

Furthermore, in considering antiracist perspectives on what makes an effective argument, during synchronous class discussions about rhetorical appeals, students are encouraged to question what constitutes an effective demonstration of rhetorical appeals, especially in terms of how such an understanding might be rooted in White racial *habitus*. For example, what one might deem credible in one culture might not be viewed with the same level of credibility in another. This is why, on the assignment's grading contract, students might argue how a particular source does or does not constitute an effective demonstration of a rhetorical appeal. In furthermore supporting anti-racist perspectives in accordance with target practices, students might choose to write in Standard American English (SAE) or a language other than SAE on their essays, demonstrating linguistic competency as they so choose. In Kole's experience, students appreciate the opportunity to write in ways that reflect their lived experience and linguistic background for a graded assignment.

REFLECTION ON PRACTICE: CREATING YOUR GRADING CONTRACT

Educators interested in applying grading contracts to their courses can use this practice to create contracts that align with their values, course outcomes, and target practices of writing. First, **pedagogical values and course outcomes must be considered,** especially in terms of what students are tasked to practice. The grading contract must outline target practices and writing goals for students to demonstrate what constitutes a successful essay. These tangible goals should be reflective of disciplinary expectations and course learning outcomes.

After having considered the values or goals of a particular assignment, instructors should identify specific ways students can demonstrate pedagogical values in their knowledge making and composing practices as they complete their assignment. Importantly, the students' demonstration of knowledge making is idiosyncratic to a particular genre of writing or essay topic. To accomplish this, instructors might list a variety of ways students can be successful on a particular assignment, naming these features of writing an assignment's grading contract.

Importantly, lesson plans that build up to each assignment should be represented in the gradable values. The target practices in the grading contract must be taught to students and practiced prior to a major assignment's due date. When teaching students how to meet these contracted expectations, offer feedback as the assignment process unfolds. These target practices should be foregrounded as lessons and low-stakes assignments are introduced to students, as these practices are specific to and necessary for the successful completion of their respective assignment.

Considering Affordances of Grading Contracts in OLI

In considering affordances in OLI, to delineate the kind of affordance students experience when encountering various types of online learning materials is important. For example, when considering the affordances of grading contracts, we might clarify what grading contracts afford students and teachers in teaching, composing, and grading practices, especially as they relate to the WPA outcomes of rhetorical knowledge, information literacy, processes, and conventions.

For example, in teaching students about information literacy—guiding them through texts and encouraging their responses thereof—a number of usability affordances present themselves in online contexts in the facilitation of this learning outcome. For example, delivering reading in online contexts enhances the accessibility of course materials. Sharing readings online—especially Open Access readings—minimizes socioeconomic barriers to education. Simply put, in making readings available one click away, all students can access the course materials, provided they have a device and internet connection. Accordingly, when students are tasked to practice information literacy, the online writing course is better equipped to provide students with the necessary learning materials to integrate sources in their own writing, as per the target practice of utilizing quotations and summary of outside sources for their own purposes.

As students engage in digital composing practices, a number of rhetorical affordances are available to students, regardless of their field of interest. For example, for a major essay, students might create a multimodal feature to the written assignment such as a graphic organizer with Google drawing, a meme, or some other kind of digital image which interprets or supports the written assignment, as per the assignment's grading contract. Leveraging the rhetorical affordances of multimodal communication, arguably, creates a more rhetorically effective composition, and furthermore in doing so, demonstrates their acquisition of the target learning outcome. This is one way students can demonstrate their rhetorical knowledge in online writing contexts, while also meeting the expectations of an assignment's grading contract.

Furthermore, communicative affordances of OLI are embedded within the grading contract options for the demonstration of writing as a process. Specifically, barriers to communication must be negotiated by leveraging the communicative affordances of the online real-time and any time modes. All Kole's grading contracts encourage students to practice writing as a process by communicating with the instructor in various phases of drafting. To satisfy practices of the grading contract, students might submit a draft to the instructor for feedback asynchronously or to meet with the instructor for a real-time brainstorming session during office hours. As such, students are provided the option in the grading contract to access the instructor for feedback in the online modality that best suits their needs. Receiving feedback is one of the gradable practices from which students may choose in selecting their desired grades. In this way, the communicative affordances of online instruction are leveraged to provide students feedback while they meet the contracted expectations for demonstrating writing as a process.

Kole believes that grading contracts afford transparency, as the grading protocol is made clear to students. Specific expectations are set for students to meet in order to earn a guaranteed grade. The grading process is transparent and not left to subjective judgments about student writing, but rather agreed-upon practices and goals for student writing. Furthermore, grading contracts promote equity, as a measurable amount of labor is equal to all students, without privileging students who have been trained in cultures and education systems that reflect White habits of languaging.

Kole hopes this assessment method progressively approaches antiracist grading practice as what students do in relation to assignment goals is foregrounded, not students' linguistic practices. Furthermore, these gradable assignment goals are reflective of traditional and antiracist understandings of what writing can do in the FYC classroom and beyond. Grading contracts have the potential of encouraging students to engage online literacy as they become more confident writers. Furthermore, assessment is less about subjective judgment from the instructor and more about students' volition in composing and communicating. Accordingly, teachers might consider how they can enhance transparent and equitable grading practices by developing their own grading contracts that are reflective of pedagogical goals of disciplinary knowledge and practices.

REFLECTIONS

Even if we approach it in different ways, both of us, Kevin and Kole, value giving all our students the opportunity to succeed in our online writing classes. After being introduced to our grading contracts, students begin the semester knowing what work they must do to not only pass the class but to excel at the class. Students, who do not come to our online classes with the *habitus* often expected of writing students, are taught these expectations but given the opportunity to attempt them or to deliberately resist them. Although we both expect students to provide evidence that they can perform certain rhetorical moves—whether they are providing examples to support or illustrate claims or being able to examine a source for its topics and purpose—we leverage the technological affordances of online education to engage our students and build upon further individual instruction to provide the necessary evidence. However, our different approaches also reflect the ways that our values differ—which also probably reflects our different ranks, responsibilities, and the ways we negotiate these aspects of our lives with what we most value in the students' experience with online writing instruction. While Kevin honors students' engagement with him and with each other, Kole rewards them for choosing to demonstrate proficiencies relevant to specific types of writing assignments.

CONCLUSION

We hope that this chapter does not suggest that we have figured out the problem of grading equity. Nothing can be further from the truth. But what we have done is taken a step away from the traditional approaches used for evaluating students' work, giving us the opportunity to interrogate the old ways of assessment and explore and scrutinize new assessment methods. As you make this step, practice forgiveness with yourself. You will make misjudgments. You will continue to harm some students—both because you will not always get it right and because you cannot get some students to trust the expectations of this assessment system. But what is important is that you take that first step. Arguably this step is particularly significant in online literacy instruction where decisions have been made to design simpler courses to make them more manageable for those within the underprepared labor pools often asked to teach these courses (DePew et al., 2006). Instead, administrators and instructors need to find ways to apply GSOLE's principle of accessibility and inclusivity.

Challenging the established *habitus* of the academy, by adopting such practices as the development of critical language awareness is a threat to our established norms of schooling, both in terms of teaching philosophies and institutional norms. There will be unlearning. There will be resistance. There will be challenges to overcome. You will be doubted. You will be criticized. You will feel discouraged. While all of this is true, we ask you to work to foster a radical equity towards your students. Generations of BIPOC students have undergone a similar kind of scrutiny; however, these students did not choose to be doubted, criticized, or discouraged. Traditional systems of education have made it so. This is why it is our privilege and responsibility, as instructors, to break the racist cycles we have perpetuated every day in the writing classroom. It is our privilege and responsibility to take on the judgment, anger, and vitriol which is typically reserved for our BIPOC students when their voices enter the conversation. To create space for all students is our moral and ethical obligation, so all students, and hopefully one day all instructors, experience learning that is based on a nurtured understanding of better practices in teaching and grading.

MOVING BETTER PRACTICES ACROSS MODALITIES

- **In-Person, Real-Time Learning:** Having conversations about ungrading and its intentional differences from traditional grading systems should be held in-class. Students need activities, like reflective prompts, that help them situate their past experiences with grading and consider how this new method of assessment will differ from those experiences while also providing them with space for new areas of focus, like growth. Helping students navigate the emotional and academic reactions to new forms of grading is important in establishing trust in the new ungrading system. You might ask students, "What have your experiences with grades and grading been in the past? How do you feel about grades/grading? Along with these feelings, what thoughts or questions do you have about grades and grading?"

- **Online, Real-Time Learning:** Similar conversations summarized above can be adapted for breakout rooms, discussion boards, or collaborative whiteboard spaces.
- **Online, Any Time Learning:** Students can complete discussion board posts situating their experiences and feelings in relation to their peers. Then, they can offer feedback to peers' posts using sentence stems, like "I agree that ____." "I, too, have experienced ____." Provide students with optional or required check-ins to gauge their feelings about this new form of assessment and answer any additional questions.
- **Hybrid Learning:** You can begin conversations about ungrading in in-person meetings with options for students to continue exploring their thoughts and ideas asynchronously after the class meeting. When students come back together, you can field lingering questions and ensure all students feel confident in how their learning will be evaluated using the ungrading system.

REFERENCES

Avakian, A. N. (1974). *A guide to writing learning contracts.* ERIC. https://files.eric.ed.gov/fulltext/ED088385.pdf.

Baker-Bell, A. (2020). *Linguistic justice: Black language, literacy, identity, and pedagogy.* Routledge.

Ball, A. F. (1997). Expanding the dialogue on culture as a critical component when assessing writing. *Assessing Writing, 4*(2), 169–202. https://doi.org/10.1016/S1075-2935(97)80011-6.

Barlow, R. (1974). An experiment with learning contracts. *The Journal of Higher Education, 45*(6), 441–449. https://doi.org/10.1080/00221546.1974.11776979.

Blackstock, A. & Exton, V. (2014). "Space to grow": Grading contracts for basic writers. *Teaching English in the Two-year College, 41*(3), 278–293.

Bourdieu, P. (1990). *The logic of practice* (R. Nice, Trans.). Stanford University Press.

Conference on College Composition and Communication. (2020). *CCCC statement on second language writing and multilingual writers.* https://cccc.ncte.org/cccc/resources/positions/secondlangwriting.

Council of Writing Program Administrators. (2014). *WPA outcomes statement for first-year composition (3.0).* https://wpacouncil.org/aws/CWPA/pt/sd/news_article/243055/_PARENT/layout_details/false.

DePew, K. E., Fishman, T.A., Romberger, J. E. & Ruetenik, B. F. (2006). Designing efficiencies: The parallel narratives of distance education and composition studies. *Computers and Composition, 23*(1), 49-67. https://doi.org/10.1016/j.compcom.2005.12.005.

Elbow, P. (1999). Inviting the mother tongue: Beyond "mistakes," "bad English," and "wrong English." *JAC 19*(2), 359–388. http://www.jstor.org/stable/20866251.

Garrison, D. R., Anderson, T. & Archer, W. (1999). Critical inquiry in a text-based environment: Computer conferencing in higher education. *The Internet and Higher Education, 2*(2–3), 87–105. https://doi.org/10.1016/S1096-7516(00)00016-6.

Gibbs, L. (2020). Let's talk about grading. In S. D. Blum (Ed.), *Ungrading: Why rating students undermines learning (and what to do instead)* (pp. 91-104). West Virginia University Press.

GSOLE Executive Board. (2019, June 13). *Online literacy instruction principles and tenets*. Global Society of Online Literacy Educators. https://gsole.org/oliresources/oliprinciples.

Inoue, A. B. (2019). *Labor-based grading contracts: Building equity and inclusion in the compassionate writing classroom*. The WAC Clearinghouse; University Press of Colorado. https://doi.org/10.37514/PER-B.2019.0216.0.

Hassencahl, F. (1979). Contract grading in the classroom. *Improving College and University Teaching, 27*(1), 30–33.

Haswell, R. H. & Haswell, J. T. (1996). Gender bias and critique of student writing. *Assessing Writing, 3*(1), 31–83. https://doi.org/10.1016/S1075-2935(96)90004-5.

Laflen, A. (2020, August 4). *Using labor-based grading contracts in OWI* [Video]. YouTube. https://www.youtube.com/watch?v=km9OFMYOg10.

Laflen, A. & Sims, M. (2021). Designing a more equitable scorecard: Grading contracts and online writing instruction. In J. Borgman & C. McArdle (Eds.), *PARS in practice: More resources and strategies for online writing instructors* (pp. 119-139). The WAC Clearinghouse; University Press of Colorado. https://doi.org/10.37514/pra-b.2021.1145.2.07.

Ortmeier-Hooper, C. (2013). *The ELL writer: Moving beyond basics in the secondary classroom*. Teachers College Press.

Purdue Online Writing Lab (OWL). (n.d.). Understanding writing assignments. *Purdue University*. Retrieved January 2, 2024, from https://owl.purdue.edu/owl/general_writing/common_writing_assignments/understanding_writing_assignments.html.

Ruecker, T. (2015). *Transiciones: Pathways of Latinas and Latinos writing in high school and college*. Utah State University Press.

Weaver, M. M. (2020). *Critical language awareness pedagogy in first-year composition: A design-based research study* [Doctoral dissertation, Old Dominion University]. Old Dominion University. https://doi.org/10.25777/ghyt-v912.

Yancey, K. B. (1999). Looking back as we look forward: Historicizing writing assessment. *College Composition and Communication, 50*(3), 483–503.

CHAPTER 18.

LEARNING TO UNLEARN: GRADING CONTRACTS IN THE ONLINE CLASSROOM

Michelle Stuckey
Arizona State University

Gabriella Wilson
Syracuse University

In this chapter, the authors describe **contract grading** *used in online, any time learning. Specifically, the authors focus on the affordances, such as the valuing of students' variable knowledges and writing processes, and challenges, such as student resistance to nontraditional assessment practices, for both students and teachers in implementing contract grading in online courses. In describing their "better practice," this chapter addresses the themes of assessment and professional learning for online teachers.*

FRAMEWORKS AND PRINCIPLES IN THIS CHAPTER

- **GSOLE OLI Principle 1.1**: All stakeholders and students should be aware of and be able to engage the unique literacy features of communicating, teaching, and learning in a primarily digital environment.
- **GSOLE OLI Principle 3.5**: Instructors and tutors should research, develop, theorize, and apply appropriate reading, alphabetic writing, and multimodal composition theories to their OLI environment(s).
- **CCCC's Postsecondary Principles for Writing, 9**: Sound writing instruction provides students with the support necessary to achieve their goals.

GUIDING QUESTIONS BEFORE YOU BEGIN READING

- What are the affordances of contract grading in online writing instruction related to flexible, individualized, and transparent assessment practices?

DOI: https://doi.org/10.37514/PER-B.2024.2241.2.18

- How might contract grading support increased accessibility, equity, and inclusion in online writing courses?
- How might an instructor prepare students for the transition to contract grading? What conversations must be had and which resources must be provided in order to make this transition work?
- What assumptions about labor, entrenched ideologies around grading, and ideas about "good" writing do instructors need to reflect on and "unlearn" when transitioning to contract grading?

INTRODUCTION

As teachers of writing, and especially as teachers of online writing, we found ourselves conflicted by our feelings about grading, as have many others in this collection and across our field. We wanted to establish trust with our students, to connect with them as individuals, but the act of grading their work often created tension and exacerbated the distance between us and our students. In conversations with colleagues, we began to ask questions about grading. What is the role of grading? How do we fairly assess students in online writing classes?

As we looked for alternatives that might help us build trust and account for our students' unique needs as learners, we explored contract grading. Contract grading is a transparent, individualized method of assessment in which grading is distanced from feedback and criteria are simplified and clearly communicated to students. In exploring contract grading, we considered whether it might help us bolster the confidence of students in online, any time courses while building trust between students and instructors? Can contracts help us to unlearn harmful practices that reinforce instructors' assumptions about what makes "good writing"? These questions prompted us to develop grading contracts for our online writing classes. We dove into the process of developing contracts, revising and carefully thinking through possible issues and sources of confusion.

In doing so, we *hoped* developing grading contracts would alleviate the stress and anxiety so many students feel when confronted with a writing assignment, as we postulated that contract grading might lessen some of the cognitive overload online students in particular feel when encountering new learning situations. We *knew* that if we could break down the barriers that prevent students from just writing, if we could demonstrate that we really meant that *process* was more important than *product* through a simplified grading contract, they would embrace the new method. And they would just write because they wouldn't be worried about their grade. Right?

Not necessarily. Despite our attempts to demystify grading, students still found areas in our initial contracts that were unclear and imprecise. "What did we mean by meaningful engagement?" "What counts as 'personal insight' or 'deep reflection'?" "What counts as substantial engagement with the course content?" Beyond these more abstract questions, students suggested that our contracts reified issues that arise with traditional assessment practices. For instance, students felt contracts might leave too much room for subjective interpretation—that they might continue to encourage students to write in order to please the teacher instead of taking risks that push their learning in new directions. Moreover, students felt that the contract wasn't flexible enough in allowing for unexpected situations to arise. These responses by students elucidate common anxieties students frequently attest to about grades (the anxieties we were attempting to alleviate).

We soon came to realize that student pushback is part of the process. As Joyce Inman and Rebecca Powell (2018) argued in "In the Absence of Grades," students have complex emotional responses to grades, as typically their identities as learners have been constructed in large part through grading systems. A radical departure from the standardized grading systems they are accustomed to requires a significant cognitive shift, which, as bell hooks wrote, "may not be welcomed by students who often expect us to teach in the manner they are accustomed to" (1994, pp. 142–143). What we envisioned as a way to engage in equitable grading practices actually caused some students anxiety.

The distance between teacher and student in online, any time courses poses additional challenges to student trust. In online learning environments, these questions and anxieties can be exacerbated as students navigate potentially new online learning environments and the particular stressors and isolation that online any time learning can foster (Bawa, 2016). But student pushback can also be understood as an important way to learn about students, their relationships and orientations to learning, and the role grading plays in those. What's more, it can help us understand what assumptions we need to unlearn, and what the gaps are in our contracts.

We adopted contract grading to build a more equitable foundation in our online, any time courses, both by being transparent about how we would assess student work, and by minimizing the subjective judgment that renders so many students fearful and angry about writing. In line with Asao Inoue's critique of how instructors judge student writing, we adopted contract grading as a way to focus on developing student writing rather than *judging* student writing based on our idea of the "ideal text." Inoue (2019) writes, "when we judge [student writing] we use convenient fictions, prototypes in our heads that are cobbled together from various examples" (p. 387). These convenient fictions are usually modeled after racialized ideals about White mainstream English language practices and formal academic writing and discourse.

Given the ways these fictions infiltrate and dominate writing studies, we came to realize that we too needed to *unlearn* our focus on the product and embrace the contract as always *in process*. We have learned to approach contract grading in the spirit of unlearning. It is not just our students who are being asked to unlearn years of grade-based disciplining that shapes how and why they write; we too have been disciplined by our institutions, our fields, our own identities as scholars, and the very language we take for granted when it comes to assessment as being transparent in meaning. Jack Halberstam (2012) underscored the importance of "learning to unlearn" as a way to break with, reform, and/or reshape

> disciplinary legacies . . . and the many constraints that sometimes get in the way of our best efforts to reinvent our fields, our purpose, and our mission. Unlearning is an inevitable part of new knowledge paradigms if only because you cannot solve a problem using the same methods that created it in the first place. (pp. 9–10)

In this way, we view learning to unlearn as a productive and generative process that is beneficial in helping us to hone our teaching and grading practices. Just as we were asking our students to trust us to leave feedback that was generative and responsive to their context, we needed to view the feedback we received from students as productive moments of failure. This shift in thinking about failure is an iterative process that requires consistent revision and reflection on established practices.

Through the work of reflecting, revising, and renegotiating contract grading in our unique contexts, we have found that approaching contract grading with an understanding that it is messy, partial, and always unfinished opens us up to enjoy the process as we continue to learn how to best support our students. In addition to providing a theoretical rationale and reflections on each of our contracts, we've also composed a TILT handout located at the end of the chapter for instructors looking to engage in the process of crafting a grading contract. The TILT handout walks instructors through a series of tasks that they should consider when composing a new grading system. Through responding to these questions, instructors can review the contingencies that exist in their own classes and explore how to best accommodate the students engaging in an online space. The handout is meant to offer a reiterative, reflective process that instructors can undertake to begin the transition to contract grading and to reflect and revise their methods at the end of the semester, although the framework can be helpful at any point while teaching a class. The TILT handout does not prescribe one specific way of articulating a contract because we've learned that grading contracts must be responsive to the particular needs of individual learning environments. Instead, we offer examples of our own grading contracts and the TILT handout as a reflective framework through which to compose your own grading contract.

GRADING CONTRACTS AND EQUITABLE, INCLUSIVE, AND ACCESSIBLE PEDAGOGY

Grading contracts can be hard to define because they are highly individualized and unique to specific learning environments. In an attempt to pin down the term, we define contract grading as an approach that distances feedback from grading. As Michelle Cowan writes, "Grading contracts may be used to holistically assess work, assign grades, clearly outline the requirements to make certain grades, motivate students to take personal responsibility for their work, and/or foster democratic social engagement in the classroom" (para. 3, 2020). A grading contract can take a number of different approaches, some of the most common being Inoue's (2014, 2015) labor-based grading contracts, Jane Danielewicz and Peter Elbow's (2009) guaranteed "B" approach, and Ira Shor's (2009) negotiated contract approach. While an underexplored area in online literacy instruction (OLI), we argue that contract grading offers a better practice for approaching grading in online, any time learning environments by expanding equity, inclusion, and accessibility through a transparent and clear articulation of task expectations for specific letter grades.

Contract grading aligns with a number of OLI principles outlined by the Global Society for Online Literacy Educators (GSOLE) in *Online Literacy Instruction Principles and Tenets* (2019). First, it supports GSOLE Principle 1 (2019), which states, "Online literacy instruction should be universally accessible and inclusive." GSOLE defines inclusion and access as "using multiple teaching and learning formats, engaging students' choices, and welcoming all students in the course." Because grading contracts are adaptable and flexible, instructors can tailor their contracts to *engage student choices* and meet the specific needs of students in specific learning contexts. As Danielewicz and Elbow (2009) write, "Contract grading lends itself to variation. Teachers or programs can easily customize their contracts to fit their particular goals, priorities, and situations" (p. 257) The ability to adapt assessment to meet individual student needs and learning goals through contract grading helps to close that distance and aligns with how Beth Hewett (2015) defines the ethos of universal design principles. The ability to adapt and customize a grading contract can be especially important in online, any time courses where the distance between teacher and student and the delivery of learning may make it challenging to personalize instruction.

A well-designed grading contract can account for the needs of underrepresented and nontraditional learners in online, any time courses. This aligns with CCCC's Postsecondary Principles for Writing 9, which states, "Sound writing instruction provides students with the support necessary to achieve their goals." Principle 9 emphasizes the importance of acknowledging that "students come to postsecondary education with a wide range of writing, reading, and critical analysis experiences." In designing grading contracts, teachers can support individual student development as writers by de-emphasizing knowledge of White mainstream English (Baker-Bell, 2020), promoting instead instructor feedback that acknowledges the different experiences and literacy levels students may bring to a class. As Inoue (2014) writes,

> We know that students come to us from very different educational systems that do not equally prepare them. We know that we judge the quality of writing in most writing courses by a White, middle-class standard, one not native to poor, the working class, or many students of color. We know that students have no control over any of these factors in their lives, and yet we still say that judging writing quality, particularly for a course grade, is fair. (p. 92)

By shifting the focus from judgements of quality to individual student learning and growth, contract grading can expand equity within online writing assessment. For example, focusing assessment on student growth between drafts, giving substantive weight to student reflections and self-assessments, or using completion scores centers the individual learning of the student and gives agency to the student in the assessment process.

Students come to online learning with a wide range of preparation and experience with digital learning tools, and some space for learning new tools must be built into any course. As Jason Dockter (2016) points out, instructors frequently make generalizations about the students in their class, presuming

> that each student will possess the same knowledge of the role of an online student and the same technological, communication, and reading skills—essentially assuming that all students will react to the various elements of an online course in similar ways. (p. 81)

While online instructors often rely on technology to mediate for distance, they have to be careful to not make assumptions about students' knowledge of learning technologies. GSOLE Principle 1 (2019) emphasizes accessibility and inclusion related to technology, as follows: "to support the accessible development, design, and teaching of OLCs, all stakeholders must understand the technology use mandated by any particular institution . . . and be able to use it." Instructors should think carefully about the affordances and limitations of the technologies used in the class and what issues may arise throughout the semester, while trying to anticipate how this will impact students' abilities to fully realize the commitments and responsibilities for the class. For instance, grading contracts can support students' variable knowledge and experience related to learning technologies by building policies such as flexible due dates that allow for technology failure as students become familiar with the tools and technologies used in the course.

While the adaptability of contracts makes them attractive, the openness can be daunting and the prospect of getting it "wrong" can feel risky, especially when grades can carry so much weight for students and institutions. As Shor remarks in his 2009 essay on contract grading,

> It's easy to be a bad teacher but hard to be a good one, no matter what kind of pedagogy we use. Good teaching is labor-intensive and immensely rewarding when it "works." Of course, no pedagogy works all the time, and all face student resistances of one kind or another. (p. 6)

Certainly, no teaching practices work all the time—in all contexts and with all students—and this is especially true for online learning. Developing a contract will be an ongoing process; *teachers may feel they did not get it right the first time*, and indeed, may struggle over the grading parameters, the language used to define those parameters, and how to effectively communicate the rationale to students.

This is in line with GSOLE OLI Principle 3 (2019), which states, "Instructors and tutors should commit to regular, iterative processes of course and instructional material design, development, assessment, and revision to ensure that online literacy instruction and student support reflect current effective practices." This is precisely the kind of process our TILT handout supports for instructors developing and revising grading contracts. We emphasize in this piece that ongoing, active revision of both teaching practices and course design and content, in online courses in particular, is important for continuing to meet the needs of diverse distance learners. For new instructors especially, student feedback is integral to revising teaching practices to better accommodate student needs. Each time we use contract grading, our comfort with the methods and practices we use increases, as does our comfort with unlearning, as we become more open to ongoing revision.

COURSE CONTEXT AND LESSON

In this section, we will discuss our processes of developing and revising grading contracts in first-year composition (FYC) courses and professional writing courses. The contracts we use in these different contexts have different parameters and structures that meet the needs of different students, at different universities, and in different stages of their educational pathways. In particular, we will note the differences between how we structured our contracts and how we negotiated with tracking and valuing student work and labor. The goal of this chapter is to help readers determine a process for developing their own contracts, although readers are welcome to adapt the example contracts provided here for their own courses. In the space below, each of us will articulate our classroom contexts and how that context impacted the grading contracts we designed. It's important to recognize the similarities (mostly on the kinds of questions and concerns that we raised as we crafted our contracts) and differences between (especially related to the design and layout of our contracts and the way we negotiated with assigning point-values to assignments) each of our contracts and to interrogate the contingencies present in each of our classrooms that may have dictated the specific rhetorical and structural decisions that we made.

GRADING CONTRACTS IN AN ONLINE, ANY TIME TECHNICAL WRITING COURSE (GABBY)

As an adjunct instructor at a STEM-focused university in New Jersey, I teach an online, any time technical writing course. The course runs for 15 weeks and is a 300-level class; it is offered as a general education course to fulfill a history and humanities 300-level requirement. The course attracts students from across the university, the majority looking to fulfill a general education requirement. I sought to create a contract that was flexible, open, and accommodating. I wanted to provide students with agency in choosing how they approached the course, the assignments, and the deadlines associated with each assignment. To relieve some of the tension associated with online courses—and the physical distance between the students and instructor—I ensured that the grading expectations were transparent from the beginning. Building a trusting learning environment can be especially difficult in online, any time courses since many of us will never see some of our students face-to-face, making it harder to demonstrate our sincerity and authenticity in prioritizing revision and development over product. By clearly outlining the expectations for each letter grade, I endeavored to demystify the grading process and provide students clarity on where their grade stood throughout the semester.

I first introduced the contract to students through the syllabus. To avoid overloading students with too much information on a single document, the syllabus simply stated that students would be graded based on a contract and that they could find it by following a hyperlink. I also stressed that students should reach out to me if there was any confusion about the contract, and alerted students to the discussion board that they'd be asked to complete in which they would be reflecting on the grading contract. To further mitigate anxiety about a new grading system, I composed a preface to the grading contract to explain the rationale and reasoning behind my choice and what I hoped students would gain. I pointed to recurring anxieties that students have expressed about grading as a way to articulate what I saw as the primary benefit of using a grading contract: students' ability to take agency over their grade and a focus on revision and development. Students' awareness of the grading structure and expectations from the beginning of the semester allowed them to manage their workload appropriately according to the grade that they aimed to achieve in the class. This can be especially helpful for nontraditional students or students who are already feeling stress about online learning and succeeding in an online, any time environment, as both can present challenges and a learning curve for students.

The contract outlines the assignment and course expectations that students are expected to complete in order to receive a specific grade. I clearly defined the expectations for each grade to alleviate some anxiety that students may feel about the subjectivity involved in grading. So long as students completed the assignment expectations as outlined, they could expect to receive a completion grade for that assignment. I consistently kept up with grading to ensure that students were aware of their standing in the class throughout the semester. I marked assignments on a complete/incomplete basis and allowed students to revise assignments that did not meet the assignment expectations.

To further encourage transparency while granting students agentive moments to reach their goal grade in the course, I outlined a flexible late policy and clarified the tasks required to receive a passing grade in the preface. For instance, students only need to complete 85 percent of the reading notes (notice and focus discussion boards) to receive an A for that assignment category. This grants students the flexibility to skip a discussion assignment during a week where other stressors and material concerns may be vying for their attention. Through the flexibility offered in the grading contract and the flexible late policy, I provide students with agentive moments throughout the course.

The preface also states that students are expected to complete the assignments in the manner and spirit assigned. Because I hoped to avoid confusing students with vague language and abstract articulations of assessment, what I wanted to convey with "manner and spirit" was that students understood they should still engage with the material and topics explored in the class while balancing the freedom, flexibility, and creativity afforded by the grading contract. I don't feel I did that adequately by using "manner and spirit," given that the language does not specify, beyond the assignment expectations, how students should engage with the course material. In the future, I might change the wording to express the sentiment expressed in the previous sentence: that students should purposelessly think alongside the material in each module and the material/topics/themes engaged in the course to demonstrate that they are developing as writers and learners. Being specific about thinking alongside the material and the topics in the course provides students a grounded understanding of how they will be assessed. It's important that instructors avoid vague language in their grading contracts. Instead, instructors should aim to provide specific directions that outline the expectations and goals of individual assignments to avoid points of confusion over how students can fulfill the grading contract expectations for individual assignments.

For instance, in an earlier iteration of my grading contract, I neglected to include an explicit segment about the late policy. My intent was to maintain a flexible late policy, and I assumed that students would understand I would not wrongly penalize them for late assignments. However, while I had thought this was clear, a few comments from students suggested that the lack of clarity around the late policy was causing stress and confusion. I also struggled with knowing how to assign credit to students who completed their work consistently late in line with the contract. Thus, in a second iteration of the contract, I revised it to include a 2-point scale for major assignments that allows students to submit late and receive half credit for the assignment and made it clear that minor assignments could be made-up at any point in the semester. Though still not perfect, this version led to fewer student questions around how lates would be handled and assessed according to the grading contract.

In sum, grading contracts offer effective and impactful ways to build trust with your students through transparent grading practices and providing students with agentive moments. Grading contracts also offer a way to ease the cognitive overload students may experience as they learn to navigate digital learning environments. The next grading contract example provides an overview of a grading contract composed for an online, any time first-year composition program. Our classroom environments, students, and learning goals necessitated different approaches to our contracts, a central point we hope to stress in this chapter. In the next section, Michelle focuses on the process of revising a contract through multiple iterations as an example of the process of unlearning and productive failure that is central to using contract grading.

Grading Contracts in Online, Any Time First-Year Writing Classes (Michelle)

As a Writing Program Administrator, I direct an online, any time FYC program. The courses satisfy the general studies writing requirement for students enrolled in online, any time degree programs. The programmatic course goals include introducing students to composing in a range of genres and modalities, engaging in primary and secondary community-based research, and developing a transferable writing process. In addition, our pedagogical priorities include emphasizing process over product, giving students agency in the assessment process through meaningful and heavily weighted reflections on learning, and ensuring all students have opportunities to successfully meet their learning goals.

Students in the courses are predominantly nontraditional students with professional and familial obligations that make accelerated, 7.5-week, online any time courses appealing and convenient. However, the physical distance between instructor and student, accelerated timeframe, and personal and professional demands on students also cause a great deal of cognitive overload. As an online any time course, there is a lot of content students have to navigate on their own while being very new to both college and online learning. To help students focus on the core transferable skills of the course—writing and research in college, with an emphasis on understanding and applying feedback—I led a grading contract pilot with a small cohort of faculty in Fall 2019. The results of the pilot, which included the key finding that habits and dispositions toward grades require unlearning for both teachers and students, are detailed in an article in a special issue of the *Journal of Writing Assessment* (Stuckey et al., 2020).

As a result of the pilot and subsequent iterations of the contract, we learned that the greatest challenges for implementing grading contracts in online, any time courses were clarifying expectations for students in the rationale for the contract and aligning the assessment philosophy with the assessment structures in the learning management system, specifically the built-in rubrics and gradebook. I have come to understand the process of developing and revising the rubrics, in particular, as a moment of productive failure, which I will discuss in greater detail in this section.

The first iterations of the contract were heavily influenced by the Danielewicz and Elbow (2009) model, which is unilateral (meaning it is not negotiated with students) and uses the grade of B as a baseline, with the intention of easing student anxiety by accounting for their engagement with the writing process in a meaningful way. In the initial iteration of the contract for our online program, the purpose was communicated to students as focusing on **"learning rather than grades."** With this contract, we aimed to de-emphasize student focus on the points they received, in part by moving from a 1000-point scale to a system in which each assignment was evaluated on a scale of 0–3. This also shifted faculty's focus from judgements of quality that involved looking for "errors" to grading primarily based on completeness.

As much as the contract encouraged students to let go of their focus on grades, the previous experiences they have had with institutionalized learning made it difficult for some students to do that—and certainly it would take more than one 7.5-week class to get them there. A combination of Likert-scale and open-ended responses revealed that—while student reactions to the contract were generally favorable—they were in line with Inman and Powell's (2018) findings in "In the Absence of Grades." That is, many students rely on grades to measure their success or failure in academic contexts, which they often equate with learning, and even their sense of themselves as learners. When those traditional grades are removed from the learning environment, they can feel unmoored from their identities as students. Thus, for some students, a guaranteed "B" did not alleviate stress, and a 3-point scale did not represent the variation in the amount of labor different assignments required. In addition, the online, any time structure posed a challenge for ensuring students actively read and understood the contract.

The pilot also revealed that the language used to define criteria for A and B grades was not always clear to students or teachers. For example, one of the criteria for a B grade was that students "complete the work in a meaningful and substantive manner as outlined by the assignment rubric." Yet, in follow-up surveys, students struggled to understand what constitutes "meaningful and substantive," and indeed, we realized that what that looked like would vary significantly among different students. As part of the B baseline, we had also identified criteria for "exceeding the B" and "falling short of the B." Initial rubric categories included "exceeds expectations" (3), "meets expectations" (2), and "does not meet expectations" (1).

Surveys and focus groups with faculty informed continued revision and refinement of the grading contract, as we learned more about how faculty were interpreting and implementing the contract in their courses. The focus on the B grade was removed, and instead, the contract was structured by defining two categories of assignments: completion-graded and content-graded. What really improved the clarity were the changes made to the rubrics; specifically, the categories were changed to "meets all expectations" (3) "meets most expectations" (2), and "meets few expectations" (1). This move led to a contract that was more focused on task completion and assessed students on whether they had fully responded to the prompt with the distinguishing factor being whether the student met the listed expectations in each category and addressed all required elements of the assignment. It reduced ambiguity for students and instructors by detailing requirements for the A grade, while eliminating criteria that might force instructors to fall back on subjective judgements of quality of writing. The total score is a holistic assessment that accounts for students' work in relation to all aspects of the assignment. The original and revised versions of the contract can be found in the appendix.

The pilot and subsequent revisions of the contract were important learning experiences for both instructors and administrators, as we let go of certain assumptions and practices and adopted more flexible positions. For teachers, that meant reconsidering—unlearning—old habits and practices and being comfortable taking on new ways of thinking about student writing and grading—and risking discomfort from ambiguity and uncertainty. Instructors expressed that the contract shifted their thinking away from a deficit approach, in which they focused on looking for "errors" and justifying point deductions. For administrators, this experience required coming to terms with productive failure related especially to rubric criteria and understanding that grading contracts, and assessment more broadly, are an ongoing process of reflection and revision. The TILT framework that Gabby and I share later in this chapter is, at least in part, a way to prepare for and act on these moments of productive failure.

Overall, this process has challenged both teachers and administrators in the program to *unlearn* in various ways. The contract itself has challenged faculty to unlearn old grading habits and practices that do not account for the needs and experiences of online students. It has enabled faculty to take a more holistic view of student learning related to writing, and to consider the ideas and processes students engage in without focusing on subjective interpretations of quality. The contract revisions have also created more space for individual students to meet the criteria in their own unique ways without being overly subjected to quality-based criteria.

The process has also shifted faculty and administrators' perspectives on the contract, from seeing it as a policy that was developed and implemented, to understanding assessment methods in much the same ways we do curriculum—as always in process and requiring ongoing revision as we continue to understand students' needs and instructors' practices. With each iteration, the contract better approximates the ethos of the program's pedagogical orientation, better meets the needs of instructors, and increases assessment transparency for students. Contracts are not panaceas, and there is not one perfect solution for the complexities of writing assessment. However, embracing productive failure and understanding the value of ongoing revision and reflection can help faculty learn to design better assessments for online, any time learning contexts.

REFLECTION ON PRACTICE

What works in face-to-face classrooms does not always work in online classes, for a multitude of reasons. With so many different structures and modalities for OLI—from online real-time, online any time, hybrid, 15-week, or 8-week—determining a manageable, sustainable workload for both students and instructors can be challenging. Online students are also not monolithic; they may be first-time college students, nontraditional-aged students, and students with full-time jobs and/or caregiving responsibilities. Contract grading can offer students flexibility in the assignments they choose to focus their attention on and it also can help instructors manage how they prioritize grading and feedback. As the process of teaching well is an ongoing evolution of practice, developing an effective method of contract grading that responds to the particular online context and student population requires continual reflection, revision, and reorientation. Our approach to contracts in online, any time courses, for instance, relies on a few key points:

- Unilateral (non-negotiated) contracts that clearly and transparently outline grading criteria work better in online, any time environments, but still necessitate checkpoints to ensure students read and understand the contract. This could involve, for example, a discussion assignment in which students are required to submit a question or comment about the contract.
- Even with unilateral contracts, there is room for students to have agency in the assessment process, whether through learning reflections and self-assessments or by opportunities to choose their goal grade.
- Treating the grading contract as a foundation for an assessment ecology (Inoue, 2015) that requires alignment with other elements of the course, such as rubrics and late work policies, increases equity, inclusion, and accessibility within the course.

Thus, we are not proposing that readers take the contracts we've developed and use them in their own courses wholesale. Rather, we offer them as examples (which you are welcome to borrow from, as we have from others!) and we encourage online teachers to identify the limitations of their current assessment practices and the particular needs of their student population and consider how those might be negotiated by a grading contract. The TILT handout at the end of this chapter offers one way for instructors to engage in this reflective and reiterative process.

Through this highly individualized assessment practice, instructors can actively respond to the needs of their students. In our experiences, despite some initial hesitation, students largely perceive contract grading to be one that increases transparency by clearly outlining assessment criteria prior to the start of the semester. Contracts like Gabby's enable students to decide how to manage their workload depending on the grade they want to achieve. In fact, a common thread in her students' reflections about the contract emphasized the flexibility it afforded in terms of deadlines and completing assignments, and thus created a low-stress environment that allowed them to better engage with assignments on their own terms. Programmatic contracts like those Michelle discussed can help create greater consistency and transparency in student assessment across a program, while initiating important conversations that push instructors to examine outdated habits and practices based on error counting. Increasing transparency, encouraging student agency, and expanding inclusivity and accessibility together counter the instrumentalism and transactionality that can creep into online learning, affording more opportunities for instructors to build trust with students. Other chapters in this collection offer further variations, such as Shawn Bowers and Jennifer Smith Daniel's approach to ungrading, which emphasizes moving away from notions of "good writing" in line with White mainstream English and emphasizing iterative process; Kate Pantelides, Samira Grayson, and Erica Stone's Dialogic Assessment Agreement, which negotiates contract terms in conversation with students; or Kevin DePew and Kole Matheson's methods for developing a contract that aligns with educators' pedagogical values (see Chapter 17, this collection).

For teachers, contract grading, or other variations like simplified grading and ungrading, may at first be daunting. Some teachers may struggle with letting go of traditional scales that include plus or minus grades, or may find it challenging to give full completion credit to work that they may view as less developed. As with teaching any new assignment, it can take a semester or two to adjust to a new practice and will require active reflection on attitudes and habits of assessment. Teachers may find that using a particular method just does not work for them or their students because it is too rigid, or too flexible, or just does not meet the needs of the particular class. For example, building in opportunities for resubmission has to be considered in relation to the instructor's teaching load. Allowing multiple re-submissions won't help students if the instructor doesn't have time to re-read them. When you encounter unexpected challenges or your policies don't go as planned, we encourage you to not assume that "contract grading doesn't work for me." As we've tried to impart in this chapter—and as other authors in this collection have demonstrated—contract grading can take many forms and may require experimentation, risk, and revision.

As we've discussed throughout this chapter, using grading contracts involves a constant unlearning process and a rethinking of traditional course policies and assignments. As unpredictable issues arise throughout the semester, it is up to the instructor to continue to interrogate and revise the grading contract to reflect the class's needs. For instance, aligning the goals of the contract with the grading criteria outlined in the rubrics and making those grading structures work within the constraints of the tools available in your LMS may be challenging and may require multiple iterations. To that end, it is important for instructors to remember that grading contracts can push in ways that may feel uncomfortable in part due to the assessment habits and language biases that we hold; despite this, instructors should continue to revise and reflect on how the grading contract responds to the ebbs and flows of the online course.

CONCLUSION

Contract grading offers an accessible entry point for new instructors and students navigating online learning environments, but also a challenging and exciting path for seasoned online educators to re-envision their assessment practices. The Learning to Unlearn Assessment Revision Activity is a starting point for creating a roadmap to an individualized grading contract. We recommend beginning your journey with a clear understanding of your current assessment practices—what components of it are working for you and your students, and what parts are not? This will require some real honesty about your current approaches as well as your biases around language. We recommend you spend significant time engaging in five tasks: understand your class context; know your student population; describe your class learning goals; gauge your students' experience; and reflect on your experience as a teacher. This will involve significant time and reflection, and you may even need to gather data from your program administrators and current students. You also might consider working with a partner or a small team to engage in this work collaboratively. Being open to self-critique and feedback from others—as well as being willing to examine the habits and biases that shape your current practice—will position you to be successful in this work.

That we can continue to modify and adapt our contracts speaks to the highly individualized nature of grading contracts and the importance of consistent revision, reflection, and interrogation of our assessment practices. Remaining open to the unlearning process and embracing productive failure can help you develop a contract that works for you. This will be an ongoing endeavor, which in many ways counters the infinitely copied course model that undermines online education. Using this activity can help you situate yourself as an online educator, better understand the affordances and constraints of your current online course context, and develop assessment strategies that are more transparent, accessible, and inclusive and that grant students agency over their learning. The activity can also spark productive dialogue among online educators at a given institution or in a specific department, as it can serve as a starting point for conversations around assessment, online pedagogy, and assumptions and biases about college writing, with the goal of generating even better practices for OWI.

MOVING BETTER PRACTICES ACROSS MODALITIES

We hope our chapter and TILT Handout demonstrate the adaptability and flexibility of grading contracts to a range of teaching and learning needs. The TILT handout is designed to help instructors develop a contract that is suited for their specific modality. Below, we offer some guidance for thinking about maximizing the affordances of different contract methods in different modalities.

- **In-Person, Real-Time Learning:** This modality is well-suited to negotiated contracts in which students are able to participate in setting the terms of the contract through face-to-face conversations and as private conversations during class time or through office hours.
- **Online, Real-Time Learning:** This modality is also well-suited to negotiated contracts in which students are able to participate in setting the terms of the contract through online class conversations or a video call outside of normal class time.
- **Online, Any Time Learning:** Unilateral contracts, the terms of which are not negotiated with students, work better in this modality due to the challenges of real-time discussion. However, individual students could set up a video call for an office hours conversation about the contract.
- **Hybrid Learning:** Depending on the frequency of real-time meetings and the amount of information to be covered during that time, in this modality, instructors could opt for unilateral or negotiated contracts with the option for further discussion during office hours.

TILT HANDOUT: LEARNING TO UNLEARN ASSESSMENT REVISION ACTIVITY

Purpose

The goal of this activity is to help you 1. Understand your current assessment practice, 2. Analyze where and how your current assessment methods fall short of meeting student needs, and 3. Identify what aspects of your approach can be revised for greater clarity, transparency, and equity.

Skills

- Openness to self-critique.
- Ability to evaluate your current methods and the habits and biases that inform them.
- Willingness to revise and change your practice.

Knowledge

This practice will help you to incorporate reflection and revision into your assessment methods. It will help you improve your awareness of the practices you use in order to make deliberate decisions about how best to assess learning in your courses.

Task 1: Understand Class Context

- What is the format of the online course? In-person, real-time; online, any time; hybrid; online, real-time.
- Identify the challenges of this format as it relates to:
    - Building trust with students,
    - Assessing students' work equitably, and
    - Focusing on individual student growth and development.
- Now, flip the process. Identify the affordances of this format as it relates to:
    - Building trust with students,
    - Assessing students' work equitably, and
    - Focusing on individual student growth and development.
- What are the benefits and limitations of the LMS used?
- Identify technologies used in this class that may facilitate assessment (e.g., built-in rubrics).
- Identify technologies used in this class that may pose challenges for assessment (e.g., LMS available grading functions).
- Consider the curriculum for the course.
- What is the purpose of writing in this class, and what kind of assessment and feedback do students need to achieve the learning goals of the class?

Task 2: Know Your Student Population

- What are the demographic characteristics of the students in your online courses?
- Are your students undergraduate or graduate students?

- Are students engaging with writing as a key focus of their degree program, or is this a general education requirement?
- What particular challenges have students struggled with in your course previously?
    - How prepared are students for online learning?
    - What has your institution done to prepare these students for online learning through mandatory or suggested tutorials?
    - What have you asked them about through pre-course surveys, discussion forums, or other means?

Task 3: Describe Class Learning Goals

- What habits of mind do students need to learn or practice in this class according to the *Framework for Success in Postsecondary Writing*?
- How can individual student learning be measured through the assignments in this course?
- What assessment methods have been effective for accounting for student learning in past classes?
- On the other hand, what assessment methods have been misaligned with measuring student learning in past classes?
- Given the (mis)alignments noted above, does your current assessment method align with your stated pedagogical goals? In what ways does or does it not?

Task 4: Gauge Student Experience

- What feedback did you receive from students on how they were graded?
- Did students express confusion or concern about the grading method? If so, what did they find confusing?
- Did students say they liked or valued particular aspects of the grading method?
- Did you solicit feedback from students on the assessment method? And if so, what did you learn from that feedback?

Task 5: Reflect on Teacher Experience

- What aspects of assessing student writing do you enjoy the most? Why?
- What do you like least about assessment of student writing? Why?
- Which of the aspects you least enjoy can be eliminated or changed?
- How might they be simplified or changed to be more enjoyable for you as an instructor and meaningful for your students as well?

BACKGROUND INFORMATION

Contract grading is an approach that distances evaluation and feedback from grading. A grading contract can take a number of different approaches, some of the most common are labor-based grading contracts, the guaranteed "B" approach, and the negotiated contract approach. Labor-based grading contracts assign students a grade based on their labor output in the class. The default grade is a "B," students can achieve a higher grade by doing more work in the course. In the same respect, they can receive a lower grade if they do not submit all of the required work. The guaranteed "B" approach is exactly how it sounds. Students receive a B if they complete all required work in the course. Students can receive a higher grade based on the quality of their work or a lower grade if they do not submit all required work. Finally, the negotiated contract requires instructors to arrive at the requirements for achieving certain grades through class discussions. Instructors can read the following sources for more information on different contract grading models:

- Peter Elbow "Taking Time Out from Grading and Evaluating,"
- Shane Wood "Engaging in Resistant Genres as Antiracist Teacher Response,"
- Asao Inoue "Stories About Grading Contracts, Or How Do I Like the Violence I've Done,"
- Barret John Mandel "Teaching Without Judgement," and
- Michelle Cowan "A Legacy of Contract Grading for Composition."

REFERENCES

Baker-Bell, A. (2020). *Linguistic justice: Black language, literacy, identity, and pedagogy*. Routledge.

Bawa, P. (2016). Retention in online courses: Exploring issues and solution: A literature review. *SAGE Open, 6*(1). https://doi.org/10.1177/2158244015621777.

Brannon, L. & Knoblauch, C. H. (1982). On students' rights to their own texts: A model of teacher response. *College Composition and Communication, 33*(2), 157–166.

Conference on College Composition and Communication. (2015). Principles for the postsecondary teaching of writing [Revised]. *National Council of Teachers of English.* https://cccc.ncte.org/cccc/resources/positions/postsecondarywriting.

Cowan, M. (2020). A legacy of grading contracts for composition. *Journal of Writing Assessment, 13*(2). https://escholarship.org/uc/item/0j28w67h.

Dockter, J. (2016). The problem of teaching presence in transactional theories of distance education. *Computers and Composition, 40*, 73–86.

Danielewicz, J. & Elbow, P. (2009). A unilateral grading contract to improve learning and teaching. *College Composition and Communication, 61*(2), 244–268.

Elbow, P. (1997). Taking time out from grading and evaluating while working in a conventional system. *Assessing Writing, 4*(1), 5–27. https://doi.org/10.1016/S1075-2935(97)80003-7.

GSOLE Executive Board. (2019, June 13). Online literacy instruction principles and tenets. *Global Society of Online Literacy Educators.* https://gsole.org/oliresources/oliprinciples.

Halberstam, J. (2012). Unlearning. *Profession,* 9–16.

Hewett, B. L. (2015). Grounding principles of OWI. In B. L. Hewett & K. E. Depew (Eds.), *Foundational Practices of Online Writing Instruction,* (pp. 33–92). The WAC Clearinghouse; Parlor Press. https://doi.org/10.37514/PER-B.2015.0650.2.01.

hooks, b. (1994). *Teaching to transgress.* Taylor & Francis Group. https://ebookcentral-proquest-com.ezproxy1.lib.asu.edu/lib/asulib-ebooks/detail.action?docID=1656118.

Inman, J. O. & Powell, R. A. (2018). In the absence of grades. *College Composition and Communication, 70*(1), 30–56.

Inoue, A. B. (2014). A grade-less writing course that focuses on labor and assessing. In D. Teague & R. Lunsford (Eds.), *First-year composition: From theory to practice* (pp. 71–110). Parlor Press.

Inoue, A. B. (2015). *Antiracist writing assessment ecologies: Teaching and assessing writing for a socially just future.* The WAC Clearinghouse; Parlor Press. https://doi.org/10.37514/PER-B.2015.0698.

Inoue, A. B. (2019). Classroom writing assessment as an antiracist practice: Confronting white supremacy in the judgments of language. *Pedagogy 19*(3), 373–404. https://www.muse.jhu.edu/article/733095.

Inoue, A. B. (2020). Stories about grading contracts, or how do I like through the violence I've done? *Journal of Writing Assessment, 13*(2). https://escholarship.org/uc/item/3zw9h7p9.

Mandel, B. J. (1973). Teaching without judging. *College English, 34*(5), 623–633.

Shor, I. (2009). Critical pedagogy is too big to fail. *Journal of Basic Writing, 28*(2), 6–27.

Stuckey, M. A., Erdem, E. & Waggoner, Z. (2020). Rebuilding habits: Assessing the impact of a hybrid learning contract in online first-year composition courses. *Journal of Writing Assessment, 13*(2). https://escholarship.org/uc/item/9sp0g53j.

Wood, S. (2020). Engaging in resistant genres as antiracist teacher response. *Journal of Writing Assessment, 13*(2). https://escholarship.org/uc/item/2c45c0gf.

APPENDIX 1: GRADING CONTRACT FOR ENG 352 FALL 2021

Adapted from Asao Inoue's Labor-Based Grading Contract and Michelle Stuckey's Grading Contract

Grading is considered to be a traditional, standardized academic practice at most institutions. Most of us were first introduced to letter grades around middle school; maybe some of us felt they pushed us to be our best, maybe some of us felt they were rigid and limiting, or maybe some of us barely paid attention to them, but regardless, we all have had an experience involving grading. This semester, I'd like to turn away from the traditional grading model and its emphasis on a single standard and turn towards what I and others consider to be a more equitable assessment practice—grading contracts (Elbow, 1987; Inoue, 2014; Mandel, 1973).

A grading contract provides a clearly outlined understanding of how a student can expect to be assessed throughout the semester. This grading contract will outline the assignments that students will be expected to complete along with other expectations of the course in a clearly defined manner. I decided to utilize a grading contract this semester because I believe that it offers a way for students to take agency over the course and their grades. Traditional grading systems tend to result in students who are afraid to take risks out of fear of receiving a lower grade; moreover, they create stressful learning environments and foster competition among students.

Instead, this semester, your grade for ENG352 will be evaluated based on a grading contract that focuses on meeting explicitly defined expectations for the course. It is my hope that you will find that a grading contract offers you a clear understanding of your grade at any point in the semester. This does not mean that you will not be assessed throughout the semester; you are still expected to submit all assignments in the manner and spirit that they are assigned. You are also expected to adhere to outlined participation expectations. While you will receive feedback on your assignments, you will not receive a grade based on that feedback (just a completion mark); rather your grade will be based on your ability to fulfill the course and assignment expectations outlined below. We will use a discussion board to discuss any changes that students may wish to make to the contract. You should leave any thoughts/comments that you have about the grading contract there. Students should post a response on the discussion board by the second week of class. Take some time to look over the expectations of the course. Do any seem unfair or unreasonable? Should we raise some of the expectations? Consider your own experience with grades; how did/do grades impact your learning in the classroom? Consider the traditional grading model, and interrogate whether students are all held to an equitable standard.

The course expectations are outlined in *Table 18.1*. **Further,** assignments are expected to . . .

- Be turned in on time within the 48-hour deadline exempting extensions (students may be granted one a semester).
- Fulfill all assignment requirements as outlined in the discussion board descriptions on and on each of the major assignments.
- Engage with the course material and feedback provided by the instructor.
- Demonstrate thoughtful reflection and a deep interrogation of technical and professional writing practices.

Learning to Unlearn

Table 18.1. Grading Distribution for ENG352 Contract

Grade:	A Grade	B Grade	C Grade	D+ Below Grade
Expectations:	**6 Major Projects **All reflective questions posed at the end of major projects **85% (12) of "informal" discussion boards + minor assignments **85% (7) of notice and focus discussion boards **Collaboratively working with peers and ensuring that all peer and group work is submitted by the deadline. This includes (all) reflection discussion boards and crafting an email assignment as well as peer review for the revised proposal assignment **Attend 1 office hour sessions	**6 Major Projects—one week late **4 reflective questions posed at the end of major projects **75% (10) of "informal" discussion boards + minor assignments **75% (6) of notice and focus discussion boards **Collaboratively working with peers and ensuring that all peer and group work is submitted by the deadline. This includes completing (4) reflection discussion boards and crafting an email assignment as well as peer review for the revised proposal assignment **Attend 1 office hour session	**6 Major Projects—two weeks late **2 reflective questions posed at the end of major projects **65% (9) of "informal" discussion boards + minor assignments **65% (5) of notice and focus discussion boards **Collaboratively working with peers and ensuring that all peer and group work is submitted by the deadline. This includes completing (3) reflection discussion boards and crafting an email assignment as well as peer review for the revised proposal assignment **Attend 0 office hour sessions	**Missing a Major Project(s)—4 or more projects are two weeks late **0 reflective questions posed at the end of major projects **Less than 65% of "informal" discussion boards + minor assignments ** Less than 65% of notice and focus discussion boards **Does not collaboratively work with peers or submit peer and group work by the deadline **Attend 0 office hour sessions

Ways to move up a grade or makeup missing work, such as not attending an office hour session, not completing 90 percent of discussion boards, or not completing 85 percent of notice and focus discussion boards can possibly include:

- Attending more than one office hour sessions.
- Completing more than 85 percent of discussion board assignments or notice and focus assignments.
- Revising a major project aside from the proposal.
- Exceptional (or mediocre) work.
- Students are expected to complete all assignments according to the expectations outlined in the assignment. Consistently submitting work that does not meet the assignment expectations or does not engage with

441

the course material and feedback provided by the instructor and peers may result in a letter grade deduction at the instructor's discretion.

Should you have any questions, please feel free to contact me. By staying in this course and attending class, you accept this contract and agree to abide by it. I (Gabriella) also agree to abide by the contract and administer it fairly and equitably.

APPENDIX 2: GRADING CONTRACT FOR CISA WRITERS' STUDIO FALL 2019

Learning Contract Rationale

The Writers' Studio first-year composition courses aim to help you develop a sense of yourself as a composer, writer, reader, thinker, and learner. To accomplish this, we guide you in identifying and practicing the skills and habits you will need to be a successful composer and, more broadly, a successful learner in college, in your profession, in your community, and in your personal life. We want to help you realize that successful **rhetorical** communicators have developed a clear composing process made up of specific practices and habits. As a student in our classes, you will develop your own processes to draw on whenever you are faced with a new communication situation. We will also help you learn which of your own composing habits are strengths that you can continue to hone, and which you must work harder to improve.

Our composition classes are communities of composers and writers. Social and collaborative composing activities maximize student opportunities to engage with the concepts, habits, and processes foundational to first-year composition through the Writers' Studio. Part of this learning contract involves **committing to the community**—engaging in authentic and meaningful conversations about composing with your classmates, instructor, and writing mentor. To be an engaged and committed member of your Writers' Studio community, you also need to responsibly complete assignments and submit them in a timely manner. Your classmates need you to fully participate—their learning also depends to some extent on your learning.

We know that students find their way to first-year composition in the Writers' Studio through diverse life experiences and educational goals. We want to do our best to ensure you succeed in our courses by helping you navigate these challenges. We know every student can not only pass but also maximize your potential as writers and composers. We understand that many of you have other commitments, life goals, and motivations, and we want all students to have a path to success in our courses.

To that end, we employ the following contract, which focuses on **learning**

rather than grades. We want you to think less about your grades and more about your composing. We want you to work thoughtfully, take risks, and pursue ideas that you find compelling, without being overly distracted by your final course grade. You are guaranteed a B in the course if you complete the following activities and meet the following guidelines.

With this contract, we hope to move the focus from grades to composing. We hope you see your instructor and writing mentor as coaches who can offer support, feedback, and guidance—and who push you to excel. If you read, listen to, and act on their feedback and engage in conversation with them, you will grow as a composer while learning the valuable tool of self-assessment.

Earning a B Grade

We believe that in order for you to grow as a composer and writer, you need to develop important skills and habits through the process of developing the stages of a composing project. Completing all required assignments will help you develop these habits while meeting the course learning outcomes. Thus, if you complete the work in this class according to the criteria outlined below, **you will receive a B in the course.**

To meet the B requirement for any of the work in this course, you must do the following:

- Submit the work on time.
- Complete the work in a **meaningful and substantive manner as outlined by the assignment rubric.**
- Meet all expectations and requirements for the given assignment.
- Demonstrate **openness** to revision and consideration of previous feedback.

The majority of your work will be given a **completion grade;** that is, the grade book will reflect whether you completed the assignment in a **meaningful and substantive manner** while meeting the specific requirements of the assignment. We have provided rubrics to clarify what we mean by **meaningful and substantive** for all the major assignments.

More important than any grade you receive is your instructor and/or peer mentor's feedback. We want you to prioritize that feedback over a grade you have been assigned and hope you focus on building a conversation with the members of your composing community about your composing rather than about any specific grade.

If you engage seriously with the process approach to work in this class, you will leave with the knowledge, skills, habits, and practices you need for composing in college and beyond.

Exceeding the B Grade

We believe that improving as a composer takes practice, and so the more practice you have, the more you will improve. We acknowledge and reward those efforts to improve. You have the opportunity to exceed the B grade on every assignment. Your revision analyses and portfolio reflections also offer opportunities to argue and offer evidence for how you exceeded expectations. To achieve an "A" in this class, you must

- Consistently exceed expectations on assignments, such as making connections to the previous and upcoming assignments.
- Demonstrate deep learning, such as the ability to transfer essential skills and habits, in portfolio reflections.
- Provide evidence of substantial revision on final drafts of all major projects (Project 1, Project 2, and the Final Portfolio).

Falling Short of the B Grade

Missing assignments, unsatisfactory assignments, and turning final projects in late will reduce your grade.

Assessment and Grading

For every assignment, you will receive a score on a scale of 0–3:

- 0 = not submitted.
- 1 = submitted but does not meet expectations for a B.
- 2 = meets expectations for a B.
- 3 = exceeds expectations for a B.

Assignments will be weighted differently according to the amount of time and effort required. So, although you will receive a 0–3 score for all assignments, a final project will be weighted more than a discussion board post, for example. Please see the breakdown of the assignment weighting on the course syllabus.

Please also note that Canvas weighting always shows the total as a percentage. **In this scale from 0–3, a 66% is a B grade.**

APPENDIX 3: GRADING CONTRACT FOR CISA WRITERS' STUDIO FALL 2021

RATIONALE

The Writers' Studio composition courses are communities of composers and writers. To become stronger writers and composers, students need feedback.

That is why, in the Writers' Studio, we emphasize social and collaborative composing activities. Students need many opportunities to practice the concepts, habits, and processes foundational to first-year composition through interactions with peers, instructors, and writing mentors. Part of this learning contract involves **committing to the community**: engaging in authentic and meaningful conversations about composing with your classmates, instructor, and writing mentor. To be an engaged and committed member of your Writers' Studio community, you also need to responsibly complete assignments and submit them in a timely manner. Your classmates need you to fully participate—their learning also depends to some extent on your learning.

We know that students find their way to first-year composition in the Writers' Studio through diverse life experiences and educational goals. We want to do our best to ensure you succeed in this class by helping you navigate these life and educational challenges. We believe all of you can not only pass this class but also maximize your potential as writers and composers. We understand that many of you have other commitments, life goals, and motivations, and we want all students to have a path to success in our courses.

To help all students find a path to success in our courses, we use the following contract to assess student learning. Our approach focuses on **learning rather than grades**. We ask you to think less about your grades and more about your composing and ideas. We encourage you to work thoughtfully, take cognitive risks, and pursue ideas that you find compelling, without being overly distracted by your course grade.

With this contract, we hope to move the focus from grades to composing. We hope you see your instructor and writing mentor as coaches who can offer support, feedback, and guidance—and who encourage you to excel. If you read, listen to, and act on their feedback and engage in conversation with them, you will grow as a composer while learning the valuable tool of self-assessment.

Course Grading

In order for you to grow as a composer and writer, you need to develop important skills and habits. Completing all required assignments will help you practice these skills and habits while meeting the course goals.

For every assignment, you can earn up to 3 points, defined as follows:

- 3 = meets all requirements.
- 2 = meets most requirements.
- 1 = submitted but meets few requirements.
- 0 = not submitted or does not meet any requirements.

This class has two categories of assignments: those that are assessed on completion and those that are assessed on content.

Completion-Assessed Assignments

In this class, you will complete a number of "invention assignments," which are low-stakes assignments that help you develop your ideas for the larger projects you work on. (Details about what assignments count as invention work can be found on the syllabus.) Invention assignments in this class are assessed on completion. That is, for these assignments, you will earn a "3" if you:

- submit the assignment on time.
- complete all components for the assignment.
- demonstrate consideration of previous feedback, where applicable.

Content-Evaluated Assignments

Some assignments in this class require more time and effort; this includes your three reflections and two majors projects. To earn a "3" on these assignments, in addition to meeting the criteria above, you will also be assessed on the content of each assignment. That is, your writing will be evaluated on whether you have met the requirements listed on the rubric for the assignment.

Focus on Feedback

More important than any grade or score is the feedback you receive from your instructor, writing mentor, and peers. We want you to prioritize that feedback over any score you have been assigned. We hope you focus on building a conversation with the members of your class community about your composing rather than about any specific grade. Remember, the focus is on your learning.

If you engage seriously with the process approach to work in this course, you will leave with the knowledge, skills, habits, and practices you need for composing in college and beyond.

Assignment Weighting

Assignments will be weighted differently according to the amount of time and effort required. So, a reflection or revised draft will be weighted more than a discussion post, for example. Please see the breakdown of the assignment weighting on the course syllabus.

Please also note that Canvas weighting always shows the total as a percentage. **In this scale from 0 to 3, a score of 2/3 (67%) is the equivalent of a B grade (not a D!).**

CHAPTER 19.

DIALOGIC ASSESSMENT AGREEMENTS: A NEW GENRE FOR BUILDING TRUST AND MITIGATING RISK IN ONLINE WRITING INSTRUCTION

Kate Pantelides and Samira Grayson
Middle Tennessee State University

Erica Stone
Content Designer & UX Researcher

In this chapter, the authors describe **the implementation of Dialogic Assessment Agreements** *as an approach to assessment in online courses across modalities. Specifically, the authors provide rhetorical approaches for building trust with students and mitigating risk for faculty who choose to adopt alternative assessment practices in the online writing classroom. In describing their "better practice," the authors address the themes of assessment and professional development for online teachers.*

FRAMEWORKS AND PRINCIPLES IN THIS CHAPTER

- **GSOLE OLI Principle 3.5:** Instructors and tutors should commit to regular, iterative processes of course and instructional material design, development, assessment, and revision to ensure that online literacy instruction and student support reflect current effective practices.
- **PARS Online Writing Instruction**, Responsive: Instructors should be responsive and anticipate students' queries, needs, and requests.
- **CCCC Principles for the Postsecondary Teaching of Writing 12:** Sound writing instruction is assessed through a collaborative effort that focuses on student learning within and beyond a writing course.

DOI: https://doi.org/10.37514/PER-B.2024.2241.2.19

GUIDING QUESTIONS BEFORE YOU BEGIN READING

- How do you work to establish trust with your students in online courses? In particular, what do course materials that foreground trust look like?
- How can our online writing assessment practices reflect our values?
- What risks do you ask students to take in your class? What kinds of risks do you take in your class? How can you craft assignments to make these risks as safe as possible for both you and your students?

Throughout my life, I have learned to only go for good enough.

As early as the 2nd grade, I began to realize that my efforts in school would not always be reflected in the grade book. I have unpleasant memories of seeing red slashes across the first letters of my sentences; it felt unbearable for me at the time. Eventually, I got the hang of these skills even before my other classmates. All I got was a "Good Job" from my teacher. What I accomplished was represented the same way as the students who did less than me. **That was the first time I realized that effort would go without reward.**

> Ungrading aims to decouple these ideas, instead asking students to consider their own motivations for learning and composing.

In 4th grade, I had an incredible teacher, the kind that you remember for the rest of your life. She was good at teaching and caring for her students and making sure they felt appreciated. She fought her hardest to quell the effects of my past teachers' suffocating inspirations of mediocrity. Then the grades were passed out. I was given an A for my work. The kid to my left was given an A. The kid to my right was given an A. When everything a student has accomplished can be represented by a single letter, it begins to devalue and obscure the effort that has been provided. **That was the second time I started to realize that if the other kids didn't need to try, neither did I.**

> When grades are meant to stand-in for a judgment of quality and effort, they take on an outsize role in valuing student work, a role that runs counter to learning.

> This setup also functions to invite students to compare themselves to their colleagues and view them as competitors.

I discovered that hard work can sometimes cause you to fall behind your peers. If I were to grade my 5th grade teacher by a single letter, I would give her a C. She worked hard to connect with students. She was really into soap operas and loved to tell us about them. I quickly recognized her love of the dramatic and would try to add as much flair as possible into my writing to hide the inadequacy of my work. Unfortunately, it was effective. She loved it so much that she had me test out of the class. I no longer had to take her class simply because I wrote about her interests. I was using rhetoric without realizing it. Because I was an exceptional writer, I was punished with missing a year of instruction in one of the areas that I had enjoyed the most. **That was the third time that I realized that by working hard, I was putting myself at a disadvantage.**

> Students learn from instructors' responses to their writing, it's just not always what we're trying to teach them about writing that they learn.

-Samuel Harrison (Class of '26, Middle Tennessee State University)

Figure 19.1. A student reflection on ungrading, an alternative assessment practice, with teacher commentary.

INTRODUCTION

The excerpt in Figure 19.1 comes from a literacy narrative composed and shared with permission by Samuel Harrison, a student in Kate's first-year composition (FYC) class.[1] The literacy narrative assignment invited students to consider their own literacy practices and trace the path that had taken them to college. The FYC course itself used a Dialogic Assessment Agreement (DAA), an alternative assessment or "ungrading" practice that emphasizes student engagement with the writing process and assignment completion rather than quantitative measures of the "quality" of final products.

Rather than discerning a numerical evaluation of this writing assignment, the DAA allows us instead to turn our focus to wrestle with the ideas Sam poses to us as writing program administrators (WPAs), FYC faculty, and writing studies scholars. We are particularly struck by his **lack of trust** in the system of assessment, and his **recognition of the risks** involved in composing. We're sympathetic to both Sam and his instructors for the many systemic factors that foster this lack of trust and concern with risk, some of which we address in this chapter (these concerns require much more time and thought than one article can address, however).

Sam's ideas highlight the disconnect between what we often want students to learn about writing through our assessment, and what they actually learn. His descriptions of how traditional grading systems lead to "suffocating inspirations of mediocrity" and the "devalued" and "obscured" measures of effort are not new to us. They are depressingly consistent with what we've heard from students over the years, and what we've long tried to counter in our classrooms. They echo what we know from scholarship in writing studies about grading and feedback practices (Carillo, 2021; Elbow, 1994; Inoue, 2019; Sommers, 1980) and higher education assessment (Blum, 2020; Kohn, 2018), and particularly about the checkered history and impact of literacy sponsors (Brandt, 1998). Students are smart. They quickly differentiate what they need to do to pass a class, and students who can't do it precisely on the first try are often demoralized and don't continue to try. Students who can do it on the first try—and their ability to do so is often impacted by socioeconomics—are often not challenged further and don't continue to try or push themselves. They get the message that by doing "extra" they'll be separated, as Sam found. This disincentivizes experimentation, risk-taking, and innovation, all of which are ingredients for learning in the online writing classroom.

---

1   We are especially thankful for feedback from Amy Cicchino, Kevin DePew, Troy Hicks, Jennifer Pettit and Michelle Stuckey. Jennifer's comments went beyond enhancing and improving our ideas, introducing understandings of alternative assessment practices that extended our text. As such, we've quoted her review comments in this article. Further, we are appreciative of how the practice of including reviewer feedback in our work in some ways mimics the pedagogical practices to include student input on course design that we invite in this better practice contribution.

What we find particularly telling in Sam's narrative is how the classroom soup of kindness, caring, interest, effort, achievement, and ability being stirred together indiscriminately—and then graded—ultimately communicates the message: do as little as you can to get an A. Affect and assessment are strangely mixed. Sam describes this finding based on academic experiences that he notes as somewhat positive with an "incredible teacher, the kind you remember for the rest of your life" and a teacher that he would give a "C" were he to have to select "a single letter." Sam's narrative helps demonstrate how oversimplified, fraught assessments of student learning translate to oversimplified, fraught evaluations of faculty. Faculty, especially women like the teacher Sam mentions above, are often judged on how "nice" they are, and that becomes a lens with which students assess their teaching ability. Testimonies like Sam's have led us to invite alternative assessment practices across our FYC program. At its core, such practices attempt to separate the experience of student learning about and through writing from simplified assessments that value the products of that learning. It seeks to allow the humanness inherent in writing, reading, and assessing to function as a strength rather than a weakness.

Yet, we know that alternative assessment is a risk, one that requires trust within writing programs and between students and educators. Especially in online writing classrooms, where there may not be an opportunity to discuss assessment beyond recorded videos and syllabus language (though even in synchronous interactions, we may think that students understand things that they don't), alternative assessment practices may feel too risky for both faculty and students. In what follows, we propose a new classroom genre, a **Dialogic Assessment Agreement (DAA),** a document that provides four access points to build trust and mitigate risk for alternative assessment practices in online writing classrooms. These access points include an invitation for faculty and students to collaborate on the 1) course description, 2) course objectives, 3) course assignments, and 4) criteria for success in the course. Faculty new to alternative assessment may want to choose only one access point to negotiate or on which to invite feedback. Faculty may also limit what components are negotiable and the kinds of feedback they would like to invite from students to meet their goals for online writing instruction (OWI). Ultimately, there are many ways to customize the DAA to make it consistent with individual faculty needs in OWI.

As a responsive and feminist pedagogical practice, these access points provide faculty readers with a rhetorical approach for building trust through alternative assessment with students and rhetorical structures for mitigating risk for faculty who choose to adopt such practices in the online writing classroom. The customizable handout we include below offers access points for students to join the conversation with their online writing educators. **Alternative assessment practices in the online writing classroom are an effort to make consistent our**

pedagogical values and practices and prioritize learning for students. More personally, it's also an act of self-care and investment in our engagement with students and as feminist scholars. In writing about trust and risk, we know it is important to recognize our own subjectivities as White women: one in industry, one in a tenured position, and one in a doctoral program. We do not take lightly the invitation for students or faculty to take risks. Instead, we suggest that making trusting spaces in OWI actually reduces risk for both students and faculty. It is important pedagogically to prioritize learning, and simultaneously we prioritize labor safety and equity for faculty. We use these separate but complementary lenses to consider alternative assessment practices in the context of the DAA.

DIALOGIC ASSESSMENT AGREEMENT CUSTOMIZABLE HANDOUT

Purpose

[Suggested text below; revise to fit your course, program, and institution]. This course uses alternative assessment practices. Specifically, the work that you do in the class, the way it's evaluated, and the way I respond to your work will be collaboratively negotiated. You will not receive A–F grades on your writing projects in this class. Instead, your final grade will be based on the amount and types of work you choose to complete. The purpose of this assessment is to center learning in our class rather than achievement or unnecessary tasks. Failure, messiness, and risk-taking are essential for developing as a writer, and we hope this approach creates space for these experiences in the online writing classroom.

Task

[Suggested text below; revise to fit your course, program, and institution]. Your first task is to engage in a Dialogic Assessment Agreement. In the Knowledge section below, I detail my plan for the class using four access points:

1. Course description.
2. Course objectives.
3. Course assignments.
4. Criteria for success.

To design assessments that meet your needs, I request that you annotate and respond to these access points using the commenting feature in Word or Google Docs. Please share your ideas, requests, and needs. This exercise is meant to be invitational, to provide space for collaboration, experimentation, and active questioning, which are all central to effective research and composing practices.

Knowledge

[Suggested text below; revise to fit your course, program, and institution]. Read each *course* component carefully. Ask questions if you don't understand a concept. If you encounter an unfamiliar term, request a definition (or do some research and provide one!). Give feedback on, respond to, co-author, and customize the course description, course objectives, course assignments, and criteria for success.

Access Point 1: Course Description

[Insert your course description here].

TIP: Consider the intertextuality of course descriptions. Instead of just pasting the course description from your university's catalog, draft your own or borrow from another faculty member. Then, add and change your course description based on the iterations of your DAA.

EXAMPLE: Welcome to ENGL 1010: Expository Writing! English 1010 is the first in a two-semester first-year composition sequence that prepares you with questions and rhetorical awareness to approach the many and varied kinds of writing situations you will encounter in the future. In Expository Writing, you will gain grounded, practical experience with the conventions of academic, professional, public, and community discourse. Together, we will investigate how effective writers write in and beyond college, how compositions are rhetorically constructed, and how specific practices, strategies, and concepts will aid you in becoming a more flexible, adaptive, and skillful communicator at this university and beyond. I'm excited to write with you this semester!

[Suggested student tasks below; revise to fit your course, program, institution, and LMS constraints/affordances].

Please annotate the above course description, highlighting anything that is confusing, striking anything that is unhelpful, and adding a comment to demonstrate anything that you're particularly interested in or excited about. Finally, to meet your writing needs for the class, what sentence would you add to this course description?

Access Point 2: Course Objectives

[Insert your course objectives here].

TIP: While your program may have required objectives for your course, consider how you might explicate them or help students expand them throughout the DAA process.

EXAMPLE: In ENGL 1010: Expository Writing, students will:

1. **Conduct** primary research; Make appropriate decisions about content, form, and presentation **(Composing Processes)**;

2. **Examine** literacies across contexts; Read and analyze various types of text—print, digital, and audio **(Reading)**;
3. **Develop** genre awareness and practice genre analysis; Complete writing tasks that require an understanding of the rhetorical situation **(Rhetorical Knowledge)**;
4. **Reflect** on literacy in student lives; Develop a theory of writing that can transfer to writing situations in other classes and professions **(Integrative Thinking)**; and
5. **Learn** about discourse communities; Demonstrate understanding of ethical and primary research practices **(Information Literacy)**.

[Suggested student tasks below; revise to fit your course, program, institution, and LMS constraints/affordances]. Rate the importance of each course objective to you on a scale from 1–5 (1 being least important, 5 being most important; put NA (not applicable) next to any of the course objectives that don't make sense to you). Add at least one writing-related objective that you have for yourself for the course.

After each objective, note any experiences you have with meeting this course objective or engaging in similar activities. For example, you have likely practiced genre analysis in your daily life if you have used menus to decide on a restaurant. If you haven't completed any work toward these objectives, that's okay—that's the purpose of this class! If you have, however, please let me know so that we can together tailor our work.

Access Point 3: Course Assignments
[Insert your course assignments here].

TIP: Describe your course assignments with as much or as little detail as you deem necessary. We recognize that online any time writing classes may require more written explication while hybrid classes may require less because portions will be explained during in-person and/or Zoom class meetings.

EXAMPLE: ENGL 1010 includes Invention Assignments and Writing Projects. Invention Assignments are the daily writing opportunities that introduce you to the thinking and practices necessary to compose the major Writing Projects. As you read each assignment description, try to envision where you might begin (invention), what kinds of feedback you might like from your instructor and peers (editing, revision), and who might be interested in reading your writing (publication).

Reflect on your own literacy development. For this project, you will write a literacy narrative that connects a literacy event in your past with your literacy present.

- **Invention Assignment 1:** Audio-essay Introduction.
- **Invention Assignment 2:** Literacy Collage.

- **Invention Assignment 3:** Origin Story.

Examine the literacy development of others; this may extend beyond alphabetic literacy. For this project, you will interview a fellow student, record the interview, and analyze the transcript to craft a literacy portrait.

- **Invention Assignment 1:** Peer Interview and Transcription.
- **Invention Assignment 2:** Literacy Profile Tableau.
- **Invention Assignment 3:** Interview Proposal.

Select a genre in your community that is interesting or important to you. Analyze the genre such that you're familiar with its exigency, conventions, and deviations. Then compose a genre analysis project and develop an exemplary version of this genre to demonstrate your understanding.

- **Invention Assignment 1:** Genre Scavenger Hunt.
- **Invention Assignment 2:** Genre Reading Found Poem.
- **Invention Assignment 3:** Genre Map.

The final Ignite reflection asks you to examine your progress as a writer over the semester, and it will take the form of a highly-stylized, five-minute, fast-paced PowerPoint presentation, titled Ignite. The reflection should address your progress over the semester, questions about writing you've answered, questions about writing that you still have, and your developing theory of writing.

- **Invention Assignment 1:** Self-Analysis.
- **Invention Assignment 2:** ePortfolio Construction.
- **Invention Assignment 3:** Reflection Letter.

[Suggested student tasks below; revise to fit your course, program, institution, and LMS constraints/affordances]. Using the descriptions above, you can make an informed choice about how much work you are able to and want to complete this semester and the final grades associated with that choice. Please put an emoji response next to each project description. Select which invention assignments you plan to do, and include any requests for additions, deletions, or revisions. If you aren't sure where to begin, or if emojis don't seem like an adequate response type for you, consider answering these questions:

- What are some strategies you might use for developing these assignments?
- What are your motives and goals for completing the assignments?

Access Point 4: Criteria for Success

[Insert your criteria for success here].

TIP: We recognize that there are many approaches to ungrading and your criteria for success in your course and/or program may differ from our example. No matter your approach, be honest and clear with your students about what is needed to succeed in your course based on the course description, course objectives, and course assignments.

EXAMPLE: To pass the course all students must complete polished drafts of the major Writing Projects.

- To earn an A in the course, students must also complete at least 90 percent of invention assignments and one project revision.
- To earn a B in the course, students must also complete at least 80 percent of invention assignments and one project revision.
- To earn a C in the course, students must also complete at least 70 percent of invention assignments.
- Students who don't complete the work as noted will not pass the course.

[Suggested student tasks below; revise to fit your course, program, institution, and LMS constraints/affordances]. After reading the criteria for success in this class, consider: What will success look like for you this semester? Consider your personal and professional writing goals. Flash forward to the end of the semester and write a paragraph about what you will have done, thought, and experienced over the course of the semester if all goes well. Be creative and boundless. Don't be afraid to propose changes or think about new ways of completing the Invention Assignments and Writing Projects described above. I'll follow up on your ideas, requests, and needs with audio feedback, and you can follow up with your comments. I'll gather your ideas and that of your classmates and upload the completed DAA to which we can all refer during the semester.

SCHOLARSHIP, THEORIES, AND PRINCIPLES THAT GUIDE OUR APPROACH

In designing our DAA, we are particularly influenced by our feminist reading of GSOLE's Online Learning Principle 3: "Instructors and tutors should commit to regular, iterative processes of course and instructional material design, development, assessment, and revision to ensure that online literacy instruction and student support reflect current effective practices" (2019). We suggest that this iterative process of assessment and developing course materials should take place not just between program developers, administrators, and faculty, but also between faculty and students. Distributing decision-making and centering students in

OWI can be particularly difficult because of the intractable nature of our learning management systems and the pedagogies baked into its structures. Yet, we suggest that such pedagogies, based on a current-traditional (CTR) perception of writing and a behavior manipulation model of interacting with students, often run counter to best practices in OWI, particularly around assessment (for more on the relationship between OWI and CTR see Depew et al., 2006).

As an alternative assessment practice, ungrading offers an opportunity for the "unlearning" necessary for effective teaching in OWI (see Stuckey & Wilson, Chapter 18 this collection). Michelle Stuckey and Gabriella Wilson suggest that "ungrading" invites an opportunity for rethinking problematic structures and practices that are ingrained in the OWI classroom and reified in the learning management system (LMS). We're primarily concerned with the ways that OWI and the LMS ossify assessment structures through gradebooks, dropboxes, and graded opportunities throughout course-shells, but our concern certainly plays out in the affordances of other tools that foster student interaction. Online educators are likely familiar with the traditional gradebooks that attach a rubric and specific points to every element of student writing. The LMS makes it harder, for instance, to simply give credit for assignments, to comment on multiple student texts in the same space, for students to read and comment informally on each other's work, and to invite student comments in response to feedback. Of course, it's possible to do these things, but these behaviors are not the ones for which the LMS is built. LMS ideology is particularly visible for educators when they try to depart from CTR teaching practice. Since the online writing classroom is a shared learning space between faculty and students, a more democratic and dialogic approach to online writing instruction—one that focuses less on the structure of the LMS and more on the experiences of learning occurring within it—is a necessary next step for online writing scholarship and practice. Such work is risky, yet it provides inroads for building trust with students; such trust is necessary for students to take risks in their writing and to subsequently learn about themselves and rhetorical structures in the writing process. Further, if we concentrate our efforts on demonstrating effective learning in OWI, we can more effectively invite LMS structures that afford this learning.

At our university, online course authorship is set up to be designed by one individual, and the resulting shell must be adopted by all faculty who teach the course. This is problematic for courses such as composition, which—since this course is a requirement for general education—are taught by dozens of different faculty members. We all have shared course objectives, textbooks, and rhetorical purposes for our writing assignments, but each instructor has their own approach. We value this autonomy in the face-to-face classroom and suggest that it brings out the best in both faculty and students in the online classroom as well.

If there is only one version of the course shell, authored by only one instructor, it doesn't give faculty the opportunity to personalize their course in the ways that make them most effective and that respond to the group of students in the course. We've tried to address this by collaboratively authoring Online Educational Resources for our first-year writing curriculum, co-authoring our course shells, gathering input, and distributing labor amongst many of the faculty who will be teaching our online courses (inspired in many ways by Stuckey's work). This approach respects the university policy of developing one master course-shell, but it draws on the pedagogies and experiences of multiple educators. We suggest a similar deviation from the LMS' invitation when it comes to student assessment in the course.

Theories of Alternative Assessment

For decades, scholars in writing studies have identified the subjectivity and inequity of numerical and/or standardized writing assessment. Grade data is limited in its ability to offer an "objective" assessment of student ability. Further, increasing data suggest that assessments, both on a larger scale in regard to standardized test scores, and on a smaller scale in the context of classrooms, tell us more about a student's identity markers, including race, ethnicity, and socio-economic status, rather than student talent, potential, or most importantly, academic growth (Elsesser, 2019; Hubler, 2020; Scott-Clayton, 2018). As these concerns have been amplified by the pandemic—and its attendant, unequal impact on working-class and marginalized students—many traditional and long-used assessment methods, like the SAT, ACT, and Accuplacer, are slowly being dislodged or included as only one measure amongst others in assessing student preparation for college and various coursework. In fact, a recent study found that high school GPA (even though it is an imperfect measure) is four times a better predictor of college success than standardized tests, and standardized test scores alone are not an accurate predictor of success in postsecondary education (Scott-Clayton, 2018).

In terms of the classroom, Michelle Cowan (2020) traces contract grading, a relatively popular alternative assessment practice, to high school classrooms in the early 1920s. Contract grading took off in writing studies in the 1960s, with scholars like Peter Elbow arguing that such assessment allows faculty to evaluate student writing, an effective practice, rather than "ranking" students, a practice that—he argues and provides extensive support for—runs counter to learning (1968). Asao Inoue's (2019) construction of "labor-based contracts" was adopted by many individuals and entire programs in the last few years, though Inoue has since reconceived his own practice (Inoue, 2021), and other scholars have noted inequities in valuing classroom labor. Most recently, Ellen C. Carillo (2021) has suggested the use of "engagement-based grading contracts," which she argues are more dynamic than labor-based contracts (p. 56). Carillo's critique comes from a disability studies perspective, arguing that "One's willingness to labor is not always accompanied by one's ability to do so" (2021, p. 13) and "We do not want to put students experiencing anxiety and depression—whether long-term or temporarily—at a disadvantage by creating a standard of labor that excludes them" (2021, p. 28). Another concern is Jennifer Pettit's consideration of the economic perspective of classroom labor. She notes that "financial obstacles . . . impact economically self-supporting students' ability to complete work, particularly reflective assignments that require a greater investment of time and critical thought" (personal communication, November, 2021).

Of course, as Cowan (2020) notes, "In reality, no single ideal grading contract exists" (p. 2), and most scholars do not recommend that faculty adopt their own idiosyncratic contracts wholesale. They must, necessarily, be a locally customized document. Further, we suggest adopting "agreements" with students rather than "contracts" because we think this language is more appropriate for educational documents and we know the consequences of living our metaphors (Lakoff & Johnson, 1981). Faculty often talk about the syllabus as a "contract"—it's not. Contracts are drawn up for goods to be sold, and for services to be given and subsequently paid, a construct that further emphasizes a transactional or container model (Freire, 1972) for education. Further, Pettit notes how this language

> speaks directly to the purpose of education within liberal capitalism. Historically, the application of contractualism to the labor market was a post-emancipation, nineteenth-century innovation. However, a racially inclusive philosophical perspective on the inseparability of economic and political freedom was transformed by conservative jurists into a fictive state of equality between workers and their corporate employers. (personal communication, November, 2021)

For these reasons, we resist these business and legal metaphors for the classroom and offer the DAA as a space to dynamically negotiate work and attendant assessment in the classroom.

We argue that faculty should strategically practice alternative assessment as anti-racist, intersectional, and inclusive, and adopting a DAA invites this orientation. It is access-oriented, recognizing that all learners will bring different experiences, identities, dis/abilities, and expectations to the OWI classroom, and, coincidentally, as Rachel Donegan notes, making classroom projects "more accessible has some amazing rhetorical benefits for [students] as [. . . writers] and designer[s]" (2022). Inherent in the design of the DAA is the valuing of the different experiences, language practices, abilities, and subjectivities that impact learning. Because linguistic practices are central to all writing classrooms, we're particularly attentive to how difference manifests in the written products students complete in our OWI classrooms. DAAs invite students to claim their differences as strengths and craft assessments to best meet their individual needs.

One of the core theories of alternative assessment, like our approach to the DAA, is radically trusting students (Lynch & Alberti, 2010; Moore, 2014). For us, this means strategically democratizing the responsibility of work in the online writing classroom by decentralizing the role of the teacher and emphasizing the responsibility students have over their own learning—an idea that is easy to get behind in theory, but difficult to put into practice. Elsewhere, we've theorized radical trust as a pedagogical orientation toward the classroom, an "invitation, a purposeful feminist rupture, a mindful and strategic choice to orient to a recurrent kairotic opening: the beginning of a semester," its opportunity for newness and starting over (Pantelides, 2021). Using the DAA is a radical trust practice, and trust, broadly, is central to the work of alternative assessment. The DAA demonstrates a trust in students to make choices for themselves and to do the work of writing, not because they're being manipulated to do so through the relative carrot or stick of a numerical grade, but because they're engaged in the learning process and they choose to do work (or not) in the class that aligns with their own pedagogical needs, goals, and interests.

COURSE CONTEXT AND LESSON: THE DIALOGIC ASSESSMENT AGREEMENT (DAA): A SPACE FOR THINKING, DISCUSSING, AND NEGOTIATING ALTERNATIVE ASSESSMENT PRACTICES IN ONLINE WRITING INSTRUCTION

Because alternative assessment can initially feel risky for both students and faculty in online writing courses, we offer the DAA as an interactive, ungraded, liminal space to negotiate the course structures, build trust with students, and mitigate risk for faculty, especially those with a contingent status (~75% of the professoriate). Specifically, we offer a sample DAA—created for our university's first composition course in our two-course sequence—as a starting place for students and faculty to contextualize and apply the theories and practices of alternative assessment. The DAA is instructive for both students and faculty, as it provides an infrastructure for discussing four access points for alternative assessment in online writing instruction: course description, course objectives, course assignments, and criteria for success.

The access points in our DAA serve to build trust and knowledge between faculty and students and offer a starting point for faculty interested in alternative assessment practices in the online writing classroom. Rather than focusing on the transactional components of the LMS, our access points create opportunities for **redistributing agency,** asking students to claim choices about their personal goals, identities, and language practices. Students should be able to make choices (with guidance) about what they need to learn and compose in an online writing classroom.

Under each access point, we address how faculty might use the DAA as a space for **building trust** among students and faculty through open discussion, iterative design, and democratic negotiation of assessment criteria, as well as how this document can be used for **mitigating risk** for online writing faculty who find alternative assessment practices to be unfamiliar and risky. Initially, these orientations may seem like conflicting ways of looking at teaching materials. Rhetorical approaches to building trust are largely pedagogical and somewhat idealistic, whereas approaches for mitigating risk are largely logistical and sometimes cynical. We do not try to reconcile this apparent disconnect because it reflects the internal struggle that so many OWI faculty have: wanting to teach our values but recognizing that such work makes us vulnerable in the face of increasingly fragile labor conditions. Thus, in addressing both trust and risk in the context of alternative assessment, we offer arguments for improving the learning opportunities for students while simultaneously recognizing the precarity intrinsic for so many writing faculty. And yet, as you adopt alternative assessment practices, you might note how establishing trust in the classroom actually reduces risk. Of course, not all students will love alternative assessment practices, and not all of them will embrace the class, but by inviting conversation around these four access points across the semester, there is less opportunity for the misunderstandings and miscommunications that often bubble up at the end of the semester and put contingent faculty at risk in terms of their labor opportunities.

As a new genre, the DAA is intended to capture student attention and invite trust in alternative assessment practices from the beginning of the course. Students are so familiar with academic genres (e.g., syllabi, assignment sheets) and the associated grade expectations (e.g., rubric, checklists) that, as one of our recent writing center workshops noted, students only look for the grading expectations and often disregard the rest of the syllabus. A DAA is intended as a deviation to introductory course materials, an attempt to capture student attention and invite them into a different relationship to their writing and with their faculty and classmates than they might have had in previous courses. Given

Dialogic Assessment Agreements

this exigency, we purposely ask students and faculty to engage with the access points, further explained below, in playful ways that vary and purposefully deviate from more common ways of engaging with introductory course materials. For instance, we ask students to rank course objectives, respond with emojis, and write creatively about time travel. The DAA provides documented evidence of an iterative effort to make space for play, dialogue, and negotiation with the online writing classroom.

Access Point 1: Course Descriptions

A course description is a conflicted institutionalized genre that, in part, functions as a public-facing description of a course's primary content, degree plan orientation, inter-institutional transferability, and regional accreditation. Yet, course descriptions are also student-facing, perhaps the most conventional component of a course syllabus. In most of the institutions where we have taught, the course descriptions we circulate on our teaching materials to students go beyond the brief, transactional statements disseminated in course catalogs and departmental websites. These are often the course descriptions from the syllabi offered to us by administrators, university committees, or WPAs. And, in our roles as WPAs, we've often adapted our own course descriptions from other programs in which we've taught. Thus, they're interesting intertextual glosses of a semester, an archival amalgamation of instructors over time and their interactions with students. For online writing courses that count toward general education credits (most online writing courses!), some degree of uniformity is expected, but the DAA offers a space for coordinated deviance.

In the context of the DAA, course descriptions provide an opportunity for students and faculty to define and discuss the focus of a course. Yet, though they're the first thing on the page in most syllabi, many students (and faculty) don't necessarily read them. They're the kind of conventions that hide in plain sight because they might not be important to us, and/or students don't *need* them to take the class. The placement of the course description at the top of the DAA is meant to breathe into it new life and invite an opportunity for students and faculty to see the course description as a meaningful description in and of itself.

Building Trust in the Work of the Course

As a first step in building trust with students around alternative assessment practices, the DAA is rhetorically structured for students to collaboratively author the course documents alongside us. In our example, we ask students to add a sentence to our existing course description that will help the course meet their individual needs. Upon receiving all responses, whether structured in online real-time or online any time learning, or whether they're recorded individually or in a collaborative document, we suggest sharing the extended course description with the class. Such a simple rhetorical approach immediately demonstrates the inclusive, co-constructed nature of the class, characteristics that alternative assessment practices invite. Their words become a fundamental component of how you articulate the work of the class and make inroads toward assuring that the class will meet individual student needs. This is a starting place in building trust for alternative assessment practices, personal investment and engagement by students, and student perception of the worth of the class more broadly.

Mitigating Risk

Since many online writing courses are taught by graduate students or contingent faculty, WPAs have a responsibility to mitigate the risk associated with adopting alternative assessment practices in an online writing classroom. The course description offers a rhetorical structure to begin conversations about alternative assessment practices and processes.

Further, online writing classes can become less risky for faculty when students really engage with the purpose of the class through co-authoring the course description. The DAA offers an opportunity for students and faculty to co-construct the course. Such an orientation mitigates risk because students are actively involved in the iterative development of an institutional structure.

Access Point 2: Course Objectives

Perhaps more than course descriptions, course objectives are often not the choice of the educator and are mandated by the department, institution, or its governing body. Faculty are trained to work backward from course objectives, scaffolding the work of the class throughout the semester such that students complete the course having learned these objectives. In the DAA example we provide, we invite students to rank the ways in which they value the course objectives, share whether they've had experience with any of the course objectives, and author a course objective that meets their particular writing needs. As with all of these recommendations, if offering a numerical ranking of the course objectives is not in line with your pedagogy, we invite you to adopt a different method of response. We purposefully selected playful, non-discursive ways for students to interact with the DAA in order to demonstrate our efforts at deviation and interest in play as a purposeful strategy for student engagement. In other words, the specific ways that students interact with and respond to the DAA are less important than the fact of their engagement and their impression of these invitations as "new" and worthy of attention. Because students are used to being prompted to answer reflective discussion questions, we intentionally chose to ask students to respond in multimodal, extra-textual ways.

Building Trust in Student Writing Expertise

Many students in online writing classes, particularly first-year writing courses, have had extensive experience with research and writing processes, albeit in different contexts. Inviting explicit discussion of what students know in the Dialogic Assessment values their expertise and provides insight into prior writing experiences. This rhetorical approach shares power and demonstrates trust in students, a method that, for instance, diagnostic essays do not. Lastly, we ask students to share a course objective related to their particular needs for the course. Instead of adding these course objectives as additional work for the instructor, such objectives may become the work of individual students, ensuring that they take on responsibility for accomplishing their personal objectives and perhaps taking on leadership of these objectives for other students. We suggest that this dialogic work with the course objectives provides space for both students and faculty to build engagement and identification with the course objectives, and, further, build trust in the systems of the course. And, as we recommend with the course description, after receiving responses, share the complete list of shared course objectives alongside the official course objectives to demonstrate trust in student input and their co-authoring of the work. Perhaps most importantly, inviting students to consider their relationship to the course objectives allows faculty understanding of the rich writing experiences students bring to the classroom and concentrated information about their individual goals.

Mitigating Risk

The DAA offers a space for students and faculty to negotiate and converse about the learning objectives for an online writing course not just as a programmatic construct, but as actionable. This process mitigates risk for faculty by minimizing opportunities to misunderstand students, make assumptions about them, or spend course time in a way that runs counter to our own goals for their learning. Many classroom difficulties stem from students feeling misunderstood, unsupported, or undervalued. Articulating what they know about themselves as writers and what they need from the course ultimately asks students to take responsibility for their strengths and honestly address necessary spaces for growth. And when growth is measured through reflective, rhetorical approaches to alternative assessment practices like the DAA, the online writing classroom is refocused on transformational learning activities emplaced in rhetoric and dialogue rather than transactional interactions within an LMS (Stone & Austin, 2020).

ACCESS POINT 3: COURSE ASSIGNMENTS

Another familiar convention of many syllabi, descriptions of course assignments allow students to preview the ways in which the course objectives will be carried out. Of course, these brief descriptions only provide limited information to students, but sharing both the formal writing projects and the invention work that is intended to scaffold the formal projects offers an opportunity for preliminary engagement. Yet, course assignments differ from course descriptions and objectives in that they are traditionally the work of students in classrooms. This is where student input may be particularly helpful. Even the best-planned classes may overlook particular skills or content that students may need to successfully complete a formal project. Or, aspects of a formal project that may seem straightforward or low stakes to an instructor may need significant additional detail or may be anxiety-inducing for students. Inviting responses to—and suggestions for—these projects helps demonstrate the relationship between invention assignments (also referred to as brainstorming, scaffolding, and formative assessments) and formal writing projects to students, and it provides opportunities to refresh your course and provide new and innovative ways to scaffold writing. In the example that we provide, we list the invention assignments that are meant to scaffold the learning necessary to complete the formal writing projects alongside each other. We ask students to react to each proposed assignment by inserting emojis, planning which assignments they want to complete, and composing questions to help build their understanding of the work. We hope that by listing invention assignments and formal projects alongside each other, both students and faculty will see these writing opportunities as inextricably linked.

Building Trust in Writing as a Learning Opportunity

Inviting dialogic response around course assignments builds trust around composing processes in the class from the outset of the semester and emphasizes learning as focal. Further, incorporating recommendations from students helps build trust in the content of the course as well as the methods of instruction. Consistent deviation in the work around the course description, course objectives, and the course assignments provides a foundation for alternative assessment that culminates in the final access point, course assessments.

Mitigating Risk

Pedagogical risk is arguably higher in online and hybrid learning spaces because there are more opportunities to be misunderstood. A writer's tone can be misread; news posts can be missed; even the tiniest technical glitch can seem to throw the entire class off course. Perhaps the highest perceived risk for faculty who are reluctant to try alternative assessment practices is the fear of introducing additional, unconventional barriers to learning. While it can seem intimidating to adopt an alternative assessment practice in the online writing classroom, the DAA offers an opportunity to negotiate the rhetorical structures that guide the course iteratively at the outset of the course. The DAA can be revisited throughout the course as a strategic exercise to (re)focus the course user experience of the students (Borgman & McArdle, 2019). After all, students are the central users of our online writing courses (Stone, 2021a), and if we increase their agency through strategic and iterative activities like the DAA, major writing assignments become less focused on risk mitigation (e.g., bad grades for students and bad course evaluations for faculty) and more focused on learning activities and writing processes.

Access Point 4: Criteria for Success in the Course

In this access point, we explicitly address course assessment. In our example, we offer a simple grading system based on completion as well as an invitation for students to define what success might look like in the class in ways that go beyond numerical grades. In particular, this is an important space to invite students to consider the affective component of class—the experiences, orientations, and knowledge-building they hope to create and reflect upon during the course of the semester. Hopefully, the DAA will make inroads in drawing student attention to the many varied and complex components that might constitute "success" in a classroom—a loaded term that we hope students will spend time working through as they collaborate with us in this particular access point. We recognize that, as our peer reviewer Pettit rightly posits, "a holistic consideration of individual engagement and capacity often conflicts in practice with baseline standards determined by the class" (November 2021). Thus, for the DAA to function as we intend, as "a non-punitive method of assessment that accommodates difference," faculty must recognize and discuss the continuum of "success" that students might consider for your class. For instance, the DAA allows for student success to be earning an A in the course, or completing the minimum work required in the course while juggling caregiving, or focusing on learning rather than obsessing over grades on a non-hierarchical continuum. We urge educators to resist the discourse that associates "even minimal grading standards based on work completion [as] a meritocratic conception of equality" (Pettit, personal communication, November 2021).

Building Trust in Assessment as a Learning Practice

One of the primary goals of alternative assessment is to focus on learning rather than ranking or using grades to motivate certain behaviors. As the anecdote that begins this article demonstrates, traditional grading often motivates students to "only go for good enough." By using a DAA, we attempt to decouple the moral evaluations that are often attached to grades from the recognition of work completed. In this assessment structure, students may choose to earn Cs because that is what they're interested in, or that is what they have time for, and the instructor's perception of that choice has no bearing on the grade ultimately earned. This opens up space for students and faculty to trust their interactions and support without a grade looming over that interaction. Subsequent OWI classroom interaction may resemble the kinds of interactions we find in writing centers in which the interest in helping build better writers, not just better papers is the Stephen North mantra foundational for much of the sub-discipline (1984). Alternative assessment allows writing pedagogy to be consistent in ways that traditional grading disrupts. Contract grading is well-established in writing studies, and is addressed at length in this volume (see Bowers & Smith Daniel, Chapter 16, this collection; see DePew & Matheson, Chapter 17, this collection; see Stuckey & Wilson, Chapter 18, this collection), but, of course, choose the method of alternative assessment that is most appropriate to your classroom.

Just as importantly, we find the opportunity for students and faculty to rethink and account for what "success" in a class looks like to be particularly generative. If simply getting an A in a class translates to success, that does not tell us much about what the course offered, what course objectives the student accomplished, and what course assignments they took on and in which ways. We hope that by inviting students to think about success more broadly, particularly as it aligns with the other access points (e.g., course description, course objectives, course assignments), they may adopt a learning-focused orientation to OWI, one that trust allows.

Mitigating Risk

As a rhetorical, dialogic, and negotiated approach to alternative assessment, the DAA takes the surprise out of assessment. Surprise and lack of transparency are often central to student complaints and critical student evaluations. The DAA mitigates risk for faculty by generating discussion about assessment at the beginning of the semester rather than at the end. Of course, most faculty introduce their grading at the beginning of the semester, but the DAA asks students to respond and make meaningful relationships between the access points, particularly as they relate to their own "success" in the course. Thus, the DAA fosters transparent discussion and awareness around work completed, and students are in charge of the final grade they earn.

REFLECTION ON PRACTICE

Assessment is often the loadstone for OWI classes. In it, we can glean faculty values and beliefs about writing, and it is often what students look to first to understand how they need to navigate a course. By wading into the alternative assessment practice waters, faculty can match their pedagogical values and practices. Such assessment operationalizes best practices in OWI classrooms, not undercutting—for instance, invitations to experiment, to take risks, or to fail in our writing attempts. Instead, alternative assessment practices allow us to develop dialogic relationships with students about their work without assigning a final numerical assessment and thus closing down the conversations. Certainly, work becomes due and must be turned in, but the conversation that alternative assessment invites fundamentally changes the relationship between students and faculty that arises around compositions. For instance, you might assign due dates for formal projects but note, as we do, that extensions will always be granted upon request. The purpose of such invitations is to remain in communication and collaboration with students during their writing processes.

Yet, alternative assessment often makes both students and faculty uncomfortable, and students may complain that they don't have enough clarity or detail. We hope that the DAA is an intervention in such concerns, but it will likely not alleviate all student anxieties since students are familiar with numerical assessments of the subjective quality of their work. One of the purposes of alternative assessment is to not give students quite as much specificity when it comes to the kind of product they must develop. Instead, we draw student attention to the course objectives the assignment is to meet, the rhetorical situation in which they're composing, and the potential choices they must make. Alternative assessment asks students to take more responsibility for their decision-making. To put a finer point on it, by the end of a semester in a class that uses a DAA, we would hope that faculty should receive fewer inquiries about how many sentences should be in a paragraph and which headers they should use. Alternative assessment recognizes writing as fully rhetorical and requires students to make choices that faculty often make for them when the focus is the product rather than the rhetorical decision-making process. Yet, at the beginning of the semester, as students acclimate to alternative assessment, they may need more support than faculty may be accustomed to, and faculty may need to be more patient in repeating the methods of assessment. Because alternative assessment has ripple effects throughout the curriculum, and students may not have the footing they might expect in a traditionally graded classroom, they may have more questions and may initially be unsure. They will need support and encouragement to take the risks necessary to build their writing abilities. The purpose of the DAA is to offer a textual touchstone for these negotiations.

Alternative assessment is disruptive and problematizes classroom language practices, assumptions of the product as primary in the OWI classroom, and numerical grades as associated with those products. Because so much of the things that assessment usually stabilizes are destabilized by alternative assessment, course kairos becomes more important than ever to build trust with students and create an inclusive digital classroom space. Specifically, it's important (as possible) to respond quickly to student compositions. Quick responses to students' work will demonstrate to them that you will grade in the alternative assessment method that you've described. Even if you tell students that you will grade in a particular way, that might not mean much until you do it, and they still may not trust you until you've demonstrated this approach multiple times. You might also initially hear more requests for clarification from students. And remember—for invention assignments that cannot be revised, there is no need to provide individual feedback on every item. In traditionally graded classrooms, it's essential that students know exactly what is asked of them because their ability to do well rests on how well they can match the expectations of the faculty member. Certainly, there is use in being able to meet specific requirements, but alternative assessment instead allows for the problem solving, critical thinking, and risk-taking necessary to learn how to develop writing skills that are required in OWI classrooms, and product precision is not usually the focus.

Ultimately, our core recommendation for alternative assessment practices in the classroom, regardless of which access points you adopt, or whether or not you adopt the DAA, is to tell students what you're going to do based on their input, then show that you will do what you say. Say it; show it; say it; show it— and repeat ad nauseum. In particular, to build trust with students and mitigate risk for faculty we recommend that you consider using the DAA to negotiate the work of the class on the first day of the semester, then return to the terms of the agreement mid-semester to invite any necessary adjustments, and then re-examine the DAA as a class as the semester ends. At the end of the semester, you may want to require fewer assignments if added environmental stressors impacted the work of the class as a whole, as we all experienced in the spring of 2020, or you may want to add a course objective that was met but not noted at the outset. Some educators, particularly those new to the OWI classroom, may worry that providing this kind of flexibility and inviting such questioning may undercut their classroom ethos. We understand this concern and have felt it ourselves. Certainly, we can't tell anyone how to feel in the classroom, but we would suggest that a classroom built around the trust and respect that develops in interaction with students and in which the person "in charge" acknowledges their own humanity and fallibility has a good chance of fostering learning. We also hope that the DAA offers a structure for taking risks that may ease the discomfort for both students and faculty for whom deviation to traditional grading feels particularly vulnerable. Figure 19.2 offers a potential timeline of what labor associated with alternative assessment practices might look like across a semester.

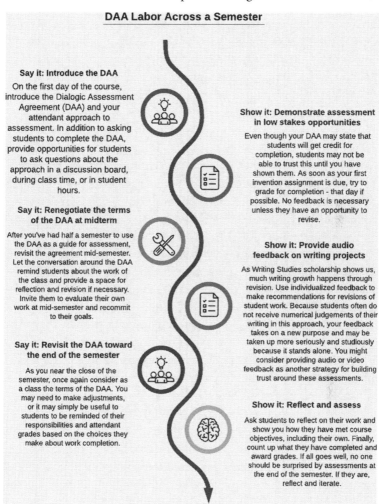

Figure 19.2. In this timeline, the left side of the diagram describes three times during the semester to talk to students about alternative assessment. On the right side of the diagram there are three different opportunities to show students what alternative assessment may look like in the OWI classroom.

CONCLUSION

Alternative assessment invites students and faculty to rethink what information we need to know and share at the beginning of the semester, and our iteration of alternative assessment—the Dialogic Assessment Agreement—is offered as a tool to negotiate this information together such that we can demonstrate to students that their ideas, experiences, and identities are central to the functioning of the course. Most importantly, this invitation demonstrates that students are necessary co-authors of the learning, which will be co-constructed in documents and in experiences across the semester. Ultimately, the DAA is a demonstration of our own commitments to antiracist, feminist pedagogy and our awareness of how the products of our pedagogy can constrain or afford the kind of equitable practice and redistributive agency for students in OWI that we value.

Alternative assessment generally deemphasizes the product, so if you are teaching a class in which what the product looks like is of primary importance (e.g., professional materials developed for an institutional partner in a technical communication course), the DAA practice may not be the best approach. Make sure that there is a consistent relationship between the course assignment and the course assessment. Also, be patient with both your students and yourself. Even if you're interested in alternative assessment, it may take a few semesters for it to make sense or feel comfortable: it's a significant change. One rule of thumb is to ensure that the assessment truly matches the expectations you have for the assignment. For example, you may *want* to be open to different approaches by students to your particular assignment, but you may actually have something pretty specific in mind. If so, have a rubric that matches this. Be honest with yourself. If the thinking and student response to the given rhetorical situation of the assignment is your focus, then the grading approach outlined in our sample DAA may be appropriate. If you're implementing an alternative assessment practice like this, the purpose of feedback changes. In traditional grading frameworks, the purpose of feedback is often primarily to explain the numerical assessment. With alternative assessment, the purpose of feedback is to engage in dialogue around the composition or to make recommendations for revision. It is about building trust rather than functioning as a defense mechanism.

The dialogue that happens in and around the DAA can be used for faculty training and as a vehicle for student attention to the learning. Using the DAA to negotiate the terms of the class creates an opportunity for every composition class to be different based on who is in the class. It offers a kairotic opportunity at the beginning of the semester and a foundation for deviation from traditional OWI interactions. The use of the DAA means that things will always be new at the beginning of a semester: it creates a space to negotiate new knowledge together, new opportunities for learning. In some ways, the DAA invites an orientation of surprise to confront reluctance and lack of engagement that we often see in the required courses that are the bread and butter for so many of us in OWI.

Of course, newness is a risk, and for faculty carrying a load of four or five classes per semester, the idea of newness in each class may seem like a liability rather than an appealing goal. To this very realistic concern we submit the following: adopting alternative assessment does not mean expanding the things that faculty need to be in charge of. Instead, it's intended to spread the work of the class such that students see themselves as important members of the community, members that are equally responsible for their learning. As with all changes to a classroom, we must always be attentive to labor. Changes must be doable and realistic to become lasting components of our course design.

Further, alternative assessment values student expertise, but it does not suggest that anything goes, and the DAA does not mean that you necessarily share in the decision-making of the course design equally with students. Faculty have expertise in the content area as well as OWI course design. Students and faculty come to a classroom with lived experiences and "learning baggage." We hope that the DAA can serve as an invitation to leave such bags at the doorway, to unlearn practices that run counter to learning, and instead invite the humanness and creativity inherent in our coursework to thrive, to be the center of our work. Certainly, these are lofty goals for one little genre, but we hope that the DAA might provide inroads for building trust and mitigating risk, two steps toward learning and engagement in OWI.

MOVING BETTER PRACTICES ACROSS MODALITIES

- **In-Person, Real-Time Learning:** In this context, you might invite students to work in groups to fill out the DAA collaboratively, or students might use different color pens and stickers to take advantage of the physical text.
- **Online, Real-Time Learning:** In this context, the DAA can function as an in-class assignment and invitation for discussion via break out groups, a Zoom whiteboard, Jamboard, Padlet, or other digital collaborative workspace.
- **Online, Any Time Learning:** In this context, students can use the "insert comment" feature, print out the document for annotation and subsequent uploading, or "handwrite" on the document with a digital pencil. Asynchronous collaboration is still possible via Jamboard, Padlet, a shared Google doc, or Perusall.

- **Hybrid Learning:** Any of the above are possible. Consider the tools available at your institution and the modalities in which students will likely compose to make choices about how you would like students to respond to the various access points. Consider the constraints and affordances of the available tools within your local context as you think through how to adopt or adapt the DAA. In any context, the DAA can be a stand-alone document, an addendum to the syllabus, or an assignment prompting discussion and reflection.

REFERENCES

Blum, S. (2020). *Ungrading: Why rating students undermines learning.* West Virginia University Press.

Borgman, J. & McArdle, C. (2019). *Personal, accessible, responsive, strategic: Resources and strategies for online writing instructors.* The WAC Clearinghouse; University Press of Colorado. https://doi.org/10.37514/PRA-B.2019.0322.

Brandt, D. (1998). Sponsors of literacy. *College Composition and Communication, 49*(2), 165–185. https://doi.org/10.2307/358929.

Carillo, E. C. (2021). *The hidden inequities in labor-based contract grading.* Utah State University Press. https://doi.org/10.7330/9781646422678.

Cowan, M. (2020). A legacy of grading contracts for composition. *Journal of Writing Assessment, 13*(2). https://escholarship.org/uc/item/0j28w67h.

DePew, K. E., Fishman, T. A., Romberger, J. E. & Ruetenik, B. F. (2006). Designing efficiencies: The parallel narratives of distance education and composition studies. *Computers and Composition, 23*(1), 49–67. https://doi.org/10.1016/j.compcom.2005.12.005.

Donegan, R. (2022). The rhetorical possibilities of accessibility. *Writing Spaces, Vol. 4.* WritingSpaces.org; Parlor Press; The WAC Clearinghouse. https://writingspaces.org/?page_id=773.

Elbow, P. (1968). A method for teaching writing. *College English 30*(2), 115–125.

Elbow, P. (1994). Ranking, evaluating, liking: Sorting out three forms of judgment. *College English, 55*(2) 187–206. https://doi.org/10.2307/378503.

Elsesser, K. (2019, Dec. 11). Lawsuit claims SAT And ACT are biased—Here's what the research says. *Forbes.* http://tinyurl.com/3862fr8e.

Freire, P. (1972). *Pedagogy of the oppressed.* Penguin Books.

GSOLE Executive Board. (2019, June 13). *Online literacy instruction principles and tenets.* Global Society of Online Literacy Educators. https://gsole.org/oliresources/oliprinciples.

Hubler, S. (2020, May 24). University of California will end use of SAT and ACT in admissions. *The New York Times.* https://www.nytimes.com/2020/05/21/us/university-california-sat-act.html.

Inoue, A. (2019). *Labor-Based grading contracts: Building equity and inclusion in the compassionate writing classroom.* The WAC Clearinghouse; University Press of Colorado. https://doi.org/10.37514/PER-B.2019.0216.0.

Inoue, A. B. (2021, January 28). *What does it mean to form an antiracist orientation to teaching writing*. University of Alabama First-Year Writing Program 2021 Keynote Address. Tuscaloosa, AL, United States. https://english.ua.edu/diversity/diversity-events/.

Kohn, A. (2018). *Punished by rewards: The trouble with gold stars, incentive plans, A's, praise, and other bribes*. Houghton Mifflin.

Lakoff, G. & Johnson, M. (1981). *Metaphors we live by*. University of Chicago Press.

Lynch, B. T. & Alberti, S. (2010). Legacies of prejudice: Racism, co-production, and radical trust in the museum. *Museum Management and Curatorship, 25*(1), 13–35. https://doi.org/10.1080/09647770903529061.

Moore, P. (2014). Radical trust. *The Incluseum*. https://incluseum.com/2014/05/07/radical-trust/.

North, S. (1984). The idea of a writing center. *College English, 46*(5), 433–446. https://doi.org/10.2307/377047.

Pantelides, K. L. (2021). *Feminism and radical trust: Plagiarism and its people*. Women's and Gender Studies Research Series at MTSU.

Porter, J. E., Sullivan, P., Blythe, S., Grabill, J. T. & Miles, L. (2000). Institutional critique: A rhetorical methodology for change. *College Composition and Communication, 51*(4), 610–642. https://doi.org/10.2307/358914.

Scott-Clayton, J. (2018). *Do high-stakes placement exams predict college success?* CCRC Community College Research Center.

Sommers, N. (1980). Revision strategies of student writers and experienced adult writers. *College Composition and Communication, 31*(4), 378–388. https://doi.org/10.2307/356588.

Stone, E. M. (2021a). Aiming for the sweet spot: A user-centered approach to migrating a community-engaged online course. In J. Borgman & C. McArdle (Eds.), *PARS in practice: More resources and strategies for online writing instructors* (pp. 317–336). The WAC Clearinghouse; University Press of Colorado. https://doi.org/10.37514/PRA-B.2021.1145.2.19.

Stone, E. M. & Austin, S. E. (2020). Writing as commodity: How neoliberalism renders the postsecondary online writing classroom transactional and ways faculty can regain agency. *Basic Writing Electronic (BWe) Journal, 16*(1), 1–23. https://tinyurl.com/stone-austin.

APPENDIX.
ALIGNMENT BETWEEN *BETTER PRACTICE* CHAPTERS AND NATIONAL POSITION STATEMENTS

ALIGNMENT BETWEEN *BETTER PRACTICES* CHAPTERS AND PARS

PARS Framework	Personal	Accessible	Responsive	Strategic
Chapter 1: "Using Push Notifications to Establish Teacher Presence in Hybrid/Online Courses"	X	X	X	X
Chapter 2: "Using Structural Examples to Promote Creativity and Engagement"	X	X	X	—
Chapter 3: "Peer Review in Synchronous Online Learning Environments"	—	—	—	—
Chapter 4: "Scaffolding for Collaboration and Multimodal Assignments"	—	—	—	—
Chapter 5: "Annotation and Rhetorical Analysis with Discussions Hosted in Flipgrid"	—	—	—	—
Chapter 6: "Collaborative Annotation in the Online Classroom"	—	—	—	—
Chapter 7: "#TeachWriteChat . . ."	—	—	—	—
Chapter 8: "Fishing for Online Engagement"	X	—	—	X
Chapter 9: "Cripping Writing Processes . . ."	—	—	—	—
Chapter 10: "Creating Cultural Awareness, Building Community . . ."	X	X	—	—
Chapter 11: "Promoting Social Justice through Multimodal Composition in the Hybrid Writing Classroom"	—	—	—	—
Chapter 12: "Open-Media Assignment Design to Address Access and Accessibility in Online Multimodal Composition"	—	—	—	—
Chapter 13: "Accessible Multimodal Social Media Projects"	—	X	—	—
Chapter 14: "Reflective Learning in Data Storytelling"	X	—	—	X
Chapter 15: "Retooling Decision-Making in A/Synchronous Online Literacy Instruction"	—	—	—	X
Chapter 16: "Iterative Processes for All . . ."	—	—	—	—
Chapter 17: "The Radical Equity of Grading Contracts in Online Writing Courses"	—	—	—	—
Chapter 18: "Learning to Unlearn . . ."	—	—	—	—
Chapter 19: "Dialogic Assessment Agreements . . ."	—	—	X	—

Appendix

ALIGNMENT BETWEEN *BETTER PRACTICES* CHAPTERS AND GSOLE'S *ONLINE LITERACY INSTRUCTION (OLI) PRINCIPLES AND TENETS*

GSOLE Principles 1: Online literacy instruction should be universally accessible and inclusive.

- All stakeholders and students should be aware of and be able to engage the unique literacy features of communicating, teaching, and learning in a primarily digital environment
- 1.2. Use of technology should support stated course objectives, thereby not presenting an undue burden for instructors and students.
- 1.3. Multimodal composition and alphabetic writing may require different technologies; therefore, those involved should be appropriately prepared to use them.
- 1.4. The student-user experience should be prioritized when designing online courses, which includes mobile-friendly content, interaction affordances, and economic needs.

GSOLE Principle 2: All program developers and institutional administrators should commit to supporting and implementing a regular, iterative process of professional development and course/program assessment for online literacy instruction.

- 2.1. All sections of the same courses should have the same learning outcomes, resources, and support regardless of educational environment.

GSOLE OLI Principles & Tenets 1 & 2	1.1	1.2	1.3	1.4	2.1
Chapter 1: "Using Push Notifications to Establish Teacher Presence in Hybrid/Online Courses"	—	X	—	—	—
Chapter 2: "Using Structural Examples to Promote Creativity and Engagement"	—	—	—	—	—
Chapter 3: "Peer Review in Synchronous Online Learning Environments"	—	—	—	—	—
Chapter 4: "Scaffolding for Collaboration and Multimodal Assignments"	—	X	X	—	—
Chapter 5: "Annotation and Rhetorical Analysis with Discussions Hosted in Flipgrid"	—	—	—	X	—
Chapter 6: "Collaborative Annotation in the Online Classroom"	—	X	—	X	—
Chapter 7: "#TeachWriteChat . . . "	—	—	—	—	—
Chapter 8: "Fishing for Online Engagement"	—	—	—	—	—

Alignment Between Chapters and National Position Statements

GSOLE OLI Principles & Tenets 1 & 2	1.1	1.2	1.3	1.4	2.1
Chapter 9: "Cripping Writing Processes . . ."	X	—	—	—	—
Chapter 10: "Creating Cultural Awareness, Building Community . . ."	X	—	—	—	—
Chapter 11: "Promoting Social Justice through Multimodal Composition in the Hybrid Writing Classroom"	—	—	X	—	—
Chapter 12: "Open-Media Assignment Design to Address Access and Accessibility in Online Multimodal Composition"	—	—	—	—	—
Chapter 13: "Accessible Multimodal Social Media Projects"	X	—	X	—	—
Chapter 14: "Reflective Learning in Data Storytelling"	—	—	—	—	—
Chapter 15: "Retooling Decision-Making in A/Synchronous Online Literacy Instruction"	X	—	—	—	—
Chapter 16: "Iterative Processes for All . . ."	—	—	—	—	—
Chapter 17: "The Radical Equity of Grading Contracts in Online Writing Courses"	—	—	—	X	—
Chapter 18: "Learning to Unlearn . . ."	X	—	—	—	—
Chapter 19: "Dialogic Assessment Agreements . . ."	—	—	—	—	X

GSOLE Principle 3: Instructors and tutors should commit to regular, iterative processes of course and instructional material design, development, assessment, and revision to ensure that online literacy instruction and student support reflect current effective practices.

- 3.1. Instructors should be familiar with online instructional delivery practices to ensure the same level and hours of instruction across all OLI settings.
- 3.4. Instructors and tutors should migrate and/or adapt appropriate reading, alphabetic writing, and multimodal composition theories from traditional instructional settings to their OLI environment(s).
- 3. 5. Instructors and tutors should research, develop, theorize, and apply appropriate reading, alphabetic writing, and multimodal composition theories to their OLI environment(s).

GSOLE Principle 4: Educators and researchers should initiate, support, and sustain online literacy instruction-related conversations and research efforts within and across institutions and disciplinary boundaries.

- 4.2. Educators and researchers should insist that various OLI delivery models (including alternative, self-paced, and experimental) comply with the principles of sound pedagogy, quality instructor/designer preparation, and appropriate oversight detailed in this document.

Appendix

GSOLE OLI Principles & Tenets 3 & 4	3.1	3.4	3.5	4.2
Chapter 1: "Using Push Notifications to Establish Teacher Presence in Hybrid/Online Courses"	—	—	—	—
Chapter 2: "Using Structural Examples to Promote Creativity and Engagement"	—	—	—	—
Chapter 3: "Peer Review in Synchronous Online Learning Environments"	—	X	X	—
Chapter 4: "Scaffolding for Collaboration and Multimodal Assignments"	—	X	X	—
Chapter 5: "Annotation and Rhetorical Analysis with Discussions Hosted in Flipgrid"	—	—	—	X
Chapter 6: "Collaborative Annotation in the Online Classroom"	—	—	—	—
Chapter 7: "#TeachWriteChat . . . "	—	—	—	—
Chapter 8: "Fishing for Online Engagement"	—	X	—	—
Chapter 9: "Cripping Writing Processes . . . "	—	—	—	—
Chapter 10: "Creating Cultural Awareness, Building Community . . . "	—	—	X	—
Chapter 11: "Promoting Social Justice through Multimodal Composition in the Hybrid Writing Classroom"	—	—	—	—
Chapter 12: "Open-Media Assignment Design to Address Access and Accessibility in Online Multimodal Composition"	—	X	—	—
Chapter 13: "Accessible Multimodal Social Media Projects"	—	—	—	—
Chapter 14: "Reflective Learning in Data Storytelling"	—	—	—	—
Chapter 15: "Retooling Decision-Making in A/Synchronous Online Literacy Instruction"	—	—	—	—
Chapter 16: "Iterative Processes for All . . . "	X	—	—	—
Chapter 17: "The Radical Equity of Grading Contracts in Online Writing Courses"	—	—	—	—
Chapter 18: "Learning to Unlearn . . . "	—	—	X	—
Chapter 19: "Dialogic Assessment Agreements . . . "	—	—	X	—

ALIGNMENT BETWEEN *BETTER PRACTICES* CHAPTERS AND THE *FRAMEWORK FOR SUCCESS IN POSTSECONDARY WRITING*

Framework for Success in Postsecondary Writing	Curiosity	Openness	Engagement	Creativity	Persistence	Flexibility	Metacognition	Rhetorical Knowledge	Critical Thinking	Writing Processes	Convention Knowledge
Chapter 1: "Using Push Notifications to Establish Teacher Presence in Hybrid/Online Courses"	—	—	—	—	X	—	—	—	—	—	—
Chapter 2: "Using Structural Examples to Promote Creativity and Engagement"	—	—	—	—	—	—	—	—	—	—	—
Chapter 3: "Peer Review in Synchronous Online Learning Environments"	—	—	X	—	—	X	X	—	—	—	—
Chapter 4: "Scaffolding for Collaboration and Multimodal Assignments"	—	—	—	—	—	—	—	—	—	—	—
Chapter 5: "Annotation and Rhetorical Analysis with Discussions Hosted in Flipgrid"	—	—	X	—	X	X	X	—	—	—	—
Chapter 6: "Collaborative Annotation in the Online Classroom"	X	X	X	—	—	X	—	—	X	—	—
Chapter 7: "#TeachWriteChat . . ."	—	—	—	—	—	—	—	—	—	—	—
Chapter 8: "Fishing for Online Engagement"	—	—	—	—	—	—	—	X	X	X	X
Chapter 9: "Cripping Writing Processes . . ."	—	—	—	—	—	—	—	—	—	—	—
Chapter 10: "Creating Cultural Awareness, Building Community . . ."	—	X	X	X	—	—	X	—	—	—	X
Chapter 11: "Promoting Social Justice through Multimodal Composition in the Hybrid Writing Classroom"	—	—	—	—	—	—	—	—	—	—	—

Appendix

Framework for Success in Postsecondary Writing	Curiosity	Openness	Engagement	Creativity	Persistence	Flexibility	Metacognition	Rhetorical Knowledge	Critical Thinking	Writing Processes	Convention Knowledge
Chapter 12: "Open-Media Assignment Design to Address Access and Accessibility in Online Multimodal Composition"	—	—	—	X	—	X	X	—	—	—	—
Chapter 13: "Accessible Multimodal Social Media Projects"	—	—	—	—	—	—	—	—	—	—	—
Chapter 14: "Reflective Learning in Data Storytelling"	—	—	—	—	—	—	X	—	—	—	—
Chapter 15: "Retooling Decision-Making in A/Synchronous Online Literacy Instruction"	—	—	—	—	—	—	—	—	—	—	—
Chapter 16: "Iterative Processes for All . . ."	—	—	X	X	—	—	—	—	—	—	—
Chapter 17: "The Radical Equity of Grading Contracts in Online Writing Courses"	—	—	—	—	—	—	—	—	—	—	—
Chapter 18: "Learning to Unlearn . . ."	—	—	—	—	—	—	—	—	—	—	—
Chapter 19: "Dialogic Assessment Agreements . . ."	—	—	—	—	—	—	—	—	—	—	—

CONTRIBUTORS

Amanda Ayers is a doctoral candidate in the English Rhetoric and Composition Program at Florida State University. Amanda teaches composition and rhetoric courses in the undergraduate Editing, Writing, and Media major. She has also served as an administrator in both the Reading Writing Center and the College Composition Program, working to train and support graduate teaching assistants. Her research focuses on care and justice in spaces where bodies and language meet both in and out of our classrooms.

Anna Barritt is Associate Director of Sooner Works at the University of Oklahoma, housed within the Zarrow Institute on Transition and Self-Determination. Sooner Works is a program that offers students with intellectual/developmental disabilities who would otherwise not have access to college a post-secondary college experience on a university campus. As a rhetorician, Anna uses her knowledge to advocate with and on behalf of people with disabilities to have greater access to education, vocational training, and social integration. Before joining Sooner Works, Anna was Assistant Director of First-Year Composition at OU. She has presented her research on the intersection of rhetorical theory and intellectual disability at national and international conferences, and her essays have appeared in numerous edited collections and *Disability Studies Quarterly*.

Jessie Borgman is an instructor in the Writers' Studio at Arizona State University. She is the co-author of *Personal, Accessible, Responsive, Strategic: Resources and Strategies for Online Writing Instructors*, which was the winner of the 2020 Computers and Composition Distinguished Book Award. She is also the co-editor of *PARS in Practice: More Resources and Strategies for Online Writing Instructors*. She is the co-creator of The Online Writing Instruction Community (www.owicommunity.org) resources website. She has served on the CCCC OWI Standing Group in multiple capacities and as the Chair, co-led a national survey on online writing instruction, and collaborated with the research group to write the 2021 State of the Art of OWI Report.

Shawn Bowers is Assistant Professor of English at Queens University of Charlotte where she serves as the first-year writing program director. Her poetry has appeared in numerous literary journals under the pen name, Anita Cantillo.

Ingrid K. Bowman is a Continuing Lecturer at the University of California Santa Barbara (UCSB). She teaches in the Linguistics Department, English for Multilingual Students Program where she specializes in academic writing and professional development.

Contributors

Christina Branson is Instructor of Humanities at Maryville University, where she serves as an instructor of composition. Her co-authored articles have appeared in *The International Journal of Open Educational Resources* and *The MLA Style Center*.

Jennifer Burke Reifman is a doctoral candidate in education/writing, rhetoric, and composition studies at the University of California, Davis, where she works as a writing instructor and writing program administrator. Her work has appeared in *College Composition & Communication*, the *Journal of Basic Writing*, and *The Learning Assistance Review*.

Amy Cicchino is Associate Director for the Center for Teaching and Learning Excellence at Embry-Riddle Aeronautical University in Daytona Beach, Florida. Her research has appeared in venues such as the *International Journal of ePortfolio*, the *Writing Center Journal*, and *WPA: Writing Program Administration*.

Brielle Campos is Assistant Professor of University Studies at Middle Tennessee State University, where she serves as the program coordinator for the university seminar program. Her research interests include composition and rhetoric, disability studies, student success, and popular culture. Her dissertation was an auto ethnographic examination of developing a disabled identity centered in current popular culture tropes. She serves on the curriculum committee for her department, and is a member of SAMLA, Phi Kappa Phi, and CCCCs. She is currently working on a collaborative piece on academic access practices spawned from the COVID pandemic restrictions.

Ana Maria Contreras is English Instructor at Harper College and doctoral student at Central Michigan University. Her research invests in a genuine commitment to student success while identifying inventive ways to use technology to enhance student success in English composition courses.

Meghalee Das is a doctoral candidate in technical communication and rhetoric at Texas Tech University (TTU), where she teaches first-year composition and technical writing courses and serves as an instructional development consultant with the TTU Graduate School. Her research interests include online pedagogy, user experience, cultural inclusivity, and digital rhetoric, and her articles have appeared in *Technical Communication, Programmatic Perspectives,* and *Intercom*. For her dissertation, she studies the user experience of international students in online learning environments to develop culturally inclusive pedagogical strategies and user-centered instructional design.

Jennifer Smith Daniel (she/her) is the director of the writing center and writing across the curriculum programs at Queens University of Charlotte. Her research areas are tutor praxis, multiliteracies, feminist rhetorics, mentorship, and writing program administration. Her work has appeared in *Praxis: A*

Writing Center Journal, Community Literacy Journal, and *MacMillan Learning Tiny Teaching Stories*.

Kevin E. DePew is Associate Professor of English at Old Dominion University. His research in online writing instruction has appeared in venues such as *Technical Communication Quarterly, Journal of Second Language Writing*, and *Computers and Composition*, among others. He co-edited *Foundational Practices in Online Writing Instruction* with Beth Hewett in 2015. He currently serves as a co-administrator of the Global Society of Online Literacy Educators' Certification Course.

Caitlin M. Donovan is Assistant Director of the Master of Arts of Teaching program at Duke University and a doctoral candidate in teacher education and learning sciences at North Carolina State University, where she works with community-based organizations and pre-service teachers to develop critical literacy practices. Her research interests center on critical digital literacies, writing communities, memes, and teacher preparation. Her articles have appeared in *English Education* and Routledge textbooks.

Jessica Eagle is a recent Ph.D. graduate of teacher education and learning science at North Carolina State University. Her research centers on computational methods in English education.

Miranda Egger is Senior Instructor of rhetoric and Assistant Director of composition at University of Colorado, Denver.

Christopher E. Etheridge is Assistant Professor in the William Allen White School of Journalism and Mass Communications at the University of Kansas, where he teaches basic data storytelling, advanced message development, and sports communication courses. His research considers how community storytellers use digital tools to reach various audiences. His work has appeared in peer-reviewed publications such as *Mass Communication and Society* and *Science Communication*.

Theresa (Tess) Evans (she/her) is Associate Teaching Professor of Professional Writing in the Department of English at Miami University (Ohio). She teaches professional and technical writing in web-enhanced, hybrid, and fully online environments. Tess has contributed chapters for two edited collections, including *PARS in Practice* and *Women's Ways of Making*. Her work also has been published in *Rhetoric Review, The Proceedings of the Computers and Writing Conference*, and the *Online Literacies Open Resource (OLOR)*. She is an active member of the Global Society of Online Literacy Educators (GSOLE), having served as secretary, treasurer, and conference co-chair.

Michelle Falter is Associate Professor of English education and director of teacher education at St. Norbert College in DePere, Wisconsin. Her work focused

Contributors

on critical, affective, and dialogic practices in English language arts. She has published several books and numerous publications in places such as *English Teaching Practice and Critique, Reading Research Quarterly,* and *The ALAN Review.*

Michael J. Faris (he/him) is Associate Professor of Technical Communication and Rhetoric in the English department at Texas Tech University. His research areas are in digital literacies and rhetorics, queer rhetorics, and writing program administration. His work has appeared in *College Composition and Communication, Kairos: A Journal of Rhetoric, Technology, and Pedagogy, Journal of Business and Technical Communication, Composition Forum, Peitho,* and *WPA: Writing Program Administration.*

Samira Grayson is a doctoral candidate in English with a concentration in rhetoric and composition at Middle Tennessee State University. Her research interests include feminist rhetorics, research methods, spatial rhetorics, writing center, and writing program administration with notions of authorship in collaborative writing. Her most recent publication can be found in *Peitho.*

Vanessa Guida Mesina is Course Director of University Writing for International Students at Columbia University. Her writing has appeared in *SALT: Studies in Applied Linguistics and TESOL.*

Troy Hicks is Professor of English and Education at Central Michigan University. He has won numerous awards and honors, including the Divergent Award for Excellence for Initiative for 21st Century Literacies Research, Teacher Educator of the Year from the Michigan Reading Association, and Excellence in Teaching Award. He has published many books on digital teaching and learning, including *Mindful Teaching with Technology* (Guildford Press), *Creating Confident Writers* (W. W. Norton), and *Ask, Explore, Write!* (Routledge). His research is also available in journals such as *Michigan Reading Journal, The Journal of Writing Teacher Education,* and the *Journal of Language and Literacy Education* and a number of edited collections.

Ada Hubrig labors as Assistant Professor of English at Sam Houston State University, where they serve as co-writing program administrator and coordinator for the English education double major. Their research centers disability and queer theory, and is featured in *College Composition and Communication, Community Literacy Journal,* and *The Journal of Multimodal Rhetorics,* among others, and their words have also found homes in *Brevity* and *Disability Visibility.* Ada is editor of the new *Journal of Disability in Writing, Rhetoric, and Literacy Studies* and managing editor of *Journal of Multimodal Rhetorics,* and they are the recipient of the 2022 NCTE Leadership Award for People with Disabilities.

Kole Matheson is a lecturer at the Old Dominion University (ODU), where he teaches general education classes in English composition. He was responsible for co-designing ODU's English Composition course for its writing program in 2023. His teaching and research interests explore intersections of rhetoric, literature, and indigenous studies.

A. Chase Mitchell is Assistant Professor of Media & Communication at East Tennessee State University, where he teaches technical communication, multimedia production, media ecology, and writing in the sciences, among other courses. He also directs ETSU's Technical & Professional Writing undergraduate minor program. His research interests include tech comm, media convergence, and religious communication. He contributes a monthly online column, called "Image to Image," for the Christianity & Communication Studies Network.

Candie Moonshower is Master Instructor of English at Middle Tennessee State University, where she serves on the Honors Faculty and the Online English Committee. Moonshower piloted the creation and implementation of online writing courses within her department. She is a co-author of MTSU's new OER textbook for freshmen expository writing classes. Several of her students have won general education English writing awards, and Moonshower has been named the General Education English Instructor of the Year. She is a published author of books for children and a frequent contributor to local and national publications. Her research interests include the Vietnam War and its aftermath and Restoration England.

Michael Neal is Associate Professor of English at Florida State University, where he has directed the Rhetoric and Composition Program and chaired the Editing, Writing, and Media undergraduate major committee. His research explores intersections between multimodal composition, digital technologies, and writing assessment. The author of *Writing Assessment and the Revolution in Digital Texts and Technologies*, his current book project explores the educational challenges and promises of composing technologies and ways they can better be integrated into college writing curricula to promote critical thinking, accessibility, cultural critique, and student engagement.

Amory Orchard is a doctoral candidate at Florida State University. Besides teaching undergraduate courses in the editing and writing major, she has served as an administrator in the reading-writing center and college composition program. Her research interests engage with academic labor scholarship to enact anti-oppression pedagogies / practices within educational settings.

Kate Pantelides is Associate Professor of English at Middle Tennessee State University. Her most recent open-access textbook, co-authored with Jennifer Clary-Lemon and Derek Mueller, is *Try This: Research Methods for Writers*.

Cecilia Ragland Perry is Academic Assistant Dean and English Composition instructor at Maryville University. Her dissertation manuscript, *Ready or Not: Examining College Readiness Among Black First-Year College Students*, will be

Contributors

published in Howard University's *Journal of Negro Education*. She is a passionate academic, lover of books and reading, college football fan, running fanatic, and most importantly, proud mother of two beautiful little boys, a kitty, and a labradoodle.

Rich Rice is Professor of English at Texas Tech University where he teaches and researches topics in composition and rhetoric, new media, intercultural communication, problem-based learning, ePortfolio assessment, online writing instruction, and service learning. He serves as director of TTU's Center for Global Communication. See http://richrice.com.

Adrian Joseph (A.J.) Rivera is Associate Director of Composition at Indiana University Bloomington. His research interests include first-year composition and its impacts on retention, writing, and revision. His work has previously appeared in the *Journal of Hispanic Higher Education*.

Heidi Skurat Harris is Associate Professor of Rhetoric and Writing and the coordinator of the Graduate Program in Professional and Technical Writing and the Graduate Certificate in Online Writing Instruction at the University of Arkansas—Little Rock. Harris currently teaches online writing instruction, technical writing, creative nonfiction, and rhetorical theory at UALR. Her publications focus primarily on research and theory related to online writing instruction, including online writing program development, online faculty professional development, and online student retention.

Mary K. Stewart is Associate Professor of Literature & Writing Studies and the general education writing coordinator at California State University San Marcos, where she teaches first-year writing and graduate-level composition pedagogy courses.

Erica M. Stone (she/her) is a content designer and researcher with experience in both academia and industry. She works at the intersection of technical communication, public rhetoric, and community organizing. Erica's writing can be found in *Journal of Technical Writing & Communication; Technical Communication; Writing Program Administration; Kairos: A Journal of Rhetoric, Technology, and Pedagogy; Forum: Issues about Part-time & Contingent Faculty; Basic Writing Electronic (BWe) Journal; Spark: A 4C4Equality Journal; Community Literacy Journal*, and various edited collections. Contact Erica via email (erica.m.stone@gmail.com).

Michelle Stuckey is Clinical Associate Professor at Arizona State University, where she serves as the writing program administrator for a fully online first-year composition program. Her essays have appeared in the *Journal of Writing Assessment* and a number of edited collections.

Valeria Tsygankova is a writing center associate at Columbia University, where she received her Ph.D. in English and comparative literature. She is also an Axinn Fellow in the MFA program in creative nonfiction at NYU. She teaches first-year writing at Columbia and creative writing at NYU.

Scott Warnock is Associate Dean of Undergraduate Education at Drexel University where he served previously as the director of the university writing program. His scholarship focuses on technology and writing instruction, especially online learning. He has authored or co-authored five books and numerous chapters and articles, and he has spoken at many institutions and conferences. He co-founded the Global Society of Online Literacy Educators in 2016 and served as president from 2018 to 2020, and he was co-chair of the Conference on College Composition and Communication Committee for Effective Practices in Online Writing Instruction from 2011 to 2016.

Briana Westmacott is a Continuing Lecturer in the English for Multilingual Students program at the University of California, Santa Barbara where she develops and instructs undergraduate and graduate level courses. In addition, she has been a columnist for over ten years and has published work in a variety of magazines and newspapers. Recently, she co-authored an article based on peer mentorship and teaching higher education in the *Chronicle of Mentoring & Coaching* (2022).

Gabriella Wilson is a doctoral student in the Composition and Cultural Rhetoric program at Syracuse University. Her essays have appeared in *Peitho, The Journal of Rhetoric, Professional Communication, and Globalization; The Journal of Multimodal Rhetoric;* and *Writers Craft & Context*.

Ashleah Wimberly is a doctoral candidate at Florida State University, where they have served as an assistant director to the college composition program, an online writing coordinator, and an instructor in the editing, writing, and media major. Their research interests include pedagogy, literacy studies, writing assessment, and graduate instructor training and mentorship.

Syndee Wood is adjunct faculty at California State University San Marcos, MiraCosta College, and Palomar College, where she teaches first-year writing and courses.

Alex Wulff is Associate Professor of English at Maryville University, where he serves as the writing program administrator and the writing studio director. He teaches writing and rhetoric courses with an emphasis on writing across the disciplines. His research interests are in writing center scholarship, composition studies, and the long nineteenth century.